DIVINE HEALTH

NEW TESTAMENT

DR. DON AND MARY COLBERT

Beloved, I pray that you may prosper in all things and be in health, just as your soul prospers.

3 JOHN 2

NKJV

NEW
KING
JAMES
VERSION®

NELSON BIBLES
A Division of Thomas Nelson Publishers
Since 1798

www.thomasnelson.com

DIVINE HEALTH
NEW TESTAMENT

SPECIAL THANKS TO

Jan Dargatz, Janene MacIvor,
and Valerie Fowler for their
valuable editorial assistance,
to Heather Dryden for her outstanding
design / illustration work,
to Jami Anderson for her exceptional
creative direction, and
to Rainbow Graphics for their
skillful typesetting.

TABLE OF CONTENTS

There's a Better Way to Live!

No matter how healthy you may be, there's always room for improvement. God's plan for health, which we call divine health, is based upon the concept of wholeness. This is health that takes into account physical factors as well as emotional, psychological, and spiritual factors. When all aspects of a person's being are strong, vibrant, filled with energy, and free of disease, that person is moving toward wholeness.

Divine health presents one of God's foremost health manuals for living a healthy, "whole" life—the New Testament. The Bible is like an owner's manual for your life. It not only addresses spiritual issues, but also practical issues related to your body, relationships, and to the ways in which you think and feel about yourself and the world around you.

In addition to Bible commentary information ("Insights into the World"), you'll find calendars that address seasonal tips for whole-person living, and short segments that provide "Wise Choices" and "Q&A" on Bible health principles. You will also find "Health Check" quizzes to help you determine your own level of wholeness. Main features about the Bible's plan for whole-person living are found in segments labeled "The Ultimate Health Resource" and "Wholeness 101."

There are a number of features that address the food you eat, including "Righteous Recipes" that use healthful foods, many of which are mentioned in the Bible. You'll also enjoy the tidbits of information found in "Bible Health and Food Factoids" and "Food Morsels." You may be surprised to learn how science is supporting the food laws of the Old Testament in a series of features titled "The Law and Science." There are features on "What Would Jesus Eat?" as well as "Bible Beverages." "The Condiment Cabinet" features present various condiments, herbs, and spices mentioned in the Bible.

Bible-inspired information related to specific ailments is found in the "Scripture Solutions" section of features. As for exercise, you'll find good tips in the "Walking the Walk" segments.

Some of the features focus on emotional health, including features titled "The Healthy Soul" and "Overcoming Obstinate Obstacles." Since many emotional and physical ailments are linked to stress, don't overlook the "Stress Busters" segments.

Specific needs of men and women are addressed in feature sections titled "Women's Issues" and "Men's Issues." Beauty and health often are closely related and you'll enjoy reading about the "beautiful people" in the Word of God ("People Called 'Beautiful' in the Bible"), as well as short bits of information under the banner "Godly 'n' Goodlookin'."

Don't miss the fun information in the special section titled "Creating Your Own Bible-Land Spa." There's also information about gardening—both as a means of growing food and herbs and as a means of creating a place of beauty for nourishment of the soul. Check out the "Gardening for Health" features.

Enjoy! But do more than enjoy the read. Start putting into practice what you learn. You'll feel better for it, and be better equipped to fulfill your purpose on this earth with the best quality of health possible!

—Dr. Don and Mary Colbert

M ATTHEW

The Gospel of Matthew was written especially for first-century Jews who were very familiar with Old Testament prophecies, commandments, and promises of God. In many ways, this Gospel account of Jesus' life emphasizes the "Jewish" nature of Jesus. More than fifty direct quotations from the Old Testament are included in it.

The Jews regarded the human being as a "whole." In fact, the words for "salvation" and "healing" have the same root word in Hebrew. The Jews did not separate the body from the soul, or the mind from the spirit. They believed that wholeness was not only what God desired for human beings, but that wholeness could be attained by keeping God's commandments. These commandments included all the laws related to the natural, material, and physical world, as well as those related to the spiritual and emotional realm. Therefore, when a person was sick, he was presumed to have broken a commandment of God, either willfully or unwittingly.

The dietary and food laws of the Old Testament were regarded as totally applicable in Jesus' time. Jesus kept those dietary laws, as did His disciples and the early Church members.

THE GENEALOGY OF JESUS CHRIST

1 The book of the genealogy of Jesus Christ, the Son of David, the Son of Abraham:

²Abraham begot Isaac, Isaac begot Jacob, and Jacob begot Judah and his brothers. ³Judah begot Perez and Zerah by Tamar, Perez begot Hezron, and Hezron begot Ram. ⁴Ram begot Amminadab, Amminadab begot Nahshon, and Nahshon begot Salmon. ⁵Salmon begot Boaz by Rahab, Boaz begot Obed by Ruth, Obed begot Jesse, ⁶and Jesse begot David the king.

David the king begot Solomon by her *who had been the wife*ᵃ of Uriah. ⁷Solomon begot Rehoboam, Rehoboam begot Abijah, and Abijah begot Asa.ᵃ ⁸Asa begot Jehoshaphat, Jehoshaphat begot Joram, and Joram begot Uzziah. ⁹Uzziah begot Jotham, Jotham begot Ahaz, and Ahaz begot Hezekiah. ¹⁰Hezekiah begot Manasseh, Manasseh begot Amon,ᵃ and Amon begot Josiah. ¹¹Josiah begot Jeconiah and his brothers about the time they were carried away to Babylon.

¹²And after they were brought to Babylon, Jeconiah begot Shealtiel, and Shealtiel begot Zerubbabel. ¹³Zerubbabel begot Abiud, Abiud begot Eliakim, and Eliakim begot Azor. ¹⁴Azor begot Zadok, Zadok begot Achim, and Achim begot Eliud. ¹⁵Eliud begot Eleazar, Eleazar begot Matthan, and Matthan begot Jacob. ¹⁶And Jacob begot Joseph the husband of Mary, of whom was born Jesus who is called Christ.

¹⁷So all the generations from Abraham to David *are* fourteen generations, from David until the captivity in Babylon *are* fourteen generations, and from the captivity in Babylon until the Christ *are* fourteen generations.

CHRIST BORN OF MARY

¹⁸Now the birth of Jesus Christ was as follows: After His mother Mary was betrothed to Joseph, before they came together, she was found with child of the Holy Spirit. ¹⁹Then Joseph her husband, being a just *man*, and not wanting to make her a public example, was minded to put her away secretly. ²⁰But while he thought about these things, behold, an angel of the Lord appeared to him in a dream, saying, "Joseph, son of David, do not be afraid to take to you Mary your wife, for that which is conceived in her is of the Holy Spirit. ²¹And she will bring forth a Son, and you shall call His name JESUS, for He will save His people from their sins."

²²So all this was done that it might be fulfilled which was spoken by the Lord through the prophet, saying: ²³"Behold, the virgin shall be with child, and bear a Son, and they shall call His name Immanuel,"ᵃ which is translated, "God with us."

²⁴Then Joseph, being aroused from sleep, did as the angel of the Lord commanded him and took to him his wife, ²⁵and did not know her till she had brought forth her firstborn Son.ᵃ And he called His name JESUS.

WISE MEN FROM THE EAST

2 Now after Jesus was born in Bethlehem of Judea in the days of Herod the king, behold, wise men from the East came to Jerusalem, ²saying, "Where is He who has been born King of the Jews? For we have seen His star in the East and have come to worship Him."

³When Herod the king heard *this*, he was troubled, and all Jerusalem with him. ⁴And when he had gathered all the chief priests and scribes

---

1:6 ᵃWords in italic type have been added for clarity. They are not found in the original Greek.   1:7 ᵃNU-Text reads *Asaph*.   1:10 ᵃNU-Text reads *Amos*.   1:23 ᵃIsaiah 7:14
1:25 ᵃNU-Text reads *a Son*.

WEIGHING Less &
ENJOYING LIFE MORE!

[Grazing Through a Day]

Many of us grew up in a time when people thought it was healthy to eat three balanced meals a day. We now know it's much healthier to have several lighter-fare meals during the day. This is also a key to weight loss that is more of a joy than a burden. Plan to have five to six small "feedings" a day, spaced two and a half to three hours apart. Do not eat within an hour of going to bed.

A "feeding" might be one of the following:

- A small bowl of whole-grain cereal with nonfat yogurt and berries
- A salad with grilled chicken and fresh veggies
- A half cup of nonfat cottage cheese with fresh pineapple
- A banana smoothie or protein shake
- A bowl of almost fat-free (no butter) popcorn sprayed lightly with olive oil
- A few almonds and an apple
- Several celery sticks and a scoop of egg salad (made with nonfat mayo)
- A bowl of homemade vegetable soup
- A portion of baked or grilled salmon with whole-grain rice and steamed vegetables

Be creative—but in small ways!

---

of the people together, he inquired of them where the Christ was to be born.

⁵So they said to him, "In Bethlehem of Judea, for thus it is written by the prophet:

⁶ 'But you, Bethlehem, in the land of Judah,
   Are not the least among the rulers of Judah;
   For out of you shall come a Ruler
   Who will shepherd My people Israel.' " ᵃ

⁷Then Herod, when he had secretly called the wise men, determined from them what time the star appeared. ⁸And he sent them to Bethlehem and said, "Go and search carefully for the young Child, and when you have found *Him*, bring back word to me, that I may come and worship Him also."

⁹When they heard the king, they departed; and behold, the star which they had seen in the East went before them, till it came and stood over where the young Child was. ¹⁰When they saw the star, they rejoiced with exceedingly great joy. ¹¹And when they had come into the house, they saw the young Child with Mary His mother, and fell down and worshiped Him. And when they had opened their treasures, they presented gifts to Him: gold, frankincense, and myrrh.

¹²Then, being divinely warned in a dream that they should not return to Herod, they departed for their own country another way.

THE FLIGHT INTO EGYPT

¹³Now when they had departed, behold, an angel of the Lord appeared to Joseph in a dream, saying, "Arise, take the young Child and His mother, flee to Egypt, and stay there until I bring you word; for Herod will seek the young Child to destroy Him."

¹⁴When he arose, he took the young Child and His mother by night and departed for Egypt, ¹⁵and was there until the death of Herod, that it might be fulfilled which was spoken by the Lord through the prophet, saying, "Out of Egypt I called My Son." ᵃ

MASSACRE OF THE INNOCENTS

¹⁶Then Herod, when he saw that he was deceived by the wise men, was exceedingly angry; and he sent forth and put to death all the male children who were in Bethlehem and in all its districts, from two years old and under, according to the time which he had determined from the wise men. ¹⁷Then was fulfilled what was spoken by Jeremiah the prophet, saying:

[ALFALFA]

FACT MORSELS

High in Potassium. Alfalfa tablets are an excellent source of potassium—helpful to the heart.

2:6 ᵃMicah 5:2   2:15 ᵃHosea 11:1

[18] "A voice was heard in Ramah,
Lamentation, weeping, and great mourning,
Rachel weeping for her children,
Refusing to be comforted,
Because they are no more."[a]

THE HOME IN NAZARETH

[19]Now when Herod was dead, behold, an angel of the Lord appeared in a dream to Joseph in Egypt, [20]saying, "Arise, take the young Child and His mother, and go to the land of Israel, for those who sought the young Child's life are dead." [21]Then he arose, took the young Child and His mother, and came into the land of Israel.

[22]But when he heard that Archelaus was reigning over Judea instead of his father Herod, he was afraid to go there. And being warned by God in a dream, he turned aside into the region of Galilee. [23]And he came and dwelt in a city called Nazareth, that it might be fulfilled which was spoken by the prophets, "He shall be called a Nazarene."

JOHN THE BAPTIST PREPARES THE WAY

3 In those days John the Baptist came preaching in the wilderness of Judea, [2]and saying, "Repent, for the kingdom of heaven is at hand!" [3]For this is he who was spoken of by the prophet Isaiah, saying:

"The voice of one crying in the wilderness:
'Prepare the way of the Lord;
Make His paths straight.' "[a]

[4]Now John himself was clothed in camel's hair, with a leather belt around his waist; and his food was locusts and wild honey. [5]Then Jerusalem, all Judea, and all the region around the Jordan went out to him [6]and were baptized by him in the Jordan, confessing their sins.

[7]But when he saw many of the Pharisees and Sadducees coming to his baptism, he said to them, "Brood of vipers! Who warned you to flee from the wrath to come? [8]Therefore bear fruits worthy of repentance, [9]and do not think to say to yourselves, 'We have Abraham as *our* father.' For I say to you that God is able to raise up children to Abraham from these stones. [10]And even now the ax is laid to the root of the trees. Therefore every tree which does not bear good fruit is cut down and thrown into the fire. [11]I indeed baptize you with water unto repentance, but He who is coming after me is mightier than I, whose sandals I am not worthy to carry. He will baptize you with the Holy Spirit and fire.[a] [12]His winnowing fan *is* in His hand, and He will thoroughly clean out His threshing floor, and gather His wheat into the barn; but He will burn up the chaff with unquenchable fire."

JOHN BAPTIZES JESUS

[13]Then Jesus came from Galilee to John at the Jordan to be baptized by him. [14]And John *tried to* prevent Him, saying, "I need to be baptized by You, and are You coming to me?"

[15]But Jesus answered and said to him, "Permit *it to be so* now, for thus it is fitting for us to fulfill all righteousness." Then he allowed Him.

SCRIPTURE SOLUTIONS

[MEMORY LOSS]

God desires you to have a sound mind! The Bible says, "God has not given us a spirit of fear, but of power and of love and of a sound mind" (2 Timothy 1:7). If you do nothing, however, to help maintain a sound mind, approximately 20 percent of all your brain cells will die over the course of your lifetime. The good news that counteracts that bad news is: much *can* be done to prevent the loss of brain cells. Even more good news: scientists have discovered in the past two decades that it is possible for the brain to produce *new* brain cells!

Here are three of the best things you can do nutritionally to keep your brain healthy:

☐ **Avoid hydrogenated fats, trans-fatty acids (often called trans fats), and saturated fats. They cause cell membranes to thicken and harden, and thus, lose their ability to absorb nutrients.**

☐ **Get enough omega-3—it is found in salmon, mackerel, sardines, tuna, herring, fish oils, and flaxseed oil. You can take omega-3 in supplement form, including very convenient fish-oil and flaxseed-oil capsules.**

☐ **Take in adequate amounts of these antioxidants: vitamin E, vitamin C, lipoic acid, glutathione, and coenzyme Q10. These extraordinary antioxidants work together in a powerful way for brain health.**

Keep your body and brain active. Aerobic exercise can help get sufficient oxygen to brain cells—the brain actually uses 25 percent of the available oxygen carried in the bloodstream. Research shows that working puzzles, diligently studying a subject (such as the Bible), writing letters, reading, and staying active in work or hobbies help prevent memory loss.

Gardening for Health

Creating a Place of Tranquility

In Bible times a garden was considered a place for delightful rest and spiritual contemplation. A garden was a place of healing for the soul. The word for garden—*gan* in the Hebrew and *kepos* in the Greek—literally means a "covered or hidden place." Gardens in Bible times often were under trellises and were sequestered behind gates and walls. They were marked by these seven characteristics:

- ☐ **Vegetation**
- ☐ **Water**
- ☐ **A place to sit**
- ☐ **Shade or "shelter"**
- ☐ **Quiet**
- ☐ **Beauty**
- ☐ **Fruitfulness**

Plants were usually arranged for aesthetic effect, but also were located close to water supplies. Fragrant flowers were emphasized, the more fragrant the better. Fruit trees, especially fig trees, and berry-producing vines were highly valued in a garden. Depending on the person's wealth, fountains and cages with exotic birds might be included.

Shelter or shade was provided by a tree, a vine arbor, latticework with reeds, or a tent.

Gardens were used as a place to meet with friends for conversation or light meals, for prayer, for feast-related social events, and for personal quiet times of reflection and meditation on Scripture. A garden was a great source of personal pleasure to those living in Bible times. The same is true today for a well-planned place of tranquility, regardless of your climate or the location of your home. A garden with the seven characteristics noted above can even be created on an apartment balcony.

[16]When He had been baptized, Jesus came up immediately from the water; and behold, the heavens were opened to Him, and He[a] saw the Spirit of God descending like a dove and alighting upon Him. [17]And suddenly a voice *came* from heaven, saying, "This is My beloved Son, in whom I am well pleased."

SATAN TEMPTS JESUS

4 Then Jesus was led up by the Spirit into the wilderness to be tempted by the devil. [2]And when He had fasted forty days and forty nights, afterward He was hungry. [3]Now when the tempter came to Him, he said, "If You are the Son of God, command that these stones become bread."

[4]But He answered and said, "It is written, 'Man shall not live by bread alone, but by every word that proceeds from the mouth of God.' "[a]

[5]Then the devil took Him up into the holy city, set Him on the pinnacle of the temple, [6]and said to Him, "If You are the Son of God, throw Yourself down. For it is written:

'He shall give His angels charge over you,'

and,

'In their hands they shall bear you up,
  Lest you dash your foot against a stone.' "[a]

[7]Jesus said to him, "It is written again, 'You shall not tempt the Lord your God.' "[a]

[8]Again, the devil took Him up on an exceedingly high mountain, and showed Him all the kingdoms of the world and their glory. [9]And he said to Him, "All these things I will give You if You will fall down and worship me."

[10]Then Jesus said to him, "Away with you,[a] Satan! For it is written, 'You shall worship the LORD your God, and Him only you shall serve.' "[b]

[11]Then the devil left Him, and behold, angels came and ministered to Him.

JESUS BEGINS HIS GALILEAN MINISTRY

[12]Now when Jesus heard that John had been put in prison, He departed to Galilee. [13]And leaving Nazareth, He came and dwelt in Capernaum, which is by the sea, in the regions of Zebulun and Naphtali, [14]that it might be fulfilled which was spoken by Isaiah the prophet, saying:

[15] "The land of Zebulun and the land of Naphtali,

By the way of the sea, beyond the Jordan,
Galilee of the Gentiles:
[16] The people who sat in darkness have seen a great light,
And upon those who sat in the region and shadow of death
Light has dawned."[a]

[17]From that time Jesus began to preach and to say, "Repent, for the kingdom of heaven is at hand."

FOUR FISHERMEN CALLED AS DISCIPLES

[18]And Jesus, walking by the Sea of Galilee, saw two brothers, Simon called Peter, and Andrew his brother, casting a net into the sea; for

3:16 [a]Or *he*   4:4 [a]Deuteronomy 8:3   4:6 [a]Psalm 91:11, 12   4:7 [a]Deuteronomy 6:16   4:10 [a]M-Text reads *Get behind Me.*   [b]Deuteronomy 6:13   4:16 [a]Isaiah 9:1, 2

they were fishermen. ¹⁹Then He said to them, "Follow Me, and I will make you fishers of men." ²⁰They immediately left *their* nets and followed Him.

²¹Going on from there, He saw two other brothers, James *the son of* Zebedee, and John his brother, in the boat with Zebedee their father, mending their nets. He called them, ²²and immediately they left the boat and their father, and followed Him.

JESUS HEALS A GREAT MULTITUDE

²³And Jesus went about all Galilee, teaching in their synagogues, preaching the gospel of the kingdom, and healing all kinds of sickness and all kinds of disease among the people. ²⁴Then His fame went throughout all Syria; and they brought to Him all sick people who were afflicted with various diseases and torments, and those who were demon-possessed, epileptics, and paralytics; and He healed them. ²⁵Great multitudes followed Him—from Galilee, and *from* Decapolis, Jerusalem, Judea, and beyond the Jordan.

THE BEATITUDES

5 And seeing the multitudes, He went upon a mountain, and when He was seated His disciples came to Him. ²Then He opened His mouth and taught them, saying:

³ "Blessed *are* the poor in spirit,
For theirs is the kingdom of heaven.
⁴ Blessed *are* those who mourn,
For they shall be comforted.
⁵ Blessed *are* the meek,
For they shall inherit the earth.
⁶ Blessed *are* those who hunger and thirst for
righteousness,
For they shall be filled.
⁷ Blessed *are* the merciful,
For they shall obtain mercy.
⁸ Blessed *are* the pure in heart,
For they shall see God.

℞ PRESCRIPTIONS FOR INNER HEALTH

"Do not withhold good from those
to whom it is due,
When it is in the power of your
hand to do so."

(PROVERBS 3:27)

When you pay your bills and fulfill your obligations to others, you find that life is less stressful! People who have no debts—financial or in relationship—are people who sleep better at night!

⁹ Blessed *are* the peacemakers,
For they shall be called sons of God.
¹⁰ Blessed *are* those who are persecuted for righteousness'
sake,
For theirs is the kingdom of heaven.

¹¹"Blessed are you when they revile and persecute you, and say all kinds of evil against you falsely for My sake. ¹²Rejoice and be exceedingly glad, for great *is* your reward in heaven, for so they persecuted the prophets who were before you.

> (Matthew 5:6)

Basic Drives. Two of the most basic human drives are those that compel a person to seek sufficient water and food. Without water, a person can live for only a few days. This is especially true in an arid climate such as Israel's. Without food, a person can live for only a few weeks.

Jesus taught that we must seek to be in right relationship with God as if we are hungry and thirsty for Him. In other words, we must seek God as if our life depended upon it! Jesus promised that those who seek God in this way would be "filled," or satisfied. The Word of God, especially the Law, is described throughout the Bible in terms of food—meat, milk, bread, and so forth.

God's presence, specifically the Holy Spirit's presence, is likened to living streams of water. The person who hungers and thirsts for God, therefore, is a person who has a strong compelling desire to know God's Word, including God's commandments and promises, and to experience God's living presence. Taken together, God's Word and God's presence completely satisfy the human soul, just as food and water satisfy the human body.

INSIGHTS INTO THE WORD

CONDIMENTS

☐ Salt

People who lived at the time of Jesus were familiar with all of the wonderful properties of salt. They used it to add flavor to foods, preserve food, and cleanse and heal wounds.

Most people in the United States consume too much salt. Salt is composed of sodium and chloride. Sodium is a major culprit related to ill health. Most Americans ingest twice as much sodium as potassium. But for optimum health, a person should consume five times as much potassium as sodium. The daily amount of sodium required to maintain good health in most adults is less than 200 mg, or a tenth of a teaspoon. A typical American adult, however, consumes 6 to 25 grams of salt a day—twenty times the correct amount!

The best ways to improve a sodium–potassium ratio are: eat more fresh fruits and vegetables, which have a higher concentration of potassium than sodium; decrease dramatically the intake of processed and fast foods; and stop using a salt shaker. If you love the taste of salt, use a salt substitute, which is *potassium* chloride, such as No-Salt or Nu-Salt. If you must use salt, choose Celtic salt available in most health-food stores.

BELIEVERS ARE SALT AND LIGHT

[13]"You are the salt of the earth; but if the salt loses its flavor, how shall it be seasoned? It is then good for nothing but to be thrown out and trampled underfoot by men.

[14]"You are the light of the world. A city that is set on a hill cannot be hidden. [15]Nor do they light a lamp and put it under a basket, but on a lampstand, and it gives light to all *who are* in the house. [16]Let your light so shine before men, that they may see your good works and glorify your Father in heaven.

CHRIST FULFILLS THE LAW

[17]"Do not think that I came to destroy the Law or the Prophets. I did not come to destroy but to fulfill. [18]For assuredly, I say to you, till heaven and earth pass away, one jot or one tittle will by no means pass from the law till all is fulfilled. [19]Whoever therefore breaks one of the least of these commandments, and teaches men so, shall be called least in the kingdom of heaven; but whoever does and teaches *them,* he shall be called great in the kingdom of heaven. [20]For I say to you, that unless your righteousness exceeds *the righteousness* of the scribes and Pharisees, you will by no means enter the kingdom of heaven.

MURDER BEGINS IN THE HEART

[21]"You have heard that it was said to those of old, 'You shall not murder,[a] and whoever murders will be in danger of the judgment.' [22]But I say to you that whoever is angry with his brother without a cause[a] shall be in danger of the judgment. And whoever says to his brother, 'Raca!' shall be in danger of the council. But whoever says, 'You fool!' shall be in danger of hell fire. [23]Therefore if you bring your gift to the altar, and there remember that your brother has something against you, [24]leave your gift there before the altar, and go your way. First be reconciled to your brother, and then come and offer your gift. [25]Agree with your adversary quickly, while you are on the way with him, lest your adversary deliver you to the judge, the judge hand you over to the officer, and you be thrown into prison. [26]Assuredly, I say to you, you will by no means get out of there till you have paid the last penny.

ADULTERY IN THE HEART

[27]"You have heard that it was said to those of old,[a] 'You shall not commit adultery.'[b] [28]But I say to you that whoever looks at a woman to lust for her has already committed adultery with her in his heart. [29]If your right eye causes you to sin, pluck it out and cast *it* from you; for it is more profitable for you that one of your members perish, than for your whole body to be cast into hell. [30]And if your right hand causes you to sin, cut it off and cast *it* from you; for it is more profitable for you that one of your members perish, than for your whole body to be cast into hell.

INSIGHTS INTO THE WORD

> (Matthew 5:13)

Staying Salty. Salt loses its savor in one of two ways: dilution or pollution. Jesus warned His followers to avoid "dilution"—to avoid becoming so much like the prevailing culture that they were no longer distinctive in their faith and commitment. Jesus taught His followers to stay pure, but not aloof; to remain innocent, but not be stupid; to value relationship with Him more than religiosity; to seek every opportunity to help others; and to never become self-absorbed. He also warned His followers about the "pollution" of sin, commanding them to withstand temptations to sin.

5:21 [a]Exodus 20:13; Deuteronomy 5:17 5:22 [a]NU-Text omits *without a cause.* 5:27 [a]NU-Text and M-Text omit *to those of old.* [b]Exodus 20:14; Deuteronomy 5:18

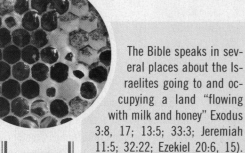

WHOLENESS 101

A Life "Flowing with Milk and Honey"

The Bible speaks in several places about the Israelites going to and occupying a land "flowing with milk and honey" Exodus 3:8, 17; 13:5; 33:3; Jeremiah 11:5; 32:22; Ezekiel 20:6, 15). What does this mean?

In the natural, a land flowing with milk refers to a land fertile enough to have great pastures capable of supporting large herds of cattle and flocks of goats and sheep. The milk of cattle was not consumed—it was used solely for nurturing calves—but the milk of goats was made into cheese and yogurt for human consumption. Herds and flocks were signs of prosperity and health to the Israelites. A land "flowing with milk" was a land blessed by God, who alone could cause flocks and herds to multiply.

A land "flowing with honey" referred to a land that could support an abundance of fruit trees and vines, their flowers being the source of nectar that bees would turn into honey. Such a land would have plenty of food for the Israelites, and have a satisfying "sweetness." It was a land conducive to farming and high yields of crops. It was a land in which man could use his talents and skills to plant, cultivate, and harvest.

In the emotional and spiritual sense, a land with many flocks, herds, and cultivated fruit trees and vineyards was a land at peace. One of the first things that warring nomadic tribes did as they invaded a territory was to consume or drive away a people's flocks and herds, and to strip the trees and vines of their fruit.

God promised His people a land filled to overflowing with prosperity, fruitfulness, and peace. The joy of living in the fullness of His Promised Land was a joy that satisfied both the body and soul. It was a joy rooted in God doing what only God can do, and man doing what God has equipped man to do. It was a land in which God and man worked together to bring about great blessings.

We know it is possible to live with great material prosperity and not be spiritually or emotionally fulfilled. We also know it is possible to feel content even in times of great material or physical need. God's desire is for His people to know material and natural fruitfulness *and* spiritual and emotional fulfillment.

Fruitfulness and fulfillment—those are the foremost hallmarks of a genuine "Promised Land."

MARRIAGE IS SACRED AND BINDING

31"Furthermore it has been said, 'Whoever divorces his wife, let him give her a certificate of divorce.' 32But I say to you that whoever divorces his wife for any reason except sexual immorality[a] causes her to commit adultery; and whoever marries a woman who is divorced commits adultery.

JESUS FORBIDS OATHS

33"Again you have heard that it was said to those of old, 'You shall not swear falsely, but shall perform your oaths to the Lord.' 34But I say to you, do not swear at all: neither by heaven, for it is God's throne; 35nor by the earth, for it is His footstool; nor by Jerusalem, for it is the city of the great King. 36Nor shall you swear by your head, because you cannot make one hair white or black. 37But let your 'Yes' be 'Yes,' and your 'No,' 'No.' For whatever is more than these is from the evil one.

GO THE SECOND MILE

38"You have heard that it was said, 'An eye for an eye and a tooth for a tooth.'[a] 39But I tell you not to resist an evil person. But whoever slaps you on your right cheek, turn the other to him also. 40If anyone wants to sue you and take away your tunic, let him have *your* cloak also. 41And whoever compels you to go one mile, go with him two. 42Give to him who asks you, and from him who wants to borrow from you do not turn away.

LOVE YOUR ENEMIES

43"You have heard that it was said, 'You shall love your neighbor[a] and hate your enemy.' 44But I say to you, love your enemies, bless those who curse you, do good to those who hate you, and pray for those who spitefully use you and persecute you,[a] 45that you may be sons of your Father in heaven; for He makes His sun rise on the evil and on the good, and sends rain on the just and on the unjust. 46For if you love those who love you, what reward have you? Do not even the tax collectors do the same? 47And if you greet your brethren[a] only, what do you do more *than others*? Do not even the tax collectors[b] do so? 48Therefore you shall be perfect, just as your Father in heaven is perfect.

DO GOOD TO PLEASE GOD

6 "Take heed that you do not do your charitable deeds before men, to be seen by them. Otherwise you have no reward from your Father in heaven. 2Therefore, when you do a charitable deed, do not sound a trumpet before you as the hypocrites do in the synagogues and in the streets, that they may have glory from men. Assuredly, I say to you, they have their reward. 3But when you do a charitable deed, do not let your left hand know what your right hand is doing, 4that your charitable deed may be in secret; and your Father who sees in secret will Himself reward you openly.[a]

THE MODEL PRAYER

5"And when you pray, you shall not be like the hypocrites. For they love to pray standing

5:32 [a]Or *fornication*   5:38 [a]Exodus 21:24; Leviticus 24:20; Deuteronomy 19:21   5:43 [a]Compare Leviticus 19:18   5:44 [a]NU-Text omits three clauses from this verse, leaving, *"But I say to you, love your enemies and pray for those who persecute you."*   5:47 [a]M-Text reads *friends.* [b]NU-Text reads *Gentiles.*   6:4 [a]NU-Text omits *openly.*

> (Matthew 6:11)

All We Need. "Bread" to the Jew in Jesus' time was a term that included far more than food. It referred to *all* the substance that was considered necessary for life, including emotional and spiritual nourishment. Jesus pointed out in the Sermon on the Mount that life encompasses far more than food, drink, and clothing (Matthew 6:31). The true necessities of life are those things that must be acquired or used on a *daily* basis.

Spending time *daily* with the Lord in prayer and reading the Bible is vital to a healthy spiritual life. Spending time *daily* with a spouse and children is vital to the health of a marriage and family. Spending time *daily* using your mind to be creative, to solve problems, and to learn something new is vital to your mental health. Giving *daily* of yourself to others is vital to your emotional health.

in the synagogues and on the corners of the streets, that they may be seen by men. Assuredly, I say to you, they have their reward. ⁶But you, when you pray, go into your room, and when you have shut your door, pray to your Father who *is* in the secret *place;* and your Father who sees in secret will reward you openly.*ª* ⁷And when you pray, do not use vain repetitions as the heathen *do.* For they think that they will be heard for their many words.

⁸"Therefore do not be like them. For your Father knows the things you have need of before you ask Him. ⁹In this manner, therefore, pray:

Our Father in heaven,
Hallowed be Your name.
¹⁰ Your kingdom come.
Your will be done
On earth as *it is* in heaven.
¹¹ Give us this day our daily bread.
¹² And forgive us our debts,
As we forgive our debtors.
¹³ And do not lead us into temptation,
But deliver us from the evil one.

For Yours is the kingdom and the power and the glory forever.
Amen.*ª*

¹⁴"For if you forgive men their trespasses, your heavenly Father will also forgive you. ¹⁵But if you do not forgive men their trespasses, neither will your Father forgive your trespasses.

FASTING TO BE SEEN ONLY BY GOD

¹⁶"Moreover, when you fast, do not be like the hypocrites, with a sad countenance. For they disfigure their faces that they may appear to men to be fasting. Assuredly, I say to you, they have their reward. ¹⁷But you, when you fast, anoint your head and wash your face, ¹⁸so that you do not appear to men to be fasting, but to your Father who *is* in the secret *place;* and your Father who sees in secret will reward you openly.*ª*

LAY UP TREASURES IN HEAVEN

¹⁹"Do not lay up for yourselves treasures on earth, where moth and rust destroy and where thieves break in and steal; ²⁰but lay up for yourselves treasures in heaven, where neither moth nor rust destroys and

> (Matthew 6:16–18)

Biblical Fasting. Fasting in the Bible is usually accompanied by prayer, and at times by doing good works. It is a matter meant to be exclusively between a person and God. The Hebrew word for *fasting (tsum)* means "to cover over"—as in covering the mouth. The Greek word for *fasting (nesteia)* means "to abstain from food."

The ancient Israelites fasted on the Day of Atonement. (See Leviticus 16:29–31.) In other places in the

Bible, people fasted as a sign of mourning (1 Samuel 31:13); as an act of repentance (Daniel 9:3–19); as a means of seeking God on behalf of those who were suffering or sick (2 Samuel 12:16–23); or as a means of clearing the mind in a time of important decision making (2 Chronicles 20:1–18). Fasting was thought to have both spiritual and physical *recuperative* and *therapeutic* value—as a means of cleansing body and soul, and bringing about greater wholeness.

6:6 ªNU-Text omits *openly.*   6:13 ªNU-Text omits *For Yours* through *Amen.*   6:18 ªNU-Text and M-Text omit *openly.*

Yogurt Sauce

Here's a great sauce to use with grilled chicken, lamb, or fish!

Ingredients:

- ☐ 8 ounces yogurt
- ☐ 1 chopped garlic clove
- ☐ 1 tablespoon vinegar
- ☐ ½ teaspoon salt
- ☐ ½ teaspoon cumin
- ☐ 1 cup chopped coriander (cilantro) leaves

Blend all ingredients together well. Chill thoroughly before serving.

than th... ...cubit to his statur...

fi...

things. ...
all these things s... ...
tomorrow, for tomorrow wil... ...
the day *is* its own trouble.

DO NOT JUDGE

7 "Judge not, that you be not judged. ²For with what j... you judge, you will be judged; and with the measure you us..., it will be measured back to you. ³And why do you look at the speck in your brother's eye, but do not consider the plank in your own eye? ⁴Or how can you say to your brother, 'Let me remove the speck from your eye'; and look, a plank *is* in your own eye? ⁵Hypocrite! First remove the plank from your own eye, and then you will see clearly to remove the speck from your brother's eye.

⁶"Do not give what is holy to the dogs; nor cast your pearls before swine, lest they trample them under their feet, and turn and tear you in pieces.

KEEP ASKING, SEEKING, KNOCKING

⁷"Ask, and it will be given to you; seek, and you will find; knock, and it will be opened to you. ⁸For everyone who asks receives, and he who seeks finds, and to him who knocks it will be opened. ⁹Or what man is there among you who, if his son asks for bread, will give him a stone? ¹⁰Or if he asks for a fish, will he give him a serpent? ¹¹If you then, being evil, know how to give good gifts to your children, how much more will your Father who is in heaven give good things to those who ask Him!

where thieves do not break in and steal. ²¹For where your treasure is, there your heart will be also.

THE LAMP OF THE BODY

²²"The lamp of the body is the eye. If therefore your eye is good, your whole body will be full of light. ²³But if your eye is bad, your whole body will be full of darkness. If therefore the light that is in you is darkness, how great *is* that darkness!

YOU CANNOT SERVE GOD AND RICHES

²⁴"No one can serve two masters; for either he will hate the one and love the other, or else he will be loyal to the one and despise the other. You cannot serve God and mammon.

DO NOT WORRY

²⁵"Therefore I say to you, do not worry about your life, what you will eat or what you will drink; nor about your body, what you will put on. Is not life more than food and the body more than clothing? ²⁶Look at the birds of the air, for they neither sow nor reap nor gather into barns; yet your heavenly Father feeds them. Are you not of more value

> **(Matthew 6:22, 23)**

Food Cues. In our culture the strongest impulse to eat comes by way of the eyes. We *see* a television commercial, billboard, supermarket display, or a sign for a restaurant and we begin to *want* the food or beverage offered. What we *perceive* as being good or satisfying is what we will *pursue*. Take stock of what you watch and what you focus your attention on. Your viewing habits, to a great extent, will determine your eating habits, as well as all the other habits in your life.

INSIGHTS INTO THE WORD

Overcoming Anxiety and Worry

OVERCOMING OBSTINATE OBSTACLES • OVERCOMING OBSTINATE OBSTACLES • OVERCOMING OBSTINATE OBSTACLES •

Anxiety is a form of "abiding fear"—a feeling that lingers long after an actual threat has passed. Worry is a form of anxiety that anticipates a *potential* threat. Both anxiety and worry can be chronic or short-term. They can be as intense as a panic attack or as mild as a little fretting. Anxiety can become pathological, leading to an anxiety disorder that may take the form of generalized anxiety (no specific focus), post-traumatic stress disorder (related generally to a specific incident), a panic disorder (overwhelming feelings of terror that may come without warn-

ing), or an obsessive-compulsive disorder (use of repeated rituals to try to rid the mind of an image or disturbing idea). If you struggle with a pathological form of anxiety, seek counseling.

People who worry usually go through a series of "what if" possibilities in their minds—this gives a certain feeling of control that if something has been anticipated, it can be endured. In reality, worriers rarely reach the end of "what if" scenarios, so they are always in a state of anxiety! This anxiety leads to release of stress hormones and the elevated levels of adrenaline and cortisol can eventually cause serious damage in the body.

A key to overcoming worry is learning which worries are productive and which aren't. Write down the things you worry about. Next to each worry identify one practical step that you might take to keep the reality you fear from occurring. For example, if you worry that you are losing touch with a grown child, you might choose to send a funny greeting card to that child—and do it immediately!

Another key to overcoming worry and anxiety is memorizing Bible verses that address anxiety. When you begin to worry, quote one of these verses to yourself and then say: "I will not worry. God's Word is true for me!" Here are three verses and anti-worry lines you might use:

☐ "He who trusts in his riches will fall, But the righteous will flourish like foliage" (Proverbs 11:28). Say: "I will not worry! I will trust in God and I will flourish! God's Word is true for me!"
☐ "Seek first the kingdom of God and His righteousness, and all these things shall be added to you" (Matthew 6:33). Say: "I will not worry! I will seek God's best for me and trust Him to provide all I need. God's Word is true for me!"
☐ "[Cast] all your care upon Him, for He cares for you" (1 Peter 5:7). Say: "I will not worry! God cares about me. God's Word is true for me!"

Finally, when you begin to worry, start to pray! Voice thanksgiving and praise to God, and then ask the Lord to deal with the situation or potential situation about which you are anxious. Ask Him to fill you with His peace.

---

¹²Therefore, whatever you want men to do to you, do also to them, for this is the Law and the Prophets.

THE NARROW WAY

¹³"Enter by the narrow gate; for wide *is* the gate and broad *is* the way that leads to destruction, and there are many who go in by it. ¹⁴Be-cause" narrow *is* the gate and difficult *is* the way which leads to life, and there are few who find it.

YOU WILL KNOW THEM BY THEIR FRUITS

¹⁵"Beware of false prophets, who come to you in sheep's clothing, but inwardly they are ravenous wolves. ¹⁶You will know them by their fruits. Do men gather grapes from thornbushes or figs from thistles? ¹⁷Even so, every good tree bears good fruit, but a bad tree bears bad fruit. ¹⁸A good tree cannot bear bad fruit, nor *can* a bad tree bear good fruit. ¹⁹Every tree that does not bear good fruit is cut down and thrown into the fire. ²⁰Therefore by their fruits you will know them.

I NEVER KNEW YOU

²¹"Not everyone who says to Me, 'Lord, Lord,' shall enter the kingdom of heaven, but he who does the will of My Father in heaven. ²²Many will say to Me in that day, 'Lord, Lord, have we not prophesied in Your name, cast out demons in Your name, and done many wonders in Your name?' ²³And then I will declare to them, 'I never knew you; depart from Me, you who practice lawlessness!'

BUILD ON THE ROCK

²⁴"Therefore whoever hears these sayings of Mine, and does them, I will liken him to a wise man who built his house on the rock: ²⁵and the rain descended, the floods came, and the winds blew and beat on that house; and it did not fall, for it was founded on the rock.

²⁶"But everyone who hears these sayings of Mine, and does not do them, will be like a foolish man who built his house on the sand: ²⁷and the rain descended, the floods came, and the winds blew and beat on that house; and it fell. And great was its fall."

7:14 ªNU-Text and M-Text read *How . . . !*

²⁸And so it was, when Jesus had ended these sayings, that the people were astonished at His teaching, ²⁹for He taught them as one having authority, and not as the scribes.

JESUS CLEANSES A LEPER

8 When He had come down from the mountain, great multitudes followed Him. ²And behold, a leper came and worshiped Him, saying, "Lord, if You are willing, You can make me clean."

³Then Jesus put out *His* hand and touched him, saying, "I am willing; be cleansed." Immediately his leprosy was cleansed.

⁴And Jesus said to him, "See that you tell no one; but go your way, show yourself to the priest, and offer the gift that Moses commanded, as a testimony to them."

JESUS HEALS A CENTURION'S SERVANT

⁵Now when Jesus had entered Capernaum, a centurion came to Him, pleading with Him, ⁶saying, "Lord, my servant is lying at home paralyzed, dreadfully tormented."

⁷And Jesus said to him, "I will come and heal him."

⁸The centurion answered and said, "Lord, I am not worthy that You should come under my roof. But only speak a word, and my servant will be healed. ⁹For I also am a man under authority, having soldiers under me. And I say to this *one,* 'Go,' and he goes; and to another, 'Come,' and he comes; and to my servant, 'Do this,' and he does *it.*"

¹⁰When Jesus heard *it,* He marveled, and said to those who followed, "Assuredly, I say to you, I have not found such great faith, not even in Israel. ¹¹And I say to you that many will come from east and west, and sit down with Abraham, Isaac, and Jacob in the kingdom of heaven. ¹²But the sons of the kingdom will be cast out into outer darkness. There will be weeping and gnashing of teeth." ¹³Then Jesus said to the centurion, "Go your way; and as you have believed, *so* let it be done for you." And his servant was healed that same hour.

PETER'S MOTHER-IN-LAW HEALED

¹⁴Now when Jesus had come into Peter's house, He saw his wife's mother lying sick with a fever. ¹⁵So He touched her hand, and the fever left her. And she arose and served them.ᵃ

MANY HEALED IN THE EVENING

¹⁶When evening had come, they brought to Him many who were demon-possessed. And He cast out the spirits with a word, and healed all who were sick, ¹⁷that it might be fulfilled which was spoken by Isaiah the prophet, saying:

"He Himself took our infirmities
And bore our sicknesses."ᵃ

THE COST OF DISCIPLESHIP

¹⁸And when Jesus saw great multitudes about Him, He gave a command to depart to the other side. ¹⁹Then a certain scribe came and said to Him, "Teacher, I will follow You wherever You go."

²⁰And Jesus said to him, "Foxes have holes and birds of the air *have* nests, but the Son of Man has nowhere to lay *His* head."

Stress Busters
Laugh More!

Are you aware that children laugh an average of 146 times a day, but adults laugh only an average of 4 times a day? Children smile an average of 400 times a day and adults average only 25 times. Most of us need to put more laughter and smiles into our lives! Laughter is one of the best stress busters available to every person. It costs nothing and nobody ever died of an overdose.

Research shows that a good belly laugh can reduce levels of the stress hormone cortisol in the body, and at the same time, increase levels of the feel-good hormone endorphin and dramatically increase the growth hormone (the "youth hormone") as much as 87 percent. Laughter also bolsters the immune system. It can even have an aerobic benefit—a hundred laughs a day can equal ten minutes of rowing or jogging.

Laughter is not just for the body. The brain benefits, too. Laughter and humor allow you to use both sides of your brain simultaneously, and in some studies, people who laughed more were more creative and more flexible in their problem solving.

Have you lost your ability to laugh? Do your best to regain it! Learn to develop a sense of play, to take delight in humorous stories, and to cut out criticism, sarcasm, ridicule, and negative jokes. Find a child or a pet to play with daily. Make an active choice to change your attitude toward work—and yes, it's possible! Begin to see your job as something fun to do. Learn to see the world as a child does—a place to explore and enjoy.

The Bible has it right: "A merry heart does good, like medicine" (Proverbs 17:22).

The LAW AND THE SCIENCE

[DON'T PIG OUT!]

>**SCIENCE**

tells us that pork is a food that digests improperly in the human digestive system—the fat portion of the meat is digested but the remainder of the meat is left to ferment in the intestines. Eating pork products slows down the body's ability to fight diseases and impairs the immune system. Many pork products remain very high in fat, especially ham, bologna, and franks in the luncheon-meats category, as well as bacon, pepperoni, and sausage. In addition, bacon and other pork products are loaded with sodium nitrite, which become nitrosamines in the stomach—one of the most potent cancer-causing agents known to man. A second chemical also used frequently in the processing of meats is polycyclic hydrocarbon, also linked to cancer.

>**THE LAW**

says: "These you shall not eat . . . the swine, though it divides the hoof, having cloven hooves, yet does not chew the cud, is unclean to you. Their flesh you shall not eat, and their carcasses you shall not touch. They are unclean to you" (Leviticus 11:4, 7, 8).

²¹Then another of His disciples said to Him, "Lord, let me first go and bury my father."

²²But Jesus said to him, "Follow Me, and let the dead bury their own dead."

WIND AND WAVE OBEY JESUS

²³Now when He got into a boat, His disciples followed Him. ²⁴And suddenly a great tempest arose on the sea, so that the boat was covered with the waves. But He was asleep. ²⁵Then His disciples came to *Him* and awoke Him, saying, "Lord, save us! We are perishing!"

²⁶But He said to them, "Why are you fearful, O you of little faith?" Then He arose and rebuked the winds and the sea, and there was a great calm. ²⁷So the men marveled, saying, "Who can this be, that even the winds and the sea obey Him?"

TWO DEMON-POSSESSED MEN HEALED

²⁸When He had come to the other side, to the country of the Gergesenes,ᵃ there met Him two demon-possessed *men,* coming out of the tombs, exceedingly fierce, so that no one could pass that way. ²⁹And suddenly they cried out, saying, "What have we to do with You, Jesus, You Son of God? Have You come here to torment us before the time?"

³⁰Now a good way off from them there was a herd of many swine feeding. ³¹So the demons begged Him, saying, "If You cast us out, permit us to go awayᵃ into the herd of swine."

³²And He said to them, "Go." So when they had come out, they went into the herd of swine. And suddenly the whole herd of swine ran violently down the steep place into the sea, and perished in the water. ³³Then those who kept *them* fled; and they went away into the city and told everything, including what *had happened* to the demon-possessed *men.* ³⁴And behold, the whole city came out to meet Jesus. And when they saw Him, they begged *Him* to depart from their region.

JESUS FORGIVES AND HEALS A PARALYTIC

9 So He got into a boat, crossed over, and came to His own city. ²Then behold, they brought to Him a paralytic lying on a bed. When Jesus saw their faith, He said to the paralytic, "Son, be of good cheer; your sins are forgiven you."

³And at once some of the scribes said within themselves, "This Man blasphemes!"

⁴But Jesus, knowing their thoughts, said, "Why do you think evil in your hearts? ⁵For which is easier, to say, 'Your sins are forgiven you,' or to say, 'Arise and walk'? ⁶But that you may know that the Son of Man has power on earth to forgive sins"—then He said to the paralytic, "Arise, take up your bed, and go to your house." ⁷And he arose and departed to his house.

⁸Now when the multitudes saw *it,* they marveledᵃ and glorified God, who had given such power to men.

MATTHEW THE TAX COLLECTOR

⁹As Jesus passed on from there, He saw a man named Matthew sitting at the tax office. And He said to him, "Follow Me." So he arose and followed Him.

¹⁰Now it happened, as Jesus sat at the table in the house, *that* behold, many tax collectors and sinners came and sat down with Him and His disciples. ¹¹And when the Pharisees saw *it,* they said to His disciples, "Why does your Teacher eat with tax collectors and sinners?"

¹²When Jesus heard *that,* He said to them, "Those who are well have no need of a physician, but those who are sick. ¹³But go and learn what *this* means: 'I desire mercy and not sacrifice.'ᵃ For I did not come to call the righteous, but sinners, to repentance."ᵇ

JESUS IS QUESTIONED ABOUT FASTING

¹⁴Then the disciples of John came to Him, saying, "Why do we and the Pharisees fast often,ᵃ but Your disciples do not fast?"

¹⁵And Jesus said to them, "Can the friends of the bridegroom mourn as long as the bridegroom is with them? But the days will come when the bridegroom will be taken away from them, and then they will fast. ¹⁶No one puts a piece of unshrunk cloth on an old garment; for the patch pulls away from the garment, and the tear is made worse. ¹⁷Nor do they put new wine into old wineskins, or else the wineskins break, the wine is spilled, and the wineskins are ruined. But they put new wine into new wineskins, and both are preserved."

8:28 ᵃNU-Text reads *Gadarenes.*   8:31 ᵃNU-Text reads *send us.*   9:8 ᵃNU-Text reads *were afraid.*   9:13 ᵃHosea 6:6   ᵇNU-Text omits *to repentance.*   9:14 ᵃNU-Text brackets *often* as disputed.

January

Let's Celebrate

1   2   3   4   5   6   7

☐ Set goals for the new year! Include goals for your finances, family, and health. Swing into the new year with a healthy eating plan and a new workout regimen. ☐ **Epiphany**—also called Twelfth Night. In traditional churches this is the celebration of the arrival of the wise men in Bethlehem. Light some candles and spend an evening of reflection with your family members or friends about your best memories of this and past holiday seasons. ☐ **Distaff Day and Plow Monday.** These are old English holidays. Women were expected to return to their spinning on January 7, and men to their plowing on the first Monday after Epiphany. Determine in your own heart and mind to "celebrate" the opportunities that God has given you to work—with good physical and emotional health.

8   9   10   11   12   13   14

Now Is the Time To...

☐ Step it up a notch in your workout, especially if you're at a lull in your workout or you've hit a peak in your weight after the holidays. ☐ If your pantry contains items that aren't healthful for you or your family, throw those items out! ☐ Go outdoors and run and play in the snow. ☐ Soak in a whirlpool tub on a cold night.

15   16   17   18   19   20   21

Seasonal Tips

☐ Plant or transplant trees and shrubs while they are dormant.
☐ Begin clearing out your gardening area for the spring.
☐ Prolong the life of your Christmas plants—keep them cool and moist.

22   23   24   25   26   27   28

In the Garden

☐ Protect your trees and shrubs from the snow. ☐ Start thinking about the plants you'll need for the spring. Begin plotting out your spring and summer flower and vegetable gardens.

29   30   31   ## Table Fresh

☐ Serve a fresh green salad with a bowl of lentil soup for lunch or dinner. ☐ Do you have turkey left from holiday feasting? Prepare a big pot of turkey chili! ☐ Add more vegetables to this month's menus. This will provide your digestive system a break from the fats and sweets of holiday snacking and desserts.

SCRIPTURE SOLUTIONS

[COLDS, FLU, AND SINUS INFECTIONS]

According to the New Testament, the Christian's body is "the temple of the Holy Spirit" (1 Corinthians 6:19). Why then, if the body is intended to house the Spirit of the almighty God, are people constantly bombarded with physical attacks such as colds, influenzas, and sinus infections? First, we live in a fallen world in which disease abounds and every person is subject to bacterial and viral attack. We also are subject to excess stress and poor nutrition. To enjoy the health God desires for us, we must practice the principles that are necessary for good health. We may not be able to eliminate all contact with viruses and bacteria, but we can take significant nutritional steps to build up the body's immunity to fight these attackers, and we *can* pursue good nutrition and eliminate stress.

Here are some ways to improve immunity:

☐ Eliminate or greatly lower sugar intake. Consumption of sugar can lower immunity. Although it is obvious to avoid cakes and cookies when watching sugar intake, we must also watch out for sugar as a hidden ingredient in many condiments and breads, as well a common ingredient in most processed foods.

☐ Eliminate bad fats in the diet, primarily hydrogenated and partially hydrogenated fats. Avoid the following:

- Vegetable shortening
- Margarine
- Fried foods
- Many salad dressings
- Cakes, pies, and cookies
- Most processed foods

☐ Like Mom said, "Eat your vegetables!" Each day we should be eating at least five servings of fruits and vegetables. When possible, select items that are organically grown, and eat the freshest produce available.

Also remember to wash your hands frequently, take a comprehensive multivitamin or mineral supplement on a daily basis, get enough rest, and continually look to Jesus Christ as your Healer and strength.

A GIRL RESTORED TO LIFE AND A WOMAN HEALED

¹⁸While He spoke these things to them, behold, a ruler came and worshiped Him, saying, "My daughter has just died, but come and lay Your hand on her and she will live." ¹⁹So Jesus arose and followed him, and so *did* His disciples.

²⁰And suddenly, a woman who had a flow of blood for twelve years came from behind and touched the hem of His garment. ²¹For she said to herself, "If only I may touch His garment, I shall be made well." ²²But Jesus turned around, and when He saw her He said, "Be of good cheer, daughter; your faith has made you well." And the woman was made well from that hour.

²³When Jesus came into the ruler's house, and saw the flute players and the noisy crowd wailing, ²⁴He said to them, "Make room, for the girl is not dead, but sleeping." And they ridiculed Him. ²⁵But when the crowd was put outside, He went in and took her by the hand, and the girl arose. ²⁶And the report of this went out into all that land.

TWO BLIND MEN HEALED

²⁷When Jesus departed from there, two blind men followed Him, crying out and saying, "Son of David, have mercy on us!"

²⁸And when He had come into the house, the blind men came to Him. And Jesus said to them, "Do you believe that I am able to do this?"

They said to Him, "Yes, Lord."

²⁹Then He touched their eyes, saying, "According to your faith let it be to you." ³⁰And their eyes were opened. And Jesus sternly warned them, saying, "See *that* no one knows *it*." ³¹But when they had departed, they spread the news about Him in all that country.

A MUTE MAN SPEAKS

³²As they went out, behold, they brought to Him a man, mute and demon-possessed. ³³And when the demon was cast out, the mute spoke. And the multitudes marveled, saying, "It was never seen like this in Israel!"

³⁴But the Pharisees said, "He casts out demons by the ruler of the demons."

THE COMPASSION OF JESUS

³⁵Then Jesus went about all the cities and villages, teaching in their synagogues, preaching the gospel of the kingdom, and healing every sickness and every disease among the people.ᵃ ³⁶But when He saw the multitudes, He was moved with compassion for them, because they were wearyᵃ and scattered, like sheep having no shepherd. ³⁷Then He said to His disciples, "The harvest truly *is* plentiful, but the laborers *are* few. ³⁸Therefore pray the Lord of the harvest to send out laborers into His harvest."

THE TWELVE APOSTLES

10 And when He had called His twelve disciples to *Him*, He gave them power *over* unclean spirits, to cast them out, and to heal all kinds of sickness and all kinds of disease. ²Now the names of the twelve apostles are these: first, Simon, who is

9:35 ᵃNU-Text omits *among the people.*   9:36 ᵃNU-Text and M-Text read *harassed.*

Kitchen Gardens

Bible Health + Food Facts

During New Testament times, most rural and village families had kitchen gardens. The people grew a wide variety of produce, including onions, beans, leeks, peppers, and melons.

called Peter, and Andrew his brother; James the *son* of Zebedee, and John his brother; ³Philip and Bartholomew; Thomas and Matthew the tax collector; James the *son* of Alphaeus, and Lebbaeus, whose surname was^a Thaddaeus; ⁴Simon the Cananite,^a and Judas Iscariot, who also betrayed Him.

SENDING OUT THE TWELVE

⁵These twelve Jesus sent out and commanded them, saying: "Do not go into the way of the Gentiles, and do not enter a city of the Samaritans. ⁶But go rather to the lost sheep of the house of Israel. ⁷And as you go, preach, saying, 'The kingdom of heaven is at hand.' ⁸Heal the sick, cleanse the lepers, raise the dead,^a cast out demons. Freely you have received, freely give. ⁹Provide neither gold nor silver nor copper in your money belts, ¹⁰nor bag for *your* journey, nor two tunics, nor sandals, nor staffs; for a worker is worthy of his food.

¹¹"Now whatever city or town you enter, inquire who in it is worthy, and stay there till you go out. ¹²And when you go into a household, greet it. ¹³If the household is worthy, let your peace come upon it. But if it is not worthy, let your peace return to you. ¹⁴And whoever will not receive you nor hear your words, when you depart from that house or city, shake off the dust from your feet. ¹⁵Assuredly, I say to you, it will be more tolerable for the land of Sodom and Gomorrah in the day of judgment than for that city!

PERSECUTIONS ARE COMING

¹⁶"Behold, I send you out as sheep in the midst of wolves. Therefore be wise as serpents and harmless as doves. ¹⁷But beware of men, for they will deliver you up to councils and scourge you in their synagogues. ¹⁸You will be brought before governors and kings for My sake, as a testimony to them and to the Gentiles. ¹⁹But when they deliver you up, do not worry about how or what you should speak. For it will be given to you in that hour what you should speak; ²⁰for it is not you who speak, but the Spirit of your Father who speaks in you.

²¹"Now brother will deliver up brother to death, and a father *his* child; and children will rise up against parents and cause them to be put to death. ²²And you will be hated by all for My name's sake. But he who endures to the end will be saved. ²³When they persecute you in this city, flee to another. For assuredly, I say to you, you will not have gone through the cities of Israel before the Son of Man comes.

²⁴"A disciple is not above *his* teacher, nor a servant above his master. ²⁵It is enough for a disciple that he be like his teacher, and a servant like his master. If they have called the master of the house Beelzebub,^a how much more *will they call* those of his household! ²⁶Therefore do not fear them. For there is nothing covered that will not be revealed, and hidden that will not be known.

JESUS TEACHES THE FEAR OF GOD

²⁷"Whatever I tell you in the dark, speak in the light; and what you hear in the ear, preach on the housetops. ²⁸And do not fear those who kill the body but cannot kill the soul. But rather fear Him who is able to destroy both soul and body in hell. ²⁹Are not two sparrows sold for a copper coin? And not one of them falls to the ground apart from your Father's will. ³⁰But the very hairs of your head are all numbered. ³¹Do not fear therefore; you are of more value than many sparrows.

CONFESS CHRIST BEFORE MEN

³²"Therefore whoever confesses Me before men, him I will also confess before My Father who is in heaven. ³³But whoever denies Me before men, him I will also deny before My Father who is in heaven.

CHRIST BRINGS DIVISION

³⁴"Do not think that I came to bring peace on earth. I did not come to

WISE CHOICES

Choose the right vitamin E. Choose d-tocopherol vitamin E, which is made from vegetable oils. All of the scientific studies that show health benefits from vitamin E for the heart were based on d-tocopherol studies. Another form of vitamin E, dl-tocopherol, is readily available and is cheaper, but it is made from petroleum products. To remember which to buy, think *L* for lousy—and avoid the dl-tocopherol products.

10:3 ^aNU-Text omits *Lebbaeus, whose surname was.*   10:4 ^aNU-Text reads *Cananaean.*   10:8 ^aNU-Text reads *raise the dead, cleanse the lepers;* M-Text omits *raise the dead.*   10:25 ^aNU-Text and M-Text read *Beelzebul.*

walking the walk

[ALL DRESSED UP FOR A WALK]

The good news about walking as an exercise is that it requires very little equipment. There are some basics, however:

☐ Wear shoes designed for walking exercise. They are worth the investment.

☐ Dress appropriately for the weather. You may want to dress in layers so that as you exercise and become warmed up, you can shed an outer garment and wrap it around your waist.

☐ Dress appropriately for the time of day. If you are walking before dawn or after sunset, have a strip of reflective tape on your clothing so others can readily see you.

☐ Carry your name and an emergency phone number with you. It's also a good idea to have money for a phone call, or to carry a cell phone with you.

bring peace but a sword. ³⁵For I have come to 'set a man against his father, a daughter against her mother, and a daughter-in-law against her mother-in-law'; ³⁶and 'a man's enemies will be those of his own household.'ᵃ ³⁷He who loves father or mother more than Me is not worthy of Me. And he who loves son or daughter more than Me is not worthy of Me. ³⁸And he who does not take his cross and follow after Me is not worthy of Me. ³⁹He who finds his life will lose it, and he who loses his life for My sake will find it.

A CUP OF COLD WATER

⁴⁰"He who receives you receives Me, and he who receives Me receives Him who sent Me. ⁴¹He who receives a prophet in the name of a prophet shall receive a prophet's reward. And he who receives a righteous man in the name of a righteous man shall receive a righteous man's reward. ⁴²And whoever gives one of these little ones only a cup of cold *water* in the name of a disciple, assuredly, I say to you, he shall by no means lose his reward."

JOHN THE BAPTIST SENDS MESSENGERS TO JESUS

11 Now it came to pass, when Jesus finished commanding His twelve disciples, that He departed from there to teach and to preach in their cities.

²And when John had heard in prison about the works of Christ, he sent two ofᵇ his disciples ³and said to Him, "Are You the Coming One, or do we look for another?"

⁴Jesus answered and said to them, "Go and tell John the things which you hear and see: ⁵*The* blind see and *the* lame walk; *the* lepers are cleansed and *the* deaf hear; *the* dead are raised up and *the* poor have the gospel preached to them. ⁶And blessed is he who is not offended because of Me."

⁷As they departed, Jesus began to say to the multitudes concerning John: "What did you go out into the wilderness to see? A reed shaken by the wind? ⁸But what did you go out to see? A man clothed in soft garments? Indeed, those who wear soft *clothing* are in kings' houses. ⁹But what did you go out to see? A prophet? Yes, I say to you, and more than a prophet. ¹⁰For this is *he* of whom it is written:

'Behold, I send My messenger before Your face,
Who will prepare Your way before You.'ᵃ

¹¹"Assuredly, I say to you, among those born of women there has not risen one greater than John the Baptist; but he who is least in the kingdom of heaven is greater than he. ¹²And from the days of John the Baptist until now the kingdom of heaven suffers violence, and the violent take it by force. ¹³For all the prophets and the law prophesied until John. ¹⁴And if you are willing to receive *it*, he is Elijah who is to come. ¹⁵He who has ears to hear, let him hear!

¹⁶"But to what shall I liken this generation? It is like children sitting in the marketplaces and calling to their companions, ¹⁷and saying:

'We played the flute for you,
And you did not dance;
We mourned to you,
And you did not lament.'

¹⁸For John came neither eating nor drinking, and they say, 'He has a demon.' ¹⁹The Son of Man came eating and drinking, and they say, 'Look, a glutton and a winebibber, a friend of tax collectors and sinners!' But wisdom is justified by her children."ᵃ

WOE TO THE IMPENITENT CITIES

²⁰Then He began to rebuke the cities in which most of His mighty works had been done, because they did not repent: ²¹"Woe to you, Chorazin! Woe to you, Bethsaida! For if the mighty works which were done in you had been done in Tyre and Sidon, they would have repented long ago in sackcloth and ashes. ²²But I say to you, it will be more tolerable for Tyre and Sidon in the day of judgment than for you. ²³And you, Capernaum, who are exalted to heaven, will beᵃ brought down to Hades; for if the mighty works which were done in you had been done in Sodom, it would have remained until this day. ²⁴But I say

---

10:36 ᵃMicah 7:6   11:2 ᵃNU-Text reads *by* for *two of.*   11:10 ᵃMalachi 3:1   11:19 ᵃNU-Text reads *works.*   11:23 ᵃNU-Text reads *will you be exalted to heaven? No, you will be.*

to you that it shall be more tolerable for the land of Sodom in the day of judgment than for you."

JESUS GIVES TRUE REST

²⁵At that time Jesus answered and said, "I thank You, Father, Lord of heaven and earth, that You have hidden these things from *the* wise and prudent and have revealed them to babes. ²⁶Even so, Father, for so it seemed good in Your sight. ²⁷All things have been delivered to Me by My Father, and no one knows the Son except the Father. Nor does anyone know the Father except the Son, and *the one* to whom the Son wills to reveal *Him*. ²⁸Come to Me, all *you* who labor and are heavy laden, and I will give you rest. ²⁹Take My yoke upon you and learn from Me, for I am gentle and lowly in heart, and you will find rest for your souls. ³⁰For My yoke *is* easy and My burden is light."

JESUS IS LORD OF THE SABBATH

12 At that time Jesus went through the grainfields on the Sabbath. And His disciples were hungry, and began to pluck heads of grain and to eat. ²And when the Pharisees saw *it*, they said to Him, "Look, Your disciples are doing what is not lawful to do on the Sabbath!"

³But He said to them, "Have you not read what David did when he was hungry, he and those who were with him: ⁴how he entered the house of God and ate the showbread which was not lawful for him to eat, nor for those who were with him, but only for the priests? ⁵Or have you not read in the law that on the Sabbath the priests in the temple profane the Sabbath, and are blameless? ⁶Yet I say to you that in this place there is *One* greater than the temple. ⁷But if you had known what *this* means, 'I desire mercy and not sacrifice,'ᵃ you would not have condemned the guiltless. ⁸For the Son of Man is Lord evenᵃ of the Sabbath."

HEALING ON THE SABBATH

⁹Now when He had departed from there, He went into their synagogue. ¹⁰And behold, there was a man who had a withered hand. And they asked Him, saying, "Is it lawful to heal on the Sabbath?"—that they might accuse Him.

¹¹Then He said to them, "What man is there among you who has one sheep, and if it falls into a pit on the Sabbath, will not lay hold of it and lift *it* out? ¹²Of how much more value then is a man than a sheep? Therefore it is lawful to do good on the Sabbath." ¹³Then He said to the man, "Stretch out your hand." And he stretched *it* out, and it was restored as whole as the other. ¹⁴Then the Pharisees went out and plotted against Him, how they might destroy Him.

BEHOLD, MY SERVANT

¹⁵But when Jesus knew *it*, He withdrew from there. And great multitudesᵃ followed Him, and He healed them all. ¹⁶Yet He warned them not to make Him known, ¹⁷that it might be fulfilled which was spoken by Isaiah the prophet, saying:

¹⁸ "Behold! My Servant whom I have chosen,
     My Beloved in whom My soul is well pleased!
     I will put My Spirit upon Him,
     And He will declare justice to the Gentiles.
¹⁹ He will not quarrel nor cry out,
     Nor will anyone hear His voice in the streets.
²⁰ A bruised reed He will not break,
     And smoking flax He will not quench,
     Till He sends forth justice to victory;
²¹ And in His name Gentiles will trust."ᵃ

GODLY & GOODLOOKIN'

Vitamin-ize Your Lotions

Vitamin E is a very beneficial antioxidant and cellular healer that the skin can absorb. The pure oil is great for treating scars, skin rashes, burns, and as a moisturizer. Try adding 32,000 IU of pure vitamin E oil to four ounces of 100 percent pure cold-pressed jojoba oil, or to a moisturizing lotion or cream. Or, you might squeeze ten to twenty softgels of 400 IU Vitamin E into your favorite lotion. Spread this mixture on your entire face, neck and arms at night. It is oily but absorbs quickly. In the morning, you'll have soft, moist skin. Women, consider rubbing this mixture on your legs after you have shaved. Men, try this instead of aftershave lotion.

Vitamin A is also great added to your vitamin E lotion—ten to twenty vitamin A softgels (25,000 IU) to the mixture above. The smell might be a little fishy but vitamin A is a key vitamin for skin health. (Don't use vitamin A from cod liver oil—that's *too* fishy.)

Some skin ingredients now include vitamins A, E, and C. Look for them!

12:7 ᵃHosea 6:6   12:8 ᵃNU-Text and M-Text omit *even*.   12:15 ᵃNU-Text brackets *multitudes* as disputed.   12:21 ᵃIsaiah 42:1–4

♀ Women's Issues
Childbirth and Nursing

The bearing of children was considered a tremendous blessing in Bible times. Women were expected to bear children if at all possible, and mothers were to be respected and obeyed by their children (Exodus 20:12). One of the most powerful illustrations of God's care for His people is found in these words from Isaiah 49:15:

> Can a woman forget her nursing child,
> And not have compassion on the son of her womb?
> Surely they may forget,
> Yet I will not forget you.

The Bible says that the discomfort of pregnancy and the pain of childbirth are more than compensated by the "joy that a human being has been born into the world" (John 16:21).

Childbirth in Bible times was often aided by midwives and involved the use of a birthing stool (Genesis 35:17; Exodus 1:15). Women gave birth more in a sitting/squatting position than lying down. Native Americans and many other tribal people around the world also use a birthing stool. The only downside to this appears to be a greater possibility that a woman will experience a tearing of the uterus and vaginal tissues.

It was considered normal for a mother to nurse her child, usually until the child was at least three years old. (See the example of Hannah with her son Samuel in 1 Samuel 1:22–24.) CONT. NEXT PAGE>>>

A HOUSE DIVIDED CANNOT STAND

²²Then one was brought to Him who was demon-possessed, blind and mute; and He healed him, so that the blind and*ᵃ* mute man both spoke and saw. ²³And all the multitudes were amazed and said, "Could this be the Son of David?"

²⁴Now when the Pharisees heard *it* they said, "This *fellow* does not cast out demons except by Beelzebub,*ᵃ* the ruler of the demons."

²⁵But Jesus knew their thoughts, and said to them: "Every kingdom divided against itself is brought to desolation, and every city or house divided against itself will not stand. ²⁶If Satan casts out Satan, he is divided against himself. How then will his kingdom stand? ²⁷And if I cast out demons by Beelzebub, by whom do your sons cast *them* out? Therefore they shall be your judges. ²⁸But if I cast out demons by the Spirit of God, surely the kingdom of God has come upon you. ²⁹Or how can one enter a strong man's house and plunder his goods, unless he first binds the strong man? And then he will plunder his house. ³⁰He who is not with Me is against Me, and he who does not gather with Me scatters abroad.

THE UNPARDONABLE SIN

³¹"Therefore I say to you, every sin and blasphemy will be forgiven men, but the blasphemy *against* the Spirit will not be forgiven men. ³²Anyone who speaks a word against the Son of Man, it will be forgiven him; but whoever speaks against the Holy Spirit, it will not be forgiven him, either in this age or in the *age* to come.

A TREE KNOWN BY ITS FRUIT

³³"Either make the tree good and its fruit good, or else make the tree bad and its fruit bad; for a tree is known by *its* fruit. ³⁴Brood of vipers! How can you, being evil, speak good things? For out of the abundance of the heart the mouth speaks. ³⁵A good man out of the good treasure of his heart*ᵃ* brings forth good things, and an evil man out of the evil treasure brings forth evil things. ³⁶But I say to you that for every idle word men may speak, they will give account of it in the day of judgment. ³⁷For by your words you will be justified, and by your words you will be condemned."

THE SCRIBES AND PHARISEES ASK FOR A SIGN

³⁸Then some of the scribes and Pharisees answered, saying, "Teacher, we want to see a sign from You."

³⁹But He answered and said to them, "An evil and adulterous generation seeks after a sign, and no sign will be given to it except the sign of the prophet Jonah. ⁴⁰For as Jonah was three days and three nights in the belly of the great fish, so will the Son of Man be three days and three nights in the heart of the earth. ⁴¹The men of Nineveh will rise up in the judgment with this generation and condemn it, because they repented at the preaching of Jonah; and indeed a greater than Jonah *is* here. ⁴²The queen of the South will rise up in the judgment with this generation and condemn it, for she came from the ends of the earth to hear the wisdom of Solomon; and indeed a greater than Solomon *is* here.

12:22 ᵃNU-Text omits *blind and.*   12:24 ᵃNU-Text and M-Text read *Beelzebul.*   12:35 ᵃNU-Text and M-Text omit *of his heart.*

Women's Issues Cont.>>>

If a mother died or was not be able to produce enough milk for her child, "wet nurses" were used to feed babies in Bible times. Moses was given to a wet nurse after Pharaoh's daughter found him floating in the Nile River. Fortunately for Moses, that wet nurse was his real mother! (See Exodus 2:1–9.) It wasn't until the twentieth century that formulas were manufactured for feeding infants.

Breast-feeding and weaning are mentioned several times in the Bible. Breast-feeding was regarded as a means of bonding a mother and child (Isaiah 66:11). It was considered a natural form of birth control. (See the example of Gomer in Hosea 2.) While a woman is breast-feeding, her ovulation is usually suppressed—although this isn't always the case! Women *can* become pregnant while breast-feeding.

Weaning was regarded as a time for celebrating a milestone in a child's life (Genesis 21:8). It was after weaning that a child was expected to receive teaching (Isaiah 28:9).

AN UNCLEAN SPIRIT RETURNS

43"When an unclean spirit goes out of a man, he goes through dry places, seeking rest, and finds none. 44Then he says, 'I will return to my house from which I came.' And when he comes, he finds *it* empty, swept, and put in order. 45Then he goes and takes with him seven other spirits more wicked than himself, and they enter and dwell there; and the last *state* of that man is worse than the first. So shall it also be with this wicked generation."

JESUS' MOTHER AND BROTHERS SEND FOR HIM

46While He was still talking to the multitudes, behold, His mother and brothers stood outside, seeking to speak with Him. 47Then one said to Him, "Look, Your mother and Your brothers are standing outside, seeking to speak with You."

48But He answered and said to the one who told Him, "Who is My mother and who are My brothers?" 49And He stretched out His hand toward His disciples and said, "Here are My mother and My brothers! 50For whoever does the will of My Father in heaven is My brother and sister and mother."

THE PARABLE OF THE SOWER

13 On the same day Jesus went out of the house and sat by the sea. 2And great multitudes were gathered together to Him, so that He got into a boat and sat; and the whole multitude stood on the shore.

3Then He spoke many things to them in parables, saying: "Behold, a sower went out to sow. 4And as he sowed, some *seed* fell by the wayside; and the birds came and devoured them. 5Some fell on stony places, where they did not have much earth; and they immediately sprang up because they had no depth of earth. 6But when the sun was up they were scorched, and because they had no root they withered away. 7And some fell among thorns, and the thorns sprang up and choked them. 8But others fell on good ground and yielded a crop: some a hundredfold, some sixty, some thirty. 9He who has ears to hear, let him hear!"

THE PURPOSE OF PARABLES

10And the disciples came and said to Him, "Why do You speak to them in parables?"

11He answered and said to them, "Because it has been given to you to know the mysteries of the kingdom of heaven, but to them it has not been given. 12For whoever has, to him more will be given, and he will have abundance; but whoever does not have, even what he has will be taken away from him. 13Therefore I speak to them in parables, because seeing they do not see, and hearing they do not hear, nor do they understand. 14And in them the prophecy of Isaiah is fulfilled, which says:

'Hearing you will hear and shall not understand,
And seeing you will see and not perceive;
15 For the hearts of this people have grown dull.
Their ears are hard of hearing,
And their eyes they have closed,
Lest they should see with their eyes and hear with their ears,
Lest they should understand with their hearts and turn,
So that I should^a heal
them.'^b

16But blessed *are* your eyes for they see, and your ears for they hear; 17for assuredly, I say to you that many prophets and righteous *men* desired to see what you see, and did not see *it*, and to hear what you hear, and did not hear *it*.

THE PARABLE OF THE SOWER EXPLAINED

18"Therefore hear the parable of the sower: 19When anyone hears the word of the kingdom, and does not understand *it*, then the wicked *one* comes and snatches away what was sown in his heart. This is he who received seed by the wayside. 20But he who received the seed on stony places, this is he who hears the word and immediately receives it with joy; 21yet he

WISE CHOICES

Choose fresh vegetables over canned vegetables. Fresh vegetables have more valuable potassium and other nutrients—and less sodium—than canned vegetables.

13:15 ^aNU-Text and M-Text read *would*. ^bIsaiah 6:9, 10

has no root in himself, but endures only for a while. For when tribulation or persecution arises because of the word, immediately he stumbles. ²²Now he who received seed among the thorns is he who hears the word, and the cares of this world and the deceitfulness of riches choke the word, and he becomes unfruitful. ²³But he who received seed on the good ground is he who hears the word and understands *it*, who indeed bears fruit and produces: some a hundredfold, some sixty, some thirty."

THE PARABLE OF THE WHEAT AND THE TARES

²⁴Another parable He put forth to them, saying: "The kingdom of heaven is like a man who sowed good seed in his field; ²⁵but while men slept, his enemy came and sowed tares among the wheat and went his way. ²⁶But when the grain had sprouted and produced a crop, then the tares also appeared. ²⁷So the servants of the owner came and said to him, 'Sir, did you not sow good seed in your field? How then does it have tares?' ²⁸He said to them, 'An enemy has done this.' The servants said to him, 'Do you want us then to go and gather them up?' ²⁹But he said, 'No, lest while you gather up the tares you also uproot the wheat with them. ³⁰Let both grow together until the harvest, and at the time of harvest I will say to the reapers, "First gather together the tares and bind them in bundles to burn them, but gather the wheat into my barn." ' "

THE PARABLE OF THE MUSTARD SEED

³¹Another parable He put forth to them, saying: "The kingdom of heaven is like a mustard seed, which a man took and sowed in his field, ³²which indeed is the least of all the seeds; but when it is grown it is greater than the herbs and becomes a tree, so that the birds of the air come and nest in its branches."

THE PARABLE OF THE LEAVEN

³³Another parable He spoke to them: "The kingdom of heaven is like leaven, which a woman took and hid in three measures" of meal till it was all leavened."

PROPHECY AND THE PARABLES

³⁴All these things Jesus spoke to the multitude in parables; and without a parable He did not speak to them, ³⁵that it might be fulfilled which was spoken by the prophet, saying:

"I will open My mouth in parables;
I will utter things kept secret from the
    foundation of the world."ᵃ

THE PARABLE OF THE TARES EXPLAINED

³⁶Then Jesus sent the multitude away and went into the house. And His disciples came to Him, saying, "Explain to us the parable of the tares of the field."

Flee, Fight, or Stew

ULTIMATE HEALTH RESOURCE • ULTIMATE HEALTH RESOURCE • ULTIMATE HEALTH RESOURCE •

God, our Creator, has built into each one of us a remarkable mechanism for staying alive. Even if we do not consciously activate this mechanism, our bodies respond intuitively and instinctively to danger. We were designed to flee or to fight.

☐ *Flee*—get away *now!*
☐ *Fight*—stand and fight to *win!*

This flee-or-fight mechanism was designed by God to work quickly. When we take the position of just coping with danger, we are messing with God's plan. Those who attempt to cope with danger often end of "stewing" in their own mixed emotions. Perhaps they know they *should* flee but they choose instead to accommodate the danger. Or, perhaps they know they *should* fight but they simply lack the courage to fight in a definitively winner-takes-all manner.

The hormones that were designed to be released quickly and for a very limited time become something of a drip, drip, drip into the body's system. That steady drip can raise cortisol levels, and in turn, lead to serious physical ailments.

What was your usual response to crisis situations you have encountered?

☐ Those who *flee* remove themselves physically and emotionally from the immediate situation as quickly as possible.
☐ Those who *fight* stay where they are and stand up for themselves or face the situation head-on.
☐ Those who *stew* may flee or fight in the short term, but discover later that they are reliving the event and experiencing the emotions they felt at the time of the event.

If you routinely stew, recognize that you are setting yourself up for a chronic stress response!

13:33 ᵃGreek *sata*, approximately two pecks in all   13:35 ᵃPsalm 78:2

³⁷He answered and said to them: "He who sows the good seed is the Son of Man. ³⁸The field is the world, the good seeds are the sons of the kingdom, but the tares are the sons of the wicked *one*. ³⁹The enemy who sowed them is the devil, the harvest is the end of the age, and the reapers are the angels. ⁴⁰Therefore as the tares are gathered and burned in the fire, so it will be at the end of this age. ⁴¹The Son of Man will send out His angels, and they will gather out of His kingdom all things that offend, and those who practice lawlessness, ⁴²and will cast them into the furnace of fire. There will be wailing and gnashing of teeth. ⁴³Then the righteous will shine forth as the sun in the kingdom of their Father. He who has ears to hear, let him hear!

THE PARABLE OF THE HIDDEN TREASURE

⁴⁴"Again, the kingdom of heaven is like treasure hidden in a field, which a man found and hid; and for joy over it he goes and sells all that he has and buys that field.

THE PARABLE OF THE PEARL OF GREAT PRICE

⁴⁵"Again, the kingdom of heaven is like a merchant seeking beautiful pearls, ⁴⁶who, when he had found one pearl of great price, went and sold all that he had and bought it.

THE PARABLE OF THE DRAGNET

⁴⁷"Again, the kingdom of heaven is like a dragnet that was cast into the sea and gathered some of every kind, ⁴⁸which, when it was full, they drew to shore; and they sat down and gathered the good into vessels, but threw the bad away. ⁴⁹So it will be at the end of the age. The angels will come forth, separate the wicked from among the just, ⁵⁰and cast them into the furnace of fire. There will be wailing and gnashing of teeth."

⁵¹Jesus said to them,^a "Have you understood all these things?"

They said to Him, "Yes, Lord."^b

⁵²Then He said to them, "Therefore every scribe instructed concerning^a the kingdom of heaven is like a householder who brings out of his treasure *things* new and old."

JESUS REJECTED AT NAZARETH

⁵³Now it came to pass, when Jesus had finished these parables, that He departed from there. ⁵⁴When He had come to His own country, He taught them in their synagogue, so that they were astonished and said, "Where did this *Man* get this wisdom and *these* mighty works? ⁵⁵Is this not the carpenter's son? Is not His mother called Mary? And His brothers James, Joses,^a Simon, and Judas? ⁵⁶And His sisters, are they not all with us? Where then did this *Man* get all these things?" ⁵⁷So they were offended at Him.

But Jesus said to them, "A prophet is not without honor except in his own country and in his own house." ⁵⁸Now He did not do many mighty works there because of their unbelief.

JOHN THE BAPTIST BEHEADED

14 At that time Herod the tetrarch heard the report about Jesus ²and said to his servants, "This is John the Baptist; he is risen from the dead, and therefore these powers are

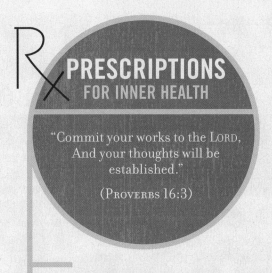

PRESCRIPTIONS FOR INNER HEALTH

"Commit your works to the LORD, And your thoughts will be established."

(PROVERBS 16:3)

Once you really know what it is that the Lord has assigned for you to do in any given area or task—an assignment in accordance with His Word and in keeping with your talents, personality, and skills—your thoughts will be *focused*. You'll find it easier to plan and schedule, and you will be much more productive.

at work in him." ³For Herod had laid hold of John and bound him, and put *him* in prison for the sake of Herodias, his brother Philip's wife. ⁴Because John had said to him, "It is not lawful for you to have her." ⁵And although he wanted to put him to death, he feared the multitude, because they counted him as a prophet.

⁶But when Herod's birthday was celebrated, the daughter of Herodias danced before them and pleased Herod. ⁷Therefore he promised with an oath to give her whatever she might ask.

⁸So she, having been prompted by her mother, said, "Give me John the Baptist's head here on a platter."

⁹And the king was sorry; nevertheless, because of the oaths and because of those who sat with him, he commanded *it* to be given to *her*. ¹⁰So he sent and had John beheaded in prison. ¹¹And his head was brought on a platter and given to the girl, and she brought *it* to her mother. ¹²Then his disciples came and took away the body and buried it, and went and told Jesus.

FEEDING THE FIVE THOUSAND

¹³When Jesus heard *it*, He departed from there by boat to a deserted place by Himself. But when the multitudes heard it, they followed Him on foot from the cities. ¹⁴And when Jesus went out He saw a great multitude; and He was moved with compassion for them, and healed their sick. ¹⁵When it was evening, His disciples came to Him, saying, "This is a deserted place, and the hour is already late. Send the multitudes away, that they may go into the villages and buy themselves food."

13:51 ^aNU-Text omits *Jesus said to them*. ^bNU-Text omits *Lord*. 13:52 ^aOr *for* 13:55 ^aNU-Text reads *Joseph*.

PEOPLE CALLED "BEAUTIFUL" IN THE BIBLE

Beautiful and Desirable

Only a very few people in the Bible are described as beautiful or handsome. Women described as beautiful are Abigail, Sarah, Rebekah, Rachel, Bathsheba, Tamar, Vashti, and Esther. Men described as being of handsome or distinguished in appearance include David, Saul, and Absalom. The stories of these people cover far more than the fact that they were of beautiful countenance. If anything, they are examples that people who are "good-looking" are as complex in personality and as prone to flaws as those who are not beautiful or handsome.

At the same time, the Bible clearly recognizes that being beautiful is a part of what makes a woman attractive to a man so that he might want to marry her. Being handsome as a man also seems to have had some "political merit." Certainly we see both of these social conclusions in place today. Men want to marry supermodels; voters seem more prone to vote for good-looking politicians!

A little-known law in the Bible covers the rules for how the Israelites were to treat beautiful women they might take captive after a war. Deuteronomy 21:10–14 says:

When you go out to war against your enemies, and the LORD your God delivers them into your hand, and you take them captive, and you see among the captives a beautiful woman, and desire her and would take her for your wife, then you shall bring her home to your house, and she shall shave her head and trim her nails. She shall put off the clothes of her captivity, remain in your house, and mourn her father and her mother a full month; after that you may go in to her and be her husband, and she shall be your wife. And it shall be, if you have no delight in her, then you shall set her free, but you certainly shall not sell her for money; you shall not treat her brutally, because you have humbled her.

These rules were set up so that a captive female would have time to mourn the loss of her home and relatives. To have her head shaved and nails trimmed were acts associated with mourning. Putting on the clothing of the Israelites was a sign of identification with her new family. It was only after a full month of mourning that a captive woman could enter into sexual relations with her husband. This law helped restrain Jewish men from rape. If the man no longer desired the woman during the mourning period, he could dismiss her, but not sell her, thus keeping some degree of her esteem intact. The full month of mourning not only allowed the woman time to adjust to a new reality and home situation, but also allowed the man time for his lust to cool and for him to reappraise his desire for a "beautiful captive."

[16]But Jesus said to them, "They do not need to go away. You give them something to eat."

[17]And they said to Him, "We have here only five loaves and two fish."

[18]He said, "Bring them here to Me." [19]Then He commanded the multitudes to sit down on the grass. And He took the five loaves and the two fish, and looking up to heaven, He blessed and broke and gave the loaves to the disciples; and the disciples gave to the multitudes. [20]So they all ate and were filled, and they took up twelve baskets full of the fragments that remained. [21]Now those who had eaten were about five thousand men, besides women and children.

JESUS WALKS ON THE SEA

[22]Immediately Jesus made His disciples get into the boat and go before Him to the other side, while He sent the multitudes away. [23]And when He had sent the multitudes away, He went up on the mountain by Himself to pray. Now when evening came, He was alone there. [24]But the boat was now in the middle of the sea,[a] tossed by the waves, for the wind was contrary.

[25]Now in the fourth watch of the night Jesus went to them, walking on the sea. [26]And when the disciples saw Him walking on the sea, they were troubled, saying, "It is a ghost!" And they cried out for fear.

[27]But immediately Jesus spoke to them, saying, "Be of good cheer! It is I; do not be afraid."

[28]And Peter answered Him and said, "Lord, if it is You, command me to come to You on the water."

[29]So He said, "Come." And when Peter had come down out of the boat, he walked on the water to go to Jesus. [30]But when he saw that the wind *was* boisterous,[a] he was afraid; and beginning to sink he cried out, saying, "Lord, save me!"

[31]And immediately Jesus stretched out *His* hand and caught him, and said to him, "O you of little faith, why did you doubt?" [32]And when they got into the boat, the wind ceased.

[33]Then those who were in the boat came and[a] worshiped Him, saying, "Truly You are the Son of God."

14:24 [a]NU-Text reads *many furlongs away from the land.*   14:30 [a]NU-Text brackets *that* and *boisterous* as disputed.   14:33 [a]NU-Text omits *came and.*

MANY TOUCH HIM AND ARE MADE WELL

[34]When they had crossed over, they came to the land of[a] Gennesaret. [35]And when the men of that place recognized Him, they sent out into all that surrounding region, brought to Him all who were sick, [36]and begged Him that they might only touch the hem of His garment. And as many as touched *it* were made perfectly well.

DEFILEMENT COMES FROM WITHIN

15 Then the scribes and Pharisees who were from Jerusalem came to Jesus, saying, [2]"Why do Your disciples transgress the tradition of the elders? For they do not wash their hands when they eat bread."

[3]He answered and said to them, "Why do you also transgress the commandment of God because of your tradition? [4]For God commanded, saying, 'Honor your father and your mother';[a] and, 'He who curses father or mother, let him be put to death.'[b] [5]But you say, 'Whoever says to his father or mother, "Whatever profit you might have received from me *is a gift to God*"— [6]then he need not honor his father or mother.'[a] Thus you have made the commandment[b] of God of no effect by your tradition. [7]Hypocrites! Well did Isaiah prophesy about you, saying:

[8] 'These people draw near to Me with their mouth,
And[a] honor Me with their lips,
But their heart is far from Me.
[9] And in vain they worship Me,
Teaching as doctrines the commandments of men.' "[a]

[10]When He had called the multitude to *Himself*, He said to them, "Hear and understand: [11]Not what goes into the mouth defiles a man; but what comes out of the mouth, this defiles a man."

[12]Then His disciples came and said to Him, "Do You know that the Pharisees were offended when they heard this saying?"

[13]But He answered and said, "Every plant which My heavenly Father has not planted will be uprooted. [14]Let them alone. They are blind leaders of the blind. And if the blind leads the blind, both will fall into a ditch."

[15]Then Peter answered and said to Him, "Explain this parable to us."

[16]So Jesus said, "Are you also still without understanding? [17]Do you not yet understand that whatever enters the mouth goes into the stomach and is eliminated? [18]But those things which proceed out of the mouth come from the heart, and they defile a man. [19]For out of the heart proceed evil thoughts, murders, adulteries, fornications, thefts, false witness, blasphemies. [20]These are *the things* which defile a man, but to eat with unwashed hands does not defile a man."

A GENTILE SHOWS HER FAITH

[21]Then Jesus went out from there and departed to the region of Tyre and Sidon. [22]And behold, a woman of Canaan came from that region and cried out to Him, saying, "Have mercy on me, O Lord, Son of David! My daughter is severely demon-possessed."

[23]But He answered her not a word.

And His disciples came and urged Him, saying, "Send her away, for she cries out after us."

[24]But He answered and said, "I was not sent except to the lost sheep of the house of Israel."

Bible Beverages
Pure Water

Perhaps the most important beverage you can drink—and certainly one that Jesus drank—is *pure water*. So-called "drinking water" in Jesus' time came from wells, some of them quite deep and some of them connected to artesian springs. The water was much purer and cooler from these wells than the tap water in many homes today.

Water is the most important nutrient for the human body. In fact, the human body consists primarily of water—approximately two-thirds of a person's body weight is water. Water is necessary for nearly every bodily function, including circulation, digestion, absorption, and excretion. Water is the major constituent of all bodily fluids, including saliva, gastric juices, bile, pancreatic juices, intestinal secretions, synovial fluid, and blood. It is vital for carrying nutrients to all cells of the body.

A person needs to drink at least two to three quarts of filtered or distilled water a day—or at least half of your body weight in ounces. In other words, a person who weighs 160 pounds should drink 80 ounces of water, which is equal to ten 8-ounce cups of water, or two quarts.

Drink a cup or two of water thirty minutes before a meal. At mealtimes, limit your consumption of fluids to 4 to 8 ounces. Digestion is delayed if you drink iced beverages at mealtimes, so drink water without ice at meals.

14:34 [a]NU-Text reads *came to land at.*   **15:4** [a]Exodus 20:12; Deuteronomy 5:16 [b]Exodus 21:17   **15:6** [a]NU-Text omits *or mother.* [b]NU-Text reads *word.*   **15:8** [a]NU-Text omits *draw near to Me with their mouth, And.*   **15:9** [a]Isaiah 29:13

²⁵Then she came and worshiped Him, saying, "Lord, help me!"

²⁶But He answered and said, "It is not good to take the children's bread and throw *it* to the little dogs."

²⁷And she said, "Yes, Lord, yet even the little dogs eat the crumbs which fall from their masters' table."

²⁸Then Jesus answered and said to her, "O woman, great *is* your faith! Let it be to you as you desire." And her daughter was healed from that very hour.

JESUS HEALS GREAT MULTITUDES

²⁹Jesus departed from there, skirted the Sea of Galilee, and went up on the mountain and sat down there. ³⁰Then great multitudes came to Him, having with them *the* lame, blind, mute, maimed, and many others; and they laid them down at Jesus' feet, and He healed them. ³¹So the multitude marveled when they saw *the* mute speaking, *the* maimed made whole, *the* lame walking, and *the* blind seeing; and they glorified the God of Israel.

FEEDING THE FOUR THOUSAND

³²Now Jesus called His disciples to *Himself* and said, "I have compassion on the multitude, because they have now continued with Me three days and have nothing to eat. And I do not want to send them away hungry, lest they faint on the way."

³³Then His disciples said to Him, "Where could we get enough bread in the wilderness to fill such a great multitude?"

³⁴Jesus said to them, "How many loaves do you have?"

And they said, "Seven, and a few little fish."

³⁵So He commanded the multitude to sit down on the ground. ³⁶And He took the seven loaves and the fish and gave thanks, broke *them* and gave *them* to His disciples; and the disciples *gave* to the multitude. ³⁷So they all ate and were filled, and they took up seven large baskets full of the fragments that were left. ³⁸Now those who ate were four thousand men, besides women and children. ³⁹And He sent away the multitude, got into the boat, and came to the region of Magdala.ᵃ

THE PHARISEES AND SADDUCEES SEEK A SIGN

16 Then the Pharisees and Sadducees came, and testing Him asked that He would show them a sign from heaven. ²He answered and said to them, "When it is

[VALERIAN]

FACT MORSELS

Natural Help for Sleep. Valerian is an herb that can improve the quality of sleep, decrease the time it takes to fall asleep, and decrease awakening at night.

PEACE LOVE JOY KINDNESS

The Healthy Soul
>Soul Fruit

Fruits and vegetables are sometimes called *pro*duce in a grocery store—in truth, they are what fruit trees, vines, and vegetable plants pro*duce*! The apostle Paul used the metaphor of fruit to describe what the Holy Spirit produces as virtues in the person who has accepted Jesus as Savior and is seeking to follow Him as Lord.

The "fruit of the Spirit" described by Paul is singular—it is one *set* of character traits that is regarded as being descriptive of the overall character Jesus had as a human being on this earth. In other words, love is not one fruit and joy another fruit. The *fruit* of the Spirit is exhibited as love, joy, peace, patience, kindness, goodness, faithfulness, gentleness, and self-control (Galatians 5:22, 23).

Just as a grapevine cannot produce any other kind of fruit besides grapes, and an apple tree cannot produce fruit other than apples, so the Holy Spirit does not produce in the Christian's character anything that is not virtuous. That's why the apostle Paul pointed out that there is *nothing* that stands against any of the virtues in Christ's character. Nobody is going to pass a law against being loving, joyful, kind, and so forth.

We also are wise to know that it is the Holy Spirit's work to produce this character in the believer. It isn't something we can do ourselves. If we believe we are lacking in love, short on joy, or out of control, then the goal we need to set is not to try to drum up love, joy, or self-control, but rather, to invite the Holy Spirit to fill us fully with His presence. We must ask Him to convict us, lead us, guide us, and empower us to display the nature of Jesus Christ. Only the Holy Spirit can do the work, but He waits for us to invite Him to do the work *in* us—and then *through* us.

---

evening you say, '*It will be* fair weather, for the sky is red'; ³and in the morning, '*It will be* foul weather today, for the sky is red and threatening.' Hypocrites!ᵃ You know how to discern the face of the sky, but you cannot *discern* the signs of the times. ⁴A wicked and adulterous generation seeks after a sign, and no sign shall be given to it except the sign of the prophetᵃ Jonah." And He left them and departed.

15:39 ᵃNU-Text reads *Magadan*.   16:3 ᵃNU-Text omits *Hypocrites*.   16:4 ᵃNU-Text omits *the prophet*.

THE LEAVEN OF THE PHARISEES AND SADDUCEES

[5]Now when His disciples had come to the other side, they had forgotten to take bread. [6]Then Jesus said to them, "Take heed and beware of the leaven of the Pharisees and the Sadducees."

[7]And they reasoned among themselves, saying, "It is because we have taken no bread."

[8]But Jesus, being aware of it, said to them, "O you of little faith, why do you reason among yourselves because you have brought no bread?[a] [9]Do you not yet understand, or remember the five loaves of the five thousand and how many baskets you took up? [10]Nor the seven loaves of the four thousand and how many large baskets you took up? [11]How is it you do not understand that I did not speak to you concerning bread?—but to beware of the leaven of the Pharisees and Sadducees." [12]Then they understood that He did not tell them to beware of the leaven of bread, but of the doctrine of the Pharisees and Sadducees.

PETER CONFESSES JESUS AS THE CHRIST

[13]When Jesus came into the region of Caesarea Philippi, He asked His disciples, saying, "Who do men say that I, the Son of Man, am?"

[14]So they said, "Some say John the Baptist, some Elijah, and others Jeremiah or one of the prophets."

[15]He said to them, "But who do you say that I am?"

[16]Simon Peter answered and said, "You are the Christ, the Son of the living God."

[17]Jesus answered and said to him, "Blessed are you, Simon Bar-Jonah, for flesh and blood has not revealed this to you, but My Father who is in heaven. [18]And I also say to you that you are Peter, and on this rock I will build My church, and the gates of Hades shall not prevail against it. [19]And I will give you the keys of the kingdom of heaven, and whatever you bind on earth will be bound in heaven, and whatever you loose on earth will be loosed[a] in heaven."

[20]Then He commanded His disciples that they should tell no one that He was Jesus the Christ.

JESUS PREDICTS HIS DEATH AND RESURRECTION

[21]From that time Jesus began to show to His disciples that He must go to Jerusalem, and suffer many things from the elders and chief priests and scribes, and be killed, and be raised the third day.

[22]Then Peter took Him aside and began to rebuke Him, saying, "Far be it from You, Lord; this shall not happen to You!"

[23]But He turned and said to Peter, "Get behind Me, Satan! You are an offense to Me, for you are not mindful of the things of God, but the things of men."

TAKE UP THE CROSS AND FOLLOW HIM

[24]Then Jesus said to His disciples, "If anyone desires to come after Me, let him deny himself, and take up his cross, and follow Me. [25]For whoever desires to save his life will lose it, but whoever loses his life for My sake will find it. [26]For what profit is it to a man if he gains the whole world, and loses his own soul? Or what will a man give in exchange for his soul? [27]For the Son of Man will come in the glory of His Father with His angels, and then He will reward each according to his works.

JESUS TRANSFIGURED ON THE MOUNT

[28]Assuredly, I say to you, there are some standing here who shall not taste death till they see the Son of Man coming in His kingdom."

17 Now after six days Jesus took Peter, James, and John his brother, led them up on a high mountain by themselves; [2]and He was transfigured before them. His face shone like the sun, and His clothes became as white as the light. [3]And behold, Moses and Elijah appeared to them, talking with Him. [4]Then Peter answered and said to Jesus, "Lord, it is good for us to be here; if You wish, let us[a] make here three tabernacles: one for You, one for Moses, and one for Elijah."

[5]While he was still speaking, behold, a bright cloud overshadowed them; and suddenly a voice came out of the cloud, saying, "This is My beloved Son, in whom I am well pleased. Hear Him!" [6]And when the disciples heard it, they fell on their faces and were greatly afraid. [7]But Jesus came and touched them and said, "Arise, and do not be afraid." [8]When they had lifted up their eyes, they saw no one but Jesus only.

[9]Now as they came down from the mountain, Jesus commanded

A Really Good Salad Dressing

Righteous Recipes

This salad dressing is easy to make and tastes delicious.

Ingredients:
- ☐ 2 tablespoons extra-virgin olive oil
- ☐ 1 tablespoon freshly squeezed lemon juice (or apple cider vinegar or balsamic vinegar)
- ☐ 1 tablespoon purified water
- ☐ 1 teaspoon tarragon
- ☐ 1 teaspoon garlic salt
- ☐ 1 teaspoon parsley flakes
- ☐ Dash of pepper
- ☐ Dash of salt
- ☐ 2–3 drops of Stevia (natural sweetener)

Shake all ingredients together in a cruet or jar and pour over salad greens.

16:8 [a]NU-Text reads *you have no bread.*   16:19 [a]Or *will have been bound . . . will have been loosed*   17:4 [a]NU-Text reads *I will.*

WEIGHING Less & ENJOYING LIFE MORE!

[Staying on the Wagon]

You probably will find it easier to stay on a weight-loss program if these things are in place:

- Every day, choose a balance of foods that covers every food group. This will help you avoid cravings.
- Eat sufficient fresh fruit. The fructose (sugar) in fruit is readily absorbed by the body and is not nearly as addictive or damaging to a diet as sucrose (white sugar).
- Have an "accountability partner"—someone who is also dieting and who is willing to encourage you, and vice versa.
- Weigh only once a week—that way you won't be subject to water-weight fluctuations that can occur from day to day.

them, saying, "Tell the vision to no one until the Son of Man is risen from the dead."

[10]And His disciples asked Him, saying, "Why then do the scribes say that Elijah must come first?"

[11]Jesus answered and said to them, "Indeed, Elijah is coming first[a] and will restore all things. [12]But I say to you that Elijah has come already, and they did not know him but did to him whatever they wished. Likewise the Son of Man is also about to suffer at their hands." [13]Then the disciples understood that He spoke to them of John the Baptist.

A BOY IS HEALED

[14]And when they had come to the multitude, a man came to Him, kneeling down to Him and saying, [15]"Lord, have mercy on my son, for he is an epileptic[a] and suffers severely; for he often falls into the fire and often into the water. [16]So I brought him to Your disciples, but they could not cure him."

[17]Then Jesus answered and said, "O faithless and perverse genera-tion, how long shall I be with you? How long shall I bear with you? Bring him here to Me." [18]And Jesus rebuked the demon, and it came out of him; and the child was cured from that very hour.

[19]Then the disciples came to Jesus privately and said, "Why could we not cast it out?"

[20]So Jesus said to them, "Because of your unbelief;[a] for assuredly, I say to you, if you have faith as a mustard seed, you will say to this mountain, 'Move from here to there,' and it will move; and nothing will be impossible for you. [21]However, this kind does not go out except by prayer and fasting."[a]

JESUS AGAIN PREDICTS HIS DEATH AND RESURRECTION

[22]Now while they were staying[a] in Galilee, Jesus said to them, "The Son of Man is about to be betrayed into the hands of men, [23]and they will kill Him, and the third day He will be raised up." And they were exceedingly sorrowful.

PETER AND HIS MASTER PAY THEIR TAXES

[24]When they had come to Capernaum,[a] those who received the *temple* tax came to Peter and said, "Does your Teacher not pay the *temple* tax?"

[25]He said, "Yes."

And when he had come into the house, Jesus anticipated him, saying, "What do you think, Simon? From whom do the kings of the earth take customs or taxes, from their sons or from strangers?"

[26]Peter said to Him, "From strangers."

Jesus said to him, "Then the sons are free. [27]Nevertheless, lest we offend them, go to the sea, cast in a hook, and take the fish that comes up first. And when you have opened its mouth, you will find a piece of money;[a] take that and give it to them for Me and you."

WHO IS THE GREATEST?

18 At that time the disciples came to Jesus, saying, "Who then is greatest in the kingdom of heaven?"

Bible Health + Food Facts

Fig Trees

During New Testament times, many gardens of rural and village people had fig trees. Besides bearing two crops of fruit a year, the fig trees were especially valuable in providing shade during hot weather.

17:11 [a]NU-Text omits *first*.   17:15 [a]Literally *moonstruck*   17:20 [a]NU-Text reads *little faith*.   17:21 [a]NU-Text omits this verse.   17:22 [a]NU-Text reads *gathering together*.   17:24 [a]NU-Text reads *Capharnaum* (here and elsewhere).   17:27 [a]Greek *stater*, the exact amount to pay the temple tax (didrachma) for two

²Then Jesus called a little child to Him, set him in the midst of them, ³and said, "Assuredly, I say to you, unless you are converted and become as little children, you will by no means enter the kingdom of heaven. ⁴Therefore whoever humbles himself as this little child is the greatest in the kingdom of heaven. ⁵Whoever receives one little child like this in My name receives Me.

JESUS WARNS OF OFFENSES

⁶"Whoever causes one of these little ones who believe in Me to sin, it would be better for him if a millstone were hung around his neck, and he were drowned in the depth of the sea. ⁷Woe to the world because of offenses! For offenses must come, but woe to that man by whom the offense comes!

⁸"If your hand or foot causes you to sin, cut it off and cast *it* from you. It is better for you to enter into life lame or maimed, rather than having two hands or two feet, to be cast into the everlasting fire. ⁹And if your eye causes you to sin, pluck it out and cast *it* from you. It is better for you to enter into life with one eye, rather than having two eyes, to be cast into hell fire.

THE PARABLE OF THE LOST SHEEP

¹⁰"Take heed that you do not despise one of these little ones, for I say to you that in heaven their angels always see the face of My Father who is in heaven. ¹¹For the Son of Man has come to save that which was lost.ᵃ

¹²"What do you think? If a man has a hundred sheep, and one of them goes astray, does he not leave the ninety-nine and go to the mountains to seek the one that is straying? ¹³And if he should find it, assuredly, I say to you, he rejoices more over that *sheep* than over the ninety-nine that did not go astray. ¹⁴Even so it is not the will of your Father who is in heaven that one of these little ones should perish.

DEALING WITH A SINNING BROTHER

¹⁵"Moreover if your brother sins against you, go and tell him his fault between you and him alone. If he hears you, you have gained your brother. ¹⁶But if he will not hear, take with you one or two more, that 'by the mouth of two or three witnesses every word may be established.'ᵃ ¹⁷And if he refuses to hear them, tell *it* to the church. But if he refuses even to hear the church, let him be to you like a heathen and a tax collector.

¹⁸"Assuredly, I say to you, whatever you bind on earth will be bound in heaven, and whatever you loose on earth will be loosed in heaven.

¹⁹"Again I sayᵃ to you that if two of you agree on earth concerning anything that they ask, it will be done for them by My Father in heaven. ²⁰For where two or three are gathered together in My name, I am there in the midst of them."

THE PARABLE OF THE UNFORGIVING SERVANT

²¹Then Peter came to Him and said, "Lord, how often shall my brother sin against me, and I forgive him? Up to seven times?"

²²Jesus said to him, "I do not say to you, up to seven times, but up to seventy times seven. ²³Therefore the kingdom of heaven is like a certain

---

SCRIPTURE SOLUTIONS

[CHRONIC FATIGUE AND FIBROMYALGIA]

Are strength, vigor, energy, and rest foreign to you? Are you continually depleted and drained of physical and emotional energy? Has fatigue seemingly become a routine part of your lifestyle? If so, you are not alone. Nearly one million people nationwide suffer from chronic fatigue syndrome. Of those, many also suffer from fibromyalgia, a muscular skeletal pain that often accompanies chronic fatigue.

If you are experiencing chronic fatigue, you may notice one or more of the following areas in excess in your life: chronic candida (yeast) infection and other infections, excessive stress, and depression.

With fibromyalgia you will notice muscular skeletal pains. These pains are often known as trigger points or tender points. Sleep disturbances and fatigue tend to accompany them. Other conditions associated with fibromyalgia include depression, irritable bowl, joint symptoms, and anxiety.

The following steps can help in the fight against chronic fatigue and fibromyalgia:

☐ **Proper nutrition is the first key in restoring your energy and strength.**
☐ **Exercise will help relieve the stress and assist in more restful sleep.**

☐ **Try deep, abdominal, slow breathing.**
☐ **Give your body the correct amounts of vitamins and supplements it needs.**

☐ **Take a look at your spiritual life, and allow God to come into the picture. (See Psalms 46:1, 2.) Consider God's thoughts toward you in Isaiah 40:28–31.**

God's desire for us is that we find rest in Him and allow Him to give us refreshment and restoration (Matthew 11:28, 29).

18:11 ᵃNU-Text omits this verse.   18:16 ᵃDeuteronomy 19:15   18:19 ᵃNU-Text and M-Text read *Again, assuredly, I say.*

WWJE?

[WHAT WOULD JESUS EAT]

[VEGETABLES]

Vegetables were among the most common foods eaten in the Mediterranean area where Jesus lived. The Israelites craved cucumbers, leeks, onions, and garlic when they wandered in the wilderness. These were foods they enjoyed in abundance in Egypt. (See Numbers 11:5.) These vegetables are all very healthy foods, totally approved by God in the dietary laws given to Moses.

Cucumbers, especially, were a major food of the poor in the centuries before Jesus lived (See Numbers 11:4–6; Isaiah 1:8). The melons mentioned in Numbers 11:5 may have been a kind of cucumber. The melons we know as muskmelon or watermelon were also widely grown in Egypt as a food consumed mostly by the poor. They were used as an alternative to water, which was often scarce.

Although they were not known in the Middle East in Jesus' time, cruciferous vegetables and carotenoid vegetables are extremely healthful. Cruciferous vegetables include broccoli, cauliflower, Brussels sprouts, bok choy, collard greens, kale, mustard greens, watercress, turnip greens, radishes, rutabaga, horseradish, and cabbage. They have a number of anticancer compounds in addition to being valuable sources of vitamins and minerals.

Carotenoid vegetables are the orange, yellow, and red vegetables, such as carrots, squash, and sweet potatoes or yams. Green leafy vegetables that are rich in health benefits include spinach, parsley, and beet tops.

The Bible mentions the vegetables chicory, dandelion, endive, lettuce, sorrel, and watercress as "bitter herbs." We would call them "salad greens"!

Choose a variety of vegetables. Eat vegetables daily. Eat them fresh or lightly steamed, not boiled or fried. Experiment with dishes that combine whole grains and vegetables—you might find that you don't even miss meat.

king who wanted to settle accounts with his servants. [24]And when he had begun to settle accounts, one was brought to him who owed him ten thousand talents. [25]But as he was not able to pay, his master commanded that he be sold, with his wife and children and all that he had, and that payment be made. [26]The servant therefore fell down before him, saying, 'Master, have patience with me, and I will pay you all.' [27]Then the master of that servant was moved with compassion, released him, and forgave him the debt.

[28]"But that servant went out and found one of his fellow servants who owed him a hundred denarii; and he laid hands on him and took *him* by the throat, saying, 'Pay me what you owe!' [29]So his fellow servant fell down at his feet[a] and begged him, saying, 'Have patience with me, and I will pay you all.'[b] [30]And he would not, but went and threw him into prison till he should pay the debt. [31]So when his fellow servants saw what had been done, they were very grieved, and came and told their master all that had been done. [32]Then his master, after he had called him, said to him, 'You wicked servant! I forgave

you all that debt because you begged me. [33]Should you not also have had compassion on your fellow servant, just as I had pity on you?' [34]And his master was angry, and delivered him to the torturers until he should pay all that was due to him.

[35]"So My heavenly Father also will do to you if each of you, from his heart, does not forgive his brother his trespasses."[a]

MARRIAGE AND DIVORCE

19 Now it came to pass, when Jesus had finished these sayings, *that* He departed from Galilee and came to the region of Judea beyond the Jordan. [2]And great multitudes followed Him, and He healed them there.

[3]The Pharisees also came to Him, testing Him, and saying to Him, "Is it lawful for a man to divorce his wife for *just* any reason?"

[4]And He answered and said to them, "Have you not read that He who made[a] *them* at the beginning 'made them male and female,'[b] [5]and said, 'For this reason a man shall leave his father and mother and be joined to his wife, and the two shall become one flesh'?[a] [6]So then, they are no longer two but one flesh. Therefore what God has joined together, let not man separate."

[7]They said to Him, "Why then did Moses command to give a certificate of divorce, and to put her away?"

[8]He said to them, "Moses, because of the hardness of your hearts, permitted you to divorce your wives, but from the beginning it was not so. [9]And I say to you, whoever divorces his wife, except for sexual immorality,[a] and marries another, commits adultery; and whoever marries her who is divorced commits adultery."

[10]His disciples said to Him, "If such is the case of the man with *his* wife, it is better not to marry."

JESUS TEACHES ON CELIBACY

[11]But He said to them, "All cannot accept this saying, but only *those* to whom it has been given: [12]For there are eunuchs who were born thus from *their* mother's womb, and there are eunuchs who were made eunuchs by men, and there are eunuchs who have made themselves eunuchs for the kingdom of

---

18:29 [a]NU-Text omits *at his feet.* [b]NU-Text and M-Text omit *all.* **18:35** [a]NU-Text omits *his trespasses.* **19:4** [a]NU-Text reads *created.* [b]Genesis 1:27; 5:2 **19:5** [a]Genesis 2:24 **19:9** [a]Or *fornication*

PREACHING HEALTH

heaven's sake. He who is able to accept *it*, let him accept *it*."

JESUS BLESSES LITTLE CHILDREN

¹³Then little children were brought to Him that He might put *His* hands on them and pray, but the disciples rebuked them. ¹⁴But Jesus said, "Let the little children come to Me, and do not forbid them; for of such is the kingdom of heaven." ¹⁵And He laid *His* hands on them and departed from there.

JESUS COUNSELS THE RICH YOUNG RULER

¹⁶Now behold, one came and said to Him, "Good[a] Teacher, what good thing shall I do that I may have eternal life?"

¹⁷So He said to him, "Why do you call Me good?[a] No one *is* good but One, *that is*, God.[b] But if you want to enter into life, keep the commandments."

¹⁸He said to Him, "Which ones?"

Jesus said, " 'You shall not murder,' 'You shall not commit adultery,' 'You shall not steal,' 'You shall not bear false witness,' ¹⁹'Honor your father and your mother,'[a] and, 'You shall love your neighbor as yourself.' "[b]

²⁰The young man said to Him, "All these things I have kept from my youth.[a] What do I still lack?"

²¹Jesus said to him, "If you want to be perfect, go, sell what you have and give to the poor, and you will have treasure in heaven; and come, follow Me."

²²But when the young man heard that saying, he went away sorrowful, for he had great possessions.

WITH GOD ALL THINGS ARE POSSIBLE

²³Then Jesus said to His disciples, "Assuredly, I say to you that it is hard for a rich man to enter the kingdom of heaven. ²⁴And again I say to you, it is easier for a camel to go through the eye of a needle than for a rich man to enter the kingdom of God."

²⁵When His disciples heard *it*, they were greatly astonished, saying, "Who then can be saved?"

²⁶But Jesus looked at *them* and said to them, "With men this is impossible, but with God all things are possible."

²⁷Then Peter answered and said to Him, "See, we have left all and followed You. Therefore what shall we have?"

²⁸So Jesus said to them, "Assuredly I say to you, that in the regeneration, when the Son of Man sits on the throne of His glory, you who have followed Me will also sit on twelve thrones, judging the twelve tribes of Israel. ²⁹And everyone who has left houses or brothers or sisters or father or mother or wife[a] or children or lands, for My name's sake, shall receive a hundredfold, and inherit eternal life. ³⁰But many *who are* first will be last, and the last first.

THE PARABLE OF THE WORKERS IN THE VINEYARD

20 "For the kingdom of heaven is like a landowner who went out early in the morning to hire laborers for his vineyard. ²Now when he had agreed with the laborers for a denarius a day, he sent them into his vineyard. ³And he went out about the third hour and saw others standing idle in the marketplace, ⁴and said to them, 'You also go into the vineyard, and whatever is right I will give you.' So they went. ⁵Again he went out about the sixth and the ninth hour, and did likewise. ⁶And about the eleventh hour he went out and found others standing idle,[a] and said to them, 'Why have you been standing here idle all day?' ⁷They said to him, 'Because no one hired us.'

He said to them, 'You also go into the vineyard, and whatever is right you will receive.'[a]

⁸"So when evening had come, the owner of the vineyard said to his steward, 'Call the laborers and give them *their* wages, beginning with the last to the first.' ⁹And when those came who *were hired* about the eleventh hour, they each received a denarius. ¹⁰But when the first came, they supposed that they would receive more; and they likewise received each a denarius. ¹¹And when they had received *it*, they complained against the landowner, ¹²saying, 'These last *men* have worked *only* one hour, and you made them equal to us who have borne the burden and the heat of the day.' ¹³But he answered one of them and said, 'Friend, I am doing you no wrong. Did you

WISE CHOICES

Choose soy products.
Drink soy milk. Use soy cheese instead of regular cheese. Make a soy shake for breakfast. Eat soy nuts as a snack. Use tempeh, tofu, or soy flour. Eat soy burgers instead of regular hamburgers. Soy has great health properties!

Super Soy Shake
1 cup soy milk
1–2 tablespoons soy protein powder
¼ to ½ cup fresh or frozen blueberries, strawberries, or other berries
5 ice cubes (optional)
Add a very small amount of Stevia natural sweetener to taste. Blend until smooth.

19:16 ᵃNU-Text omits *Good*.   **19:17** ᵃNU-Text reads *Why do you ask Me about what is good?* ᵇNU-Text reads *There is One who is good*.   **19:19** ᵃExodus 20:12–16; Deuteronomy 5:16–20 ᵇLeviticus 19:18
19:20 ᵃNU-Text omits *from my youth*.   **19:29** ᵃNU-Text omits *or wife*.   **20:6** ᵃNU-Text omits *idle*.   **20:7** ᵃNU-Text omits the last clause of this verse.

not agree with me for a denarius? [14]Take *what is* yours and go your way. I wish to give to this last man *the same* as to you. [15]Is it not lawful for me to do what I wish with my own things? Or is your eye evil because I am good?' [16]So the last will be first, and the first last. For many are called, but few chosen."[a]

JESUS A THIRD TIME PREDICTS HIS DEATH AND RESURRECTION

[17]Now Jesus, going up to Jerusalem, took the twelve disciples aside on the road and said to them, [18]"Behold, we are going up to Jerusalem, and the Son of Man will be betrayed to the chief priests and to the scribes; and they will condemn Him to death, [19]and deliver Him to the Gentiles to mock and to scourge and to crucify. And the third day He will rise again."

GREATNESS IS SERVING

[20]Then the mother of Zebedee's sons came to Him with her sons, kneeling down and asking something from Him.

[21]And He said to her, "What do you wish?"

She said to Him, "Grant that these two sons of mine may sit, one on Your right hand and the other on the left, in Your kingdom."

[22]But Jesus answered and said, "You do not know what you ask. Are you able to drink the cup that I am about to drink, and be baptized with the baptism that I am baptized with?"[a]

They said to Him, "We are able."

[23]So He said to them, "You will indeed drink My cup, and be baptized with the baptism that I am baptized with;[a] but to sit on My right hand and on My left is not Mine to give, but *it is for those* for whom it is prepared by My Father."

[24]And when the ten heard *it,* they were greatly displeased with the two brothers. [25]But Jesus called them to *Himself* and said, "You know that the rulers of the Gentiles lord it over them, and those who are great exercise authority over them. [26]Yet it shall not be so among you; but whoever desires to become great among you, let him be your servant. [27]And whoever desires to be first among you, let him be your slave— [28]just as the Son of Man did not come to be served, but to serve, and to give His life a ransom for many."

TWO BLIND MEN RECEIVE THEIR SIGHT

[29]Now as they went out of Jericho, a great multitude followed Him. [30]And behold, two blind men sitting by the road, when they heard that Jesus was passing by, cried out, saying, "Have mercy on us, O Lord, Son of David!"

[31]Then the multitude warned them that they should be quiet; but they cried out all the more, saying, "Have mercy on us, O Lord, Son of David!"

[32]So Jesus stood still and called them, and said, "What do you want Me to do for you?"

[33]They said to Him, "Lord, that our eyes may be opened." [34]So Jesus had compassion and touched their eyes. And immediately their eyes received sight, and they followed Him.

♂ Men's Issues
Circumcision

Circumcision is the surgical removal of the foreskin of the penis. Baby boys today are often circumcised for reasons of health and hygiene, but in Bible times and even today in modern Jewish communities, circumcision is a religious ritual. When God first made a covenant with Abraham, He commanded circumcision as a sign of the faith relationship that Abraham had with Him (Genesis 17:9–14). Circumcision is also regarded in the Scriptures as an act of obedience and a sign that a person is "putting away evil." (See Jeremiah 4:4 and Deuteronomy 10:16.) Moses was required by God to circumcise his son before returning to Pharaoh to demand that the Israelites be set free from Egyptian bondage. Since Moses was to speak before Pharaoh on behalf of all those who were in covenant relationship with God through Abraham, it was vitally important that Moses and all the males in his family be perceived as having a part of that covenant relationship. (See Exodus 4:24–26.)

For the Christian, who is in a covenant relationship with God through the shed blood of Jesus Christ, circumcision is not a ritual requirement. Many Christians continue to circumcise primarily for perceived hygiene reasons, not religious reasons. The apostle Paul wrote that for a Christian there is a circumcision of the *heart*—the sinful nature of man is replaced by Christ's presence and therefore, "putting away evil" and willfully submitting to God's commandments becomes a matter of the heart. (See Romans 2:29 and Colossians 2:11.)

20:16 [a]NU-Text omits the last sentence of this verse.   20:22 [a]NU-Text omits *and be baptized with the baptism that I am baptized with.*   20:23 [a]NU-Text omits *and be baptized with the baptism that I am baptized with.*

THE TRIUMPHAL ENTRY

21 Now when they drew near Jerusalem, and came to Bethphage,[a] at the Mount of Olives, then Jesus sent two disciples, [2]saying to them, "Go into the village opposite you, and immediately you will find a donkey tied, and a colt with her. Loose *them* and bring *them* to Me. [3]And if anyone says anything to you, you shall say, 'The Lord has need of them,' and immediately he will send them."

[4]All[a] this was done that it might be fulfilled which was spoken by the prophet, saying:

[5] "Tell the daughter of Zion,
'Behold, your King is coming to you,
Lowly, and sitting on a donkey,
A colt, the foal of a donkey.' "[a]

[6]So the disciples went and did as Jesus commanded them. [7]They brought the donkey and the colt, laid their clothes on them, and set *Him*[a] on them. [8]And a very great multitude spread their clothes on the road; others cut down branches from the trees and spread *them* on the road. [9]Then the multitudes who went before and those who followed cried out, saying:

"Hosanna to the Son of David!
'Blessed is He who comes in the name of the LORD!'[a]
Hosanna in the highest!"

[10]And when He had come into Jerusalem, all the city was moved, saying, "Who is this?"

[11]So the multitudes said, "This is Jesus, the prophet from Nazareth of Galilee."

JESUS CLEANSES THE TEMPLE

[12]Then Jesus went into the temple of God[a] and drove out all those who bought and sold in the temple, and overturned the tables of the money changers and the seats of those who sold doves. [13]And He said to them, "It is written, 'My house shall be called a house of prayer,'[a] but you have made it a 'den of thieves.' "[b]

[14]Then *the* blind and *the* lame came to Him in the temple, and He healed them. [15]But when the chief priests and scribes saw the wonderful things that He did, and the children crying out in the temple and saying, "Hosanna to the Son of David!" they were indignant [16]and said to Him, "Do You hear what these are saying?"

And Jesus said to them, "Yes. Have you never read,

'Out of the mouth of babes and nursing infants
You have perfected praise'? "[a]

[17]Then He left them and went out of the city to Bethany, and He lodged there.

THE FIG TREE WITHERED

[18]Now in the morning, as He returned to the city, He was hungry. [19]And seeing a fig tree by the road, He came to it and found nothing on it but leaves, and said to it, "Let no fruit grow on you ever again." Immediately the fig tree withered away.

THE LESSON OF THE WITHERED FIG TREE

[20]And when the disciples saw *it,* they marveled, saying, "How did the fig tree wither away so soon?"

[21]So Jesus answered and said to them, "Assuredly, I say to you, if you have faith and do not doubt, you will not only do what was done to the fig tree, but also if you say to this mountain, 'Be removed and be cast into the sea,' it will be done. [22]And whatever things you ask in prayer, believing, you will receive."

JESUS' AUTHORITY QUESTIONED

[23]Now when He came into the temple, the chief priests and the elders of the people confronted Him as He was teaching, and said, "By what authority are You doing these things? And who gave You this authority?"

[24]But Jesus answered and said to them, "I also will ask you one thing, which if you tell Me, I likewise will tell you by what authority I do these things: [25]The baptism of John—where was it from? From heaven or from men?"

And they reasoned among themselves, saying, "If we say, 'From heaven,' He will say to us, 'Why then did you not believe him?' [26]But if we say, 'From men,' we fear the multitude, for all count John as a prophet." [27]So they answered Jesus and said, "We do not know."

And He said to them, "Neither will I tell you by what authority I do these things.

THE PARABLE OF THE TWO SONS

[28]"But what do you think? A man had two sons, and he came to the first and said, 'Son, go, work today in my vineyard.' [29]He answered and said, 'I will not,' but afterward he regretted it and went. [30]Then he

"If men gave three times as much attention as they now do to ventilation, ablution, and exercise in the open air, and only one third as much to eating, luxury, and late hours, the number of doctors, dentists, and apothecaries, and the amount of neuralgia, dyspepsia, gout, fever, and consumption, would be changed in a corresponding ratio. Never hurry; take plenty of exercise; always be cheerful, and take all the sleep you need, and you may expect to be well."
—*J. F. Clarke, American clergyman (1810–1888)*

PREACHING HEALTH

21:1 [a]M-Text reads *Bethsphage.* 21:4 [a]NU-Text omits *All.* 21:5 [a]Zechariah 9:9 21:7 [a]NU-Text reads *and He sat.* 21:9 [a]Psalm 118:26 21:12 [a]NU-Text omits *of God.* 21:13 [a]Isaiah 56:7 [b]Jeremiah 7:11 21:16 [a]Psalm 8:2

Women's Issues
Yeast Infections

Yeast—also called candida—is a single-celled organism found everywhere: water, air, and land. When yeast is allowed to "overgrow," it can affect nearly every organ in the body and particularly the GI tract, nervous system, genital/urinary tract, endocrine system, and immune system. Sometimes roots of normal yeast bacteria in the body can put out rootlike tentacles that penetrate through the lining of the GI tract and cause a painful condition known as "leaky gut." Toxic waste becomes built up in the bloodstream and a number of conditions can result—from fatigue to mental confusion, from headaches to depression.

Both men and women can suffer from yeast infections, although the problem is more common in women. Here are some things you can do if you struggle with candida:

☐ **Cut out refined carbohydrates and sugar. Candida thrives on sugar, including milk sugar (lactose). Choose whole grains instead.**

☐ **Avoid foods with yeast and mold, such as all cheeses and yeast breads. Avoid mushrooms of all types since yeast is simply a form of fungus and mushrooms are fungi.**

☐ **Avoid vinegary foods and condiments, especially salad dressings, mayonnaise and mayonnaise products, as well as most condiments (including mustard, ketchup, barbecue sauce, soy sauce, pickles, sauerkraut, horseradish, and relishes). The only exception is apple cider vinegar, which actually contains good bacteria to fight yeast proliferation.**

CONT. NEXT PAGE >>>

came to the second and said likewise. And he answered and said, 'I go, sir,' but he did not go. ³¹Which of the two did the will of *his* father?"

They said to Him, "The first."

Jesus said to them, "Assuredly, I say to you that tax collectors and harlots enter the kingdom of God before you. ³²For John came to you in the way of righteousness, and you did not believe him; but tax collectors and harlots believed him; and when you saw *it,* you did not afterward relent and believe him.

THE PARABLE OF THE WICKED VINEDRESSERS

³³"Hear another parable: There was a certain landowner who planted a vineyard and set a hedge around it, dug a winepress in it and built a tower. And he leased it to vinedressers and went into a far country. ³⁴Now when vintage-time drew near, he sent his servants to the vinedressers, that they might receive its fruit. ³⁵And the vinedressers took his servants, beat one, killed one, and stoned another. ³⁶Again he sent other servants, more than the first, and they did likewise to them. ³⁷Then last of all he sent his son to them, saying, 'They will respect my son.' ³⁸But when the vinedressers saw the son, they said among themselves, 'This is the heir. Come, let us kill him and seize his inheritance.' ³⁹So they took him and cast *him* out of the vineyard and killed *him.*

⁴⁰"Therefore, when the owner of the vineyard comes, what will he do to those vinedressers?"

⁴¹They said to Him, "He will destroy those wicked men miserably, and lease *his* vineyard to other vinedressers who will render to him the fruits in their seasons."

⁴²Jesus said to them, "Have you never read in the Scriptures:

'The stone which the builders rejected
Has become the chief cornerstone.
This was the LORD's doing,
And it is marvelous in our eyes'?ᵃ

⁴³"Therefore I say to you, the kingdom of God will be taken from you and given to a nation bearing the fruits of it. ⁴⁴And whoever falls on this stone will be broken; but on whomever it falls, it will grind him to powder."

⁴⁵Now when the chief priests and Pharisees heard His parables, they perceived that He was speaking of them. ⁴⁶But when they sought to lay hands on Him, they feared the multitudes, because they took Him for a prophet.

THE PARABLE OF THE WEDDING FEAST

22 And Jesus answered and spoke to them again by parables and said: ²"The kingdom of heaven is like a certain king who arranged a marriage for his son, ³and sent out his servants to call those who were invited to the wedding; and they were not willing to come. ⁴Again, he sent out other servants, saying, 'Tell those who are invited, "See, I have prepared my dinner; my oxen and fatted cattle *are* killed, and all things *are* ready. Come to the wedding." ' ⁵But they made light of it and went their ways, one to his own farm, another to his business. ⁶And the rest seized his servants, treated

Women's Issues Cont.>>>

☐ Avoid preserved and processed meats, alcoholic beverages (especially beer), and any foods to which you have an allergy.

☐ Make sure you have enough soluble fiber in your diet. Good sources are psyllium seed, fruit pectin, oat bran, and rice brain. Insoluble fiber is also very helpful, especially methylcellulose, a tasteless powder that inactivates toxins in the GI tract. Eat high-fiber foods.

☐ Take supplements that fight candida, such as garlic, goldenseal, grapefruit seed extract, caprylic acid, oil of oregano, and chlorophyll supplements (green food).

☐ Finally, take supplements of lactobacillus acidophilus and bifidus bacteria to add good forms of bacteria to the intestinal tract.

them spitefully, and killed *them.* ⁷But when the king heard *about it,* he was furious. And he sent out his armies, destroyed those murderers, and burned up their city. ⁸Then he said to his servants, 'The wedding is ready, but those who were invited were not worthy. ⁹Therefore go into the highways, and as many as you find, invite to the wedding.' ¹⁰So those servants went out into the highways and gathered together all whom they found, both bad and good. And the wedding *hall* was filled with guests.

¹¹"But when the king came in to see the guests, he saw a man there who did not have on a wedding garment. ¹²So he said to him, 'Friend, how did you come in here without a wedding garment?' And he was speechless. ¹³Then the king said to the servants, 'Bind him hand and foot, take him away, and*ᵃ* cast *him* into outer darkness; there will be weeping and gnashing of teeth.'

¹⁴"For many are called, but few *are* chosen."

THE PHARISEES: IS IT LAWFUL TO PAY TAXES TO CAESAR?

¹⁵Then the Pharisees went and plotted how they might entangle Him in *His* talk. ¹⁶And they sent to Him their disciples with the Herodians, saying, "Teacher, we know that You are true, and teach the way of God in truth; nor do You care about anyone, for You do not regard the person of men. ¹⁷Tell us, therefore, what do You think? Is it lawful to pay taxes to Caesar, or not?"

¹⁸But Jesus perceived their wickedness, and said, "Why do you test Me, *you* hypocrites? ¹⁹Show Me the tax money."

So they brought Him a denarius.

²⁰And He said to them, "Whose image and inscription *is* this?"

²¹They said to Him, "Caesar's."

And He said to them, "Render therefore to Caesar the things that are Caesar's, and to God the things that are God's." ²²When they had heard *these words,* they marveled, and left Him and went their way.

THE SADDUCEES: WHAT ABOUT THE RESURRECTION?

²³The same day the Sadducees, who say there is no resurrection, came to Him and asked Him, ²⁴saying: "Teacher, Moses said that if a man dies, having no children, his brother shall marry his wife and raise up offspring for his brother. ²⁵Now there were with us seven brothers. The first died after he had married, and having no offspring, left his wife to his brother. ²⁶Likewise the second also, and the third, even to the seventh. ²⁷Last of all the woman died also. ²⁸Therefore, in the resurrection, whose wife of the seven will she be? For they all had her."

²⁹Jesus answered and said to them, "You are mistaken, not knowing the Scriptures nor the power of God. ³⁰For in the resurrection they neither marry nor are given in marriage, but are like angels of God*ᵃ* in heaven. ³¹But concerning the resurrection of the dead, have you not read what was spoken to you by God, saying, ³²'I am the God of Abraham, the God of Isaac, and the God of Jacob'?*ᵃ* God is not the God of the dead, but of the living." ³³And when the multitudes heard *this,* they were astonished at His teaching.

THE SCRIBES: WHICH IS THE FIRST COMMANDMENT OF ALL?

³⁴But when the Pharisees heard that He had silenced the Sadducees, they gathered together. ³⁵Then one of them, a lawyer, asked *Him a question,* testing Him, and saying, ³⁶"Teacher, which *is* the great commandment in the law?"

³⁷Jesus said to him, " 'You shall love the Lᴏʀᴅ your God with all your heart, with all your soul, and with all your mind.'*ᵃ* ³⁸This is *the* first and great commandment. ³⁹And *the* second *is* like it: 'You shall love your neighbor as yourself.'*ᵃ* ⁴⁰On these two commandments hang all the Law and the Prophets."

JESUS: HOW CAN DAVID CALL HIS DESCENDANT LORD?

⁴¹While the Pharisees were gathered together, Jesus asked them, ⁴²saying, "What do you think about the Christ? Whose Son is He?"

They said to Him, "*The Son* of David."

⁴³He said to them, "How then does David in the Spirit call Him '*Lord*,' saying:

⁴⁴ 'The Lᴏʀᴅ said to my Lord,
"Sit at My right hand,
  Till I make Your enemies Your footstool" '?*ᵃ*

⁴⁵If David then calls Him '*Lord*,' how is He his Son?" ⁴⁶And no one was able to answer Him a word, nor from that day on did anyone dare question Him anymore.

WOE TO THE SCRIBES AND PHARISEES

23 Then Jesus spoke to the multitudes and to His disciples, ²saying: "The scribes and the Pharisees sit in Moses' seat. ³Therefore whatever they tell you to observe,*ᵃ* *that* observe and do, but do not do according to their works; for they say,

22:13 ᵃNU-Text omits *take him away, and.*   22:30 ᵃNU-Text omits *of God.*   22:32 ᵃExodus 3:6, 15   22:37 ᵃDeuteronomy 6:5   22:39 ᵃLeviticus 19:18   22:44 ᵃPsalm 110:1
23:3 ᵃNU-Text omits *to observe.*

DIVINE HEALTH   35

PEOPLE CALLED "BEAUTIFUL" IN THE BIBLE

Abigail

Beautiful and Wise

The Bible describes Abigail as "a woman of good understanding and beautiful appearance" (1 Samuel 25:3).

Many people seem to believe that just because a woman is beautiful, she can get any man she wants—the richest, smartest, most handsome, and most godly. Not always!

Although Abigail probably had very little opportunity to *choose* Nabal as her husband, given the times in which she lived, she is not unlike many women today who find themselves as the beautiful and intelligent wives of men who are not worthy of them. Nabal is described in the Bible as "harsh and evil in his doings," as well as a "scoundrel." From his story in the Bible we can also conclude that he had real anger issues and was a man who could not be confronted about his decisions. (See 1 Samuel 25:3, 17.)

Nabal was a wealthy man with a flock of three thousand sheep and a thousand goats. As these flocks grazed on the hills of Carmel, the animals and their shepherds were protected in part by a roaming band of men under David's leadership. This was a common custom in those days. At shearing time it was considered an act of goodwill and good business for the owners of flocks to reward those who had helped protect their investment. David sent men to collect from Nabal, and they were rudely sent away empty-handed. David's first thoughts turned to revenge.

Abigail learned about what happened and took it upon herself to send a gracious gift of food and wine to David and his men. She also boldly and courageously chose to deliver the gift herself and to plead for the safety of her husband and all in her household. She knew that the consequences for her husband's rudeness would not be good!

Abigail spoke to David with humility, warm hospitality, and reason. He agreed to spare her and her household.

In going to David, Abigail was going against her husband's wishes. She wisely waited to tell Nabal what she had done so she might speak to him while he was sober. Even so, when Nabal learned what had happened, his "heart died within him, and he became like a stone" (1 Samuel 25:37). He apparently had a heart attack or stroke. The Bible tells us he died about ten days later.

When David learned that Nabal was dead, he remembered Abigail's beauty—her external beauty, and her inner beauty of graciousness and reason—and proposed to her and took her as his wife. David said to her: "I . . . respected your person" (1 Samuel 25:35).

Q The Bible says the Lord will do this for a certain type of person: "strengthen him on his bed of illness" and "sustain him on his sickbed." What type of person qualifies for this help?

A "He who considers the poor" *(Psalm 41:1, 3).*

< ABIGAIL'S GIFT >

Question: What was the food gift that Abigail sent to David and his four hundred men?

Answer: It was enough food for a nice "feast meal." It included the following:

☐ One hundred loaves of bread (each about six inches in diameter and an inch thick)

☐ Two skins of wine (the wine containers were made of whole goat skins, each "skin" would hold several gallons of wine)

☐ Five sheep already dressed

☐ Five seahs of roasted grain (about five pecks of dry roasted grain that would have tasted to us like roasted nuts)

☐ One hundred clusters of raisins (no doubt large clusters of grapes, with the grapes allowed to "dry on the vine")

☐ Two hundred cakes of figs (these were made of figs that were pressed together, perhaps with honey, to form cakelike shapes)

Each of David's men would have received a piece of bread, a cup of wine, a few bites of meat, a small handful of grain, a dozen or so raisins, and a small square of fig cake.

and do not do. ⁴For they bind heavy burdens, hard to bear, and lay *them* on men's shoulders; but they *themselves* will not move them with one of their fingers. ⁵But all their works they do to be seen by men. They make their phylacteries broad and enlarge the borders of their garments. ⁶They love the best places at feasts, the best seats in the synagogues, ⁷greetings in the marketplaces, and to be called by men, 'Rabbi, Rabbi.' ⁸But you, do not be called 'Rabbi'; for One is your Teacher, the Christ,ᵃ and you are all brethren. ⁹Do not call anyone on earth your father; for One is your Father, He who is in heaven. ¹⁰And do not be called teachers; for One is your Teacher, the Christ. ¹¹But he who is greatest among you shall be your servant. ¹²And whoever exalts himself will be humbled, and he who humbles himself will be exalted.

¹³"But woe to you, scribes and Pharisees, hypocrites! For you shut up the kingdom of heaven against men; for you neither go in *yourselves,* nor do you allow those who are entering to go in. ¹⁴Woe to you, scribes and Pharisees, hypocrites! For you devour widows' houses, and for a pretense make long prayers. Therefore you will receive greater condemnation.ᵃ

whitewashed tombs which indeed appear beautiful outwardly, but inside are full of dead *men's* bones and all uncleanness. ²⁸Even so you also outwardly appear righteous to men, but inside you are full of hypocrisy and lawlessness.

²⁹"Woe to you, scribes and Pharisees, hypocrites! Because you build the tombs of the prophets and adorn the monuments of the righteous, ³⁰and say, 'If we had lived in the days of our fathers, we would not have been partakers with them in the blood of the prophets.' ³¹"Therefore you are witnesses against yourselves that you are sons of those who murdered the prophets. ³²Fill up, then, the measure of your fathers' *guilt.* ³³Serpents, brood of vipers! How can you escape the condemnation of hell? ³⁴Therefore, indeed, I send you prophets, wise men, and scribes: *some* of them you will kill and crucify, and *some* of them you will scourge in your synagogues and persecute from city to city, ³⁵that on you may come all the righteous blood shed on the earth, from the blood of righteous Abel to the blood of Zechariah, son of Berechiah, whom you murdered between the temple and the altar. ³⁶Assuredly, I say to you, all these things will come upon this generation.

> "There is this difference between the two temporal blessings—health and money; money is the most envied, but the least enjoyed; health is the most enjoyed, but the least envied; and this superiority of the latter is still more obvious when we reflect that the poorest man would not part with health for money, but that the richest would gladly part with all his money for health."
> —*Caleb Colton, English clergyman (1780–1832)*

PREACHING HEALTH

¹⁵"Woe to you, scribes and Pharisees, hypocrites! For you travel land and sea to win one proselyte, and when he is won, you make him twice as much a son of hell as yourselves.

¹⁶"Woe to you, blind guides, who say, 'Whoever swears by the temple, it is nothing; but whoever swears by the gold of the temple, he is obliged *to perform it.*' ¹⁷Fools and blind! For which is greater, the gold or the temple that sanctifiesᵃ the gold? ¹⁸And, 'Whoever swears by the altar, it is nothing; but whoever swears by the gift that is on it, he is obliged *to perform it.*' ¹⁹Fools and blind! For which is greater, the gift or the altar that sanctifies the gift? ²⁰Therefore he who swears by the altar, swears by it and by all things on it. ²¹He who swears by the temple, swears by it and by Him who dwellsᵃ in it. ²²And he who swears by heaven, swears by the throne of God and by Him who sits on it.

²³"Woe to you, scribes and Pharisees, hypocrites! For you pay tithe of mint and anise and cummin, and have neglected the weightier *matters* of the law: justice and mercy and faith. These you ought to have done, without leaving the others undone. ²⁴Blind guides, who strain out a gnat and swallow a camel!

²⁵"Woe to you, scribes and Pharisees, hypocrites! For you cleanse the outside of the cup and dish, but inside they are full of extortion and self-indulgence.ᵃ ²⁶Blind Pharisee, first cleanse the inside of the cup and dish, that the outside of them may be clean also.

²⁷"Woe to you, scribes and Pharisees, hypocrites! For you are like

JESUS LAMENTS OVER JERUSALEM

³⁷"O Jerusalem, Jerusalem, the one who kills the prophets and stones those who are sent to her! How often I wanted to gather your children together, as a hen gathers her chicks under *her* wings, but you were not willing! ³⁸See! Your house is left to you desolate; ³⁹for I say to you, you shall see Me no more till you say, 'Blessed is He who comes in the name of the LORD!' "ᵃ

JESUS PREDICTS THE DESTRUCTION OF THE TEMPLE

24 Then Jesus went out and departed from the temple, and His disciples came up to show Him the buildings of the temple. ²And Jesus said to them, "Do you not see all these things? Assuredly, I say to you, not *one* stone shall be left here upon another, that shall not be thrown down."

THE SIGNS OF THE TIMES AND THE END OF THE AGE

³Now as He sat on the Mount of Olives, the disciples came to Him privately, saying, "Tell us, when will these things be? And what *will be* the sign of Your coming, and of the end of the age?"

⁴And Jesus answered and said to them: "Take heed that no one deceives

---

23:8 ᵃNU-Text omits *the Christ.*   23:14 ᵃNU-Text omits this verse.   23:17 ᵃNU-Text reads *sanctified.*   23:21 ᵃM-Text reads *dwelt.*   23:25 ᵃM-Text reads *unrighteousness.*   23:39 ᵃPsalm 118:26

you. ⁵For many will come in My name, saying, 'I am the Christ,' and will deceive many. ⁶And you will hear of wars and rumors of wars. See that you are not troubled; for all[ᵃ] *these things* must come to pass, but the end is not yet. ⁷For nation will rise against nation, and kingdom against kingdom. And there will be famines, pestilences,[ᵃ] and earthquakes in various places. ⁸All these *are* the beginning of sorrows.

⁹"Then they will deliver you up to tribulation and kill you, and you will be hated by all nations for My name's sake. ¹⁰And then many will be offended, will betray one another, and will hate one another. ¹¹Then many false prophets will rise up and deceive many. ¹²And because lawlessness will abound, the love of many will grow cold. ¹³But he who endures to the end shall be saved. ¹⁴And this gospel of the kingdom will be preached in all the world as a witness to all the nations, and then the end will come.

THE GREAT TRIBULATION

¹⁵"Therefore when you see the 'abomination of desolation,'[ᵃ] spoken of by Daniel the prophet, standing in the holy place" (whoever reads, let him understand), ¹⁶"then let those who are in Judea flee to the mountains. ¹⁷Let him who is on the housetop not go down to take anything out of his house. ¹⁸And let him who is in the field not go back to get his clothes. ¹⁹But woe to those who are pregnant and to those who are nursing babies in those days! ²⁰And pray that your flight may not be in winter or on the Sabbath. ²¹For then there will be great tribulation, such as has not been since the beginning of the world until this time, no, nor ever shall be. ²²And unless those days were shortened, no flesh would be saved; but for the elect's sake those days will be shortened.

²³"Then if anyone says to you, 'Look, here *is* the Christ!' or 'There!' do not believe *it*. ²⁴For false christs and false prophets will rise and show great signs and wonders to deceive, if possible, even the elect. ²⁵See, I have told you beforehand.

²⁶"Therefore if they say to you, 'Look, He is in the desert!' do not go out; *or* 'Look, *He is* in the inner rooms!' do not believe *it*. ²⁷For as the lightning comes from the east and flashes to the west, so also will the coming of the Son of Man be. ²⁸For wherever the carcass is, there the eagles will be gathered together.

THE COMING OF THE SON OF MAN

²⁹"Immediately after the tribulation of those days the sun will be darkened, and the moon will not give its light; the stars will fall from heaven, and the powers of the heavens will be shaken. ³⁰Then the sign of the Son of Man will appear in heaven, and then all the tribes of the earth will mourn, and they will see the Son of Man coming on the clouds of heaven with power and great glory. ³¹And He will send His angels with a great sound of a trumpet, and they will gather together His elect from the four winds, from one end of heaven to the other.

THE PARABLE OF THE FIG TREE

³²"Now learn this parable from the fig tree: When its branch has already become tender and puts forth leaves, you know that summer *is* near. ³³So you also, when you see all these things, know that it[ᵃ] is near—at the doors! ³⁴Assuredly, I say to you, this generation will by no means pass away till all these things take place. ³⁵Heaven and earth will pass away, but My words will by no means pass away.

NO ONE KNOWS THE DAY OR HOUR

³⁶"But of that day and hour no one knows, not even the angels of heaven,[ᵃ] but My Father only. ³⁷But as the days of Noah *were*, so also will the coming of the Son of Man be. ³⁸For as in the days before the flood, they were eating and drinking, marrying and giving in marriage, until the day that Noah entered the ark, ³⁹and did not know until the flood came and took them all away, so also will the coming of the Son of Man be. ⁴⁰Then two *men* will be in the field: one will be taken and the other left. ⁴¹Two *women will be* grinding at the mill: one will be taken and the other left. ⁴²Watch therefore, for you do not know what hour[ᵃ] your Lord is coming. ⁴³But know this, that if the master of the house had known what hour the thief would come, he would have watched and not allowed his house to be broken into. ⁴⁴Therefore you also be ready, for the Son of Man is coming at an hour you do not expect.

THE FAITHFUL SERVANT AND THE EVIL SERVANT

⁴⁵"Who then is a faithful and wise servant, whom his master made ruler over his household, to give them food in due season? ⁴⁶Blessed *is* that servant whom his master, when he comes, will find so doing. ⁴⁷Assuredly, I say to you that he will make him ruler over all his goods. ⁴⁸But if that evil servant says in his heart, 'My master is delaying his coming,'[ᵃ] ⁴⁹and begins to beat *his* fellow servants, and to eat and drink with the drunkards, ⁵⁰the master of that servant will come on a day when he is not looking for *him* and at an hour that he is not aware of, ⁵¹and will cut him in two and appoint *him* his portion with the hypocrites. There shall be weeping and gnashing of teeth.

THE PARABLE OF THE WISE AND FOOLISH VIRGINS

25 "Then the kingdom of heaven shall be likened to ten virgins who took their lamps and went out to meet the bridegroom. ²Now five of them were wise, and five *were* foolish. ³Those who *were* foolish took their lamps and took no oil with them, ⁴but the wise took oil in their vessels with their lamps. ⁵But while the bridegroom was delayed, they all slumbered and slept.

⁶"And at midnight a cry was *heard:* 'Behold, the bridegroom is coming;'[ᵃ] go out to meet him!' ⁷Then all those virgins arose and trimmed their lamps. ⁸And the foolish said to the wise, 'Give us *some* of your oil, for our lamps are going out.' ⁹But the wise answered, saying, '*No*, lest there should not be enough for us and you; but go rather to those who sell, and buy for yourselves.' ¹⁰And while they went to buy, the bridegroom came, and those who were ready went in with him to the wedding; and the door was shut.

¹¹"Afterward the other virgins came also, saying, 'Lord, Lord, open to us!' ¹²But he answered and said, 'Assuredly, I say to you, I do not know you.'

¹³"Watch therefore, for you know neither the day nor the hour[ᵃ] in which the Son of Man is coming.

THE PARABLE OF THE TALENTS

¹⁴"For *the kingdom of heaven is* like a man traveling to a far country, *who* called his own servants and delivered his goods to them. ¹⁵And to one he gave five talents, to another two, and to another one, to each according to his own ability; and immediately he went on

24:6 ᵃNU-Text omits *all*.   24:7 ᵃNU-Text omits *pestilences*.   24:15 ᵃDaniel 11:31; 12:11   24:33 ᵃOr *He*   24:36 ᵃNU-Text adds *nor the Son*.   24:42 ᵃNU-Text reads *day*.   24:48 ᵃNU-Text omits *his coming*.   25:6 ᵃNU-Text omits *is coming*.   25:13 ᵃNU-Text omits the rest of this verse.

Throughout the Bible, God presents Himself as the foremost protector and provider of His people. In turn, He asks that His people help to protect the innocent and provide for the needy. Christians are called to live in a way that *nourishes* and *nurtures*.

Nourishing. To nourish is to recognize what is lacking or needed, and then to do one's best to provide that. What is lacking for a person emotionally may be a sense of security. It may be that a person needs to receive the gift of touch—a display of physical affection in the form of gentle touches and bold hugs. A person may be lacking in "fun." A person may need more laughs and more opportunities to relax.

In the physical arena, a person may be lacking adequate shelter or clothing. A person may be lacking sufficient nutrients or food. Certainly we as Christians bear a great responsibility to see that we are doing everything possible to feed those who are physically hungry, to clothe those who don't have adequate clothing, and to provide shelter for the homeless. A person may also have the lack of the *right* nutrients. We bear a responsibility for learning what it is that our bodies need, and then supplying those nutrients to our cells, tissues, and organs. We also are to help others gain more information about their physical health and to provide healthful meals for our children—not only those in our immediate family, but also the children whose parents either don't know or don't care about the health of their offspring. All of these actions, and more, fall into the category of providing "nourishment" to the world.

Certainly from a spiritual standpoint, the world is in great need of good spiritual nourishment. There's plenty of spiritual junk food floating around in our society these days—so-called "spiritual" beliefs and practices that do not lead to eternal life, genuine forgiveness of sins, or a flow of godly character and behavior between people. We need to be people who nourish the world with truth and love.

In providing good nourishment, we are *protecting*

The Two N's: Nourish and Nurture

people from the ills associated with lack—a lack of emotional support, a lack of correct teaching, a lack of sufficient income or material goods, or a lack of sufficient food, water, clothing, or shelter. Lack puts a person in danger. Nourishing seeks to remove a person from danger by providing what is needed.

Nurturing. To nurture is to do whatever is necessary to promote good growth and development toward wholeness. In the physical sense, we nurture a child to adulthood by providing those good things that are beneficial and necessary for a child to develop his full potential—we nurture by providing good food, a good physical environment, a loving family, a good education, and an atmosphere in which a child can hear the gospel and come to accept Jesus Christ as his or her personal Savior. In the emotional sense, we do whatever we can to build up other people and in doing that, we build up friendships, marriages, and a community or church as a whole.

In the physical realm, we nurture ourselves by giving our bodies the right food, right amount of exercise, right amount of sleep, and the right relationships for emotional growth and health.

Spiritually, we nurture others when we express our spiritual gifts with love, when we give of our resources, and when we speak words of encouragement and enrichment. We provide nurture when we help a new believer "grow up" by teaching him or her what the Bible says and helping him or her develop the disciplines of prayer, praise and thanksgiving, ministry gifts, opportunities for outreach to the needy and lost, and regular worship of God in the church of his or her choice.

In providing good nurture, we are providing what will build up our society and the kingdom of God around the world. We are going from strength to strength, and from glory to glory.

Choose today to become a person who embodies the "Two *N's*." Do what you can to provide nourishment and nurture—not only to your family and yourself, but to others you encounter in your workplace, neighborhood, and church community.

WHOLENESS 101

a journey. ¹⁶Then he who had received the five talents went and traded with them, and made another five talents. ¹⁷And likewise he who *had received* two gained two more also. ¹⁸But he who had received one went and dug in the ground, and hid his lord's money. ¹⁹After a long time the lord of those servants came and settled accounts with them.

²⁰"So he who had received five talents came and brought five other talents, saying, 'Lord, you delivered to me five talents; look, I have gained five more talents besides them.' ²¹His lord said to him, 'Well *done*, good and faithful servant; you were faithful over a few things, I will make you ruler over many things. Enter into the joy of your lord.' ²²He also who had received two talents came and said, 'Lord, you delivered to me two talents; look, I have gained two more talents besides them.' ²³His lord said to him, 'Well *done*, good and faithful servant; you have been faithful over a few things, I will make you ruler over many things. Enter into the joy of your lord.'

²⁴"Then he who had received the one talent came and said, 'Lord, I knew you to be a hard man, reaping where you have not sown, and gathering where you have not scattered seed. ²⁵And I was afraid, and went and hid your talent in the ground. Look, *there* you have *what is* yours.'

²⁶"But his lord answered and said to him, 'You wicked and lazy servant, you knew that I reap where I have not sown, and gather where I have not scattered seed. ²⁷So you ought to have deposited my money with the bankers, and at my coming I would have received back my own with interest. ²⁸So take the talent from him, and give *it* to him who has ten talents.

²⁹'For to everyone who has, more will be given, and he will have abundance; but from him who does not have, even what he has will be taken away. ³⁰And cast the unprofitable servant into the outer darkness. There will be weeping and gnashing of teeth.'

THE SON OF MAN WILL JUDGE THE NATIONS

³¹"When the Son of Man comes in His glory, and all the holy* angels with Him, then He will sit on the throne of His glory. ³²All the nations will be gathered before Him, and He will separate them one from another, as a shepherd divides *his* sheep from the goats. ³³And He will set the sheep on His right hand, but the goats on the left. ³⁴Then the King will say to those on His right hand, 'Come, you blessed of My Father, inherit the kingdom prepared for you from the foundation of the world: ³⁵for I was hungry and you gave Me food; I was thirsty and you gave Me drink; I was a stranger and you took Me in; ³⁶I *was* naked and you clothed Me; I was sick and you visited Me; I was in prison and you came to Me.'

³⁷"Then the righteous will answer Him, saying, 'Lord, when did we see You hungry and feed *You*, or thirsty and give *You* drink? ³⁸When did we see You a stranger and take *You* in, or naked and clothe *You?* ³⁹Or when did we see You sick, or in prison, and come to You?' ⁴⁰And the King will answer and say to them, 'Assuredly, I say to you, inasmuch as you did *it* to one of the least of these My brethren, you did *it* to Me.'

⁴¹"Then He will also say to those on the left hand, 'Depart from Me, you cursed, into the everlasting fire prepared for the devil and his angels: ⁴²for I was hungry and you gave Me no food; I was thirsty and you gave Me no drink; ⁴³I was a stranger and you did not take Me in, naked and you did not clothe Me, sick and in prison and you did not visit Me.'

⁴⁴"Then they also will answer Him,* saying, 'Lord, when did we see You hungry or thirsty or a stranger or naked or sick or in prison, and did not minister to You?' ⁴⁵Then He will answer them, saying, 'Assuredly, I say to you, inasmuch as you did not do *it* to one of the least of these, you did not do *it* to Me.' ⁴⁶And these will go away into everlasting punishment, but the righteous into eternal life."

THE PLOT TO KILL JESUS

26 Now it came to pass, when Jesus had finished all these sayings, *that* He said to His disciples, ²"You know that after two days is the Passover, and the Son of Man will be delivered up to be crucified."

³Then the chief priests, the scribes,* and the elders of the people assembled at the palace of the high priest, who was called Caiaphas, ⁴and plotted to take Jesus by trickery and kill *Him.* ⁵But they said, "Not during the feast, lest there be an uproar among the people."

THE ANOINTING AT BETHANY

⁶And when Jesus was in Bethany at the house of Simon the leper, ⁷a woman came to Him having an alabaster flask of very costly fragrant oil, and she poured *it* on His head as He sat *at the table.* ⁸But when His disciples saw *it,* they were indignant, saying, "Why this waste? ⁹For this fragrant oil might have been sold for much and given to *the* poor."

¹⁰But when Jesus was aware of *it,* He said to them, "Why do you trouble the woman? For she has done a good work for Me. ¹¹For you have the poor with you always, but Me you do not have always. ¹²For in pouring this fragrant oil on My body, she did *it* for My burial. ¹³Assuredly, I say to you, wherever this gospel is preached in the whole world, what this woman has done will also be told as a memorial to her."

JUDAS AGREES TO BETRAY JESUS

¹⁴Then one of the twelve, called Judas Iscariot, went to the chief priests ¹⁵and said, "What are you willing to give me if I deliver Him to you?" And they counted out to him thirty pieces of silver. ¹⁶So from that time he sought opportunity to betray Him.

JESUS CELEBRATES PASSOVER WITH HIS DISCIPLES

¹⁷Now on the first *day of the Feast* of the Unleavened Bread the disciples came to Jesus, saying to Him, "Where do You want us to prepare for You to eat the Passover?"

¹⁸And He said, "Go into the city to a certain man, and say to him, 'The Teacher says, "My time is at hand; I will keep the Passover at your house with My disciples." ' "

¹⁹So the disciples did as Jesus had directed them; and they prepared the Passover.

²⁰When evening had come, He sat down with the twelve. ²¹Now as they were eating, He said, "Assuredly, I say to you, one of you will betray Me."

²²And they were exceedingly sorrowful, and each of them began to say to Him, "Lord, is it I?"

²³He answered and said, "He who dipped *his* hand with Me in the dish will betray Me. ²⁴The Son of Man indeed goes just as it is written of Him, but woe to that man by whom the Son of Man is betrayed! It would have been good for that man if he had not been born."

²⁵Then Judas, who was betraying Him, answered and said, "Rabbi, is it I?"

He said to him, "You have said it."

25:31 *NU-Text omits *holy*.   25:44 *NU-Text and M-Text omit *Him*.   26:3 *NU-Text omits *the scribes*.

QUIZ 1

ARE YOU STRESSED OUT?

Can stress be measured medically? Yes!

When the body shifts into a stressful "I hate this situation but I just have to cope" state, a number of chemicals are released into the bloodstream. The end result is nearly always the production of an excessive amount of cortisol. Elevated cortisol levels are associated with a number of ailments, although not all people manifest precisely the same number or mix of conditions when they have elevated cortisol.

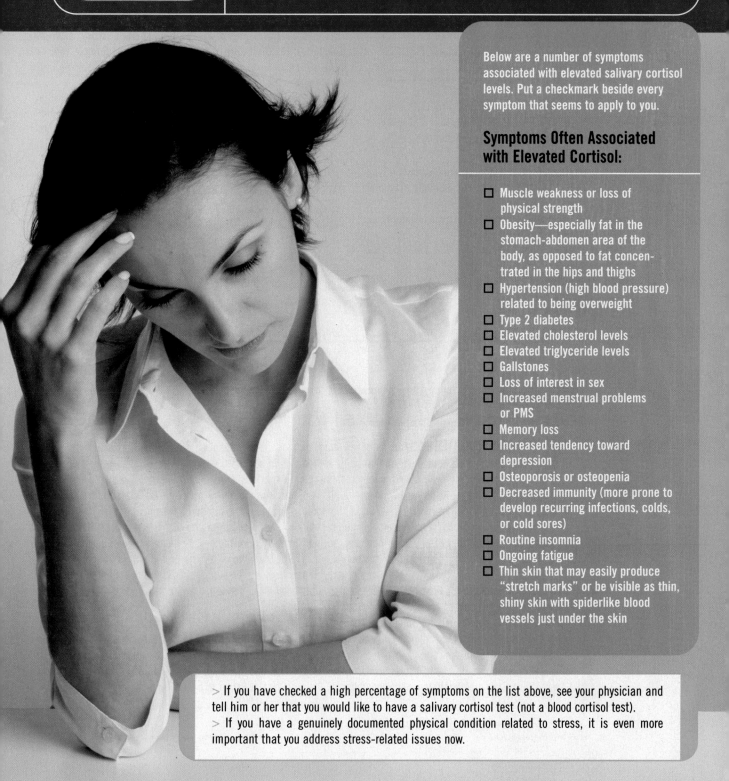

Below are a number of symptoms associated with elevated salivary cortisol levels. Put a checkmark beside every symptom that seems to apply to you.

Symptoms Often Associated with Elevated Cortisol:

☐ Muscle weakness or loss of physical strength
☐ Obesity—especially fat in the stomach-abdomen area of the body, as opposed to fat concentrated in the hips and thighs
☐ Hypertension (high blood pressure) related to being overweight
☐ Type 2 diabetes
☐ Elevated cholesterol levels
☐ Elevated triglyceride levels
☐ Gallstones
☐ Loss of interest in sex
☐ Increased menstrual problems or PMS
☐ Memory loss
☐ Increased tendency toward depression
☐ Osteoporosis or osteopenia
☐ Decreased immunity (more prone to develop recurring infections, colds, or cold sores)
☐ Routine insomnia
☐ Ongoing fatigue
☐ Thin skin that may easily produce "stretch marks" or be visible as thin, shiny skin with spiderlike blood vessels just under the skin

> If you have checked a high percentage of symptoms on the list above, see your physician and tell him or her that you would like to have a salivary cortisol test (not a blood cortisol test).
> If you have a genuinely documented physical condition related to stress, it is even more important that you address stress-related issues now.

JESUS INSTITUTES THE LORD'S SUPPER

²⁶And as they were eating, Jesus took bread, blessed" and broke *it*, and gave *it* to the disciples and said, "Take, eat; this is My body."

²⁷Then He took the cup, and gave thanks, and gave *it* to them, saying, "Drink from it, all of you. ²⁸For this is My blood of the new" covenant, which is shed for many for the remission of sins. ²⁹But I say to you, I will not drink of this fruit of the vine from now on until that day when I drink it new with you in My Father's kingdom."

³⁰And when they had sung a hymn, they went out to the Mount of Olives.

JESUS PREDICTS PETER'S DENIAL

³¹Then Jesus said to them, "All of you will be made to stumble because of Me this night, for it is written:

'I will strike the Shepherd,
And the sheep of the flock will be scattered.'"

³²But after I have been raised, I will go before you to Galilee."

³³Peter answered and said to Him, "Even if all are made to stumble because of You, I will never be made to stumble."

³⁴Jesus said to him, "Assuredly, I say to you that this night, before the rooster crows, you will deny Me three times."

³⁵Peter said to Him, "Even if I have to die with You, I will not deny You!"

And so said all the disciples.

THE PRAYER IN THE GARDEN

³⁶Then Jesus came with them to a place called Gethsemane, and said to the disciples, "Sit here while I go and pray over there." ³⁷And He took with Him Peter and the two sons of Zebedee, and He began to be sorrowful and deeply distressed. ³⁸Then He said to them, "My soul is exceedingly sorrowful, even to death. Stay here and watch with Me."

³⁹He went a little farther and fell on His face, and prayed, saying, "O My Father, if it is possible, let this cup pass from Me; nevertheless, not as I will, but as You *will.*"

⁴⁰Then He came to the disciples and found them sleeping, and said to Peter, "What! Could you not watch with Me one hour? ⁴¹Watch and pray, lest you enter into temptation. The spirit indeed *is* willing, but the flesh *is* weak."

⁴²Again, a second time, He went away and prayed, saying, "O My Father, if this cup cannot pass away from Me unless" I drink it, Your will be done." ⁴³And He came and found them asleep again, for their eyes were heavy.

⁴⁴So He left them, went away again, and prayed the third time, saying the same words. ⁴⁵Then He came to His disciples and said to them, "Are *you* still sleeping and resting? Behold, the hour is at hand, and the Son of Man is being betrayed into the hands of sinners. ⁴⁶Rise, let us be going. See, My betrayer is at hand."

BETRAYAL AND ARREST IN GETHSEMANE

⁴⁷And while He was still speaking, behold, Judas, one of the twelve, with a great multitude with swords and clubs, came from the chief priests and elders of the people.

⁴⁸Now His betrayer had given them a sign, saying, "Whomever I kiss, He is the One; seize Him." ⁴⁹Immediately he went up to Jesus and said, "Greetings, Rabbi!" and kissed Him.

⁵⁰But Jesus said to him, "Friend, why have you come?"

Then they came and laid hands on Jesus and took Him. ⁵¹And suddenly, one of those *who were* with Jesus stretched out *his* hand and drew his sword, struck the servant of the high priest, and cut off his ear.

INSIGHTS INTO THE WORD

> (Matthew 26:67)

He Should Have Died. From a purely medical standpoint, Jesus *could* have died, and probably *should* have died long before He was nailed to the cross. In the Garden of Gethsemane, Jesus was in such a heightened state of inner turmoil that blood came out of the pores in His skin. This condition has been documented several times—the stress level in a person becomes so high that the capillaries of the blood-vessel system begin to break, including the capillaries in the brain. A person almost always dies from a stroke within minutes after bleeding from the skin's pores.

During His trial before the Sanhedrin, Jesus was severely beaten. During His handling by Pilate's soldiers, He had a crown of thorns—some likely two to three inches long—crushed into His skull. He was struck on the head repeatedly. Brain hemorrhaging was very probable.

Other Gospel accounts tell how Jesus was flogged *and* scourged with thirty-nine stripes, just one shy of what was considered a lethal beating. Flogging was administered with heavy leather straps. Stones and pieces of glass and metal embedded the leather whips used in scourging so that the skin was literally ripped away from the person being whipped. Jesus was given no water to drink and probably was not only weakened from the bleeding, but also dehydrated by the time He was compelled to carry a heavy wooden yokelike crosspiece.

From a physical standpoint, He was bloodied and bruised beyond recognition. Nevertheless, Jesus endured all the way to the Cross—to fulfill the necessary atonement as the Lamb who was pure and spotless, chosen by God the Father to become the sacrifice for sin.

26:26 "M-Text reads *gave thanks for.* 26:28 "NU-Text omits *new.* 26:31 "Zechariah 13:7 26:42 "NU-Text reads *if this may not pass away unless.*

[52]But Jesus said to him, "Put your sword in its place, for all who take the sword will perish[a] by the sword. [53]Or do you think that I cannot now pray to My Father, and He will provide Me with more than twelve legions of angels? [54]How then could the Scriptures be fulfilled, that it must happen thus?"

[55]In that hour Jesus said to the multitudes, "Have you come out, as against a robber, with swords and clubs to take Me? I sat daily with you, teaching in the temple, and you did not seize Me. [56]But all this was done that the Scriptures of the prophets might be fulfilled."

Then all the disciples forsook Him and fled.

JESUS FACES THE SANHEDRIN

[57]And those who had laid hold of Jesus led *Him* away to Caiaphas the high priest, where the scribes and the elders were assembled. [58]But Peter followed Him at a distance to the high priest's courtyard. And he went in and sat with the servants to see the end.

[59]Now the chief priests, the elders,[a] and all the council sought false testimony against Jesus to put Him to death, [60]but found none. Even though many false witnesses came forward, they found none.[a] But at last two false witnesses[b] came forward [61]and said, "This *fellow* said, 'I am able to destroy the temple of God and to build it in three days.' "

[62]And the high priest arose and said to Him, "Do You answer nothing? What *is it* these men testify against You?" [63]But Jesus kept silent. And the high priest answered and said to Him, "I put You under oath by the living God: Tell us if You are the Christ, the Son of God!"

[64]Jesus said to him, "*It is as* you said. Nevertheless, I say to you, hereafter you will see the Son of Man sitting at the right hand of the Power, and coming on the clouds of heaven."

[65]Then the high priest tore his clothes, saying, "He has spoken blasphemy! What further need do we have of witnesses? Look, now you have heard His blasphemy! [66]What do you think?"

They answered and said, "He is deserving of death."

[67]Then they spat in His face and beat Him; and others struck *Him* with the palms of their hands, [68]saying, "Prophesy to us, Christ! Who is the one who struck You?"

PETER DENIES JESUS, AND WEEPS BITTERLY

[69]Now Peter sat outside in the courtyard. And a servant girl came to him, saying, "You also were with Jesus of Galilee."

[70]But he denied it before *them* all, saying, "I do not know what you are saying."

[71]And when he had gone out to the gateway, another *girl* saw him and said to those *who were* there, "This *fellow* also was with Jesus of Nazareth."

[72]But again he denied with an oath, "I do not know the Man!"

[73]And a little later those who stood by came up and said to Peter, "Surely you also are *one* of them, for your speech betrays you."

[74]Then he began to curse and swear, *saying,* "I do not know the Man!"

Immediately a rooster crowed. [75]And Peter remembered the word of Jesus who had said to him, "Before the rooster crows, you will deny Me three times." So he went out and wept bitterly.

JESUS HANDED OVER TO PONTIUS PILATE

27 When morning came, all the chief priests and elders of the people plotted against Jesus to put Him to death. [2]And when they had bound Him, they led Him away and delivered Him to Pontius[a] Pilate the governor.

JUDAS HANGS HIMSELF

[3]Then Judas, His betrayer, seeing that He had been condemned, was remorseful and brought back the thirty pieces of silver to the chief priests and elders, [4]saying, "I have sinned by betraying innocent blood."

And they said, "What *is that* to us? You see *to it!*"

[5]Then he threw down the pieces of silver in the temple and departed, and went and hanged himself.

[6]But the chief priests took the silver pieces and said, "It is not lawful to put them into the treasury, because they are the price of blood." [7]And they consulted together and bought with them the potter's field, to bury strangers in. [8]Therefore that field has been called the Field of Blood to this day.

[9]Then was fulfilled what was spoken by Jeremiah the prophet, saying, "And they took the thirty pieces of silver, the value of Him who was priced, whom they of the children of Israel priced, [10]and gave them for the potter's field, as the LORD directed me."[a]

JESUS FACES PILATE

[11]Now Jesus stood before the governor. And the governor asked Him, saying, "Are You the King of the Jews?"

Jesus said to him, "*It is as* you say." [12]And while He was being accused by the chief priests and elders, He answered nothing.

[13]Then Pilate said to Him, "Do You not hear how many things they testify against You?" [14]But He answered him not one word, so that the governor marveled greatly.

TAKING THE PLACE OF BARABBAS

[15]Now at the feast the governor was accustomed to releasing to the multitude one prisoner whom they wished. [16]And at that time they had a notorious prisoner called Barabbas.[a] [17]Therefore, when they had gathered together, Pilate said to them, "Whom do you want me to release to you? Barabbas, or Jesus who is called Christ?" [18]For he knew that they had handed Him over because of envy.

[19]While he was sitting on the judgment seat, his wife sent to him, saying, "Have nothing to do with that just Man, for I have suffered many things today in a dream because of Him."

[20]But the chief priests and elders persuaded the multitudes that they should ask for Barabbas and destroy Jesus. [21]The governor answered and said to them, "Which of the two do you want me to release to you?"

They said, "Barabbas!"

[22]Pilate said to them, "What then shall I do with Jesus who is called Christ?"

They all said to him, "Let Him be crucified!"

[23]Then the governor said, "Why, what evil has He done?"

But they cried out all the more, saying, "Let Him be crucified!"

[24]When Pilate saw that he could not prevail at all, but rather *that* a

26:52 [a]M-Text reads *die.*   26:59 [a]NU-Text omits *the elders.*   26:60 [a]NU-Text puts a comma after *but found none,* does not capitalize *Even,* and omits *they found none.*   [b]NU-Text omits *false witnesses.* 27:2 [a]NU-Text omits *Pontius.*   27:10 [a]Jeremiah 32:6–9   27:16 [a]NU-Text reads *Jesus Barabbas.*

tumult was rising, he took water and washed *his* hands before the multitude, saying, "I am innocent of the blood of this just Person.ᵃ You see *to it.*"

²⁵And all the people answered and said, "His blood *be* on us and on our children."

²⁶Then he released Barabbas to them; and when he had scourged Jesus, he delivered *Him* to be crucified.

THE SOLDIERS MOCK JESUS

²⁷Then the soldiers of the governor took Jesus into the Praetorium and gathered the whole garrison around Him. ²⁸And they stripped Him and put a scarlet robe on Him. ²⁹When they had twisted a crown of thorns, they put *it* on His head, and a reed in His right hand. And they bowed the knee before Him and mocked Him, saying, "Hail, King of the Jews!" ³⁰Then they spat on Him, and took the reed and struck Him on the head. ³¹And when they had mocked Him, they took the robe off Him, put His *own* clothes on Him, and led Him away to be crucified.

THE KING ON A CROSS

³²Now as they came out, they found a man of Cyrene, Simon by name. Him they compelled to bear His cross. ³³And when they had come to a place called Golgotha, that is to say, Place of a Skull, ³⁴they gave Him sourᵃ wine mingled with gall to drink. But when He had tasted *it,* He would not drink.

³⁵Then they crucified Him, and divided His garments, casting lots,ᵃ that it might be fulfilled which was spoken by the prophet:

"They divided My garments among them,
And for My clothing they cast lots."ᵇ

³⁶Sitting down, they kept watch over Him there. ³⁷And they put up over His head the accusation written against Him:

THIS IS JESUS
THE KING OF THE JEWS.

³⁸Then two robbers were crucified with Him, one on the right and another on the left.

³⁹And those who passed by blasphemed Him, wagging their heads ⁴⁰and saying, "You who destroy the temple and build *it* in three days, save Yourself! If You are the Son of God, come down from the cross."

⁴¹Likewise the chief priests also, mocking with the scribes and elders,ᵃ said, ⁴²"He saved others; Himself He cannot save. If He is the King of Israel,ᵃ let Him now come down from the cross, and we will believe Him.ᵇ ⁴³He trusted in God; let Him deliver Him now if He will have Him; for He said, 'I am the Son of God.' "

⁴⁴Even the robbers who were crucified with Him reviled Him with the same thing.

JESUS DIES ON THE CROSS

⁴⁵Now from the sixth hour until the ninth hour there was darkness over all the land. ⁴⁶And about the ninth hour Jesus cried out with a loud voice, saying, "Eli, Eli, lama sabachthani?" that is, "My God, My God, why have You forsaken Me?"ᵃ

⁴⁷Some of those who stood there, when they heard *that,* said, "This Man is calling for Elijah!" ⁴⁸Immediately one of them ran and took a sponge, filled *it* with sour wine and put *it* on a reed, and offered it to Him to drink.

⁴⁹The rest said, "Let Him alone; let us see if Elijah will come to save Him."

⁵⁰And Jesus cried out again with a loud voice, and yielded up His spirit.

⁵¹Then, behold, the veil of the temple was torn in two from top to bottom; and the earth quaked, and the rocks were split, ⁵²and the graves were opened; and many bodies of the saints who had fallen asleep were raised; ⁵³and coming out of the graves after His resurrection, they went into the holy city and appeared to many.

> (Matthew 27:45, 46, 50)

The Ninth Hour. The Bible is very precise about timing! Jesus was on the cross from noon until three o'clock in the afternoon. It was precisely at three o'clock that the last lamb was slain in the temple for the Passover Feast—this last lamb was the one sacrificed by the High Priest for all of Israel, especially those who had not been able to come up to Jerusalem for the feast. Jesus, as the Lamb of God, died at precisely that moment, completely fulfilling all of the sacrificial laws related to sin offerings.

He died as "the Lamb slain from the foundation of the world" (Revelation 13:8) and precisely at that moment, Jesus became the only sacrifice for salvation. (See Hebrews 10:10.) Also at that moment, the veil of the temple was torn in two from top to bottom. The rending of the veil was a sign that God was giving full access to the Most Holy Place, the place where Jews experienced an intimate relationship with a forgiving God.

It tore from bottom to top, which meant that the veil did not come apart because of the weight of the fabric, which would have been a rending from top to bottom. Jesus' death created full access to heaven—from earth to heaven—at precisely the moment He yielded up His spirit. When all of the details of the Crucifixion come into focus, surely we must exclaim as the Roman centurion and others at the Cross exclaimed: "Truly this was the Son of God!"

INSIGHTS INTO THE WORD

27:24 ᵃNU-Text omits *just.*   27:34 ᵃNU-Text omits *sour.*   27:35 ᵃNU-Text and M-Text omit the rest of this verse.   ᵇPsalm 22:18   27:41 ᵃM-Text reads *with the scribes, the Pharisees, and the elders.*   27:42 ᵃNU-Text reads *He is the King of Israel!*   ᵇNU-Text and M-Text read *we will believe in Him.*   27:46 ᵃPsalm 22:1

44   DIVINE HEALTH

[54]So when the centurion and those with him, who were guarding Jesus, saw the earthquake and the things that had happened, they feared greatly, saying, "Truly this was the Son of God!"

[55]And many women who followed Jesus from Galilee, ministering to Him, were there looking on from afar, [56]among whom were Mary Magdalene, Mary the mother of James and Joses,[a] and the mother of Zebedee's sons.

JESUS BURIED IN JOSEPH'S TOMB

[57]Now when evening had come, there came a rich man from Arimathea, named Joseph, who himself had also become a disciple of Jesus. [58]This man went to Pilate and asked for the body of Jesus. Then Pilate commanded the body to be given to him. [59]When Joseph had taken the body, he wrapped it in a clean linen cloth, [60]and laid it in his new tomb which he had hewn out of the rock; and he rolled a large stone against the door of the tomb, and departed. [61]And Mary Magdalene was there, and the other Mary, sitting opposite the tomb.

PILATE SETS A GUARD

[62]On the next day, which followed the Day of Preparation, the chief priests and Pharisees gathered together to Pilate, [63]saying, "Sir, we remember, while He was still alive, how that deceiver said, 'After three days I will rise.' [64]Therefore command that the tomb be made secure until the third day, lest His disciples come by night[a] and steal Him *away*, and say to the people, 'He has risen from the dead.' So the last deception will be worse than the first."

[65]Pilate said to them, "You have a guard; go your way, make *it* as secure as you know how." [66]So they went and made the tomb secure, sealing the stone and setting the guard.

HE IS RISEN

28

Now after the Sabbath, as the first *day* of the week began to dawn, Mary Magdalene and the other Mary came to see the tomb. [2]And behold, there was a great earthquake; for an angel of the Lord descended from heaven, and came and rolled back the stone from the door,[a] and sat on it. [3]His countenance was like lightning, and his clothing as white as snow. [4]And the guards shook for fear of him, and became like dead *men*.

[5]But the angel answered and said to the women, "Do not be afraid, for I know that you seek Jesus who was crucified. [6]He is not here; for He is risen, as He said. Come, see the place where the Lord lay. [7]And go quickly and tell His disciples that He is risen from the dead, and indeed He is going before you into Galilee; there you will see Him. Behold, I have told you."

[8]So they went out quickly from the tomb with fear and great joy, and ran to bring His disciples word.

THE WOMEN WORSHIP THE RISEN LORD

[9]And as they went to tell His disciples,[a] behold, Jesus met them, saying, "Rejoice!" So they came and held Him by the feet and worshiped Him. [10]Then Jesus said to them, "Do not be afraid. Go *and* tell My brethren to go to Galilee, and there they will see Me."

CONDIMENTS

☐ Coriander

We know coriander better as cilantro. Historically called "the healer from heaven," it has been used for centuries to treat minor digestive ailments, including indigestion, flatulence, and diarrhea. It has also been applied topically to ease muscle and joint pain. Research shows that it may function as an anti-inflammatory suitable for treating arthritis, and as a blood-sugar-reducing agent useful in managing diabetes.

Coriander is an annual plant in the parsley or carrot family. The "fruit" of the plant consists of grayish-white, globular seeds, which have a pleasant, aromatic oil. Coriander has been used to flavor pastries, meats, candies, salads, curries, soups, and even wine.

THE SOLDIERS ARE BRIBED

[11]Now while they were going, behold, some of the guard came into the city and reported to the chief priests all the things that had happened. [12]When they had assembled with the elders and consulted together, they gave a large sum of money to the soldiers, [13]saying, "Tell them, 'His disciples came at night and stole Him *away* while we slept.' [14]And if this comes to the governor's ears, we will appease him and make you secure." [15]So they took the money and did as they were instructed; and this saying is commonly reported among the Jews until this day.

THE GREAT COMMISSION

[16]Then the eleven disciples went away into Galilee, to the mountain which Jesus had appointed for them. [17]When they saw Him, they worshiped Him; but some doubted.

[18]And Jesus came and spoke to them, saying, "All authority has been given to Me in heaven and on earth. [19]Go therefore[a] and make disciples of all the nations, baptizing them in the name of the Father and of the Son and of the Holy Spirit, [20]teaching them to observe all things that I have commanded you; and lo, I am with you always, *even* to the end of the age." Amen.[a]

27:56 [a]NU-Text reads *Joseph.*   27:64 [a]NU-Text omits *by night.*   28:2 [a]NU-Text omits *from the door.*   28:9 [a]NU-Text omits the first clause of this verse.   28:19 [a]M-Text omits *therefore.*   28:20 [a]NU-Text omits *Amen.*

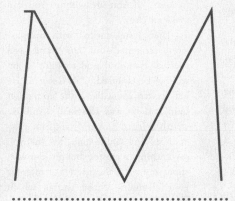

MARK

The Gospel of Mark is an "action" book—it is the shortest of the four Gospels, the stories of miracles are directly to the point, and the language is simple with strong, active verbs. The word "immediately" begins several sections of the book, conveying a sense of urgency!

The Gospel was written by John Mark (John his Hebrew name, Mark his Greek name). He was the son of a woman named Mary, whose home may have been the location of the Last Supper. John Mark was also related to Barnabas and he traveled with Paul and Barnabas. Mark also knew the apostle Peter, an eyewitness to Jesus' ministry in the Galilee. Mark himself was as an eyewitness of Jesus' ministry in Jerusalem.

Mark captures the fact that Jesus lived a very active life. Jesus didn't sit in one place and wait for people to come to Him. He went from town to town, teaching as he walked. Jesus was on the "move." To many of us who work in sedentary jobs and lead couch-potato lives, this Gospel is a challenge to get moving and go where the people are so we might share the love of Christ with them.

JOHN THE BAPTIST PREPARES THE WAY

1 The beginning of the gospel of Jesus Christ, the Son of God. [2]As it is written in the Prophets:[a]

"Behold, I send My messenger before Your face,
Who will prepare Your way before You."[b]
[3] "The voice of one crying in the wilderness:
'Prepare the way of the LORD;
Make His paths straight.' "[a]

[4]John came baptizing in the wilderness and preaching a baptism of repentance for the remission of sins. [5]Then all the land of Judea, and those from Jerusalem, went out to him and were all baptized by him in the Jordan River, confessing their sins.

[6]Now John was clothed with camel's hair and with a leather belt around his waist, and he ate locusts and wild honey. [7]And he preached, saying, "There comes One after me who is mightier than I, whose sandal strap I am not worthy to stoop down and loose. [8]I indeed baptized you with water, but He will baptize you with the Holy Spirit."

JOHN BAPTIZES JESUS

[9]It came to pass in those days *that* Jesus came from Nazareth of Galilee, and was baptized by John in the Jordan. [10]And immediately, coming up from[a] the water, He saw the heavens parting and the Spirit descending upon Him like a dove. [11]Then a voice came from heaven, "You are My beloved Son, in whom I am well pleased."

SATAN TEMPTS JESUS

[12]Immediately the Spirit drove Him into the wilderness. [13]And He was there in the wilderness forty days, tempted by Satan, and was with the wild beasts; and the angels ministered to Him.

JESUS BEGINS HIS GALILEAN MINISTRY

[14]Now after John was put in prison, Jesus came to Galilee, preaching the gospel of the kingdom[a] of God, [15]and saying, "The time is fulfilled, and the kingdom of God is at hand. Repent, and believe in the gospel."

FOUR FISHERMEN CALLED AS DISCIPLES

[16]And as He walked by the Sea of Galilee, He saw Simon and Andrew his brother casting a net into the sea; for they were fishermen. [17]Then Jesus said to them, "Follow Me, and I will make you become fishers of men." [18]They immediately left their nets and followed Him.

[19]When He had gone a little farther from there, He saw James the *son* of Zebedee, and John his brother, who also *were* in the boat mending their nets. [20]And immediately He called them, and they left their father Zebedee in the boat with the hired servants, and went after Him.

JESUS CASTS OUT AN UNCLEAN SPIRIT

[21]Then they went into Capernaum, and immediately on the Sabbath He entered the synagogue and taught. [22]And they were astonished at His teaching, for He taught them as one having authority, and not as the scribes.

1:2 [a]NU-Text reads *Isaiah the prophet.* [b]Malachi 3:1   1:3 [a]Isaiah 40:3   1:10 [a]NU-Text reads *out of.*   1:14 [a]NU-Text omits *of the kingdom.*

INSIGHTS INTO THE WORD

> (Mark 1:30, 31)

The Picture of Health. Returning to Peter's house after a synagogue service, Jesus received word that Peter's mother-in-law was lying in bed sick with a fever. Jesus went to her, and took her by the hand and lifted her up. Immediately she began to help with meal preparations for Jesus, Peter, and the other disciples traveling with them.

Not only did this woman's fever break immediately, but also she had sufficient physical strength and energy to *work*. That isn't at all the norm after a fever. Most people with a high fever feel weak and sapped of energy after a fever breaks. They prefer to sleep, not fix a meal for a group of hungry men. This healing miracle gives us a snapshot of the type of health God desires for His people: strength, energy, freedom from disease, and a motivation to serve.

²³Now there was a man in their synagogue with an unclean spirit. And he cried out, ²⁴saying, "Let *us* alone! What have we to do with You, Jesus of Nazareth? Did You come to destroy us? I know who You are—the Holy One of God!"

²⁵But Jesus rebuked him, saying, "Be quiet, and come out of him!" ²⁶And when the unclean spirit had convulsed him and cried out with a loud voice, he came out of him. ²⁷Then they were all amazed, so that they questioned among themselves, saying, "What is this? What new doctrine *is* this? For with authority[a] He commands even the unclean spirits, and they obey Him." ²⁸And immediately His fame spread throughout all the region around Galilee.

PETER'S MOTHER-IN-LAW HEALED

²⁹Now as soon as they had come out of the synagogue, they entered the house of Simon and Andrew, with James and John. ³⁰But Simon's wife's mother lay sick with a fever, and they told Him about her at once. ³¹So He came and took her by the hand and lifted her up, and immediately the fever left her. And she served them.

MANY HEALED AFTER SABBATH SUNSET

³²At evening, when the sun had set, they brought to Him all who were sick and those who were demon-possessed. ³³And the whole city was gathered together at the door. ³⁴Then He healed many who were sick with various diseases, and cast out many demons; and He did not allow the demons to speak, because they knew Him.

PREACHING IN GALILEE

³⁵Now in the morning, having risen a long while before daylight, He went out and departed to a solitary place; and there He prayed. ³⁶And Simon and those *who were* with Him searched for Him. ³⁷When they found Him, they said to Him, "Everyone is looking for You."

³⁸But He said to them, "Let us go into the next towns, that I may preach there also, because for this purpose I have come forth." ³⁹And He was preaching in their synagogues throughout all Galilee, and casting out demons.

JESUS CLEANSES A LEPER

⁴⁰Now a leper came to Him, imploring Him, kneeling down to Him and saying to Him, "If You are willing, You can make me clean."

⁴¹Then Jesus, moved with compassion, stretched out *His* hand and touched him, and said to him, "I am willing; be cleansed." ⁴²As soon as He had spoken, immediately the leprosy left him, and he was cleansed. ⁴³And He strictly warned him and sent him away at once, ⁴⁴and said to him, "See that you say nothing to anyone; but go your way, show yourself to the priest, and offer for your cleansing those things which Moses commanded, as a testimony to them."

⁴⁵However, he went out and began to proclaim *it* freely, and to spread the matter, so that Jesus could no longer openly enter the city, but was outside in deserted places; and they came to Him from every direction.

JESUS FORGIVES AND HEALS A PARALYTIC

2 And again He entered Capernaum after *some* days, and it was heard that He was in the house. ²Immediately[a] many gathered together, so that there was no longer room to receive *them*, not even near the door. And He preached the word to them. ³Then they came to Him, bringing a paralytic who was carried by four *men*. ⁴And when they could not come near Him because of the crowd, they uncovered the roof where He was. So when they had broken through, they let down the bed on which the paralytic was lying.

⁵When Jesus saw their faith, He said to the paralytic, "Son, your sins are forgiven you."

⁶And some of the scribes were sitting there and reasoning in their hearts, ⁷"Why does this *Man* speak blasphemies like this? Who can forgive sins but God alone?"

⁸But immediately, when Jesus perceived in His spirit that they reasoned thus within themselves, He said to them, "Why do you reason about these things in your hearts? ⁹Which is easier, to say to the paralytic, '*Your* sins are forgiven you,' or to say, 'Arise, take up your bed and walk'? ¹⁰But that you may know that the Son of Man has power on earth to forgive sins"—He said to the paralytic, ¹¹"I say to you, arise, take up your bed, and go to your house." ¹²Immediately he arose, took up the bed, and went out in the presence of them all, so that all were amazed and glorified God, saying, "We never saw *anything* like this!"

MATTHEW THE TAX COLLECTOR

¹³Then He went out again by the sea; and all the multitude came to Him, and He taught them. ¹⁴As He passed by, He saw Levi the *son* of Alphaeus sitting at the tax office. And He said to him, "Follow Me." So he arose and followed Him.

¹⁵Now it happened, as He was dining in *Levi's* house, that many tax collectors and sinners also sat together with Jesus and His disciples;

1:27 [a]NU-Text reads *What is this? A new doctrine with authority.*   **2:2** [a]NU-Text omits *Immediately.*

for there were many, and they followed Him. [16]And when the scribes and[a] Pharisees saw Him eating with the tax collectors and sinners, they said to His disciples, "How *is it* that He eats and drinks with tax collectors and sinners?"

[17]When Jesus heard *it,* He said to them, "Those who are well have no need of a physician, but those who are sick. I did not come to call *the* righteous, but sinners, to repentance."[a]

JESUS IS QUESTIONED ABOUT FASTING

[18]The disciples of John and of the Pharisees were fasting. Then they came and said to Him, "Why do the disciples of John and of the Pharisees fast, but Your disciples do not fast?"

[19]And Jesus said to them, "Can the friends of the bridegroom fast while the bridegroom is with them? As long as they have the bridegroom with them they cannot fast. [20]But the days will come when the bridegroom will be taken away from them, and then they will fast in those days. [21]No one sews a piece of unshrunk cloth on an old garment; or else the new piece pulls away from the old, and the tear is made worse. [22]And no one puts new wine into old wineskins; or else the new wine bursts the wineskins, the wine is spilled, and the wineskins are ruined. But new wine must be put into new wineskins."

JESUS IS LORD OF THE SABBATH

[23]Now it happened that He went through the grainfields on the Sabbath; and as they went His disciples began to pluck the heads of grain. [24]And the Pharisees said to Him, "Look, why do they do what is not lawful on the Sabbath?"

[25]But He said to them, "Have you never read what David did when he was in need and hungry, he and those with him: [26]how he went into the house of God *in the days* of Abiathar the high priest, and ate the showbread, which is not lawful to eat except for the priests, and also gave some to those who were with him?"

[27]And He said to them, "The Sabbath was made for man, and not man for the Sabbath. [28]Therefore the Son of Man is also Lord of the Sabbath."

PRESCRIPTIONS FOR INNER HEALTH

"The mouth of the righteous is a well of life,
But violence covers the mouth of the wicked."

(PROVERBS 10:11)

If you love what is good and right in God's sight in your *heart,* you will be quick to speak words that promote what is good and right—all things that contribute to a higher quality of life for yourself and other people. If you love what is evil, even the so-called "good words" you speak will be perceived as evil, cynical, sarcastic, or negative. What you say, and how you say it, reveals much about your character and the degree to which you possess God's wisdom.

HEALING ON THE SABBATH

3 And He entered the synagogue again, and a man was there who had a withered hand. [2]So they watched Him closely, whether He would heal him on the Sabbath, so that they might accuse Him. [3]And He said to the man who had the withered hand, "Step forward." [4]Then He said to them, "Is it lawful on the Sabbath to do good or to do evil, to save life or to kill?" But they kept

> (Mark 2:3, 4)

Four Friends Rally to Help. Perhaps nothing is more encouraging to a sick person than to have friends who care enough to help in practical ways beyond offering words of sympathy or encouragement. The paralyzed man who was lowered through a roof into Jesus' presence had four such friends. We don't know what caused this man's paralysis. He may have suffered an injury or illness, or he may have become so fearful about something that he lost physical control over his large muscles. Intense fear can paralyze a person!

What we do know is that there was a spiritual component to his paralysis because the *first* thing that Jesus did was pronounce forgiveness of sins to this man. For whatever reason, this man and the others who heard Jesus needed to hear this pronouncement. Jesus made it clear to all gathered there that He had the authority to forgive *and* to heal. Both are required for wholeness and Jesus had the power and authority to make people *whole.* Jesus also made it clear that it was no more difficult to do one than the other. God's power and desire to heal is just as strong as His power and desire to forgive.

INSIGHTS INTO THE WORD

Hummus

Righteous Recipes

This is a great dip to have with fresh vegetables or pieces of pita bread. It is also good as a condiment for whole grains.

Ingredients:

- ☐ 2 cups dried chickpeas (garbanzo beans)
- ☐ ½ cup tahini (or less depending on taste)
- ☐ 2 tablespoons extra-virgin olive oil
- ☐ 1 garlic clove, minced
- ☐ ½ to 1 teaspoon Celtic salt
- ☐ ½ teaspoon cumin
- ☐ Juice of 2 medium lemons

Cover the chickpeas with water and soak for 8 to 10 hours. Drain well. Then place the drained chickpeas in 1 quart fresh water and bring to a boil. Reduce the heat and simmer for 1 to 2 hours or until the chickpeas are tender. Drain well. Puree the chickpeas in a blender or food processor. Add the tahini, olive oil, garlic, salt, cumin, and lemon juice. Blend until smooth. Adjust the seasoning to taste. Serve immediately, or store in an airtight container in the refrigerator until serving time. The dip will keep about 5 days.

Yield: about 4 cups. The recipe is easily doubled.

Idumea and beyond the Jordan; and those from Tyre and Sidon, a great multitude, when they heard how many things He was doing, came to Him. [9]So He told His disciples that a small boat should be kept ready for Him because of the multitude, lest they should crush Him. [10]For He healed many, so that as many as had afflictions pressed about Him to touch Him. [11]And the unclean spirits, whenever they saw Him, fell down before Him and cried out, saying, "You are the Son of God." [12]But He sternly warned them that they should not make Him known.

THE TWELVE APOSTLES

[13]And He went up on the mountain and called to *Him* those He Himself wanted. And they came to Him. [14]Then He appointed twelve,[a] that they might be with Him and that He might send them out to preach, [15]and to have power to heal sicknesses and[a] to cast out demons: [16]Simon,[a] to whom He gave the name Peter; [17]James the *son* of Zebedee and John the brother of James, to whom He gave the name Boanerges, that is, "Sons of Thunder"; [18]Andrew, Philip, Bartholomew, Matthew, Thomas, James the *son* of Alphaeus, Thaddaeus, Simon the Cananite; [19]and Judas Iscariot, who also betrayed Him. And they went into a house.

A HOUSE DIVIDED CANNOT STAND

[20]Then the multitude came together again, so that they could not so much as eat bread. [21]But when His own people heard *about this*, they went out to lay hold of Him, for they said, "He is out of His mind."

[22]And the scribes who came down from Jerusalem said, "He has Beelzebub," and, "By the ruler of the demons He casts out demons."

[23]So He called them to *Himself* and said to them in parables: "How can Satan cast out Satan? [24]If a kingdom is divided against itself, that kingdom cannot stand. [25]And if a house is divided against itself, that house cannot stand. [26]And if Satan has risen up against himself, and is divided, he cannot stand, but has an end. [27]No one can enter a strong man's house and plunder his goods, unless he first binds the strong man. And then he will plunder his house.

THE UNPARDONABLE SIN

[28]"Assuredly, I say to you, all sins will be forgiven the sons of men, and whatever blasphemies they may utter; [29]but he who blasphemes against the Holy Spirit never has forgiveness, but is subject to eternal condemnation"— [30]because they said, "He has an unclean spirit."

JESUS' MOTHER AND BROTHERS SEND FOR HIM

[31]Then His brothers and His mother came, and standing outside they sent to Him, calling Him. [32]And a multitude was sitting around Him; and they said to Him, "Look, Your mother and Your brothers[a] are outside seeking You."

[33]But He answered them, saying, "Who is My mother, or My brothers?" [34]And He looked around in a circle at those who sat about Him,

silent. [5]And when He had looked around at them with anger, being grieved by the hardness of their hearts, He said to the man, "Stretch out your hand." And he stretched *it* out, and his hand was restored as whole as the other.[a] [6]Then the Pharisees went out and immediately plotted with the Herodians against Him, how they might destroy Him.

A GREAT MULTITUDE FOLLOWS JESUS

[7]But Jesus withdrew with His disciples to the sea. And a great multitude from Galilee followed Him, and from Judea [8]and Jerusalem and

3:5 [a]NU-Text omits *as whole as the other.*   3:14 [a]NU-Text adds *whom He also named apostles.*   3:15 [a]NU-Text omits *to heal sicknesses and.*   3:16 [a]NU-Text reads *and He appointed the twelve: Simon. . . .*
3:32 [a]NU-Text and M-Text add *and Your sisters.*

February

1   **3**   **4**   **5**   **6**   **7**

Now Is the Time To...

☐ Write a letter to a longstanding friend—or give that friend a call.   ☐ Read a book in front of the fireplace on a quiet evening.   ☐ Take a walk in the cool, brisk air.   ☐ Take a soothing bubble bath; light some candles and just relax.   ☐ Invite a friend to the gym as your guest and enjoy working out together.   ☐ Begin reading a new book today. Consider selecting a nonfiction book on a subject of interest that you have not yet explored. Learn something new!

Seasonal Tips

8   **9**   **10**   **11**   **12**

☐ Inspect your lawn mower and garden tools to see if they need oiling, servicing, repairing, or replacing.   ☐ Prune your shade, flowering, or fruit trees.   ☐ Keep your outdoor birdseed containers filled and check your birdbath to make sure the water hasn't frozen.

13   **14**

In the Garden

15   **16**   **17**   **18**   **19**   **20**   **21**

☐ Plant seeds in containers indoors to jumpstart herbs and vegetable plants.   ☐ If it's not too cold, begin tilling and spading your vegetable garden area.   ☐ Consider sowing early vegetable seeds in your garden, and then covering the ground of your vegetable plot with a thick plastic sheet.   ☐ Plant your favorite fruit tree.

Table Fresh

22   **23**   **24**   **25**   **26**   **27**   **28**

☐ Try grilled chicken on your salad tonight. Serve hummus and pita bread on the side.   ☐ Make soft tacos for dinner using ground turkey and whole-wheat tortillas.   ☐ Juice today: 2 celery stalks, 2 carrots, and 2 apples.

Let's Celebrate

☐ Do something special as a surprise for someone you love!   ☐ Call someone just to say "I love you!"   ☐ **Lent.** Beginning with Ash Wednesday, Lent is a time for sober reflection on life's priorities. Originally a preparation time for the baptism of adults, Lent is a time to determine if there are things in your life that you need to get rid of, or perhaps new spiritual disciplines that you need to add or emphasize. Lent begins forty days before Easter—with Sundays omitted—and ends the night before Easter.

WALKING THE WALK

[TRAINING FOR A MARATHON]

If you are no longer being challenged in the sport of walking, you might consider signing up for a marathon. With proper training you can be ready to walk a half or full marathon in just five months.

Here are a few things to consider as you train:

☐ *Schedule.* Set apart the necessary hours each week to train consistently.

☐ *Have a Plan.* Walk at least three or four days a week and cross train two days a week. Give your body at least one day a week to rest.

☐ *Lift Weights.* By lifting weights in addition to your walking and cross training, you can increase muscle mass and strength in your legs.

☐ *Diet.* A good nutrition plan can play a key role in marathon training. Work with knowledgeable trainers.

☐ *Race.* As you select your race, be aware that not all marathons offer a "half marathon" finish line. If you are interested in a race that is less than a marathon, check for races that have 5K or 10K options. Some "fun walks" are only one or two miles.

☐ *Coaches.* Most cities have organizations, groups, or clubs that will help you train. Sometimes this is in exchange for fund-raising for a charity. In some cases, you may need to pay a small fee to become a member of the group.

Once you're trained and are ready to go, here are some things to remember for race day:

☐ *Gear.* Gather everything you'll need two days before the race. If you wait until the night before the race to get your gear organized, you'll probably get to bed later than planned. CONT. NEXT PAGE>>>

---

and said, "Here are My mother and My brothers! ³⁵For whoever does the will of God is My brother and My sister and mother."

THE PARABLE OF THE SOWER

4 And again He began to teach by the sea. And a great multitude was gathered to Him, so that He got into a boat and sat *in it* on the sea; and the whole multitude was on the land facing the sea. ²Then He taught them many things by parables, and said to them in His teaching:

³"Listen! Behold, a sower went out to sow. ⁴And it happened, as he sowed, *that* some *seed* fell by the wayside; and the birds of the airᵃ came and devoured it. ⁵Some fell on stony ground, where it did not have much earth; and immediately it sprang up because it had no depth of earth. ⁶But when the sun was up it was scorched, and because it had no root it withered away. ⁷And some *seed* fell among thorns; and the thorns grew up and choked it, and it yielded no crop. ⁸But other *seed* fell on good ground and yielded a crop that sprang up, increased and produced: some thirtyfold, some sixty, and some a hundred."

⁹And He said to them,ᵃ "He who has ears to hear, let him hear!"

THE PURPOSE OF PARABLES

¹⁰But when He was alone, those around Him with the twelve asked Him about the parable. ¹¹And He said to them, "To you it has been given to know the mystery of the kingdom of God; but to those who are outside, all things come in parables, ¹²so that

'Seeing they may see and not perceive,
And hearing they may hear and not understand;
Lest they should turn,
And their sins be forgiven them.' "ᵃ

THE PARABLE OF THE SOWER EXPLAINED

¹³And He said to them, "Do you not understand this parable? How then will you understand all the parables? ¹⁴The sower sows the word. ¹⁵And these are the ones by the wayside where the word is sown. When they hear, Satan comes immediately and takes away the word that was sown in their hearts. ¹⁶These likewise are the ones sown on stony ground who, when they hear the word, immediately receive it with gladness; ¹⁷and they have no root in themselves, and so endure only for a time. Afterward, when tribulation or persecution arises for the word's sake, immediately they stumble. ¹⁸Now these are the ones sown among thorns; *they are* the ones who hear the word, ¹⁹and the cares of this world, the deceitfulness of riches, and the desires for other things entering in choke the word, and it becomes unfruitful. ²⁰But these are the ones sown on good ground, those who hear the word, accept *it*, and bear fruit: some thirtyfold, some sixty, and some a hundred."

LIGHT UNDER A BASKET

²¹Also He said to them, "Is a lamp brought to be put under a basket or under a bed? Is it not to be set on a lampstand? ²²For there is nothing hidden which will not be revealed, nor has anything been kept secret but that it should come to light. ²³If anyone has ears to hear, let him hear."

4:4 ᵃNU-Text and M-Text omit *of the air*.   4:9 ᵃNU-Text and M-Text omit *to them*.   4:12 ᵃIsaiah 6:9, 10

☐ *Breakfast.* Eat breakfast before leaving your house. Do not eat anything on race day that you've not already eaten on a training day. Avoid all citrus the morning of a race. A bagel with peanut butter and a banana makes a good race-day breakfast.

☐ *Arrive early.* Well-publicized marathons usually attract a large group of fans and participants. Be prepared for road closures and detours—map out the route you'll need to take to get to the starting line. If you park at the starting line, have a plan for getting back to that point so you can retrieve your car. Start and finish lines for many races are in the same location.

☐ *Stretch,* stretch, and then stretch some more.

☐ *Port-a-potty.* Seasoned marathon runners often say, "Get in line early, have someone save your place and go, and then get back in line." Although the lines at the port-a-potty may be long, they generally move quickly.

☐ *Check unnecessary gear.* If you have a jacket or belongings with you that you don't want to carry during the race, check them at the "gear check," and you will be able to pick them up at the finish line.

☐ *Starting line.* Find your corral ahead of the starting gun being fired, so you can start on time.

Just as in any sport, it is important that you continually challenge yourself to go to the next level!

[24]Then He said to them, "Take heed what you hear. With the same measure you use, it will be measured to you; and to you who hear, more will be given. [25]For whoever has, to him more will be given; but whoever does not have, even what he has will be taken away from him."

THE PARABLE OF THE GROWING SEED

[26]And He said, "The kingdom of God is as if a man should scatter seed on the ground, [27]and should sleep by night and rise by day, and the seed should sprout and grow, he himself does not know how. [28]For the earth yields crops by itself: first the blade, then the head, after that the full grain in the head. [29]But when the grain ripens, immediately he puts in the sickle, because the harvest has come."

THE PARABLE OF THE MUSTARD SEED

[30]Then He said, "To what shall we liken the kingdom of God? Or with what parable shall we picture it? [31]*It is* like a mustard seed which, when it is sown on the ground, is smaller than all the seeds on earth; [32]but when it is sown, it grows up and becomes greater than all herbs, and shoots out large branches, so that the birds of the air may nest under its shade."

JESUS' USE OF PARABLES

[33]And with many such parables He spoke the word to them as they were able to hear *it.* [34]But without a parable He did not speak to them. And when they were alone, He explained all things to His disciples.

WIND AND WAVE OBEY JESUS

[35]On the same day, when evening had come, He said to them, "Let us cross over to the other side." [36]Now when they had left the multitude, they took Him along in the boat as He was. And other little boats were also with Him. [37]And a great windstorm arose, and the waves beat into the boat, so that it was already filling. [38]But He was in the stern, asleep on a pillow. And they awoke Him and said to Him, "Teacher, do You not care that we are perishing?"

[39]Then He arose and rebuked the wind, and said to the sea, "Peace, be still!" And the wind ceased and there was a great calm. [40]But He said to them, "Why are you so fearful? How *is it* that you have no faith?"[a] [41]And they feared exceedingly, and said to one another, "Who can this be, that even the wind and the sea obey Him!"

A DEMON-POSSESSED MAN HEALED

5 Then they came to the other side of the sea, to the country of the Gadarenes.[a] [2]And when He had come out of the boat, immediately there met Him out of the tombs a man with an unclean spirit, [3]who had *his* dwelling among the tombs; and no one could bind him,[a] not even with chains, [4]because he had often been bound with shackles and chains. And the chains had been pulled apart by him, and the shackles broken in pieces; neither could anyone tame him. [5]And always, night and day, he was in the mountains and in the tombs, crying out and cutting himself with stones.

[6]When he saw Jesus from afar, he ran and worshiped Him. [7]And he cried out with a loud voice and said, "What have I to do with You, Jesus, Son of the Most High God? I implore You by God that You do not torment me."

[8]For He said to him, "Come out of the man, unclean spirit!" [9]Then He asked him, "What *is* your name?"

And he answered, saying, "My name *is* Legion; for we are many." [10]Also he begged Him earnestly that He would not send them out of the country.

[11]Now a large herd of

WISE CHOICES

Choose Celtic salt over regular salt.
Celtic salt is a sea salt. It is a natural salt with all its nutrients still intact. Common table salt has been processed and is often mixed with aluminum to make it more soluble. Avoid the intake of aluminum whenever possible!

4:40 [a]NU-Text reads *Have you still no faith?* 5:1 [a]NU-Text reads *Gerasenes.* 5:3 [a]NU-Text adds *anymore.*

SCRIPTURE SOLUTIONS

[SKIN DISORDERS]

At some point in life, nearly every person experiences some type of skin disorder, such as acne, psoriasis, or eczema. To keep your skin glowing with health, check your diet and rid your body and skin of toxins.

When you hear the word *toxic* you may picture a garbage dump. If so, you're not too far off. If we continually feed our body garbage, it will become toxic. When toxins seek to escape the body, they sometimes travel through the skin. The connection between skin problems and toxicity is very high.

The liver is the main cleaning filter that eliminates up to 99 percent of harmful toxins, poisons, and anything else that would be of danger to your body. To keep the liver clean and working properly, here are four things to consider:

Water. Since water is the best cleanser for the body, drink plenty of pure water every day. Decrease your consumption of other drinks such as coffee and sodas and drink more water.

Food. Be aware of what you are eating. Are you eating at least five servings of fruits and vegetables a day? Are you following a properly balanced carbohydrate-protein-fat eating plan? The more healthful your diet, the better your liver will function, and the clearer your skin will be.

Allergies. Know what you may be allergic to and refrain from eating it.

Additives, preservatives, and exposure to chemicals. Avoid known environmental toxins and you'll have a jumpstart on eliminating the toxicity level of your own body.

As your liver health improves, it is very likely you will have fresher, cleaner, clearer skin.

---

swine was feeding there near the mountains. [12]So all the demons begged Him, saying, "Send us to the swine, that we may enter them." [13]And at once Jesus[a] gave them permission. Then the unclean spirits went out and entered the swine (there were about two thousand); and the herd ran violently down the steep place into the sea, and drowned in the sea.

[14]So those who fed the swine fled, and they told *it* in the city and in the country. And they went out to see what it was that had happened. [15]Then they came to Jesus, and saw the one *who had been* demon-possessed and had the legion, sitting and clothed and in his right mind. And they were afraid. [16]And those who saw it told them how it happened to him *who had been* demon-possessed, and about the swine. [17]Then they began to plead with Him to depart from their region.

[18]And when He got into the boat, he who had been demon-possessed begged Him that he might be with Him. [19]However, Jesus did not permit him, but said to him, "Go home to your friends, and tell them what great things the Lord has done for you, and how He has had compassion on you." [20]And he departed and began to proclaim in Decapolis all that Jesus had done for him; and all marveled.

A GIRL RESTORED TO LIFE AND A WOMAN HEALED

[21]Now when Jesus had crossed over again by boat to the other side, a great multitude gathered to Him; and He was by the sea. [22]And behold, one of the rulers of the synagogue came, Jairus by name. And when he saw Him, he fell at His feet [23]and begged Him earnestly, saying, "My little daughter lies at the point of death. Come and lay Your hands on her, that she may be healed, and she will live." [24]So *Jesus* went with him, and a great multitude followed Him and thronged Him.

[25]Now a certain woman had a flow of blood for twelve years, [26]and had suffered many things from many physicians. She had spent all that she had and was no better, but rather grew worse. [27]When she heard about Jesus, she came behind *Him* in the crowd and touched His garment. [28]For she said, "If only I may touch His clothes, I shall be made well."

[29]Immediately the fountain of her blood was dried up, and she felt in *her* body that she was healed of the affliction. [30]And Jesus, immediately knowing in Himself that power had gone out of Him, turned around in the crowd and said, "Who touched My clothes?"

[31]But His disciples said to Him, "You see the multitude thronging You, and You say, 'Who touched Me?' "

[32]And He looked around to see her who had done this thing. [33]But the woman, fearing and trembling, knowing what had happened to her, came and fell down before Him and told Him the whole truth. [34]And He said to her, "Daughter, your faith has made you well. Go in peace, and be healed of your affliction."

[35]While He was still speaking, *some* came from the ruler of the synagogue's *house* who said, "Your daughter is dead. Why trouble the Teacher any further?"

[36]As soon as Jesus heard the word that was spoken, He said to the ruler of the synagogue, "Do not be afraid; only believe." [37]And He permitted no one to follow Him except Peter, James, and John the brother of James. [38]Then He came to the house of the ruler of the synagogue, and saw a tumult and those who wept and wailed loudly. [39]When He

5:13 [a]NU-Text reads *And He gave.*

came in, He said to them, "Why make this commotion and weep? The child is not dead, but sleeping."

⁴⁰And they ridiculed Him. But when He had put them all outside, He took the father and the mother of the child, and those *who were* with Him, and entered where the child was lying. ⁴¹Then He took the child by the hand, and said to her, "Talitha, cumi," which is translated, "Little girl, I say to you, arise." ⁴²Immediately the girl arose and walked, for she was twelve years *of age.* And they were overcome with great amazement. ⁴³But He commanded them strictly that no one should know it, and said that *something* should be given her to eat.

JESUS REJECTED AT NAZARETH

6 Then He went out from there and came to His own country, and His disciples followed Him. ²And when the Sabbath had come, He began to teach in the synagogue. And many hearing *Him* were astonished, saying, "Where *did* this Man *get* these things? And what wisdom *is* this which is given to Him, that such mighty works are performed by His hands! ³Is this not the carpenter, the Son of Mary, and brother of James, Joses, Judas, and Simon? And are not His sisters here with us?" So they were offended at Him.

⁴But Jesus said to them, "A prophet is not without honor except in his own country, among his own relatives, and in his own house." ⁵Now He could do no mighty work there, except that He laid His hands on a few sick people and healed *them.* ⁶And He marveled because of their unbelief. Then He went about the villages in a circuit, teaching.

SENDING OUT THE TWELVE

⁷And He called the twelve to *Himself,* and began to send them out two *by* two, and gave them power over unclean spirits. ⁸He commanded them to take nothing for the journey except a staff—no bag, no bread, no copper in *their* money belts— ⁹but to wear sandals, and not to put on two tunics.

¹⁰Also He said to them, "In whatever place you enter a house, stay there till you depart from that place. ¹¹And whoeverᵃ will not receive you nor hear you, when you depart from

▼ Can Emotions Kill? ▲

ULTIMATE HEALTH RESOURCE • ULTIMATE HEALTH RESOURCE • ULTIMATE HEALTH RESOURCE •

According to the American Institute of Stress, between 75 and 90 percent of all visits to primary care physicians result from *stress-related disorders.* Many of these visits are associated with obvious symptoms of stress: headaches, digestive-tract problems, and skin eruptions. If the core ailments that are giving rise to these symptoms are not addressed, additional symptoms can appear: sleeplessness, weight loss or gain, muscle aches, feelings of exhaustion, sluggish thinking, and a lack of ambition. Core causes of stress *can* turn into outright disease— the kinds that require surgery, chemotherapy, radiation therapy, heavy-duty medication, and other serious treatment protocols.

Stress is the body and mind's response to any pressure that disrupts the balance of physical systems. The cause may be something in the environment, or it may be something in the mind or emotions. The body does not differentiate between environmental and psychological stress! Studies show that those who have ongoing stress reactions have

☐ a 40 percent higher death rate than non-stressed individuals;
☐ a significantly increased risk of coronary heart disease;
☐ a greater risk of heart attack.

They also are much more prone to increased bone loss, reduced muscle mass, inhibited skin regeneration, increased fat accumulation, and impaired learning and memory.

In addition, stress triggers a chemical reaction in the body that releases elevated amounts of adrenaline and cortisone. Over time, too much of these hormones in the body can "sear" the body so that higher and higher amounts are required for the same effect. Long-term chronic stress—including such emotions as pent-up hatred, seething anger, slow-smoldering resentment, and ongoing bitterness— cause burnout of the systems that produce adrenaline and cortisone. At that point, the body has much lower immunity and is much more prone to infections and autoimmune diseases, including cancer.

What must we do? We must recognize that ongoing emotions such as rage, unforgiveness, depression, anger, worry, frustration, fear, grief, and guilt *can* put a person's health into a "higher risk" category. We also need to learn how to turn off stress in our lives. Stress can and does kill.

6:11 ᵃNU-Text reads *whatever place.*

there, shake off the dust under your feet as a testimony against them.[b] Assuredly, I say to you, it will be more tolerable for Sodom and Gomorrah in the day of judgment than for that city!"

[12]So they went out and preached that *people* should repent. [13]And they cast out many demons, and anointed with oil many who were sick, and healed *them*.

JOHN THE BAPTIST BEHEADED

[14]Now King Herod heard *of Him*, for His name had become well known. And he said, "John the Baptist is risen from the dead, and therefore these powers are at work in him."

[15]Others said, "It is Elijah."

And others said, "It is the Prophet, or[a] like one of the prophets."

[16]But when Herod heard, he said, "This is John, whom I beheaded; he has been raised from the dead!" [17]For Herod himself had sent and laid hold of John, and bound him in prison for the sake of Herodias, his brother Philip's wife; for he had married her. [18]Because John had said to Herod, "It is not lawful for you to have your brother's wife."

[19]Therefore Herodias held it against him and wanted to kill him, but she could not; [20]for Herod feared John, knowing that he *was* a just and holy man, and he protected him. And when he heard him, he did many things, and heard him gladly.

[21]Then an opportune day came when Herod on his birthday gave a feast for his nobles, the high officers, and the chief *men* of Galilee. [22]And when Herodias' daughter herself came in and danced, and pleased Herod and those who sat with him, the king said to the girl, "Ask me whatever you want, and I will give *it* to you." [23]He also swore to her, "Whatever you ask me, I will give you, up to half my kingdom."

[24]So she went out and said to her mother, "What shall I ask?"

And she said, "The head of John the Baptist!"

[25]Immediately she came in with haste to the king and asked, saying, "I want you to give me at once the head of John the Baptist on a platter."

[26]And the king was exceedingly sorry; *yet*, because of the oaths and because of those who sat with him, he did not want to refuse her. [27]Immediately the king sent an executioner and commanded his head to be brought. And he went and beheaded him in prison, [28]brought his head on a platter, and gave it to the girl; and the girl gave it to her mother. [29]When his disciples heard *of it*, they came and took away his corpse and laid it in a tomb.

FEEDING THE FIVE THOUSAND

[30]Then the apostles gathered to Jesus and told Him all things, both what they had done and what they had taught. [31]And He said to them, "Come aside by yourselves to a deserted place and rest a while." For there were many coming and going, and they did not even have time to eat. [32]So they departed to a deserted place in the boat by themselves.

[33]But the multitudes[a] saw them departing, and many knew Him and ran there on foot from all the cities. They arrived before them and came together to Him. [34]And Jesus, when He came out, saw a great multitude and was moved with compassion for them, because they were like sheep not having a shepherd. So He began to teach them many things. [35]When the day was now far spent, His disciples came to Him and said, "This is a deserted place, and already the hour *is* late. [36]Send them away, that they may go into the surrounding country and villages and buy themselves bread;[a] for they have nothing to eat."

[37]But He answered and said to them, "You give them something to eat."

And they said to Him, "Shall we go and buy two hundred denarii worth of bread and give them *something* to eat?"

[38]But He said to them, "How many loaves do you have? Go and see." And when they found out they said, "Five, and two fish."

[39]Then He commanded them to make them all sit down in groups on the green grass. [40]So they sat down in ranks, in hundreds and in fifties. [41]And when He had taken the five loaves and the two fish, He looked up to heaven, blessed and broke the loaves, and gave *them* to His disciples to set before them; and the two fish He divided among *them* all. [42]So they all ate and were filled. [43]And they took up twelve baskets full of fragments and of the fish. [44]Now those who had eaten the loaves were about[a] five thousand men.

JESUS WALKS ON THE SEA

[45]Immediately He made His disciples get into the boat and go before Him to the other side, to Bethsaida, while He sent the multitude away. [46]And when He had sent them away, He departed to the mountain to pray. [47]Now when evening came, the boat was in the middle of the sea; and He *was* alone on the land. [48]Then He saw them straining at rowing, for the wind was against them. Now about the fourth watch of the night He came to them, walking on the sea, and would have passed them by. [49]And when they saw Him walking on the sea, they sup-

INSIGHTS INTO THE WORD

> (Mark 6:38)

Barley Bread. The loaves that Jesus multiplied were barley loaves. The prophet Elisha also multiplied barley loaves—in his case, twenty loaves of barley bread were multiplied to feed a hundred men. (See 2 Kings 4:42–44.) In the Middle East, barley has been called the "medicine for the heart." It contains fiber that can lower the risk of heart disease by reducing artery-clogged LDL (bad) cholesterol. The same high fiber content keeps a person regular, relieving constipation and warding off a variety of digestive problems. It may also help block the development of cancer. Today, barley bread is virtually nonexistent—you would have to make this bread for yourself from barley grain that can be found in some health-food stores. Barley is sometimes used as an ingredient in soups.

6:11 [b]NU-Text omits the rest of this verse.   6:15 [a]NU-Text and M-Text omit *or*.   6:33 [a]NU-Text and M-Text read *they*.   6:36 [a]NU-Text reads *something to eat* and omits the rest of this verse.   6:44 [a]NU-Text and M-Text omit *about*.

56   DIVINE HEALTH

posed it was a ghost, and cried out; [50]for they all saw Him and were troubled. But immediately He talked with them and said to them, "Be of good cheer! It is I; do not be afraid." [51]Then He went up into the boat to them, and the wind ceased. And they were greatly amazed in themselves beyond measure, and marveled. [52]For they had not understood about the loaves, because their heart was hardened.

MANY TOUCH HIM AND ARE MADE WELL

[53]When they had crossed over, they came to the land of Gennesaret and anchored there. [54]And when they came out of the boat, immediately the people recognized Him, [55]ran through that whole surrounding region, and began to carry about on beds those who were sick to wherever they heard He was. [56]Wherever He entered, into villages, cities, or the country, they laid the sick in the marketplaces, and begged Him that they might just touch the hem of His garment. And as many as touched Him were made well.

DEFILEMENT COMES FROM WITHIN

7 Then the Pharisees and some of the scribes came together to Him, having come from Jerusalem. [2]Now when[a] they saw some of His disciples eat bread with defiled, that is, with unwashed hands, they found fault. [3]For the Pharisees and all the Jews do not eat unless they wash *their* hands in a special way, holding the tradition of the elders. [4]*When they come* from the marketplace, they do not eat unless they wash. And there are many other things which they have received and hold, *like* the washing of cups, pitchers, copper vessels, and couches.

[5]Then the Pharisees and scribes asked Him, "Why do Your disciples not walk according to the tradition of the elders, but eat bread with unwashed hands?"

[6]He answered and said to them, "Well did Isaiah prophesy of you hypocrites, as it is written:

'This people honors Me with their lips,
But their heart is far from Me.
[7] And in vain they worship Me,
Teaching as doctrines the commandments of men.'[a]

[8]For laying aside the commandment of God, you hold the tradition of men[a]—the washing of pitchers and cups, and many other such things you do."

[9]He said to them, "*All too* well you reject the commandment of God, that you may keep your tradition. [10]For Moses said, 'Honor your father and your mother';[a] and, 'He who curses father or mother, let him be put to death.'[b] [11]But you say, 'If a man says to his father or mother,

---

> ## (Mark 6:45–52)

Walking in Water.
Jesus—and the apostle Peter—may have been successful in walking on water, but for most of us, walking *in* water is something we can do readily and should consider doing frequently! Water aerobics exercises, including walking or jogging in place in the shallow end of a swimming pool, are especially good exercises for those who are overweight, have joint problems, are pregnant, or don't know how to swim. Swimming or jogging in warm water is also helpful for those who have arthritis. Walking in water, however, will not do much to help osteoporosis. There's not enough resistance placed on the body in water. Supplement your water aerobics with weight training to build up the strength of your bones.

INSIGHTS INTO THE WORD

"Whatever profit you might have received from me *is* Corban"—' (that is, a gift *to God*), [12]then you no longer let him do anything for his father or his mother, [13]making the word of God of no effect through your tradition which you have handed down. And many such things you do."

[14]When He had called all the multitude to *Himself,* He said to them, "Hear Me, everyone, and understand: [15]There is nothing that enters a man from outside which can defile him; but the things which come out of him, those are the things that defile a man. [16]If anyone has ears to hear, let him hear!"[a]

[17]When He had entered a house away from the crowd, His disciples asked Him concerning the parable. [18]So He said to them, "Are you thus without understanding also? Do you not perceive that whatever enters a man from outside cannot defile him, [19]because it does not enter his heart but his stomach, and is eliminated, *thus* purifying all foods?"[a] [20]And He said, "What comes out of a man, that defiles a man. [21]For from within, out of the heart of men, proceed evil thoughts, adulteries, fornications, murders, [22]thefts, covetousness, wickedness, deceit, lewdness, an evil eye, blasphemy, pride, foolishness. [23]All these evil things come from within and defile a man."

A GENTILE SHOWS HER FAITH

[24]From there He arose and went to the region of Tyre and Sidon.[a] And He entered a house and wanted no one to know *it*, but He could not be hidden. [25]For a woman whose young daughter had an unclean spirit heard about Him, and she came and fell at His feet. [26]The woman was a Greek, a Syro-Phoenician by birth, and she kept asking Him to cast the demon out of her daughter. [27]But Jesus said to her, "Let the children be filled first, for it is not good to take the children's bread and throw *it* to the little dogs."

[28]And she answered and said to Him, "Yes, Lord, yet even the little dogs under the table eat from the children's crumbs."

[29]Then He said to her, "For this saying go your way; the demon has gone out of your daughter."

[30]And when she had come to her house, she found the demon gone out, and her daughter lying on the bed.

7:2 [a]NU-Text omits *when* and *they found fault.*   7:7 [a]Isaiah 29:13   7:8 [a]NU-Text omits the rest of this verse.   7:10 [a]Exodus 20:12; Deuteronomy 5:16 [b]Exodus 21:17   7:16 [a]NU-Text omits this verse.
7:19 [a]NU-Text ends quotation with *eliminated,* setting off the final clause as Mark's comment that Jesus has declared all foods clean.   7:24 [a]NU-Text omits *and Sidon.*

WEIGHING Less & ENJOYING LIFE MORE!

[10 Tips for Eating Out]

Here are tips to help you maintain a weight-loss program as you dine out:

1. Go out to eat with at least one friend who is also trying to lose weight. Encourage each other to order the right foods
2. Choose a low-fat dressing and ask for it to be served "on the side." Dip your fork in the dressing and take a bite of salad, rather than pouring the dressing over your salad.
3. Look for low-fat, low-calorie, and heart-healthy items on a menu.
4. Order everything á la carte.
5. Ask for steamed vegetables rather than the "starch portion" that comes with many meals.
6. Order any sauces or gravies to be served on the side or left off.
7. Ask for a lunch portion. Many menus now have the option of a lunch-size or dinner-size entrée. At times, even this amount of food can be shared!
8. Ask for a to-go box at the time you order. Before you take a bite of your dinner, put half of the meal into the to-go box. You'll save money as well as calories!
9. Instead of fried foods, choose baked or grilled.
10. If you are going to a party, eat healthful foods first so you are full when you arrive. Then, put only veggies on your plate.

JESUS HEALS A DEAF-MUTE

³¹Again, departing from the region of Tyre and Sidon, He came through the midst of the region of Decapolis to the Sea of Galilee. ³²Then they brought to Him one who was deaf and had an impediment in his speech, and they begged Him to put His hand on him. ³³And He took him aside from the multitude, and put His fingers in his ears, and He spat and touched his tongue. ³⁴Then, looking up to heaven, He sighed, and said to him, "Ephphatha," that is, "Be opened."

³⁵Immediately his ears were opened, and the impediment of his tongue was loosed, and he spoke plainly. ³⁶Then He commanded them that they should tell no one; but the more He commanded them, the more widely they proclaimed it. ³⁷And they were astonished beyond measure, saying, "He has done all things well. He makes both the deaf to hear and the mute to speak."

FEEDING THE FOUR THOUSAND

8 In those days, the multitude being very great and having nothing to eat, Jesus called His disciples to Him and said to them, ²"I have compassion on the multitude, because they have now continued with Me three days and have nothing to eat. ³And if I send them away hungry to their own houses, they will faint on the way; for some of them have come from afar."

⁴Then His disciples answered Him, "How can one satisfy these people with bread here in the wilderness?"

⁵He asked them, "How many loaves do you have?"

And they said, "Seven."

⁶So He commanded the multitude to sit down on the ground. And He took the seven loaves and gave thanks, broke *them* and gave *them* to His disciples to set before *them;* and they set *them* before the multitude. ⁷They also had a few small fish; and having blessed them, He said to set them also before *them.* ⁸So they ate and were filled, and they took up seven large baskets of leftover fragments. ⁹Now those who had eaten were about four thousand. And He sent them away, ¹⁰immediately got into the boat with His disciples, and came to the region of Dalmanutha.

THE PHARISEES SEEK A SIGN

¹¹Then the Pharisees came out and began to dispute with Him, seeking from Him a sign from heaven, testing Him. ¹²But He sighed deeply in His spirit, and said, "Why does this generation seek a sign? Assuredly, I say to you, no sign shall be given to this generation."

BEWARE OF THE LEAVEN OF THE PHARISEES AND HEROD

¹³And He left them, and getting into the boat again, departed to the other side. ¹⁴Now the disciplesᵃ had forgotten to take bread, and they did not have more than one loaf with them in the boat. ¹⁵Then He charged them, saying, "Take heed, beware of the leaven of the Pharisees and the leaven of Herod."

¹⁶And they reasoned among themselves, saying, "*It is* because we have no bread."

¹⁷But Jesus, being aware of *it,* said to them, "Why do you reason because you have no bread? Do you not yet perceive nor understand? Is your heart stillᵃ hardened? ¹⁸Having eyes, do you not see? And having ears, do you not hear? And do you not remember? ¹⁹When I broke the

8:14 ᵃNU-Text and M-Text read *they.*   8:17 ᵃNU-Text omits *still.*

five loaves for the five thousand, how many baskets full of fragments did you take up?"

They said to Him, "Twelve."

²⁰"Also, when I broke the seven for the four thousand, how many large baskets full of fragments did you take up?"

And they said, "Seven."

²¹So He said to them, "How *is it* you do not understand?"

A BLIND MAN HEALED AT BETHSAIDA

²²Then He came to Bethsaida; and they brought a blind man to Him, and begged Him to touch him. ²³So He took the blind man by the hand and led him out of the town. And when He had spit on his eyes and put His hands on him, He asked him if he saw anything.

²⁴And he looked up and said, "I see men like trees, walking."

²⁵Then He put *His* hands on his eyes again and made him look up. And he was restored and saw everyone clearly. ²⁶Then He sent him away to his house, saying, "Neither go into the town, nor tell anyone in the town."ᵃ

PETER CONFESSES JESUS AS THE CHRIST

²⁷Now Jesus and His disciples went out to the towns of Caesarea Philippi; and on the road He asked His disciples, saying to them, "Who do men say that I am?"

²⁸So they answered, "John the Baptist; but some *say*, Elijah; and others, one of the prophets."

²⁹He said to them, "But who do you say that I am?"

Peter answered and said to Him, "You are the Christ."

³⁰Then He strictly warned them that they should tell no one about Him.

JESUS PREDICTS HIS DEATH AND RESURRECTION

³¹And He began to teach them that the Son of Man must suffer many things, and be rejected by the elders and chief priests and scribes, and be killed, and after three days rise again. ³²He spoke this word openly. Then Peter took Him aside and began to rebuke Him. ³³But when He had turned around and looked at His disciples, He rebuked Peter, saying, "Get behind Me, Satan! For you are not mindful of the things of God, but the things of men."

TAKE UP THE CROSS AND FOLLOW HIM

³⁴When He had called the people to *Himself*, with His disciples also, He said to them, "Whoever desires to come after Me, let him deny himself, and take up his cross, and follow Me. ³⁵For whoever desires to save his life will lose it, but whoever loses his life for My sake and the gospel's will save it. ³⁶For what will it profit a man if he gains the whole world, and loses his own soul? ³⁷Or what will a man give in exchange for his soul? ³⁸For whoever is ashamed of Me and My words in this adulterous and sinful generation, of him the Son of Man also will be ashamed when He comes in the glory of His Father with the holy angels."

JESUS TRANSFIGURED ON THE MOUNT

9 And He said to them, "Assuredly, I say to you that there are some standing here who will not taste death till they see the kingdom of God present with power."

²Now after six days Jesus took Peter, James, and John, and led them up on a high mountain apart by themselves; and He was transfigured before them. ³His clothes became shining, exceedingly white, like snow, such as no launderer on earth can whiten them. ⁴And Elijah appeared to them with Moses, and they were talking with Jesus. ⁵Then Peter answered and said to Jesus, "Rabbi, it is good for us to be here; and let us make three tabernacles: one for You, one for Moses, and one for Elijah"— ⁶because he did not know what to say, for they were greatly afraid.

⁷And a cloud came and overshadowed them; and a voice came out of the cloud, saying, "This is My beloved Son. Hear Him!" ⁸Suddenly, when they had looked around, they saw no one anymore, but only Jesus with themselves.

⁹Now as they came down from the mountain, He commanded them that they should tell no one the things they had seen, till the Son of Man had risen from the dead. ¹⁰So they kept this word to themselves, questioning what the rising from the dead meant.

¹¹And they asked Him, saying, "Why do the scribes say that Elijah must come first?"

¹²Then He answered and told them, "Indeed, Elijah is coming first and restores all things. And how is it written concerning the Son of Man, that He must suffer many things and be treated with contempt? ¹³But I say to you that Elijah has also come, and they did to him whatever they wished, as it is written of him."

A BOY IS HEALED

¹⁴And when He came to the disciples, He saw a great multitude around them, and scribes disputing with them. ¹⁵Immediately, when they saw Him, all the people were greatly amazed, and running to *Him*, greeted Him. ¹⁶And He asked the scribes, "What are you discussing with them?"

¹⁷Then one of the crowd answered and said, "Teacher, I brought You my son, who has a mute spirit. ¹⁸And wherever it seizes him, it throws him down; he foams at the mouth, gnashes his teeth, and becomes rigid. So I spoke to Your disciples, that they should cast it out, but they could not."

Bible Health + Food Facts

Manna

The Israelites described the manna they ate in the wilderness as being like coriander. The word *manna* means "What is it?" The Israelites didn't know—and we don't know! Whatever its nature, a steady diet of manna kept the Israelites alive for almost four decades.

8:26 ᵃNU-Text reads *"Do not even go into the town."*

[ICE WATER]

FACT MORSELS

When a person drinks ice water, the body needs to use up to 30 calories just to warm itself to body temperature to absorb the water. People who are watching their weight often drink only ice water to help cleanse toxins from the body and increase metabolic output.

¹⁹He answered him and said, "O faithless generation, how long shall I be with you? How long shall I bear with you? Bring him to Me." ²⁰Then they brought him to Him. And when he saw Him, immediately the spirit convulsed him, and he fell on the ground and wallowed, foaming at the mouth.

²¹So He asked his father, "How long has this been happening to him?"

And he said, "From childhood. ²²And often he has thrown him both into the fire and into the water to destroy him. But if You can do anything, have compassion on us and help us."

²³Jesus said to him, "If you can believe,ᵃ all things *are* possible to him who believes."

²⁴Immediately the father of the child cried out and said with tears, "Lord, I believe; help my unbelief!"

²⁵When Jesus saw that the people came running together, He rebuked the unclean spirit, saying to it, "Deaf and dumb spirit, I command you, come out of him and enter him no more!" ²⁶Then *the spirit* cried out, convulsed him greatly, and came out of him. And he became as one dead, so that many said, "He is dead." ²⁷But Jesus took him by the hand and lifted him up, and he arose.

²⁸And when He had come into the house, His disciples asked Him privately, "Why could we not cast it out?"

²⁹So He said to them, "This kind can come out by nothing but prayer and fasting."ᵃ

JESUS AGAIN PREDICTS HIS DEATH AND RESURRECTION

³⁰Then they departed from there and passed through Galilee, and He did not want anyone to know *it.* ³¹For He taught His disciples and said to them, "The Son of Man is being betrayed into the hands of men, and they will kill Him. And after He is killed, He will rise the third day." ³²But they did not understand this saying, and were afraid to ask Him.

WHO IS THE GREATEST?

³³Then He came to Capernaum. And when He was in the house He asked them, "What was it you disputed among yourselves on the road?"

³⁴But they kept silent, for on the road they had disputed among themselves who *would be the* greatest. ³⁵And He sat down, called the twelve, and said to them, "If anyone desires to be first, he shall be last of all and servant of all." ³⁶Then He took a little child and set him in the midst of them. And when He had taken him in His arms, He said to them, ³⁷"Whoever receives one of these little children in My name receives Me; and whoever receives Me, receives not Me but Him who sent Me."

JESUS FORBIDS SECTARIANISM

³⁸Now John answered Him, saying, "Teacher, we saw someone who does not follow us casting out demons in Your name, and we forbade him because he does not follow us."

³⁹But Jesus said, "Do not forbid him, for no one who works a miracle in My name can soon afterward speak evil of Me. ⁴⁰For he who is not against us is on ourᵃ side. ⁴¹For whoever gives you a cup of water to drink in My name, because you belong to Christ, assuredly, I say to you, he will by no means lose his reward.

JESUS WARNS OF OFFENSES

⁴²"But whoever causes one of these little ones who believe in Me to stumble, it would be better for him if a millstone were hung around his neck, and he were thrown into the sea. ⁴³If your hand causes you to sin, cut it off. It is better for you to enter into life maimed, rather than having two hands, to go to hell, into the fire that shall never be quenched— ⁴⁴where

'Their worm does not die
And the fire is not quenched.'ᵃ

⁴⁵And if your foot causes you to sin, cut it off. It is better for you to enter life lame, rather than having two feet, to be cast into hell, into the fire that shall never be quenched— ⁴⁶where

'Their worm does not die
And the fire is not quenched.'ᵃ

⁴⁷And if your eye causes you to sin, pluck it out. It is better for you to enter the kingdom of God with one eye, rather than having two eyes, to be cast into hell fire— ⁴⁸where

'Their worm does not die
And the fire is not quenched.'ᵃ

TASTELESS SALT IS WORTHLESS

⁴⁹"For everyone will be seasoned with fire,ᵃ and every sacrifice will be seasoned with salt. ⁵⁰Salt *is* good, but if the salt loses its flavor, how will you season it? Have salt in yourselves, and have peace with one another."

MARRIAGE AND DIVORCE

10 Then He arose from there and came to the region of Judea by the other side of the Jordan. And multitudes gathered to Him again, and as He was accustomed, He taught them again.

9:23 ᵃNU-Text reads *"If You can!" All things. . . ."*   9:29 ᵃNU-Text omits *and fasting.*   9:40 ᵃM-Text reads *against you is on your side.*   9:44 ᵃNU-Text omits this verse.   9:46 ᵃNU-Text omits the last clause of verse 45 and all of verse 46.   9:48 ᵃIsaiah 66:24   9:49 ᵃNU-Text omits the rest of this verse.

[2]The Pharisees came and asked Him, "Is it lawful for a man to divorce *his* wife?" testing Him.

[3]And He answered and said to them, "What did Moses command you?"

[4]They said, "Moses permitted *a man* to write a certificate of divorce, and to dismiss *her*."

[5]And Jesus answered and said to them, "Because of the hardness of your heart he wrote you this precept. [6]But from the beginning of the creation, God 'made them male and female.'[a] [7]For this reason a man shall leave his father and mother and be joined to his wife, [8]and the two shall become one flesh';[a] so then they are no longer two, but one flesh. [9]Therefore what God has joined together, let not man separate."

[10]In the house His disciples also asked Him again about the same *matter*. [11]So He said to them, "Whoever divorces his wife and marries another commits adultery against her. [12]And if a woman divorces her husband and marries another, she commits adultery."

JESUS BLESSES LITTLE CHILDREN

[13]Then they brought little children to Him, that He might touch them; but the disciples rebuked those who brought *them*. [14]But when Jesus saw *it*, He was greatly displeased and said to them, "Let the little children come to Me, and do not forbid them; for of such is the kingdom of God. [15]Assuredly, I say to you, whoever does not receive the kingdom of God as a little child will by no means enter it." [16]And He took them up in His arms, laid *His* hands on them, and blessed them.

JESUS COUNSELS THE RICH YOUNG RULER

[17]Now as He was going out on the road, one came running, knelt before Him, and asked Him, "Good Teacher, what shall I do that I may inherit eternal life?"

[18]So Jesus said to him, "Why do you call Me good? No one *is* good but One, *that is,* God. [19]You know the commandments: 'Do not commit adultery,' 'Do not murder,' 'Do not steal,' 'Do not bear false witness,' 'Do not defraud,' 'Honor your father and your mother.' "[a]

[20]And he answered and said to Him, "Teacher, all these things I have kept from my youth."

[21]Then Jesus, looking at him, loved him, and said to him, "One thing you lack: Go your way, sell whatever you have and give to the poor, and you will have treasure in heaven; and come, take up the cross, and follow Me."

[22]But he was sad at this word, and went away sorrowful, for he had great possessions.

WITH GOD ALL THINGS ARE POSSIBLE

[23]Then Jesus looked around and said to His disciples, "How hard it is for those who have riches to enter the kingdom of God!" [24]And the disciples were astonished at His words. But Jesus answered again and said to them, "Children, how hard it is for those who trust in riches[a] to enter the kingdom of God! [25]It is easier for a camel to go through the eye of a needle than for a rich man to enter the kingdom of God."

[26]And they were greatly astonished, saying among themselves, "Who then can be saved?"

walking the walk

[A SAFE AND STEADY WALKING ROUTINE]

Walking is probably the most universally easy and effective exercise. You can walk just about any place at some time during the day, without expensive or elaborate equipment or team players. Even a ten-minute walk can be beneficial to cardiovascular health, and researchers have discovered that three ten-minute walks a day are as beneficial to the heart and lungs as one thirty-minute walk. Walking can fit into just about any person's schedule!

Here are six tips for a safe and steady walking program:

☐ Don't walk too far or too fast the first day. You'll become discouraged. Increase both the speed of your walking and the length of your walk gradually.

☐ Choose to walk on surfaces that do not have loose gravel (chat) and that are fairly even. Watch out for holes in grassy areas or loose clay areas. Especially choose surfaces that have been designed for walking—many city parks and athletic clubs have designated walking paths.

☐ The best warm-up for walking is to walk! Walk slowly for five minutes. Then increase your pace to elevate your heart rate. At the end of your walk, walk slowly for five minutes to cool down.

☐ People who walk with a partner—someone with whom they can converse and be accountable—are more likely to stick with a walking program.

☐ Choose to walk in areas that are safe—especially on frequently used well-lit walkways.

☐ If you develop pain in your legs or feet while walking, slow your pace.

Is It Worth It? It takes walking one hundred yards to burn the calories gained by eating one M&M.

10:6 [a]Genesis 1:27; 5:2   10:8 [a]Genesis 2:24   10:19 [a]Exodus 20:12–16; Deuteronomy 5:16–20   10:24 [a]NU-Text omits *for those who trust in riches.*

PEOPLE CALLED "BEAUTIFUL" IN THE BIBLE

Bathsheba

Beautiful Manipulator or Victim?

Bathsheba was a woman "very beautiful to behold." At least that was the opinion of King David as he saw her one evening while he was out on a stroll on the rooftop balconies of his palace. (See 2 Samuel 11:2.) He looked down into the courtyard of one of his trusted warriors, Uriah, and saw a woman bathing there. Rather than look the other direction, it appears that David enjoyed what he saw to the point that he asked who the woman was and then sent messengers to her, summoning her to spend the evening with him in his palace.

Bathsheba became pregnant as the result of their encounter. Upon hearing this news, David had Uriah sent to the front lines of battle, knowing that he would probably be killed there. Uriah did die in battle, and David then took Bathsheba as his wife. Their first child died, but Bathsheba later became the mother of King Solomon, whom she insisted be named as David's successor.

Was Bathsheba a manipulator or a victim of a king's lust? We can't know with certainty from what we read in the Bible. We do know that all of the dwellings of the key people in David's life were below his palace—his home was the highest on the hillside on which the City of David had been built. David could look down on every home and into every courtyard. Bathsheba would have known the king was in residence and that any of her actions—including a nighttime bath—were subject to his view.

Bathsheba apparently did nothing to resist David or to argue against his invitation to the palace or his advances to her. Abigail, in contrast, was a woman who reasoned with David when she thought David was about to do something wrong, and David was persuaded. We also know that Bathsheba did nothing to rebuff David when he came to her after her first child had died. She openly accepted his attempts to comfort her and again had sex with him. We also know that Bathsheba lobbied hard and long to have her son recognized as "next in line" to David's throne.

The implications can be drawn from these examples that Bathsheba *wanted* to be noticed by David on that infamous night he saw her bathing. She may have desired for some time that David seek her out and make her a queen. She may very well have used her great beauty to entice David so that she might elevate her position in his kingdom. Although few make the association, Bathsheba was the granddaughter of Ahithophel, one of David's trusted counselors who had tremendous personal political aspirations and eventually sided with Absalom and turned against David.

Beauty can be a tool of manipulation. That certainly isn't to say that all beautiful women are manipulators—not at all! It is to say that a beautiful woman can use her beauty to manipulate men who are drawn to beauty and prone to lust. The end result is always marked by emotional turmoil and sometimes tragedy, not only for the man involved, but also for the woman. Manipulation never produces lasting good.

[27]But Jesus looked at them and said, "With men *it is* impossible, but not with God; for with God all things are possible."

[28]Then Peter began to say to Him, "See, we have left all and followed You."

[29]So Jesus answered and said, "Assuredly, I say to you, there is no one who has left house or brothers or sisters or father or mother or wife[a] or children or lands, for My sake and the gospel's, [30]who shall not receive a hundredfold now in this time—houses and brothers and sisters and mothers and children and lands, with persecutions—and in the age to come, eternal life. [31]But many *who are* first will be last, and the last first."

JESUS A THIRD TIME PREDICTS HIS DEATH AND RESURRECTION

[32]Now they were on the road, going up to Jerusalem, and Jesus was going before them; and they were amazed. And as they followed they were afraid. Then He took the twelve aside again and began to tell them the things that would happen to Him: [33]"Behold, we are going up to Jerusalem, and the Son of Man will be betrayed to the chief priests and to the scribes; and they will condemn Him to death and deliver Him to the Gentiles; [34]and they will mock Him, and scourge Him, and spit on Him, and kill Him. And the third day He will rise again."

GREATNESS IS SERVING

[35]Then James and John, the sons of Zebedee, came to Him, saying, "Teacher, we want You to do for us whatever we ask."

[36]And He said to them, "What do you want Me to do for you?"

[37]They said to Him, "Grant us that we may sit, one on Your right hand and the other on Your left, in Your glory."

[38]But Jesus said to them, "You do not know what you ask. Are you able to drink the cup that I drink, and be baptized with the baptism that I am baptized with?"

10:29 [a]NU-Text omits *or wife*.

[39]They said to Him, "We are able."

So Jesus said to them, "You will indeed drink the cup that I drink, and with the baptism I am baptized with you will be baptized; [40]but to sit on My right hand and on My left is not Mine to give, but *it is for those* for whom it is prepared."

[41]And when the ten heard *it,* they began to be greatly displeased with James and John. [42]But Jesus called them to *Himself* and said to them, "You know that those who are considered rulers over the Gentiles lord it over them, and their great ones exercise authority over them. [43]Yet it shall not be so among you; but whoever desires to become great among you shall be your servant. [44]And whoever of you desires to be first shall be slave of all. [45]For even the Son of Man did not come to be served, but to serve, and to give His life a ransom for many."

JESUS HEALS BLIND BARTIMAEUS

[46]Now they came to Jericho. As He went out of Jericho with His disciples and a great multitude, blind Bartimaeus, the son of Timaeus, sat by the road begging. [47]And when he heard that it was Jesus of Nazareth, he began to cry out and say, "Jesus, Son of David, have mercy on me!"

[48]Then many warned him to be quiet; but he cried out all the more, "Son of David, have mercy on me!"

[49]So Jesus stood still and commanded him to be called.

Then they called the blind man, saying to him, "Be of good cheer. Rise, He is calling you."

[50]And throwing aside his garment, he rose and came to Jesus.

[51]So Jesus answered and said to him, "What do you want Me to do for you?"

The blind man said to Him, "Rabboni, that I may receive my sight."

[52]Then Jesus said to him, "Go your way; your faith has made you well." And immediately he received his sight and followed Jesus on the road.

THE TRIUMPHAL ENTRY

11 Now when they drew near Jerusalem, to Bethphage[a] and Bethany, at the Mount of Olives, He sent two of His disciples; [2]and He said to them, "Go into the village opposite you; and as soon as you have entered it you will find a colt tied, on which no one has sat. Loose it and bring *it.* [3]And if anyone says to you, 'Why are you doing this?' say, 'The Lord has need of it,' and immediately he will send it here."

[4]So they went their way, and found the[a] colt tied by the door outside on the street, and they loosed it. [5]But some of those who stood there said to them, "What are you doing, loosing the colt?"

[6]And they spoke to them just as Jesus had commanded. So they let them go. [7]Then they brought the colt to Jesus and threw their clothes on it, and He sat on it. [8]And many spread their clothes on the road, and others cut down leafy branches from the trees and spread *them* on the road. [9]Then those who went before and those who followed cried out, saying:

"Hosanna!
'Blessed is He who comes in the name of the LORD!'[a]

[10] Blessed *is* the kingdom of our father David
That comes in the name of the Lord![a]
Hosanna in the highest!"

[11]And Jesus went into Jerusalem and into the temple. So when He had looked around at all things, as the hour was already late, He went out to Bethany with the twelve.

THE FIG TREE WITHERED

[12]Now the next day, when they had come out from Bethany, He was hungry. [13]And seeing from afar a fig tree having leaves, He went to see if perhaps He would find something on it. When He came to it, He found nothing but leaves, for it was not the season for figs. [14]In response Jesus said to it, "Let no one eat fruit from you ever again."

And His disciples heard *it.*

JESUS CLEANSES THE TEMPLE

[15]So they came to Jerusalem. Then Jesus went into the temple and began to drive out those who bought and sold in the temple, and overturned the tables of the money changers and the seats of those who sold doves. [16]And He would not allow anyone to carry wares through the temple. [17]Then He taught, saying to them, "Is it not written, 'My house shall be called a house of prayer for all nations'?[a] But you have made it a 'den of thieves.'"[b]

[18]And the scribes and chief priests heard it and sought how they might destroy Him; for they feared Him, because all the people were astonished at His teaching. [19]When evening had come, He went out of the city.

Q What does the Bible refer to as the "fountain of life" that turns a person away from the snares of death?

A Wisdom or "the law of the wise" *(Proverbs 13:14).*

THE LESSON OF THE WITHERED FIG TREE

[20]Now in the morning, as they passed by, they saw the fig tree dried up from the roots. [21]And Peter, remembering, said to Him, "Rabbi, look! The fig tree which You cursed has withered away."

[22]So Jesus answered and said to them, "Have faith in God. [23]For assuredly, I say to you, whoever says to this mountain, 'Be removed and be cast into the sea,' and does not doubt in his heart, but believes that those things he says will be done, he will have whatever he says. [24]Therefore I say to you, whatever things you ask when you pray, believe that you receive *them,* and you will have *them.*

11:1 [a]M-Text reads *Bethsphage.*   11:4 [a]NU-Text and M-Text read *a.*   11:9 [a]Psalm 118:26   11:10 [a]NU-Text omits *in the name of the Lord.*   11:17 [a]Isaiah 56:7 [b]Jeremiah 7:11

FORGIVENESS AND PRAYER

²⁵"And whenever you stand praying, if you have anything against anyone, forgive him, that your Father in heaven may also forgive you your trespasses. ²⁶But if you do not forgive, neither will your Father in heaven forgive your trespasses."ᵃ

JESUS' AUTHORITY QUESTIONED

²⁷Then they came again to Jerusalem. And as He was walking in the temple, the chief priests, the scribes, and the elders came to Him. ²⁸And they said to Him, "By what authority are You doing these things? And who gave You this authority to do these things?"

²⁹But Jesus answered and said to them, "I also will ask you one question; then answer Me, and I will tell you by what authority I do these things: ³⁰The baptism of John—was it from heaven or from men? Answer Me."

³¹And they reasoned among themselves, saying, "If we say, 'From heaven,' He will say, 'Why then did you not believe him?' ³²But if we say, 'From men' "—they feared the people, for all counted John to have been a prophet indeed. ³³So they answered and said to Jesus, "We do not know."

And Jesus answered and said to them, "Neither will I tell you by what authority I do these things."

THE PARABLE OF THE WICKED VINEDRESSERS

12 Then He began to speak to them in parables: "A man planted a vineyard and set a hedge around it, dug *a place for* the wine vat and built a tower. And he leased it to vinedressers and went into a far country. ²Now at vintage-time he sent a servant to the vinedressers, that he might receive some of the fruit of the vineyard from the vinedressers. ³And they took *him* and beat him and sent *him* away empty-handed. ⁴Again he sent them another servant, and at him they threw stones,ᵃ wounded *him* in the head, and sent *him* away shamefully treated. ⁵And again he sent another, and him they killed; and many others, beating some and killing some. ⁶Therefore still having one son, his beloved, he also sent him to them last, saying, 'They will respect my son.' ⁷But those vinedressers said among themselves, 'This is the heir. Come, let us kill him, and the inheritance will be ours.' ⁸So they took him and killed *him* and cast *him* out of the vineyard.

⁹Therefore what will the owner of the vineyard do? He will come and destroy the vinedressers, and give the vineyard to others. ¹⁰Have you not even read this Scripture:

'The stone which the builders rejected
Has become the chief cornerstone.
¹¹ This was the Lord's doing,
And it is marvelous in our eyes'? "ᵃ

¹²And they sought to lay hands on Him, but feared the multitude, for they knew He had spoken the parable against them. So they left Him and went away.

THE PHARISEES: IS IT LAWFUL TO PAY TAXES TO CAESAR?

¹³Then they sent to Him some of the Pharisees and the Herodians, to catch Him in *His* words. ¹⁴When they had come, they said to Him, "Teacher, we know that You are true, and care about no one; for You do not regard the person of men, but teach the way of God in truth. Is it lawful to pay taxes to Caesar, or not? ¹⁵Shall we pay, or shall we not pay?"

But He, knowing their hypocrisy, said to them, "Why do you test Me? Bring Me a denarius that I may see *it.*" ¹⁶So they brought *it.*

And He said to them, "Whose image and inscription *is* this?" They said to Him, "Caesar's."

¹⁷And Jesus answered and said to them, "Render to Caesar the things that are Caesar's, and to God the things that are God's."

And they marveled at Him.

THE SADDUCEES: WHAT ABOUT THE RESURRECTION?

¹⁸Then *some* Sadducees, who say there is no resurrection, came to Him; and they asked Him, saying: ¹⁹"Teacher, Moses wrote to us that if a man's brother dies, and leaves *his* wife behind, and leaves no children, his brother should take his wife and raise up offspring for his brother. ²⁰Now there were seven brothers. The first took a wife; and dying, he left no offspring. ²¹And the second took her, and he died; nor did he leave any offspring. And the third likewise. ²²So the seven had her and left no offspring. Last of all the woman died also. ²³Therefore, in the resurrection, when they rise, whose wife will she be? For all seven had her as wife."

²⁴Jesus answered and said to them, "Are you not therefore mistaken, because you do not know the Scriptures nor the power of

> (Mark 11:25, 26)

INSIGHTS INTO THE WORD

Forgiving Others. Prayer is an amazingly powerful resource for healing and wholeness. Prayer becomes impotent, however, in the presence of unforgiveness. (See also Matthew 6:13, 14; Luke 11:9.) The Bible presents two types of forgiveness. There is forgiveness that brings salvation from sin. This forgiveness is once-and-for-all, accomplished solely by Jesus on the cross, and is received through the act of believing in and accepting Jesus as Savior.

The second aspect is forgiveness among believers, which preserves fellowship and helps create a wonderful sense of security in belonging to a "family" of believers.

It is this type of forgiveness that Jesus described in Mark 11:25, 26. He is speaking to those who have a relationship with the Father. If a person does not forgive other people for the hurts they may have caused—as in cases of rejection, willful criticism or ridicule, abuse, or even unintentional acts that inflicted emotional pain—then the unforgiving person cannot be *healed* of the hurts he or she feels. To feel true freedom from emotional baggage, a person must *first* forgive, or release to God, the person who has caused him or her pain. Be quick to forgive. It's the only way to be truly free.

11:26 ᵃNU-Text omits this verse. 12:4 ᵃNU-Text omits *and at him they threw stones.* 12:11 ᵃPsalm 118:22, 23

God? 25For when they rise from the dead, they neither marry nor are given in marriage, but are like angels in heaven. 26But concerning the dead, that they rise, have you not read in the book of Moses, in the *burning* bush *passage,* how God spoke to him, saying, 'I *am* the God of Abraham, the God of Isaac, and the God of Jacob'?" 27He is not the God of the dead, but the God of the living. You are therefore greatly mistaken."

THE SCRIBES: WHICH IS THE FIRST COMMANDMENT OF ALL?

28Then one of the scribes came, and having heard them reasoning together, perceiving[a] that He had answered them well, asked Him, "Which is the first commandment of all?"

29Jesus answered him, "The first of all the commandments *is:* 'Hear, O Israel, the LORD our God, the LORD is one. 30And you shall love the LORD your God with all your heart, with all your soul, with all your mind, and with all your strength.'[a] This *is* the first commandment.[b] 31And the second, like *it, is* this: 'You shall love your neighbor as yourself.'[a] There is no other commandment greater than these."

32So the scribe said to Him, "Well *said,* Teacher. You have spoken the truth, for there is one God, and there is no other but He. 33And to love Him with all the heart, with all the understanding, with all the soul,[a] and with all the strength, and to love one's neighbor as oneself, is more than all the whole burnt offerings and sacrifices."

34Now when Jesus saw that he answered wisely, He said to him, "You are not far from the kingdom of God."

But after that no one dared question Him.

JESUS: HOW CAN DAVID CALL HIS DESCENDANT LORD?

35Then Jesus answered and said, while He taught in the temple, "How *is it* that the scribes say that the Christ is the Son of David? 36For David himself said by the Holy Spirit:

'The LORD said to my Lord,
"Sit at My right hand,
Till I make Your enemies Your footstool." '[a]

37Therefore David himself calls Him 'Lord'; how is He *then* his Son?"

And the common people heard Him gladly.

BEWARE OF THE SCRIBES

38Then He said to them in His teaching, "Beware of the scribes, who desire to go around in long robes, *love* greetings in the marketplaces, 39the best seats in the synagogues, and the best places at feasts, 40who devour widows' houses, and for a pretense make long prayers. These will receive greater condemnation."

THE WIDOW'S TWO MITES

41Now Jesus sat opposite the treasury and saw how the people put money into the treasury. And many *who were* rich put in much. 42Then one poor widow came and threw in two mites,[a] which make a quadrans. 43So He called His disciples to *Himself* and said to them, "Assuredly, I say to you that this poor widow has put in more than all those who have given to the treasury; 44for they all put in out of their abundance, but she out of her poverty put in all that she had, her whole livelihood."

JESUS PREDICTS THE DESTRUCTION OF THE TEMPLE

13 Then as He went out of the temple, one of His disciples said to Him, "Teacher, see what manner of stones and what buildings *are here!*"

2And Jesus answered and said to him, "Do you see these great buildings? Not *one* stone shall be left upon another, that shall not be thrown down."

THE SIGNS OF THE TIMES AND THE END OF THE AGE

3Now as He sat on the Mount of Olives opposite the temple, Peter, James, John, and Andrew asked Him privately, 4"Tell us, when will these things be? And what *will be* the sign when all these things will be fulfilled?"

5And Jesus, answering them, began to say: "Take heed that no one deceives you. 6For many will come in My name, saying, 'I am He,' and will deceive many. 7But when you hear of wars and rumors of wars, do not be troubled; for *such things* must happen, but the end *is* not yet. 8For nation will rise against nation, and kingdom against kingdom. And there will be earthquakes in various places, and there will be famines and troubles.[a] These *are* the beginnings of sorrows.

9"But watch out for yourselves, for they will deliver you up to councils, and you will be beaten in the synagogues. You will be brought[a] before rulers and kings for My sake, for a testimony to them. 10And the gospel must first be preached to all the nations. 11But when they arrest *you* and deliver you up, do not worry beforehand, or premeditate[a] what you will speak. But whatever is given you in that hour, speak that; for it is not you who speak, but the Holy Spirit. 12Now brother will betray brother to death, and a father *his* child; and children will rise up against parents and cause them to be put to death. 13And you will be hated by all for My name's sake. But he who endures to the end shall be saved.

THE GREAT TRIBULATION

14"So when you see the 'abomination of desolation,'[a] spoken of by Daniel the prophet,[b] standing where it ought not" (let the reader

12:26 [a]Exodus 3:6, 15   12:28 [a]NU-Text reads *seeing.*   12:30 [a]Deuteronomy 6:4, 5   [b]NU-Text omits this sentence.   12:31 [a]Leviticus 19:18   12:33 [a]NU-Text omits *with all the soul.*   12:36 [a]Psalm 110:1   12:42 [a]Greek *lepta,* very small copper coins worth a fraction of a penny   13:8 [a]NU-Text omits *and troubles.*   13:9 [a]NU-Text and M-Text read *will stand.*   13:11 [a]NU-Text omits *or premeditate.*   13:14 [a]Daniel 11:31; 12:11   [b]NU-Text omits *spoken of by Daniel the prophet.*

WWJE?

[WHAT WOULD JESUS EAT]

[BEEF AND LAMB]

During Jesus' time, red meat was reserved primarily for feasts—weddings, holidays, banquets, parties, and religious festivals. One of the most famous stories in the New Testament is the story of the Prodigal Son (Luke 15:11–31). The father was so happy his son returned home that he celebrated by killing the "fatted calf." This calf was being reserved for a special occasion, probably a religious feast time. Beef was considered a luxury in ancient Israel and was consumed only by the more affluent people.

The more common red meats consumed by people in Jesus' day were lamb and goat. These tender and more plentiful animals grazed in open pastures. Today we would call them "range-fed" animals. The Jews, of course, did not eat *any* pork products since pork was considered an unclean food.

In the Jesus' time, people grilled, baked, or stewed their meat. They did not bread it or fry it. Fresh herbs, onions, and garlic were often used in cooking meat to add flavor. Some meats were marinated in wine or yogurt to tenderize them. Meat was generally served in portions no more than two to four ounces per serving.

Make sure that the red meat you buy and consume is

☐ trimmed of all fat;

☐ labeled as extra-lean, range-fed, or kosher;

☐ kept in the coldest part of your refrigerator and used within two to five days of purchase. Ground beef should be thrown out after two days. Frozen meats should be defrosted either in a refrigerator or microwave oven.

Cooked meats should not be left outside a refrigerator for more than two hours. If food is left out even for a few hours, the bacteria rapidly multiply. Reheat all food containing meat to at least 106 degrees.

Kiwifruit Tenderizes Meat
Thin slices of kiwifruit placed on a coarse cut of red meat will tenderize the meat overnight in a refrigerator!

understand), "then let those who are in Judea flee to the mountains. ¹⁵Let him who is on the housetop not go down into the house, nor enter to take anything out of his house. ¹⁶And let him who is in the field not go back to get his clothes. ¹⁷But woe to those who are pregnant and to those who are nursing babies in those days! ¹⁸And pray that your flight may not be in winter. ¹⁹For *in* those days there will be tribulation, such as has not been since the beginning of the creation which God created until this time, nor ever shall be. ²⁰And unless the Lord had shortened those days, no flesh would be saved; but for the elect's sake, whom He chose, He shortened the days.

²¹"Then if anyone says to you, 'Look, here *is* the Christ!' or, 'Look, *He is* there!' do not believe it. ²²For false christs and false prophets will rise and show signs and wonders to deceive, if possible, even the elect. ²³But take heed; see, I have told you all things beforehand.

THE COMING OF THE SON OF MAN

²⁴"But in those days, after that tribulation, the sun will be darkened, and the moon will not give its light; ²⁵the stars of heaven will fall, and the powers in the heavens will be shaken. ²⁶Then they will see the Son of Man coming in the clouds with great power and glory. ²⁷And then He will send His angels, and gather together His elect from the four winds, from the farthest part of earth to the farthest part of heaven.

THE PARABLE OF THE FIG TREE

²⁸"Now learn this parable from the fig tree: When its branch has already become tender, and puts forth leaves, you know that summer is near. ²⁹So you also, when you see these things happening, know that it^a is near—at the doors! ³⁰Assuredly, I say to you, this generation will by no means pass away till all these things take place. ³¹Heaven and earth will pass away, but My words will by no means pass away.

NO ONE KNOWS THE DAY OR HOUR

³²"But of that day and hour no one knows, not even the angels in heaven, nor the Son,

13:29 ªOr *He*

but only the Father. ³³Take heed, watch and pray; for you do not know when the time is. ³⁴*It is* like a man going to a far country, who left his house and gave authority to his servants, and to each his work, and commanded the doorkeeper to watch. ³⁵Watch therefore, for you do not know when the master of the house is coming—in the evening, at midnight, at the crowing of the rooster, or in the morning— ³⁶lest, coming suddenly, he find you sleeping. ³⁷And what I say to you, I say to all: Watch!"

THE PLOT TO KILL JESUS

14 After two days it was the Passover and *the Feast* of Unleavened Bread. And the chief priests and the scribes sought how they might take Him by trickery and put *Him* to death. ²But they said, "Not during the feast, lest there be an uproar of the people."

THE ANOINTING AT BETHANY

³And being in Bethany at the house of Simon the leper, as He sat at the table, a woman came having an alabaster flask of very costly oil of spikenard. Then she broke the flask and poured *it* on His head. ⁴But there were some who were indignant among themselves, and said, "Why was this fragrant oil wasted? ⁵For it might have been sold for more than three hundred denarii and given to the poor." And they criticized her sharply.

⁶But Jesus said, "Let her alone. Why do you trouble her? She has done a good work for Me. ⁷For you have the poor with you always, and whenever you wish you may do them good; but Me you do not have always. ⁸She has done what she could. She has come beforehand to anoint My body for burial. ⁹Assuredly, I say to you, wherever this gospel is preached in the whole world, what this woman has done will also be told as a memorial to her."

JUDAS AGREES TO BETRAY JESUS

¹⁰Then Judas Iscariot, one of the twelve, went to the chief priests to betray Him to them. ¹¹And when they heard *it*, they were glad, and promised to give him money. So he sought how he might conveniently betray Him.

JESUS CELEBRATES THE PASSOVER WITH HIS DISCIPLES

¹²Now on the first day of Unleavened Bread, when they killed the Passover *lamb*, His disciples said to Him, "Where do You want us to go and prepare, that You may eat the Passover?"

¹³And He sent out two of His disciples and said to them, "Go into the city, and a man will meet you carrying a pitcher of water; follow him. ¹⁴Wherever he goes in, say to the master of the house, 'The Teacher says, "Where is the guest room in which I may eat the Passover with My disciples?" ' ¹⁵Then he will show you a large upper room, furnished *and* prepared; there make ready for us."

¹⁶So His disciples went out, and came into the city, and found it just as He had said to them; and they prepared the Passover.

¹⁷In the evening He came with the twelve. ¹⁸Now as they sat and ate, Jesus said, "Assuredly, I say to you, one of you who eats with Me will betray Me."

¹⁹And they began to be sorrowful, and to say to Him one by one, "*Is* it I?" And another *said*, "*Is* it I?"ᵃ

²⁰He answered and said to them, "*It is* one of the twelve, who dips with Me in the dish. ²¹The Son of Man indeed goes just as it is written of Him, but woe to that man by whom the Son of Man is betrayed! It would have been good for that man if he had never been born."

JESUS INSTITUTES THE LORD'S SUPPER

²²And as they were eating, Jesus took bread, blessed and broke *it*, and gave *it* to them and said, "Take, eat;ᵃ this is My body."

²³Then He took the cup, and when He had given thanks He gave *it* to them, and they all drank from it. ²⁴And He said to them, "This is My blood of the newᵃ covenant, which is shed for many. ²⁵Assuredly, I say to you, I will no longer drink of the fruit of the vine until that day when I drink it new in the kingdom of God."

²⁶And when they had sung a hymn, they went out to the Mount of Olives.

JESUS PREDICTS PETER'S DENIAL

²⁷Then Jesus said to them, "All of you will be made to stumble because of Me this night,ᵃ for it is written:

'I will strike the Shepherd,
And the sheep will be scattered.'ᵇ

²⁸"But after I have been raised, I will go before you to Galilee."

²⁹Peter said to Him, "Even if all are made to stumble, yet I *will* not *be.*"

³⁰Jesus said to him, "Assuredly, I say to you that today, *even* this night, before the rooster crows twice, you will deny Me three times."

³¹But he spoke more vehemently, "If I have to die with You, I will not deny You!"

And they all said likewise.

THE PRAYER IN THE GARDEN

³²Then they came to a place which was named Gethsemane; and He said to His disciples, "Sit here while I pray." ³³And He took Peter, James, and John with Him, and He began to be troubled and deeply distressed. ³⁴Then He said to them, "My soul is exceedingly sorrowful, *even* to death. Stay here and watch."

³⁵He went a little farther, and fell on the

> **" But of that day and hour no one knows, not even the angels in heaven, nor the Son, but only the Father. Take heed, watch and pray; for you do not know when the time is. "** — *Mark 13:32*

14:19 ᵃNU-Text omits this sentence.   14:22 ᵃNU-Text omits *eat.*   14:24 ᵃNU-Text omits *new.*   14:27 ᵃNU-Text omits *because of Me this night.*   ᵇZechariah 13:7

ground, and prayed that if it were possible, the hour might pass from Him. ³⁶And He said, "Abba, Father, all things *are* possible for You. Take this cup away from Me; nevertheless, not what I will, but what You *will.*"

³⁷Then He came and found them sleeping, and said to Peter, "Simon, are you sleeping? Could you not watch one hour? ³⁸Watch and pray, lest you enter into temptation. The spirit indeed *is* willing, but the flesh *is* weak."

³⁹Again He went away and prayed, and spoke the same words. ⁴⁰And when He returned, He found them asleep again, for their eyes were heavy; and they did not know what to answer Him.

⁴¹Then He came the third time and said to them, "Are you still sleeping and resting? It is enough! The hour has come; behold, the Son of Man is being betrayed into the hands of sinners. ⁴²Rise, let us be going. See, My betrayer is at hand."

BETRAYAL AND ARREST IN GETHSEMANE

⁴³And immediately, while He was still speaking, Judas, one of the twelve, with a great multitude with swords and clubs, came from the chief priests and the scribes and the elders. ⁴⁴Now His betrayer had given them a signal, saying, "Whomever I kiss, He is the One; seize Him and lead *Him* away safely."

⁴⁵As soon as he had come, immediately he went up to Him and said to Him, "Rabbi, Rabbi!" and kissed Him.

⁴⁶Then they laid their hands on Him and took Him. ⁴⁷And one of those who stood by drew his sword and struck the servant of the high priest, and cut off his ear.

⁴⁸Then Jesus answered and said to them, "Have you come out, as against a robber, with swords and clubs to take Me? ⁴⁹I was daily with you in the temple teaching, and you did not seize Me. But the Scriptures must be fulfilled."

⁵⁰Then they all forsook Him and fled.

A YOUNG MAN FLEES NAKED

⁵¹Now a certain young man followed Him, having a linen cloth thrown around *his* naked *body.* And the young men laid hold of him, ⁵²and he left the linen cloth and fled from them naked.

JESUS FACES THE SANHEDRIN

⁵³And they led Jesus away to the high priest; and with him were assembled all the chief priests, the elders, and the scribes. ⁵⁴But Peter followed Him at a distance, right into the courtyard of the high priest. And he sat with the servants and warmed himself at the fire.

⁵⁵Now the chief priests and all the council sought testimony against Jesus to put Him to death, but found none. ⁵⁶For many bore false witness against Him, but their testimonies did not agree.

⁵⁷Then some rose up and bore false witness against Him, saying, ⁵⁸"We heard Him say, 'I will destroy this temple made with hands, and within three days I will build another made without hands.' " ⁵⁹But not even then did their testimony agree.

⁶⁰And the high priest stood up in the midst and asked Jesus, saying, "Do You answer nothing? What *is it* these men testify against You?" ⁶¹But He kept silent and answered nothing.

Again the high priest asked Him, saying to Him, "Are You the Christ, the Son of the Blessed?"

⁶²Jesus said, "I am. And you will see the Son of Man sitting at the right hand of the Power, and coming with the clouds of heaven."

⁶³Then the high priest tore his clothes and said, "What further need do we have of witnesses? ⁶⁴You have heard the blasphemy! What do you think?"

And they all condemned Him to be deserving of death.

⁶⁵Then some began to spit on Him, and to blindfold Him, and to beat Him, and to say to Him, "Prophesy!" And the officers struck Him with the palms of their hands.ᵃ

PETER DENIES JESUS, AND WEEPS

⁶⁶Now as Peter was below in the courtyard, one of the servant girls of the high priest came. ⁶⁷And when she saw Peter warming himself, she looked at him and said, "You also were with Jesus of Nazareth."

⁶⁸But he denied it, saying, "I neither know nor understand what you are saying." And he went out on the porch, and a rooster crowed.

⁶⁹And the servant girl saw him again, and began to say to those who stood by, "This is *one* of them." ⁷⁰But he denied it again.

And a little later those who stood by said to Peter again, "Surely you are *one* of them; for you are a Galilean, and your speech shows *it.*"ᵃ

⁷¹Then he began to curse and swear, "I do not know this Man of whom you speak!"

⁷²A second time *the* rooster crowed. Then Peter called to mind the word that Jesus had said to him, "Before the rooster crows twice, you will deny Me three times." And when he thought about it, he wept.

JESUS FACES PILATE

15 Immediately, in the morning, the chief priests held a consultation with the elders and scribes and the whole council; and they bound Jesus, led *Him* away, and delivered *Him* to Pilate. ²Then Pilate asked Him, "Are You the King of the Jews?"

He answered and said to him, "*It is as* you say."

³And the chief priests accused Him of many things, but He answered nothing. ⁴Then Pilate asked Him again, saying, "Do You answer nothing? See how many things

> " **A second time the rooster crowed. Then Peter called to mind the word that Jesus had said to him, 'Before the rooster crows twice, you will deny Me three times.' And when he thought about it, he wept.** "
>
> — *Mark 14:72*

14:65 ᵃNU-Text reads *received Him with slaps.*   14:70 ᵃNU-Text omits *and your speech shows it.*

they testify against You!"ᵃ ⁵But Jesus still answered nothing, so that Pilate marveled.

TAKING THE PLACE OF BARABBAS

⁶Now at the feast he was accustomed to releasing one prisoner to them, whomever they requested. ⁷And there was one named Barabbas, *who was* chained with his fellow rebels; they had committed murder in the rebellion. ⁸Then the multitude, crying aloud,ᵃ began to ask *him to do* just as he had always done for them. ⁹But Pilate answered them, saying, "Do you want me to release to you the King of the Jews?" ¹⁰For he knew that the chief priests had handed Him over because of envy.

¹¹But the chief priests stirred up the crowd, so that he should rather release Barabbas to them. ¹²Pilate answered and said to them again, "What then do you want me to do *with Him* whom you call the King of the Jews?"

¹³So they cried out again, "Crucify Him!"

¹⁴Then Pilate said to them, "Why, what evil has He done?"

But they cried out all the more, "Crucify Him!"

¹⁵So Pilate, wanting to gratify the crowd, released Barabbas to them; and he delivered Jesus, after he had scourged *Him,* to be crucified.

THE SOLDIERS MOCK JESUS

¹⁶Then the soldiers led Him away into the hall called Praetorium, and they called together the whole garrison. ¹⁷And they clothed Him with purple; and they twisted a crown of thorns, put it on His *head,* ¹⁸and began to salute Him, "Hail, King of the Jews!" ¹⁹Then they struck Him on the head with a reed and spat on Him; and bowing the knee, they worshiped Him. ²⁰And when they had mocked Him, they took the purple off Him, put His own clothes on Him, and led Him out to crucify Him.

THE KING ON A CROSS

²¹Then they compelled a certain man, Simon a Cyrenian, the father of Alexander and Rufus, as he was coming out of the country and passing by, to bear His cross. ²²And they brought Him to the place Golgotha, which is translated, Place of a Skull. ²³Then they gave Him wine mingled with myrrh to drink, but He did not take *it.* ²⁴And when they crucified Him, they divided His garments, casting lots for them to determine what every man should take.

²⁵Now it was the third hour, and they crucified Him. ²⁶And the inscription of His accusation was written above:

THE KING OF THE JEWS.

²⁷With Him they also crucified two robbers, one on His right and the other on His left. ²⁸So the Scripture was fulfilledᵃ which says, "And He was numbered with the transgressors."ᵇ

²⁹And those who passed by blasphemed Him, wagging their heads and saying, "Aha! *You* who destroy the temple and build *it* in three days, ³⁰save Yourself, and come down from the cross!"

³¹Likewise the chief priests also, mocking among themselves with the scribes, said, "He saved others; Himself He cannot save. ³²Let the Christ, the King of Israel, descend now from the cross, that we may see and believe."ᵃ

Even those who were crucified with Him reviled Him.

PRESCRIPTIONS FOR INNER HEALTH

"The labor of the righteous leads to life,
The wages of the wicked to sin."

(Proverbs 10:16)

People who are in right standing with God seek to do work that contributes to, encourages, and promotes all things pertaining to *life*—physical life, good relationships in life, emotional life, and spiritual life. Evil people generally tear down, destroy, and defame what is good. They diminish and disregard other people. They are poison in the soul of society.

JESUS DIES ON THE CROSS

³³Now when the sixth hour had come, there was darkness over the whole land until the ninth hour. ³⁴And at the ninth hour Jesus cried out with a loud voice, saying, "Eloi, Eloi, lama sabachthani?" which is translated, "My God, My God, why have You forsaken Me?"ᵃ

³⁵Some of those who stood by, when they heard *that,* said, "Look, He is calling for Elijah!" ³⁶Then someone ran and filled a sponge full of sour wine, put *it* on a reed, and offered *it* to Him to drink, saying, "Let Him alone; let us see if Elijah will come to take Him down."

³⁷And Jesus cried out with a loud voice, and breathed His last.

³⁸Then the veil of the temple was torn in two from top to bottom. ³⁹So when the centurion, who stood opposite Him, saw that He cried out like this and breathed His last,ᵃ he said, "Truly this Man was the Son of God!"

⁴⁰There were also women looking on from afar, among whom were Mary Magdalene, Mary the mother of James the Less and of Joses, and Salome, ⁴¹who also followed Him and ministered to Him when He was in Galilee, and many other women who came up with Him to Jerusalem.

JESUS BURIED IN JOSEPH'S TOMB

⁴²Now when evening had come, because it was the Preparation Day, that is, the day before the Sabbath, ⁴³Joseph of Arimathea, a prominent

15:4 ᵃNU-Text reads *of which they accuse You.* 15:8 ᵃNU-Text reads *going up.* 15:28 ᵃIsaiah 53:12 ᵇNU-Text omits this verse. 15:32 ᵃM-Text reads *believe Him.* 15:34 ᵃPsalm 22:1 15:39 ᵃNU-Text reads *that He thus breathed His last.*

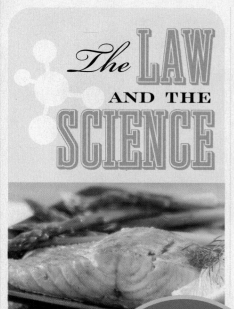

The LAW AND THE SCIENCE

[RICH IN OMEGA OILS]

>SCIENCE tells us that fish with fins and scales are very healthy foods! Among the fish that are excellent choices for a low-fat, high-energy, high-protein eating plan are grouper, red snapper, orange roughy, salmon, and albacore tuna. Fish are also high in Omega 3 fatty acids, which are valuable to good nutrition and the health of brain tissue. Cold-water fish and cod liver oil are especially high in the essential fatty acids EPA and DHA. (You can find fish oil in capsules at your health-food store.) Be sure to eat your fish baked, grilled, or poached—not breaded and fried.

>THE LAW says: "These you may eat of all that are in the water: whatever in the water has fins and scales, whether in the seas or in the rivers—that you may eat" (Leviticus 11:9).

council member, who was himself waiting for the kingdom of God, coming and taking courage, went in to Pilate and asked for the body of Jesus. ⁴⁴Pilate marveled that He was already dead; and summoning the centurion, he asked him if He had been dead for some time. ⁴⁵So when he found out from the centurion, he granted the body to Joseph. ⁴⁶Then he bought fine linen, took Him down, and wrapped Him in the linen. And he laid Him in a tomb which had been hewn out of the rock, and rolled a stone against the door of the tomb. ⁴⁷And Mary Magdalene and Mary *the mother* of Joses observed where He was laid.

HE IS RISEN

16 Now when the Sabbath was past, Mary Magdalene, Mary *the mother* of James, and Salome bought spices, that they might come and anoint Him. ²Very early in the morning, on the first *day* of the week, they came to the tomb when the sun had risen. ³And they said among themselves, "Who will roll away the stone from the door of the tomb for us?" ⁴But when they looked up, they saw that the stone had been rolled away—for it was very large. ⁵And entering the tomb, they saw a young man clothed in a long white robe sitting on the right side; and they were alarmed.

⁶But he said to them, "Do not be alarmed. You seek Jesus of Nazareth, who was crucified. He is risen! He is not here. See the place where they laid Him. ⁷But go, tell His disciples—and Peter—that He is going before you into Galilee; there you will see Him, as He said to you."

⁸So they went out quicklyᵃ and fled from the tomb, for they trembled and were amazed. And they said nothing to anyone, for they were afraid.

MARY MAGDALENE SEES THE RISEN LORD

⁹Now when *He* rose early on the first *day* of the week, He appeared first to Mary Magdalene, out of whom He had cast seven demons. ¹⁰She went and told those who had been with Him, as they mourned and wept. ¹¹And when they heard that He was alive and had been seen by her, they did not believe.

JESUS APPEARS TO TWO DISCIPLES

¹²After that, He appeared in another form to two of them as they walked and went into the country. ¹³And they went and told *it* to the rest, *but* they did not believe them either.

THE GREAT COMMISSION

¹⁴Later He appeared to the eleven as they sat at the table; and He rebuked their unbelief and hardness of heart, because they did not believe those who had seen Him after He had risen. ¹⁵And He said to them, "Go into all the world and preach the gospel to every creature. ¹⁶He who believes and is baptized will be saved; but he who does not believe will be condemned. ¹⁷And these signs will follow those who believe: In My name they will cast out demons; they will speak with new tongues; ¹⁸theyᵃ will take up serpents; and if they drink anything deadly, it will by no means hurt them; they will lay hands on the sick, and they will recover."

CHRIST ASCENDS TO GOD'S RIGHT HAND

¹⁹So then, after the Lord had spoken to them, He was received up into heaven, and sat down at the right hand of God. ²⁰And they went out and preached everywhere, the Lord working with *them* and confirming the word through the accompanying signs. Amenᵃ

16:8 ᵃNU-Text and M-Text omit *quickly.* 16:18 ᵃNU-Text reads *and in their hands they will.* 16:20 ᵃVerses 9–20 are bracketed in NU-Text as not original. They are lacking in Codex Sinaiticus and Codex Vaticanus, although nearly all other manuscripts of Mark contain them.

HEALTH NOTES

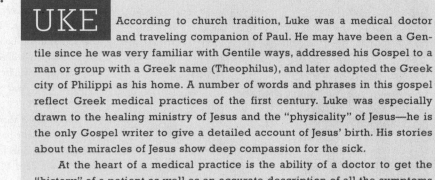

UKE

According to church tradition, Luke was a medical doctor and traveling companion of Paul. He may have been a Gentile since he was very familiar with Gentile ways, addressed his Gospel to a man or group with a Greek name (Theophilus), and later adopted the Greek city of Philippi as his home. A number of words and phrases in this gospel reflect Greek medical practices of the first century. Luke was especially drawn to the healing ministry of Jesus and the "physicality" of Jesus—he is the only Gospel writer to give a detailed account of Jesus' birth. His stories about the miracles of Jesus show deep compassion for the sick.

At the heart of a medical practice is the ability of a doctor to get the "history" of a patient as well as an accurate description of all the symptoms a patient may be experiencing. In these ways, Luke is an excellent physician! While his friend Paul was imprisoned in Caesarea, Luke apparently interviewed a large number of people who knew Jesus. He wove these into a history that revealed a compassionate, kind, tender, healing Christ.

DEDICATION TO THEOPHILUS

1 Inasmuch as many have taken in hand to set in order a narrative of those things which have been fulfilled[a] among us, ²just as those who from the beginning were eyewitnesses and ministers of the word delivered them to us, ³it seemed good to me also, having had perfect understanding of all things from the very first, to write to you an orderly account, most excellent Theophilus, ⁴that you may know the certainty of those things in which you were instructed.

JOHN'S BIRTH ANNOUNCED TO ZACHARIAS

⁵There was in the days of Herod, the king of Judea, a certain priest named Zacharias, of the division of Abijah. His wife *was* of the daughters of Aaron, and her name *was* Elizabeth. ⁶And they were both righteous before God, walking in all the commandments and ordinances of the Lord blameless. ⁷But they had no child, because Elizabeth was barren, and they were both well advanced in years.

⁸So it was, that while he was serving as priest before God in the order of his division, ⁹according to the custom of the priesthood, his lot fell to burn incense when he went into the temple of the Lord. ¹⁰And the whole multitude of the people was praying outside at the hour of incense. ¹¹Then an angel of the Lord appeared to him, standing on the right side of the altar of incense. ¹²And when Zacharias saw *him,* he was troubled, and fear fell upon him.

¹³But the angel said to him, "Do not be afraid, Zacharias, for your prayer is heard; and your wife Elizabeth will bear you a son, and you shall call his name John. ¹⁴And you will have joy and gladness, and many will rejoice at his birth. ¹⁵For he will be great in the sight of the Lord, and shall drink neither wine nor strong drink. He will also be filled with the Holy Spirit, even from his mother's womb. ¹⁶And he will turn many of the children of Israel to the Lord their God. ¹⁷He will also go before Him in the spirit and power of Elijah, 'to turn the hearts of the fathers to the children,'[a] and the disobedient to the wisdom of the just, to make ready a people prepared for the Lord."

¹⁸And Zacharias said to the angel, "How shall I know this? For I am an old man, and my wife is well advanced in years."

¹⁹And the angel answered and said to him, "I am Gabriel, who stands in the presence of God, and was sent to speak to you and bring you these glad tidings. ²⁰But behold, you will be mute and not able to speak until the day these things take place, because you did not believe my words which will be fulfilled in their own time."

²¹And the people waited for Zacharias, and marveled that he lingered so long in the temple. ²²But when he came out, he could not speak to them; and they perceived that he had seen a vision in the temple, for he beckoned to them and remained speechless.

²³So it was, as soon as the days of his service were completed, that he departed to his own house. ²⁴Now after those days his wife Elizabeth conceived; and she hid herself five months, saying, ²⁵"Thus the Lord has dealt with me, in the days when He looked on *me,* to take away my reproach among people."

CHRIST'S BIRTH ANNOUNCED TO MARY

²⁶Now in the sixth month the angel Gabriel was sent by God to a city of Galilee named Nazareth, ²⁷to a virgin betrothed to a man whose name was Joseph, of the house of David. The virgin's name *was* Mary. ²⁸And having come in, the angel said to her, "Rejoice, highly favored *one,* the Lord *is* with you; blessed *are* you among women!"[a]

1:1 [a]Or *are most surely believed*   1:17 [a]Malachi 4:5, 6   1:28 [a]NU-Text omits *blessed are you among women.*

Women's Issues
A Pregnant Mother's Song

It was customary in Bible times for a young woman to "go away" for several weeks shortly after she knew that she was pregnant for the expressed purpose of devoting herself to the spiritual formation of her child. Many times a girl went to the home of an older and trusted aunt, cousin, grandmother, or other relative—someone who knew what she was going through, but who had no expectations about what she should or shouldn't do in the way of household chores or work. This may have been the reason that the Virgin Mary went to visit her older cousin Elizabeth for three months.

How did a woman encourage the spiritual formation of the baby growing in her womb? She talked to it about the goodness of God, the love of the mother for the child, and her hopes and dreams for her child's life. The foremost way for her to encourage the spiritual formation of the fetus was to *sing* to the baby.

The songs included the ancient songs about God's provision and protection that had been handed down through thousands of years of Judaism. The songs were also to include an *original* song that the mother would compose specifically for her child. This is an example of the "new song" that the psalmist described in Psalm 144:9: "I will sing a new song to You, O God." New songs were sung to indicate not only the creativity of a songwriter but to reflect times of new hope, new dreams, new courage, a new attitude, or a *new life!*　　　CONT. NEXT PAGE>>>

[29]But when she saw *him*,[a] she was troubled at his saying, and considered what manner of greeting this was. [30]Then the angel said to her, "Do not be afraid, Mary, for you have found favor with God. [31]And behold, you will conceive in your womb and bring forth a Son, and shall call His name Jesus. [32]He will be great, and will be called the Son of the Highest; and the Lord God will give Him the throne of His father David. [33]And He will reign over the house of Jacob forever, and of His kingdom there will be no end."

[34]Then Mary said to the angel, "How can this be, since I do not know a man?"

[35]And the angel answered and said to her, "*The* Holy Spirit will come upon you, and the power of the Highest will overshadow you; therefore, also, that Holy One who is to be born will be called the Son of God. [36]Now indeed, Elizabeth your relative has also conceived a son in her old age; and this is now the sixth month for her who was called barren. [37]For with God nothing will be impossible."

[38]Then Mary said, "Behold the maidservant of the Lord! Let it be to me according to your word." And the angel departed from her.

MARY VISITS ELIZABETH

[39]Now Mary arose in those days and went into the hill country with haste, to a city of Judah, [40]and entered the house of Zacharias and greeted Elizabeth. [41]And it happened, when Elizabeth heard the greeting of Mary, that the babe leaped in her womb; and Elizabeth was filled with the Holy Spirit. [42]Then she spoke out with a loud voice and said, "Blessed *are* you among women, and blessed *is* the fruit of your womb! [43]But why *is* this *granted* to me, that the mother of my Lord should come to me? [44]For indeed, as soon as the voice of your greeting sounded in my ears, the babe leaped in my womb for joy. [45]Blessed *is* she who believed, for there will be a fulfillment of those things which were told her from the Lord."

THE SONG OF MARY

[46]And Mary said:

> "My soul magnifies the Lord,
> [47] And my spirit has rejoiced in God my Savior.
> [48] For He has regarded the lowly state of His maidservant;
> For behold, henceforth all generations will call me blessed.
> [49] For He who is mighty has done great things for me,
> And holy *is* His name.
> [50] And His mercy *is* on those who fear Him
> From generation to generation.
> [51] He has shown strength with His arm;
> He has scattered *the* proud in the imagination of their hearts.
> [52] He has put down the mighty from *their* thrones,
> And exalted *the* lowly.
> [53] He has filled *the* hungry with good things,
> And *the* rich He has sent away empty.
> [54] He has helped His servant Israel,
> In remembrance of *His* mercy,
> [55] As He spoke to our fathers,
> To Abraham and to his seed forever."

1:29 [a]NU-Text omits *when she saw him.*

⁵⁶And Mary remained with her about three months, and returned to her house.

BIRTH OF JOHN THE BAPTIST

⁵⁷Now Elizabeth's full time came for her to be delivered, and she brought forth a son. ⁵⁸When her neighbors and relatives heard how the Lord had shown great mercy to her, they rejoiced with her.

CIRCUMCISION OF JOHN THE BAPTIST

⁵⁹So it was, on the eighth day, that they came to circumcise the child; and they would have called him by the name of his father, Zacharias. ⁶⁰His mother answered and said, "No; he shall be called John."

⁶¹But they said to her, "There is no one among your relatives who is called by this name." ⁶²So they made signs to his father—what he would have him called.

⁶³And he asked for a writing tablet, and wrote, saying, "His name is John." So they all marveled. ⁶⁴Immediately his mouth was opened and his tongue *loosed*, and he spoke, praising God. ⁶⁵Then fear came on all who dwelt around them; and all these sayings were discussed throughout all the hill country of Judea. ⁶⁶And all those who heard *them* kept *them* in their hearts, saying, "What kind of child will this be?" And the hand of the Lord was with him.

ZACHARIAS' PROPHECY

⁶⁷Now his father Zacharias was filled with the Holy Spirit, and prophesied, saying:

⁶⁸ "Blessed *is* the Lord God of Israel,
For He has visited and redeemed His people,
⁶⁹ And has raised up a horn of salvation for us
In the house of His servant David,
⁷⁰ As He spoke by the mouth of His holy prophets,
Who *have been* since the world began,

⁷¹ That we should be saved from our enemies
And from the hand of all who hate us,
⁷² To perform the mercy *promised* to our fathers
And to remember His holy covenant,
⁷³ The oath which He swore to our father Abraham:
⁷⁴ To grant us that we,
Being delivered from the hand of our enemies,
Might serve Him without fear,
⁷⁵ In holiness and righteousness before Him all the days of our life.

⁷⁶ "And you, child, will be called the prophet of the Highest;
For you will go before the face of the Lord to prepare His ways,
⁷⁷ To give knowledge of salvation to His people
By the remission of their sins,
⁷⁸ Through the tender mercy of our God,
With which the Dayspring from on high has visited[a] us;
⁷⁹ To give light to those who sit in darkness and the shadow of death,
To guide our feet into the way of peace."

⁸⁰So the child grew and became strong in spirit, and was in the deserts till the day of his manifestation to Israel.

CHRIST BORN OF MARY

2 And it came to pass in those days *that* a decree went out from Caesar Augustus that all the world should be registered. ²This census first took place while Quirinius was governing Syria. ³So all went to be registered, everyone to his own city.

⁴Joseph also went up from Galilee, out of the city of Nazareth, into Judea, to the city of David, which is called Bethlehem, because he was of the house and lineage of David, ⁵to be registered with Mary, his betrothed wife,[a] who was with child. ⁶So it was, that while they were there, the days were completed for her to be delivered. ⁷And she brought forth her firstborn Son, and wrapped Him in swaddling cloths, and laid Him in a manger, because there was no room for them in the inn.

[TURKEY JERKY]

FACT MORSELS

A stick of natural turkey jerky has only about 1 gram of fat and 75 calories. The good news it that it takes about twenty minutes to chew a stick of turkey jerky completely, which makes it a satisfying and low-calorie protein source. It may be one of the finest forms of "fast food."

1:78 ᵃNU-Text reads *shall visit.*   2:5 ᵃNU-Text omits *wife.*

GODLY & GOODLOOKIN'

Aloe Vera for Your Skin

Aloe vera is a plant that has been used since Bible times. It has remarkable healing abilities and has properties for promoting removal of dead skin and stimulating normal growth of living cells. It can help tighten pores and has antibacterial qualities for fighting infection. It can also stop pain and reduce the chances of scarring. It is especially valuable for minor cuts, as well as first- and second-degree burns.

Aloe has a composition similar to that of human blood plasma and seawater—its pH is the same as human skin. In gel form, especially from a cut fresh leaf, aloe can be used directly as an aftershave lotion or moisturizer.

GLORY IN THE HIGHEST

[8]Now there were in the same country shepherds living out in the fields, keeping watch over their flock by night. [9]And behold,[a] an angel of the Lord stood before them, and the glory of the Lord shone around them, and they were greatly afraid. [10]Then the angel said to them, "Do not be afraid, for behold, I bring you good tidings of great joy which will be to all people. [11]For there is born to you this day in the city of David a Savior, who is Christ the Lord. [12]And this *will be* the sign to you: You will find a Babe wrapped in swaddling cloths, lying in a manger."

[13]And suddenly there was with the angel a multitude of the heavenly host praising God and saying:

[14] "Glory to God in the highest,
And on earth peace, goodwill toward men!"[a]

[15]So it was, when the angels had gone away from them into heaven, that the shepherds said to one another, "Let us now go to Bethlehem and see this thing that has come to pass, which the Lord has made known to us." [16]And they came with haste and found Mary and Joseph, and the Babe lying in a manger. [17]Now when they had seen *Him,* they made widely[a] known the saying which was told them concerning this Child. [18]And all those who heard *it* marveled at those things which were told them by the shepherds. [19]But Mary kept all these things and pondered *them* in her heart. [20]Then the shepherds returned, glorifying and praising God for all the things that they had heard and seen, as it was told them.

CIRCUMCISION OF JESUS

[21]And when eight days were completed for the circumcision of the Child,[a] His name was called JESUS, the name given by the angel before He was conceived in the womb.

JESUS PRESENTED IN THE TEMPLE

[22]Now when the days of her purification according to the law of Moses were completed, they brought Him to Jerusalem to present *Him* to the Lord [23](as it is written in the law of the Lord, "Every male who opens the womb shall be called holy to the LORD"),[a] [24]and to offer a sacrifice according to what is said in the law of the Lord, "A pair of turtledoves or two young pigeons."[a]

SIMEON SEES GOD'S SALVATION

[25]And behold, there was a man in Jerusalem whose name *was* Simeon, and this man *was* just and devout, waiting for the Consolation of Israel, and the Holy Spirit was upon him. [26]And it had been revealed to him by the Holy Spirit that he would not see death before he had seen the Lord's Christ. [27]So he came by the Spirit into the temple. And when the parents brought in the Child Jesus, to do for Him according to the custom of the law, [28]he took Him up in his arms and blessed God and said:

[29] "Lord, now You are letting Your servant depart in peace,
According to Your word;
[30] For my eyes have seen Your salvation
[31] Which You have prepared before the face of all peoples,
[32] A light to *bring* revelation to the Gentiles,
And the glory of Your people Israel."

[33]And Joseph and His mother[a] marveled at those things which were spoken of Him. [34]Then Simeon blessed them, and said to Mary His mother, "Behold, this *Child* is destined for the fall and rising of many in Israel, and for a sign which will be spoken against [35](yes, a sword will pierce through your own soul also), that the thoughts of many hearts may be revealed."

ANNA BEARS WITNESS TO THE REDEEMER

[36]Now there was one, Anna, a prophetess, the daughter of Phanuel, of the tribe of Asher. She was of a great age, and had lived with a husband seven years from her virginity; [37]and this woman *was* a widow of about eighty-four years,[a] who did not depart from the temple, but served *God* with fastings and prayers night and day. [38]And coming in that instant she gave thanks to the Lord,[a] and spoke of Him to all those who looked for redemption in Jerusalem.

THE FAMILY RETURNS TO NAZARETH

[39]So when they had performed all things according to the law of the Lord, they returned to Galilee, to their *own* city, Nazareth. [40]And the

---

2:9 [a]NU-Text omits *behold.*   2:14 [a]NU-Text reads *toward men of goodwill.*   2:17 [a]NU-Text omits *widely.*   2:21 [a]NU-Text reads *for His circumcision.*   2:23 [a]Exodus 13:2, 12, 15   2:24 [a]Leviticus 12:8

2:33 [a]NU-Text reads *And His father and mother.*   2:37 [a]NU-Text reads *a widow until she was eighty-four.*   2:38 [a]NU-Text reads *to God.*

Child grew and became strong in spirit,[a] filled with wisdom; and the grace of God was upon Him.

THE BOY JESUS AMAZES THE SCHOLARS

[41]His parents went to Jerusalem every year at the Feast of the Passover. [42]And when He was twelve years old, they went up to Jerusalem according to the custom of the feast. [43]When they had finished the days, as they returned, the Boy Jesus lingered behind in Jerusalem. And Joseph and His mother[a] did not know *it;* [44]but supposing Him to have been in the company, they went a day's journey, and sought Him among *their* relatives and acquaintances. [45]So when they did not find Him, they returned to Jerusalem, seeking Him. [46]Now so it was *that* after three days they found Him in the temple, sitting in the midst of the teachers, both listening to them and asking them questions. [47]And all who heard Him were astonished at His understanding and answers. [48]So when they saw Him, they were amazed; and His mother said to Him, "Son, why have You done this to us? Look, Your father and I have sought You anxiously."

[49]And He said to them, "Why did you seek Me? Did you not know that I must be about My Father's business?" [50]But they did not understand the statement which He spoke to them.

JESUS ADVANCES IN WISDOM AND FAVOR

[51]Then He went down with them and came to Nazareth, and was subject to them, but His mother kept all these things in her heart. [52]And Jesus increased in wisdom and stature, and in favor with God and men.

JOHN THE BAPTIST PREPARES THE WAY

3 Now in the fifteenth year of the reign of Tiberius Caesar, Pontius Pilate being governor of Judea, Herod being tetrarch of Galilee, his brother Philip tetrarch of Iturea and the region of Trachonitis, and Lysanias tetrarch of Abilene, [2]while Annas and Caiaphas were high priests,[a] the word of God came to John the son of Zacharias in the wilderness. [3]And he went into all the region around the Jordan, preaching a baptism of repentance for the remission of sins, [4]as it is written in the book of the words of Isaiah the prophet, saying:

"The voice of one crying in the wilderness:
'Prepare the way of the Lord;
Make His paths straight.
[5] Every valley shall be filled
And every mountain and hill brought low;
The crooked places shall be made straight
And the rough ways smooth;
[6] And all flesh shall see the salvation of God.' "[a]

JOHN PREACHES TO THE PEOPLE

[7]Then he said to the multitudes that came out to be baptized by him, "Brood of vipers! Who warned you to flee from the wrath to come? [8]Therefore bear fruits worthy of repentance, and do not begin to say to yourselves, 'We have Abraham as *our* father.' For I say to you that God

---

Righteous Recipes

Mediterranean Lentil Soup

Ingredients:
- ☐ 5 cups lentils, sorted and washed
- ☐ 2 quarts water
- ☐ 1½ large onion, chopped
- ☐ 2 tablespoons extra-virgin olive oil
- ☐ 1 green bell pepper, chopped
- ☐ 1 teaspoon Celtic salt
- ☐ ⅓ teaspoon freshly ground black pepper
- ☐ 1 teaspoon cumin
- ☐ 1 cup fresh cilantro, chopped
- ☐ 5 garlic cloves, minced
- ☐ ½ cup fresh lime juice

Combine the lentils and water and bring to a boil. Reduce heat and simmer while preparing other ingredients. Sauté the onions in half of the olive oil in a saucepan over medium heat for about 8 minutes. Add the bell pepper and sauté for a minute or two longer. Add the onion mixture to the lentils. Simmer 30 minutes. Season with salt, pepper, and cumin. Simmer 20 minutes longer. Stir in the cilantro and remove the kettle from the heat.

Combine the garlic, lime juice, and the remaining 1 tablespoon olive oil in a food processor or blender and blend well. Add garlic mixture and lime juice to the lentil mixture. Mix well and serve.

Yield: 6 servings

---

is able to raise up children to Abraham from these stones. [9]And even now the ax is laid to the root of the trees. Therefore every tree which does not bear good fruit is cut down and thrown into the fire."

[10]So the people asked him, saying, "What shall we do then?"

[11]He answered and said to them, "He who has two tunics, let him

---

2:40 [a]NU-Text omits *in spirit.*   **2:43** [a]NU-Text reads *And His parents.*   **3:2** [a]NU-Text and M-Text read *in the high priesthood of Annas and Caiaphas.*   **3:6** [a]Isaiah 40:3–5

WWJE? [FISH]

[WHAT WOULD JESUS EAT]

Fish was the most common source of protein in the days of Jesus. It was an inexpensive and daily part of the average person's diet. The fish that Jesus and His disciples consumed was "clean" according to the Old Testament dietary laws.

Unfortunately, much of the fish consumed in the modern American diet is fried, which actually cancels out the beneficial health-promoting effects of the natural oil in fish. Also, many fish dishes served in American restaurants are made with "unclean" fish, such as catfish.

Fish is low in saturated fat. The lower-fat fish include cod, flounder, haddock, halibut, perch, Pollack, red snapper, sea bass, rainbow trout, and yellow fin tuna. High-fat fish include herring, mackerel, pompano, salmon, and sardines. These fish, however, are also very high in the essential omega-3 fatty acids.

In addition to protein, fish is a good source of essential nutrients such as zinc, copper, magnesium, B vitamins, and iodine, as well as various minerals. One major medical study involving thirteen thousand men revealed that the men who ate the most fish had an approximately 40 percent lower risk of dying from a heart attack.

Studies have shown that eating fish has the following health benefits:

- ☐ Thins the blood and protects arteries from damage
- ☐ Inhibits the formation of blood clots
- ☐ Lowers LDL (bad) cholesterol, lowers blood pressure, and reduces triglycerides
- ☐ Reduces the risk of lupus
- ☐ Fights inflammation
- ☐ Eases symptoms of rheumatoid arthritis
- ☐ Relieves migraine headaches
- ☐ Helps regulate the immune system
- ☐ Sooths bronchial asthma
- ☐ Combats early kidney disease
- ☐ Inhibits the growth of cancerous tumors in animals

The fish eaten in Bible times was grilled, baked, broiled, or poached.

Do your best to ensure that your fish comes from unpolluted waters, that it is fresh, and that it has been stored and cooked in a way that maintains maximum nutritional benefit.

anyone or accuse falsely, and be content with your wages."

[15]Now as the people were in expectation, and all reasoned in their hearts about John, whether he was the Christ or not, [16]John answered, saying to all, "I indeed baptize you with water; but One mightier than I is coming, whose sandal strap I am not worthy to loose. He will baptize you with the Holy Spirit and fire. [17]His winnowing fan is in His hand, and He will thoroughly clean out His threshing floor, and gather the wheat into His barn; but the chaff He will burn with unquenchable fire."

[18]And with many other exhortations he preached to the people. [19]But Herod the tetrarch, being rebuked by him concerning Herodias, his brother Philip's wife,[a] and for all the evils which Herod had done, [20]also added this, above all, that he shut John up in prison.

JOHN BAPTIZES JESUS

[21]When all the people were baptized, it came to pass that Jesus also was baptized; and while He prayed, the heaven was opened. [22]And the Holy Spirit descended in bodily form like a dove upon Him, and a voice came from heaven which said, "You are My beloved Son; in You I am well pleased."

THE GENEALOGY OF JESUS CHRIST

[23]Now Jesus Himself began His ministry at about thirty years of age, being (as was supposed) the son of Joseph, the son of Heli, [24]the son of Matthat,[a] the son of Levi, the son of Melchi, the son of Janna, the son of Joseph, [25]the son of Mattathiah, the son of Amos, the son of Nahum, the son of Esli, the son of Naggai, [26]the son of Maath, the son of Mattathiah, the son of Semei, the son of Joseph, the son of Judah, [27]the son of Joannas, the son of Rhesa, the son of Zerubbabel, the son of Shealtiel, the son of Neri, [28]the son of Melchi, the son of Addi, the son of Cosam, the son of Elmodam, the son of Er, [29]the son of Jose, the son of Eliezer, the son of Jorim, the son of Matthat, the son of Levi, [30]the son of Simeon, the son of Judah, the son of Joseph, the son of Jonan, the son of Eliakim, [31]the son of Melea, the son of Menan, the son of Mattathah, the son of Nathan, the son of David, [32]the son of Jesse, the son of Obed, the son of Boaz, the son of Salmon, the son of

give to him who has none; and he who has food, let him do likewise."

[12]Then tax collectors also came to be baptized, and said to him, "Teacher, what shall we do?"

[13]And he said to them, "Collect no more than what is appointed for you."

[14]Likewise the soldiers asked him, saying, "And what shall we do?"

So he said to them, "Do not intimidate

3:19 [a]NU-Text reads his brother's wife. 3:24 [a]This and several other names in the genealogy are spelled somewhat differently in the NU-Text. Since the New King James Version uses the Old Testament spelling for persons mentioned in the New Testament, these variations, which come from the Greek, have not been footnoted.

78 DIVINE HEALTH

Nahshon, [33]*the son of* Amminadab, *the son of* Ram, *the son of* Hezron, *the son of* Perez, *the son of* Judah, [34]*the son of* Jacob, *the son of* Isaac, *the son of* Abraham, *the son of* Terah, *the son of* Nahor, [35]*the son of* Serug, *the son of* Reu, *the son of* Peleg, *the son of* Eber, *the son of* Shelah, [36]*the son of* Cainan, *the son of* Arphaxad, *the son of* Shem, *the son of* Noah, *the son of* Lamech, [37]*the son of* Methuselah, *the son of* Enoch, *the son of* Jared, *the son of* Mahalalel, *the son of* Cainan, [38]*the son of* Enosh, *the son of* Seth, *the son of* Adam, *the son of* God.

SATAN TEMPTS JESUS

4 Then Jesus, being filled with the Holy Spirit, returned from the Jordan and was led by the Spirit into[a] the wilderness, [2]being tempted for forty days by the devil. And in those days He ate nothing, and afterward, when they had ended, He was hungry.

[3]And the devil said to Him, "If You are the Son of God, command this stone to become bread."

[4]But Jesus answered him, saying,[a] "It is written, 'Man shall not live by bread alone, but by every word of God.' "[b]

[5]Then the devil, taking Him up on a high mountain, showed Him[a] all the kingdoms of the world in a moment of time. [6]And the devil said to Him, "All this authority I will give You, and their glory; for *this* has been delivered to me, and I give it to whomever I wish. [7]Therefore, if You will worship before me, all will be Yours."

[8]And Jesus answered and said to him, "Get behind Me, Satan![a] For[b] it is written, 'You shall worship the Lord your God, and Him only you shall serve.' "[c]

[9]Then he brought Him to Jerusalem, set Him on the pinnacle of the temple, and said to Him, "If You are the Son of God, throw Yourself down from here. [10]For it is written:

'He shall give His angels charge over you,
 To keep you,'

[11]and,

'In their hands they shall bear you up,
 Lest you dash your foot against a stone.' "[a]

[12]And Jesus answered and said to him, "It has been said, 'You shall not tempt the LORD your God.' "[a]

[13]Now when the devil had ended every temptation, he departed from Him until an opportune time.

◄ Overcoming Anger and Hostility ▼

OVERCOMING OBSTINATE OBSTACLES • OVERCOMING OBSTINATE OBSTACLES • OVERCOMING OBSTINATE OBSTACLES

If you have periodic times in which you feel as if you are going to explode with anger, or if you recognize that you are nearly always angry deep within—harboring a smoldering, ongoing anger—*face up to your anger and determine to overcome it!* If you need help with this, seek help.

Seething anger, often labeled *hostility*, is one of the most deadly emotions you can harbor in your soul. You need to find a healthful and helpful way of releasing this emotion. Spewing it out in verbal tirades or acting out your anger in vengeful ways does no real good—to you or to others. The Bible clearly commands that we are never to give full vent to our anger, nor are we to take revenge (Proverbs 29:11 and Romans 12:19).

Here are several things to consider as your confront your own anger and hostility:

☐ Adjust your expectations of other people. If you are expecting perfection from others, or are expecting others to treat you in a kind and considerate way at all times, you are going to live in a constant state of disappointment! Never expect perfection from others, and for that matter, never expect perfection from yourself. Perfection in human beings is simply not possible. Doing one's best is possible. (See Romans 3:10, 23.)
☐ Choose to think first and speak second (James 1:19, 20). You *can* change your behavioral patterns and give pause to speak if you are angry.

☐ Refuse to get caught up in name-calling (Matthew 5:22). It does nothing to release anger—it fuels it.
☐ Seek out the source of your seething anger. Ask yourself, *Why do I respond this way?* (See Psalms 139:23, 24.) Never fall into the trap of thinking, *God made me this way.* He didn't.
☐ Release your right to stay angry (Colossians 3:8). You do *not* have a right to hold on to hostility or anger. It is an ungodly trait that God desires for you to overcome.
☐ Turn to God when you feel angry and give your anger to Him (1 Peter 5:7).
☐ Ask God for His wisdom in how to deal with your anger (James 1:5).

The ultimate answer to long-held anger is nearly always forgiveness. If you have a deep anger issue, ask the Lord to reveal whom you need to forgive, and then ask Him to give you the courage to forgive them.

4:1 [a]NU-Text reads *in.*   4:4 [a]Deuteronomy 8:3   [b]NU-Text omits *but by every word of God.*   4:5 [a]NU-Text reads *And taking Him up, he showed Him.*   4:8 [a]NU-Text omits *Get behind Me, Satan.*   [b]NU-Text and M-Text omit *For.*   [c]Deuteronomy 6:13   4:11 [a]Psalm 91:11, 12   4:12 [a]Deuteronomy 6:16

Feasting

Bible Health + Food Facts

The Jewish people loved feasts. Feasts often lasted five to six hours, and were usually accompanied by music and dancing. They were usually associated with religious holidays and weddings.

JESUS BEGINS HIS GALILEAN MINISTRY

¹⁴Then Jesus returned in the power of the Spirit to Galilee, and news of Him went out through all the surrounding region. ¹⁵And He taught in their synagogues, being glorified by all.

JESUS REJECTED AT NAZARETH

¹⁶So He came to Nazareth, where He had been brought up. And as His custom was, He went into the synagogue on the Sabbath day, and stood up to read. ¹⁷And He was handed the book of the prophet Isaiah. And when He had opened the book, He found the place where it was written:

¹⁸ "The Spirit of the Lord is upon Me,
Because He has anointed Me
To preach the gospel to the poor;
He has sent Me to heal the brokenhearted,ᵃ
To proclaim liberty to the captives
And recovery of sight to the blind,
To set at liberty those who are oppressed;
¹⁹ To proclaim the acceptable year of the Lord." ᵃ

²⁰Then He closed the book, and gave *it* back to the attendant and sat down. And the eyes of all who were in the synagogue were fixed on Him. ²¹And He began to say to them, "Today this Scripture is fulfilled in your hearing." ²²So all bore witness to Him, and marveled at the gracious words which proceeded out of His mouth. And they said, "Is this not Joseph's son?"

²³He said to them, "You will surely say this proverb to Me, 'Physician, heal yourself! Whatever we have heard done in Capernaum,ᵃ do also here in Your country.' " ²⁴Then He said, "Assuredly, I say to you, no prophet is accepted in his own country. ²⁵But I tell you truly, many widows were in Israel in the days of Elijah, when the heaven was shut up three years and six months, and there was a great famine throughout all the land; ²⁶but to none of them was Elijah sent except to Zarephath,ᵃ *in the region* of Sidon, to a woman *who was* a widow. ²⁷And

many lepers were in Israel in the time of Elisha the prophet, and none of them was cleansed except Naaman the Syrian."

²⁸So all those in the synagogue, when they heard these things, were filled with wrath, ²⁹and rose up and thrust Him out of the city; and they led Him to the brow of the hill on which their city was built, that they might throw Him down over the cliff. ³⁰Then passing through the midst of them, He went His way.

JESUS CASTS OUT AN UNCLEAN SPIRIT

³¹Then He went down to Capernaum, a city of Galilee, and was teaching them on the Sabbaths. ³²And they were astonished at His teaching, for His word was with authority. ³³Now in the synagogue there was a man who had a spirit of an unclean demon. And he cried out with a loud voice, ³⁴saying, "Let *us* alone! What have we to do with You, Jesus of Nazareth? Did You come to destroy us? I know who You are—the Holy One of God!"

³⁵But Jesus rebuked him, saying, "Be quiet, and come out of him!" And when the demon had thrown him in *their* midst, it came out of him and did not hurt him. ³⁶Then they were all amazed and spoke among themselves, saying, "What a word this *is!* For with authority and power He commands the unclean spirits, and they come out." ³⁷And the report about Him went out into every place in the surrounding region.

PETER'S MOTHER-IN-LAW HEALED

³⁸Now He arose from the synagogue and entered Simon's house. But Simon's wife's mother was sick with a high fever, and they made request of Him concerning her. ³⁹So He stood over her and rebuked the fever, and it left her. And immediately she arose and served them.

MANY HEALED AFTER SABBATH SUNSET

⁴⁰When the sun was setting, all those who had any that were sick with various diseases brought them to Him; and He laid His hands on every one of them and healed them. ⁴¹And demons also came

WISE CHOICES

Choose fructose over sucrose.

Fructose—the sugar found in fresh fruit—breaks down differently in the body than sucrose, which is found in white sugar, syrups, and other processed-sugar products. Avoid sucrose products. They are directly linked to a breakdown of the immune system.

4:18 ᵃNU-Text omits *to heal the brokenhearted*.　4:19 ᵃIsaiah 61:1, 2　4:23 ᵃHere and elsewhere the NU-Text spelling is *Capharnaum*.　4:26 ᵃGreek *Sarepta*

out of many, crying out and saying, "You are the Christ,ᵃ the Son of God!"

And He, rebuking *them,* did not allow them to speak, for they knew that He was the Christ.

JESUS PREACHES IN GALILEE

⁴²Now when it was day, He departed and went into a deserted place. And the crowd sought Him and came to Him, and tried to keep Him from leaving them; ⁴³but He said to them, "I must preach the kingdom of God to the other cities also, because for this purpose I have been sent." ⁴⁴And He was preaching in the synagogues of Galilee.ᵃ

FOUR FISHERMEN CALLED AS DISCIPLES

5 So it was, as the multitude pressed about Him to hear the word of God, that He stood by the Lake of Gennesaret, ²and saw two boats standing by the lake; but the fishermen had gone from them and were washing *their* nets. ³Then He got into one of the boats, which was Simon's, and asked him to put out a little from the land. And He sat down and taught the multitudes from the boat.

⁴When He had stopped speaking, He said to Simon, "Launch out into the deep and let down your nets for a catch."

⁵But Simon answered and said to Him, "Master, we have toiled all night and caught nothing; nevertheless at Your word I will let down the net." ⁶And when they had done this, they caught a great number of fish, and their net was breaking. ⁷So they signaled to *their* partners in the other boat to come and help them. And they came and filled both the boats, so that they began to sink. ⁸When Simon Peter saw *it,* he fell down at Jesus' knees, saying, "Depart from me, for I am a sinful man, O Lord!"

⁹For he and all who were with him were astonished at the catch of fish which they had taken; ¹⁰and so also *were* James and John, the sons of Zebedee, who were partners with Simon. And Jesus said to Simon, "Do not be afraid. From now on you will catch men." ¹¹So when they had brought their boats to land, they forsook all and followed Him.

JESUS CLEANSES A LEPER

¹²And it happened when He was in a certain city, that behold, a man who was full of leprosy saw Jesus; and he fell on *his* face and implored Him, saying, "Lord, if You are willing, You can make me clean."

¹³Then He put out *His* hand and touched him, saying, "I am willing; be cleansed." Immediately the leprosy left him. ¹⁴And He charged him to tell no one, "But go and show yourself to the priest, and make an offering for your cleansing, as a testimony to them, just as Moses commanded."

¹⁵However, the report went around concerning Him all the more; and great multitudes came together to hear, and to be healed by Him of their infirmities. ¹⁶So He Himself *often* withdrew into the wilderness and prayed.

JESUS FORGIVES AND HEALS A PARALYTIC

¹⁷Now it happened on a certain day, as He was teaching, that there were Pharisees and teachers of the law sitting by, who had come out of every town of Galilee, Judea, and Jerusalem. And the power of the Lord

Stress Busters
Adjust Your Priorities

Take the "one-year-to-live" test. Pretend that you have only one year to live. What would you do during that time? Make a list and then put the things on your list into one of three categories:

1. Activities you *must* do.
2. Things you *enjoy* doing.
3. Activities you neither enjoy nor are required to do.

Eliminate everything in category three! For the remainder of your life, focus only on those things in the first two categories.

was *present* to heal them.ᵃ ¹⁸Then behold, men brought on a bed a man who was paralyzed, whom they sought to bring in and lay before Him. ¹⁹And when they could not find how they might bring him in, because of the crowd, they went up on the housetop and let him down with *his* bed through the tiling into the midst before Jesus.

²⁰When He saw their faith, He said to him, "Man, your sins are forgiven you."

²¹And the scribes and the Pharisees began to reason, saying, "Who is this who speaks blasphemies? Who can forgive sins but God alone?"

²²But when Jesus perceived their thoughts, He answered and said to them, "Why are you reasoning in your hearts? ²³Which is easier, to say, 'Your sins are forgiven you,' or to say, 'Rise up and walk'? ²⁴But that you may know that the Son of Man has power on earth to forgive sins"—He said to the man who was paralyzed, "I say to you, arise, take up your bed, and go to your house."

4:41 ᵃNU-Text omits *the Christ.*   4:44 ᵃNU-Text reads *Judea.*   5:17 ᵃNU-Text reads *present with Him to heal.*

²⁵Immediately he rose up before them, took up what he had been lying on, and departed to his own house, glorifying God. ²⁶And they were all amazed, and they glorified God and were filled with fear, saying, "We have seen strange things today!"

MATTHEW THE TAX COLLECTOR

²⁷After these things He went out and saw a tax collector named Levi, sitting at the tax office. And He said to him, "Follow Me." ²⁸So he left all, rose up, and followed Him.

²⁹Then Levi gave Him a great feast in his own house. And there were a great number of tax collectors and others who sat down with them. ³⁰And their scribes and the Pharisees*ᵃ* complained against His disciples, saying, "Why do You eat and drink with tax collectors and sinners?"

³¹Jesus answered and said to them, "Those who are well have no need of a physician, but those who are sick. ³²I have not come to call *the* righteous, but sinners, to repentance."

JESUS IS QUESTIONED ABOUT FASTING

³³Then they said to Him, "Why do*ᵃ* the disciples of John fast often and make prayers, and likewise those of the Pharisees, but Yours eat and drink?"

³⁴And He said to them, "Can you make the friends of the bridegroom fast while the bridegroom is with them? ³⁵But the days will come when the bridegroom will be taken away from them; then they will fast in those days."

³⁶Then He spoke a parable to them: "No one puts a piece from a new garment on an old one;*ᵃ* otherwise the new makes a tear, and also the piece that was *taken* out of the new does not match the old. ³⁷And no one puts new wine into old wineskins; or else the new wine will burst the wineskins and be spilled, and the wineskins will be ruined. ³⁸But new wine must be put into new wineskins, and both are preserved.*ᵃ* ³⁹And no one, having drunk old *wine*, immediately*ᵃ* desires new; for he says, 'The old is better.' "*ᵇ*

JESUS IS LORD OF THE SABBATH

6 Now it happened on the second Sabbath after the first*ᵃ* that He went through the grainfields. And His disciples plucked the heads of grain and ate *them*, rubbing *them* in *their* hands.

²And some of the Pharisees said to them, "Why are you doing what is not lawful to do on the Sabbath?"

³But Jesus answering them said, "Have you not even read this, what David did when he was hungry, he and those who were with him: ⁴how he went into the house of God, took and ate the showbread, and also gave some to those with him, which is not lawful for any but the priests to eat?" ⁵And He said to them, "The Son of Man is also Lord of the Sabbath."

HEALING ON THE SABBATH

⁶Now it happened on another Sabbath, also, that He entered the synagogue and taught. And a man was there whose right hand was withered. ⁷So the scribes and Pharisees watched Him closely, whether He would heal on the Sabbath, that they might find an accusation against Him. ⁸But He knew their thoughts, and said to the man who had the withered hand, "Arise and stand here." And he arose and stood. ⁹Then Jesus said to them, "I will ask you one thing: Is it lawful on the Sabbath to do good or to do evil, to save life or to destroy?"*ᵃ* ¹⁰And when He had looked around at them all, He said to the man,*ᵃ* "Stretch out your hand." And he did so, and his hand was restored as whole as the other.*ᵇ* ¹¹But they were filled with rage, and discussed with one another what they might do to Jesus.

THE TWELVE APOSTLES

¹²Now it came to pass in those days that He went out to the mountain to pray, and continued all night in prayer to God. ¹³And when it was day, He called His disciples to *Himself;* and from them He chose twelve whom He also named apostles: ¹⁴Simon, whom He also named Peter, and Andrew his brother; James and John; Philip and Bartholomew; ¹⁵Matthew and Thomas; James the *son* of Alphaeus, and Simon called the Zealot; ¹⁶Judas *the son* of James, and Judas Iscariot who also became a traitor.

JESUS HEALS A GREAT MULTITUDE

¹⁷And He came down with them and stood on a level place with a crowd of His disciples and a great multitude of people from all Judea

> (Luke 5:31)

The Counsel of a Godly Physician. Many people do not seek out a physician until they are sick, which means that they rarely see a physician unless they already know that they need medical help. For many people, the first real step toward *wholeness* comes when a person admits to himself, *I may not be sick right now, but I know I'm not in the best health I can have.*

Admitting that you have room to improve physically, as well as in all other areas of life, is the most important first step toward growth and change. That's the ideal time to seek out a physician who not only is well trained to help a person overcome disease or injury, but who is also trained to help a person grow toward maximum wellness.

Generally speaking, the best physician to choose is one who understands the connections between body and mind, body and emotions, and body and spirit. A physician who believes that God desires a person to be *whole* is a physician not limited to the use of medication and surgery, but who also understands nutrition, exercise physiology, basic psychological principles, has a sound theology, and believes in the power of faith and prayer.

INSIGHTS INTO THE WORD

5:30 *ᵃNU-Text reads But the Pharisees and their scribes.* 5:33 *ᵃNU-Text omits Why do, making the verse a statement.* 5:36 *ᵃNU-Text reads No one tears a piece from a new garment and puts it on an old one.* 5:38 *ᵃNU-Text omits and both are preserved.* 5:39 *ᵃNU-Text omits immediately.* *ᵇNU-Text reads good.* 6:1 *ᵃNU-Text reads on a Sabbath.* 6:9 *ᵃM-Text reads to kill.* 6:10 *ᵃNU-Text and M-Text read to him.* *ᵇNU-Text omits as whole as the other.*

82   DIVINE HEALTH

> (Luke 6:36, 37)

Judging and Condemning. To judge is to draw a conclusion based upon an evaluation of evidence, which might be objective or subjective. As Christians we are to judge acts of behavior (speech and deeds), and to determine if the behavior and stated beliefs are right or wrong. We are *not*, however, to judge the degree of righteousness, or unrighteousness, in another human being. Why? Because we can never know *all* the evidence! We cannot know a person's innermost motives, desires, or intentions. We do not know the beginning from the ending of their life. Only God does, and therefore, we are to leave the judgment of people to Him.

To condemn is to put a person beyond the reaches of God's redemptive power or to conclude that a person is unworthy of salvation and therefore, is destined for eternal damnation. Only God has the authority to determine a person's eternal destiny, and therefore, we are to leave all condemnation to Him.

Judgmental or condemning attitudes, words, or deeds are often linked to the highly unhealthy emotions of hate, anger, bitterness, and resentment. Choose to forgive instead!

INSIGHTS INTO THE WORD

and Jerusalem, and from the seacoast of Tyre and Sidon, who came to hear Him and be healed of their diseases, [18] as well as those who were tormented with unclean spirits. And they were healed. [19] And the whole multitude sought to touch Him, for power went out from Him and healed *them* all.

THE BEATITUDES

[20] Then He lifted up His eyes toward His disciples, and said:

"Blessed *are you* poor,
> For yours is the kingdom of God.
[21] Blessed *are you* who hunger now,
> For you shall be filled.
Blessed *are you* who weep now,
> For you shall laugh.
[22] Blessed are you when men hate you,
> And when they exclude you,
> And revile *you,* and cast out your name as evil,
> For the Son of Man's sake.
[23] Rejoice in that day and leap for joy!
> For indeed your reward *is* great in heaven,
> For in like manner their fathers did to the prophets.

JESUS PRONOUNCES WOES

[24] "But woe to you who are rich,
> For you have received your consolation.
[25] Woe to you who are full,
> For you shall hunger.
Woe to you who laugh now,
> For you shall mourn and weep.
[26] Woe to you[a] when all[b] men speak well of you,
> For so did their fathers to the false prophets.

LOVE YOUR ENEMIES

[27] "But I say to you who hear: Love your enemies, do good to those who hate you, [28] bless those who curse you, and pray for those who spitefully use you. [29] To him who strikes you on the *one* cheek, offer the other also. And from him who takes away your cloak, do not withhold *your* tunic either. [30] Give to everyone who asks of you. And from him who takes away your goods do not ask *them* back. [31] And just as you want men to do to you, you also do to them likewise.

[32] "But if you love those who love you, what credit is that to you? For even sinners love those who love them. [33] And if you do good to those who do good to you, what credit is that to you? For even sinners do the same. [34] And if you lend *to those* from whom you hope to receive back, what credit is that to you? For even sinners lend to sinners to receive as much back. [35] But love your enemies, do good, and lend, hoping for nothing in return; and your reward will be great, and you will be sons of the Most High. For He is kind to the unthankful and evil. [36] Therefore be merciful, just as your Father also is merciful.

DO NOT JUDGE

[37] "Judge not, and you shall not be judged. Condemn not, and you shall not be condemned. Forgive, and you will be forgiven. [38] Give, and it will be given to you: good measure, pressed down, shaken together, and running over will be put into your bosom. For with the same measure that you use, it will be measured back to you."

[39] And He spoke a parable to them: "Can the blind lead the blind? Will they not both fall into the ditch? [40] A disciple is not above his teacher, but everyone who is perfectly trained will be like his teacher. [41] And why do you look at the speck in your brother's eye, but do not perceive the plank in your own eye? [42] Or how can you say to your brother, 'Brother, let me remove the speck that *is* in your eye,' when you yourself do not see the plank that *is* in your own eye? Hypocrite! First remove the plank from your own eye, and then you will see clearly to remove the speck that is in your brother's eye.

A TREE IS KNOWN BY ITS FRUIT

[43] "For a good tree does not bear bad fruit, nor does a bad tree bear good fruit. [44] For every tree is known by its own fruit. For *men* do not gather figs from thorns, nor do they gather grapes from a bramble bush. [45] A good man out of the good treasure of his heart brings forth good; and an evil man out of the evil treasure of his heart[a] brings forth evil. For out of the abundance of the heart his mouth speaks.

SCRIPTURE SOLUTIONS

[ARTHRITIS]

Arthritis is an affliction. Although there are many forms and varieties of arthritis, the symptoms nearly always include stiffness, pain, swelling, or creaking of the joints.

Although proper nutrition, a correct spiritual viewpoint, and taking vitamins and supplements are all very beneficial in overcoming arthritis, people sometimes overlook *exercise* as an aid in their recovery and healing.

Exercise may be very painful and difficult at first, but exercise and losing weight can greatly help those with arthritis by keeping the joints free and moving, and by reducing the weight load on the joints. Here are three helpful hints to make exercise more productive and beneficial:

Do aerobic exercise within your "heart rate zone." How do you know when you're training in your heart rate zone? Take your current age and subtract that number from 220. Take that number and multiply by 0.65. Write that number on a piece of paper. Then, go back and take the first number again (age subtracted from 220), and multiply it by 0.80. These two numbers give the range that your heart should be beating per minute. This is called the *heart rate zone*. Try to work out as much within this zone as possible.

Drink plenty of water. You need sufficient water to keep the synovial fluid flowing freely in and out of the cartilage throughout your body.

Do weight-bearing exercises, also known as "using weights." Weight-bearing exercises aid in the growth of stronger and thicker bones.

Also immerse yourself in these encouraging Scriptures that relate to healing: Psalms 34:1–6; 1 Peter 2:24; and Romans 8:23.

BUILD ON THE ROCK

⁴⁶"But why do you call Me 'Lord, Lord,' and not do the things which I say? ⁴⁷Whoever comes to Me, and hears My sayings and does them, I will show you whom he is like: ⁴⁸He is like a man building a house, who dug deep and laid the foundation on the rock. And when the flood arose, the stream beat vehemently against that house, and could not shake it, for it was founded on the rock.ᵃ ⁴⁹But he who heard and did nothing is like a man who built a house on the earth without a foundation, against which the stream beat vehemently; and immediately it fell.ᵃ And the ruin of that house was great."

JESUS HEALS A CENTURION'S SERVANT

7 Now when He concluded all His sayings in the hearing of the people, He entered Capernaum. ²And a certain centurion's servant, who was dear to him, was sick and ready to die. ³So when he heard about Jesus, he sent elders of the Jews to Him, pleading with Him to come and heal his servant. ⁴And when they came to Jesus, they begged Him earnestly, saying that the one for whom He should do this was deserving, ⁵"for he loves our nation, and has built us a synagogue."

⁶Then Jesus went with them. And when He was already not far from the house, the centurion sent friends to Him, saying to Him, "Lord, do not trouble Yourself, for I am not worthy that You should enter under my roof. ⁷Therefore I did not even think myself worthy to come to You. But say the word, and my servant will be healed. ⁸For I also am a man placed under authority, having soldiers under me. And I say to one, 'Go,' and he goes; and to another, 'Come,' and he comes; and to my servant, 'Do this,' and he does *it*."

⁹When Jesus heard these things, He marveled at him, and turned around and said to the crowd that followed Him, "I say to you, I have not found such great faith, not even in Israel!" ¹⁰And those who were sent, returning to the house, found the servant well who had been sick.ᵃ

JESUS RAISES THE SON OF THE WIDOW OF NAIN

¹¹Now it happened, the day after, *that* He went into a city called Nain; and many of His disciples went with Him, and a large crowd. ¹²And when He came near the gate of the city, behold, a dead man was being carried out, the only son of his mother; and she was a widow. And a large crowd from the city was with her. ¹³When the Lord saw her, He had compassion on her and said to her, "Do not weep." ¹⁴Then He came and touched the open coffin, and those who carried *him* stood still. And He said, "Young man, I say to you, arise." ¹⁵So he who was dead sat up and began to speak. And He presented him to his mother.

¹⁶Then fear came upon all, and they glorified God, saying, "A great prophet has risen up among us"; and, "God has visited His people." ¹⁷And this report about Him went throughout all Judea and all the surrounding region.

JOHN THE BAPTIST SENDS MESSENGERS TO JESUS

¹⁸Then the disciples of John reported to him concerning all these things. ¹⁹And John, calling two of his disciples to *him*, sent *them* to Je-

sus," saying, "Are You the Coming One, or do we look for another?"

²⁰When the men had come to Him, they said, "John the Baptist has sent us to You, saying, 'Are You the Coming One, or do we look for another?' " ²¹And that very hour He cured many of infirmities, afflictions, and evil spirits; and to many blind He gave sight.

²²Jesus answered and said to them, "Go and tell John the things you have seen and heard: that *the* blind see, *the* lame walk, *the* lepers are cleansed, *the* deaf hear, *the* dead are raised, *the* poor have the gospel preached to them. ²³And blessed is *he* who is not offended because of Me."

²⁴When the messengers of John had departed, He began to speak to the multitudes concerning John: "What did you go out into the wilderness to see? A reed shaken by the wind? ²⁵But what did you go out to see? A man clothed in soft garments? Indeed those who are gorgeously appareled and live in luxury are in kings' courts. ²⁶But what did you go out to see? A prophet? Yes, I say to you, and more than a prophet. ²⁷This is *he* of whom it is written:

'Behold, I send My messenger before Your face,
Who will prepare Your way before You.'ᵃ

²⁸For I say to you, among those born of women there is not a greater prophet than John the Baptist;ᵃ but he who is least in the kingdom of God is greater than he."

²⁹And when all the people heard *Him,* even the tax collectors justified God, having been baptized with the baptism of John. ³⁰But the Pharisees and lawyers rejected the will of God for themselves, not having been baptized by him.

³¹And the Lord said;ᵃ "To what then shall I liken the men of this generation, and what are they like? ³²They are like children sitting in the marketplace and calling to one another, saying:

'We played the flute for you,
    And you did not dance;
We mourned to you,
    And you did not weep.'

³³For John the Baptist came neither eating bread nor drinking wine, and you say, 'He has a demon.' ³⁴The Son of Man has come eating and drinking, and you say, 'Look, a glutton and a winebibber, a friend of tax collectors and sinners!' ³⁵But wisdom is justified by all her children."

A SINFUL WOMAN FORGIVEN

³⁶Then one of the Pharisees asked Him to eat with him. And He went to the Pharisee's house, and sat down to eat. ³⁷And behold, a woman in the city who was a sinner, when she knew that *Jesus* sat at the table in the Pharisee's house, brought an alabaster flask of fragrant oil, ³⁸and stood at His feet behind *Him* weeping; and she began to wash His feet with her tears, and wiped *them* with the hair of her head; and she kissed His feet and anointed *them* with the fragrant oil. ³⁹Now when the Pharisee who had invited Him saw *this,* he spoke to himself, saying, "This Man, if He were a prophet, would know who and what manner of woman *this is* who is touching Him, for she is a sinner."

⁴⁰And Jesus answered and said to him, "Simon, I have something to say to you."

So he said, "Teacher, say it."

⁴¹"There was a certain creditor who had two debtors. One owed five hundred denarii, and the other fifty. ⁴²And when they had nothing with which to repay, he freely forgave them both. Tell Me, therefore, which of them will love him more?"

⁴³Simon answered and said, "I suppose the *one* whom he forgave more."

And He said to him, "You have rightly judged." ⁴⁴Then He turned to the woman and said to Simon, "Do you see this woman? I entered your house; you gave Me no water for My feet, but she has washed My feet with her tears and wiped *them* with the hair of her head. ⁴⁵You gave Me no kiss, but this woman has not ceased to kiss My feet since the time I came in. ⁴⁶You did not anoint My head with oil, but this woman has anointed My feet with fragrant oil. ⁴⁷Therefore I say to you, her sins, *which are* many, are forgiven, for she loved much. But to whom little is forgiven, *the same* loves little."

⁴⁸Then He said to her, "Your sins are forgiven."

⁴⁹And those who sat at the table with Him began to say to themselves, "Who is this who even forgives sins?"

⁵⁰Then He said to the woman, "Your faith has saved you. Go in peace."

MANY WOMEN MINISTER TO JESUS

8 Now it came to pass, afterward, that He went through every city and village, preaching and bringing the glad tidings of the kingdom of God. And the twelve *were* with Him, ²and certain women who had been healed of evil spirits and infirmities—Mary called Magdalene, out of whom had come seven demons, ³and Joanna the wife of Chuza, Herod's steward, and Susanna, and many others who provided for Himᵃ from their substance.

> **(Luke 7:46)**

Anointing the Head with Oil. It was a common practice of hospitality in Bible times to provide a little scented olive oil for a guest to put on his own hair, face, and hands—something of a hair and skin "dressing" prior to the partaking of a meal. The washing of hands and feet, and the anointing of oil on hair and skin, signaled the beginning of a proper meal. Oil is considered a symbol throughout the Bible of the presence of God's Spirit. Using oil to anoint those partaking of a meal signaled that all parties present at the meal were in the presence of God's Spirit. An atmosphere of congeniality, faith, and love was expected.

INSIGHTS INTO THE WORD

7:19 ᵃNU-Text reads *the Lord.*   7:27 ᵃMalachi 3:1   7:28 ᵃNU-Text reads *there is none greater than John.*   7:31 ᵃNU-Text and M-Text omit *And the Lord said.*   8:3 ᵃNU-Text and M-Text read *them.*

WEIGHING Less & ENJOYING LIFE MORE!

[Start Your Day with Fresh Fruit!]

Fresh fruit for breakfast is something of a jump-starter for a day of healthful eating. Sugar comes in lots of varieties but the least offensive and most healthful variety for the human body is fructose, the sugar found in fresh fruit. Fructose gives a person an energy lift, and for most people, a portion of fresh fruit provides a sense of satisfaction and freshness at the start of a new day.

In addition, fresh fruit is a good source of fiber. Choose fresh fruit over fruit juice if you can—fresh fruit has fewer calories per portion and more fiber. Frozen fruit, partially thawed, mixed into a smoothie or added to a protein drink makes a great breakfast beverage.

THE PARABLE OF THE SOWER

⁴And when a great multitude had gathered, and they had come to Him from every city, He spoke by a parable: ⁵"A sower went out to sow his seed. And as he sowed, some fell by the wayside; and it was trampled down, and the birds of the air devoured it. ⁶Some fell on rock; and as soon as it sprang up, it withered away because it lacked moisture. ⁷And some fell among thorns, and the thorns sprang up with it and choked it. ⁸But others fell on good ground, sprang up, and yielded a crop a hundredfold." When He had said these things He cried, "He who has ears to hear, let him hear!"

THE PURPOSE OF PARABLES

⁹Then His disciples asked Him, saying, "What does this parable mean?"

¹⁰And He said, "To you it has been given to know the mysteries of the kingdom of God, but to the rest *it is given* in parables, that

'Seeing they may not see,
And hearing they may not understand.'ᵃ

THE PARABLE OF THE SOWER EXPLAINED

¹¹"Now the parable is this: The seed is the word of God. ¹²Those by the wayside are the ones who hear; then the devil comes and takes away the word out of their hearts, lest they should believe and be saved. ¹³But the ones on the rock *are those* who, when they hear, receive the word with joy; and these have no root, who believe for a while and in time of temptation fall away. ¹⁴Now the ones *that* fell among thorns are those who, when they have heard, go out and are choked with cares, riches, and pleasures of life, and bring no fruit to maturity. ¹⁵But the ones *that* fell on the good ground are those who, having heard the word with a noble and good heart, keep *it* and bear fruit with patience.

THE PARABLE OF THE REVEALED LIGHT

¹⁶"No one, when he has lit a lamp, covers it with a vessel or puts *it* under a bed, but sets *it* on a lampstand, that those who enter may see the light. ¹⁷For nothing is secret that will not be revealed, nor *anything* hidden that will not be known and come to light. ¹⁸Therefore take heed how you hear. For whoever has, to him *more* will be given; and whoever does not have, even what he seems to have will be taken from him."

JESUS' MOTHER AND BROTHERS COME TO HIM

¹⁹Then His mother and brothers came to Him, and could not approach Him because of the crowd. ²⁰And it was told Him *by some,* who said, "Your mother and Your brothers are standing outside, desiring to see You."

²¹But He answered and said to them, "My mother and My brothers are these who hear the word of God and do it."

WIND AND WAVE OBEY JESUS

²²Now it happened, on a certain day, that He got into a boat with His disciples. And He said to them, "Let us cross over to the other side of the lake." And they launched out. ²³But as they sailed He fell asleep. And a windstorm came down on the lake, and they were filling *with water,* and were in jeopardy. ²⁴And they came to Him and awoke Him, saying, "Master, Master, we are perishing!"

Then He arose and rebuked the wind and the raging of the water. And they ceased, and there was a calm. ²⁵But He said to them, "Where is your faith?"

And they were afraid, and marveled, saying to one another, "Who can this be? For He commands even the winds and water, and they obey Him!"

A DEMON-POSSESSED MAN HEALED

²⁶Then they sailed to the country of the Gadarenes,ᵃ which is opposite Galilee. ²⁷And when He stepped out on the land, there met Him a certain man from the city who had demons for a long time. And he wore no clothes,ᵃ nor did he live in a house but in the tombs. ²⁸When he saw Jesus, he cried out, fell down before Him, and with a loud voice

8:10 ᵃIsaiah 6:9   8:26 ᵃNU-Text reads *Gerasenes.*   8:27 ᵃNU-Text reads *who had demons and for a long time wore no clothes.*

said, "What have I to do with You, Jesus, Son of the Most High God? I beg You, do not torment me!" [29]For He had commanded the unclean spirit to come out of the man. For it had often seized him, and he was kept under guard, bound with chains and shackles; and he broke the bonds and was driven by the demon into the wilderness.

[30]Jesus asked him, saying, "What is your name?"

And he said, "Legion," because many demons had entered him. [31]And they begged Him that He would not command them to go out into the abyss.

[32]Now a herd of many swine was feeding there on the mountain. So they begged Him that He would permit them to enter them. And He permitted them. [33]Then the demons went out of the man and entered the swine, and the herd ran violently down the steep place into the lake and drowned.

[34]When those who fed *them* saw what had happened, they fled and told *it* in the city and in the country. [35]Then they went out to see what had happened, and came to Jesus, and found the man from whom the demons had departed, sitting at the feet of Jesus, clothed and in his right mind. And they were afraid. [36]They also who had seen *it* told them by what means he who had been demon-possessed was healed. [37]Then the whole multitude of the surrounding region of the Gadarenes[a] asked Him to depart from them, for they were seized with great fear. And He got into the boat and returned.

[38]Now the man from whom the demons had departed begged Him that he might be with Him. But Jesus sent him away, saying, [39]"Return to your own house, and tell what great things God has done for you." And he went his way and proclaimed throughout the whole city what great things Jesus had done for him.

A GIRL RESTORED TO LIFE AND A WOMAN HEALED

[40]So it was, when Jesus returned, that the multitude welcomed Him, for they were all waiting for Him. [41]And behold, there came a man named Jairus, and he was a ruler of the synagogue. And he fell down at Jesus' feet and begged Him to come to his house, [42]for he had an only daughter about twelve years of age, and she was dying.

But as He went, the multitudes thronged Him. [43]Now a woman, having a flow of blood for twelve years, who had spent all her livelihood on physicians and could not be healed by any, [44]came from behind and touched the border of His garment. And immediately her flow of blood stopped.

[45]And Jesus said, "Who touched Me?"

When all denied it, Peter and those with him[a] said, "Master, the multitudes throng and press You, and You say, 'Who touched Me?' "[b]

[46]But Jesus said, "Somebody touched Me, for I perceived power going out from Me." [47]Now when the woman saw that she was not hidden, she came trembling; and falling down before Him, she declared to Him in the presence of all the people the reason she had touched Him and how she was healed immediately.

[48]And He said to her, "Daughter, be of good cheer;[a] your faith has made you well. Go in peace."

▲ **What Did Jesus Eat?** ▼

ULTIMATE HEALTH RESOURCE • ULTIMATE HEALTH RESOURCE • ULTIMATE HEALTH RESOURCE

We don't know everything about Jesus' eating patterns but we do know this:

☐ Jesus kept the dietary laws of the Old Testament.

☐ Jesus ate primarily what people today would call a "Mediterranean diet"—an eating plan that includes lots of fresh fruits and vegetables, very little red meat, and plenty of olives and olive oil. The Mediterranean diet also includes whole grains, very few milk products, and lots of fish.

☐ Jesus ate primarily whole foods and fresh foods—in many cases eaten raw.

☐ Jesus ate foods that were free of pesticides, fungicides, and any type of additives.

☐ Jesus ate foods that for the most part had not been laced with any sugar or infused with fat, salt, additives, or chemical preservatives.

The vegetables and fruits in Jesus' time probably had at least four times the amount of minerals and water-soluble vitamins, and about ten times the amount of fat-soluble vitamins, as identical fruits and vegetables in our American diet. The soil had not been depleted of valuable nutrients.

What we also know is that Jesus did *not* eat deep-fried foods, white sugar or white flour, canned foods high in sodium, hydrogenated or refined vegetable oils, or pasteurized or homogenized milk.

Jesus valued the way God the Father had created the earth as well as our bodies. He valued good health and those things that contributed to wholeness.

One of the best questions we can ask about every bite of food that goes into our mouths: *Would Jesus eat this?* If the substance has any potential to harm the body, the answer is a resounding "no."

8:37 [a]NU-Text reads *Gerasenes.*   8:45 [a]NU-Text omits *and those with him.* [b]NU-Text omits *and You say, 'Who touched Me?'*   8:48 [a]NU-Text omits *be of good cheer.*

Q Who was told by the Angel of the Lord, "You are barren and have borne no children, but you shall conceive and bear a son. Now, therefore, please be careful not to drink wine or similar drink, and not to eat anything unclean. For behold, you shall conceive and bear a son. And no razor shall come upon his head, for the child shall be a Nazirite to God from the womb; and he shall begin to deliver Israel out of the hand of the Philistines"?

A Samson's mother *(Judges 13:3–5)*.

⁴⁹While He was still speaking, someone came from the ruler of the synagogue's *house,* saying to him, "Your daughter is dead. Do not trouble the Teacher."ᵃ

⁵⁰But when Jesus heard *it,* He answered him, saying, "Do not be afraid; only believe, and she will be made well." ⁵¹When He came into the house, He permitted no one to go inᵃ except Peter, James, and John,ᵇ and the father and mother of the girl. ⁵²Now all wept and mourned for her; but He said, "Do not weep; she is not dead, but sleeping." ⁵³And they ridiculed Him, knowing that she was dead.

⁵⁴But He put them all outside,ᵃ took her by the hand and called, saying, "Little girl, arise." ⁵⁵Then her spirit returned, and she arose immediately. And He commanded that she be given *something* to eat. ⁵⁶And her parents were astonished, but He charged them to tell no one what had happened.

SENDING OUT THE TWELVE

9 Then He called His twelve disciples together and gave them power and authority over all demons, and to cure diseases. ²He sent them to preach the kingdom of God and to heal the sick. ³And He said to them, "Take nothing for the journey, neither staffs nor bag nor bread nor money; and do not have two tunics apiece.

⁴"Whatever house you enter, stay there, and from there depart. ⁵And whoever will not receive you, when you go out of that city, shake off the very dust from your feet as a testimony against them."

⁶So they departed and went through the towns, preaching the gospel and healing everywhere.

HEROD SEEKS TO SEE JESUS

⁷Now Herod the tetrarch heard of all that was done by Him; and he was perplexed, because it was said by some that John had risen from the dead, ⁸and by some that Elijah had appeared, and by others that one of the old prophets had risen again. ⁹Herod said, "John I have beheaded, but who is this of whom I hear such things?" So he sought to see Him.

FEEDING THE FIVE THOUSAND

¹⁰And the apostles, when they had returned, told Him all that they had done. Then He took them and went aside privately into a deserted place belonging to the city called Bethsaida. ¹¹But when the multitudes knew *it,* they followed Him; and He received them and spoke to them about the kingdom of God, and healed those who had need of healing. ¹²When the day began to wear away, the twelve came and said to Him, "Send the multitude away, that they may go into the surrounding towns and country, and lodge and get provisions; for we are in a deserted place here."

¹³But He said to them, "You give them something to eat."

And they said, "We have no more than five loaves and two fish, unless we go and buy food for all these people." ¹⁴For there were about five thousand men.

Then He said to His disciples, "Make them sit down in groups of fifty." ¹⁵And they did so, and made them all sit down.

¹⁶Then He took the five loaves and the two fish, and looking up to heaven, He blessed and broke *them,* and gave *them* to the disciples to set before the multitude. ¹⁷So they all ate and were filled, and twelve baskets of the leftover fragments were taken up by them.

PETER CONFESSES JESUS AS THE CHRIST

¹⁸And it happened, as He was alone praying, *that* His disciples joined Him, and He asked them, saying, "Who do the crowds say that I am?"

¹⁹So they answered and said, "John the Baptist, but some *say* Elijah; and others *say* that one of the old prophets has risen again."

²⁰He said to them, "But who do you say that I am?"

Peter answered and said, "The Christ of God."

JESUS PREDICTS HIS DEATH AND RESURRECTION

²¹And He strictly warned and commanded them to tell this to no one, ²²saying, "The Son of Man must suffer many things, and be rejected by the elders and chief priests and scribes, and be killed, and be raised the third day."

TAKE UP THE CROSS AND FOLLOW HIM

²³Then He said to *them* all, "If anyone desires to come after Me, let him deny himself, and take up his cross daily,ᵃ and follow Me. ²⁴For whoever desires to save his life will lose it, but whoever loses his life for My sake will save it. ²⁵For what profit is it to a man if he gains the whole world, and is himself destroyed or lost? ²⁶For whoever is ashamed of Me and My words, of him the Son of Man will be ashamed when He comes in His *own* glory, and in *His* Father's, and of the holy angels.

JESUS TRANSFIGURED ON THE MOUNT

²⁷But I tell you truly, there are some standing here who shall not taste death till they see the kingdom of God."

8:49 ᵃNU-Text adds *anymore.*   8:51 ᵃNU-Text adds *with Him.*   ᵇNU-Text and M-Text read *Peter, John, and James.*   8:54 ᵃNU-Text omits *put them all outside.*   9:23 ᵃM-Text omits *daily.*

March

1　2　3　4　5　6　7

Now Is the Time To...

☐ Sit out under the stars and relax, if the weather is nice. ☐ Spend 10 minutes stretching today. ☐ Clean out and reorganize your kitchen cupboards. ☐ Try a new aerobics exercise class at the gym. ☐ Invite a friend to dinner at a restaurant neither of you has tried.

Seasonal Tips

8　9　10　11　12　13　14

☐ Remember that even if a day is warm, the night can be cold. Snow and freezing temperatures are likely in the majority of the U.S. Be prepared to cover young plants and shrubs.

In the Garden

15　16　17　18　19　20　21

☐ This is the best time to apply pre-emergent weed killers on your lawn. ☐ If you live in the south or west, plant more seeds in your vegetable garden. Thin plants out when they are 2–3 inches tall to give more room for growth. ☐ Begin planning your summer flower garden. Consider planting a few flowers solely for the purpose of making bouquets for your home. Fresh floral arrangements, even small ones, can be food for the soul—the touch of beauty can turn a house into a home.

22　23　24　25　26　27　28

Table Fresh

☐ Try using tarragon, one of the strongest herbs, in cooking and decorating. ☐ Cook with fresh garlic tonight.

29　30　31

Let's Celebrate

☐ Consider fasting—partially or completely from all food—on the Fridays leading up to Easter. (If Easter falls in March this year, check out the April calendar later in this publication.)

CONDIMENTS

☐ Yogurt Has Dozens of Uses

Although yogurt might not be considered a condiment in the American diet, it is used in a wide variety of ways in Mediterranean cooking:

- ☐ Served as a side dish
- ☐ Used as a salad base. A very popular salad in the Middle East is simply small pieces of cucumber in yogurt, with a little fresh mint and garlic added.
- ☐ Used as a dip or dressing. A popular dip is made with yogurt and dill.
- ☐ Used in making a sauce for meat
- ☐ Used as an alternative to sour cream or butter in seasoning or adding to the flavor of vegetables, including baked potatoes

Yogurt is very high in bone-building calcium. It has been linked to the prevention of colds, allergies, and cancer. It helps lower LDL (bad) cholesterol, fights dangerous intestinal infections, improves bowel function, and blocks ulcers.

One cup of yogurt contains 11.9 grams of protein, 415 mg of calcium, and 531 mg potassium (a good balance to the 149 mg sodium in the same amount of yogurt). It is also a good source of vitamins A and B.

It is best to choose nonfat, plain yogurt that does not have any sugar, fruit, or artificial flavoring or color added. The yogurt should contain live good-bacteria cultures, especially lactobacillus acidophilus and bifidobacterium. You can find this kind of yogurt at a health-food store or in the health-food section of a local grocery.

[28]Now it came to pass, about eight days after these sayings, that He took Peter, John, and James and went up on the mountain to pray. [29]As He prayed, the appearance of His face was altered, and His robe *became* white *and* glistening. [30]And behold, two men talked with Him, who were Moses and Elijah, [31]who appeared in glory and spoke of His decease which He was about to accomplish at Jerusalem. [32]But Peter and those with him were heavy with sleep; and when they were fully awake, they saw His glory and the two men who stood with Him. [33]Then it happened, as they were parting from Him, *that* Peter said to Jesus, "Master, it is good for us to be here; and let us make three tabernacles: one for You, one for Moses, and one for Elijah"—not knowing what he said.

[34]While he was saying this, a cloud came and overshadowed them; and they were fearful as they entered the cloud. [35]And a voice came out of the cloud, saying, "This is My beloved Son.[a] Hear Him!" [36]When the voice had ceased, Jesus was found alone. But they kept quiet, and told no one in those days any of the things they had seen.

A BOY IS HEALED

[37]Now it happened on the next day, when they had come down from the mountain, that a great multitude met Him. [38]Suddenly a man from the multitude cried out, saying, "Teacher, I implore You, look on my son, for he is my only child. [39]And behold, a spirit seizes him, and he suddenly cries out; it convulses him so that he foams *at the mouth;* and it departs from him with great difficulty, bruising him. [40]So I implored Your disciples to cast it out, but they could not."

[41]Then Jesus answered and said, "O faithless and perverse generation, how long shall I be with you and bear with you? Bring your son here." [42]And as he was still coming, the demon threw him down and convulsed *him.* Then Jesus rebuked the unclean spirit, healed the child, and gave him back to his father.

JESUS AGAIN PREDICTS HIS DEATH

[43]And they were all amazed at the majesty of God.

But while everyone marveled at all the things which Jesus did, He said to His disciples, [44]"Let these words sink down into your ears, for the Son of Man is about to be betrayed into the hands of men." [45]But they did not understand this saying, and it was hidden from them so that they did not perceive it; and they were afraid to ask Him about this saying.

WHO IS THE GREATEST?

[46]Then a dispute arose among them as to which of them would be greatest. [47]And Jesus, perceiving the thought of their heart, took a little child and set him by Him, [48]and said to them, "Whoever receives this little child in My name receives Me; and whoever receives Me receives Him who sent Me. For he who is least among you all will be great."

JESUS FORBIDS SECTARIANISM

[49]Now John answered and said, "Master, we saw someone casting out demons in Your name, and we forbade him because he does not follow with us."

[50]But Jesus said to him, "Do not forbid *him,* for he who is not against us[a] is on our[b] side."

A SAMARITAN VILLAGE REJECTS THE SAVIOR

[51]Now it came to pass, when the time had come for Him to be received up, that He steadfastly set His face to go to Jerusalem, [52]and sent messen-

9:35 [a]NU-Text reads *This is My Son, the Chosen One.*   9:50 [a]NU-Text reads *you.*   [b]NU-Text reads *your.*

WEIGHING Less & ENJOYING LIFE MORE!

[Avoid Using Diuretics for Weight Loss]

Many fad diets offer the promise of losing up to ten pounds in a few days. They generally do this by removing water from the tissues and bloodstream. Then, when a person quits taking the diuretic herbs or supplements, the weight reappears. This is not healthful for the body over time, nor is it genuine *fat* loss.

Sufficient water intake is critically important to a person who begins a fat-loss plan. If you do not take in sufficient water, the body will store the water it has and it will also keep any fat that is released into the bloodstream. Arteries are *not* a good place for fat to be deposited! The body needs water to flush away fat globules and other toxins.

gers before His face. And as they went, they entered a village of the Samaritans, to prepare for Him. ⁵³But they did not receive Him, because His face was *set* for the journey to Jerusalem. ⁵⁴And when His disciples James and John saw *this*, they said, "Lord, do You want us to command fire to come down from heaven and consume them, just as Elijah did?"ᵃ

⁵⁵But He turned and rebuked them,ᵃ and said, "You do not know what manner of spirit you are of. ⁵⁶For the Son of Man did not come to destroy men's lives but to save *them*."ᵃ And they went to another village.

THE COST OF DISCIPLESHIP

⁵⁷Now it happened as they journeyed on the road, *that* someone said to Him, "Lord, I will follow You wherever You go."

⁵⁸And Jesus said to him, "Foxes have holes and birds of the air *have* nests, but the Son of Man has nowhere to lay *His* head."

⁵⁹Then He said to another, "Follow Me."

But he said, "Lord, let me first go and bury my father."

⁶⁰Jesus said to him, "Let the dead bury their own dead, but you go and preach the kingdom of God."

⁶¹And another also said, "Lord, I will follow You, but let me first go *and* bid them farewell who are at my house."

⁶²But Jesus said to him, "No one, having put his hand to the plow, and looking back, is fit for the kingdom of God."

THE SEVENTY SENT OUT

10 After these things the Lord appointed seventy others also,ᵃ and sent them two by two before His face into every city and place where He Himself was about to go. ²Then He said to them, "The harvest truly *is* great, but the laborers *are* few; therefore pray the Lord of the harvest to send out laborers into His harvest. ³Go your way; behold, I send you out as lambs among wolves. ⁴Carry neither money bag, knapsack, nor sandals; and greet no one along the road. ⁵But whatever house you enter, first say, 'Peace to this house.' ⁶And if a son of peace is there, your peace will rest on it; if

not, it will return to you. ⁷And remain in the same house, eating and drinking such things as they give, for the laborer is worthy of his wages. Do not go from house to house. ⁸Whatever city you enter, and they receive you, eat such things as are set before you. ⁹And heal the sick there, and say to them, 'The kingdom of God has come near to you.' ¹⁰But whatever city you enter, and they do not receive you, go out into its streets and say, ¹¹'The very dust of your city which clings to usᵃ we wipe off against you. Nevertheless know this, that the kingdom of God has come near you.' ¹²Butᵃ I say to you that it will be more tolerable in that Day for Sodom than for that city.

WOE TO THE IMPENITENT CITIES

¹³"Woe to you, Chorazin! Woe to you, Bethsaida! For if the mighty works which were done in you had been done in Tyre and Sidon, they would have repented long ago, sitting in sackcloth and ashes. ¹⁴But it will be more tolerable for Tyre and Sidon at the judgment than for you. ¹⁵And you, Capernaum, who are exalted to heaven, will be brought down to Hades.ᵃ ¹⁶He who hears you hears Me, he who rejects you rejects Me, and he who rejects Me rejects Him who sent Me."

THE SEVENTY RETURN WITH JOY

¹⁷Then the seventyᵃ returned with joy, saying, "Lord, even the demons are subject to us in Your name."

¹⁸And He said to them, "I saw Satan fall like lightning from heaven. ¹⁹Behold, I give you the authority to trample on serpents and scorpions, and over all the power of the enemy, and nothing shall by any means hurt you. ²⁰Nevertheless do not rejoice in this, that the spirits are subject to you, but ratherᵃ rejoice because your names are written in heaven."

JESUS REJOICES IN THE SPIRIT

²¹In that hour Jesus rejoiced in the Spirit and said, "I thank You, Father, Lord of heaven and earth, that You have hidden these things from *the* wise and prudent and revealed them to babes. Even so, Father, for so it seemed good in Your sight. ²²Allᵃ things have been delivered to Me by

---

9:54 ᵃNU-Text omits *just as Elijah did.*   9:55 ᵃNU-Text omits the rest of this verse.   9:56 ᵃNU-Text omits the first sentence of this verse.   10:1 ᵃNU-Text reads *seventy-two others.*   10:11 ᵃNU-Text reads *our feet.*   10:12 ᵃNU-Text and M-Text omit *But.*   10:15 ᵃNU-Text reads *will you be exalted to heaven? You will be thrust down to Hades!*   10:17 ᵃNU-Text reads *seventy-two.*   10:20 ᵃNU-Text and M-Text omit *rather.*   10:22 ᵃM-Text reads *And turning to the disciples He said, "All . . .*

The Glory of a King's Courtyard

The ancient Middle East was not necessarily a place of great scenic beauty. The soil was rocky, the climate arid. Although much of the area we know as Israel today was once covered with forest, there were also vast areas of desert and mountainous areas marked by deep crevices that flowed with water only after thunderstorms. Apart from flowering plants, there was very little in the way of color in the ancient world—the clothing and homes and utensils of all kinds were generally drab among the common people, with only small touches of embroidery or ornamentation providing color. Except for the Jordan River, there were not many areas in which water flowed freely from artesian springs to create streams or ponds.

The most beautiful places in this ancient world were the courtyards of kings and the wealthy. Most courtyards were separated from busy thoroughfares by high walls. Access was through a gate. The courtyard separated the main living quarters from the street. In many ways, the courtyard was like a very large indoor-outdoor room.

What might be found in a king's courtyard?

- ☐ Exotic plants of many varieties, especially flowering plants, vines on trellises and arbors; and small fruit trees, especially fig, apricot, and miniature citrus trees
- ☐ Exotic species of birds in cages or on tethers
- ☐ Fountains of flowing water
- ☐ Mosaic tiled garden containers, water pools, and pathways
- ☐ Overstuffed colorful embroidered pillows and small benches for seating
- ☐ Small canopies to provide shade as necessary
- ☐ Brass or gold-covered pitchers and basins near the gate so a visitor coming in from the street might wash his hands, feet, and face
- ☐ Shelving for sandals
- ☐ Small, lush Persian-style carpets in sitting areas

Everything about the courtyard was designed to evoke pleasure and peace. The walls provided a buffer from the sounds of traffic. The bubbling CONT. NEXT PAGE>>>

My Father, and no one knows who the Son is except the Father, and who the Father is except the Son, and *the one* to whom the Son wills to reveal *Him.*"

²³Then He turned to *His* disciples and said privately, "Blessed *are* the eyes which see the things you see; ²⁴for I tell you that many prophets and kings have desired to see what you see, and have not seen *it,* and to hear what you hear, and have not heard *it.*"

THE PARABLE OF THE GOOD SAMARITAN

²⁵And behold, a certain lawyer stood up and tested Him, saying, "Teacher, what shall I do to inherit eternal life?"

²⁶He said to him, "What is written in the law? What is your reading *of it?*"

²⁷So he answered and said, " 'You shall love the Lord your God with all your heart, with all your soul, with all your strength, and with all your mind,'ᵃ and 'your neighbor as yourself.' "ᵇ

²⁸And He said to him, "You have answered rightly; do this and you will live."

²⁹But he, wanting to justify himself, said to Jesus, "And who is my neighbor?"

³⁰Then Jesus answered and said: "A certain *man* went down from Jerusalem to Jericho, and fell among thieves, who stripped him of his clothing, wounded *him,* and departed, leaving *him* half dead. ³¹Now by chance a certain priest came down that road. And when he saw him, he passed by on the other side. ³²Likewise a Levite, when he arrived at the place, came and looked, and passed by on the other side. ³³But a certain Samaritan, as he journeyed, came where he was. And when he saw him, he had compassion. ³⁴So he went to *him* and bandaged his wounds, pouring on oil and wine; and he set him on his own animal, brought him to an inn, and took care of him. ³⁵On the next day, when he departed,ᵃ he took out two denarii, gave *them* to the innkeeper, and said to him, 'Take care of him; and whatever more you spend, when I come again, I will repay you.' ³⁶So which of these three do you think was neighbor to him who fell among the thieves?"

³⁷And he said, "He who showed mercy on him."

Then Jesus said to him, "Go and do likewise."

MARY AND MARTHA WORSHIP AND SERVE

³⁸Now it happened as they went that He entered a certain village; and a certain woman named Martha welcomed Him into her house. ³⁹And she had a sister called Mary, who also sat at Jesus'ᵃ feet and heard His word. ⁴⁰But Martha was distracted with much serving, and she approached Him and said, "Lord, do You not care that my sister has left me to serve alone? Therefore tell her to help me."

⁴¹And Jesusᵃ answered and said to her, "Martha, Martha, you are worried and troubled about many things. ⁴²But one thing is needed, and Mary has chosen that good part, which will not be taken away from her."

THE MODEL PRAYER

11 Now it came to pass, as He was praying in a certain place, when He ceased, *that* one of His disciples said to Him, "Lord, teach us to pray, as John also taught his disciples."

10:27 ᵃDeuteronomy 6:5 ᵇLeviticus 19:18   10:35 ᵃNU-Text omits *when he departed.*   10:39 ᵃNU-Text reads *the Lord's.*   10:41 ᵃNU-Text reads *the Lord.*

fountains and the songs of birds generated soothing lyrical sounds. The plants were arranged to be in bloom as much of the time as possible, and vines and trees were carefully pruned and cultivated to provide year-round produce. The foliage, pillows, and tiled surfaces provided a great variety of texture. The water for washing provided immediate refreshment.

A person entering a king's courtyard was likely to be filled with an overwhelming sense of awe—an immediate flooding of the senses of sight, sound, smell, and touch. Very quickly upon arrival a visitor was likely to be presented with a bowl of fresh fruit so that the sense of taste could also be satisfied.

No place was more inviting or luxurious than the courtyard of a king's dwelling. Those who had the privilege of enjoying a king's courtyard had little desire to leave its beauty.

Now—what might *you* do with your yard or garden space? What might you do with your balcony or patio? Think like a king in the ancient world!

²So He said to them, "When you pray, say:

Our Father in heaven,*
Hallowed be Your name.
Your kingdom come.*
Your will be done
On earth as *it is* in heaven.
³ Give us day by day our daily bread.
⁴ And forgive us our sins,
For we also forgive everyone who is indebted to us.
And do not lead us into temptation,
But deliver us from the evil one." *

A FRIEND COMES AT MIDNIGHT

⁵And He said to them, "Which of you shall have a friend, and go to him at midnight and say to him, 'Friend, lend me three loaves; ⁶for a friend of mine has come to me on his journey, and I have nothing to set before him'; ⁷and he will answer from within and say, 'Do not trouble me; the door is now shut, and my children are with me in bed; I cannot rise and give to you'? ⁸I say to you, though he will not rise and give to him because he is his friend, yet because of his persistence he will rise and give him as many as he needs.

KEEP ASKING, SEEKING, KNOCKING

⁹"So I say to you, ask, and it will be given to you; seek, and you will find; knock, and it will be opened to you. ¹⁰For everyone who asks receives, and he who seeks finds, and to him who knocks it will be opened. ¹¹If a son asks for bread* from any father among you, will he give him a stone? Or if *he asks* for a fish, will he give him a serpent instead of a fish? ¹²Or if he asks for an egg, will he offer him a scorpion? ¹³If you then, being evil, know how to give good gifts to your children, how much more will *your* heavenly Father give the Holy Spirit to those who ask Him!"

A HOUSE DIVIDED CANNOT STAND

¹⁴And He was casting out a demon, and it was mute. So it was, when the demon had gone out, that the mute spoke; and the multitudes marveled. ¹⁵But some of them said, "He casts out demons by Beelzebub,* the ruler of the demons."

¹⁶Others, testing *Him,* sought from Him a sign from heaven. ¹⁷But He, knowing their thoughts, said to them: "Every kingdom divided against itself is brought to desolation, and a house *divided* against a house falls. ¹⁸If Satan also is divided against himself, how will his kingdom stand? Because you say I cast out demons by Beelzebub. ¹⁹And if I cast out demons by Beelzebub, by whom do your sons cast *them* out? Therefore they will be your judges. ²⁰But if I cast out demons with the finger of God, surely the kingdom of God has come upon you. ²¹When a strong man, fully armed, guards his own palace, his goods are in peace. ²²But when a stronger than he comes upon him and overcomes him, he takes from him all his armor in which he trusted, and divides his spoils. ²³He who is not with Me is against Me, and he who does not gather with Me scatters.

AN UNCLEAN SPIRIT RETURNS

²⁴"When an unclean spirit goes out of a man, he goes through dry places, seeking rest; and finding none, he says, 'I will return to my house from which I came.' ²⁵And when he comes, he finds *it* swept and put in order. ²⁶Then he goes and takes with *him* seven other spirits more wicked than himself, and they enter and dwell there; and the last *state* of that man is worse than the first."

KEEPING THE WORD

²⁷And it happened, as He spoke these things, that a certain woman from the crowd raised her voice and said to Him, "Blessed *is* the womb that bore You, and *the* breasts which nursed You!"

²⁸But He said, "More than that, blessed *are* those who hear the word of God and keep it!"

SEEKING A SIGN

²⁹And while the crowds were thickly gathered together, He began to say, "This is an evil generation. It seeks a sign, and no sign will be given to it except the sign of Jonah the prophet.* ³⁰For as Jonah became a sign to the Ninevites, so also the Son of Man will be to this generation. ³¹The queen of the South will rise up in the judgment with the men of this generation and condemn them, for she came from the ends of the earth to hear the wisdom of Solomon; and indeed a greater than Solomon *is* here. ³²The men of Nineveh will rise up in the judgment with this generation and condemn it, for they repented at the preaching of Jonah; and indeed a greater than Jonah *is* here.

THE LAMP OF THE BODY

³³"No one, when he has lit a lamp, puts *it* in a secret place or under a basket, but on a lampstand, that those who come in may see the

---

11:2 *NU-Text omits *Our* and *in heaven.* *NU-Text omits the rest of this verse. **11:4** *NU-Text omits *But deliver us from the evil one.* **11:11** *NU-Text omits the words from *bread* through *for* in the next sentence. **11:15** *NU-Text and M-Text read *Beelzebul.* **11:29** *NU-Text omits *the prophet.*

WISE CHOICES

Choose extra-virgin olive oil.

Extra-virgin olive oil is oil from the first pressing of olives. The oil is extracted, filtered, and undergoes no further refining. It is the highest quality olive oil available on the market. If olive oil is not labeled extra-virgin or virgin, it has been processed in some way.

light. ³⁴The lamp of the body is the eye. Therefore, when your eye is good, your whole body also is full of light. But when *your eye* is bad, your body also *is* full of darkness. ³⁵Therefore take heed that the light which is in you is not darkness. ³⁶If then your whole body *is* full of light, having no part dark, *the* whole *body* will be full of light, as when the bright shining of a lamp gives you light."

WOE TO THE PHARISEES AND LAWYERS

³⁷And as He spoke, a certain Pharisee asked Him to dine with him. So He went in and sat down to eat. ³⁸When the Pharisee saw *it*, he marveled that He had not first washed before dinner.

³⁹Then the Lord said to him, "Now you Pharisees make the outside of the cup and dish clean, but your inward part is full of greed and wickedness. ⁴⁰Foolish ones! Did not He who made the outside make the inside also? ⁴¹But rather give alms of such things as you have; then indeed all things are clean to you.

⁴²"But woe to you Pharisees! For you tithe mint and rue and all manner of herbs, and pass by justice and the love of God. These you ought to have done, without leaving the others undone. ⁴³Woe to you Pharisees! For you love the best seats in the synagogues and greetings in the marketplaces. ⁴⁴Woe to you, scribes and Pharisees, hypocrites!ᵃ For you are like graves which are not seen, and the men who walk over *them* are not aware *of them*."

⁴⁵Then one of the lawyers answered and said to Him, "Teacher, by saying these things You reproach us also."

⁴⁶And He said, "Woe to you also, lawyers! For you load men with burdens hard to bear, and you yourselves do not touch the burdens with one of your fingers. ⁴⁷Woe to you! For you build the tombs of the prophets, and your fathers killed them. ⁴⁸In fact, you bear witness that you approve the deeds of your fathers; for they indeed killed them, and you build their tombs. ⁴⁹Therefore the wisdom of God also said, 'I will send them prophets and apostles, and *some* of them they will kill and persecute,' ⁵⁰that the blood of all the prophets which was shed from the foundation of the world may be required of this generation, ⁵¹from the blood of Abel to the blood of Zechariah who perished between the altar and the temple. Yes, I say to you, it shall be required of this generation.

⁵²"Woe to you lawyers! For you have taken away the key of knowledge. You did not enter in yourselves, and those who were entering in you hindered."

⁵³And as He said these things to them,ᵃ the scribes and the Pharisees began to assail *Him* vehemently, and to cross-examine Him about many things, ⁵⁴lying in wait for Him, and seeking to catch Him in something He might say, that they might accuse Him.ᵃ

BEWARE OF HYPOCRISY

12 In the meantime, when an innumerable multitude of people had gathered together, so that they trampled one another, He began to say to His disciples first *of all*, "Beware of the leaven of the Pharisees, which is hypocrisy. ²For there is nothing covered that will not be revealed, nor hidden that will not be known. ³Therefore whatever you have spoken in the dark will be heard in the light, and what you have spoken in the ear in inner rooms will be proclaimed on the housetops.

JESUS TEACHES THE FEAR OF GOD

⁴"And I say to you, My friends, do not be afraid of those who kill the body, and after that have no more that they can do. ⁵But I will show you whom you should fear: Fear Him who, after He has killed, has power to cast into hell; yes, I say to you, fear Him!

⁶"Are not five sparrows sold for two copper coins?ᵃ And not one of them is forgotten before God. ⁷But the very hairs of your head are all numbered. Do not fear therefore; you are of more value than many sparrows.

CONFESS CHRIST BEFORE MEN

⁸"Also I say to you, whoever confesses Me before men, him the Son of Man also will confess before the angels of God. ⁹But he who denies Me before men will be denied before the angels of God.

¹⁰"And anyone who speaks a word against the Son of Man, it will be forgiven him; but to him who blasphemes against the Holy Spirit, it will not be forgiven.

¹¹"Now when they bring you to the synagogues and magistrates and authorities, do not worry about how or what you should answer, or what you should say. ¹²For the Holy Spirit will teach you in that very hour what you ought to say."

THE PARABLE OF THE RICH FOOL

¹³Then one from the crowd said to Him, "Teacher, tell my brother to divide the inheritance with me."

¹⁴But He said to him, "Man, who made Me a judge or an arbitrator over you?" ¹⁵And He said to them, "Take heed and beware of covetousness,ᵃ for one's life does not consist in the abundance of the things he possesses."

¹⁶Then He spoke a parable to them, saying: "The ground of a certain rich man yielded plentifully. ¹⁷And he thought within himself, saying,

---

11:44 ᵃNU-Text omits *scribes and Pharisees, hypocrites*.   **11:53** ᵃNU-Text reads *And when He left there*.   **11:54** ᵃNU-Text omits *and seeking* and *that they might accuse Him*.   **12:6** ᵃGreek *assarion*, a coin of very small value   **12:15** ᵃNU-Text reads *all covetousness*.

'What shall I do, since I have no room to store my crops?' [18]So he said, 'I will do this: I will pull down my barns and build greater, and there I will store all my crops and my goods. [19]And I will say to my soul, "Soul, you have many goods laid up for many years; take your ease; eat, drink, *and* be merry." ' [20]But God said to him, 'Fool! This night your soul will be required of you; then whose will those things be which you have provided?'

[21]"So *is* he who lays up treasure for himself, and is not rich toward God."

DO NOT WORRY

[22]Then He said to His disciples, "Therefore I say to you, do not worry about your life, what you will eat; nor about the body, what you will put on. [23]Life is more than food, and the body *is more* than clothing. [24]Consider the ravens, for they neither sow nor reap, which have neither storehouse nor barn; and God feeds them. Of how much more value are you than the birds? [25]And which of you by worrying can add one cubit to his stature? [26]If you then are not able to do *the* least, why are you anxious for the rest? [27]Consider the lilies, how they grow: they neither toil nor spin; and yet I say to you, even Solomon in all his glory was not arrayed like one of these. [28]If then God so clothes the grass, which today is in the field and tomorrow is thrown into the oven, how much more *will He clothe* you, O *you* of little faith?

[29]"And do not seek what you should eat or what you should drink, nor have an anxious mind. [30]For all these things the nations of the world seek after, and your Father knows that you need these things. [31]But seek the kingdom of God, and all these things[a] shall be added to you.

[32]"Do not fear, little flock, for it is your Father's good pleasure to give you the kingdom. [33]Sell what you have and give alms; provide yourselves money bags which do not grow old, a treasure in the heavens that does not fail, where no thief approaches nor moth destroys. [34]For where your treasure is, there your heart will be also.

THE FAITHFUL SERVANT AND THE EVIL SERVANT

[35]"Let your waist be girded and *your* lamps burning; [36]and you yourselves be like men who wait for their master, when he will return from the wedding, that when he comes and knocks they may open to him immediately. [37]Blessed *are* those servants whom the master, when he comes, will find watching. Assuredly, I say to you that he will gird himself and have them sit down *to eat,* and will come and serve them. [38]And if he should come in the second watch, or come in the third watch, and find *them* so, blessed are those servants. [39]But know this, that if the master of the house had known what hour the thief would come, he would have watched and[a] not allowed his house to be broken into. [40]Therefore you also be ready, for the Son of Man is coming at an hour you do not expect."

[41]Then Peter said to Him, "Lord, do You speak this parable *only* to us, or to all *people?*"

[42]And the Lord said, "Who then is that faithful and wise steward, whom *his* master will make ruler over his household, to give *them their* portion of food in due season? [43]Blessed *is* that servant whom his master will find so doing when he comes. [44]Truly, I say to you that he will make him ruler over all that he has. [45]But if that servant says in his heart, 'My master is delaying his coming,' and begins to beat the male and female servants, and to eat and drink and be drunk, [46]the master of that servant will come on a day when he is not looking for

---

> (Luke 12:18)

The Dangers of Excess. The harm associated with excess is well documented in the Bible. Excess comes in many forms.

- ☐ Excess in eating produces the storage of nutrients in the form of fat, which in turn creates weight problems.
- ☐ Excess in drinking alcohol produces drunkenness and can result in alcoholism.
- ☐ Excess in spending produces debt; excess in hoarding produces a greedy spirit.
- ☐ Excessive devotion to good works or ministry can have a negative side, especially when the excessive time given to a career or ministry results in neglected family relationships.
- ☐ An excess of emotion—negative or positive—can be unhealthful. Even highly positive emotions such as joy and love can produce such an endorphin high that people artificially try to keep

that high going by consuming of substances, continual spending, overworking, excessive care, or too much stimulation the senses.

- ☐ Excessive negative emotions, of course, can drive a person to depression, despair, and even suicide.

The Bible's answer to excess is twofold: *generosity*, including a generous spirit called a "cheerful" spirit when it comes to giving to God and to others; and *moderation*, taking things into our bodies and lives in a measured, intentional, conscientious way. The two should be in balance. We must be generous, but within God's guidelines. For example, God requires a tithe, and then offerings. He doesn't require "excess" that leaves a person in poverty. We must live in moderation, but even if we have few resources, we must be generous toward others. We must never lose sight of the eternal consequences of our consumption. The excesses of this earthly life do not produce eternal rewards.

INSIGHTS | INTO THE WORD

12:31 [a]NU-Text reads *His kingdom, and these things.*   12:39 [a]NU-Text reads *he would not have allowed.*

him, and at an hour when he is not aware, and will cut him in two and appoint *him* his portion with the unbelievers. ⁴⁷And that servant who knew his master's will, and did not prepare *himself* or do according to his will, shall be beaten with many *stripes.* ⁴⁸But he who did not know, yet committed things deserving of stripes, shall be beaten with few. For everyone to whom much is given, from him much will be required; and to whom much has been committed, of him they will ask the more.

CHRIST BRINGS DIVISION

⁴⁹"I came to send fire on the earth, and how I wish it were already kindled! ⁵⁰But I have a baptism to be baptized with, and how distressed I am till it is accomplished! ⁵¹Do *you* suppose that I came to give peace on earth? I tell you, not at all, but rather division. ⁵²For from now on five in one house will be divided: three against two, and two against three. ⁵³Father will be divided against son and son against father, mother against daughter and daughter against mother, mother-in-law against her daughter-in-law and daughter-in-law against her mother-in-law."

DISCERN THE TIME

⁵⁴Then He also said to the multitudes, "Whenever you *see* a cloud rising out of the west, immediately you say, 'A shower is coming'; and so it is. ⁵⁵And when you see the south wind blow, you say, 'There will be hot weather'; and there is. ⁵⁶Hypocrites! You can discern the face of the sky and of the earth, but how *is it* you do not discern this time?

MAKE PEACE WITH YOUR ADVERSARY

⁵⁷"Yes, and why, even of yourselves, do you not judge what is right? ⁵⁸When you go with your adversary to the magistrate, make every effort along the way to settle with him, lest he drag you to the judge, the judge deliver you to the officer, and the officer throw you into prison. ⁵⁹I tell you, you shall not depart from there till you have paid the very last mite."

REPENT OR PERISH

13 There were present at that season some who told Him about the Galileans whose blood Pilate had mingled with their sacrifices. ²And Jesus answered and said to them, "Do you suppose that these Galileans were worse sinners than all *other* Galileans, because they suffered such things? ³I tell you, no; but unless you repent you will all likewise perish. ⁴Or those eighteen on whom the tower in Siloam fell and killed them, do you think that they were worse sinners than all *other* men who dwelt in Jerusalem? ⁵I tell you, no; but unless you repent you will all likewise perish."

THE PARABLE OF THE BARREN FIG TREE

⁶He also spoke this parable: "A certain *man* had a fig tree planted in his vineyard, and he came seeking fruit on it and found none. ⁷Then he said to the keeper of his vineyard, 'Look, for three years I have come seeking fruit on this fig tree and find none. Cut it down; why does it use up the ground?' ⁸But he answered and said to him, 'Sir, let it alone this year also, until I dig around it and fertilize *it.* ⁹And if it bears fruit, *well.* But if not, after that* you can cut it down.' "

A SPIRIT OF INFIRMITY

¹⁰Now He was teaching in one of the synagogues on the Sabbath. ¹¹And behold, there was a woman who had a spirit of infirmity eighteen years, and was bent over and could in no way raise *herself* up. ¹²But when Jesus saw her, He called *her* to *Him* and said to her, "Woman, you are loosed from your infirmity." ¹³And He laid *His* hands on her, and immediately she was made straight, and glorified God.

¹⁴But the ruler of the synagogue answered with indignation, because Jesus had healed on the Sabbath; and he said to the crowd, "There are six days on which men ought to work; therefore come and be healed on them, and not on the Sabbath day."

¹⁵The Lord then answered him and said, "Hypocrite!* Does not each one of you on the Sabbath loose his ox or donkey from the stall, and lead *it* away to water it? ¹⁶So ought not this woman, being a daughter of Abraham, whom Satan has bound—think of it—for eighteen years, be loosed from this bond on the Sabbath?" ¹⁷And when He said these things, all His adversaries were put to shame; and all the multitude rejoiced for all the glorious things that were done by Him.

THE PARABLE OF THE MUSTARD SEED

¹⁸Then He said, "What is the kingdom of God like? And to what shall I compare it? ¹⁹It is like a mustard seed, which a man took and put in his garden; and it grew and became a large* tree, and the birds of the air nested in its branches."

INSIGHTS INTO THE WORD

> (Luke 13:6–9)

Looking for Fruit. God is looking for fruit from our lives—not just our dreams, desires, hopes, plans, or good intentions. He judges us on the basis of what we believe and *do.* Jesus told a parable about this fig tree in the context of *repentance*—turning away from sin and turning toward God in obedience. He revealed God's nature as being very patient, but not *eternally* patient. God expects His people to embrace changes that are for the good—not to resist them. He expects His people to receive all that He offers to them—not reject His blessings and His plan of salvation.

Fig trees yield their sweet fruit in the summer. Excess figs were usually dried and stored for the future. God expects us to be fruitful in our lives, generously giving to others in a way that is sweet now, but also beneficial for eternity.

13:9 ªNU-Text reads *And if it bears fruit after that, well. But if not, you can cut it down.*   13:15 ªNU-Text and M-Text read *Hypocrites.*   13:19 ªNU-Text omits *large.*

> (Luke 13:11)

A Spirit of Infirmity. One Sabbath Jesus encountered a woman in the synagogue who had suffered from a "spirit of infirmity" for eighteen years! She was hunched over and could not straighten her body. We are not told the exact nature of this spinal condition—it may have been a serious scoliosis, a severe example of osteoporosis, or a form of spinal fusion.

The Bible tells us that she was "bound" by Satan (Luke 13:16). Apparently there was some form of *spiritual* cause at the root of her difficulty. This is just one of many examples in the Bible in which a physical condition and a spiritual condition are linked. Whatever the exact cause or medical outcome of her condition, we know this: seven words spoken by Jesus completely cured the spiritual *and* physical infirmity. When Jesus said, "Woman, you are loosed from your infirmity" as He laid His hands on her, "immediately she was made straight, and glorified God"

(Luke 13:13). Her body was released so that she could stand upright, and praise came from her lips.

Those who refuse to praise God, but rather blame God for their infirmities, nearly always experience something of a "bent-over spirit." They lose a degree of their confidence as they stop trusting God in all things. They become more negative and pessimistic. The words and phrases in our language to convey a negative spirit are numerous. People are perceived to be downcast, down in the mouth, down in spirit, down-and-out, or in a downward spiral, to give just a few examples. If this continues, a person can also experience a downward trend in his or her physical health!

One of the great turn-around remedies offered by the Bible is joy, or regularly voicing praise and thanksgiving. As the psalmist said: "Unto You I lift up my eyes, O You who dwell in the heavens" (Psalm 123:1).

INSIGHTS INTO THE WORD

THE PARABLE OF THE LEAVEN

²⁰And again He said, "To what shall I liken the kingdom of God? ²¹It is like leaven, which a woman took and hid in three measures* of meal till it was all leavened."

THE NARROW WAY

²²And He went through the cities and villages, teaching, and journeying toward Jerusalem. ²³Then one said to Him, "Lord, are there few who are saved?"

And He said to them, ²⁴"Strive to enter through the narrow gate, for many, I say to you, will seek to enter and will not be able. ²⁵When once the Master of the house has risen up and shut the door, and you begin to stand outside and knock at the door, saying, 'Lord, Lord, open for us,' and He will answer and say to you, 'I do not know you, where you are from,' ²⁶then you will begin to say, 'We ate and drank in Your presence, and You taught in our streets.' ²⁷But He will say, 'I tell you I do not know you, where you are from. Depart from Me, all you workers of iniquity.' ²⁸There will be weeping and gnashing of teeth, when you see Abraham and Isaac and Jacob and all the prophets in the kingdom of God, and yourselves thrust out. ²⁹They will come from the east and the west, from the north and the south, and sit down in the kingdom of God. ³⁰And indeed there are last who will be first, and there are first who will be last."

³¹On that very day* some Pharisees came, saying to Him, "Get out and depart from here, for Herod wants to kill You."

³²And He said to them, "Go, tell that fox, 'Behold, I cast out demons and perform cures today and tomorrow, and the third *day* I shall be perfected.' ³³Nevertheless I must journey today, tomorrow, and the *day* following; for it cannot be that a prophet should perish outside of Jerusalem.

JESUS LAMENTS OVER JERUSALEM

³⁴"O Jerusalem, Jerusalem, the one who kills the prophets and stones those who are sent to her! How often I wanted to gather your children together, as a hen *gathers* her brood under *her* wings, but you were not willing! ³⁵See! Your house is left to you desolate; and assuredly,* I say to you, you shall not see Me until *the time* comes when you say, 'Blessed is He who comes in the name of the LORD!' "ᵇ

A MAN WITH DROPSY HEALED ON THE SABBATH

14 Now it happened, as He went into the house of one of the rulers of the Pharisees to eat bread on the Sabbath, that they watched Him closely. ²And behold, there was a certain man before Him who had dropsy. ³And Jesus, answering, spoke to the lawyers and Pharisees, saying, "Is it lawful to heal on the Sabbath?"ᵃ

⁴But they kept silent. And He took *him* and healed him, and let him go. ⁵Then He answered them, saying, "Which of you, having a donkey* or an ox that has fallen into a pit, will not immediately pull him out on the Sabbath day?" ⁶And they could not answer Him regarding these things.

TAKE THE LOWLY PLACE

⁷So He told a parable to those who were invited, when He noted how they chose the best places, saying to them: ⁸"When you are invited by anyone to a wedding feast, do not sit down in the best place, lest one more honorable than you be invited by him; ⁹and he who invited you and him come and say to you, 'Give place to this man,' and then you begin with shame to take the lowest place. ¹⁰But when you are invited, go and sit down in the lowest place, so that when he who invited you

---

13:21 ªGreek *sata*, approximately two pecks in all **13:31** ªNU-Text reads *In that very hour.* **13:35** ªNU-Text and M-Text omit *assuredly.* ᵇPsalm 118:26 **14:3** ªNU-Text adds *or not.* **14:5** ªNU-Text and M-Text read *son.*

Women's Issues
Osteoporosis

Osteoporosis, which means "porous bones," is a condition that impacts twenty million people in the United States, mostly women. One in four women after menopause develop this condition of significant bone loss. This makes them more susceptible to bone and hip fractures, developing a "dowager's hump," and having dental problems.

A number of things can be done nutritionally to help prevent or slow the development of osteoporosis:

Increase your intake of calcium-rich foods. Milk and milk products are high sources of calcium. An eight-ounce glass of milk has 300 mg of calcium. Choose low-fat dairy products. Vegetables such as broccoli, cauliflower, peas, and beans are high in calcium, as are almonds and sunflower seeds.

Avoid foods that rob you of calcium. Asparagus, spinach, chard, rhubarb and beet greens are foods high in oxalic acid, which inhibits calcium absorption. Don't eat too much of these foods. Also avoid carbonated beverages, caffeine, alcohol, sugar, and excessive red meat.

Eat foods rich in vitamin D. The best sources are egg yolks, salmon, and fish oil, which can be taken in capsule form.

Eat foods rich in magnesium, which helps the body absorb calcium. Some of the many foods rich in magnesium are whole grains, apples, apricots, CONT. NEXT PAGE>>>

comes he may say to you, 'Friend, go up higher.' Then you will have glory in the presence of those who sit at the table with you. [11]For whoever exalts himself will be humbled, and he who humbles himself will be exalted."

[12]Then He also said to him who invited Him, "When you give a dinner or a supper, do not ask your friends, your brothers, your relatives, nor rich neighbors, lest they also invite you back, and you be repaid. [13]But when you give a feast, invite *the* poor, *the* maimed, *the* lame, *the* blind. [14]And you will be blessed, because they cannot repay you; for you shall be repaid at the resurrection of the just."

THE PARABLE OF THE GREAT SUPPER

[15]Now when one of those who sat at the table with Him heard these things, he said to Him, "Blessed *is* he who shall eat bread[a] in the kingdom of God!"

[16]Then He said to him, "A certain man gave a great supper and invited many, [17]and sent his servant at supper time to say to those who were invited, 'Come, for all things are now ready.' [18]But they all with one *accord* began to make excuses. The first said to him, 'I have bought a piece of ground, and I must go and see it. I ask you to have me excused.' [19]And another said, 'I have bought five yoke of oxen, and I am going to test them. I ask you to have me excused.' [20]Still another said, 'I have married a wife, and therefore I cannot come.' [21]So that servant came and reported these things to his master. Then the master of the house, being angry, said to his servant, 'Go out quickly into the streets and lanes of the city, and bring in here *the* poor and *the* maimed and *the* lame and *the* blind.' [22]And the servant said, 'Master, it is done as you commanded, and still there is room.' [23]Then the master said to the servant, 'Go out into the highways and hedges, and compel *them* to come in, that my house may be filled. [24]For I say to you that none of those men who were invited shall taste my supper.' "

LEAVING ALL TO FOLLOW CHRIST

[25]Now great multitudes went with Him. And He turned and said to them, [26]"If anyone comes to Me and does not hate his father and mother, wife and children, brothers and sisters, yes, and his own life also, he cannot be My disciple. [27]And whoever does not bear his cross and come after Me cannot be My disciple. [28]For which of you, intending to build a tower, does not sit down first and count the cost, whether he has *enough* to finish *it*— [29]lest, after he has laid the foundation, and is not able to finish, all who see *it* begin to mock him, [30]saying, 'This man began to build and was not able to finish'? [31]Or what king, going to make war against another king, does not sit down first and consider whether he is able with ten thousand to meet him who comes against him with twenty thousand? [32]Or else, while the other is still a great way off, he sends a delegation and asks conditions of peace. [33]So likewise, whoever of you does not forsake all that he has cannot be My disciple.

TASTELESS SALT IS WORTHLESS

[34]"Salt *is* good; but if the salt has lost its flavor, how shall it be seasoned? [35]It is neither fit for the land nor for the dunghill, *but* men throw it out. He who has ears to hear, let him hear!"

14:15 [a]M-Text reads *dinner.*

avocados, bananas, cantaloupes, grapefruit, soy products, garlic, lemons, lima beans, and peaches.

Have sufficient hydrochloric acid. Make sure you have enough hydrochloric acid in your stomach to absorb calcium.

Take chelated forms of calcium. If you take calcium supplements, the best ones are "chelated" forms of calcium—such as calcium citrate, calcium aspartate, or calcium fumarate. Premenopausal women should consider taking 1,000 mg of chelated calcium a day, and post-menopausal women should take 1,500 mg a day. Be sure to take a multivitamin that includes B_6, B_{12}, and folic acid in sufficient quantities. Your mineral supplement should include boron and silicon.

Stay active! One of the best things you can do is stay active. Weight-bearing exercises and calisthenics are the two forms of exercise that stimulate the growth of new bone cells. You can buy dumbbells at a department store or athletic supply store to begin a basic weightlifting program at home.

Reduce stress. Finally, stay encouraged and reduce the stress level in your life. The Bible says: "A broken spirit dries [up] the bones" (Proverbs 17:22).

THE PARABLE OF THE LOST SHEEP

15 Then all the tax collectors and the sinners drew near to Him to hear Him. ²And the Pharisees and scribes complained, saying, "This Man receives sinners and eats with them." ³So He spoke this parable to them, saying:

⁴"What man of you, having a hundred sheep, if he loses one of them, does not leave the ninety-nine in the wilderness, and go after the one which is lost until he finds it? ⁵And when he has found *it*, he lays *it* on his shoulders, rejoicing. ⁶And when he comes home, he calls together *his* friends and neighbors, saying to them, 'Rejoice with me, for I have found my sheep which was lost!' ⁷I say to you that likewise there will be more joy in heaven over one sinner who repents than over ninety-nine just persons who need no repentance.

THE PARABLE OF THE LOST COIN

⁸"Or what woman, having ten silver coins,ᵃ if she loses one coin, does not light a lamp, sweep the house, and search carefully until she finds *it*? ⁹And when she has found *it*, she calls *her* friends and neighbors together, saying, 'Rejoice with me, for I have found the piece which I lost!' ¹⁰Likewise, I say to you, there is joy in the presence of the angels of God over one sinner who repents."

THE PARABLE OF THE LOST SON

¹¹Then He said: "A certain man had two sons. ¹²And the younger of them said to *his* father, 'Father, give me the portion of goods that falls to me.' So he divided to them *his* livelihood. ¹³And not many days after, the younger son gathered all together, journeyed to a far country, and there wasted his possessions with prodigal living. ¹⁴But when he had spent all, there arose a severe famine in that land, and he began to be in want. ¹⁵Then he went and joined himself to a citizen of that country, and he sent him into his fields to feed swine. ¹⁶And he would gladly have filled his stomach with the pods that the swine ate, and no one gave him *anything*.

¹⁷"But when he came to himself, he said, 'How many of my father's hired servants have bread enough and to spare, and I perish with hunger! ¹⁸I will arise and go to my father, and will say to him, "Father, I have sinned against heaven and before you, ¹⁹and I am no longer worthy to be called your son. Make me like one of your hired servants."'

²⁰"And he arose and came to his father. But when he was still a great way off, his father saw him and had compassion, and ran and fell on his neck and kissed him. ²¹And the son said to him, 'Father, I have sinned against heaven and in your sight, and am no longer worthy to be called your son.'

²²"But the father said to his servants, 'Bringᵃ out the best robe and put *it* on him, and put a ring on his hand and sandals on *his* feet. ²³And bring the fatted calf here and kill *it*, and let us eat and be merry; ²⁴for this my son was dead and is alive again; he was lost and is found.' And they began to be merry.

²⁵"Now his older son was in the field. And as he came and drew near to the house, he heard music and dancing. ²⁶So he called one of the servants and asked what these things meant. ²⁷And he said to him, 'Your brother has come, and because he has received him safe and sound, your father has killed the fatted calf.'

²⁸"But he was angry and would not go in. Therefore his father came out and pleaded with him. ²⁹So he answered and said to *his* father, 'Lo, these many years I have been serving you; I never transgressed your commandment at any time; and yet you never gave me a young goat, that I might make merry with my friends. ³⁰But as soon as this son of yours came, who has devoured your livelihood with harlots, you killed the fatted calf for him.'

³¹"And he said to him, 'Son, you are always with me, and all that I have is yours. ³²It was right that we should make merry and be glad, for your brother was dead and is alive again, and was lost and is found.'"

THE PARABLE OF THE UNJUST STEWARD

16 He also said to His disciples: "There was a certain rich man who had a steward, and an accusation was brought to him that this man was wasting his goods. ²So he called him and said to him, 'What is this I hear about you? Give an account of your stewardship, for you can no longer be steward.'

³"Then the steward said within himself, 'What shall I do? For my master is taking the stewardship away from me. I cannot dig; I am ashamed to beg. ⁴I have resolved what to do, that when I am put out of the stewardship, they may receive me into their houses.'

⁵"So he called every one of his master's debtors to *him*, and said to the first, 'How much do you owe my master?' ⁶And he said, 'A hundred measuresᵃ of oil.' So he said to him, 'Take your bill, and sit down quickly and write fifty.' ⁷Then he said to another, 'And how much do

---

15:8 ᵃGreek *drachma*, a valuable coin often worn in a ten-piece garland by married women   **15:22** ᵃNU-Text reads *Quickly bring.*   **16:6** ᵃGreek *batos*, eight or nine gallons each (Old Testament *bath*)

SCRIPTURE SOLUTIONS

[HEARTBURN AND INDIGESTION]

More than 60 million Americans are diagnosed each year with digestive problems. Many of these problems are painful. Some can lead to deadly diseases. If you routinely suffer from heartburn and indigestion, seek medical help. Don't rely on over-the-counter medications that often provide only temporary relief or that mask the true nature of the problem. You will also be wise to do the following:

☐ Eliminate stress as much as possible from your life.

☐ Don't eat after an outburst of anger or other negative emotion.

☐ Slow down—eat in a more relaxed way and in a relaxed environment.

☐ Eat with a fork. If you sit and eat with a fork—as opposed to "man-handling" a hamburger and fries, or eating other fast foods with your hands or fingers—you will eat less and probably eat more healthful foods. Even if you are having a burger, eat it with a fork!

Also give serious consideration to fasting for a period of time to rid your body of toxins. Here is a basic detox fast:

1. When you first get up in the morning make a drink combining wheat grass, barley grass, alfalfa, spirulina, chlorella, and blue-green algae. Or, you can drink a glass of orange or grapefruit juice and take nine capsules of chlorella.

2. About 45 minutes later, make a protein shake with 2 cups filtered water, CONT. NEXT PAGE>>>

you owe?' So he said, 'A hundred measures*ᵃ* of wheat.' And he said to him, 'Take your bill, and write eighty.' ⁸So the master commended the unjust steward because he had dealt shrewdly. For the sons of this world are more shrewd in their generation than the sons of light.

⁹"And I say to you, make friends for yourselves by unrighteous mammon, that when you fail,*ᵃ* they may receive you into an everlasting home. ¹⁰He who *is* faithful in *what is* least is faithful also in much; and he who is unjust in *what is* least is unjust also in much. ¹¹Therefore if you have not been faithful in the unrighteous mammon, who will commit to your trust the true *riches?* ¹²And if you have not been faithful in what is another man's, who will give you what is your own?

¹³"No servant can serve two masters; for either he will hate the one and love the other, or else he will be loyal to the one and despise the other. You cannot serve God and mammon."

THE LAW, THE PROPHETS, AND THE KINGDOM

¹⁴Now the Pharisees, who were lovers of money, also heard all these things, and they derided Him. ¹⁵And He said to them, "You are those who justify yourselves before men, but God knows your hearts. For what is highly esteemed among men is an abomination in the sight of God.

¹⁶"The law and the prophets *were* until John. Since that time the kingdom of God has been preached, and everyone is pressing into it. ¹⁷And it is easier for heaven and earth to pass away than for one tittle of the law to fail.

¹⁸"Whoever divorces his wife and marries another commits adultery; and whoever marries her who is divorced from *her* husband commits adultery.

THE RICH MAN AND LAZARUS

¹⁹"There was a certain rich man who was clothed in purple and fine linen and fared sumptuously every day. ²⁰But there was a certain beggar named Lazarus, full of sores, who was laid at his gate, ²¹desiring to be fed with the crumbs which fell*ᵃ* from the rich man's table. Moreover the dogs came and licked his sores. ²²So it was that the beggar died, and was carried by the angels to Abraham's bosom. The rich man also died and was buried. ²³And being in torments in Hades, he lifted up his eyes and saw Abraham afar off, and Lazarus in his bosom.

²⁴"Then he cried and said, 'Father Abraham, have mercy on me, and send Lazarus that he may dip the tip of his finger in water and cool my tongue; for I am tormented in this flame.' ²⁵But Abraham said, 'Son, remember that in your lifetime you received your good things, and likewise Lazarus evil things; but now he is comforted and you are tormented. ²⁶And besides all this, between us and you there is a great gulf fixed, so that those who want to pass from here to you cannot, nor can those from there pass to us.'

²⁷"Then he said, 'I beg you therefore, father, that you would send him to my father's house, ²⁸for I have five brothers, that he may testify to them, lest they also come to this place of torment.' ²⁹Abraham said to him, 'They have Moses and the prophets; let them hear them.' ³⁰And he said, 'No, father Abraham; but if one goes to them from the dead, they will repent.' ³¹But he said to him, 'If they do not hear Moses and the prophets, neither will they be persuaded though one rise from the dead.' "

16:7 *ᵃGreek koros, ten or twelve bushels each (Old Testament kor)*   16:9 *ᵃNU-Text reads it fails.*   16:21 *ᵃNU-Text reads with what fell.*

Scripture Solutions Cont.>>>

5 teaspoons ground flaxseed (you can grind this in the coffee grinder), 1 cup fresh fruit, and 2 tablespoons flaxseed oil. Add 1 teaspoon lactobacillus acidophilus and bifidus. Then add 2 large scoops of a hypoallergenic protein mix, and sweeten the drink to taste with Stevia, if necessary. Blend for 2 minutes and let sit for 5 minutes before drinking. Have this shake for breakfast, and then make another shake for lunch and a third shake for dinner.

Some people use this approach to fasting for three days, some for a week, some for as long as three weeks. This is not a fast designed for losing weight—it is aimed at ridding your body of toxins. In addition to the drinks above, you need to be drinking at least two quarts of water a day, and possibly more. The goal is to flush toxins from your system while still maintaining the health of your muscles and key body tissues and organs.

JESUS WARNS OF OFFENSES

17 Then He said to the disciples, "It is impossible that no offenses should come, but woe *to him* through whom they do come! ²It would be better for him if a millstone were hung around his neck, and he were thrown into the sea, than that he should offend one of these little ones. ³Take heed to yourselves. If your brother sins against you,ᵃ rebuke him; and if he repents, forgive him. ⁴And if he sins against you seven times in a day, and seven times in a day returns to you,ᵃ saying, 'I repent,' you shall forgive him."

FAITH AND DUTY

⁵And the apostles said to the Lord, "Increase our faith."

⁶So the Lord said, "If you have faith as a mustard seed, you can say to this mulberry tree, 'Be pulled up by the roots and be planted in the sea,' and it would obey you. ⁷And which of you, having a servant plowing or tending sheep, will say to him when he has come in from the field, 'Come at once and sit down to eat'? ⁸But will he not rather say to him, 'Prepare something for my supper, and gird yourself and serve me till I have eaten and drunk, and afterward you will eat and drink'? ⁹Does he thank that servant because he did the things that were commanded him? I think not.ᵃ ¹⁰So likewise you, when you have done all those things which you are commanded, say, 'We are unprofitable servants. We have done what was our duty to do.' "

TEN LEPERS CLEANSED

¹¹Now it happened as He went to Jerusalem that He passed through the midst of Samaria and Galilee. ¹²Then as He entered a certain village, there met Him ten men who were lepers, who stood afar off. ¹³And

> (Luke 17:12–14)

Cleansed! Leprosy and other skin diseases, including psoriasis and eczema, were common in the Middle East in Bible times. All of these skin diseases made the person who had them "unclean," which meant they needed to be separated from the general population until their condition was healed. In the case of leprosy, of course, the condition was terminal, often a slow and agonizingly painful progression over many years. Those who were "unclean" were required to keep their distance from "clean" individuals. Lepers specifically were required to keep the distance that a voice could carry.

The lepers who shouted to Jesus were, by Jewish law, keeping the required distance but nevertheless, "lifted up their voices" to ask for God's mercy. Jesus recognized that they would not have called out to Him if they had not had faith to believe He could heal them. He therefore had no need to pronounce any type of healing message, but shouted back to them, "Go, show yourselves to the priests." This was also in keeping with Mosaic Law, which gave the priests the responsibility for declaring that a leper, or any person with a skin disorder, could be allowed to reenter society.

As these ten lepers made their way to the priests, they were all cured of their disease. Only one, however, returned to Jesus to give thanks. Jesus was saddened that the other nine had not done so. He said to the Samaritan leper who had been healed, "Arise, go your way. Your faith has made you well" (Luke 17:19). This statement was not made about the leprosy alone. To be made "well" meant to be made "whole."

This man experienced a whole-person healing from Jesus. His thanksgiving and praise put him in a spiritually right relationship with Jesus; and through Jesus, to God the Father. This spiritual aspect of healing meant that the leper had truly been made *whole*—spirit, mind, and body. The implication is that the other nine, although they were Jews and not "foreigners" like the Samaritan, may have experienced a physical healing, but they had not been made truly *well*. They still lacked a complete spiritual healing.

INSIGHTS | **INTO THE WORD**

17:3 ᵃNU-Text omits *against you*.   17:4 ᵃM-Text omits *to you*.   17:9 ᵃNU-Text ends verse with *commanded;* M-Text omits *him*.

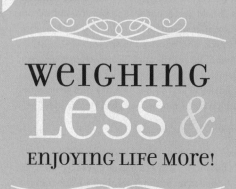

WEIGHING Less &
ENJOYING LIFE MORE!

[Fruit in the Frig]

Keep a bowl of chopped-up fruit in the refrigerator for a quick and healthful snack. Good fruits to include are pineapple (fresh preferred but canned in light syrup acceptable), cantaloupe, honeydew melon, apples, seedless grapes, oranges, and perhaps a canned of "natural syrup" mixed fruits.

Be sure to add enough citrus to keep the apples from turning brown. Do *not* add bananas, papayas, mangos, kiwifruit, watermelon, pears, peaches, or strawberries because these fruits tend to become mushy. If you want to add any of these to your fruit salad, add them at the time of serving.

You may want to add dried cranberries, raspberries, strawberries, or cherries to your fruit salad at the time of serving to add a little bit of "texture difference" from time to time.

---

they lifted up *their* voices and said, "Jesus, Master, have mercy on us!"

[14]So when He saw *them,* He said to them, "Go, show yourselves to the priests." And so it was that as they went, they were cleansed.

[15]And one of them, when he saw that he was healed, returned, and with a loud voice glorified God, [16]and fell down on *his* face at His feet, giving Him thanks. And he was a Samaritan.

[17]So Jesus answered and said, "Were there not ten cleansed? But where *are* the nine? [18]Were there not any found who returned to give glory to God except this foreigner?" [19]And He said to him, "Arise, go your way. Your faith has made you well."

THE COMING OF THE KINGDOM

[20]Now when He was asked by the Pharisees when the kingdom of God would come, He answered them and said, "The kingdom of God does not come with observation; [21]nor will they say, 'See here!' or 'See there!'[a] For indeed, the kingdom of God is within you."

[22]Then He said to the disciples, "The days will come when you will desire to see one of the days of the Son of Man, and you will not see *it.* [23]And they will say to you, 'Look here!' or 'Look there!'[a] Do not go after *them* or follow *them.* [24]For as the lightning that flashes out of one *part* under heaven shines to the other *part* under heaven, so also the Son of Man will be in His day. [25]But first He must suffer many things and be rejected by this generation. [26]And as it was in the days of Noah, so it will be also in the days of the Son of Man: [27]They ate, they drank, they married wives, they were given in marriage, until the day that Noah entered the ark, and the flood came and destroyed them all. [28]Likewise as it was also in the days of Lot: They ate, they drank, they bought, they sold, they planted, they built; [29]but on the day that Lot went out of Sodom it rained fire and brimstone from heaven and destroyed *them* all. [30]Even so will it be in the day when the Son of Man is revealed.

[31]"In that day, he who is on the housetop, and his goods *are* in the house, let him not come down to take them away. And likewise the one who is in the field, let him not turn back. [32]Remember Lot's wife. [33]Whoever seeks to save his life will lose it, and whoever loses his life

will preserve it. [34]I tell you, in that night there will be two *men* in one bed: the one will be taken and the other will be left. [35]Two *women* will be grinding together: the one will be taken and the other left. [36]Two *men* will be in the field: the one will be taken and the other left."[a]

[37]And they answered and said to Him, "Where, Lord?"

So He said to them, "Wherever the body is, there the eagles will be gathered together."

THE PARABLE OF THE PERSISTENT WIDOW

18 Then He spoke a parable to them, that men always ought to pray and not lose heart, [2]saying: "There was in a certain city a judge who did not fear God nor regard man. [3]Now there was a widow in that city; and she came to him, saying, 'Get justice for me from my adversary.' [4]And he would not for a while; but afterward he said within himself, 'Though I do not fear God nor regard man, [5]yet because this widow troubles me I will avenge her, lest by her continual coming she weary me.' "

[6]Then the Lord said, "Hear what the unjust judge said. [7]And shall God not avenge His own elect who cry out day and night to Him, though He bears long with them? [8]I tell you that He will avenge them speedily. Nevertheless, when the Son of Man comes, will He really find faith on the earth?"

THE PARABLE OF THE PHARISEE AND THE TAX COLLECTOR

[9]Also He spoke this parable to some who trusted in themselves that they were righteous, and despised others: [10]"Two men went went up to the temple to pray, one a Pharisee and the other a tax collector. [11]The Pharisee stood and prayed thus with himself, 'God, I thank You that I am not like other men—extortioners, unjust, adulterers, or even as this tax collector. [12]I fast twice a week; I give tithes of all that I possess.' [13]And the tax collector, standing afar off, would not so much as raise *his* eyes to heaven, but beat his breast, saying, 'God, be merciful to me a sinner!' [14]I tell you, this man went down to his house

---

17:21 [a]NU-Text reverses *here* and *there*.   **17:23** [a]NU-Text reverses *here* and *there*.   **17:36** [a]NU-Text and M-Text omit verse 36.

justified *rather* than the other; for everyone who exalts himself will be humbled, and he who humbles himself will be exalted."

JESUS BLESSES LITTLE CHILDREN

[15]Then they also brought infants to Him that He might touch them; but when the disciples saw *it,* they rebuked them. [16]But Jesus called them to *Him* and said, "Let the little children come to Me, and do not forbid them; for of such is the kingdom of God. [17]Assuredly, I say to you, whoever does not receive the kingdom of God as a little child will by no means enter it."

JESUS COUNSELS THE RICH YOUNG RULER

[18]Now a certain ruler asked Him, saying, "Good Teacher, what shall I do to inherit eternal life?"

[19]So Jesus said to him, "Why do you call Me good? No one *is* good but One, *that is,* God. [20]You know the commandments: 'Do not commit adultery,' 'Do not murder,' 'Do not steal,' 'Do not bear false witness,' 'Honor your father and your mother.' "[a]

[21]And he said, "All these things I have kept from my youth."

[22]So when Jesus heard these things, He said to him, "You still lack one thing. Sell all that you have and distribute to the poor, and you will have treasure in heaven; and come, follow Me."

[23]But when he heard this, he became very sorrowful, for he was very rich.

WITH GOD ALL THINGS ARE POSSIBLE

[24]And when Jesus saw that he became very sorrowful, He said, "How hard it is for those who have riches to enter the kingdom of God! [25]For it is easier for a camel to go through the eye of a needle than for a rich man to enter the kingdom of God."

[26]And those who heard it said, "Who then can be saved?"

[27]But He said, "The things which are impossible with men are possible with God."

[28]Then Peter said, "See, we have left all[a] and followed You."

[29]So He said to them, "Assuredly, I say to you, there is no one who has left house or parents or brothers or wife or children, for the sake of the kingdom of God, [30]who shall not receive many times more in this present time, and in the age to come eternal life."

JESUS A THIRD TIME PREDICTS HIS DEATH AND RESURRECTION

[31]Then He took the twelve aside and said to them, "Behold, we are going up to Jerusalem, and all things that are written by the prophets concerning the Son of Man will be accomplished. [32]For He will be delivered to the Gentiles and will be mocked and insulted and spit upon. [33]They will scourge *Him* and kill Him. And the third day He will rise again."

[34]But they understood none of these things; this saying was hidden from them, and they did not know the things which were spoken.

A BLIND MAN RECEIVES HIS SIGHT

[35]Then it happened, as He was coming near Jericho, that a certain blind man sat by the road begging. [36]And hearing a multitude passing by, he asked what it meant. [37]So they told him that Jesus of Nazareth was passing by. [38]And he cried out, saying, "Jesus, Son of David, have mercy on me!"

[39]Then those who went before warned him that he should be quiet; but he cried out all the more, "Son of David, have mercy on me!"

[40]So Jesus stood still and commanded him to be brought to Him. And when he had come near, He asked him, [41]saying, "What do you want Me to do for you?"

He said, "Lord, that I may receive my sight."

[42]Then Jesus said to him, "Receive your sight; your faith has made you well." [43]And immediately he received his sight, and followed Him, glorifying God. And all the people, when they saw *it,* gave praise to God.

JESUS COMES TO ZACCHAEUS' HOUSE

19 Then *Jesus* entered and passed through Jericho. [2]Now behold, *there was* a man named Zacchaeus who was a chief tax collector, and he was rich. [3]And he sought to see who Jesus was, but could not because of the crowd, for he was of short stature. [4]So he ran ahead and climbed up into a sycamore tree to see Him, for He was going to pass that *way.* [5]And when Jesus came to the place, He looked up and saw him,[a] and said to him, "Zacchaeus, make haste and come down, for today I must stay at your house." [6]So he made haste and came down, and received Him joyfully. [7]But when they saw *it,* they all complained, saying, "He has gone to be a guest with a man who is a sinner."

[8]Then Zacchaeus stood and said to the Lord, "Look, Lord, I give half of my goods to the poor; and if I have taken anything from anyone by false accusation, I restore fourfold."

[9]And Jesus said to him, "Today salvation has come to this house, because he also is a son of Abraham; [10]for the Son of Man has come to seek and to save that which was lost."

THE PARABLE OF THE MINAS

[11]Now as they heard these things, He spoke another parable, because He

WISE CHOICES

Choose bright colors for your salads.

To a bowl of dark green lettuce (such as Romaine), choose vegetables that are as brilliantly colored as possible: carrots, red onions, tomatoes, cucumbers, green (or red, orange, or yellow) bell peppers, and marinated beans (black, green, kidney, or other beans).

18:20 [a]Exodus 20:12–16; Deuteronomy 5:16–20 18:28 [a]NU-Text reads *our own.* 19:5 [a]NU-Text omits *and saw him.*

PEOPLE CALLED "BEAUTIFUL" IN THE BIBLE

Vashti and Esther

Queens with Different Roles

Vashti, the queen of King Ahasuerus, was "beautiful to behold." In fact, King Ahasuerus thought she was so beautiful that he sought to show her off to all of his top officials. King Ahasuerus gave a feast during a major conference to which he summoned the leaders of the 127 provinces in his kingdom,. The feast lasted seven days and featured the best of everything served in the most lavish way. The king's feast was only for men. Vashti, his queen, gave a feast for the women in another area of the royal palace. (See Esther 1.)

On the seventh day of the feast, after the men were thoroughly "merry" with wine, King Ahasuerus sent for Queen Vashti. He wanted her to come in her royal apparel to "show her beauty" to his officials. Queen Vashti had no desire to be ogled by drunken men. She may have had other reasons for not coming—some have even speculated that she was pregnant. Vashti's failure to obey her husband's request cost her the crown. Her refusal was humiliating to the king and in his anger he gave in to his advisors' counsel that she be removed as queen. Later, the king regretted this decision, but the decree that demoted Vashti was not reversed.

"Beautiful young virgins" were sought for the king, one of whom was to be chosen as queen in Vashti's place. Esther, a young Jewish woman, was eventually chosen. In her position as queen, Esther was able to save her people in a time of need. Although the Bible does not specifically describe Esther as beautiful, she certainly was one of the "beautiful young virgins" chosen for special treatment within the king's court.

The Bible tells us that she underwent a year of preparation. During that year she was taught how to dress and was given special clothing. She received training in protocol should she be chosen queen. She also received six months of treatment with oil of myrrh and six months of treatment with perfumes and preparations for "beautifying women" (Esther 2:12). Her year of preparation was like spending a year in a thoroughly pampering spa, with finishing school courses on the side! Each of the virgins was given only one night with the king and the Bible says that "the king loved Esther more than all the other women, and she obtained grace and favor in his sight more than all the virgins" (Esther 2:17).

No amount of beauty can overcome the ugliness of prideful behavior.

No amount of beauty can *cause* a person to fall in love.

Nevertheless, countless stories through the ages link beauty with pride and love. Those who are beautiful and those who are easily swayed by beauty need to take note!

---

was near Jerusalem and because they thought the kingdom of God would appear immediately. [12]Therefore He said: "A certain nobleman went into a far country to receive for himself a kingdom and to return. [13]So he called ten of his servants, delivered to them ten minas,ᵃ and said to them, 'Do business till I come.' [14]But his citizens hated him, and sent a delegation after him, saying, 'We will not have this *man* to reign over us.'

[15]"And so it was that when he returned, having received the kingdom, he then commanded these servants, to whom he had given the money, to be called to him, that he might know how much every man had gained by trading. [16]Then came the first, saying, 'Master, your mina has earned ten minas.' [17]And he said to him, 'Well *done*, good servant; because you were faithful in a very little, have authority over ten cities.' [18]And the second came, saying, 'Master, your mina has earned five minas.' [19]Likewise he said to him, 'You also be over five cities.'

[20]"Then another came, saying, 'Master, here is your mina, which I have kept put away in a handkerchief. [21]For I feared you, because you are an austere man. You collect what you did not deposit, and reap what you did not sow.' [22]And he said to him, 'Out of your own mouth I will judge you, *you* wicked servant. You knew that I was an austere man, collecting what I did not deposit and reaping what I did not sow. [23]Why then did you not put my money in the bank, that at my coming I might have collected it with interest?'

[24]"And he said to those who stood by, 'Take the mina from him, and give *it* to him who has ten minas.' [25](But they said to him, 'Master, he has ten minas.') [26]For I say to you, that to everyone who has will be given; and from him who does not have, even what he has will be taken away from him. [27]But bring here those enemies of mine, who did not want me to reign over them, and slay *them* before me.' "

THE TRIUMPHAL ENTRY

[28]When He had said this, He went on ahead, going up to Jerusalem. [29]And it came to pass, when He drew near to Bethphageᵃ and Bethany, at the mountain called Olivet, *that* He sent two of His disciples, [30]saying, "Go into the village opposite *you*, where as you enter you will find a colt tied, on which no one has ever sat. Loose it and bring *it* here.

19:13 ᵃThe *mina* (Greek *mna*, Hebrew *minah*) was worth about three months' salary.   19:29 ᵃM-Text reads *Bethsphage*.

³¹And if anyone asks you, 'Why are you loosing *it*?' thus you shall say to him, 'Because the Lord has need of it.' "

³²So those who were sent went their way and found *it* just as He had said to them. ³³But as they were loosing the colt, the owners of it said to them, "Why are you loosing the colt?"

³⁴And they said, "The Lord has need of him." ³⁵Then they brought him to Jesus. And they threw their own clothes on the colt, and they set Jesus on him. ³⁶And as He went, *many* spread their clothes on the road.

³⁷Then, as He was now drawing near the descent of the Mount of Olives, the whole multitude of the disciples began to rejoice and praise God with a loud voice for all the mighty works they had seen, ³⁸saying:

" 'Blessed is the *King* who comes in the name of the LORD!'ᵃ
Peace in heaven and glory in the highest!"

³⁹And some of the Pharisees called to Him from the crowd, "Teacher, rebuke Your disciples."

⁴⁰But He answered and said to them, "I tell you that if these should keep silent, the stones would immediately cry out."

JESUS WEEPS OVER JERUSALEM

⁴¹Now as He drew near, He saw the city and wept over it, ⁴²saying, "If you had known, even you, especially in this your day, the things *that make* for your peace! But now they are hidden from your eyes. ⁴³For days will come upon you when your enemies will build an embankment around you, surround you and close you in on every side, ⁴⁴and level you, and your children within you, to the ground; and they will not leave in you one stone upon another, because you did not know the time of your visitation."

JESUS CLEANSES THE TEMPLE

⁴⁵Then He went into the temple and began to drive out those who bought and sold in it,ᵃ ⁴⁶saying to them, "It is written, 'My house isᵇ a house of prayer,'ᵇ but you have made it a 'den of thieves.' "ᶜ

⁴⁷And He was teaching daily in the temple. But the chief priests, the scribes, and the leaders of the people sought to destroy Him, ⁴⁸and were unable to do anything; for all the people were very attentive to hear Him.

JESUS' AUTHORITY QUESTIONED

20 Now it happened on one of those days, as He taught the people in the temple and preached the gospel, *that* the chief priests and the scribes, together with the elders, confronted *Him* ²and spoke to Him, saying, "Tell us, by what authority are You doing these things? Or who is he who gave You this authority?"

³But He answered and said to them, "I also will ask you one thing, and answer Me: ⁴The baptism of John—was it from heaven or from men?"

⁵And they reasoned among themselves, saying, "If we say, 'From heaven,' He will say, 'Why thenᵃ did you not believe him?' ⁶But if we say, 'From men,' all the people will stone us, for they are persuaded that John was a prophet." ⁷So they answered that they did not know where *it was* from.

⁸And Jesus said to them, "Neither will I tell you by what authority I do these things."

THE PARABLE OF THE WICKED VINEDRESSERS

⁹Then He began to tell the people this parable: "A certain man planted a vineyard, leased it to vinedressers, and went into a far country for a long time. ¹⁰Now at vintage-time he sent a servant to the vinedressers, that they might give him some of the fruit of the vineyard. But the vinedressers beat him and sent *him* away empty-handed. ¹¹Again he sent another servant; and they beat him also, treated *him*

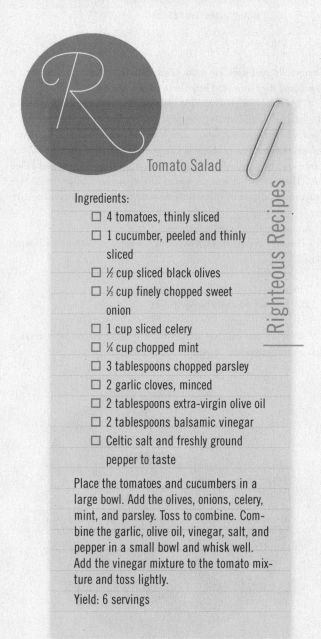

Righteous Recipes

Tomato Salad

Ingredients:

☐ 4 tomatoes, thinly sliced
☐ 1 cucumber, peeled and thinly sliced
☐ ½ cup sliced black olives
☐ ⅓ cup finely chopped sweet onion
☐ 1 cup sliced celery
☐ ¼ cup chopped mint
☐ 3 tablespoons chopped parsley
☐ 2 garlic cloves, minced
☐ 2 tablespoons extra-virgin olive oil
☐ 2 tablespoons balsamic vinegar
☐ Celtic salt and freshly ground pepper to taste

Place the tomatoes and cucumbers in a large bowl. Add the olives, onions, celery, mint, and parsley. Toss to combine. Combine the garlic, olive oil, vinegar, salt, and pepper in a small bowl and whisk well. Add the vinegar mixture to the tomato mixture and toss lightly.

Yield: 6 servings

19:38 ᵃPsalm 118:26   **19:45** ᵃNU-Text reads *those who were selling.*   **19:46** ᵃNU-Text reads *shall be.* ᵇIsaiah 56:7 ᶜJeremiah 7:11   **20:5** ᵃNU-Text and M-Text omit *then.*

DIVINE HEALTH   105

[APPLE CIDER VINEGAR]

This is a great blood purifier when a tablespoon is added to a cup of hot water as a "tonic" drink. Apple cider vinegar can also be used as an astringent for both face (toner) and hair (rinse to remove residue).

shamefully, and sent *him* away empty-handed. ¹²And again he sent a third; and they wounded him also and cast *him* out.

¹³"Then the owner of the vineyard said, 'What shall I do? I will send my beloved son. Probably they will respect *him* when they see him.' ¹⁴But when the vinedressers saw him, they reasoned among themselves, saying, 'This is the heir. Come, let us kill him, that the inheritance may be ours.' ¹⁵So they cast him out of the vineyard and killed *him.* Therefore what will the owner of the vineyard do to them? ¹⁶He will come and destroy those vinedressers and give the vineyard to others."

And when they heard *it* they said, "Certainly not!"

¹⁷Then He looked at them and said, "What then is this that is written:

'The stone which the builders rejected
Has become the chief cornerstone'?ᵃ

¹⁸Whoever falls on that stone will be broken; but on whomever it falls, it will grind him to powder."

Mealtime Rituals

Bible Health + Food Facts

Religious laws required that at least the right hand of a person be washed before eating. The food was blessed *before* a meal and thanks was offered *after* the meal.

¹⁹And the chief priests and the scribes that very hour sought to lay hands on Him, but they feared the peopleᵃ—for they knew He had spoken this parable against them.

THE PHARISEES: IS IT LAWFUL TO PAY TAXES TO CAESAR?

²⁰So they watched *Him,* and sent spies who pretended to be righteous, that they might seize on His words, in order to deliver Him to the power and the authority of the governor. ²¹Then they asked Him, saying, "Teacher, we know that You say and teach rightly, and You do not show personal favoritism, but teach the way of God in truth: ²²Is it lawful for us to pay taxes to Caesar or not?"

²³But He perceived their craftiness, and said to them, "Why do you test Me?ᵃ ²⁴Show Me a denarius. Whose image and inscription does it have?"

They answered and said, "Caesar's."

²⁵And He said to them, "Render therefore to Caesar the things that are Caesar's, and to God the things that are God's."

²⁶But they could not catch Him in His words in the presence of the people. And they marveled at His answer and kept silent.

THE SADDUCEES: WHAT ABOUT THE RESURRECTION?

²⁷Then some of the Sadducees, who deny that there is a resurrection, came to *Him* and asked Him, ²⁸saying: "Teacher, Moses wrote to us *that* if a man's brother dies, having a wife, and he dies without children, his brother should take his wife and raise up offspring for his brother. ²⁹Now there were seven brothers. And the first took a wife, and died without children. ³⁰And the secondᵃ took her as wife, and he died childless. ³¹Then the third took her, and in like manner the seven also; and they left no children,ᵃ and died. ³²Last of all the woman died also. ³³Therefore, in the resurrection, whose wife does she become? For all seven had her as wife."

³⁴Jesus answered and said to them, "The sons of this age marry and are given in marriage. ³⁵But those who are counted worthy to attain that age, and the resurrection from the dead, neither marry nor are given in marriage; ³⁶nor can they die anymore, for they are equal to the angels and are sons of God, being sons of the resurrection. ³⁷But even Moses showed in the *burning* bush *passage* that the dead are raised, when he called the Lord 'the God of Abraham, the God of Isaac, and the God of Jacob.'ᵃ ³⁸For He is not the God of the dead but of the living, for all live to Him."

³⁹Then some of the scribes answered and said, "Teacher, You have spoken well." ⁴⁰But after that they dared not question Him anymore.

JESUS: HOW CAN DAVID CALL HIS DESCENDANT LORD?

⁴¹And He said to them, "How can they say that the Christ is the Son of David? ⁴²Now David himself said in the Book of Psalms:

'The Lord said to my Lord,
"Sit at My right hand,
⁴³ Till I make Your enemies Your footstool." 'ᵃ

20:17 ᵃPsalm 118:22   20:19 ᵃM-Text reads *but they were afraid.*   20:23 ᵃNU-Text omits *Why do you test Me?*   20:30 ᵃNU-Text ends verse 30 here.   20:31 ᵃNU-Text and M-Text read *the seven also left no children.*   20:37 ᵃExodus 3:6, 15   20:43 ᵃPsalm 110:1

[44]"Therefore David calls Him 'Lord'; how is He then his Son?"

BEWARE OF THE SCRIBES

[45]Then, in the hearing of all the people, He said to His disciples, [46]"Beware of the scribes, who desire to go around in long robes, love greetings in the marketplaces, the best seats in the synagogues, and the best places at feasts, [47]who devour widows' houses, and for a pretense make long prayers. These will receive greater condemnation."

THE WIDOW'S TWO MITES

21 And He looked up and saw the rich putting their gifts into the treasury, [2]and He saw also a certain poor widow putting in two mites. [3]So He said, "Truly I say to you that this poor widow has put in more than all; [4]for all these out of their abundance have put in offerings for God,[a] but she out of her poverty put in all the livelihood that she had."

JESUS PREDICTS THE DESTRUCTION OF THE TEMPLE

[5]Then, as some spoke of the temple, how it was adorned with beautiful stones and donations, He said, [6]"These things which you see—the days will come in which not *one* stone shall be left upon another that shall not be thrown down."

THE SIGNS OF THE TIMES AND THE END OF THE AGE

[7]So they asked Him, saying, "Teacher, but when will these things be? And what sign *will there be* when these things are about to take place?"

[8]And He said: "Take heed that you not be deceived. For many will come in My name, saying, 'I am *He*,' and, 'The time has drawn near.' Therefore[a] do not go after them. [9]But when you hear of wars and commotions, do not be terrified; for these things must come to pass first, but the end *will* not *come* immediately."

[10]Then He said to them, "Nation will rise against nation, and kingdom against kingdom. [11]And there will be great earthquakes in various places, and famines and pestilences; and there will be fearful sights and great signs from heaven. [12]But before all these things, they will lay their hands on you and persecute *you*, delivering *you* up to the synagogues and prisons. You will be brought before kings and rulers for My name's sake. [13]But it will turn out for you as an occasion for testimony. [14]Therefore settle *it* in your hearts not to meditate beforehand on what you will answer; [15]for I will give you a mouth and wisdom which all your adversaries will not be able to contradict or resist. [16]You will be betrayed even by parents and brothers, relatives and friends; and they will put *some* of you to death. [17]And you will be hated by all for My name's sake. [18]But not a hair of your head shall be lost. [19]By your patience possess your souls.

THE DESTRUCTION OF JERUSALEM

[20]"But when you see Jerusalem surrounded by armies, then know that its desolation is near. [21]Then let those who are in Judea flee to the mountains, let those who are in the midst of her depart, and let not those who are in the country enter her. [22]For these are the days of vengeance, that all things which are written may be fulfilled. [23]But woe to those who are pregnant and to those who are nursing babies in those days! For there will be great distress in the land and wrath upon this people. [24]And they will fall by the edge of the sword, and be led away captive into all nations. And Jerusalem will be trampled by Gentiles until the times of the Gentiles are fulfilled.

THE COMING OF THE SON OF MAN

[25]"And there will be signs in the sun, in the moon, and in the stars; and on the earth distress of nations, with perplexity, the sea and the waves roaring; [26]men's hearts failing them from fear and the expectation of those things which are coming on the earth, for the powers of the heavens will be shaken. [27]Then they will see the Son of Man coming in a cloud with power and great glory. [28]Now when these things begin to happen, look up and lift up your heads, because your redemption draws near."

21:4 [a]NU-Text omits *for God*.   21:8 [a]NU-Text omits *Therefore*.

The LAW AND THE SCIENCE

>THE LAW

says: "All in the seas or in the rivers that do not have fins and scales, all that move in the water or any living thing which is in the water, they are an abomination to you" (Leviticus 11:10).

[AVOID THE BOTTOM FEEDERS]

>SCIENCE tells us that shellfish—scavengers that were designed by God to cleanse the waters and the ocean floor—tend to be loaded with toxins. Shellfish include shrimp, lobster, crab, oysters, scallops, mussels, and clams. They are easily contaminated with mercury, lead, arsenic, carcinogens, and hundreds of chemical and synthetic contaminants. The more polluted the waters, the more likely the shellfish in them are dangerous.

Shellfish have a unique ability to carry deadly carcinogens in their bodies without dying, but they pass these carcinogens upward through the food chain. Shellfish are also highly susceptible to a bacteria named *Vibrio vulnificus*, which thrives in warm seas and is very dangerous to human beings. Always keep in mind that fish and shellfish are two different classes of seafood!

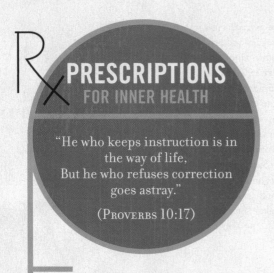

PRESCRIPTIONS
FOR INNER HEALTH

"He who keeps instruction is in
the way of life,
But he who refuses correction
goes astray."

(PROVERBS 10:17)

People who follow the commandments of God in the Bible are doing what God has said is good for our lives. People who know the commandments and then refuse to do them put themselves outside the blessings and promises of God.

THE PARABLE OF THE FIG TREE

²⁹Then He spoke to them a parable: "Look at the fig tree, and all the trees. ³⁰When they are already budding, you see and know for yourselves that summer is now near. ³¹So you also, when you see these things happening, know that the kingdom of God is near. ³²Assuredly, I say to you, this generation will by no means pass away till all things take place. ³³Heaven and earth will pass away, but My words will by no means pass away.

THE IMPORTANCE OF WATCHING

³⁴"But take heed to yourselves, lest your hearts be weighed down with carousing, drunkenness, and cares of this life, and that Day come on you unexpectedly. ³⁵For it will come as a snare on all those who dwell on the face of the whole earth. ³⁶Watch therefore, and pray always that you may be counted worthy* to escape all these things that will come to pass, and to stand before the Son of Man."

³⁷And in the daytime He was teaching in the temple, but at night He went out and stayed on the mountain called Olivet. ³⁸Then early in the morning all the people came to Him in the temple to hear Him.

THE PLOT TO KILL JESUS

22 Now the Feast of Unleavened Bread drew near, which is called Passover. ²And the chief priests and the scribes sought how they might kill Him, for they feared the people.

³Then Satan entered Judas, surnamed Iscariot, who was numbered among the twelve. ⁴So he went his way and conferred with the chief priests and captains, how he might betray Him to them. ⁵And they were glad, and agreed to give him money. ⁶So he promised and sought opportunity to betray Him to them in the absence of the multitude.

JESUS AND HIS DISCIPLES PREPARE THE PASSOVER

⁷Then came the Day of Unleavened Bread, when the Passover must be killed. ⁸And He sent Peter and John, saying, "Go and prepare the Passover for us, that we may eat."

⁹So they said to Him, "Where do You want us to prepare?"

¹⁰And He said to them, "Behold, when you have entered the city, a man will meet you carrying a pitcher of water; follow him into the house which he enters. ¹¹Then you shall say to the master of the house, 'The Teacher says to you, "Where is the guest room where I may eat the Passover with My disciples?" ' ¹²Then he will show you a large, furnished upper room; there make ready."

¹³So they went and found it just as He had said to them, and they prepared the Passover.

JESUS INSTITUTES THE LORD'S SUPPER

¹⁴When the hour had come, He sat down, and the twelve* apostles with Him. ¹⁵Then He said to them, "With *fervent* desire I have desired to eat this Passover with you before I suffer; ¹⁶for I say to you, I will no longer eat of it until it is fulfilled in the kingdom of God."

¹⁷Then He took the cup, and gave thanks, and said, "Take this and divide *it* among yourselves; ¹⁸for I say to you,* I will not drink of the fruit of the vine until the kingdom of God comes."

¹⁹And He took bread, gave thanks and broke *it*, and gave *it* to them, saying, "This is My body which is given for you; do this in remembrance of Me."

²⁰Likewise He also *took* the cup after supper, saying, "This cup *is* the new covenant in My blood, which is shed for you. ²¹But behold, the hand of My betrayer *is* with Me on the table. ²²And truly the Son of Man goes as it has been determined, but woe to that man by whom He is betrayed!"

²³Then they began to question among themselves, which of them it was who would do this thing.

THE DISCIPLES ARGUE ABOUT GREATNESS

²⁴Now there was also a dispute among them, as to which of them should be considered the greatest. ²⁵And He said to them, "The kings of the Gentiles exercise lordship over them, and those who exercise authority over them are called 'benefactors.' ²⁶But not so *among* you; on the contrary, he who is greatest among you, let him be as the younger, and he who governs as he who serves. ²⁷For who *is* greater, he who sits at the table, or he who serves? *Is* it not he who sits at the table? Yet I am among you as the One who serves.

²⁸"But you are those who have continued with Me in My trials. ²⁹And I bestow upon you a kingdom, just as My Father bestowed *one* upon Me, ³⁰that you may eat and drink at My table in My kingdom, and sit on thrones judging the twelve tribes of Israel."

21:36 *NU-Text reads *may have strength.*   22:14 *NU-Text omits *twelve.*   22:18 *NU-Text adds *from now on.*

JESUS PREDICTS PETER'S DENIAL

³¹And the Lord said,ᵃ "Simon, Simon! Indeed, Satan has asked for you, that he may sift *you* as wheat. ³²But I have prayed for you, that your faith should not fail; and when you have returned to *Me*, strengthen your brethren."

³³But he said to Him, "Lord, I am ready to go with You, both to prison and to death."

³⁴Then He said, "I tell you, Peter, the rooster shall not crow this day before you will deny three times that you know Me."

SUPPLIES FOR THE ROAD

³⁵And He said to them, "When I sent you without money bag, knapsack, and sandals, did you lack anything?"

So they said, "Nothing."

³⁶Then He said to them, "But now, he who has a money bag, let him take *it*, and likewise a knapsack; and he who has no sword, let him sell his garment and buy one. ³⁷For I say to you that this which is written must still be accomplished in Me: 'And He was numbered with the transgressors.'ᵃ For the things concerning Me have an end."

³⁸So they said, "Lord, look, here *are* two swords."

And He said to them, "It is enough."

THE PRAYER IN THE GARDEN

³⁹Coming out, He went to the Mount of Olives, as He was accustomed, and His disciples also followed Him. ⁴⁰When He came to the place, He said to them, "Pray that you may not enter into temptation."

⁴¹And He was withdrawn from them about a stone's throw, and He knelt down and prayed, ⁴²saying, "Father, if it is Your will, take this cup away from Me; nevertheless not My will, but Yours, be done." ⁴³Then an angel appeared to Him from heaven, strengthening Him. ⁴⁴And being in agony, He prayed more earnestly. Then His sweat became like great drops of blood falling down to the ground.ᵃ

⁴⁵When He rose up from prayer, and had come to His disciples, He found them sleeping from sorrow. ⁴⁶Then He said to them, "Why do you sleep? Rise and pray, lest you enter into temptation."

BETRAYAL AND ARREST IN GETHSEMANE

⁴⁷And while He was still speaking, behold, a multitude; and he who was called Judas, one of the twelve, went before them and drew near to Jesus to kiss Him. ⁴⁸But Jesus said to him, "Judas, are you betraying the Son of Man with a kiss?"

⁴⁹When those around Him saw what was going to happen, they said to Him, "Lord, shall we strike with the sword?" ⁵⁰And one of them struck the servant of the high priest and cut off his right ear.

⁵¹But Jesus answered and said, "Permit even this." And He touched his ear and healed him.

⁵²Then Jesus said to the chief priests, captains of the temple, and the elders who had come to Him, "Have you come out, as against a robber, with swords and clubs? ⁵³When I was with you daily in the temple, you did not try to seize Me. But this is your hour, and the power of darkness."

PETER DENIES JESUS, AND WEEPS BITTERLY

⁵⁴Having arrested Him, they led *Him* and brought Him into the high priest's house. But Peter followed at a distance. ⁵⁵Now when they had kindled a fire in the midst of the courtyard and sat down together, Peter sat among them. ⁵⁶And a certain servant girl, seeing him as he sat by the fire, looked intently at him and said, "This man was also with Him."

⁵⁷But he denied Him,ᵃ saying, "Woman, I do not know Him."

⁵⁸And after a little while another saw him and said, "You also are of them."

But Peter said, "Man, I am not!"

⁵⁹Then after about an hour had passed, another confidently affirmed, saying, "Surely this *fellow* also was with Him, for he is a Galilean."

⁶⁰But Peter said, "Man, I do not know what you are saying!"

Immediately, while he was still speaking, the roosterᵃ crowed. ⁶¹And

---

> ## > (Luke 22:24)

Climbing the Corporate Ladder. Although

God desires us to become all He created us to be—and to do all that He has prepared and called us to do—God does not shower with favor those who are highly competitive or who seek status. God does not play corporate politics! A great deal of stress in our society is generated because people are striving to be recognized, valued, and rewarded by their peers as well as by their "superiors" in a business setting.

God does not bless jockeying for position, manipulating one's way to the next rung up the corporate ladder, and forming alliances for the benefit of some and the detriment of others. He calls His people to *serve*, not to seek to be served. He elevates into greater and greater positions of authority those who are humble and generous toward others.

Envy, jealousy, greed, and the desire for personal power are all attitudes contradictory to a Christlike nature. They can lead to deep-seated anxiety and frustration, discouragement and depression. These emotions, in turn, release harmful stress hormones into the physical body and create a physical environment that is ideal for chronic illness. Seek to do all you can do, as well as you can do it, with maximum personal productivity and quality; and to work in a way that is a blessing to your company, your superiors, your peers, and those who work under you. God will make sure you are amply rewarded!

INSIGHTS | **INTO THE WORD**

22:31 ᵃNU-Text omits *And the Lord said.* 22:37 ᵃIsaiah 53:12 22:44 ᵃNU-Text brackets verses 43 and 44 as not in the original text. 22:57 ᵃNU-Text reads *denied it.* 22:60 ᵃNU-Text and M-Text read *a rooster.*

the Lord turned and looked at Peter. Then Peter remembered the word of the Lord, how He had said to him, "Before the rooster crows," you will deny Me three times." ⁶²So Peter went out and wept bitterly.

JESUS MOCKED AND BEATEN

⁶³Now the men who held Jesus mocked Him and beat Him. ⁶⁴And having blindfolded Him, they struck Him on the face and asked Him," saying, "Prophesy! Who is the one who struck You?" ⁶⁵And many other things they blasphemously spoke against Him.

JESUS FACES THE SANHEDRIN

⁶⁶As soon as it was day, the elders of the people, both chief priests and scribes, came together and led Him into their council, saying, ⁶⁷"If You are the Christ, tell us."

But He said to them, "If I tell you, you will by no means believe. ⁶⁸And if I also ask *you,* you will by no means answer Me or let *Me* go." ⁶⁹Hereafter the Son of Man will sit on the right hand of the power of God."

⁷⁰Then they all said, "Are You then the Son of God?"

So He said to them, "You *rightly* say that I am."

⁷¹And they said, "What further testimony do we need? For we have heard it ourselves from His own mouth."

JESUS HANDED OVER TO PONTIUS PILATE

23 Then the whole multitude of them arose and led Him to Pilate. ²And they began to accuse Him, saying, "We found this *fellow* perverting the" nation, and forbidding to pay taxes to Caesar, saying that He Himself is Christ, a King."

³Then Pilate asked Him, saying, "Are You the King of the Jews?"

He answered him and said, "*It is as* you say."

⁴So Pilate said to the chief priests and the crowd, "I find no fault in this Man."

⁵But they were the more fierce, saying, "He stirs up the people, teaching throughout all Judea, beginning from Galilee to this place."

JESUS FACES HEROD

⁶When Pilate heard of Galilee," he asked if the Man were a Galilean. ⁷And as soon as he knew that He belonged to Herod's jurisdiction, he sent Him to Herod, who was also in Jerusalem at that time. ⁸Now when Herod saw Jesus, he was exceedingly glad; for he had desired for a long *time* to see Him, because he had heard many things about Him, and he hoped to see some miracle done by Him. ⁹Then he questioned Him with many words, but He answered him nothing. ¹⁰And the chief priests and scribes stood and vehemently accused Him. ¹¹Then Herod, with his men of war, treated Him with contempt and mocked *Him,* arrayed Him in a gorgeous robe, and sent Him back to Pilate. ¹²That very day Pilate and Herod became friends with each other, for previously they had been at enmity with each other.

TAKING THE PLACE OF BARABBAS

¹³Then Pilate, when he had called together the chief priests, the rulers, and the people, ¹⁴said to them, "You have brought this Man to me, as one who misleads the people. And indeed, having examined *Him* in your presence, I have found no fault in this Man concerning those things of which you accuse Him; ¹⁵no, neither did Herod, for I sent you back to him;" and indeed nothing deserving of death has been done by Him. ¹⁶I will therefore chastise Him and release *Him*" ¹⁷(for it was necessary for him to release one to them at the feast)."

¹⁸And they all cried out at once, saying, "Away with this *Man,* and re-

> (Luke 23:33)

INSIGHTS INTO THE WORD

Death by Crucifixion. Crucifixion is one of the cruelest forms of punishment ever devised. It was feared and hated by the Jews, who saw it as the ultimate form of Roman oppression. From a medical standpoint, crucifixion was a slow and painful way to die. A crucified person did not die from loss of blood. In many cases, the person was not nailed to a cross but merely tied to it with thick ropes at their hands and feet. Nails were generally used to prevent the person's supporters from causing a skirmish, quickly cutting the ropes, and pulling the crucified person away to safety.

Death by crucifixion was ultimately death by suffocation. The weight of a person hanging from a cross pulled the body down so that inhaled air could not be expelled. For the lungs to expel air, the person had to hoist himself up a little, somewhat like doing pull-ups, at times with the aid of a small ledge on the upright part of the cross. Over hours, and sometimes days, the person became exhausted and unable to release the air in his lungs. Death was usually slow.

The experience was even more agonizing for the crucified person because most of the time his feet were only inches from the ground. The person was low enough to the ground so that passersby could spit in his face. The Roman soldiers intended to break Jesus' legs, which would have completely disabled Him from pulling Himself up to expel air.

The soldiers discovered as they approached Him that Jesus had willfully expelled all His air in a great cry to God, "It is finished!" He was already dead. The sword thrust into Jesus' side caused blood and water to flow, which was a sure sign that He had already died. Jesus had "given up" His life voluntarily as a sacrifice for sin. (See also John 19:28–37.)

22:61 ªNU-Text adds *today.*   **22:64** ªNU-Text reads *And having blindfolded Him, they asked Him.*   **22:68** ªNU-Text omits *also* and *Me or let Me go.*   **23:2** ªNU-Text reads *our.*   **23:6** ªNU-Text omits *of Galilee.*   **23:15** ªNU-Text reads *for he sent Him back to us.*   **23:17** ªNU-Text omits verse 17.

lease to us Barabbas"— [19]who had been thrown into prison for a certain rebellion made in the city, and for murder.

[20]Pilate, therefore, wishing to release Jesus, again called out to them. [21]But they shouted, saying, "Crucify *Him*, crucify Him!"

[22]Then he said to them the third time, "Why, what evil has He done? I have found no reason for death in Him. I will therefore chastise Him and let *Him* go."

[23]But they were insistent, demanding with loud voices that He be crucified. And the voices of these men and of the chief priests prevailed.ᵃ [24]So Pilate gave sentence that it should be as they requested. [25]And he released to themᵃ the one they requested, who for rebellion and murder had been thrown into prison; but he delivered Jesus to their will.

THE KING ON A CROSS

[26]Now as they led Him away, they laid hold of a certain man, Simon a Cyrenian, who was coming from the country, and on him they laid the cross that he might bear *it* after Jesus.

[27]And a great multitude of the people followed Him, and women who also mourned and lamented Him. [28]But Jesus, turning to them, said, "Daughters of Jerusalem, do not weep for Me, but weep for yourselves and for your children. [29]For indeed the days are coming in which they will say, 'Blessed *are* the barren, wombs that never bore, and breasts which never nursed!' [30]Then they will begin 'to say to the mountains, "Fall on us!" and to the hills, "Cover us!" 'ᵃ [31]For if they do these things in the green wood, what will be done in the dry?"

[32]There were also two others, criminals, led with Him to be put to death. [33]And when they had come to the place called Calvary, there they crucified Him, and the criminals, one on the right hand and the other on the left. [34]Then Jesus said, "Father, forgive them, for they do not know what they do."ᵃ

And they divided His garments and cast lots. [35]And the people stood looking on. But even the rulers with them sneered, saying, "He saved others; let Him save Himself if He is the Christ, the chosen of God."

[36]The soldiers also mocked Him, coming and offering Him sour wine, [37]and saying, "If You are the King of the Jews, save Yourself."

[38]And an inscription also was written over Him in letters of Greek, Latin, and Hebrew:ᵃ

THIS IS THE KING OF THE JEWS.

[39]Then one of the criminals who were hanged blasphemed Him, saying, "If You are the Christ,ᵃ save Yourself and us."

[40]But the other, answering, rebuked him, saying, "Do you not even fear God, seeing you are under the same condemnation? [41]And we indeed justly, for we receive the due reward of our deeds; but this Man has done nothing wrong." [42]Then he said to Jesus, "Lord,ᵃ remember me when You come into Your kingdom."

[43]And Jesus said to him, "Assuredly, I say to you, today you will be with Me in Paradise."

JESUS DIES ON THE CROSS

[44]Now it wasᵃ about the sixth hour, and there was darkness over all the earth until the ninth hour. [45]Then the sun was darkened,ᵃ and the veil of the temple was torn in two. [46]And when Jesus had cried out with a loud voice, He said, "Father, 'into Your hands I commit My spirit.' "ᵃ Having said this, He breathed His last.

[47]So when the centurion saw what had happened, he glorified God, saying, "Certainly this was a righteous Man!"

[48]And the whole crowd who came together to that sight, seeing what had been done, beat their breasts and returned. [49]But all His acquaintances, and the women who followed Him from Galilee, stood at a distance, watching these things.

> " **As soon as it was day, the elders of the people, both chief priests and scribes, came together and led Him into their council, saying, 'If You are the Christ, tell us.'** "
> — *Luke 22:66-67*

JESUS BURIED IN JOSEPH'S TOMB

[50]Now behold, *there was* a man named Joseph, a council member, a good and just man. [51]He had not consented to their decision and deed. *He was* from Arimathea, a city of the Jews, who himself was also waitingᵃ for the kingdom of God. [52]This man went to Pilate and asked for the body of Jesus. [53]Then he took it down, wrapped it in linen, and laid it in a tomb *that was* hewn out of the rock, where no one had ever lain before. [54]That day was the Preparation, and the Sabbath drew near.

[55]And the women who had come with Him from Galilee followed after, and they observed the tomb and how His body was laid. [56]Then they returned and prepared spices and fragrant oils. And they rested on the Sabbath according to the commandment.

HE IS RISEN

24 Now on the first *day* of the week, very early in the morning, they, and certain *other women* with them,ᵃ came to the tomb bringing the spices which they had prepared. [2]But they found the stone rolled away from the tomb. [3]Then they went in and did not find the body of the Lord Jesus. [4]And it happened, as they were greatlyᵃ perplexed about this, that behold, two men stood by them in shining garments. [5]Then, as they were afraid and bowed *their* faces to the earth, they said to them, "Why do you seek the living among the dead? [6]He is not here, but is risen! Remember how He spoke to you when He was still in Galilee, [7]saying, 'The Son of Man must be delivered into the hands of sinful men, and be crucified, and the third day rise again.' "

[8]And they remembered His words. [9]Then they returned from the tomb and told all these things to the eleven and to all the rest. [10]It was Mary Magdalene, Joanna, Mary *the mother* of James, and the other

---

23:23 ᵃNU-Text omits *and of the chief priests.*   23:25 ᵃNU-Text and M-Text omit *to them.*   23:30 ᵃHosea 10:8   23:34 ᵃNU-Text brackets the first sentence as a later addition.   23:38 ᵃNU-Text omits *written* and *in letters of Greek, Latin, and Hebrew.*   23:39 ᵃNU-Text reads *Are You not the Christ?*   23:42 ᵃNU-Text reads *And he said, "Jesus, remember me.*   23:44 ᵃNU-Text adds *already.*   23:45 ᵃNU-Text reads *obscured.*   23:46 ᵃPsalm 31:5   23:51 ᵃNU-Text reads *who was waiting.*   24:1 ᵃNU-Text omits *and certain other women with them.*   24:4 ᵃNU-Text omits *greatly.*

walking the walk

[BALANCED AND BENEFICIAL EXERCISE]

There are seven major advantages of exercise for every person:

☐ Exercise burns fat.
☐ Exercise increases the percentage of lean body tissue.
☐ Exercise raises the body's metabolic rate.
☐ Exercise increases the sensitivity of cells to insulin, which means that the pancreas needs to produce less insulin.
☐ Exercise (strength building) is the only way to reshape a person's genetically predisposed body type.
☐ Exercise releases endorphin neuropeptides in the brain—these are the so-called "feel good" hormones. Endorphins have very beneficial effects on the immune system.
☐ Exercise reduces the level of stress hormones in the body. The immune system also benefits by having lower levels of cortisol.

Include the following kinds of exercise every week:

Aerobic exercise—walking, running, cycling, or swimming. This exercise is great for the cardiovascular system.

Flexibility exercises—these are stretching exercises that can help keep you limber.

Strength-building exercises—weight training or resistance training exercises to build muscle.

THE ROAD TO EMMAUS

[13]Now behold, two of them were traveling that same day to a village called Emmaus, which was seven miles[a] from Jerusalem. [14]And they talked together of all these things which had happened. [15]So it was, while they conversed and reasoned, that Jesus Himself drew near and went with them. [16]But their eyes were restrained, so that they did not know Him.

[17]And He said to them, "What kind of conversation *is* this that you have with one another as you walk and are sad?"[a]

[18]Then the one whose name was Cleopas answered and said to Him, "Are You the only stranger in Jerusalem, and have You not known the things which happened there in these days?"

[19]And He said to them, "What things?"

So they said to Him, "The things concerning Jesus of Nazareth, who was a Prophet mighty in deed and word before God and all the people, [20]and how the chief priests and our rulers delivered Him to be condemned to death, and crucified Him. [21]But we were hoping that it was He who was going to redeem Israel. Indeed, besides all this, today is the third day since these things happened. [22]Yes, and certain women of our company, who arrived at the tomb early, astonished us. [23]When they did not find His body, they came saying that they had also seen a vision of angels who said He was alive. [24]And certain of those *who were* with us went to the tomb and found *it* just as the women had said; but Him they did not see."

[25]Then He said to them, "O foolish ones, and slow of heart to believe in all that the prophets have spoken! [26]Ought not the Christ to have suffered these things and to enter into His glory?" [27]And beginning at Moses and all the Prophets, He expounded to them in all the Scriptures the things concerning Himself.

THE DISCIPLES' EYES OPENED

[28]Then they drew near to the village where they were going, and He indicated that He would have gone farther. [29]But they constrained Him, saying, "Abide with us, for it is toward evening, and the day is far spent." And He went in to stay with them.

[30]Now it came to pass, as He sat at the table with them, that He took bread, blessed and broke *it*, and gave it to them. [31]Then their eyes were opened and they knew Him; and He vanished from their sight.

[32]And they said to one another, "Did not our heart burn within us while He talked with us on the road, and while He opened the Scriptures to us?" [33]So they rose up that very hour and returned to Jerusalem, and found the eleven and those *who were* with them gathered together, [34]saying, "The Lord is risen indeed, and has appeared to Simon!" [35]And they told about the things *that had happened* on the road, and how He was known to them in the breaking of bread.

JESUS APPEARS TO HIS DISCIPLES

[36]Now as they said these things, Jesus Himself stood in the midst of them, and said to them, "Peace to you." [37]But they were terrified and frightened, and supposed they had seen a spirit. [38]And He said to them, "Why are you troubled? And why do doubts arise in your hearts? [39]Behold My hands and My feet, that it is I Myself. Handle Me and see, for a spirit does not have flesh and bones as you see I have."

women with them, who told these things to the apostles. [11]And their words seemed to them like idle tales, and they did not believe them. [12]But Peter arose and ran to the tomb; and stooping down, he saw the linen cloths lying[a] by themselves; and he departed, marveling to himself at what had happened.

24:12 [a]NU-Text omits *lying.*   24:13 [a]Literally *sixty stadia*   24:17 [a]NU-Text reads *as you walk? And they stood still, looking sad.*

[40]When He had said this, He showed them His hands and His feet.[a] [41]But while they still did not believe for joy, and marveled, He said to them, "Have you any food here?" [42]So they gave Him a piece of a broiled fish and some honeycomb.[a] [43]And He took *it* and ate in their presence.

THE SCRIPTURES OPENED

[44]Then He said to them, "These *are* the words which I spoke to you while I was still with you, that all things must be fulfilled which were written in the Law of Moses and *the* Prophets and *the* Psalms concerning Me." [45]And He opened their understanding, that they might comprehend the Scriptures.

[46]Then He said to them, "Thus it is written, and thus it was necessary for the Christ to suffer and to rise[a] from the dead the third day, [47]and that repentance and remission of sins should be preached in His name to all nations, beginning at Jerusalem. [48]And you are witnesses of these things. [49]Behold, I send the Promise of My Father upon you; but tarry in the city of Jerusalem[a] until you are endued with power from on high."

THE ASCENSION

[50]And He led them out as far as Bethany, and He lifted up His hands and blessed them. [51]Now it came to pass, while He blessed them, that He was parted from them and carried up into heaven. [52]And they worshiped Him, and returned to Jerusalem with great joy, [53]and were continually in the temple praising and[a] blessing God. Amen.[b]

Bible Health + Food Facts

Bible Grains

The two foremost grains used in Old Testament times were barley and wheat. Wheat is mentioned fifty-one times in the Bible.

24:40 [a]Some printed New Testaments omit this verse. It is found in nearly all Greek manuscripts.   **24:42** [a]NU-Text omits *and some honeycomb.*   **24:46** [a]NU-Text reads *written, that the Christ should suffer and rise.*   **24:49** [a]NU-Text omits *of Jerusalem.*   **24:53** [a]NU-Text omits *praising and.* [b]NU-Text omits *Amen.*

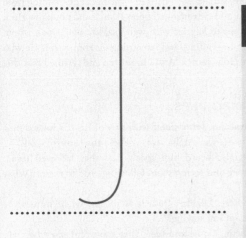

OHN John knew Jesus. He was one of the twelve disciples and along with Peter and James, was in Jesus' inner circle. John was an eyewitness to the life and ministry of Jesus, and after Jesus rose from the dead and ascended to heaven, John ministered longer than any other disciple.

John also knew without doubt that Jesus was the Son of God and that the Father and Son were One. John knew Jesus had existed as the Word of God from Creation. Perhaps most importantly, John knew that Jesus loved him. He refers to himself repeatedly as the "beloved disciple." The foremost fact of John's life was that Jesus had loved him and called him.

One of the greatest hallmarks of emotional health is knowing who you are, and knowing who you are flows directly from knowing who has loved you, does love you, and will always love you. John would be the first to say, "The One who loves you the most and the best is God. He loves you so much He gave His only begotten Son, Jesus, to die for you so that you might be forgiven of your sins and live forever with Him in heaven!" (See *John 3:16.*)

THE ETERNAL WORD

1 In the beginning was the Word, and the Word was with God, and the Word was God. ²He was in the beginning with God. ³All things were made through Him, and without Him nothing was made that was made. ⁴In Him was life, and the life was the light of men. ⁵And the light shines in the darkness, and the darkness did not comprehend" it.

JOHN'S WITNESS: THE TRUE LIGHT

⁶There was a man sent from God, whose name *was* John. ⁷This man came for a witness, to bear witness of the Light, that all through him might believe. ⁸He was not that Light, but *was sent* to bear witness of that Light. ⁹That was the true Light which gives light to every man coming into the world."

¹⁰He was in the world, and the world was made through Him, and the world did not know Him. ¹¹He came to His own," and His own^b did not receive Him. ¹²But as many as received Him, to them He gave the right to become children of God, to those who believe in His name: ¹³who were born, not of blood, nor of the will of the flesh, nor of the will of man, but of God.

THE WORD BECOMES FLESH

¹⁴And the Word became flesh and dwelt among us, and we beheld His glory, the glory as of the only begotten of the Father, full of grace and truth.

¹⁵John bore witness of Him and cried out, saying, "This was He of whom I said, 'He who comes after me is preferred before me, for He was before me.' "

¹⁶And" of His fullness we have all received, and grace for grace. ¹⁷For the law was given through Moses, *but* grace and truth came through Jesus Christ. ¹⁸No one has seen God at any time. The only begotten Son," who is in the bosom of the Father, He has declared *Him.*

A VOICE IN THE WILDERNESS

¹⁹Now this is the testimony of John, when the Jews sent priests and Levites from Jerusalem to ask him, "Who are you?"

²⁰He confessed, and did not deny, but confessed, "I am not the Christ."

²¹And they asked him, "What then? Are you Elijah?"

He said, "I am not."

"Are you the Prophet?"

And he answered, "No."

²²Then they said to him, "Who are you, that we may give an answer to those who sent us? What do you say about yourself?"

²³He said: "I *am*

'The voice of one crying in the wilderness:
"Make straight the way of the Lord," ' "

as the prophet Isaiah said."

²⁴Now those who were sent were from the Pharisees. ²⁵And they asked him, saying, "Why then do you baptize if you are not the Christ, nor Elijah, nor the Prophet?"

²⁶John answered them, saying, "I baptize with water, but there stands One among you whom you do not know. ²⁷It is He who, coming after me, is preferred before me, whose sandal strap I am not worthy to loose."

1:5 "Or *overcome*   1:9 "Or *That was the true Light which, coming into the world, gives light to every man.*   1:11 "That is, His own things or domain ᵇThat is, His own people   1:16 "NU-Text reads *For.*
1:18 "NU-Text reads *only begotten God.*   1:23 "Isaiah 40:3

SCRIPTURE SOLUTIONS

[THYROID DISORDERS]

Do you gain weight or remain the same weight even though you are sticking to a diet and exercise program? Do you commonly experience unexplained fatigue, weakness, unwanted weight gain, dry skin, hair loss, depression, cold hands and feet, memory loss, or a hoarse voice? If so, you might be suffering from hypothyroidism.

Hypothyroidism is a condition in which the thyroid gland isn't producing enough thyroid hormones. Many people who are overweight and are unable to successfully lose weight, likely have hypothyroidism. The primary hormone produced by the thyroid is thyroxin, which is responsible for regulating the body's metabolism.

Iodine and the amino acid tyrosine are essential to healthy thyroid hormones. We usually get plenty of iodine in the salt we eat. Amino acids, such as tyrosine, are the important factors that make up protein. Choose soy products, chicken breast, turkey, and fish as your main sources of protein.

Certain vitamins are needed in moderate amounts for thyroid hormones. A good comprehensive multivitamin should provide adequate amounts of these nutrients. A regular exercise program is also needed to promote a healthy thyroid. Walk briskly three to four times a week for twenty minutes.

In addition, begin drinking at least two quarts of pure water every day.

²⁸These things were done in Bethabara^a beyond the Jordan, where John was baptizing.

THE LAMB OF GOD

²⁹The next day John saw Jesus coming toward him, and said, "Behold! The Lamb of God who takes away the sin of the world! ³⁰This is He of whom I said, 'After me comes a Man who is preferred before me,

for He was before me.' ³¹I did not know Him; but that He should be revealed to Israel, therefore I came baptizing with water."

³²And John bore witness, saying, "I saw the Spirit descending from heaven like a dove, and He remained upon Him. ³³I did not know Him, but He who sent me to baptize with water said to me, 'Upon whom you see the Spirit descending, and remaining on Him, this is He who baptizes with the Holy Spirit.' ³⁴And I have seen and testified that this is the Son of God."

THE FIRST DISCIPLES

³⁵Again, the next day, John stood with two of his disciples. ³⁶And looking at Jesus as He walked, he said, "Behold the Lamb of God!"

³⁷The two disciples heard him speak, and they followed Jesus. ³⁸Then Jesus turned, and seeing them following, said to them, "What do you seek?"

They said to Him, "Rabbi" (which is to say, when translated, Teacher), "where are You staying?"

³⁹He said to them, "Come and see." They came and saw where He was staying, and remained with Him that day (now it was about the tenth hour).

⁴⁰One of the two who heard John *speak,* and followed Him, was Andrew, Simon Peter's brother. ⁴¹He first found his own brother Simon, and said to him, "We have found the Messiah" (which is translated, the Christ). ⁴²And he brought him to Jesus.

Now when Jesus looked at him, He said, "You are Simon the son of Jonah.^a You shall be called Cephas" (which is translated, A Stone).

PHILIP AND NATHANAEL

⁴³The following day Jesus wanted to go to Galilee, and He found Philip and said to him, "Follow Me." ⁴⁴Now Philip was from Bethsaida, the city of Andrew and Peter. ⁴⁵Philip found Nathanael and said to him, "We have found Him of whom Moses in the law, and also the prophets, wrote—Jesus of Nazareth, the son of Joseph."

⁴⁶And Nathanael said to him, "Can anything good come out of Nazareth?"

Philip said to him, "Come and see."

⁴⁷Jesus saw Nathanael coming toward Him, and said of him, "Behold, an Israelite indeed, in whom is no deceit!"

⁴⁸Nathanael said to Him, "How do You know me?"

Jesus answered and said to him, "Before Philip called you, when you were under the fig tree, I saw you."

⁴⁹Nathanael answered and said to Him, "Rabbi, You are the Son of God! You are the King of Israel!"

⁵⁰Jesus answered and said to him, "Because I said to you, 'I saw you under the fig tree,' do you believe? You will see greater things than these." ⁵¹And He said to him, "Most assuredly, I say to you, hereafter^a you shall see heaven open, and the angels of God ascending and descending upon the Son of Man."

WATER TURNED TO WINE

2 On the third day there was a wedding in Cana of Galilee, and the mother of Jesus was there. ²Now both Jesus and His disciples were invited to the wedding. ³And when they ran out of wine, the mother of Jesus said to Him, "They have no wine."

1:28 ^aNU-Text and M-Text read *Bethany.*   1:42 ^aNU-Text reads *John.*   1:51 ^aNU-Text omits *hereafter.*

PREACHING HEALTH

⁴Jesus said to her, "Woman, what does your concern have to do with Me? My hour has not yet come."

⁵His mother said to the servants, "Whatever He says to you, do *it.*"

⁶Now there were set there six waterpots of stone, according to the manner of purification of the Jews, containing twenty or thirty gallons apiece. ⁷Jesus said to them, "Fill the waterpots with water." And they filled them up to the brim. ⁸And He said to them, "Draw *some* out now, and take *it* to the master of the feast." And they took *it.* ⁹When the master of the feast had tasted the water that was made wine, and did not know where it came from (but the servants who had drawn the water knew), the master of the feast called the bridegroom. ¹⁰And he said to him, "Every man at the beginning sets out the good wine, and when the *guests* have well drunk, then the inferior. You have kept the good wine until now!"

¹¹This beginning of signs Jesus did in Cana of Galilee, and manifested His glory; and His disciples believed in Him.

¹²After this He went down to Capernaum, He, His mother, His brothers, and His disciples; and they did not stay there many days.

JESUS CLEANSES THE TEMPLE

¹³Now the Passover of the Jews was at hand, and Jesus went up to Jerusalem. ¹⁴And He found in the temple those who sold oxen and sheep and doves, and the money changers doing business. ¹⁵When He had made a whip of cords, He drove them all out of the temple, with the sheep and the oxen, and poured out the changers' money and overturned the tables. ¹⁶And He said to those who sold doves, "Take these things away! Do not make My Father's house a house of merchandise!" ¹⁷Then His disciples remembered that it was written, "Zeal for Your house has eaten[a] Me up."[b]

¹⁸So the Jews answered and said to Him, "What sign do You show to us, since You do these things?"

¹⁹Jesus answered and said to them, "Destroy this temple, and in three days I will raise it up."

²⁰Then the Jews said, "It has taken forty-six years to build this temple, and will You raise it up in three days?"

²¹But He was speaking of the temple of His body. ²²Therefore, when He had risen from the dead, His disciples remembered that He had said this to them;[a] and they believed the Scripture and the word which Jesus had said.

THE DISCERNER OF HEARTS

²³Now when He was in Jerusalem at the Passover, during the feast, many believed in His name when they saw the signs which He did. ²⁴But Jesus did not commit Himself to them, because He knew all *men,* ²⁵and had no need that anyone should testify of man, for He knew what was in man.

THE NEW BIRTH

3 There was a man of the Pharisees named Nicodemus, a ruler of the Jews. ²This man came to Jesus by night and said to Him, "Rabbi, we know that You are a teacher come from God; for no one can do these signs that You do unless God is with him."

³Jesus answered and said to him, "Most assuredly, I say to you, unless one is born again, he cannot see the kingdom of God."

⁴Nicodemus said to Him, "How can a man be born when he is old? Can he enter a second time into his mother's womb and be born?"

⁵Jesus answered, "Most assuredly, I say to you, unless one is born of water and the Spirit, he cannot enter the kingdom of God. ⁶That which is born of the flesh is flesh, and that which is born of the Spirit is spirit. ⁷Do not marvel that I said to you, 'You must be born again.' ⁸The wind blows where it wishes, and you hear the sound of it, but cannot tell where it comes from and where it goes. So is everyone who is born of the Spirit."

⁹Nicodemus answered and said to Him, "How can these things be?"

¹⁰Jesus answered and said to him, "Are you the teacher of Israel, and do not know these things? ¹¹Most assuredly, I say to you, We speak what We know and testify what We have seen, and you do not receive Our witness. ¹²If I have told you earthly things and you do not believe, how will you believe if I tell you heavenly things? ¹³No one has ascended to heaven but He who came down from heaven, *that is,* the Son of Man who is in heaven.[a] ¹⁴And as Moses lifted up the serpent in the

[LEMONS]

FACT MORSELS

Eating lemons helps maintain the elasticity of skin. Vitamin C, plentiful in lemons and limes, aids in the manufacture of collagen. Be sure to brush your teeth immediately after eating lemons, however, since the acid can damage tooth enamel.

2:17 ᵃNU-Text and M-Text read *will eat.* ᵇPsalm 69:9 2:22 ᵃNU-Text and M-Text omit *to them.* 3:13 ᵃNU-Text omits *who is in heaven.*

ULTIMATE HEALTH RESOURCE • ULTIMATE HEALTH RESOURCE • ULTIMATE HEALTH RESOURCE

In the beginning, God created the heavens and the earth and populated the earth with broccoli, cauliflower, spinach, and many other green and yellow and red vegetables of all kinds so Man and Woman might live long and healthy lives. He gave grains for fiber and milk for the growth of children. Then using God's creations, Satan prompted the invention of luxury ice creams and oh-so-delectable donuts. And Satan asked, "You want chocolate with that?" Man said, "Yes!" and Woman added, "As long as you're at it, add some sprinkles." And they gained ten pounds. Satan smiled.

God created healthful yogurt so that Woman might keep the figure that Man found so fair. Satan brought forth processed white flour from the wheat and processed white sugar from the cane and combined them. And Woman increased four dress sizes.

God said, "Try my fresh green salad!" Satan added Thousand Island dressing, buttery croutons, and garlic toast on the side. And Man and Woman unfastened their belts and opted for elastic waistbands.

God said, "I have given you heart-healthy vegetables, and olive oil and wine vinegar to add flavor to them." Satan offered his own forms of hydrogenated oils and a method for deep-frying fish and chicken, and came up with a chicken fried steak so big it needed its own platter. And Man gained more weight and his cholesterol count went through the roof.

God brought forth the potato, naturally low in fat and brimming with nutrition. Satan peeled off the healthful skin of the potato, and sliced the starchy center into chips and strips and deep-fried them in the same oil that had been used for the fish and chicken. And Man and Woman gained even more.

God created a light, fluffy white cake and named it "Angel Food Cake." Satan countered with a chocolate cake and named it "Devil's Food."

God brought forth running shoes so His children might lose the extra pounds they had gained. Satan presented cable TV with a remote control so Man would not have to toil changing the channels while sitting on the sofa hour after hour. And Man and Woman laughed and cried before the flickering blue light of their television set and their fat became flab.

God gave lean beef so Man might consume fewer calories and still satisfy his appetite. Satan came up with the double-cheeseburger and said, "Surely you want a shake and some fries with that?" And Man replied, "Yes, and supersize them!" And Satan winked and asked, "Isn't this good?" And Man went into cardiac arrest.

God sighed and created quadruple bypass surgery. And Satan offered even higher health insurance premiums.

—Author unknown

wilderness, even so must the Son of Man be lifted up, [15]that whoever believes in Him should not perish but[a] have eternal life. [16]For God so loved the world that He gave His only begotten Son, that whoever believes in Him should not perish but have everlasting life. [17]For God did not send His Son into the world to condemn the world, but that the world through Him might be saved.

[18]"He who believes in Him is not condemned; but he who does not believe is condemned already, because he has not believed in the name of the only begotten Son of God. [19]And this is the condemnation, that the light has come into the world, and men loved darkness rather than light, because their deeds were evil. [20]For everyone practicing evil hates the light and does not come to the light, lest his deeds should be exposed. [21]But he who does the truth comes to the light, that his deeds may be clearly seen, that they have been done in God."

JOHN THE BAPTIST EXALTS CHRIST

[22]After these things Jesus and His disciples came into the land of Judea, and there He remained with them and baptized. [23]Now John also was baptizing in Aenon near Salim, because there was much water there. And they came and were baptized. [24]For John had not yet been thrown into prison.

[25]Then there arose a dispute between *some* of John's disciples and the Jews about purification. [26]And they came to John and said to him, "Rabbi, He who was with you beyond the Jordan, to whom you have testified—behold, He is baptizing, and all are coming to Him!"

[27]John answered and said, "A man can receive nothing unless it has been given to him from heaven. [28]You yourselves bear me witness, that I said, 'I am not the Christ,' but, 'I have been sent before Him.' [29]He who has the bride is the bridegroom; but the friend of the bridegroom, who stands and hears him, rejoices greatly because of the bridegroom's voice. Therefore this joy of mine is fulfilled. [30]He must increase, but I *must* decrease. [31]He who comes from above is above all; he who is of the earth is earthly and speaks of the earth. He who comes from heaven is above all. [32]And what He has seen and heard, that He testifies; and no one receives His testimony. [33]He who has received His testimony has certified that

3:15 aNU-Text omits *not perish but.*

God is true. ³⁴For He whom God has sent speaks the words of God, for God does not give the Spirit by measure. ³⁵The Father loves the Son, and has given all things into His hand. ³⁶He who believes in the Son has everlasting life; and he who does not believe the Son shall not see life, but the wrath of God abides on him."

A SAMARITAN WOMAN MEETS HER MESSIAH

4 Therefore, when the Lord knew that the Pharisees had heard that Jesus made and baptized more disciples than John ²(though Jesus Himself did not baptize, but His disciples), ³He left Judea and departed again to Galilee. ⁴But He needed to go through Samaria.

WISE CHOICES

Choose skim or nonfat milk over whole milk products.

Whole milk and whole milk products are high in fat content and are not for adults. Skim or nonfat milk and milk products may be. Researchers have found that skim milk seems to lower the liver's output of LDL (bad) cholesterol. The calcium in skim milk may also have beneficial effects in controlling high blood pressure.

GODLY & GOODLOOKIN'

Natural "Peels" for Wrinkles

Alpha Hydroxy Acid (AHA) products have flooded the market in the last decade. They work as a natural peel, similar in results over the long run but more gentle than the chemical peels used by many dermatologists. They have an advantage over the stronger chemical peels in that they do not result in extreme sun sensitivity. They are an effective way for many people to treat wrinkles.

AHA removes dead skin by loosening the intracellular "cement" between old and new skin cells, and dissolving dead surface cells. Several kinds of AHA's are available, especially: *citric acid* from oranges, lemons, limes; *glycolic acid* from sugar cane; *lactic acid* from milk; *malic acid* from apples; and *tartaric acid* from wine grapes.

Glycolic acid has the smallest molecules and is very effective in exfoliating skin. Products with lactic acid are more moisturizing. If you have sensitive or fair skin, use these products with great caution. Start with a product that has a low percentage of AHA (2–4 percent) and work up to higher percentage levels.

---

⁵So He came to a city of Samaria which is called Sychar, near the plot of ground that Jacob gave to his son Joseph. ⁶Now Jacob's well was there. Jesus therefore, being wearied from *His* journey, sat thus by the well. It was about the sixth hour.

⁷A woman of Samaria came to draw water. Jesus said to her, "Give Me a drink." ⁸For His disciples had gone away into the city to buy food.

⁹Then the woman of Samaria said to Him, "How is it that You, being a Jew, ask a drink from me, a Samaritan woman?" For Jews have no dealings with Samaritans.

¹⁰Jesus answered and said to her, "If you knew the gift of God, and who it is who says to you, 'Give Me a drink,' you would have asked Him, and He would have given you living water."

¹¹The woman said to Him, "Sir, You have nothing to draw with, and the well is deep. Where then do You get that living water? ¹²Are You greater than our father Jacob, who gave us the well, and drank from it himself, as well as his sons and his livestock?"

¹³Jesus answered and said to her, "Whoever drinks of this water will thirst again, ¹⁴but whoever drinks of the water that I shall give him will never thirst. But the water that I shall give him will become in him a fountain of water springing up into everlasting life."

¹⁵The woman said to Him, "Sir, give me this water, that I may not thirst, nor come here to draw."

¹⁶Jesus said to her, "Go, call your husband, and come here."

¹⁷The woman answered and said, "I have no husband."

Jesus said to her, "You have well said, 'I have no husband,' ¹⁸for you have had five husbands, and the one whom you now have is not your husband; in that you spoke truly."

¹⁹The woman said to Him, "Sir, I perceive that You are a prophet. ²⁰Our fathers worshiped

Olive Oil

Bible Health + Food Facts

One tablespoon of olive oil has 119 calories and as much as 30 mg of vitamin E. Olive oil is 56–82 percent monounsaturated fatty acids (oleic), and 3.5–20 percent polyunsaturated unfatty acids (linoleic). It is among the most healthful oils a person can consume.

on this mountain, and you *Jews* say that in Jerusalem is the place where one ought to worship."

²¹Jesus said to her, "Woman, believe Me, the hour is coming when you will neither on this mountain, nor in Jerusalem, worship the Father. ²²You worship what you do not know; we know what we worship, for salvation is of the Jews. ²³But the hour is coming, and now is, when the true worshipers will worship the Father in spirit and truth; for the Father is seeking such to worship Him. ²⁴God *is* Spirit, and those who worship Him must worship in spirit and truth."

²⁵The woman said to Him, "I know that Messiah is coming" (who is called Christ). "When He comes, He will tell us all things."

²⁶Jesus said to her, "I who speak to you am *He.*"

THE WHITENED HARVEST

²⁷And at this *point* His disciples came, and they marveled that He talked with a woman; yet no one said, "What do You seek?" or, "Why are You talking with her?"

²⁸The woman then left her waterpot, went her way into the city, and said to the men, ²⁹"Come, see a Man who told me all things that I ever did. Could this be the Christ?" ³⁰Then they went out of the city and came to Him.

³¹In the meantime His disciples urged Him, saying, "Rabbi, eat."

³²But He said to them, "I have food to eat of which you do not know."

³³Therefore the disciples said to one another, "Has anyone brought Him *anything* to eat?"

³⁴Jesus said to them, "My food is to do the will of Him who sent Me, and to finish His work. ³⁵Do you not say, 'There are still four months and *then* comes the harvest'? Behold, I say to you, lift up your eyes and look at the fields, for they are already white for harvest! ³⁶And he who reaps receives wages, and gathers fruit for eternal life, that both he who sows and he who reaps may rejoice together. ³⁷For in this the saying is true: 'One sows and another reaps.' ³⁸I sent you to reap that for which you have not labored; others have labored, and you have entered into their labors."

THE SAVIOR OF THE WORLD

³⁹And many of the Samaritans of that city believed in Him because of the word of the woman who testified, "He told me all that I *ever* did." ⁴⁰So when the Samaritans had come to Him, they urged Him to stay with them; and He stayed there two days. ⁴¹And many more believed because of His own word.

⁴²Then they said to the woman, "Now we believe, not because of what you said, for we ourselves have heard *Him* and we know that this is indeed the Christ,ᵃ the Savior of the world."

WELCOME AT GALILEE

⁴³Now after the two days He departed from there and went to Galilee. ⁴⁴For Jesus Himself testified that a prophet has no honor in his own country. ⁴⁵So when He came to Galilee, the Galileans received Him, having seen all the things He did in Jerusalem at the feast; for they also had gone to the feast.

A NOBLEMAN'S SON HEALED

⁴⁶So Jesus came again to Cana of Galilee where He had made the water wine. And there was a certain nobleman whose son was sick at Capernaum. ⁴⁷When he heard that Jesus had come out of Judea into Galilee, he went to Him and implored Him to come down and heal his son, for he was at the point of death. ⁴⁸Then Jesus said to him, "Unless you *people* see signs and wonders, you will by no means believe."

⁴⁹The nobleman said to Him, "Sir, come down before my child dies!"

⁵⁰Jesus said to him, "Go your way; your son lives." So the man believed the word that Jesus spoke to him, and he went his way. ⁵¹And as he was now going down, his servants met him and told *him,* saying, "Your son lives!"

⁵²Then he inquired of them the hour when he got better. And they said to him, "Yesterday at the seventh hour the fever left him." ⁵³So the father knew that *it was* at the same hour in which Jesus said to him, "Your son lives." And he himself believed, and his whole household.

⁵⁴This again *is* the second sign Jesus did when He had come out of Judea into Galilee.

Q Who was described as the most handsome man in all of Israel?

A Absalom *(2 Samuel 14:25).*

A MAN HEALED AT THE POOL OF BETHESDA

5 After this there was a feast of the Jews, and Jesus went up to Jerusalem. ²Now there is in Jerusalem by the Sheep *Gate* a pool, which is called in Hebrew, Bethesda,ᵃ having five porches. ³In these lay a great multitude of sick people, blind, lame, paralyzed,

4:42 ᵃNU-Text omits *the Christ.* 5:2 ᵃNU-Text reads *Bethzatha.*

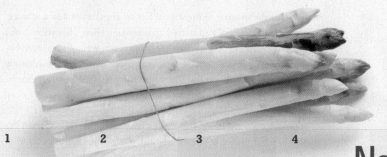

April

| 1 | 2 | 3 | 4 | 5 | 6 | 7 |

Now Is the Time To...

☐ Begin planning your summer vacation. Mark out a time for the renewal of your health, family relationships, and your perspective on life. A key tip for planning a great vacation: choose to spend a few days in the least stressful manner possible! ☐ Scout out summer activities and camps for your children. Get your kids "outside" and "moving"! The more physical activity the better!

Let's Celebrate

| 8 | 9 | 10 | 11 | 12 | 13 | 14 |

☐ **Palm Sunday.** The Sunday before Easter marks the beginning of "Holy Week," which generally falls in April but sometimes comes in March. Palm Sunday celebrates the day that Jesus entered Jerusalem and was hailed as a triumphant king with the waving of palm branches and shouts of "Hosanna!" ☐ **Maundy Thursday.** This day is a time to remember what Jesus said and did at the Last Supper—before His arrest and crucifixion. Consider having a family dinner focused on reading and discussing what Jesus said in John 14–17. ☐ **Good Friday.** This day should be solemn and reflective—the way to mark Good Friday is with fasting rather than feasting. Nevertheless, it is a day worth celebrating for a Christian. It is the day that Jesus took on the sins of the world and made the supreme sacrifice so that all who believe in Him might experience forgiveness and eternal life.

| 15 | 16 | 17 | 18 | 19 | 20 | 21 |

☐ **Easter!** Christ's resurrection should be a joyous celebration. Do something special—perhaps attend a sunrise service or a passion play.

Seasonal Tips

☐ Spring clean! This is not only therapeutic for the soul, but can be healthful for the body as well—you likely will be clearing away a number of allergens from your home. Consider buying a water-purification system and air purifiers if you don't already have them. Sort closets and give away unused items. ☐ Check for holes in the screens over your windows or doors. ☐ Check your outdoor grill. Now is the time to make sure your grill is clean and in good working order.

| 22 | 23 | 24 | 25 | 26 | 27 | 28 |

In the Garden

☐ Overseed your lawn.

| 29 | 30 |

Table Fresh

☐ Asparagus and April go together. Try grilling this spring vegetable, basting it with a small amount of fat-free Italian dressing. Or, try marinating it with a little olive oil, white vinegar, garlic, and a teaspoon of crushed red pepper. ☐ Instead of cooking a ham for Easter, consider grilling burgers made from ground lamb. Serve with pineapple salsa on the side.

Gardening for Health

Plant a Biblical Herb Garden

Both the medicinal and culinary properties of herbs have been known for thousands of years. Herbs are also planted for their ornamental beauty. You may want to consider planting a section of your yard or garden as a biblical herb garden. Or, you may want to plant clusters of herbs in containers or pots that you place on a deck, patio, or in a sunny area of your kitchen.

Fifteen herbs are mentioned specifically in the Bible. Herbs called "tithing herbs" from Matthew 23:23 were cumin, dill, mint, and rue. Gums and resins from herbs were used for religious purposes, such as frankincense and myrrh, and some herbs are mentioned symbolically (such as wormwood referring to sorrow or bitterness). The Bible herbs most readily grown in American herb gardens are listed below with Bible references and a brief description about their use.

☐ **Aloes** (John 19:39)   Sap from the leaves is added to other spices to make anointing oil. (See Matthew 26:7.) This is called "aloes" in the Bible (Psalms 45:8) as well as "fragrant oil" (Mark 14:4, 5).

☐ **Coriander** (Exodus 16:31)   One of the most ancient herbs, used for seasoning and medicine. It is called "coriander seed" in the Bible (Numbers 11:7).

☐ **Cumin** (Isaiah 28:25–27)   This herb has been used since the days of the prophet Isaiah. It is used in making unleavened bread and for digestive disorders. It is spelled "cummin" in the Book of Isaiah and in Matthew 23:23.

☐ **Dill** (Matthew 23:23)   This herb is called "anise" in the Bible, but Bible scholars agree that it is what we know as dill. It has been used for centuries for flavoring and in medicine.

☐ **Fennel** (Isaiah 28:25–27)   The aromatic hot-tasting seeds of this herb were an Eastern substitution for black pepper. The oil from the seeds increase appetite and saliva flow. It is called "black cummin" in the Bible.

☐ **Marjoram** (Exodus 12:21, 22; Numbers 19:6, 18; Psalms 51:7)   Bible scholars believe the herb called "hyssop" is actually Syrian marjoram, a bushy herb widely used by ancient peoples to cleanse and purify.   CONT. NEXT PAGE>>>

waiting for the moving of the water. ⁴For an angel went down at a certain time into the pool and stirred up the water; then whoever stepped in first, after the stirring of the water, was made well of whatever disease he had.ᵃ ⁵Now a certain man was there who had an infirmity thirty-eight years. ⁶When Jesus saw him lying there, and knew that he already had been *in that condition* a long time, He said to him, "Do you want to be made well?"

⁷The sick man answered Him, "Sir, I have no man to put me into the pool when the water is stirred up; but while I am coming, another steps down before me."

⁸Jesus said to him, "Rise, take up your bed and walk." ⁹And immediately the man was made well, took up his bed, and walked.

And that day was the Sabbath. ¹⁰The Jews therefore said to him who was cured, "It is the Sabbath; it is not lawful for you to carry your bed."

¹¹He answered them, "He who made me well said to me, 'Take up your bed and walk.' "

¹²Then they asked him, "Who is the Man who said to you, 'Take up your bed and walk'?" ¹³But the one who was healed did not know who it was, for Jesus had withdrawn, a multitude being in *that* place. ¹⁴Afterward Jesus found him in the temple, and said to him, "See, you have been made well. Sin no more, lest a worse thing come upon you."

¹⁵The man departed and told the Jews that it was Jesus who had made him well.

HONOR THE FATHER AND THE SON

¹⁶For this reason the Jews persecuted Jesus, and sought to kill Him,ᵃ because He had done these things on the Sabbath. ¹⁷But Jesus answered them, "My Father has been working until now, and I have been working."

¹⁸Therefore the Jews sought all the more to kill Him, because He not only broke the Sabbath, but also said that God was His Father, making Himself equal with God. ¹⁹Then Jesus answered and said to them, "Most assuredly, I say to you, the Son can do nothing of Himself, but what He sees the Father do; for whatever He does, the Son also does in like manner. ²⁰For the Father loves the Son, and shows Him all things that He Himself does; and He will show Him greater works than these, that you may marvel. ²¹For as the Father raises the dead and gives life to *them,* even so the Son gives life to whom He will. ²²For the Father judges no one, but has committed all judgment to the Son, ²³that all should honor the Son just as they honor the Father. He who does not honor the Son does not honor the Father who sent Him.

LIFE AND JUDGMENT ARE THROUGH THE SON

²⁴"Most assuredly, I say to you, he who hears My word and believes in Him who sent Me has everlasting life, and shall not come into judgment, but has passed from death into life. ²⁵Most assuredly, I say to you, the hour is coming, and now is, when the dead will hear the voice of the Son of God; and those who hear will live. ²⁶For as the Father has life in Himself, so He has granted the Son to have life in Himself, ²⁷and has given Him authority to execute judgment also, because He is the Son of Man. ²⁸Do not marvel at this; for the hour is coming in which all who are in the graves will hear His voice ²⁹and come forth—those

5:4 ᵃNU-Text omits *waiting for the moving of the water* at the end of verse 3, and all of verse 4.   5:16 ᵃNU-Text omits *and sought to kill Him.*

☐ **Mint** (Luke 11:42)   This was probably "horsemint," which was used in cooking, medicine, and worship rituals. It was sometimes scattered in synagogues to reduce bad odors.

☐ **Rue** (Luke 11:42)   This has been called the "herb of grace" because it was scattered in buildings for protection against disease. It has been valued for centuries for its strong unusual taste and medicinal properties.

☐ **Sage** (Exodus 37:17, 18)   Sage was used in Bible times as a cure for many ailments and was cultivated for its fragrant oil. The blossoms are similar to the designs on the golden lampstand in the temple and sage is called *lampstand* in the Bible.

who have done good, to the resurrection of life, and those who have done evil, to the resurrection of condemnation. ³⁰I can of Myself do nothing. As I hear, I judge; and My judgment is righteous, because I do not seek My own will but the will of the Father who sent Me.

THE FOURFOLD WITNESS

³¹"If I bear witness of Myself, My witness is not true. ³²There is another who bears witness of Me, and I know that the witness which He witnesses of Me is true. ³³You have sent to John, and he has borne witness to the truth. ³⁴Yet I do not receive testimony from man, but I say these things that you may be saved. ³⁵He was the burning and shining lamp, and you were willing for a time to rejoice in his light. ³⁶But I have a greater witness than John's; for the works which the Father has given Me to finish—the very works that I do—bear witness of Me, that the Father has sent Me. ³⁷And the Father Himself, who sent Me, has testified of Me. You have neither heard His voice at any time, nor seen His form. ³⁸But you do not have His word abiding in you, because whom He sent, Him you do not believe. ³⁹You search the Scriptures, for in them you think you have eternal life; and these are they which testify of Me. ⁴⁰But you are not willing to come to Me that you may have life.

⁴¹"I do not receive honor from men. ⁴²But I know you, that you do not have the love of God in you. ⁴³I have come in My Father's name, and you do not receive Me; if another comes in his own name, him you will receive. ⁴⁴How can you believe, who receive honor from one another, and do not seek the honor that *comes* from the only God? ⁴⁵Do not think that I shall accuse you to the Father; there is *one* who accuses you—Moses, in whom you trust. ⁴⁶For if you believed Moses, you would believe Me; for he wrote about Me. ⁴⁷But if you do not believe his writings, how will you believe My words?"

FEEDING THE FIVE THOUSAND

6 After these things Jesus went over the Sea of Galilee, which is *the Sea* of Tiberias. ²Then a great multitude followed Him, because they saw His signs which He performed on those who were diseased. ³And Jesus went up on the mountain, and there He sat with His disciples.

⁴Now the Passover, a feast of the Jews, was near. ⁵Then Jesus lifted up *His* eyes, and seeing a great multitude coming toward Him, He said to Philip, "Where shall we buy bread, that these may eat?" ⁶But this He said to test him, for He Himself knew what He would do.

⁷Philip answered Him, "Two hundred denarii worth of bread is not sufficient for them, that every one of them may have a little."

⁸One of His disciples, Andrew, Simon Peter's brother, said to Him, ⁹"There is a lad here who has five barley loaves and two small fish, but what are they among so many?"

¹⁰Then Jesus said, "Make the people sit down." Now there was much grass in the place. So the men sat down, in number about five thousand. ¹¹And Jesus took the loaves, and when He had given thanks He distributed *them* to the disciples, and the disciplesᵃ to those sitting down; and likewise of the fish, as much as they wanted. ¹²So when they were filled, He said to His disciples, "Gather up the fragments that remain, so that nothing is lost." ¹³Therefore they gathered *them* up, and filled twelve baskets with the fragments of the five barley loaves which were left over by those who had eaten. ¹⁴Then those men, when they had seen the sign that Jesus did, said, "This is truly the Prophet who is to come into the world."

JESUS WALKS ON THE SEA

¹⁵Therefore when Jesus perceived that they were about to come and take Him by force to make Him king, He departed again to the mountain by Himself alone.

¹⁶Now when evening came, His disciples went down to the sea, ¹⁷got into the boat, and went over the sea toward Capernaum. And it was already dark, and Jesus had not come to them. ¹⁸Then the sea arose because a great wind was blowing. ¹⁹So when they had rowed about three or four miles,ᵃ they saw Jesus walking on the sea and drawing near the

> **(John 6:9)**

The Blessing of Barley Bread. The bread that Jesus broke and multiplied was barley bread. Barley bread was the bread of the poor. Wheat was worth three times what barley was worth in Jesus' time. Barley, however, is very high in nutritional value. It is one of three balanced starches that are rich in complex carbohydrates and give the body a steady flow of energy. (Rice and potatoes are the other two.) Unfortunately, barley bread is virtually nonexistent today—you'd have to make it yourself from barley grain from a health-food store. Perhaps it's time to "multiply" once again the use of barley bread! It certainly is a whole grain worth blessing.

INSIGHTS | **INTO THE WORD**

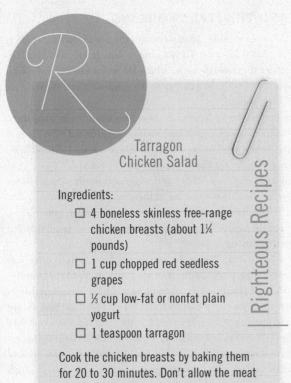

Tarragon Chicken Salad

Righteous Recipes

Ingredients:

- ☐ 4 boneless skinless free-range chicken breasts (about 1¼ pounds)
- ☐ 1 cup chopped red seedless grapes
- ☐ ⅓ cup low-fat or nonfat plain yogurt
- ☐ 1 teaspoon tarragon

Cook the chicken breasts by baking them for 20 to 30 minutes. Don't allow the meat to be overcooked and to become dry. Chop the meat into bite-size pieces. Combine the chicken, grapes, yogurt, and tarragon in a bowl and mix well. Cover and refrigerate until chilled.

Serve with lettuce and sliced tomatoes. Or, you may want to make a pita-bread sandwich with the chicken mixture and lettuce.

Yield: 6 servings

boat; and they were afraid. ²⁰But He said to them, "It is I; do not be afraid." ²¹Then they willingly received Him into the boat, and immediately the boat was at the land where they were going.

THE BREAD FROM HEAVEN

²²On the following day, when the people who were standing on the other side of the sea saw that there was no other boat there, except that one which His disciples had entered,ᵃ and that Jesus had not entered the boat with His disciples, but His disciples had gone away alone— ²³however, other boats came from Tiberias, near the place where they ate bread after the Lord had given thanks— ²⁴when the people therefore saw that Jesus was not there, nor His disciples, they also got into boats and came to Capernaum, seeking Jesus. ²⁵And when they found Him on the other side of the sea, they said to Him, "Rabbi, when did You come here?"

²⁶Jesus answered them and said, "Most assuredly, I say to you, you seek Me, not because you saw the signs, but because you ate of the loaves and were filled. ²⁷Do not labor for the food which perishes, but for the food which endures to everlasting life, which the Son of Man will give you, because God the Father has set His seal on Him."

²⁸Then they said to Him, "What shall we do, that we may work the works of God?"

²⁹Jesus answered and said to them, "This is the work of God, that you believe in Him whom He sent."

³⁰Therefore they said to Him, "What sign will You perform then, that we may see it and believe You? What work will You do? ³¹Our fathers ate the manna in the desert; as it is written, 'He gave them bread from heaven to eat.' "ᵃ

³²Then Jesus said to them, "Most assuredly, I say to you, Moses did not give you the bread from heaven, but My Father gives you the true bread from heaven. ³³For the bread of God is He who comes down from heaven and gives life to the world."

³⁴Then they said to Him, "Lord, give us this bread always."

³⁵And Jesus said to them, "I am the bread of life. He who comes to Me shall never hunger, and he who believes in Me shall never thirst. ³⁶But I said to you that you have seen Me and yet do not believe. ³⁷All that the Father gives Me will come to Me, and the one who comes to Me I will by no means cast out. ³⁸For I have come down from heaven, not to do My own will, but the will of Him who sent Me. ³⁹This is the will of the Father who sent Me, that of all He has given Me I should lose nothing, but should raise it up at the last day. ⁴⁰And this is the will of Him who sent Me, that everyone who sees the Son and believes in Him may have everlasting life; and I will raise him up at the last day."

REJECTED BY HIS OWN

⁴¹The Jews then complained about Him, because He said, "I am the bread which came down from heaven." ⁴²And they said, "Is not this Jesus, the son of Joseph, whose father and mother we know? How is it then that He says, 'I have come down from heaven'?"

⁴³Jesus therefore answered and said to them, "Do not murmur among yourselves. ⁴⁴No one can come to Me unless the Father who sent Me draws him; and I will raise him up at the last day. ⁴⁵It is written in the prophets, 'And they shall all be taught by God.'ᵃ Therefore everyone who has heard and learnedᵇ from the Father comes to Me. ⁴⁶Not that anyone has seen the Father, except He who is from God; He has seen the Father. ⁴⁷Most assuredly, I say to you, he who believes in Meᵃ has everlasting life. ⁴⁸I am the bread of life. ⁴⁹Your fathers ate the manna in the wilderness, and are dead. ⁵⁰This is the bread which comes down from heaven, that one may eat of it and not die. ⁵¹I am the living bread which came down from heaven. If anyone eats of this bread, he will live forever; and the bread that I shall give is My flesh, which I shall give for the life of the world."

⁵²The Jews therefore quarreled among themselves, saying, "How can this Man give us His flesh to eat?"

⁵³Then Jesus said to them, "Most assuredly, I say to you, unless you eat the flesh of the Son of Man and drink His blood, you have no life in you. ⁵⁴Whoever eats My flesh and drinks My blood has eternal life, and I will raise him up at the last day. ⁵⁵For My flesh is food indeed,ᵃ and My blood is drink indeed. ⁵⁶He who eats My flesh and drinks My

---

6:22 ᵃNU-Text omits *that* and *which His disciples had entered.*   6:31 ᵃExodus 16:4; Nehemiah 9:15; Psalm 78:24   6:45 ᵃIsaiah 54:13   ᵇM-Text reads *hears and has learned.*   6:47 ᵃNU-Text omits *in Me.*
6:55 ᵃNU-Text reads *true food* and *true drink.*

blood abides in Me, and I in him. ⁵⁷As the living Father sent Me, and I live because of the Father, so he who feeds on Me will live because of Me. ⁵⁸This is the bread which came down from heaven—not as your fathers ate the manna, and are dead. He who eats this bread will live forever."

⁵⁹These things He said in the synagogue as He taught in Capernaum.

MANY DISCIPLES TURN AWAY

⁶⁰Therefore many of His disciples, when they heard *this*, said, "This is a hard saying; who can understand it?"

⁶¹When Jesus knew in Himself that His disciples complained about this, He said to them, "Does this offend you? ⁶²*What* then if you should see the Son of Man ascend where He was before? ⁶³It is the Spirit who gives life; the flesh profits nothing. The words that I speak to you are spirit, and *they* are life. ⁶⁴But there are some of you who do not believe." For Jesus knew from the beginning who they were who did not believe, and who would betray Him. ⁶⁵And He said, "Therefore I have said to you that no one can come to Me unless it has been granted to him by My Father."

⁶⁶From that *time* many of His disciples went back and walked with Him no more. ⁶⁷Then Jesus said to the twelve, "Do you also want to go away?"

⁶⁸But Simon Peter answered Him, "Lord, to whom shall we go? You have the words of eternal life. ⁶⁹Also we have come to believe and know that You are the Christ, the Son of the living God."ᵃ

⁷⁰Jesus answered them, "Did I not choose you, the twelve, and one of you is a devil?" ⁷¹He spoke of Judas Iscariot, *the son* of Simon, for it was he who would betray Him, being one of the twelve.

JESUS' BROTHERS DISBELIEVE

7 After these things Jesus walked in Galilee; for He did not want to walk in Judea, because the Jewsᵃ sought to kill Him. ²Now the Jews' Feast of Tabernacles was at hand. ³His brothers therefore said to Him, "Depart from here and go into Judea, that Your disciples also may see the works that You are doing. ⁴For no one does anything in secret while he himself seeks to be known openly. If You do these things, show Yourself to the world." ⁵For even His brothers did not believe in Him.

⁶Then Jesus said to them, "My time has not yet come, but your time is always ready. ⁷The world cannot hate you, but it hates Me because I testify of it that its works are evil. ⁸You go up to this feast. I am not yetᵃ going up to this feast, for My time has not yet fully come." ⁹When He had said these things to them, He remained in Galilee.

THE HEAVENLY SCHOLAR

¹⁰But when His brothers had gone up, then He also went up to the feast, not openly, but as it were in secret. ¹¹Then the Jews sought Him at the feast, and said, "Where is He?" ¹²And there was much complaining among the people concerning Him. Some said, "He is good"; others said, "No, on the contrary, He deceives the people." ¹³However, no one spoke openly of Him for fear of the Jews.

¹⁴Now about the middle of the feast Jesus went up into the temple and taught. ¹⁵And the Jews marveled, saying, "How does this Man know letters, having never studied?"

¹⁶Jesusᵃ answered them and said, "My doctrine is not Mine, but His who sent Me. ¹⁷If anyone wills to do His will, he shall know concerning the doctrine, whether it is from God or *whether* I speak on My own *authority*. ¹⁸He who speaks from himself seeks his own glory; but He who seeks the glory of the One who sent Him is true, and no unrighteousness is in Him. ¹⁹Did not Moses give you the law, yet none of you keeps the law? Why do you seek to kill Me?"

²⁰The people answered and said, "You have a demon. Who is seeking to kill You?"

²¹Jesus answered and said to them, "I did one work, and you all marvel. ²²Moses therefore gave you circumcision (not that it is from Moses, but from the fathers), and you circumcise a man on the Sabbath. ²³If a man receives circumcision on the Sabbath, so that the law of Moses should not be broken, are you angry with Me because I made a man completely well on the Sabbath? ²⁴Do not judge according to appearance, but judge with righteous judgment."

COULD THIS BE THE CHRIST?

²⁵Now some of them from Jerusalem said, "Is this not He whom they seek to kill? ²⁶But look! He speaks boldly, and they say nothing to Him. Do the rulers know indeed that this is trulyᵃ the Christ? ²⁷However, we know where this Man is from; but when the Christ comes, no one knows where He is from."

²⁸Then Jesus cried out, as He taught in the temple, saying, "You

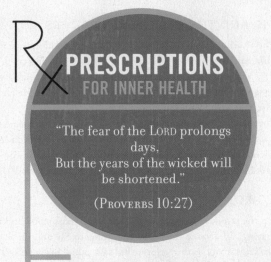

R℞ PRESCRIPTIONS FOR INNER HEALTH

"The fear of the LORD prolongs days,
But the years of the wicked will be shortened."
(PROVERBS 10:27)

The righteous live longer than the wicked, as a whole, because the lifestyle of the person who seeks to do what is right in God's eyes leads to peace, security, and less anxiety. These contribute to health and longevity. Those who are involved in crime are much more prone to a violent demise earlier in life!

6:69 ᵃNU-Text reads *You are the Holy One of God.*   7:1 ᵃThat is, the ruling authorities   7:8 ᵃNU-Text omits *yet.*   7:16 ᵃNU-Text and M-Text read *So Jesus.*   7:26 ᵃNU-Text omits *truly.*

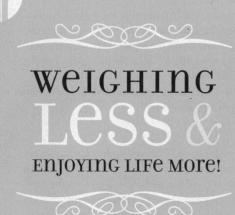

WEIGHING Less & ENJOYING LIFE MORE!

[Frozen Grapes—a Great Snack!]

A delicious snack or dessert item: frozen grapes! Simply wash and then freeze a bunch of grapes in a baggie or two. You may want to remove the stems from the grapes. A handful of frozen grapes is like eating bits of grape-flavored Popsicles. Be sure to choose seedless grapes. If you have frozen grapes in the freezer, you may be less tempted to reach for the ice-cream as a late-evening snack. The grapes will be just as satisfying in their sweetness, and they have a lot fewer calories!

both know Me, and you know where I am from; and I have not come of Myself, but He who sent Me is true, whom you do not know. ²⁹But[ᵃ] I know Him, for I am from Him, and He sent Me."

³⁰Therefore they sought to take Him; but no one laid a hand on Him, because His hour had not yet come. ³¹And many of the people believed in Him, and said, "When the Christ comes, will He do more signs than these which this *Man* has done?"

JESUS AND THE RELIGIOUS LEADERS

³²The Pharisees heard the crowd murmuring these things concerning Him, and the Pharisees and the chief priests sent officers to take Him. ³³Then Jesus said to them,[ᵃ] "I shall be with you a little while longer, and *then* I go to Him who sent Me. ³⁴You will seek Me and not find *Me,* and where I am you cannot come."

³⁵Then the Jews said among themselves, "Where does He intend to go that we shall not find Him? Does He intend to go to the Dispersion among the Greeks and teach the Greeks? ³⁶What is this thing that He said, 'You will seek Me and not find Me, and where I am you cannot come'?"

THE PROMISE OF THE HOLY SPIRIT

³⁷On the last day, that great *day* of the feast, Jesus stood and cried out, saying, "If anyone thirsts, let him come to Me and drink. ³⁸He who believes in Me, as the Scripture has said, out of his heart will flow rivers of living water." ³⁹But this He spoke concerning the Spirit, whom those believing[ᵃ] in Him would receive; for the Holy[ᵇ] Spirit was not yet *given,* because Jesus was not yet glorified.

WHO IS HE?

⁴⁰Therefore many[ᵃ] from the crowd, when they heard this saying, said, "Truly this is the Prophet." ⁴¹Others said, "This is the Christ."

But some said, "Will the Christ come out of Galilee? ⁴²Has not the Scripture said that the Christ comes from the seed of David and from the town of Bethlehem, where David was?" ⁴³So there was a division

among the people because of Him. ⁴⁴Now some of them wanted to take Him, but no one laid hands on Him.

REJECTED BY THE AUTHORITIES

⁴⁵Then the officers came to the chief priests and Pharisees, who said to them, "Why have you not brought Him?"

⁴⁶The officers answered, "No man ever spoke like this Man!"

⁴⁷Then the Pharisees answered them, "Are you also deceived? ⁴⁸Have any of the rulers or the Pharisees believed in Him? ⁴⁹But this crowd that does not know the law is accursed."

⁵⁰Nicodemus (he who came to Jesus by night,[ᵃ] being one of them) said to them, ⁵¹"Does our law judge a man before it hears him and knows what he is doing?"

⁵²They answered and said to him, "Are you also from Galilee? Search and look, for no prophet has arisen[ᵃ] out of Galilee."

AN ADULTERESS FACES THE LIGHT OF THE WORLD

⁵³And everyone went to his *own* house.[ᵃ]

8 But Jesus went to the Mount of Olives. ²Now early[ᵃ] in the morning He came again into the temple, and all the people came to Him; and He sat down and taught them. ³Then the scribes and Pharisees brought to Him a woman caught in adultery. And when they had set her in the midst, ⁴they said to Him, "Teacher, this woman was caught[ᵃ] in adultery, in the very act. ⁵Now Moses, in the law, commanded[ᵃ] us that such should be stoned.[ᵇ] But what do You say?"[ᶜ] ⁶This they said, testing Him, that they might have *something* of which to accuse Him. But Jesus stooped down and wrote on the ground with *His* finger, as though He did not hear.[ᵃ]

⁷So when they continued asking Him, He raised Himself up[ᵃ] and said to them, "He who is without sin among you, let him throw a stone at her first." ⁸And again He stooped down and wrote on the ground. ⁹Then those who heard *it,* being convicted by *their* conscience,[ᵃ] went out one by

one, beginning with the oldest *even* to the last. And Jesus was left alone, and the woman standing in the midst. ¹⁰When Jesus had raised Himself up and saw no one but the woman, He said to her,ᵃ "Woman, where are those accusers of yours?ᵇ Has no one condemned you?"

"She said, "No one, Lord."

And Jesus said to her, "Neither do I condemn you; go andᵃ sin no more."

¹²Then Jesus spoke to them again, saying, "I am the light of the world. He who follows Me shall not walk in darkness, but have the light of life."

JESUS DEFENDS HIS SELF-WITNESS

¹³The Pharisees therefore said to Him, "You bear witness of Yourself; Your witness is not true."

¹⁴Jesus answered and said to them, "Even if I bear witness of Myself, My witness is true, for I know where I came from and where I am going; but you do not know where I come from and where I am going. ¹⁵You judge according to the flesh; I judge no one. ¹⁶And yet if I do judge, My judgment is true; for I am not alone, but I *am* with the Father who sent Me. ¹⁷It is also written in your law that the testimony of two men is true. ¹⁸I am One who bears witness of Myself, and the Father who sent Me bears witness of Me."

¹⁹Then they said to Him, "Where is Your Father?"

Jesus answered, "You know neither Me nor My Father. If you had known Me, you would have known My Father also."

²⁰These words Jesus spoke in the treasury, as He taught in the temple; and no one laid hands on Him, for His hour had not yet come.

JESUS PREDICTS HIS DEPARTURE

²¹Then Jesus said to them again, "I am going away, and you will seek Me, and will die in your sin. Where I go you cannot come."

²²So the Jews said, "Will He kill Himself, because He says, 'Where I go you cannot come'?"

²³And He said to them, "You are from beneath; I am from above. You are of this world; I am not of this world. ²⁴Therefore I said to you that you will die in your sins; for if you do not believe that I am *He,* you will die in your sins."

²⁵Then they said to Him, "Who are You?"

And Jesus said to them, "Just what I have been saying to you from the beginning. ²⁶I have many things to say and to judge concerning you, but He who sent Me is true; and I speak to the world those things which I heard from Him."

²⁷They did not understand that He spoke to them of the Father.

²⁸Then Jesus said to them, "When you lift up the Son of Man, then you will know that I am *He,* and *that* I do nothing of Myself; but as My Father taught Me, I speak these things. ²⁹And He who sent Me is with Me. The Father has not left Me alone, for I always do those things that please Him." ³⁰As He spoke these words, many believed in Him.

THE TRUTH SHALL MAKE YOU FREE

³¹Then Jesus said to those Jews who believed Him, "If you abide in My word, you are My disciples indeed. ³²And you shall know the truth, and the truth shall make you free."

³³They answered Him, "We are Abraham's descendants, and have never been in bondage to anyone. How *can* You say, 'You will be made free'?"

³⁴Jesus answered them, "Most assuredly, I say to you, whoever commits sin is a slave of sin. ³⁵And a slave does not abide in the house forever, *but* a son abides forever. ³⁶Therefore if the Son makes you free, you shall be free indeed.

ABRAHAM'S SEED AND SATAN'S

³⁷"I know that you are Abraham's descendants, but you seek to kill Me, because My word has no place in you. ³⁸I speak what I have seen with My Father, and you do what you have seen withᵃ your father."

³⁹They answered and said to Him, "Abraham is our father."

Jesus said to them, "If you were Abraham's children, you would do the works of Abraham. ⁴⁰But now you seek to kill Me, a Man who has told you the truth which I heard from God. Abraham did not do this. ⁴¹You do the deeds of your father."

Then they said to Him, "We were not born of fornication; we have one Father—God."

⁴²Jesus said to them, "If God were your Father, you would love Me, for I proceeded forth and came from God; nor have I come of Myself, but He sent Me. ⁴³Why do you not understand My speech? Because you are not able to listen to My word. ⁴⁴You are of *your* father the devil, and the desires of your father you want to do. He was a murderer from the beginning, and does not stand in the truth, because there is no truth in him. When he speaks a lie, he speaks from his own *resources,* for he is a liar and the father of it. ⁴⁵But because I tell the truth, you do not believe Me. ⁴⁶Which of you convicts Me of sin? And if I tell the truth, why do you not believe Me? ⁴⁷He who is of God hears God's words; therefore you do not hear, because you are not of God."

BEFORE ABRAHAM WAS, I AM

⁴⁸Then the Jews answered and said to Him, "Do we not say rightly that You are a Samaritan and have a demon?"

⁴⁹Jesus answered, "I do not have a demon; but I honor My Father,

Super Yogurt

Yogurt is highly regarded around the world as a "super food." Known since ancient times, it has been a mainstay in the diets of people who have traditionally lived very long lives, especially people living in Turkey, Armenia, and remote regions of the Caucasus Mountains.

Bible Health + Food Facts

8:10 ᵃNU-Text omits *and saw no one but the woman;* M-Text reads *He saw her and said.* ᵇNU-Text and M-Text omit *of yours.* 8:11 ᵃNU-Text and M-Text add *from now on.* 8:38 ᵃNU-Text reads *heard from.*

and you dishonor Me. [50]And I do not seek My *own* glory; there is One who seeks and judges. [51]Most assuredly, I say to you, if anyone keeps My word he shall never see death."

[52]Then the Jews said to Him, "Now we know that You have a demon! Abraham is dead, and the prophets; and You say, 'If anyone keeps My word he shall never taste death.' [53]Are You greater than our father Abraham, who is dead? And the prophets are dead. Who do You make Yourself out to be?"

[54]Jesus answered, "If I honor Myself, My honor is nothing. It is My Father who honors Me, of whom you say that He is your[a] God. [55]Yet you have not known Him, but I know Him. And if I say, 'I do not know Him,' I shall be a liar like you; but I do know Him and keep His word. [56]Your father Abraham rejoiced to see My day, and he saw *it* and was glad."

[57]Then the Jews said to Him, "You are not yet fifty years old, and have You seen Abraham?"

[58]Jesus said to them, "Most assuredly, I say to you, before Abraham was, I AM."

[59]Then they took up stones to throw at Him; but Jesus hid Himself and went out of the temple,[a] going through the midst of them, and so passed by.

A MAN BORN BLIND RECEIVES SIGHT

9 Now as *Jesus* passed by, He saw a man who was blind from birth. [2]And His disciples asked Him, saying, "Rabbi, who sinned, this man or his parents, that he was born blind?"

[3]Jesus answered, "Neither this man nor his parents sinned, but that the works of God should be revealed in him. [4]I[a] must work the works of Him who sent Me while it is day; *the* night is coming when no one can work. [5]As long as I am in the world, I am the light of the world."

[6]When He had said these things, He spat on the ground and made clay with the saliva; and He anointed the eyes of the blind man with the clay. [7]And He said to him, "Go, wash in the pool of Siloam" (which is translated, Sent). So he went and washed, and came back seeing.

[8]Therefore the neighbors and those who previously had seen that he was blind[a] said, "Is not this he who sat and begged?"

[9]Some said, "This is he." Others *said,* "He is like him."[a] He said, "I am *he.*"

[10]Therefore they said to him, "How were your eyes opened?"

[11]He answered and said, "A Man called Jesus made clay and anointed my eyes and said to me, 'Go to the pool of[a] Siloam and wash.' So I went and washed, and I received sight."

[12]Then they said to him, "Where is He?"

He said, "I do not know."

> " **Therefore they said to him, 'How were your eyes opened?' He answered and said, 'A Man called Jesus made clay and anointed my eyes and said to me, 'Go to the pool of Siloam and wash.' So I went and washed, and I received sight.' "**
>
> — *John 9:10–11*

THE PHARISEES EXCOMMUNICATE THE HEALED MAN

[13]They brought him who formerly was blind to the Pharisees. [14]Now it was a Sabbath when Jesus made the clay and opened his eyes. [15]Then the Pharisees also asked him again how he had received his sight. He said to them, "He put clay on my eyes, and I washed, and I see."

[16]Therefore some of the Pharisees said, "This Man is not from God, because He does not keep the Sabbath."

Others said, "How can a man who is a sinner do such signs?" And there was a division among them.

[17]They said to the blind man again, "What do you say about Him because He opened your eyes?"

INSIGHTS INTO THE WORD

> (John 9:6, 7)

Combining the Natural and Supernatural. Jesus clearly combined the natural and the supernatural in His healing ministry. In this particular case, He made a poultice from the clay of the earth and His own spittle. While we might think of this as an unhealthful thing to do, the people in Jesus' day believed that saliva—especially the saliva of a godly person—had healing properties. Certainly the earth's minerals have healing properties—today many medicines are made from earth's chemicals.

Jesus told the man to wash in the pool of Siloam, which was a pool constructed through God's miraculous guidance during the days of King Hezekiah. Sending the man to this pool was a clear signal that he was to *expect* a miracle—that his blind eyes might see the light of day, just as those who tunneled through the solid rock broke through to the light and to the flow of water that saved Jerusalem.

When you visit a godly physician, do what the physician advises. Take the medicines that he or she may prescribe. At the same time, trust God for the miracle of your healing and wholeness. Physicians can help you but only God can truly *heal* you. Seek to combine the natural and the spiritual in your health care. It's what Jesus did!

He said, "He is a prophet."

[18]But the Jews did not believe concerning him, that he had been blind and received his sight, until they called the parents of him who had received his sight. [19]And they asked them, saying, "Is this your son, who you say was born blind? How then does he now see?"

[20]His parents answered them and said, "We know that this is our son, and that he was born blind; [21]but by what means he now sees we do not know, or who opened his eyes we do not know. He is of age; ask him. He will speak for himself." [22]His parents said these *things* because they feared the Jews, for the Jews had agreed already that if anyone confessed *that* He *was* Christ, he would be put out of the synagogue. [23]Therefore his parents said, "He is of age; ask him."

[24]So they again called the man who was blind, and said to him, "Give God the glory! We know that this Man is a sinner."

[25]He answered and said, "Whether He is a sinner *or not* I do not know. One thing I know: that though I was blind, now I see."

[26]Then they said to him again, "What did He do to you? How did He open your eyes?"

[27]He answered them, "I told you already, and you did not listen. Why do you want to hear *it* again? Do you also want to become His disciples?"

[28]Then they reviled him and said, "You are His disciple, but we are Moses' disciples. [29]We know that God spoke to Moses; *as for* this *fellow*, we do not know where He is from."

[30]The man answered and said to them, "Why, this is a marvelous thing, that you do not know where He is from; yet He has opened my eyes! [31]Now we know that God does not hear sinners; but if anyone is a worshiper of God and does His will, He hears him. [32]Since the world began it has been unheard of that anyone opened the eyes of one who was born blind. [33]If this Man were not from God, He could do nothing."

[34]They answered and said to him, "You were completely born in sins, and are you teaching us?" And they cast him out.

TRUE VISION AND TRUE BLINDNESS

[35]Jesus heard that they had cast him out; and when He had found him, He said to him, "Do you believe in the Son of God?"[a]

[36]He answered and said, "Who is He, Lord, that I may believe in Him?"

[37]And Jesus said to him, "You have both seen Him and it is He who is talking with you."

[38]Then he said, "Lord, I believe!" And he worshiped Him.

[39]And Jesus said, "For judgment I have come into this world, that those who do not see may see, and that those who see may be made blind."

[40]Then *some* of the Pharisees who were with Him heard these words, and said to Him, "Are we blind also?"

[41]Jesus said to them, "If you were blind, you would have no sin; but now you say, 'We see.' Therefore your sin remains.

JESUS THE TRUE SHEPHERD

10 "Most assuredly, I say to you, he who does not enter the sheepfold by the door, but climbs up some other way, the same is a thief and a robber. [2]But he who en-

WHOLENESS 101

How Toxic Are You?

Medical research studies have shown that the average person might be storing from fifty to one hundred harmful toxins in their fat cells (adipose tissue). Many poisonous pollutants seep into the body through the skin. The various lists of toxins include chlorine, bromine, gasoline, additives, pesticides, herbicides, wood preservatives, heavy metals (lead, cadmium, and so forth), household chemicals, residues of prescription drugs, and mercury from amalgam fillings.

A wide variety of toxins also impact a person's soul—negative remarks, cutting criticism, statements that signal rejection, and words that condemn. We say that sticks and stones hurt our bones and words never hurt us, but the truth is that words can often hurt us longer and in more unhealthful ways than a bruise from a stone or a broken bone!

Just as we need to flush physical toxins from our systems with pure water, colonic flushes, and perhaps even a blood-cleansing system of purification, we also need to flush emotional toxins from our souls. Seek counseling and work your way to total forgiveness of those who have hurt you emotionally—your soul needs to be cleansed as much as your body or spirit!

ters by the door is the shepherd of the sheep. [3]To him the doorkeeper opens, and the sheep hear his voice; and he calls his own sheep by name and leads them out. [4]And when he brings out his own sheep, he goes before them; and the sheep follow him, for they know his voice. [5]Yet they will by no means follow a stranger, but will flee from him, for they do not know the voice of strangers." [6]Jesus used this illustration, but they did not understand the things which He spoke to them.

JESUS THE GOOD SHEPHERD

[7]Then Jesus said to them again, "Most assuredly, I say to you, I am the door of the sheep. [8]All who *ever* came before Me[a] are thieves and robbers, but the sheep did not hear them. [9]I am the door. If anyone enters by Me, he will be saved, and will go in and out and find pasture. [10]The thief does

Men's Issues
Looking Deeper

"Beauty is only skin deep" is a well-known saying. But the truth is, most men don't like that saying. They like beauty, and it doesn't really matter if it is skin deep!

Is the beauty of a woman a bad thing? Not at all! Beauty, by whatever definition a man may have, is what initially attracts a man to a woman. It may be a beautiful face, a beautiful figure, a beautiful smile, a beautiful way of walking or moving or gesturing. A man finds something in a woman's appearance and demeanor that is appealing to him, and if not appealing in a way that inspires lust, at least appealing in the sense that he would like to see her or be around her again.

Without a certain degree of beauty, it is unlikely that the human race would continue. Men are creatures that are moved by what they *see* more than by any other factor. The problem with outward beauty, however, is that it never lasts. Beauty always fades. Even the most beautiful woman in her youth can be the victim of wrinkles, sags, bags, and weight gain, and especially so if she has children. No amount of cosmetic surgery can keep a woman from aging.

The challenge every man faces is to look beyond the physical appearance of a woman and to see her inside character. Is she someone who can be trusted? Is she a woman who will be faithful, kind, loving, nurturing, reliable, honest, comforting in crises, encouraging in what she says and does, and a good "cheerleader" for the battles of life? Is she a woman who thinks of others more than CONT. NEXT PAGE>>>

not come except to steal, and to kill, and to destroy. I have come that they may have life, and that they may have *it* more abundantly.

¹¹"I am the good shepherd. The good shepherd gives His life for the sheep. ¹²But a hireling, *he who is* not the shepherd, one who does not own the sheep, sees the wolf coming and leaves the sheep and flees; and the wolf catches the sheep and scatters them. ¹³The hireling flees because he is a hireling and does not care about the sheep. ¹⁴I am the good shepherd; and I know My *sheep,* and am known by My own. ¹⁵As the Father knows Me, even so I know the Father; and I lay down My life for the sheep. ¹⁶And other sheep I have which are not of this fold; them also I must bring, and they will hear My voice; and there will be one flock *and* one shepherd.

¹⁷"Therefore My Father loves Me, because I lay down My life that I may take it again. ¹⁸No one takes it from Me, but I lay it down of Myself. I have power to lay it down, and I have power to take it again. This command I have received from My Father."

¹⁹Therefore there was a division again among the Jews because of these sayings. ²⁰And many of them said, "He has a demon and is mad. Why do you listen to Him?"

²¹Others said, "These are not the words of one who has a demon. Can a demon open the eyes of the blind?"

THE SHEPHERD KNOWS HIS SHEEP

²²Now it was the Feast of Dedication in Jerusalem, and it was winter. ²³And Jesus walked in the temple, in Solomon's porch. ²⁴Then the Jews surrounded Him and said to Him, "How long do You keep us in doubt? If You are the Christ, tell us plainly."

²⁵Jesus answered them, "I told you, and you do not believe. The works that I do in My Father's name, they bear witness of Me. ²⁶But you do not believe, because you are not of My sheep, as I said to you.ᵃ ²⁷My sheep hear My voice, and I know them, and they follow Me. ²⁸And I give them eternal life, and they shall never perish; neither shall anyone snatch them out of My hand. ²⁹My Father, who has given *them* to Me, is greater than all; and no one is able to snatch *them* out of My Father's hand. ³⁰I and *My* Father are one."

RENEWED EFFORTS TO STONE JESUS

³¹Then the Jews took up stones again to stone Him. ³²Jesus answered them, "Many good works I have shown you from My Father. For which of those works do you stone Me?"

³³The Jews answered Him, saying, "For a good work we do not stone You, but for blasphemy, and because You, being a Man, make Yourself God."

³⁴Jesus answered them, "Is it not written in your law, 'I said, "You are gods" '?ᵃ ³⁵If He called them gods, to whom the word of God came (and the Scripture cannot be broken), ³⁶do you say of Him whom the Father sanctified and sent into the world, 'You are blaspheming,' because I said, 'I am the Son of God'? ³⁷If I do not do the works of My Father, do not believe Me; ³⁸but if I do, though you do not believe Me, believe the works, that you may know and believeᵃ that the Father *is* in Me, and I in Him." ³⁹Therefore they sought again to seize Him, but He escaped out of their hand.

10:26 ᵃNU-Text omits *as I said to you.*   10:34 ᵃPsalm 82:6   10:38 ᵃNU-Text reads *understand.*

herself, keeps a confidence, is loyal, refuses to gossip, and does not readily complain, criticize, or think negatively? Is she a woman who loves the Lord and desires to obey God's commandments? These traits are ones that create a rare form of beauty within a woman—a beauty that grows with experience and longevity of relationship, a beauty that doesn't fade with age, a beauty that doesn't *need* a makeover!

Men should also recognize that although a handful of women in the Bible are described as being physically beautiful, some of the most admired women in the Bible—including the Virgin Mary, Hannah, Lydia, and even Eve—have nothing mentioned about their physical appearance. Leah, a woman considered *not* attractive, became the mother of half of the tribes of Israel and was one of the most influential women in all of Jewish history.

Look beyond the physical. You may be amazed at what you really "see" in a woman.

THE BELIEVERS BEYOND JORDAN

40And He went away again beyond the Jordan to the place where John was baptizing at first, and there He stayed. 41Then many came to Him and said, "John performed no sign, but all the things that John spoke about this Man were true." 42And many believed in Him there.

THE DEATH OF LAZARUS

11 Now a certain *man* was sick, Lazarus of Bethany, the town of Mary and her sister Martha. 2It was *that* Mary who anointed the Lord with fragrant oil and wiped His feet with her hair, whose brother Lazarus was sick. 3Therefore the sisters sent to Him, saying, "Lord, behold, he whom You love is sick."

4When Jesus heard *that,* He said, "This sickness is not unto death, but for the glory of God, that the Son of God may be glorified through it."

5Now Jesus loved Martha and her sister and Lazarus. 6So, when He heard that he was sick, He stayed two more days in the place where He was. 7Then after this He said to *the* disciples, "Let us go to Judea again."

8*The* disciples said to Him, "Rabbi, lately the Jews sought to stone You, and are You going there again?"

9Jesus answered, "Are there not twelve hours in the day? If anyone walks in the day, he does not stumble, because he sees the light of this world. 10But if one walks in the night, he stumbles, because the light is not in him." 11These things He said, and after that He said to them, "Our friend Lazarus sleeps, but I go that I may wake him up."

12Then His disciples said, "Lord, if he sleeps he will get well." 13However, Jesus spoke of his death, but they thought that He was speaking about taking rest in sleep.

14Then Jesus said to them plainly, "Lazarus is dead. 15And I am glad for your sakes that I was not there, that you may believe. Nevertheless let us go to him."

16Then Thomas, who is called the Twin, said to his fellow disciples, "Let us also go, that we may die with Him."

I AM THE RESURRECTION AND THE LIFE

17So when Jesus came, He found that he had already been in the tomb four days. 18Now Bethany was near Jerusalem, about two miles*a* away. 19And many of the Jews had joined the women around Martha and Mary, to comfort them concerning their brother.

20Now Martha, as soon as she heard that Jesus was coming, went and met Him, but Mary was sitting in the house. 21Now Martha said to Jesus, "Lord, if You had been here, my brother would not have died. 22But even now I know that whatever You ask of God, God will give You."

23Jesus said to her, "Your brother will rise again."

24Martha said to Him, "I know that he will rise again in the resurrection at the last day."

25Jesus said to her, "I am the resurrection and the life. He who believes in Me, though he may die, he shall live. 26And whoever lives and believes in Me shall never die. Do you believe this?"

27She said to Him, "Yes, Lord, I believe that You are the Christ, the Son of God, who is to come into the world."

JESUS AND DEATH, THE LAST ENEMY

28And when she had said these things, she went her way and secretly called Mary her sister, saying, "The Teacher has come and is calling for you." 29As soon as she heard *that,* she arose quickly and came to Him. 30Now Jesus had not yet come into the town, but was*a* in the place where Martha met Him. 31Then the Jews who were with her in the house, and comforting her, when they saw that Mary rose up quickly and went out, followed her, saying, "She is going to the tomb to weep there."*a*

32Then, when Mary came where Jesus was, and saw Him, she fell down at His feet, saying to Him, "Lord, if You had been here, my brother would not have died."

[KELP]

FACT MORSELS

Kelp—yes, the seaweed—can help speed up a person's metabolism. It comes in tablet form and is available at health-food stores and drugstores. Kelp, along with algae, is also a good detoxifier. It helps "sponge up" and carry heavy metals out of the body. It is excellent for skin care.

11:18 *a*Literally *fifteen stadia*   11:30 *a*NU-Text adds *still.*   11:31 *a*NU-Text reads *supposing that she was going to the tomb to weep there.*

DIVINE HEALTH   131

WWJE? [NUTS]

[WHAT WOULD JESUS EAT]

When Judah sent his sons, including Benjamin, to see Joseph in Egypt, he said, "Take some of the best fruits of the land in your vessels and carry down a present for the man—a little balm and a little honey, spices and myrrh, pistachio nuts and almonds" (Genesis 43:11).

Pistachios, almonds, and walnuts were plentiful in Jesus' day. King Solomon had a "garden of nuts"—probably a grove of walnut trees grown mainly for walnut oil, which was prized as second best to olive oil. Walnuts are considered a delicacy even today.

Nuts are more commonly served as a dessert than an appetizer in the Middle East. They are often served with honey, yogurt, and tea.

Nuts have been associated with cancer prevention, a lower risk of heart disease, and help for diabetes. They are rich in important minerals such as zinc, iron, copper, calcium, magnesium, and phosphorus.

Here's a quick comparison of three of the most popular nuts available today. (Peanuts are included, but are actually legumes.)

	Almonds (blanched)	Peanuts (dry roasted)	Walnuts
PER ONE-OUNCE SERVING			
Calories	174	164	172
Fat grams	16	14	17.6
Carbohydrate grams	9.5	6	3.4
Potassium	95 mg	180 mg	
Magnesium			57.4 mg
Protein grams	1	6.6	6.9

[33]Therefore, when Jesus saw her weeping, and the Jews who came with her weeping, He groaned in the spirit and was troubled. [34]And He said, "Where have you laid him?"

They said to Him, "Lord, come and see."

[35]Jesus wept. [36]Then the Jews said, "See how He loved him!"

[37]And some of them said, "Could not this Man, who opened the eyes of the blind, also have kept this man from dying?"

LAZARUS RAISED FROM THE DEAD

[38]Then Jesus, again groaning in Himself, came to the tomb. It was a cave, and a stone lay against it. [39]Jesus said, "Take away the stone."

Martha, the sister of him who was dead, said to Him, "Lord, by this time there is a stench, for he has been *dead* four days."

[40]Jesus said to her, "Did I not say to you that if you would believe you would see the glory of God?" [41]Then they took away the stone *from the place* where the dead man was lying.[a] And Jesus lifted up *His* eyes and said, "Father, I thank You that You have heard Me. [42]And I know that You always hear Me, but because of the people who are standing by I said *this*, that they may believe that You sent Me." [43]Now when He had said these things, He cried with a loud voice, "Lazarus, come forth!" [44]And he who had died came out bound hand and foot with graveclothes, and his face was wrapped with a cloth. Jesus said to them, "Loose him, and let him go."

THE PLOT TO KILL JESUS

[45]Then many of the Jews who had come to Mary, and had seen the things Jesus did, believed in Him. [46]But some of them went away to the Pharisees and told them the things Jesus did. [47]Then the chief priests and the Pharisees gathered a council and said, "What shall we do? For this Man works many signs. [48]If we let Him alone like this, everyone will believe in Him, and the Romans will come and take away both our place and nation."

[49]And one of them, Caiaphas, being high priest that year, said to them, "You know nothing at all, [50]nor do you consider that it is expedient for us[a] that one man should die for the people, and not that the whole nation should perish." [51]Now this he did not say on his own *authority;* but being high priest that year he prophesied that Jesus would die for the nation, [52]and not for that nation only, but also that He would gather together in one the children of God who were scattered abroad.

[53]Then, from that day on, they plotted to put Him to death. [54]Therefore Jesus no longer walked openly among the Jews, but went from there into the country near the wilderness, to a city called Ephraim, and there remained with His disciples.

[55]And the Passover of the Jews was near, and many went from the country up to Jerusalem before the Passover, to purify themselves. [56]Then they sought Jesus, and spoke among themselves as they stood in the temple, "What

11:41 [a]NU-Text omits *from the place where the dead man was lying.* 11:50 [a]NU-Text reads *you.*

do you think—that He will not come to the feast?" ⁵⁷Now both the chief priests and the Pharisees had given a command, that if anyone knew where He was, he should report *it*, that they might seize Him.

THE ANOINTING AT BETHANY

12 Then, six days before the Passover, Jesus came to Bethany, where Lazarus was who had been dead,ᵃ whom He had raised from the dead. ²There they made Him a supper; and Martha served, but Lazarus was one of those who sat at the table with Him. ³Then Mary took a pound of very costly oil of spikenard, anointed the feet of Jesus, and wiped His feet with her hair. And the house was filled with the fragrance of the oil.

⁴But one of His disciples, Judas Iscariot, Simon's *son*, who would betray Him, said, ⁵"Why was this fragrant oil not sold for three hundred denariiᵃ and given to the poor?" ⁶This he said, not that he cared for the poor, but because he was a thief, and had the money box; and he used to take what was put in it.

⁷But Jesus said, "Let her alone; she has keptᵃ this for the day of My burial. ⁸For the poor you have with you always, but Me you do not have always."

THE PLOT TO KILL LAZARUS

⁹Now a great many of the Jews knew that He was there; and they came, not for Jesus' sake only, but that they might also see Lazarus, whom He had raised from the dead. ¹⁰But the chief priests plotted to put Lazarus to death also, ¹¹because on account of him many of the Jews went away and believed in Jesus.

THE TRIUMPHAL ENTRY

¹²The next day a great multitude that had come to the feast, when they heard that Jesus was coming to Jerusalem, ¹³took branches of palm trees and went out to meet Him, and cried out:

"Hosanna!
'Blessed is He who comes in the name of the Lord!'ᵃ
The King of Israel!"

¹⁴Then Jesus, when He had found a young donkey, sat on it; as it is written:

¹⁵ "Fear not, daughter of Zion;
Behold, your King is coming,
Sitting on a donkey's colt."ᵃ

¹⁶His disciples did not understand these things at first; but when Jesus was glorified, then they remembered that these things were written about Him and *that* they had done these things to Him.

¹⁷Therefore the people, who were with Him when He called Lazarus out of his tomb and raised him from the dead, bore witness. ¹⁸For this reason the people also met Him, because they heard that He had done this sign. ¹⁹The Pharisees therefore said among themselves, "You see that you are accomplishing nothing. Look, the world has gone after Him!"

THE FRUITFUL GRAIN OF WHEAT

²⁰Now there were certain Greeks among those who came up to worship at the feast. ²¹Then they came to Philip, who was from Bethsaida of Galilee, and asked him, saying, "Sir, we wish to see Jesus."

²²Philip came and told Andrew, and in turn Andrew and Philip told Jesus.

²³But Jesus answered them, saying, "The hour has come that the Son of Man should be glorified. ²⁴Most assuredly, I say to you, unless a grain of wheat falls into the ground and dies, it remains alone; but if it dies, it produces much grain. ²⁵He who loves his life will lose it, and he who hates his life in this world will keep it for eternal life. ²⁶If anyone serves Me, let him follow Me; and where I am, there My servant will be also. If anyone serves Me, him *My* Father will honor.

JESUS PREDICTS HIS DEATH ON THE CROSS

²⁷"Now My soul is troubled, and what shall I say? 'Father, save Me from this hour'? But for this purpose I came to this hour. ²⁸Father, glorify Your name."

Then a voice came from heaven, *saying*, "I have both glorified *it* and will glorify *it* again."

²⁹Therefore the people who stood by and heard *it* said that it had thundered. Others said, "An angel has spoken to Him."

³⁰Jesus answered and said, "This voice did not come because of Me, but for your sake. ³¹Now is the judgment of this world; now the ruler of this world will be cast out. ³²And I, if I am lifted up from the

WISE CHOICES

Choose whole-grain flour over white flour.
When whole grains are processed to make white flour, the two outer layers of the grain are destroyed—along with 80 percent of the grain's nutrients! The two outer layers, called the bran and the wheat germ, are rich sources of B vitamins, minerals, vitamin E, and fiber. The inner part of the grain kernel is called the endosperm. This is the part that remains after the refining process and is pure starch. In addition, the refining process includes a bleaching step to make the flour white. The bleaches used can cause free-radical reactions, dangerous to the human body.

12:1 ᵃNU-Text omits *who had been dead*. 12:5 ᵃAbout one year's wages for a worker 12:7 ᵃNU-Text reads *that she may keep*. 12:13 ᵃPsalm 118:26 12:15 ᵃZechariah 9:9

PEOPLE CALLED "BEAUTIFUL" IN THE BIBLE

Saul

Head and Shoulders Above the Rest

We don't know if Saul was handsome, but we do know that the phrase "head and shoulders above the rest" certainly applied to him. According to the Bible, Saul literally was "taller than any of the people from his shoulders upward" (1 Samuel 10:23). There's a little bit of irony in this. Saul was from the tribe of Benjamin, considered to be the "least" of the twelve tribes, and yet God chose him through the prophet Samuel, to be the first king of Israel.

For all his height, Saul was apparently a shy man. When Samuel came to examine the people he found Saul hiding among the equipment—the various wagons and carts that the people had used to travel to Samuel. He was reluctant at the outset to be a leader.

Later, however, Saul was all too quick to take the reins of power and even to extend his power beyond the boundaries that God had established. He erred greatly in taking on some of the duties and responsibilities reserved only for the high priest. In so doing, he lost God's favor. In losing God's favor, Saul also eventually lost his mind—he became consumed with jealousy of the one God had chosen to be the next king after him—David.

Being good-looking is not a requirement for rising to political power or achieving fame or social status, although good looks often seem to become linked with leadership positions, fame, and status. This is true not only in our society but in other cultures as well. Perhaps people universally want to believe that "what you see is what you get." Unfortunately, what we see is very often only a fraction of the whole story about a person. Handsome men can become entrusted with authority and responsibilities for which they are not remotely equipped in skills or quality of character.

---

earth, will draw all *peoples* to Myself." [33]This He said, signifying by what death He would die.

[34]The people answered Him, "We have heard from the law that the Christ remains forever; and how *can* You say, 'The Son of Man must be lifted up'? Who is this Son of Man?"

[35]Then Jesus said to them, "A little while longer the light is with you. Walk while you have the light, lest darkness overtake you; he who walks in darkness does not know where he is going. [36]While you have the light, believe in the light, that you may become sons of light." These things Jesus spoke, and departed, and was hidden from them.

WHO HAS BELIEVED OUR REPORT?

[37]But although He had done so many signs before them, they did not believe in Him, [38]that the word of Isaiah the prophet might be fulfilled, which he spoke:

"Lord, who has believed our report?
And to whom has the arm of the LORD been revealed?"[a]

[39]Therefore they could not believe, because Isaiah said again:

[40]"He has blinded their eyes and hardened their hearts,
Lest they should see with their eyes,
Lest they should understand with their hearts and turn,
So that I should heal them."[a]

[41]These things Isaiah said when[a] he saw His glory and spoke of Him.

WALK IN THE LIGHT

[42]Nevertheless even among the rulers many believed in Him, but because of the Pharisees they did not confess *Him,* lest they should be put out of the synagogue; [43]for they loved the praise of men more than the praise of God.

[44]Then Jesus cried out and said, "He who believes in Me, believes not in Me but in Him who sent Me. [45]And he who sees Me sees Him who sent Me. [46]I have come *as* a light into the world, that whoever believes in Me should not abide in darkness. [47]And if anyone hears My words and does not believe,[a] I do not judge him; for I did not come to judge the world but to save the world. [48]He who rejects Me, and does not receive My words, has that which judges him—the word that I have spoken will judge him in the last day. [49]For I have not spoken on My own *authority;* but the Father who sent Me gave Me a command, what I should say and what I should speak. [50]And I know that His command is everlasting life. Therefore, whatever I speak, just as the Father has told Me, so I speak."

JESUS WASHES THE DISCIPLES' FEET

13 Now before the Feast of the Passover, when Jesus knew that His hour had come that He should depart from this world to the Father, having loved His own who were in the world, He loved them to the end.

12:38 [a]Isaiah 53:1   12:40 [a]Isaiah 6:10   12:41 [a]NU-Text reads *because.*   12:47 [a]NU-Text reads *keep them.*

²And supper being ended,ᵃ the devil having already put it into the heart of Judas Iscariot, Simon's *son,* to betray Him, ³Jesus, knowing that the Father had given all things into His hands, and that He had come from God and was going to God, ⁴rose from supper and laid aside His garments, took a towel and girded Himself. ⁵After that, He poured water into a basin and began to wash the disciples' feet, and to wipe *them* with the towel with which He was girded. ⁶Then He came to Simon Peter. And *Peter* said to Him, "Lord, are You washing my feet?"

⁷Jesus answered and said to him, "What I am doing you do not understand now, but you will know after this."

⁸Peter said to Him, "You shall never wash my feet!"

Jesus answered him, "If I do not wash you, you have no part with Me."

⁹Simon Peter said to Him, "Lord, not my feet only, but also *my* hands and *my* head!"

¹⁰Jesus said to him, "He who is bathed needs only to wash *his* feet, but is completely clean; and you are clean, but not all of you." ¹¹For He knew who would betray Him; therefore He said, "You are not all clean."

¹²So when He had washed their feet, taken His garments, and sat down again, He said to them, "Do you know what I have done to you? ¹³You call Me Teacher and Lord, and you say well, for *so* I am. ¹⁴If I then, *your* Lord and Teacher, have washed your feet, you also ought to wash one another's feet. ¹⁵For I have given you an example, that you should do as I have done to you. ¹⁶Most assuredly, I say to you, a servant is not greater than his master; nor is he who is sent greater than he who sent him. ¹⁷If you know these things, blessed are you if you do them.

JESUS IDENTIFIES HIS BETRAYER

¹⁸"I do not speak concerning all of you. I know whom I have chosen; but that the Scripture may be fulfilled, 'He who eats bread with Meᵃ has lifted up his heel against Me.'ᵇ ¹⁹Now I tell you before it comes, that when it does come to pass, you may believe that I am *He.* ²⁰Most assuredly, I say to you, he who receives whomever I send receives Me; and he who receives Me receives Him who sent Me."

²¹When Jesus had said these things, He was troubled in spirit, and testified and said, "Most assuredly, I say to you, one of you will betray Me." ²²Then the disciples looked at one another, perplexed about whom He spoke.

²³Now there was leaning on Jesus' bosom one of His disciples, whom Jesus loved. ²⁴Simon Peter therefore motioned to him to ask who it was of whom He spoke.

²⁵Then, leaning backᵃ on Jesus' breast, he said to Him, "Lord, who is it?"

²⁶Jesus answered, "It is he to whom I shall give a piece of bread when I have dipped *it.*" And having dipped the bread, He gave *it* to Judas Iscariot, *the son* of Simon. ²⁷Now after the piece of bread, Satan entered him. Then Jesus said to him, "What you do, do quickly." ²⁸But no one at the table knew for what reason He said this to him. ²⁹For some thought, because Judas had the money box, that Jesus had said to him, "Buy *those things* we need for the feast," or that he should give something to the poor.

³⁰Having received the piece of bread, he then went out immediately. And it was night.

THE NEW COMMANDMENT

³¹So, when he had gone out, Jesus said, "Now the Son of Man is glorified, and God is glorified in Him. ³²If God is glorified in Him, God will also glorify Him in Himself, and glorify Him immediately. ³³Little children, I shall be with you a little while longer. You will seek Me; and as I said to the Jews, 'Where I am going, you cannot come,' so now I say to you. ³⁴A new commandment I give to you, that you love one another; as I have loved you, that you also love one another. ³⁵By this all will know that you are My disciples, if you have love for one another."

JESUS PREDICTS PETER'S DENIAL

³⁶Simon Peter said to Him, "Lord, where are You going?"

Jesus answered him, "Where I am going you cannot follow Me now, but you shall follow Me afterward."

³⁷Peter said to Him, "Lord, why can I not follow You now? I will lay down my life for Your sake."

³⁸Jesus answered him, "Will you lay down your life for My sake? Most assuredly, I say to you, the rooster shall not crow till you have denied Me three times.

THE WAY, THE TRUTH, AND THE LIFE

14 "Let not your heart be troubled; you believe in God, believe also in Me. ²In My Father's house are many mansions;ᵃ if *it were* not *so,* I would have told you. I go to prepare a place for you.ᵇ ³And if I go and prepare a place for you, I will come again and receive you to Myself; that where I am, *there* you may be also. ⁴And where I go you know, and the way you know."

⁵Thomas said to Him, "Lord, we do not know where You are going, and how can we know the way?"

⁶Jesus said to him, "I am the way, the truth, and the life. No one comes to the Father except through Me.

"Every one should be his own physician. We ought to assist, and not to force nature. Eat with moderation what agrees with your constitution. Nothing is good for the body but what we can digest. What medicine can procure digestion? Exercise. What will recruit strength? Sleep. What will alleviate incurable evils? Patience."
—*Francois Marie de Voltaire, French poet and dramatist (1694–1773)*

PREACHING HEALTH

13:2 ᵃNU-Text reads *And during supper.*   13:18 ᵃNU-Text reads *My bread.* ᵇPsalm 41:9   13:25 ᵃNU-Text and M-Text add *thus.*   14:2 ᵃLiterally *dwellings* ᵇNU-Text adds a word which would cause the text to read either *if it were not so, would I have told you that I go to prepare a place for you?* or *if it were not so I would have told you; for I go to prepare a place for you.*

CONDIMENTS

☐ Garlic

When it comes to health benefits, garlic is one of the most important taste enhancers you can add to your foods. Garlic boosts the body's natural immunity. Studies show that it helps to slow blood coagulation and has antioxidant properties. It seems to have mild antihypertensive effects and it may lower cholesterol levels. It has been shown to reduce both systolic and diastolic blood pressure. A number of studies reported that patients using garlic were able to reduce their high blood pressure to manageable levels without using drugs. Combined, these anticoagulant, antioxidant, and antihypertensive properties make garlic a good ally in preventing atherosclerosis. Two or three cloves of garlic a day may significantly decrease a person's risk of heart attack.

Japanese scientists have distilled an antibiotic medication called *kyolic* from raw garlic. Kyolic has been used to fight influenza—including a severe outbreak in Moscow in the 1950s—as well as to ward off pneumonia, whooping cough, and various intestinal disorders. Kyolic can now be taken in extract form.

Cooking destroys or reduces some of the allicin in garlic, which weakens some of garlic's therapeutic benefits. Whether cooked, raw, or taken in extract form, however, garlic is one of the most potent natural healing foods known to man.

THE FATHER REVEALED

7 "If you had known Me, you would have known My Father also; and from now on you know Him and have seen Him."

8 Philip said to Him, "Lord, show us the Father, and it is sufficient for us."

9 Jesus said to him, "Have I been with you so long, and yet you have not known Me, Philip? He who has seen Me has seen the Father; so how can you say, 'Show us the Father'? 10 Do you not believe that I am in the Father, and the Father in Me? The words that I speak to you I do not speak on My own *authority;* but the Father who dwells in Me does the works. 11 Believe Me that I *am* in the Father and the Father in Me, or else believe Me for the sake of the works themselves.

THE ANSWERED PRAYER

12 "Most assuredly, I say to you, he who believes in Me, the works that I do he will do also; and greater *works* than these he will do, because I go to My Father. 13 And whatever you ask in My name, that I will do, that the Father may be glorified in the Son. 14 If you ask° anything in My name, I will do *it.*

JESUS PROMISES ANOTHER HELPER

15 "If you love Me, keep° My commandments. 16 And I will pray the Father, and He will give you another Helper, that He may abide with you forever— 17 the Spirit of truth, whom the world cannot receive, because it neither sees Him nor knows Him; but you know Him, for He dwells with you and will be in you. 18 I will not leave you orphans; I will come to you.

INDWELLING OF THE FATHER AND THE SON

19 "A little while longer and the world will see Me no more, but you will see Me. Because I live, you will live also. 20 At that day you will know that I *am* in My Father, and you in Me, and I in you. 21 He who has My commandments and keeps them, it is he who loves Me. And he who loves Me will be loved by My Father, and I will love him and manifest Myself to him."

22 Judas (not Iscariot) said to Him, "Lord, how is it that You will manifest Yourself to us, and not to the world?"

23 Jesus answered and said to him, "If anyone loves Me, he will keep My word; and My Father will love him, and We will come to him and make Our home with him. 24 He who does not love Me does not keep My words; and the word which you hear is not Mine but the Father's who sent Me.

THE GIFT OF HIS PEACE

25 "These things I have spoken to you while being present with you. 26 But the Helper, the Holy Spirit, whom the Father will send in My name, He will teach you all things, and bring to your remembrance all things that I said to you. 27 Peace I leave with you, My peace I give to you; not as the world gives do I give to you. Let not your heart be troubled, neither let it be afraid. 28 You have heard Me say to you, 'I am going away and coming *back* to you.' If you loved Me, you would rejoice because I said,° 'I am going to the Father,' for My Father is greater than I.

29 "And now I have told you before it comes, that when it does come to pass, you may believe. 30 I will no longer talk much with you, for the ruler of this world is coming, and he has nothing in Me. 31 But that the world may know that I love the Father, and as the Father gave Me commandment, so I do. Arise, let us go from here.

14:14 °NU-Text adds *Me.*   14:15 °NU-Text reads *you will keep.*   14:28 °NU-Text omits *I said.*

THE TRUE VINE

15 "I am the true vine, and My Father is the vinedresser. ²Every branch in Me that does not bear fruit He takes away;ᵃ and every *branch* that bears fruit He prunes, that it may bear more fruit. ³You are already clean because of the word which I have spoken to you. ⁴Abide in Me, and I in you. As the branch cannot bear fruit of itself, unless it abides in the vine, neither can you, unless you abide in Me.

⁵"I am the vine, you *are* the branches. He who abides in Me, and I in him, bears much fruit; for without Me you can do nothing. ⁶If anyone does not abide in Me, he is cast out as a branch and is withered; and they gather them and throw *them* into the fire, and they are burned. ⁷If you abide in Me, and My words abide in you, you willᵃ ask what you desire, and it shall be done for you. ⁸By this My Father is glorified, that you bear much fruit; so you will be My disciples.

LOVE AND JOY PERFECTED

⁹"As the Father loved Me, I also have loved you; abide in My love. ¹⁰If you keep My commandments, you will abide in My love, just as I have kept My Father's commandments and abide in His love.

¹¹"These things I have spoken to you, that My joy may remain in you, and *that* your joy may be full. ¹²This is My commandment, that you love one another as I have loved you. ¹³Greater love has no one than this, than to lay down one's life for his friends. ¹⁴You are My friends if you do whatever I command you. ¹⁵No longer do I call you servants, for a servant does not know what his master is doing; but I have called you friends, for all things that I heard from My Father I have made known to you. ¹⁶You did not choose Me, but I chose you and appointed you that you should go and bear fruit, and *that* your fruit should remain, that whatever you ask the Father in My name He may give you. ¹⁷These things I command you, that you love one another.

THE WORLD'S HATRED

¹⁸"If the world hates you, you know that it hated Me before *it hated* you. ¹⁹If you were of the world, the world would love its own. Yet because you are not of the world, but I chose you out of the world, therefore the world hates you. ²⁰Remember the word that I said to you, 'A servant is not greater than his master.' If they persecuted Me, they will also persecute you. If they kept My word, they will keep yours also. ²¹But all these things they will do to you for My name's sake, because they do not know Him who sent Me. ²²If I had not come and spoken to them, they would have no sin, but now they have no excuse for their sin. ²³He who hates Me hates My Father also. ²⁴If I had not done among them the works which no one else did, they would have no sin; but now they have seen and also hated both Me and My Father. ²⁵But *this happened* that the word might be fulfilled which is written in their law, 'They hated Me without a cause.'ᵃ

THE COMING REJECTION

²⁶"But when the Helper comes, whom I shall send to you from the Father, the Spirit of truth who proceeds from the Father, He will testify of Me. ²⁷And you also will bear witness, because you have been with Me from the beginning.

16 "These things I have spoken to you, that you should not be made to stumble. ²They will put you out of the synagogues; yes, the time is coming that whoever kills you will think that he offers God service. ³And these things they will do to youᵃ because they have not known the Father nor Me. ⁴But these things I have told you, that when theᵃ time comes, you may remember that I told you of them.

"And these things I did not say to you at the beginning, because I was with you.

THE WORK OF THE HOLY SPIRIT

⁵"But now I go away to Him who sent Me, and none of you asks Me, 'Where are You going?' ⁶But because I have said these things to you, sorrow has filled your heart. ⁷Nevertheless I tell you the truth. It is to your advantage that I go away; for if I do not go away, the Helper will not come to you; but if I depart, I will send Him to you. ⁸And when He has come, He will convict the world of sin, and of righteousness, and of judgment: ⁹of sin, because they do not believe in Me; ¹⁰of righteousness, because I go to My Father and you see Me no more; ¹¹of judgment, because the ruler of this world is judged.

¹²"I still have many things to say to you, but you cannot bear *them* now. ¹³However, when He, the Spirit of truth, has come, He will guide you into all truth; for He will not speak on His own *authority*, but whatever He hears He will speak; and He will tell you things to come. ¹⁴He will glorify Me, for He will take of what is Mine and declare *it* to you. ¹⁵All things that the Father has are Mine. Therefore I said that He will take of Mine and declare *it* to you.ᵃ

SORROW WILL TURN TO JOY

¹⁶"A little while, and you will not see Me; and again a little while, and you will see Me, because I go to the Father." ¹⁷Then *some* of His disciples said among themselves, "What is this

---

"It is the opinion of those who best understand the physical system, that if the physical laws were strictly observed from generation to generation, there would be an end to the frightful diseases that cut life short, and of the long list of maladies that make life a torment or a trial, and that this wonderful machine, the body—this 'goodly temple'—would gradually decay, and men would at last die as if gently falling asleep." —*Catharine Maria Sedgwick, American author (1789–1867)*

PREACHING HEALTH

15:2 ᵃOr *lifts up*   **15:7** ᵃNU-Text omits *you will.*   **15:25** ᵃPsalm 69:4   **16:3** ᵃNU-Text and M-Text omit *to you.*   **16:4** ᵃNU-Text reads *their.*   **16:15** ᵃNU-Text and M-Text read *He takes of Mine and will declare it to you.*

DIVINE HEALTH   137

QUIZ 2

ARE YOU WALKING IN DIVINE HEALTH?

What is divine health? It is living with the maximum amount of health and wholeness a person can experience—spiritually, physically, and emotionally. Many people, however, have a far better understanding of what it means to feel "sick" than to be "well." We associate sickness with having pain, disease, weakness, and a lack of energy. If that is the case, wellness must also have a set of characteristics, such as strength and stamina, energy, flexibility, and sufficient vitality to do what one desires to do. The quiz below is aimed at helping you isolate those areas of your life in which you are not experiencing optimal health.

Are you physically healthy?	Yes	No	Sometimes
1. Is your skin free from blemishes?			
2. Is your skin good in color?			
3. Is your hair shiny and full?			
4. Are your teeth free from decay?			
5. Is your posture good?			
6. Are your muscles well toned?			
7. Can you walk a mile without tiring?			
8. Can you move your joints without pain?			
9. Do you live with nearly continual pain or a physical limitation?			
10. Do you sleep well at night?			
11. Can you carry a sack of groceries 2 blocks without pain or exhaustion?			
12. Do you get frequent colds or bouts of flu?			
13. Can you get in and out of vehicles, and up from chairs easily?			
14. Do you have headaches often?			
15. Do you have periodic chest pain?			
16. Are you overweight more than twenty pounds?			
17. Do you wish you had more energy?			
18. Have you been diagnosed with a disease that is chronic or life threatening?			
19. Do you have digestion or elimination difficulties?			
20. Do you have generalized pain that seems to fill your entire body?			

PHYSICAL QUIZ: The best answer is "yes" to all of the above, except questions 9, 12, and 14–20.

EMOTIONAL QUIZ: The best answer is "no" to all of the questions above, except 2, 3, 5, 13, and 18.

SPIRITUAL QUIZ: The best answer is "yes" to all questions above, except 11.

Are you emotionally healthy?

	Yes	No	Sometimes
1. Are you sometimes haunted by painful memories associated with abusive or unhealthy relationships?			
2. Are you able to trust others easily?			
3. Are you quick to reach out to other people who are experiencing difficulties?			
4. Do you expect others to wait upon you and meet all of your needs?			
5. Do you have a balance of people-time and alone-time in your schedule?			
6. Do you have frequent bad dreams or recurring nightmares?			
7. Do you frequently feel depressed or discouraged?			
8. Are you a fretter or worrier?			
9. Do you sometimes feel so angry you don't know what to do?			
10. Do you cower rather than confront?			
11. Do you frown more than you smile?			
12. Is there a person or group of people you just cannot tolerate, even for a short while?			
13. Do you respect other people?			
14. Do you hate to get up in the morning because you don't want to deal with the responsibilities of the coming day?			
15. Do you feel guilty for spending time alone or buying something for yourself?			
16. Are you frequently jealous of other people?			
17. Do you dread new situations or meeting new people?			
18. Are you willing to take full responsibility for your behavior and attitude?			
19. Are you holding a grudge against someone who has wounded you in some way?			
20. Do you feel hopelessly rejected by someone you love?			

Are you spiritually healthy?

	Yes	No	Sometimes
1. Do you believe that you and God have a good relationship?			
2. Do you frequently ask God to forgive you and help you?			
3. Do you freely forgive others?			
4. Do you easily ask others for forgiveness?			
5. Are you quick to offer thanksgiving and praise to God?			
6. Do you have an abiding sense of joy deep inside?			
7. Do you have assurance about what will happen to you after you die?			
8. Do you have an inner confidence that God will take care of you and provide for you?			
9. Do you have hope for the future?			
10. Do you believe God hears and answers your prayers?			
11. Do you have difficulty trusting God to work on your behalf and to do for you and your loved ones what you cannot do?			
12. Do you look forward to opportunities to tell other people about Jesus?			
13. Would people around you describe you as spiritually strong?			
14. Are you in regular close contact and fellowship with other Christians?			
15. Are you growing in your relationship with the Lord?			
16. Are you influencing other people around you to follow Jesus Christ more closely?			
17. Are giving and receiving in balance in your life?			
18. Do you have a deep sense of inner peace (more than abiding fears)?			
19. Do you seek to establish peace between other people who are quarreling?			
20. Do you feel more contentment than agitation?			

that He says to us, 'A little while, and you will not see Me; and again a little while, and you will see Me'; and, 'because I go to the Father'?" [18]They said therefore, "What is this that He says, 'A little while'? We do not know what He is saying."

[19]Now Jesus knew that they desired to ask Him, and He said to them, "Are you inquiring among yourselves about what I said, 'A little while, and you will not see Me; and again a little while, and you will see Me'? [20]Most assuredly, I say to you that you will weep and lament, but the world will rejoice; and you will be sorrowful, but your sorrow will be turned into joy. [21]A woman, when she is in labor, has sorrow because her hour has come; but as soon as she has given birth to the child, she no longer remembers the anguish, for joy that a human being has been born into the world. [22]Therefore you now have sorrow; but I will see you again and your heart will rejoice, and your joy no one will take from you.

[23]"And in that day you will ask Me nothing. Most assuredly, I say to you, whatever you ask the Father in My name He will give you. [24]Until now you have asked nothing in My name. Ask, and you will receive, that your joy may be full.

JESUS CHRIST HAS OVERCOME THE WORLD

[25]"These things I have spoken to you in figurative language; but the time is coming when I will no longer speak to you in figurative language, but I will tell you plainly about the Father. [26]In that day you will ask in My name, and I do not say to you that I shall pray the Father for you; [27]for the Father Himself loves you, because you have loved Me, and have believed that I came forth from God. [28]I came forth from the Father and have come into the world. Again, I leave the world and go to the Father."

[29]His disciples said to Him, "See, now You are speaking plainly, and using no figure of speech! [30]Now we are sure that You know all things, and have no need that anyone should question You. By this we believe that You came forth from God."

[31]Jesus answered them, "Do you now believe? [32]Indeed the hour is coming, yes, has now come, that you will be scattered, each to his own, and will leave Me alone. And yet I am not alone, because the Father is with Me. [33]These things I have spoken to you, that in Me you may have peace. In the world you will[a] have tribulation; but be of good cheer, I have overcome the world."

JESUS PRAYS FOR HIMSELF

17 Jesus spoke these words, lifted up His eyes to heaven, and said: "Father, the hour has come. Glorify Your Son, that Your Son also may glorify You, [2]as You have given Him authority over all flesh, that He should[a] give eternal life to as many as You have given Him. [3]And this is eternal life, that they may know You, the only true God, and Jesus Christ whom You have sent. [4]I have glorified You on the earth. I have finished the work which You have given Me to do. [5]And now, O Father, glorify Me together with Yourself, with the glory which I had with You before the world was.

JESUS PRAYS FOR HIS DISCIPLES

[6]"I have manifested Your name to the men whom You have given Me out of the world. They were Yours, You gave them to Me, and they have kept Your word. [7]Now they have known that all things which You have given Me are from You. [8]For I have given to them the words which You have given Me; and they have received *them*, and have known surely that I came forth from You; and they have believed that You sent Me.

[9]"I pray for them. I do not pray for the world but for those whom You have given Me, for they are Yours. [10]And all Mine are Yours, and Yours are Mine, and I am glorified in them. [11]Now I am no longer in the world, but these are in the world, and I come to You. Holy Father, keep through Your name those whom You have given Me,[a] that they may be one as We *are*. [12]While I was with them in the world,[a] I kept them in Your name. Those whom You gave Me I have kept;[b] and none of them is lost except the son of perdition, that the Scripture might be fulfilled. [13]But now I come to You, and these things I speak in the world, that they may have My joy fulfilled in themselves. [14]I have given them Your word; and the world has hated them because they are not of the world,

---

INSIGHTS INTO THE WORD

> (John 16:33)

Good Cheer. God never promised His people a rose garden, only a land of "promise"—a place where potential and wholeness might be pursued and won with faith. God did tell His people they were likely to encounter tribulation— trouble, sorrow, hard times, and difficult moments. He also said that as we trusted Jesus to be with us, work in us, and then work through us, we could have victory because He has "overcome the world." We could experience emotional health to the degree that we would recover quickly from or have the ability to endure all things that might steal our joy. We could make it through the hard times, and do so victoriously. Therefore, Jesus said, "Be of good cheer!"

How do we choose to be a person of good cheer?

First, don't focus on the negative—focus on the positive. Don't dwell on your fears or give in to them—focus on your faith. Don't seek out the worst in people or build such a strong defense around your heart and life that you lose touch with other people and refuse to take the risks that are required. Instead, seek out the best in people and trust God to give you the wisdom and courage to develop healthy loving relationships.

Be of *good cheer!* Stay hopeful, believe for the best, speak positively, and offer praise and thanks to God continually. Choose to do everything with a current of joy running through your soul. People and situations that are negative or troublesome are likely to crumble away into oblivion in the presence of your positive faith.

16:33 [a]NU-Text and M-Text omit *will*.　**17:2** [a]M-Text reads *shall*.　**17:11** [a]NU-Text and M-Text read *keep them through Your name which You have given Me*.　**17:12** [a]NU-Text omits *in the world*. [b]NU-Text reads *in Your name which You gave Me. And I guarded them;* (or *it;*).

just as I am not of the world. [15]I do not pray that You should take them out of the world, but that You should keep them from the evil one. [16]They are not of the world, just as I am not of the world. [17]Sanctify them by Your truth. Your word is truth. [18]As You sent Me into the world, I also have sent them into the world. [19]And for their sakes I sanctify Myself, that they also may be sanctified by the truth.

JESUS PRAYS FOR ALL BELIEVERS

[20]"I do not pray for these alone, but also for those who will[a] believe in Me through their word; [21]that they all may be one, as You, Father, *are* in Me, and I in You; that they also may be one in Us, that the world may believe that You sent Me. [22]And the glory which You gave Me I have given them, that they may be one just as We are one: [23]I in them, and You in Me; that they may be made perfect in one, and that the world may know that You have sent Me, and have loved them as You have loved Me.

[24]"Father, I desire that they also whom You gave Me may be with Me where I am, that they may behold My glory which You have given Me; for You loved Me before the foundation of the world. [25]O righteous Father! The world has not known You, but I have known You; and these have known that You sent Me. [26]And I have declared to them Your name, and will declare *it,* that the love with which You loved Me may be in them, and I in them."

BETRAYAL AND ARREST IN GETHSEMANE

18 When Jesus had spoken these words, He went out with His disciples over the Brook Kidron, where there was a garden, which He and His disciples entered. [2]And Judas, who betrayed Him, also knew the place; for Jesus often met there with His disciples. [3]Then Judas, having received a detachment *of troops,* and officers from the chief priests and Pharisees, came there with lanterns, torches, and weapons. [4]Jesus therefore, knowing all things that would come upon Him, went forward and said to them, "Whom are you seeking?"

[5]They answered Him, "Jesus of Nazareth."

Jesus said to them, "I am *He.*" And Judas, who betrayed Him, also stood with them. [6]Now when He said to them, "I am *He,*" they drew back and fell to the ground.

[7]Then He asked them again, "Whom are you seeking?"

And they said, "Jesus of Nazareth."

[8]Jesus answered, "I have told you that I am *He.* Therefore, if you seek Me, let these go their way," [9]that the saying might be fulfilled which He spoke, "Of those whom You gave Me I have lost none."

[10]Then Simon Peter, having a sword, drew it and struck the high priest's servant, and cut off his right ear. The servant's name was Malchus.

[11]So Jesus said to Peter, "Put your sword into the sheath. Shall I not drink the cup which My Father has given Me?"

BEFORE THE HIGH PRIEST

[12]Then the detachment *of troops* and the captain and the officers of the Jews arrested Jesus and bound Him. [13]And they led Him away to Annas first, for he was the father-in-law of Caiaphas who was high priest that year. [14]Now it was Caiaphas who advised the Jews that it was expedient that one man should die for the people.

Stress Busters
Embrace a New Attitude

A person tends to feel stress if he does not truly *enjoy* his life! Choose to embrace each new season of your life with enthusiasm, faith, and grace. The Bible says, "You will keep him in perfect peace, whose mind is stayed on You" (Isaiah 26:3). Keep your focus on the Lord and ask Him not only to help you cope with change in your life, but also to see changes as exciting opportunities for growth and greater ministry.

Fix your attention on Jesus, not on your problems. Dwelling on problems only tends to enlarge those problems in your mind, and to sour your attitude toward anything and any person associated with the problems. Ask the Lord to carry your burdens.

Stay focused on uplifting thoughts. Simply turn off the great flood of negative images and words that tend to come through the media every day. Avoid people who whine or are critical all the time. Choose to associate with people who are positive and to read, hear, attend, and see things that are informational, inspirational, and positive.

See your life as a celebration—not a struggle! Having a merry heart is more powerful than any antidepressant. Seek out those things that bring a smile to your face, a belly laugh, and a joyful attitude.

Recognize that no "season" of life lasts forever. The sun *will* come up tomorrow. Circumstances *will* change. Only God's mercies, faithfulness, and love are forever, and they are renewed toward you every morning (Lamentations 3:22, 23).

17:20 [a]NU-Text and M-Text omit *will.*

SCRIPTURE SOLUTIONS

[HYPERACTIVITY AND ATTENTION-DEFICIT DISORDERS]

Tens of thousands of children these days are being diagnosed with ADD (attention-deficit disorder) and ADHD (attention-deficit hyperactivity disorder). Is there any hope for these children? Yes!

Many physicians suggest drugs for these conditions. I recommend that parents *first* try better nutrition and natural supplements. Hyperactivity and attention-deficit disorders are not caused by poor diet, but they can be triggered by an imbalance of vital chemicals in the brain. Proper nutrition can dramatically improve the function of the brain and the behavior of a child. Here are a few simple guidelines:

☐ **Don't forget protein. Protein is an important element in a child's diet.**

☐ **Limit carbohydrates and sweets. Sugar intake increases hyperactivity and a tendency to become distracted.**

☐ **Start each day with a good breakfast that includes fruit, protein, and whole grains.**

☐ **Choose good fats (omega-3s), rather than bad fats.**

The following supplements can be added to your child's diet if needed.

A good multivitamin tablet. Add to your child's daily intake.

Zinc. Many times children are low in zinc because the foods containing zinc are often on a child's "do not like" list. You may need to add zinc to your child's daily supplements if it is not included in the multivitamin. CONT. NEXT PAGE>>>

PETER DENIES JESUS

¹⁵And Simon Peter followed Jesus, and so *did* another^a disciple. Now that disciple was known to the high priest, and went with Jesus into the courtyard of the high priest. ¹⁶But Peter stood at the door outside. Then the other disciple, who was known to the high priest, went out and spoke to her who kept the door, and brought Peter in. ¹⁷Then the servant girl who kept the door said to Peter, "You are not also *one* of this Man's disciples, are you?"

He said, "I am not."

¹⁸Now the servants and officers who had made a fire of coals stood there, for it was cold, and they warmed themselves. And Peter stood with them and warmed himself.

JESUS QUESTIONED BY THE HIGH PRIEST

¹⁹The high priest then asked Jesus about His disciples and His doctrine.

²⁰Jesus answered him, "I spoke openly to the world. I always taught in synagogues and in the temple, where the Jews always meet,^a and in secret I have said nothing. ²¹Why do you ask Me? Ask those who have heard Me what I said to them. Indeed they know what I said."

²²And when He had said these things, one of the officers who stood by struck Jesus with the palm of his hand, saying, "Do You answer the high priest like that?"

²³Jesus answered him, "If I have spoken evil, bear witness of the evil; but if well, why do you strike Me?"

²⁴Then Annas sent Him bound to Caiaphas the high priest.

PETER DENIES TWICE MORE

²⁵Now Simon Peter stood and warmed himself. Therefore they said to him, "You are not also *one* of His disciples, are you?"

He denied *it* and said, "I am not!"

²⁶One of the servants of the high priest, a relative *of him* whose ear Peter cut off, said, "Did I not see you in the garden with Him?" ²⁷Peter then denied again; and immediately a rooster crowed.

IN PILATE'S COURT

²⁸Then they led Jesus from Caiaphas to the Praetorium, and it was early morning. But they themselves did not go into the Praetorium, lest they should be defiled, but that they might eat the Passover. ²⁹Pilate then went out to them and said, "What accusation do you bring against this Man?"

³⁰They answered and said to him, "If He were not an evildoer, we would not have delivered Him up to you."

³¹Then Pilate said to them, "You take Him and judge Him according to your law."

Therefore the Jews said to him, "It is not lawful for us to put anyone to death," ³²that the saying of Jesus might be fulfilled which He spoke, signifying by what death He would die.

³³Then Pilate entered the Praetorium again, called Jesus, and said to Him, "Are You the King of the Jews?"

³⁴Jesus answered him, "Are you speaking for yourself about this, or did others tell you this concerning Me?"

³⁵Pilate answered, "Am I a Jew? Your own nation and the chief priests have delivered You to me. What have You done?"

18:15 ^aM-Text reads *the other.*   **18:20** ^aNU-Text reads *where all the Jews meet.*

Scripture Solutions Cont.>>>

The complete B complex of vitamins. A lack of B vitamins in good balance can be a factor to a child's inability to learn.

Iron. You can have blood tests run to see if your child is lacking in iron. Young girls are especially prone to iron deficiency.

In addition to correcting your child's diet and nutrition, limit the amount of time a child watches television, movies, or plays video games. Make sure your child has a regular routine. Keep your child's room organized, and help your child learn to manage his or her time and homework tasks.

Ask the Lord to help you and your child experience His peace! (See John 14:27.)

[36]Jesus answered, "My kingdom is not of this world. If My kingdom were of this world, My servants would fight, so that I should not be delivered to the Jews; but now My kingdom is not from here."

[37]Pilate therefore said to Him, "Are You a king then?"

Jesus answered, "You say *rightly* that I am a king. For this cause I was born, and for this cause I have come into the world, that I should bear witness to the truth. Everyone who is of the truth hears My voice."

[38]Pilate said to Him, "What is truth?" And when he had said this, he went out again to the Jews, and said to them, "I find no fault in Him at all.

TAKING THE PLACE OF BARABBAS

[39]"But you have a custom that I should release someone to you at the Passover. Do you therefore want me to release to you the King of the Jews?"

[40]Then they all cried again, saying, "Not this Man, but Barabbas!" Now Barabbas was a robber.

THE SOLDIERS MOCK JESUS

19 So then Pilate took Jesus and scourged *Him.* [2]And the soldiers twisted a crown of thorns and put *it* on His head, and they put on Him a purple robe. [3]Then they said,[a] "Hail, King of the Jews!" And they struck Him with their hands.

[4]Pilate then went out again, and said to them, "Behold, I am bringing Him out to you, that you may know that I find no fault in Him."

PILATE'S DECISION

[5]Then Jesus came out, wearing the crown of thorns and the purple robe. And *Pilate* said to them, "Behold the Man!"

[6]Therefore, when the chief priests and officers saw Him, they cried out, saying, "Crucify *Him,* crucify *Him!* "

Pilate said to them, "You take Him and crucify *Him,* for I find no fault in Him."

[7]The Jews answered him, "We have a law, and according to our[a] law He ought to die, because He made Himself the Son of God."

[8]Therefore, when Pilate heard that saying, he was the more afraid, [9]and went again into the Praetorium, and said to Jesus, "Where are You from?" But Jesus gave him no answer.

[10]Then Pilate said to Him, "Are You not speaking to me? Do You not know that I have power to crucify You, and power to release You?"

[11]Jesus answered, "You could have no power at all against Me unless it had been given you from above. Therefore the one who delivered Me to you has the greater sin."

[12]From then on Pilate sought to release Him, but the Jews cried out, saying, "If you let this Man go, you are not Caesar's friend. Whoever makes himself a king speaks against Caesar."

[13]When Pilate therefore heard that saying, he brought Jesus out and sat down in the judgment seat in a place that is called *The* Pavement, but in Hebrew, Gabbatha. [14]Now it was the Preparation Day of the Passover, and about the sixth hour. And he said to the Jews, "Behold your King!"

[15]But they cried out, "Away with *Him,* away with *Him!* Crucify Him!"

Pilate said to them, "Shall I crucify your King?"

The chief priests answered, "We have no king but Caesar!"

[16]Then he delivered Him to them to be crucified. Then they took Jesus and led *Him* away.[a]

THE KING ON A CROSS

[17]And He, bearing His cross, went out to a place called *the Place* of a Skull, which is called in Hebrew, Golgotha, [18]where they crucified Him, and two others with Him, one on either side, and Jesus in the center. [19]Now Pilate wrote a title and put *it* on the cross. And the writing was:

JESUS OF NAZARETH, THE KING OF THE JEWS.

[20]Then many of the Jews read this title, for the place where Jesus was crucified was near the city; and it was written in Hebrew, Greek, *and* Latin.

[21]Therefore the chief priests of the Jews said to Pilate, "Do not write, 'The King of the Jews,' but, 'He said, "I am the King of the Jews." ' "

[22]Pilate answered, "What I have written, I have written."

[23]Then the soldiers, when they had crucified Jesus, took His garments and made four parts, to each soldier a part, and also the tunic. Now the tunic was without seam, woven from the top in one piece. [24]They said therefore among themselves, "Let us not tear it, but cast lots for it, whose it shall be," that the Scripture might be fulfilled which says:

"They divided My garments among them,
And for My clothing they cast lots."[a]

Therefore the soldiers did these things.

19:3 [a]NU-Text reads *And they came up to Him and said.*   19:7 [a]NU-Text reads *the law.*   19:16 [a]NU-Text omits *and led Him away.*   19:24 [a]Psalm 22:18

The LAW AND THE SCIENCE

[BIRDS ARE TO WATCH, NOT EAT]

>SCIENCE

tells us birds that prey primarily upon sick or dead animals, or upon insects or items that sink to the bottom of the seas or freshwater lakes and ponds, can carry a wide variety of diseases. Birds of prey are especially prone to carrying bacteria and viruses that are not only deadly to other animals, but also may cause serious illness in human beings. Ostrich meat has become popular in recent years, but those who eat ostrich that is harvested from the "wild" (as opposed to ostrich farms) run a risk. Ostriches bury their heads in the sand in search of food sources that are considered unclean, such as small rodents or lizards.

BEHOLD YOUR MOTHER

²⁵Now there stood by the cross of Jesus His mother, and His mother's sister, Mary the *wife* of Clopas, and Mary Magdalene. ²⁶When Je-sus therefore saw His mother, and the disciple whom He loved standing by, He said to His mother, "Woman, behold your son!" ²⁷Then He said to the disciple, "Behold your mother!" And from that hour that disciple took her to his own *home.*

IT IS FINISHED

²⁸After this, Jesus, knowing[a] that all things were now accomplished, that the Scripture might be fulfilled, said, "I thirst!" ²⁹Now a vessel full of sour wine was sitting there; and they filled a sponge with sour wine, put *it* on hyssop, and put *it* to His mouth. ³⁰So when Jesus had received the sour wine, He said, "It is finished!" And bowing His head, He gave up His spirit.

JESUS' SIDE IS PIERCED

³¹Therefore, because it was the Preparation *Day,* that the bodies should not remain on the cross on the Sabbath (for that Sabbath was a high day), the Jews asked Pilate that their legs might be broken, and *that* they might be taken away. ³²Then the soldiers came and broke the legs of the first and of the other who was crucified with Him. ³³But when they came to Jesus and saw that He was already dead, they did not break His legs. ³⁴But one of the soldiers pierced His side with a spear, and immediately blood and water came out. ³⁵And he who has seen has testified, and his testimony is true; and he knows that he is telling the truth, so that you may believe. ³⁶For these things were done that the Scripture should be fulfilled, "Not *one* of His bones shall be broken."[a] ³⁷And again another Scripture says, "They shall look on Him whom they pierced."[a]

JESUS BURIED IN JOSEPH'S TOMB

³⁸After this, Joseph of Arimathea, being a disciple of Jesus, but secretly, for fear of the Jews, asked Pilate that he might take away the body of Jesus; and Pilate gave *him* permission. So he came and took the body of Jesus. ³⁹And Nicodemus, who at first came to Jesus by night, also came, bringing a mixture of myrrh and aloes, about a hundred pounds. ⁴⁰Then they took the body of Jesus, and bound it in strips of linen with the spices, as the custom of the Jews is to bury. ⁴¹Now in the place where He was crucified there was a garden, and in the garden a new tomb in which no one had yet been laid. ⁴²So there they laid Jesus, because of the Jews' Preparation *Day,* for the tomb was nearby.

THE EMPTY TOMB

20 Now the first *day* of the week Mary Magdalene went to the tomb early, while it was still dark, and saw *that* the stone had been taken away from the tomb. ²Then she ran and came to Simon Peter, and to the other disciple, whom Jesus loved, and said to them, "They have taken away the Lord out of the tomb, and we do not know where they have laid Him."

³Peter therefore went out, and the other disciple, and were going to the tomb. ⁴So they both ran together, and the other disciple outran Peter and came to the tomb first. ⁵And he, stooping down and looking in, saw the linen cloths lying *there;* yet he did not go in. ⁶Then Simon Peter came, following him, and went into the tomb; and he saw the linen cloths lying *there,* ⁷and the handkerchief that had been around His head, not lying with the linen cloths, but folded together in a place by itself. ⁸Then the other disciple, who came to the tomb first, went in also; and he saw and believed. ⁹For as yet they did not know the Scripture, that He must rise again from the dead. ¹⁰Then the disciples went away again to their own homes.

MARY MAGDALENE SEES THE RISEN LORD

¹¹But Mary stood outside by the tomb weeping, and as she wept she stooped down *and looked* into the tomb. ¹²And she saw two angels in white sitting, one at the head and the other at the feet, where the body of Jesus had lain. ¹³Then they said to her, "Woman, why are you weeping?"

> **>THE LAW**
>
> says: "And these you shall regard as an abomination among the birds; they shall not be eaten, they are an abomination: the eagle, the vulture, the buzzard, the kite, and the falcon after its kind; every raven after its kind, the ostrich, the short-eared owl, the sea gull, and the hawk after its kind; the little owl, the fisher owl, and the screech owl; the white owl, the jackdaw, and the carrion vulture; the stork, the heron after its kind, the hoopoe, and the bat" (Leviticus 11:13–19).

19:28 ᵃM-Text reads *seeing.*　19:36 ᵃExodus 12:46; Numbers 9:12; Psalm 34:20　19:37 ᵃZechariah 12:10

She said to them, "Because they have taken away my Lord, and I do not know where they have laid Him."

[14]Now when she had said this, she turned around and saw Jesus standing *there*, and did not know that it was Jesus. [15]Jesus said to her, "Woman, why are you weeping? Whom are you seeking?"

She, supposing Him to be the gardener, said to Him, "Sir, if You have carried Him away, tell me where You have laid Him, and I will take Him away."

[16]Jesus said to her, "Mary!"

She turned and said to Him,ᵃ "Rabboni!" (which is to say, Teacher).

[17]Jesus said to her, "Do not cling to Me, for I have not yet ascended to My Father; but go to My brethren and say to them, 'I am ascending to My Father and your Father, and *to* My God and your God.' "

[18]Mary Magdalene came and told the disciples that she had seen the Lord,ᵃ and *that* He had spoken these things to her.

THE APOSTLES COMMISSIONED

[19]Then, the same day at evening, being the first *day* of the week, when the doors were shut where the disciples were assembled,ᵃ for fear of the Jews, Jesus came and stood in the midst, and said to them, "Peace *be* with you." [20]When He had said this, He showed them *His* hands and His side. Then the disciples were glad when they saw the Lord.

[21]So Jesus said to them again, "Peace to you! As the Father has sent Me, I also send you." [22]And when He had said this, He breathed on *them,* and said to them, "Receive the Holy Spirit. [23]If you forgive the sins of any, they are forgiven them; if you retain the *sins* of any, they are retained."

SEEING AND BELIEVING

[24]Now Thomas, called the Twin, one of the twelve, was not with them when Jesus came. [25]The other disciples therefore said to him, "We have seen the Lord."

So he said to them, "Unless I see in His hands the print of the nails, and put my finger into the print of the nails, and put my hand into His side, I will not believe."

[26]And after eight days His disciples were again inside, and Thomas with them. Jesus came, the doors being shut, and stood in the midst, and said, "Peace to you!" [27]Then He said to Thomas, "Reach your finger here, and look at My hands; and reach your hand *here*, and put *it* into My side. Do not be unbelieving, but believing."

[28]And Thomas answered and said to Him, "My Lord and my God!"

[29]Jesus said to him, "Thomas,ᵃ because you have seen Me, you have believed. Blessed *are* those who have not seen and *yet* have believed."

THAT YOU MAY BELIEVE

[30]And truly Jesus did many other signs in the presence of His disciples, which are not written in this book; [31]but these are written that you may believe that Jesus is the Christ, the Son of God, and that believing you may have life in His name.

BREAKFAST BY THE SEA

21 After these things Jesus showed Himself again to the disciples at the Sea of Tiberias, and in this way He showed *Himself:* [2]Simon Peter, Thomas called the Twin, Nathanael of Cana in Galilee, the *sons* of Zebedee, and two others of His disciples were together. [3]Simon Peter said to them, "I am going fishing."

They said to him, "We are going with you also." They went out and immediatelyᵃ got into the boat, and that night they caught nothing. [4]But when the morning had now come, Jesus stood on the shore; yet the disciples did not know that it was Jesus. [5]Then Jesus said to them, "Children, have you any food?"

They answered Him, "No."

[6]And He said to them, "Cast the net on the right side of the boat, and you will find *some*." So they cast, and now they were not able to draw it in because of the multitude of fish.

[7]Therefore that disciple whom Jesus loved said to Peter, "It is the Lord!" Now when Simon Peter heard that it was the Lord, he put on *his* outer garment (for he had removed it), and plunged into the sea. [8]But the other disciples came in the little boat (for they were not far from land, but about two hundred cubits), dragging the net with fish. [9]Then, as soon as they had come to land, they saw a fire of coals there, and fish laid on it, and bread. [10]Jesus said to them, "Bring some of the fish which you have just caught."

[11]Simon Peter went up and dragged the net to land, full of large fish, one hundred and fifty-three; and although there were so many, the net was not broken. [12]Jesus said to them, "Come *and* eat breakfast." Yet none of the disciples dared ask Him, "Who are You?"—knowing that it was the Lord. [13]Jesus then came and took the bread and gave it to them, and likewise the fish.

[14]This *is* now the third time Jesus showed Himself to His disciples after He was raised from the dead.

> " **He breathed on them, and said to them, 'Receive the Holy Spirit. If you forgive the sins of any, they are forgiven them; if you retain the sins of any, they are retained.' "**
>
> — *John 20:22–23*

JESUS RESTORES PETER

[15]So when they had eaten breakfast, Jesus said to Simon Peter, "Simon, *son* of Jonah,ᵃ do you love Me more than these?"

He said to Him, "Yes, Lord; You know that I love You."

He said to him, "Feed My lambs."

[16]He said to him again a second time, "Simon, *son* of Jonah,ᵃ do you love Me?"

He said to Him, "Yes, Lord; You know that I love You."

He said to him, "Tend My sheep."

20:16 ᵃNU-Text adds *in Hebrew.*   20:18 ᵃNU-Text reads *disciples, "I have seen the Lord,"* . . .   20:19 ᵃNU-Text omits *assembled.*   20:29 ᵃNU-Text and M-Text omit *Thomas.*   21:3 ᵃNU-Text omits *immediately.*   21:15 ᵃNU-Text reads *John.*   21:16 ᵃNU-Text reads *John.*

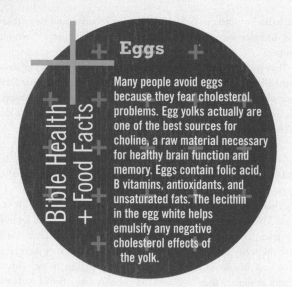

Bible Health + Food Facts

Eggs

Many people avoid eggs because they fear cholesterol problems. Egg yolks actually are one of the best sources for choline, a raw material necessary for healthy brain function and memory. Eggs contain folic acid, B vitamins, antioxidants, and unsaturated fats. The lecithin in the egg white helps emulsify any negative cholesterol effects of the yolk.

[17] He said to him the third time, "Simon, *son* of Jonah,* do you love Me?" Peter was grieved because He said to him the third time, "Do you love Me?"

And he said to Him, "Lord, You know all things; You know that I love You."

Jesus said to him, "Feed My sheep. [18] Most assuredly, I say to you, when you were younger, you girded yourself and walked where you wished; but when you are old, you will stretch out your hands, and another will gird you and carry *you* where you do not wish." [19] This He spoke, signifying by what death he would glorify God. And when He had spoken this, He said to him, "Follow Me."

THE BELOVED DISCIPLE AND HIS BOOK

[20] Then Peter, turning around, saw the disciple whom Jesus loved following, who also had leaned on His breast at the supper, and said, "Lord, who is the one who betrays You?" [21] Peter, seeing him, said to Jesus, "But Lord, what *about* this man?"

[22] Jesus said to him, "If I will that he remain till I come, what *is that* to you? You follow Me."

[23] Then this saying went out among the brethren that this disciple would not die. Yet Jesus did not say to him that he would not die, but, "If I will that he remain till I come, what *is that* to you?"

[24] This is the disciple who testifies of these things, and wrote these things; and we know that his testimony is true.

[25] And there are also many other things that Jesus did, which if they were written one by one, I suppose that even the world itself could not contain the books that would be written. Amen.

21:17 *NU-Text reads *John.*

HEALTH NOTES

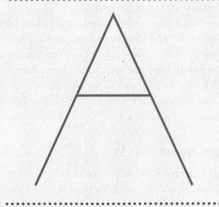

CTS

This book is the sequel to Luke—it tells what the disciples of Jesus did after Jesus ascended to heaven. One thing is clear: The apostles of Jesus said and did what Jesus had said and done. They preached the good news, healed the sick, delivered people from demons, and were willing to suffer and die for the Gospel of Christ. In many cases, they used the exact words and did precisely the same things Jesus had done in His earthly ministry. This was true of Paul, too, even though he never met Jesus in the flesh.

In today's world, we like to think we are independent thinkers, free to be "ourselves." In truth, we all follow and copy someone in every area of our life—a parent, teacher, coach, pastor, mentor. How we think and feel about God, ourselves, and other people is the result of what we have learned from someone. How we relate to God and to others is also the result of what we have learned—directly or indirectly, consciously or subconsciously.

Who do you love and admire—who are you following? Those who love and follow Jesus will seek to act like Him.

PROLOGUE

1 The former account I made, O Theophilus, of all that Jesus began both to do and teach, ²until the day in which He was taken up, after He through the Holy Spirit had given commandments to the apostles whom He had chosen, ³to whom He also presented Himself alive after His suffering by many infallible proofs, being seen by them during forty days and speaking of the things pertaining to the kingdom of God.

THE HOLY SPIRIT PROMISED

⁴And being assembled together with *them,* He commanded them not to depart from Jerusalem, but to wait for the Promise of the Father, "which," *He said,* "you have heard from Me; ⁵for John truly baptized with water, but you shall be baptized with the Holy Spirit not many days from now." ⁶Therefore, when they had come together, they asked Him, saying, "Lord, will You at this time restore the kingdom to Israel?" ⁷And He said to them, "It is not for you to know times or seasons which the Father has put in His own authority. ⁸But you shall receive power when the Holy Spirit has come upon you; and you shall be witnesses to Me^a in Jerusalem, and in all Judea and Samaria, and to the end of the earth."

JESUS ASCENDS TO HEAVEN

⁹Now when He had spoken these things, while they watched, He was taken up, and a cloud received Him out of their sight. ¹⁰And while they looked steadfastly toward heaven as He went up, behold, two men stood by them in white apparel, ¹¹who also said, "Men of Galilee, why do you stand gazing up into heaven? This *same* Jesus, who was taken up from you into heaven, will so come in like manner as you saw Him go into heaven."

THE UPPER ROOM PRAYER MEETING

¹²Then they returned to Jerusalem from the mount called Olivet, which is near Jerusalem, a Sabbath day's journey. ¹³And when they had entered, they went up into the upper room where they were staying: Peter, James, John, and Andrew; Philip and Thomas; Bartholomew and Matthew; James *the son* of Alphaeus and Simon the Zealot; and Judas *the son* of James. ¹⁴These all continued with one accord in prayer and supplication,^a with the women and Mary the mother of Jesus, and with His brothers.

MATTHIAS CHOSEN

¹⁵And in those days Peter stood up in the midst of the disciples^a (altogether the number of names was about a hundred and twenty), and said, ¹⁶"Men *and* brethren, this Scripture had to be fulfilled, which the Holy Spirit spoke before by the mouth of David concerning Judas, who became a guide to those who arrested Jesus; ¹⁷for he was numbered with us and obtained a part in this ministry."

¹⁸(Now this man purchased a field with the wages of iniquity; and falling headlong, he burst open in the middle and all his entrails gushed out. ¹⁹And it became known to all those dwelling in Jerusalem; so that field is called in their own language, Akel Dama, that is, Field of Blood.)

²⁰"For it is written in the Book of Psalms:

'Let his dwelling place be desolate,
And let no one live in it';^a

and,

'Let^b another take his office.'^c

1:8 ^aNU-Text reads *My witnesses.*   1:14 ^aNU-Text omits *and supplication.*   1:15 ^aNU-Text reads *brethren.*   1:20 ^aPsalm 69:25 ^bPsalm 109:8 ^cGreek *episkopen,* position of overseer

Your Garden—A Refuge for Meditation

Make your garden a place for reflective thought as well as a place for emotional rest. One way to do this is to make your garden the place where you spend quiet time with the Lord—a place to pray, read Scripture, and sit to meditate on or memorize Scripture.

Another way to make your garden a place for thought is to choose to spend time in your garden as you face important decisions or ponder critical choices. A garden setting is often much more conducive to focused and creative thinking than the walls of an office cubicle or the distractions associated with a room inside a house. It often is a place where you can retreat for quiet moments alone in the early morning or early evening.

It is important for you to have a comfortable place to sit if you want your garden to become a place for meditation or reflection. A bench or chair is easily added to most gardens. Place your garden seating so you can enjoy a vista or an especially beautiful area of your garden, eliminating as many distractions as possible. If you like to read in the garden or make notes as you reflect or meditate, consider adding a table that is the right height for writing.

Some gardeners add "words" to their gardens as spiritual reminders or to give them ongoing encouragement or inspiration. Often these messages are carved into stone (or *faux* stone) or concrete. The messages might be single words, such as *hope, rejoice, love,* or *peace.* The message might be a favorite verse of Scripture, one of the "I am" statements made by Jesus such as, "I am the Way, the Truth, and the Life", or one of the names or attributes of God, for example, God is Omnipresent, God is Holy, or God is Creator. These messages do not necessarily need to be large—they can be "hidden" among foliage and flowers. Finding them as you pull weeds or stroll casually along a garden path can be like finding a spiritual Easter egg—a life-giving word of blessing.

Consider adding a water feature with a fountain or pond to your garden. The sound of flowing water is not only soothing, but it also evokes many spiritual and creative images associated with life, renewal, rejuvenation, replenishment, nourishment, and refreshment.

²¹"Therefore, of these men who have accompanied us all the time that the Lord Jesus went in and out among us, ²²beginning from the baptism of John to that day when He was taken up from us, one of these must become a witness with us of His resurrection."

²³And they proposed two: Joseph called Barsabas, who was surnamed Justus, and Matthias. ²⁴And they prayed and said, "You, O Lord, who know the hearts of all, show which of these two You have chosen ²⁵to take part in this ministry and apostleship from which Judas by transgression fell, that he might go to his own place." ²⁶And they cast their lots, and the lot fell on Matthias. And he was numbered with the eleven apostles.

COMING OF THE HOLY SPIRIT

2 When the Day of Pentecost had fully come, they were all with one accord[a] in one place. ²And suddenly there came a sound from heaven, as of a rushing mighty wind, and it filled the whole house where they were sitting. ³Then there appeared to them divided tongues, as of fire, and *one* sat upon each of them. ⁴And they were all filled with the Holy Spirit and began to speak with other tongues, as the Spirit gave them utterance.

THE CROWD'S RESPONSE

⁵And there were dwelling in Jerusalem Jews, devout men, from every nation under heaven. ⁶And when this sound occurred, the multitude came together, and were confused, because everyone heard them speak in his own language. ⁷Then they were all amazed and marveled, saying to one another, "Look, are not all these who speak Galileans? ⁸And how *is it that* we hear, each in our own language in which we were born? ⁹Parthians and Medes and Elamites, those dwelling in Mesopotamia, Judea and Cappadocia, Pontus and Asia, ¹⁰Phrygia and Pamphylia, Egypt and the parts of Libya adjoining Cyrene, visitors from Rome, both Jews and proselytes, ¹¹Cretans and Arabs—we hear them speaking in our own tongues the wonderful works of God." ¹²So they were all amazed and perplexed, saying to one another, "Whatever could this mean?"

¹³Others mocking said, "They are full of new wine."

PETER'S SERMON

¹⁴But Peter, standing up with the eleven, raised his voice and said to them, "Men of Judea and all who dwell in Jerusalem, let this be known to you, and heed my words. ¹⁵For these are not drunk, as you suppose, since it is *only* the third hour of the day. ¹⁶But this is what was spoken by the prophet Joel:

¹⁷ 'And it shall come to pass in the last days, says God,
  That I will pour out of My Spirit on all flesh;
  Your sons and your daughters shall prophesy,
  Your young men shall see visions,
  Your old men shall dream dreams.
¹⁸ And on My menservants and on My maidservants
  I will pour out My Spirit in those days;
  And they shall prophesy.

2:1 ªNU-Text reads *together.*

WISE CHOICES

Choose grapes over raisins.

Raisins have a much higher concentration of sugar than fresh grapes. They are also more subject to pesticide residue. If you choose to eat raisins, I recommend organic raisins.

[19] I will show wonders in
heaven above
And signs in the earth
beneath:
Blood and fire and vapor
of smoke.
[20] The sun shall be turned
into darkness,
And the moon into blood,
Before the coming of the
great and awesome
day of the LORD.
[21] And it shall come to
pass
That whoever calls on the
name of the LORD
Shall be saved.'[a]

[22]"Men of Israel, hear these words: Jesus of Nazareth, a Man attested by God to you by miracles, wonders, and signs which God did through Him in your midst, as you yourselves also know— [23] Him, being delivered by the determined purpose and foreknowledge of God, you have taken[a] by lawless hands, have crucified, and put to death; [24] whom God raised up, having loosed the pains of death, because it was not possible that He should be held by it. [25] For David says concerning Him:

'I foresaw the LORD always before my face,
For He is at my right hand, that I may not be shaken.
[26] Therefore my heart rejoiced, and my tongue was glad;
Moreover my flesh also will rest in hope.
[27] For You will not leave my soul in Hades,
Nor will You allow Your Holy One to see corruption.
[28] You have made known to me the ways of life;
You will make me full of joy in Your presence.'[a]

[29]"Men and brethren, let me speak freely to you of the patriarch David, that he is both dead and buried, and his tomb is with us to this day. [30] Therefore, being a prophet, and knowing that God had sworn with an oath to him that of the fruit of his body, according to the flesh, He would raise up the Christ to sit on his throne,[a] [31] he, foreseeing this, spoke concerning the resurrection of the Christ, that His soul was not left in Hades, nor did His flesh see corruption. [32] This Jesus God has raised up, of which we are all witnesses. [33] Therefore being exalted to the right hand of God, and having received from the Father the promise of the Holy Spirit, He poured out this which you now see and hear. [34]"For David did not ascend into the heavens, but he says himself:

'The Lord said to my Lord,
"Sit at My right hand,
[35] Till I make Your enemies Your footstool." '[a]

[36]"Therefore let all the house of Israel know assuredly that God has made this Jesus, whom you crucified, both Lord and Christ."

[37] Now when they heard this, they were cut to the heart, and said to Peter and the rest of the apostles, "Men and brethren, what shall we do?"

[38] Then Peter said to them, "Repent, and let every one of you be baptized in the name of Jesus Christ for the remission of sins; and you shall receive the gift of the Holy Spirit. [39] For the promise is to you and to your children, and to all who are afar off, as many as the Lord our God will call."

A VITAL CHURCH GROWS

[40] And with many other words he testified and exhorted them, saying, "Be saved from this perverse generation." [41] Then those who gladly[a] received his word were baptized; and that day about three thousand souls were added to them. [42] And they continued steadfastly in the apostles' doctrine and fellowship, in the breaking of bread, and in prayers. [43] Then fear came upon every soul, and many wonders and signs were done through the apostles. [44] Now all who believed were together, and

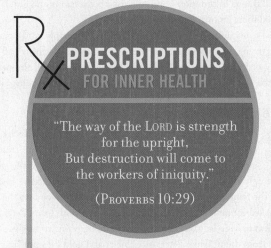

PRESCRIPTIONS
FOR INNER HEALTH

"The way of the LORD is strength
for the upright,
But destruction will come to
the workers of iniquity."

(PROVERBS 10:29)

When you follow God's commandments for living, you can walk with your head up and shoulders back—confidently, boldly, and in strength. You will be admired by others and have a greater opportunity for influence in your world. Those who behave contrary to God's laws reap scorn, ridicule, and denunciation from other people. Their reputations are destroyed, and in the end, so are their careers and their emotional health.

2:21 [a]Joel 2:28–32   2:23 [a]NU-Text omits *have taken.*   2:28 [a]Psalm 16:8–11   2:30 [a]NU-Text omits *according to the flesh, He would raise up the Christ* and completes the verse with *He would seat one on his throne.*   2:35 [a]Psalm 110:1   2:41 [a]NU-Text omits *gladly.*

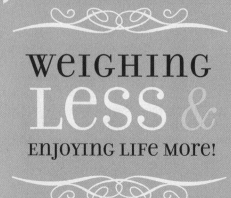

WEIGHING LESS & ENJOYING LIFE MORE!

[Eat V-E-R-Y Slowly]

One of the best things you can do for digestion and a weight-loss plan is to chew your food *v-e-r-y* slowly. This is especially important for red meat. Chewing a bite of meat approximately twenty to thirty times before swallowing allows the meat to be digested much better. The result of eating meat too quickly and washing it down with a beverage is often heartburn and indigestion.

In addition to chewing slowly, try putting your fork down between each bite. Don't use this "time out" to drink—too much liquid at a meal is not healthful. Rather, use this time to look around and enjoy the scenery or to "people watch."

It takes about fifteen minutes for your digestive system to send a signal to your brain that you are full. If you eat slowly, your brain will have more time to register a "that's enough" signal to you. I recommend you eat a small portion of food—perhaps 200–300 calories in a good balance of protein and carbohydrate—and then sit back and relax for a while to see if you are still hungry. Many times you will discover you aren't!

By relaxing and slowing down your eating, you can choose to make dining an enjoyable social experience. You'll find that you like eating good foods—even "diet foods"—if the meal is both enjoyable socially and satisfying physically.

had all things in common, [45]and sold their possessions and goods, and divided them among all, as anyone had need.

[46]So continuing daily with one accord in the temple, and breaking bread from house to house, they ate their food with gladness and simplicity of heart, [47]praising God and having favor with all the people. And the Lord added to the church[a] daily those who were being saved.

A LAME MAN HEALED

3 Now Peter and John went up together to the temple at the hour of prayer, the ninth *hour*. [2]And a certain man lame from his mother's womb was carried, whom they laid daily at the gate of the temple which is called Beautiful, to ask alms from those who entered the temple; [3]who, seeing Peter and John about to go into the temple, asked for alms. [4]And fixing his eyes on him, with John, Peter said, "Look at us." [5]So he gave them his attention, expecting to receive something from them. [6]Then Peter said, "Silver and gold I do not have, but what I do have I give you: In the name of Jesus Christ of Nazareth, rise up and walk." [7]And he took him by the right hand and lifted *him* up, and immediately his feet and ankle bones received strength. [8]So he, leaping up, stood and walked and entered the temple with them—walking, leaping, and praising God. [9]And all the people saw him walking and praising God. [10]Then they knew that it was he who sat begging alms at the Beautiful Gate of the temple; and they were filled with wonder and amazement at what had happened to him.

PREACHING IN SOLOMON'S PORTICO

[11]Now as the lame man who was healed held on to Peter and John, all the people ran together to them in the porch which is called Solomon's, greatly amazed. [12]So when Peter saw *it*, he responded to the people: "Men of Israel, why do you marvel at this? Or why look so intently at us, as though by our own power or godliness we had made this man walk? [13]The God of Abraham, Isaac, and Jacob, the God of our fathers, glorified His Servant Jesus, whom you delivered up and denied in the presence of Pilate, when he was determined to let *Him* go. [14]But you denied the Holy One and the Just, and asked for a murderer to be granted to you, [15]and killed the Prince of life, whom God raised from the dead, of which we are witnesses. [16]And His name, through faith in His name, has made this man strong, whom you see and know. Yes, the faith which *comes* through Him has given him this perfect soundness in the presence of you all.

[17]"Yet now, brethren, I know that you did *it* in ignorance, as *did* also your rulers. [18]But those things which God foretold by the mouth of all His prophets, that the Christ would suffer, He has thus fulfilled. [19]Repent therefore and be converted, that your sins may be blotted out, so that times of refreshing may come from the presence of the Lord, [20]and that He may send Jesus Christ, who was preached to you before,[a] [21]whom heaven must receive until the times of restoration of all things, which God has spoken by the mouth of all His holy prophets since the world began. [22]For Moses truly said to the fathers, 'The LORD your God will raise up for you a Prophet like me from your brethren. Him you shall hear in all things, whatever He says to you. [23]And it shall be that every soul who will not hear that Prophet shall be utterly destroyed from among the people.'[a] [24]Yes, and all the prophets, from Samuel and those who follow, as many as have spoken, have also foretold[a] these days. [25]You are sons of the prophets, and of the covenant which God made with our fathers, saying to Abraham, 'And in your seed all the families of the earth shall be blessed.'[a] [26]To you first, God, having raised up His Servant Jesus, sent Him to bless you, in turning away every one *of you* from your iniquities."

2:47 [a]NU-Text omits *to the church*. **3:20** [a]NU-Text and M-Text read *Christ Jesus, who was ordained for you before*. **3:23** [a]Deuteronomy 18:15, 18, 19 **3:24** [a]NU-Text and M-Text read *proclaimed*.
3:25 [a]Genesis 22:18; 26:4; 28:14

PETER AND JOHN ARRESTED

4 Now as they spoke to the people, the priests, the captain of the temple, and the Sadducees came upon them, ²being greatly disturbed that they taught the people and preached in Jesus the resurrection from the dead. ³And they laid hands on them, and put *them* in custody until the next day, for it was already evening. ⁴However, many of those who heard the word believed; and the number of the men came to be about five thousand.

ADDRESSING THE SANHEDRIN

⁵And it came to pass, on the next day, that their rulers, elders, and scribes, ⁶as well as Annas the high priest, Caiaphas, John, and Alexander, and as many as were of the family of the high priest, were gathered together at Jerusalem. ⁷And when they had set them in the midst, they asked, "By what power or by what name have you done this?"

⁸Then Peter, filled with the Holy Spirit, said to them, "Rulers of the people and elders of Israel: ⁹If we this day are judged for a good deed *done* to a helpless man, by what means he has been made well, ¹⁰let it be known to you all, and to all the people of Israel, that by the name of Jesus Christ of Nazareth, whom you crucified, whom God raised from the dead, by Him this man stands here before you whole. ¹¹This is the 'stone which was rejected by you builders, which has become the chief cornerstone.'ª ¹²Nor is there salvation in any other, for there is no other name under heaven given among men by which we must be saved."

Q Who is the first person in the Bible described as a farmer—"a tiller of the ground"?

A **Cain** *(Genesis 4:2).*

THE NAME OF JESUS FORBIDDEN

¹³Now when they saw the boldness of Peter and John, and perceived that they were uneducated and untrained men, they marveled. And they realized that they had been with Jesus. ¹⁴And seeing the man who had been healed standing with them, they could say nothing against it. ¹⁵But when they had commanded them to go aside out of the council, they conferred among themselves, ¹⁶saying, "What shall we do to these men? For, indeed, that a notable miracle has been done through them *is* evident to all who dwell in Jerusalem, and we cannot deny *it*. ¹⁷But so that it spreads no further among the people, let us severely threaten them, that from now on they speak to no man in this name."

¹⁸So they called them and commanded them not to speak at all nor teach in the name of Jesus. ¹⁹But Peter and John answered and said to them, "Whether it is right in the sight of God to listen to you more than to God, you judge. ²⁰For we cannot but speak the things which we have seen and heard." ²¹So when they had further threatened them, they let them go, finding no way of punishing them, because of the people, since they all glorified God for what had been done. ²²For the man was over forty years old on whom this miracle of healing had been performed.

PRAYER FOR BOLDNESS

²³And being let go, they went to their own *companions* and reported all that the chief priests and elders had said to them. ²⁴So when they heard that, they raised their voice to God with one accord and said:

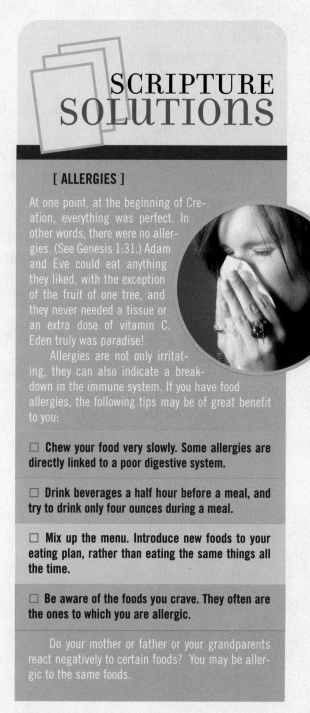

SCRIPTURE SOLUTIONS

[ALLERGIES]

At one point, at the beginning of Creation, everything was perfect. In other words, there were no allergies. (See Genesis 1:31.) Adam and Eve could eat anything they liked, with the exception of the fruit of one tree, and they never needed a tissue or an extra dose of vitamin C. Eden truly was paradise!

Allergies are not only irritating, they can also indicate a breakdown in the immune system. If you have food allergies, the following tips may be of great benefit to you:

☐ **Chew your food very slowly. Some allergies are directly linked to a poor digestive system.**

☐ **Drink beverages a half hour before a meal, and try to drink only four ounces during a meal.**

☐ **Mix up the menu. Introduce new foods to your eating plan, rather than eating the same things all the time.**

☐ **Be aware of the foods you crave. They often are the ones to which you are allergic.**

Do your mother or father or your grandparents react negatively to certain foods? You may be allergic to the same foods.

Ezekiel's Bread

Righteous Recipes

Ingredients:

- ☐ 4 envelopes dry yeast
- ☐ 1 tablespoon honey
- ☐ 1 cup warm water
- ☐ 8 cups whole-wheat flour
- ☐ 4 cups barley flour
- ☐ 2 cups soy flour
- ☐ ½ cup millet flour
- ☐ ⅓ cup rye flour
- ☐ 1 cup mashed *cooked* lentils
- ☐ 4–5 tablespoons extra-virgin olive oil
- ☐ ½–¾ cup honey
- ☐ 4 cups water
- ☐ 1 tablespoon Celtic salt

Stir the yeast and 1 tablespoon honey into 1 cup warm water and let stand for 10 minutes. Place the whole-wheat flour, barley flour, soy flour, millet flour, and rye flour in a large bowl and stir to combine. Combine the lentils, olive-oil, ½–¾ cup honey, and ½ cup water in a blender and process until smooth. Combine the lentil mixture and the remaining 3½ cups water in a large bowl. Stir until well mixed. Stir in 2 cups of the flour mixture. Stir in the yeast mixture. Add the salt and the remaining flour mixture.

Knead until smooth on a floured board. Place in an oiled bowl. Cover and let rise in a warm place until doubled in bulk. Knead again. Divide into 4 equal portions. Shape each portion into a large loaf. Place in greased loaf pans. Cover and let rise in a warm place until doubled in bulk.

Bake at 375 degrees for 45 minutes to 1 hour, or until the bread tests done.

Yield: 4 loaves

"Lord, You *are* God, who made heaven and earth and the sea, and all that is in them, [25]who by the mouth of Your servant David[a] have said:

> 'Why did the nations rage,
> And the people plot vain things?
> [26] The kings of the earth took their stand,
> And the rulers were gathered together
> Against the LORD and against His Christ.'[a]

[27]"For truly against Your holy Servant Jesus, whom You anointed, both Herod and Pontius Pilate, with the Gentiles and the people of Israel, were gathered together [28]to do whatever Your hand and Your purpose determined before to be done. [29]Now, Lord, look on their threats, and grant to Your servants that with all boldness they may speak Your word, [30]by stretching out Your hand to heal, and that signs and wonders may be done through the name of Your holy Servant Jesus."

[31]And when they had prayed, the place where they were assembled together was shaken; and they were all filled with the Holy Spirit, and they spoke the word of God with boldness.

SHARING IN ALL THINGS

[32]Now the multitude of those who believed were of one heart and one soul; neither did anyone say that any of the things he possessed was his own, but they had all things in common. [33]And with great power the apostles gave witness to the resurrection of the Lord Jesus. And great grace was upon them all. [34]Nor was there anyone among them who lacked; for all who were possessors of lands or houses sold them, and brought the proceeds of the things that were sold, [35]and laid *them* at the apostles' feet; and they distributed to each as anyone had need.

[36]And Joses,[a] who was also named Barnabas by the apostles (which is translated Son of Encouragement), a Levite of the country of Cyprus, [37]having land, sold *it*, and brought the money and laid *it* at the apostles' feet.

LYING TO THE HOLY SPIRIT

5 But a certain man named Ananias, with Sapphira his wife, sold a possession. [2]And he kept back *part* of the proceeds, his wife also being aware *of it*, and brought a certain part and laid *it* at the apostles' feet. [3]But Peter said, "Ananias, why has Satan filled your heart to lie to the Holy Spirit and keep back *part* of the price of the land for yourself? [4]While it remained, was it not your own? And after it was sold, was it not in your own control? Why have you conceived this thing in your heart? You have not lied to men but to God."

[5]Then Ananias, hearing these words, fell down and breathed his last. So great fear came upon all those who heard these things. [6]And the young men arose and wrapped him up, carried *him* out, and buried *him*.

[7]Now it was about three hours later when his wife came in, not knowing what had happened. [8]And Peter answered her, "Tell me whether you sold the land for so much?"

She said, "Yes, for so much."

[9]Then Peter said to her, "How is it that you have agreed together to

4:25 [a]NU-Text reads *who through the Holy Spirit, by the mouth of our father, Your servant David.*   4:26 [a]Psalm 2:1, 2   4:36 [a]NU-Text reads *Joseph.*

test the Spirit of the Lord? Look, the feet of those who have buried your husband *are* at the door, and they will carry you out." [10]Then immediately she fell down at his feet and breathed her last. And the young men came in and found her dead, and carrying *her* out, buried *her* by her husband. [11]So great fear came upon all the church and upon all who heard these things.

CONTINUING POWER IN THE CHURCH

[12]And through the hands of the apostles many signs and wonders were done among the people. And they were all with one accord in Solomon's Porch. [13]Yet none of the rest dared join them, but the people esteemed them highly. [14]And believers were increasingly added to the Lord, multitudes of both men and women, [15]so that they brought the sick out into the streets and laid *them* on beds and couches, that at least the shadow of Peter passing by might fall on some of them. [16]Also a multitude gathered from the surrounding cities to Jerusalem, bringing sick people and those who were tormented by unclean spirits, and they were all healed.

IMPRISONED APOSTLES FREED

[17]Then the high priest rose up, and all those who *were* with him (which is the sect of the Sadducees), and they were filled with indignation, [18]and laid their hands on the apostles and put them in the common prison. [19]But at night an angel of the Lord opened the prison doors and brought them out, and said, [20]"Go, stand in the temple and speak to the people all the words of this life."

[21]And when they heard *that,* they entered the temple early in the morning and taught. But the high priest and those with him came and called the council together, with all the elders of the children of Israel, and sent to the prison to have them brought.

APOSTLES ON TRIAL AGAIN

[22]But when the officers came and did not find them in the prison, they returned and reported, [23]saying, "Indeed we found the prison shut securely, and the guards standing outside[a] before the doors; but when we opened them, we found no one inside!" [24]Now when the high priest,[a] the captain of the temple, and the chief priests heard these things, they wondered what the outcome would be. [25]So one came and told them, saying,[a] "Look, the men whom you put in prison are standing in the temple and teaching the people!"

[26]Then the captain went with the officers and brought them without violence, for they feared the people, lest they should be stoned. [27]And when they had brought them, they set *them* before the council.

Barley Eaters

Bible Health + Food Facts

Roman gladiators in New Testament times were sometimes called *hordearii,* which means "barley eaters." Barley was added to their diet to give them bursts of strength before their contests.

And the high priest asked them, [28]saying, "Did we not strictly command you not to teach in this name? And look, you have filled Jerusalem with your doctrine, and intend to bring this Man's blood on us!"

[29]But Peter and the *other* apostles answered and said: "We ought to obey God rather than men. [30]The God of our fathers raised up Jesus whom you murdered by hanging on a tree. [31]Him God has exalted to His right hand *to be* Prince and Savior, to give repentance to Israel and forgiveness of sins. [32]And we are His witnesses to these things, and *so* also *is* the Holy Spirit whom God has given to those who obey Him."

GAMALIEL'S ADVICE

[33]When they heard *this,* they were furious and plotted to kill them. [34]Then one in the council stood up, a Pharisee named Gamaliel, a teacher of the law held in respect by all the people, and commanded them to put the apostles outside for a little while. [35]And he said to them: "Men of Israel, take heed to yourselves what you intend to do regarding these men. [36]For some time ago Theudas rose up, claiming to be somebody. A number of men, about four hundred, joined him. He was slain, and all who obeyed him were scattered and came to nothing. [37]After this man, Judas of Galilee rose up in the days of the census, and drew away many people after him. He also perished, and all who obeyed him were dispersed. [38]And now I say to you, keep away from these men and let them alone; for if this plan or this work is of men, it will come to nothing; [39]but if it is of God, you cannot overthrow it—

ULTIMATE HEALTH RESOURCE • ULTIMATE HEALTH RESOURCE • ULTIMATE HEALTH RESOURCE

In many ways, the Passover Feast—celebrated in Old Testament times as well as in Jesus' time and today—is a whole-person feast. Associated with it are customs that feed the body, the soul, and the spirit. (See Exodus 12—13.)

Passover was established to remember the way God supernaturally delivered the Israelites from slavery in Egypt. The celebration lasts seven days. It is held at the full moon of the first month in the Jewish calendar—the "fullness of the first." The exact date usually falls in March or April on the Roman calendar.

Four dishes are traditionally part of a Passover meal:

1. Roasted lamb. The whole lamb is to be roasted, according to the Old Testament.
2. Unleavened bread. Passover is also called the Feast of Unleavened Bread. Unleavened bread is to be eaten for the entire seven-day feast.
3. Bitter herbs. These are greens, generally what we call "salad greens." The bitterness represents the bitterness of slavery.
4. Haroset. This mixture of fruits and nuts represents the mortar that the Hebrew slaves used in building Pharaoh's pyramids.

The foods in the Passover meal cover the major nondairy foods: meat, grains, vegetables, fruit, and nuts.

How did this meal address the "soul" needs of the Israelites? The meal was to be served in family units. If one family could not consume an entire lamb, then other families were invited to the meal. God recognized the social needs of His people to be together in times of celebration and remembrance.

And what about the spiritual aspects of the meal? The meal was to be celebrated annually throughout history—to be a regular reminder of God's power to deliver those who trust in Him. All aspects of the meal have spiritually symbolic meaning.

The Lord does not merely call His people to celebrate—He gives His people the "how" and "why" of celebration. We celebrate His love, His power, His manifestations of provision and protection, His presence, and His call on our lives.

HAROSET

¼ cup chopped almonds
¾ cup chopped walnuts
3 cups chopped apples
½ cup raisins
½ cup chopped dates
½ teaspoon cinnamon
¾ cup grape juice or red wine
Combine all ingredients and serve chilled.
Yield: 8–12 servings

---

lest you even be found to fight against God."

[40]And they agreed with him, and when they had called for the apostles and beaten *them,* they commanded that they should not speak in the name of Jesus, and let them go. [41]So they departed from the presence of the council, rejoicing that they were counted worthy to suffer shame for His[a] name. [42]And daily in the temple, and in every house, they did not cease teaching and preaching Jesus *as* the Christ.

SEVEN CHOSEN TO SERVE

6 Now in those days, when *the number of* the disciples was multiplying, there arose a complaint against the Hebrews by the Hellenists,[a] because their widows were neglected in the daily distribution. [2]Then the twelve summoned the multitude of the disciples and said, "It is not desirable that we should leave the word of God and serve tables. [3]Therefore, brethren, seek out from among you seven men of *good* reputation, full of the Holy Spirit and wisdom, whom we may appoint over this business; [4]but we will give ourselves continually to prayer and to the ministry of the word."

[5]And the saying pleased the whole multitude. And they chose Stephen, a man full of faith and the Holy Spirit, and Philip, Prochorus, Nicanor, Timon, Parmenas, and Nicolas, a proselyte from Antioch, [6]whom they set before the apostles; and when they had prayed, they laid hands on them.

[7]Then the word of God spread, and the number of the disciples multiplied greatly in Jerusalem, and a great many of the priests were obedient to the faith.

STEPHEN ACCUSED OF BLASPHEMY

[8]And Stephen, full of faith[a] and power, did great wonders and signs among the people. [9]Then there arose some from what is called the Synagogue of the Freedmen (Cyrenians, Alexandrians, and those from Cilicia and Asia), disputing with Stephen. [10]And they were not able to resist the wisdom and the Spirit by which he spoke. [11]Then they secretly induced men to say, "We have heard him speak blasphemous words against Moses and God." [12]And they stirred up the people, the elders, and the scribes; and they came upon *him,* seized him, and brought *him* to the coun-

---

5:41 [a]NU-Text reads *the name;* M-Text reads *the name of Jesus.*   6:1 [a]That is, Greek-speaking Jews   6:8 [a]NU-Text reads *grace.*

cil. [13]They also set up false witnesses who said, "This man does not cease to speak blasphemous[a] words against this holy place and the law; [14]for we have heard him say that this Jesus of Nazareth will destroy this place and change the customs which Moses delivered to us." [15]And all who sat in the council, looking steadfastly at him, saw his face as the face of an angel.

STEPHEN'S ADDRESS: THE CALL OF ABRAHAM

7 Then the high priest said, "Are these things so?"

[2]And he said, "Brethren and fathers, listen: The God of glory appeared to our father Abraham when he was in Mesopotamia, before he dwelt in Haran, [3]and said to him, 'Get out of your country and from your relatives, and come to a land that I will show you.'[a] [4]Then he came out of the land of the Chaldeans and dwelt in Haran. And from there, when his father was dead, He moved him to this land in which you now dwell. [5]And *God* gave him no inheritance in it, not even *enough* to set his foot on. But even when *Abraham* had no child, He promised to give it to him for a possession, and to his descendants after him. [6]But God spoke in this way: that his descendants would dwell in a foreign land, and that they would bring them into bondage and oppress *them* four hundred years. [7]And the nation to whom they will be in bondage I will judge,'[a] said God, 'and after that they shall come out and serve Me in this place.'[b] [8]Then He gave him the covenant of circumcision; and so *Abraham* begot Isaac and circumcised him on the eighth day; and Isaac *begot* Jacob, and Jacob *begot* the twelve patriarchs.

THE PATRIARCHS IN EGYPT

[9]"And the patriarchs, becoming envious, sold Joseph into Egypt. But God was with him [10]and delivered him out of all his troubles, and gave him favor and wisdom in the presence of Pharaoh, king of Egypt; and he made him governor over Egypt and all his house. [11]Now a famine and great trouble came over all the land of Egypt and Canaan, and our fathers found no sustenance. [12]But when Jacob heard that there was grain in Egypt, he sent out our fathers first. [13]And the second *time* Joseph was made known to his brothers, and Joseph's family became known to the Pharaoh. [14]Then Joseph sent and called his father Jacob and all his relatives to *him,* seventy-five[a] people. [15]So Jacob went down to Egypt; and he died, he and our fathers. [16]And they were carried back to Shechem and laid in the tomb that Abraham bought for a sum of money from the sons of Hamor, *the father* of Shechem.

GOD DELIVERS ISRAEL BY MOSES

[17]"But when the time of the promise drew near which God had sworn to Abraham, the people grew and multiplied in Egypt [18]till another king arose who did not know Joseph. [19]This man dealt treacherously with our people, and oppressed our forefathers, making them expose their babies, so that they might not live. [20]At this time Moses was born, and was well pleasing to God; and he was brought up in his father's house for three months. [21]But when he was set out, Pharaoh's daughter took him away and brought him up as her own son. [22]And Moses was learned in all the wisdom of the Egyptians, and was mighty in words and deeds.

Bible Beverages
Wine

Wine in Bible times was most commonly made from grapes, but it was also made from figs, dates, and even pomegranates.

Certain people in Bible times were specifically forbidden to drink wine:

☐ Men who took a Nazirite vow and were dedicated to special, sacred service for a period of time.

☐ Israelite priests who were on duty in the tabernacle or temple.

The Bible also recommends that kings not drink wine or intoxicating beverages so they might maintain clarity of mind, memory, and judgment (Proverbs 31:4, 5).

Most of the wine consumed in Bible times was made from the juice of red grapes that had been put in small vats and fermented for about six weeks. The juice was then put in goatskin flasks (wineskins). Red wine is by far the most common wine produced throughout history. It has been consumed at meals and used medicinally for thousands of years.

Today we know that red grapes and the juice of red grapes are rich in a substance called flavonoids—especially quercetin, catechin, epicatechin, and resveratrol. These flavonoids are powerful antioxidants and anti-inflammatory agents. They also help decrease the clumping of blood platelets in the blood stream, and in so doing, help prevent blood clots. Red wine is rich in phenolic compounds that also help protect against cardiovascular disease and ischemic strokes. Red wine also helps stimulate digestion, and helps to prevent gastroenteritis and traveler's diarrhea.

The Bible warns against excessive consumption of wine. The benefits of red wine can be achieved without the alcohol by taking red wine capsules available in health-food stores, or by drinking natural purple grape juice with no sugar added.

Detoxifying Your Entire Life

Detoxification is the removal of dangerous, sometimes poisonous, chemical substances—called *toxins*—that detract from normal physical, mental, or spiritual functioning. Toxins are capable of producing disease, although in many cases they contribute more to a sense of ill-being—fatigue, a generalized "depressed" feeling, lack of motivation, and various allergic reactions.

Every aspect of a person's being is prone to toxins of one sort or another. The process of detoxification is generally a three-staged process: first, the recognition and release of the toxic substance; second, the elimination of the toxic substance; and third, an infusion of life-giving substances to restore any damage the toxin caused.

Mentally speaking, one of the first steps to detoxification is to recognize negative, harmful, or faulty thinking—in many cases, this means to own up to the lies that you have internalized. The lies must be named if they are ever to be released. Then, you need to willfully and intentionally *refuse* to verbalize or think about the lie. This means monitoring your speech, as well as putting a stop to an inflow of lies that another person may continue to speak. In the third step, you need to focus on "truth statements," including verses of the Bible that state the truth about your value, forgiven state, eternal life, and God's outpouring of blessings.

In the emotional realm, some relationships are toxic. They need to be recognized and a toxic relationship either needs to be severed or the parties involved need to seek godly counseling about how to cleanse their communication of toxic statements and their relationship of toxic behaviors. New friendships or healthy affiliations may need to be established.

Spiritually speaking, many people have been fed toxic beliefs about the nature of God, the nature of human beings, and the relationship God desires to have with His people. These toxic beliefs and any practices or rituals associated with them need to be recognized. A person needs to ask forgiveness for believing incorrectly or engaging in rituals that are forbidden by God or are hurtful to a good relationship with Him. New spiritual disciplines need to be put into place. To experience a renewed perspective, a person needs to read and study the Scriptures. Physically, you need to recognize that toxins have been taken into your body and take steps to detoxify the liver and digestive tract in order to thoroughly cleanse the blood system and all organs of your body. Some supplements can be taken to release toxins, and others to bind and eliminate the toxins from your body. New health practices need to be put in place.

Detoxification is an ongoing process. The end result is increased immunity and better overall health!

WHOLENESS 101

---

²³"Now when he was forty years old, it came into his heart to visit his brethren, the children of Israel. ²⁴And seeing one of *them* suffer wrong, he defended and avenged him who was oppressed, and struck down the Egyptian. ²⁵For he supposed that his brethren would have understood that God would deliver them by his hand, but they did not understand. ²⁶And the next day he appeared to two of them as they were fighting, and *tried to* reconcile them, saying, 'Men, you are brethren; why do you wrong one another?' ²⁷But he who did his neighbor wrong pushed him away, saying, 'Who made you a ruler and a judge over us? ²⁸Do you want to kill me as you did the Egyptian yesterday?'ᵃ ²⁹Then, at this saying, Moses fled and became a dweller in the land of Midian, where he had two sons.

³⁰"And when forty years had passed, an Angel of the Lordᵃ appeared to him in a flame of fire in a bush, in the wilderness of Mount Sinai. ³¹When Moses saw *it*, he marveled at the sight; and as he drew near to observe, the voice of the Lord came to him, ³²saying, 'I am the God of your fathers—the God of Abraham, the God of Isaac, and the God of Jacob.'ᵃ And Moses trembled and dared not look. ³³Then the Lord said to him, "Take your sandals off your feet, for the place where you stand is holy ground. ³⁴I have surely seen the oppression of My people who are in Egypt; I have heard their groaning and have come down to deliver them. And now come, I will send you to Egypt." 'ᵃ

³⁵"This Moses whom they rejected, saying, 'Who made you a ruler and a judge?'ᵃ is the one God sent *to be* a ruler and a deliverer by the hand of the Angel who appeared to him in the bush. ³⁶He brought them out, after he had shown wonders and signs in the land of Egypt, and in the Red Sea, and in the wilderness forty years.

ISRAEL REBELS AGAINST GOD

³⁷"This is that Moses who said to the children of Israel,ᵃ 'The Lord your God will raise up for you a Prophet like me from your brethren. Him you shall hear.'ᵇ

³⁸"This is he who was in the congregation in the wilderness with the Angel who spoke to him on Mount Sinai, and *with* our fathers, the one who received the living oracles to give to us, ³⁹whom our fathers would not obey, but rejected. And in their hearts they turned back to Egypt, ⁴⁰saying to Aaron, 'Make us gods to go before us; as for this Moses who brought us out of the land of Egypt, we do not know what has become of him.'ᵃ ⁴¹And they made a calf in those days, offered sacrifices to the idol, and rejoiced in the works of their own hands. ⁴²Then God turned

7:28 ᵃExodus 2:14   7:30 ᵃNU-Text omits *of the Lord*.   7:32 ᵃExodus 3:6, 15   7:34 ᵃExodus 3:5, 7, 8, 10   7:35 ᵃExodus 2:14   7:37 ᵃDeuteronomy 18:15   ᵇNU-Text and M-Text omit *Him you shall hear.*
7:40 ᵃExodus 32:1, 23

and gave them up to worship the host of heaven, as it is written in the book of the Prophets:

> 'Did you offer Me slaughtered animals and sacrifices during forty
> years in the wilderness,
> O house of Israel?
> [43] You also took up the tabernacle of Moloch,
> And the star of your god Remphan,
> Images which you made to worship;
> And I will carry you away beyond Babylon.'[a]

GOD'S TRUE TABERNACLE

[44]"Our fathers had the tabernacle of witness in the wilderness, as He appointed, instructing Moses to make it according to the pattern that he had seen, [45]which our fathers, having received it in turn, also brought with Joshua into the land possessed by the Gentiles, whom God drove out before the face of our fathers until the days of David, [46]who found favor before God and asked to find a dwelling for the God of Jacob. [47]But Solomon built Him a house.

[48]"However, the Most High does not dwell in temples made with hands, as the prophet says:

> [49] 'Heaven is My throne,
> And earth is My footstool.
> What house will you build for Me? says the LORD,
> Or what is the place of My rest?
> [50] Has My hand not made all these things?'[a]

ISRAEL RESISTS THE HOLY SPIRIT

[51]"*You* stiff-necked and uncircumcised in heart and ears! You always resist the Holy Spirit; as your fathers *did,* so *do* you. [52]Which of the prophets did your fathers not persecute? And they killed those who foretold the coming of the Just One, of whom you now have become the betrayers and murderers, [53]who have received the law by the direction of angels and have not kept *it.*"

STEPHEN THE MARTYR

[54]When they heard these things they were cut to the heart, and they gnashed at him with *their* teeth. [55]But he, being full of the Holy Spirit, gazed into heaven and saw the glory of God, and Jesus standing at the right hand of God, [56]and said, "Look! I see the heavens opened and the Son of Man standing at the right hand of God!"

[57]Then they cried out with a loud voice, stopped their ears, and ran at him with one accord; [58]and they cast *him* out of the city and stoned *him.* And the witnesses laid down their clothes at the feet of a young man named Saul. [59]And they stoned Stephen as he was calling on *God* and saying, "Lord Jesus, receive my spirit." [60]Then he knelt down and cried out with a loud voice, "Lord, do not charge them with this sin." And when he had said this, he fell asleep.

SAUL PERSECUTES THE CHURCH

8 Now Saul was consenting to his death. At that time a great persecution arose against the church which was at Jerusalem; and they were all scattered throughout the regions of Judea and Samaria, except the apostles. [2]And devout men carried Stephen *to his burial,* and made great lamentation over him.

[3]As for Saul, he made havoc of the church, entering every house, and dragging off men and women, committing *them* to prison.

CHRIST IS PREACHED IN SAMARIA

[4]Therefore those who were scattered went everywhere preaching the word. [5]Then Philip went down to the[a] city of Samaria and preached Christ to them. [6]And the multitudes with one accord heeded the things spoken by Philip, hearing and seeing the miracles which he did. [7]For unclean spirits, crying with a loud voice, came out of many who were possessed; and many who were paralyzed and lame were healed. [8]And there was great joy in that city.

THE SORCERER'S PROFESSION OF FAITH

[9]But there was a certain man called Simon, who previously practiced sorcery in the city and astonished the people of Samaria, claiming that he was someone great, [10]to whom they all gave heed, from the

---

> (Acts 7:51)

Do You Have a Stiff Neck? To be stiff-necked in Jesus' day did *not* mean that a person was rigid or inflexible. It meant that a person willfully and consciously chose *not* to obey God's commands. The person might be in open rebellion, pursuing evil activities that God prohibited. Or, the person might be in latent rebellion, simply choosing not to do the *good* things that God commanded. Either way, the person was in error.

Today in the liturgical church various confessions of sin acknowledge sins of "commission" and sins of "omission." Sins of commission are bad things done;

sins of omission are good things left undone. A person who has a "stiff neck" is a person who is likely to *choose* to ignore God's laws and commandments, and willfully neglect what he knows he should do and pursue instead what he knows he shouldn't do.

Are you stiff necked when it comes to eating and exercising? The failure to eat and exercise correctly may not be a sin, but a failure to do what you know you *should* do may be a subtle form of rebellion symptomatic of a bigger problem.

INSIGHTS INTO THE WORD

---

least to the greatest, saying, "This man is the great power of God." [11]And they heeded him because he had astonished them with his sorceries for a long time. [12]But when they believed Philip as he preached the things concerning the kingdom of God and the name of Jesus Christ, both men and women were baptized. [13]Then Simon himself also believed; and when he was baptized he continued with Philip, and was amazed, seeing the miracles and signs which were done.

THE SORCERER'S SIN

[14]Now when the apostles who were at Jerusalem heard that Samaria had received the word of God, they sent Peter and John to them, [15]who, when they had come down, prayed for them that they might receive the Holy Spirit. [16]For as yet He had fallen upon none of them. They had only been baptized in the name of the Lord Jesus. [17]Then they laid hands on them, and they received the Holy Spirit.

[18]And when Simon saw that through the laying on of the apostles' hands the Holy Spirit was given, he offered them money, [19]saying, "Give me this power also, that anyone on whom I lay hands may receive the Holy Spirit."

[20]But Peter said to him, "Your money perish with you, because you thought that the gift of God could be purchased with money! [21]You have neither part nor portion in this matter, for your heart is not right in the sight of God. [22]Repent therefore of this your wickedness, and pray God if perhaps the thought of your heart may be forgiven you. [23]For I see that you are poisoned by bitterness and bound by iniquity."

[24]Then Simon answered and said, "Pray to the Lord for me, that none of the things which you have spoken may come upon me."

[25]So when they had testified and preached the word of the Lord, they returned to Jerusalem, preaching the gospel in many villages of the Samaritans.

CHRIST IS PREACHED TO AN ETHIOPIAN

[26]Now an angel of the Lord spoke to Philip, saying, "Arise and go toward the south along the road which goes down from Jerusalem to Gaza." This is desert. [27]So he arose and went. And behold, a man of Ethiopia, a eunuch of great authority under Candace the queen of the Ethiopians, who had charge of all her treasury, and had come to Jerusalem to worship, [28]was returning. And sitting in his chariot, he was reading Isaiah the prophet. [29]Then the Spirit said to Philip, "Go near and overtake this chariot."

[30]So Philip ran to him, and heard him reading the prophet Isaiah, and said, "Do you understand what you are reading?"

[31]And he said, "How can I, unless someone guides me?" And he asked Philip to come up and sit with him. [32]The place in the Scripture which he read was this:

"He was led as a sheep to the slaughter;
  And as a lamb before its shearer is silent,
  So He opened not His mouth.
[33] In His humiliation His justice was taken away,
  And who will declare His generation?
  For His life is taken from the earth."[a]

[34]So the eunuch answered Philip and said, "I ask you, of whom does the prophet say this, of himself or of some other man?" [35]Then Philip opened his mouth, and beginning at this Scripture, preached Jesus to him. [36]Now as they went down the road, they came to some water. And the eunuch said, "See, *here is* water. What hinders me from being baptized?"

[37]Then Philip said, "If you believe with all your heart, you may."

And he answered and said, "I believe that Jesus Christ is the Son of God."[a]

[38]So he commanded the chariot to stand still. And both Philip and the eunuch went down into the water, and he baptized him. [39]Now when they came up out of the water, the Spirit of the Lord caught Philip away, so that the eunuch saw him no more; and he went on his way rejoicing. [40]But Philip was found at Azotus. And passing through, he preached in all the cities till he came to Caesarea.

THE DAMASCUS ROAD: SAUL CONVERTED

9 Then Saul, still breathing threats and murder against the disciples of the Lord, went to the high priest [2]and asked letters from him to the synagogues of Damascus, so that if he found any who were of the Way, whether men or women, he might bring them bound to Jerusalem.

[3]As he journeyed he came near Damascus, and suddenly a light shone around him from heaven. [4]Then he fell to the ground, and heard a voice saying to him, "Saul, Saul, why are you persecuting Me?"

[5]And he said, "Who are You, Lord?"

Then the Lord said, "I am Jesus, whom you are persecuting.[a] It *is* hard for you to kick against the goads."

[6]So he, trembling and astonished, said, "Lord, what do You want me to do?"

Then the Lord *said* to him, "Arise and go into the city, and you will be told what you must do."

[7]And the men who journeyed with him

INSIGHTS INTO THE WORD

> (Acts 8:29, 30)

Walk or Run? Although running and jogging burn up more calories than walking—and do so in less time—walking may be a better exercise than jogging for some people, especially those who are overweight or pregnant; have joint, foot, or knee problems; or who are just beginning an exercise program. A slow rather than fast walk is now recommended for the obese—mainly because overweight people tend to walk *longer* if they walk more slowly. The extra time spent walking can be more advantageous than less time at a faster pace. If the Lord speaks to you, however, about catching up with someone in order to share the gospel, move as quickly as you can!

8:33 [a]Isaiah 53:7, 8   8:37 [a]NU-Text and M-Text omit this verse. It is found in Western texts, including the Latin tradition.   9:5 [a]NU-Text and M-Text omit the last sentence of verse 5 and begin verse 6 with *But arise and go.*

stood speechless, hearing a voice but seeing no one. [8]Then Saul arose from the ground, and when his eyes were opened he saw no one. But they led him by the hand and brought *him* into Damascus. [9]And he was three days without sight, and neither ate nor drank.

ANANIAS BAPTIZES SAUL

[10]Now there was a certain disciple at Damascus named Ananias; and to him the Lord said in a vision, "Ananias."

And he said, "Here I am, Lord."

[11]So the Lord *said* to him, "Arise and go to the street called Straight, and inquire at the house of Judas for *one* called Saul of Tarsus, for behold, he is praying. [12]And in a vision he has seen a man named Ananias coming in and putting *his* hand on him, so that he might receive his sight."

[13]Then Ananias answered, "Lord, I have heard from many about this man, how much harm he has done to Your saints in Jerusalem. [14]And here he has authority from the chief priests to bind all who call on Your name."

[15]But the Lord said to him, "Go, for he is a chosen vessel of Mine to bear My name before Gentiles, kings, and the children of Israel. [16]For I will show him how many things he must suffer for My name's sake."

[17]And Ananias went his way and entered the house; and laying his hands on him he said, "Brother Saul, the Lord Jesus,[a] who appeared to you on the road as you came, has sent me that you may receive your sight and be filled with the Holy Spirit." [18]Immediately there fell from his eyes *something* like scales, and he received his sight at once; and he arose and was baptized. [19]So when he had received food, he was strengthened. Then Saul spent some days with the disciples at Damascus.

SAUL PREACHES CHRIST

[20]Immediately he preached the Christ[a] in the synagogues, that He is the Son of God.

[21]Then all who heard were amazed, and said, "Is this not he who destroyed those who called on this name in Jerusalem, and has

come here for that purpose, so that he might bring them bound to the chief priests?"

[22]But Saul increased all the more in strength, and confounded the Jews who dwelt in Damascus, proving that this *Jesus* is the Christ.

SAUL ESCAPES DEATH

[23]Now after many days were past, the Jews plotted to kill him. [24]But their plot became known to Saul. And they watched the gates day and night, to kill him. [25]Then the disciples took him by night and let *him* down through the wall in a large basket.

SAUL AT JERUSALEM

[26]And when Saul had come to Jerusalem, he tried to join the disciples; but they were all afraid of him, and did not believe that he was a disciple. [27]But Barnabas took him and brought *him* to the apostles. And he declared to them how he had seen the Lord on the road, and that He had spoken to him, and how he had preached boldly at Damascus in the name of Jesus. [28]So he was with them at Jerusalem, coming in and going out. [29]And he spoke boldly in the name of the Lord Jesus

and disputed against the Hellenists, but they attempted to kill him. [30]When the brethren found out, they brought him down to Caesarea and sent him out to Tarsus.

THE CHURCH PROSPERS

[31]Then the churches[a] throughout all Judea, Galilee, and Samaria had peace and were edified. And walking in the fear of the Lord and in the comfort of the Holy Spirit, they were multiplied.

AENEAS HEALED

[32]Now it came to pass, as Peter went through all *parts of the country,* that he also came down to the saints who dwelt in Lydda. [33]There he found a certain man named Aeneas, who had been bedridden eight years and was paralyzed. [34]And Peter said to him, "Aeneas, Jesus the Christ heals you. Arise and make your bed." Then he arose immediately. [35]So all who dwelt at Lydda and Sharon saw him and turned to the Lord.

DORCAS RESTORED TO LIFE

[36]At Joppa there was a certain disciple named Tabitha, which is translated Dorcas.

GODLY & GOODLOOKIN'

For Better Skin and Nails . . .

For better skin and nails, think protein! Nails are made of protein, not calcium as some think. A protein deficiency is sometimes behind split or extremely thin nails. Nails that fail to grow quickly are nails without sufficient protein.

The structure of the hair follicle is protein. L-cysteine and L-methionine are the amino acids that form keratin, which is the protein structure of hair. These amino acids have been found to increase hair growth by as much as 100 percent. Egg yolk contains the highest amount of these two amino acids. Supplementation with L-cysteine may prevent hair from falling out.

Other supplements can also be helpful: Biotin has been shown to help hair growth, folic acid to restore gray hair to natural color, and inositol to prevent thinning hair and baldness.

9:17 [a]M-Text omits *Jesus.*   9:20 [a]NU-Text reads *Jesus.*   9:31 [a]NU-Text reads *church . . . was edified.*

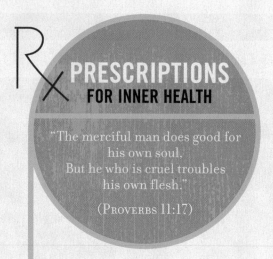

PRESCRIPTIONS
FOR INNER HEALTH

"The merciful man does good for
his own soul.
But he who is cruel troubles
his own flesh."

(PROVERBS 11:17)

When you show mercy to others, you receive mercy. You are freed emotionally to love, forgive, and be a blessing to other people. If you do not treat others with mercy, however, you are more likely to harbor bitterness, resentment, unforgiveness, and even hatred. The end result is going to be a flood of stress hormones into your physical body!

This woman was full of good works and charitable deeds which she did. ³⁷But it happened in those days that she became sick and died. When they had washed her, they laid *her* in an upper room. ³⁸And since Lydda was near Joppa, and the disciples had heard that Peter was there, they sent two men to him, imploring *him* not to delay in coming to them. ³⁹Then Peter arose and went with them. When he had come, they brought *him* to the upper room. And all the widows stood by him weeping, showing the tunics and garments which Dorcas had made while she was with them. ⁴⁰But Peter put them all out, and knelt down and prayed. And turning to the body he said, "Tabitha, arise." And she opened her eyes, and when she saw Peter she sat up. ⁴¹Then he gave her *his* hand and lifted her up; and when he had called the saints and widows, he presented her alive. ⁴²And it became known throughout all Joppa, and many believed on the Lord. ⁴³So it was that he stayed many days in Joppa with Simon, a tanner.

CORNELIUS SENDS A DELEGATION

10 There was a certain man in Caesarea called Cornelius, a centurion of what was called the Italian Regiment, ²a devout *man* and one who feared God with all his household, who gave alms generously to the people, and prayed to God always. ³About the ninth hour of the day he saw clearly in a vision an angel of God coming in and saying to him, "Cornelius!"

⁴And when he observed him, he was afraid, and said, "What is it, lord?"

So he said to him, "Your prayers and your alms have come up for a memorial before God. ⁵Now send men to Joppa, and send for Simon whose surname is Peter. ⁶He is lodging with Simon, a tanner, whose house is by the sea.ᵃ He will tell you what you must do." ⁷And when the angel who spoke to him had departed, Cornelius called two of his household servants and a devout soldier from among those who waited on him continually. ⁸So when he had explained all *these* things to them, he sent them to Joppa.

PETER'S VISION

⁹The next day, as they went on their journey and drew near the city, Peter went up on the housetop to pray, about the sixth hour. ¹⁰Then he became very hungry and wanted to eat; but while they made ready, he fell into a trance ¹¹and saw heaven opened and an object like a great sheet bound at the four corners, descending to him and let down to the earth. ¹²In it were all kinds of four-footed animals of the earth, wild beasts, creeping things, and birds of the air. ¹³And a voice came to him, "Rise, Peter; kill and eat."

¹⁴But Peter said, "Not so, Lord! For I have never eaten anything common or unclean."

¹⁵And a voice *spoke* to him again the second time, "What God has cleansed you must not call common." ¹⁶This was done three times. And the object was taken up into heaven again.

SUMMONED TO CAESAREA

¹⁷Now while Peter wondered within himself what this vision which he had seen meant, behold, the men who had been sent from Cornelius had made inquiry for Simon's house, and stood before the gate. ¹⁸And they called and asked whether Simon, whose surname was Peter, was lodging there.

¹⁹While Peter thought about the vision, the Spirit said to him, "Behold, three men are seeking you. ²⁰Arise therefore, go down and go with them, doubting nothing; for I have sent them."

²¹Then Peter went down to the men who had been sent to him from Cornelius,ᵃ and said, "Yes, I am he whom you seek. For what reason have you come?"

²²And they said, "Cornelius *the* centurion, a just man, one who fears God and has a good reputation among all the nation of the Jews, was divinely instructed by a holy angel to summon you to his house, and to hear words from you." ²³Then he invited them in and lodged *them.*

On the next day Peter went away with them, and some brethren from Joppa accompanied him.

PETER MEETS CORNELIUS

²⁴And the following day they entered Caesarea. Now Cornelius was waiting for them, and had called together his relatives and close friends. ²⁵As Peter was coming in, Cornelius met him and fell down at his feet and worshiped *him.* ²⁶But Peter lifted him up, saying, "Stand up; I myself am also a man." ²⁷And as he talked with him, he went in and found many who had come together. ²⁸Then he said to them, "You

10:6 ᵃNU-Text and M-Text omit the last sentence of this verse. **10:21** ᵃNU-Text and M-Text omit *who had been sent to him from Cornelius.*

May

1 2 3 4 5 6 7

Now Is the Time To...

☐ Anticipate summer impromptu picnics! Pack up a picnic kit to store in your car. Use a picnic hamper or a lidded box or container. Stock it with dishes, glassware, flatware, a pocketknife, and serving spoons. These can be plasticware or items you might find at a flea market or garage sale. Include salt, pepper, napkins, a roll of paper towels, a tablecloth, and moist towelettes. If a "picnic mood" strikes, you can pick up a few supplies at a grocery or farmer's market and head for a nearby beautiful location on a moment's notice.
☐ Dig out containers that you may want to use as flowering planters on your porches, patios, or walkways.

8 9 10 11 12 13 14

Seasonal Tips

☐ Be sure to store your clean gardening tools in oil-treated sand in containers that are not accessible to pets or children. The oil in the sand keeps your trowels and handheld spades from rusting. ☐ To get spring-green grass stains from gardening clothes, play clothes, or sports uniforms, pretreat the stain with this mixture: equal parts liquid detergent and white vinegar. Store this mix in a spray bottle. Apply it to a stained area and let it sit for twenty to thirty minutes. Use an old toothbrush to work the solution into the fabric, then wash. (After you've pretreated the fabric, don't let the mixture sit more than two days before washing.)

In the Garden

15 16 17 18 19 20 21

☐ Watch your weather forecasts closely. Although spring may be in the air, nighttime temperatures may not be warm enough for planting certain bedding plants, or for moving plants from the warmth of your indoor sunroom to an outdoor area. ☐ This is the time to shop for perennial blooming flowers such as daylilies—you can pick the colors, sizes, and flower forms from "real examples," not photographs. ☐ Pepper, tomato, and squash plants should be fertilized with a 10-12-12 fertilizer to improve plant growth and vegetable production. ☐ Make sure your tall-growing flowers—such as gladioli, dahlias, and lilies—have support stakes in place. ☐ This is the time to add basil and dill to your herb garden or containers. You can grow both from seeds or transplants.

Table Fresh

24 25 26 27 28

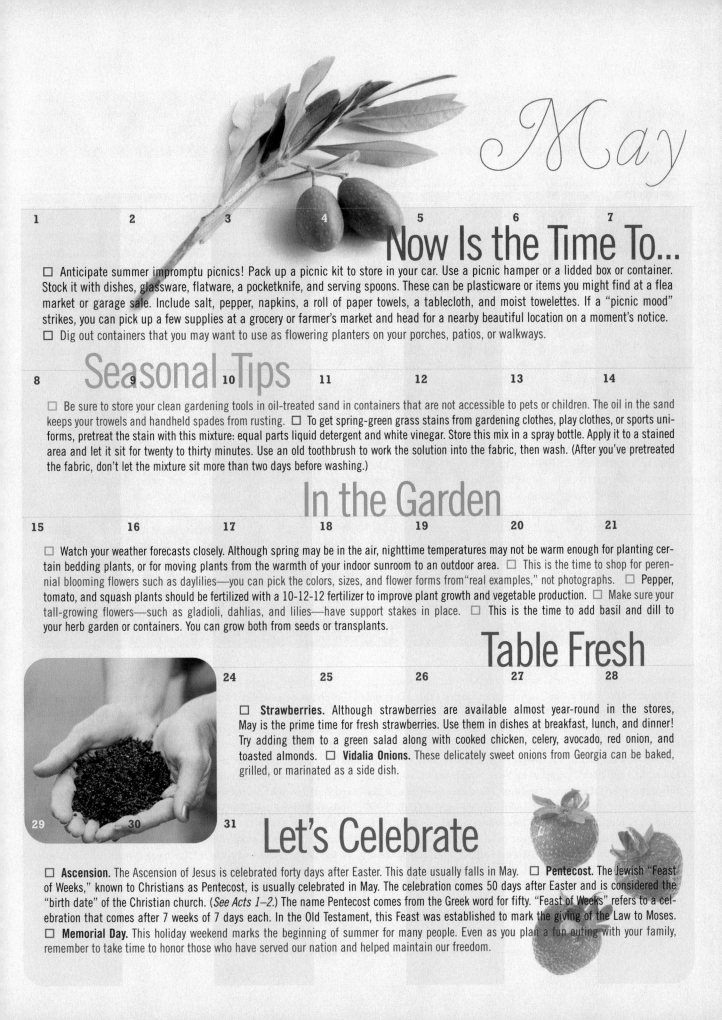

☐ **Strawberries.** Although strawberries are available almost year-round in the stores, May is the prime time for fresh strawberries. Use them in dishes at breakfast, lunch, and dinner! Try adding them to a green salad along with cooked chicken, celery, avocado, red onion, and toasted almonds. ☐ **Vidalia Onions.** These delicately sweet onions from Georgia can be baked, grilled, or marinated as a side dish.

29 30 31

Let's Celebrate

☐ **Ascension.** The Ascension of Jesus is celebrated forty days after Easter. This date usually falls in May. ☐ **Pentecost.** The Jewish "Feast of Weeks," known to Christians as Pentecost, is usually celebrated in May. The celebration comes 50 days after Easter and is considered the "birth date" of the Christian church. (*See Acts 1–2.*) The name Pentecost comes from the Greek word for fifty. "Feast of Weeks" refers to a celebration that comes after 7 weeks of 7 days each. In the Old Testament, this Feast was established to mark the giving of the Law to Moses.
☐ **Memorial Day.** This holiday weekend marks the beginning of summer for many people. Even as you plan a fun outing with your family, remember to take time to honor those who have served our nation and helped maintain our freedom.

PEOPLE CALLED "BEAUTIFUL" IN THE BIBLE

David

Handsome and Talented

Perhaps the greatest king in the history of the Jewish people and in all of the Bible is King David, described as a man after God's own heart. (See 1 Samuel 13:14.)

After Saul, the first king of Israel, rebelled and was forsaken by God, the Lord directed Samuel to go to the house of Jesse and anoint one of Jesse's sons as king. The Lord promised to show Samuel which young man was God's chosen replacement. After a time of worship and feasting, Samuel began to examine Jesse's sons. He thought surely the eldest son, Eliab, was the chosen one. God said very specifically, however, "Do not look at his appearance or at his physical stature, because I have refused him. For the LORD does not see as man sees; for man looks at the outward appearance, but the LORD looks at the heart" (1 Samuel 16:7).

Samuel then evaluated Abinadab, then Shammah, and then four more of Jesse's sons. About each one the Lord spoke to Samuel's spirit, "Not this one." Finally Samuel asked Jesse, "Are all the young men here?" Jesse replied that the youngest son was out in the pasture, keeping the sheep. Samuel asked that the young man be brought in from the fields and Jesse sent for him. The Bible tells us about David: "Now he was ruddy, with bright eyes, and good-looking." The LORD said to Samuel, "Arise, anoint him; for this is the one!" (See 1 Samuel 16:8–12.)

Bible scholars have speculated that David was a handsome redhead (ruddy), with blue eyes (bright eyes). If so, he certainly wasn't very Semitic in appearance. His physical appearance is noted in the Bible at this point, but it has absolutely nothing to do with what really mattered the rest of David's life. What mattered was that David was chosen and anointed by the Lord for the task of being king.

He had remarkable musical ability to sing, to play instruments, and to compose music. He was able to use this ability to inspire and comfort others. He was the author of many of the psalms. David had great skill with a slingshot, became a skilled warrior, and showed great courage in the face of danger. He developed a great ability to lead and inspire other people. He knew how to serve, how to be a friend, and how to worship. He was a man willing to praise and worship God with utter abandon. David trusted God in good times and bad. David wanted in his life, and in the life of Israel, what God wanted for Israel and for him. These were the traits that mattered to God, and the traits that mattered most in David's success as king.

What about you? Are you a person who knows you have been chosen and anointed by God? Are you using your talents to give praise to God and to inspire and help others? Are you manifesting courage? Are you doing what you can to inspire other people to obey God? Are you a loyal friend? Are you willing to worship God with all of your heart, mind, soul, and strength? These are the qualities God honors!

know how unlawful it is for a Jewish man to keep company with or go to one of another nation. But God has shown me that I should not call any man common or unclean. ²⁹Therefore I came without objection as soon as I was sent for. I ask, then, for what reason have you sent for me?"

³⁰So Cornelius said, "Four days ago I was fasting until this hour; and at the ninth hour^a I prayed in my house, and behold, a man stood before me in bright clothing, ³¹and said, 'Cornelius, your prayer has been heard, and your alms are remembered in the sight of God. ³²Send therefore to Joppa and call Simon here, whose surname is Peter. He is lodging in the house of Simon, a tanner, by the sea.^a When he comes, he will speak to you.' ³³So I sent to you immediately, and you have done well to come. Now therefore, we are all present before God, to hear all the things commanded you by God."

PREACHING TO CORNELIUS' HOUSEHOLD

³⁴Then Peter opened *his* mouth and said: "In truth I perceive that God shows no partiality. ³⁵But in every nation whoever fears Him and works righteousness is accepted by Him. ³⁶The word which *God* sent to the children of Israel, preaching peace through Jesus Christ—He is Lord of all— ³⁷that word you know, which was proclaimed throughout all Judea, and began from Galilee after the baptism which John preached: ³⁸how God anointed Jesus of Nazareth with the Holy Spirit and with power, who went about doing good and healing all who were oppressed by the devil, for God was with Him. ³⁹And we are witnesses of all things which He did both in the land of the Jews and in Jerusalem, whom they^a killed by hanging on a tree. ⁴⁰Him God raised up on the third day, and showed Him openly, ⁴¹not to all the people, but to witnesses chosen before by God, *even* to us who ate and drank with Him after He arose from the dead. ⁴²And He commanded us to preach to the people, and to testify that it is He who was ordained by God *to be* Judge of the living and the dead. ⁴³To Him all the prophets

---

10:30 ^aNU-Text reads *Four days ago to this hour, at the ninth hour.*   10:32 ^aNU-Text omits the last sentence of this verse.   10:39 ^aNU-Text and M-Text add *also.*

witness that, through His name, whoever believes in Him will receive remission of sins."

THE HOLY SPIRIT FALLS ON THE GENTILES

⁴⁴While Peter was still speaking these words, the Holy Spirit fell upon all those who heard the word. ⁴⁵And those of the circumcision who believed were astonished, as many as came with Peter, because the gift of the Holy Spirit had been poured out on the Gentiles also. ⁴⁶For they heard them speak with tongues and magnify God.

Then Peter answered, ⁴⁷"Can anyone forbid water, that these should not be baptized who have received the Holy Spirit just as we *have?*" ⁴⁸And he commanded them to be baptized in the name of the Lord. Then they asked him to stay a few days.

PETER DEFENDS GOD'S GRACE

11 Now the apostles and brethren who were in Judea heard that the Gentiles had also received the word of God. ²And when Peter came up to Jerusalem, those of the circumcision contended with him, ³saying, "You went in to uncircumcised men and ate with them!"

⁴But Peter explained *it* to them in order from the beginning, saying: ⁵"I was in the city of Joppa praying; and in a trance I saw a vision, an object descending like a great sheet, let down from heaven by four corners; and it came to me. ⁶When I observed it intently and considered, I saw four-footed animals of the earth, wild beasts, creeping things, and birds of the air. ⁷And I heard a voice saying to me, 'Rise, Peter; kill and eat.' ⁸But I said, 'Not so, Lord! For nothing common or unclean has at any time entered my mouth.' ⁹But the voice answered me again from heaven, 'What God has cleansed you must not call common.' ¹⁰Now this was done three times, and all were drawn up again into heaven. ¹¹At that very moment, three men stood before the house where I was, having been sent to me from Caesarea. ¹²Then the Spirit told me to go with them, doubting nothing. Moreover these six brethren accompanied me, and we entered the man's house. ¹³And he told us how he had seen an angel standing in his house, who said to

him, 'Send men to Joppa, and call for Simon whose surname is Peter, ¹⁴who will tell you words by which you and all your household will be saved.' ¹⁵And as I began to speak, the Holy Spirit fell upon them, as upon us at the beginning. ¹⁶Then I remembered the word of the Lord, how He said, 'John indeed baptized with water, but you shall be baptized

with the Holy Spirit.' ¹⁷If therefore God gave them the same gift as *He gave* us when we believed on the Lord Jesus Christ, who was I that I could withstand God?"

¹⁸When they heard these things they became silent; and they glorified God, saying, "Then God has also granted to the Gentiles repentance to life."

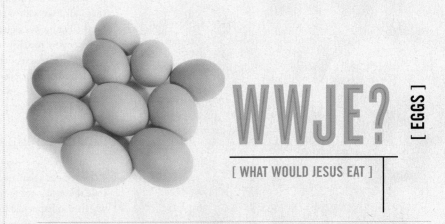

WWJE? [EGGS]

[WHAT WOULD JESUS EAT]

The eating of eggs was fairly common during Jesus' time. Eggs were prepared in several ways, including boiling and frying. Some people cooked fish under a layer of eggs.

In teaching His followers, Jesus placed eggs in a positive light. He said, "Ask, and it will be given to you; seek, and you will find; knock, and it will be opened to you . . . If a son . . . asks for an egg, will he offer him a scorpion? If you then, being evil, know how to give good gifts to your children, how much more will your heavenly Father give the Holy Spirit to those who ask Him!" (Luke 11:9, 11–13).

Eggs from free-range chickens are eggs from animals that have not been given hormones, antibiotics, or pesticides—all of which can impact the nutritional value of an egg. Free-range chickens usually feed on grass or grain that has been organically grown.

Eggs with blood spots are forbidden under kosher food laws.

Some people refuse eggs because they think they are high in cholesterol. Actually, the studies that found eggs to be high in cholesterol have been overturned. Whole eggs are high in lecithin—an agent that emulsifies, or breaks up, the cholesterol of the egg yolk. A study done at Harvard University in 1999 showed that eating one egg a day was unlikely to increase a person's risk of either heart disease or stroke.

Eggs are high in protein, folic acid, B vitamins, antioxidants, unsaturated fats, and choline, which is a raw material for the production of acetylcholine, one of the most important neurotransmitters associated with brain function and memory.

Do not use raw eggs. Make sure your eggs are cooked until the yolk is firm. Keep eggs in the coldest part of a refrigerator and in their original containers. Use eggs within three weeks of purchase.

SCRIPTURE SOLUTIONS

[HEPATITIS]

Hepatitis and hepatitis C are conditions related to improper liver function. Here are some dietary suggestions to improve liver health:

Eat organic foods. As much as possible, choose foods that are pesticide-free. Don't add toxins to your body—that means extra work for the liver.

Select free-range meats. Free-range meats contain no hormones, antibiotics, or other chemicals that can add stress to the liver.

Add detoxifying proteins to your eating plan. Salmon, halibut, mackerel, herring, and tuna are some of the best sources of detoxifying protein.

Choose liver-friendly fats. Most fats are difficult for the liver to digest. Fats such as those found in avocados, fresh nuts, and seeds (except peanuts and cashews), fish oil, flaxseed oil, and extra-virgin olive oil will support liver function.

Choose healthful starches. Try eating brown rice, wild rice, rice pasta, and brown-rice bread since the liver can usually tolerate these starches well.

Juice vegetables, and drink herbal and green teas and plenty of filtered water. These fluids assist liver function.

Avoid the following:

- ☐ **Hydrogenated fats, fried foods, and refined vegetable oils**
- ☐ **Peanuts, peanut oil, and peanut butter**
- ☐ **Dairy products**
- ☐ **Foods high in sugar**
- ☐ **Processed foods**
- ☐ **Sugar substitutes**
- ☐ **Coffee and black teas**

BARNABAS AND SAUL AT ANTIOCH

¹⁹Now those who were scattered after the persecution that arose over Stephen traveled as far as Phoenicia, Cyprus, and Antioch, preaching the word to no one but the Jews only. ²⁰But some of them were men from Cyprus and Cyrene, who, when they had come to Antioch, spoke to the Hellenists, preaching the Lord Jesus. ²¹And the hand of the Lord was with them, and a great number believed and turned to the Lord.

²²Then news of these things came to the ears of the church in Jerusalem, and they sent out Barnabas to go as far as Antioch. ²³When he came and had seen the grace of God, he was glad, and encouraged them all that with purpose of heart they should continue with the Lord. ²⁴For he was a good man, full of the Holy Spirit and of faith. And a great many people were added to the Lord.

²⁵Then Barnabas departed for Tarsus to seek Saul. ²⁶And when he had found him, he brought him to Antioch. So it was that for a whole year they assembled with the church and taught a great many people. And the disciples were first called Christians in Antioch.

RELIEF TO JUDEA

²⁷And in these days prophets came from Jerusalem to Antioch. ²⁸Then one of them, named Agabus, stood up and showed by the Spirit that there was going to be a great famine throughout all the world, which also happened in the days of Claudius Caesar. ²⁹Then the disciples, each according to his ability, determined to send relief to the brethren dwelling in Judea. ³⁰This they also did, and sent it to the elders by the hands of Barnabas and Saul.

HEROD'S VIOLENCE TO THE CHURCH

12 Now about that time Herod the king stretched out *his* hand to harass some from the church. ²Then he killed James the brother of John with the sword. ³And because he saw that it pleased the Jews, he proceeded further to seize Peter also. Now it was *during* the Days of Unleavened Bread. ⁴So when he had arrested him, he put *him* in prison, and delivered *him* to four squads of soldiers to keep him, intending to bring him before the people after Passover.

PETER FREED FROM PRISON

⁵Peter was therefore kept in prison, but constant* prayer was offered to God for him by the church. ⁶And when Herod was about to bring him out, that night Peter was sleeping, bound with two chains between two soldiers; and the guards before the door were keeping the prison. ⁷Now behold, an angel of the Lord stood by *him,* and a light shone in the prison; and he struck Peter on the side and raised him up, saying, "Arise quickly!" And his chains fell off *his* hands. ⁸Then the angel said to him, "Gird yourself and tie on your sandals"; and so he did. And he said to him, "Put on your garment and follow me." ⁹So he went out and followed him, and did not know that what was done by the angel was real, but thought he was seeing a vision. ¹⁰When they were past the first and the second guard posts, they came to the iron gate that leads to the city, which opened to them of its own accord; and

12:5 *NU-Text reads *constantly* (or *earnestly*).

[ROSEMARY OIL]

FACT MORSELS

Rosemary oil can be rubbed into the temples to help relieve headaches that come from constricted muscles.

they went out and went down one street, and immediately the angel departed from him.

[11]And when Peter had come to himself, he said, "Now I know for certain that the Lord has sent His angel, and has delivered me from the hand of Herod and *from* all the expectation of the Jewish people."

[12]So, when he had considered *this*, he came to the house of Mary, the mother of John whose surname was Mark, where many were gathered together praying. [13]And as Peter knocked at the door of the gate, a girl named Rhoda came to answer. [14]When she recognized Peter's voice, because of *her* gladness she did not open the gate, but ran in and announced that Peter stood before the gate. [15]But they said to her, "You are beside yourself!" Yet she kept insisting that it was so. So they said, "It is his angel."

[16]Now Peter continued knocking; and when they opened *the door* and saw him, they were astonished. [17]But motioning to them with his hand to keep silent, he declared to them how the Lord had brought him out of the prison. And he said, "Go, tell these things to James and to the brethren." And he departed and went to another place.

[18]Then, as soon as it was day, there was no small stir among the soldiers about what had become of Peter. [19]But when Herod had searched for him and not found him, he examined the guards and commanded that *they* should be put to death.

And he went down from Judea to Caesarea, and stayed *there*.

HEROD'S VIOLENT DEATH

[20]Now Herod had been very angry with the people of Tyre and Sidon; but they came to him with one accord, and having made Blastus the king's personal aide their friend, they asked for peace, because their country was supplied with food by the king's *country*.

[21]So on a set day Herod, arrayed in royal apparel, sat on his throne and gave an oration to them. [22]And the people kept shouting, "The voice of a god and not of a man!" [23]Then immediately an angel of the Lord struck him, because he did not give glory to God. And he was eaten by worms and died.

[24]But the word of God grew and multiplied.

BARNABAS AND SAUL APPOINTED

[25]And Barnabas and Saul returned from[a] Jerusalem when they had fulfilled *their* ministry, and they also took with them John whose surname was Mark.

13 Now in the church that was at Antioch there were certain prophets and teachers: Barnabas, Simeon who was called Niger, Lucius of Cyrene, Manaen who had been brought up with Herod the tetrarch, and Saul. [2]As they ministered to the Lord and fasted, the Holy Spirit said, "Now separate to Me Barnabas and Saul for the work to which I have called them." [3]Then, having fasted and prayed, and laid hands on them, they sent *them* away.

PREACHING IN CYPRUS

[4]So, being sent out by the Holy Spirit, they went down to Seleucia, and from there they sailed to Cyprus. [5]And when they arrived in Salamis, they preached the word of God in the synagogues of the Jews. They also had John as *their* assistant.

[6]Now when they had gone through the island[a] to Paphos, they found a certain sorcerer, a false prophet, a Jew whose name *was* Bar-Jesus, [7]who was with the proconsul, Sergius Paulus, an intelligent man. This man called for Barnabas and Saul and sought to hear the word of God. [8]But Elymas the sorcerer (for so his name is translated) withstood them, seeking to turn the proconsul away from the faith. [9]Then Saul, who also *is called* Paul, filled with the Holy Spirit, looked intently at him [10]and said, "O full of all deceit and all fraud, *you* son of the devil, *you* enemy of all righteousness, will you not cease perverting the straight ways of the Lord? [11]And now, indeed, the hand of the Lord *is* upon you, and you shall be blind, not seeing the sun for a time."

And immediately a dark mist fell on him, and he went around seeking someone to lead him by the hand. [12]Then the proconsul believed, when he saw what had been done, being astonished at the teaching of the Lord.

WISE CHOICES

Choose a healthy sweetener.
Avoid saccharin and products made with aspartic acid (such as NutraSweet and Equal). Instead, choose Splenda or even better, Stevia. Stevia is a natural sweetener that is sweeter than sugar—fifty to four hundred times sweeter! It can be used in baking and cooking, is safe for diabetics, and is calorie-free. It is made from the "sweet herb" or "honey leaf" plant, *Stevia rebaudianada*. In various nations around the world, Stevia has been used for hundreds of years without any recorded side effects. Clinical research studies have even shown that Stevia increases glucose tolerance and decreases blood sugar levels.

12:25 [a]NU-Text and M-Text read *to*.   13:6 [a]NU-Text reads *the whole island*.

[Split an Entrée]

Here's a new twist on "portion control"—making sure you eat only the portion of food that you need, which is not necessarily the portion of food served to you!

Food portions have grown to extravagant sizes in many restaurants these days. What was once served on a plate now arrives on a personal *platter*! Two people can easily share most restaurant entrées. You and a friend, or your spouse, may want to take turns deciding who is going to choose the entrée as you dine out. Consider it similar to deciding who is going to cook.

Ask your waitress for a second plate at the time you place your order. If you don't want to split a salad or bowl of soup that may come as part of the meal, you can always order another first-course item on an á la carte basis. Or, you may want to choose a specialty dinner-size salad that you also split. If there are more than two of you dining out, you may want to order a salad for each person and then share several appetizers, creating something of a one-table buffet selection.

WEIGHING LESS & ENJOYING LIFE MORE!

AT ANTIOCH IN PISIDIA

[13]Now when Paul and his party set sail from Paphos, they came to Perga in Pamphylia; and John, departing from them, returned to Jerusalem. [14]But when they departed from Perga, they came to Antioch in Pisidia, and went into the synagogue on the Sabbath day and sat down. [15]And after the reading of the Law and the Prophets, the rulers of the synagogue sent to them, saying, "Men *and* brethren, if you have any word of exhortation for the people, say on."

[16]Then Paul stood up, and motioning with *his* hand said, "Men of Israel, and you who fear God, listen: [17]The God of this people Israel[a] chose our fathers, and exalted the people when they dwelt as strangers in the land of Egypt, and with an uplifted arm He brought them out of it. [18]Now for a time of about forty years He put up with their ways in the wilderness. [19]And when He had destroyed seven nations in the land of Canaan, He distributed their land to them by allotment.

[20]"After that He gave *them* judges for about four hundred and fifty years, until Samuel the prophet. [21]And afterward they asked for a king; so God gave them Saul the son of Kish, a man of the tribe of Benjamin, for forty years. [22]And when He had removed him, He raised up for them David as king, to whom also He gave testimony and said, 'I have found David[a] the son of Jesse, a man after My own heart, who will do all My will.'[b] [23]From this man's seed, according to *the* promise, God raised up for Israel a Savior—Jesus—[a] [24]after John had first preached, before His coming, the baptism of repentance to all the people of Israel. [25]And as John was finishing his course, he said, 'Who do you think I am? I am not *He*. But behold, there comes One after me, the sandals of whose feet I am not worthy to loose.'

[26]"Men *and* brethren, sons of the family of Abraham, and those among you who fear God, to you the word of this salvation has been sent. [27]For those who dwell in Jerusalem, and their rulers, because they did not know Him, nor even the voices of the Prophets which are read every Sabbath, have fulfilled *them* in condemning *Him*. [28]And though they found no cause for death *in Him*, they asked Pilate that He should be put to death. [29]Now when they had fulfilled all that was written concerning Him, they took *Him* down from the tree and laid *Him* in a tomb. [30]But God raised Him from the dead. [31]He was seen for many days by those who came up with Him from Galilee to Jerusalem, who are His witnesses to the people. [32]And we declare to you glad tidings—that promise which was made to the fathers. [33]God has fulfilled this for us their children, in that He has raised up Jesus. As it is also written in the second Psalm:

'You are My Son,
  Today I have begotten You.'[a]

[34]And that He raised Him from the dead, no more to return to corruption, He has spoken thus:

'I will give you the sure mercies of David.'[a]

[35]Therefore He also says in another *Psalm:*

'You will not allow Your Holy One to see corruption.'[a]

[36]"For David, after he had served his own generation by the will of God, fell asleep, was buried with his fathers, and saw corruption; [37]but He whom God raised up saw no corruption. [38]Therefore let it be known to you, brethren, that through this Man is preached to you the forgiveness of sins; [39]and by Him everyone who believes is justified from all things from which you could not be justified by the law of Moses. [40]Beware therefore, lest what has been spoken in the prophets come upon you:

[41] 'Behold, you despisers,
  Marvel and perish!
  For I work a work in your days,

13:17 [a]M-Text omits *Israel*.   13:22 [a]Psalm 89:20   [b]1 Samuel 13:14   13:23 [a]M-Text reads *for Israel salvation*.   13:33 [a]Psalm 2:7   13:34 [a]Isaiah 55:3   13:35 [a]Psalm 16:10

A work which you will by no means believe,
Though one were to declare it to you.' "ᵃ

BLESSING AND CONFLICT AT ANTIOCH

⁴²So when the Jews went out of the synagogue,ᵃ the Gentiles begged that these words might be preached to them the next Sabbath. ⁴³Now when the congregation had broken up, many of the Jews and devout proselytes followed Paul and Barnabas, who, speaking to them, persuaded them to continue in the grace of God.

⁴⁴On the next Sabbath almost the whole city came together to hear the word of God. ⁴⁵But when the Jews saw the multitudes, they were filled with envy; and contradicting and blaspheming, they opposed the things spoken by Paul. ⁴⁶Then Paul and Barnabas grew bold and said, "It was necessary that the word of God should be spoken to you first; but since you reject it, and judge yourselves unworthy of everlasting life; behold, we turn to the Gentiles. ⁴⁷For so the Lord has commanded us:

'I have set you as a light to the Gentiles,
That you should be for salvation to the ends of the earth.' "ᵃ

⁴⁸Now when the Gentiles heard this, they were glad and glorified the word of the Lord. And as many as had been appointed to eternal life believed.

⁴⁹And the word of the Lord was being spread throughout all the region. ⁵⁰But the Jews stirred up the devout and prominent women and the chief men of the city, raised up persecution against Paul and Barnabas, and expelled them from their region. ⁵¹But they shook off the dust from their feet against them, and came to Iconium. ⁵²And the disciples were filled with joy and with the Holy Spirit.

AT ICONIUM

14 Now it happened in Iconium that they went together to the synagogue of the Jews, and so spoke that a great multitude both of the Jews and of the Greeks believed. ²But the unbelieving Jews stirred up the Gentiles and poisoned their minds against the brethren. ³Therefore they stayed there a long time, speaking boldly in the Lord, who was bearing witness to the word of His grace, granting signs and wonders to be done by their hands. ⁴But the multitude of the city was divided: part sided with the Jews, and part with the apostles. ⁵And when a violent attempt was made by both the Gentiles and Jews, with their rulers, to abuse and stone them, ⁶they became aware of it and fled to Lystra and Derbe, cities of Lycaonia, and to the surrounding region. ⁷And they were preaching the gospel there.

IDOLATRY AT LYSTRA

⁸And in Lystra a certain man without strength in his feet was sitting, a cripple from his mother's womb, who had never walked. ⁹This man heard Paul speaking. Paul, observing him intently and seeing that he had faith to be healed, ¹⁰said with a loud voice, "Stand up straight on your feet!" And he leaped and walked. ¹¹Now when the people saw what Paul had done, they raised their voices, saying in the Lycaonian *language*, "The gods have come down to us in the likeness of men!"

¹²And Barnabas they called Zeus, and Paul, Hermes, because he was the chief speaker. ¹³Then the priest of Zeus, whose temple was in front of their city, brought oxen and garlands to the gates, intending to sacrifice with the multitudes.

¹⁴But when the apostles Barnabas and Paul heard this, they tore their clothes and ran in among the multitude, crying out ¹⁵and saying, "Men, why are you doing these things? We also are men with the same nature as you, and preach to you that you should turn from these useless things to the living God, who made the heaven, the earth, the sea, and all things that are in them, ¹⁶who in bygone generations allowed all nations to walk in their own ways. ¹⁷Nevertheless He did not leave Himself without witness, in that He did good, gave us rain from heaven and fruitful seasons, filling our hearts with food and gladness." ¹⁸And with these sayings they could scarcely restrain the multitudes from sacrificing to them.

STONING, ESCAPE TO DERBE

¹⁹Then Jews from Antioch and Iconium came there; and having persuaded the multitudes, they stoned Paul *and* dragged *him* out of the city, supposing him to be dead. ²⁰However, when the disciples gathered around him, he rose up and went into the city. And the next day he departed with Barnabas to Derbe.

STRENGTHENING THE CONVERTS

²¹And when they had preached the gospel to that city and made many disciples, they returned to Lystra, Iconium, and Antioch, ²²strengthening the souls of the disciples, exhorting *them* to continue in the faith, and *saying*, "We must through many tribulations enter the kingdom of God." ²³So when they had appointed elders in every church, and prayed with fasting, they commended them to the Lord in whom they had believed. ²⁴And after they had passed through Pisidia, they came to Pamphylia. ²⁵Now when they had preached the word in Perga, they went down to Attalia. ²⁶From there they sailed to Antioch, where they had been commended to the grace of God for the work which they had completed.

Bible Health + Food Facts

Fish-Buying Tips

When purchasing fresh fish, look at the eyes of the fish. They should be bright and shiny, bulging, firm, and clear. Then look at the scales—they should also be shiny. Touch the fish—the flesh should spring back to the touch. If you can make a dent in the flesh, don't buy it. The gills of the fish should be pink and firm. If the fish smells "fishy" don't buy it—fresh fish has almost no odor!

13:41 ᵃHabakkuk 1:5   13:42 ᵃOr *And when they went out of the synagogue of the Jews;* NU-Text reads *And when they went out, they begged.*   13:47 ᵃIsaiah 49:6

walking the WALK

[THE VALUE OF AN ACCOUNTABILITY PARTNER]

The key to establishing a new habit and to sticking with it is the same: have an accountability partner! This seems to be especially true if a person is trying to establish a new habit of exercise, or a new eating plan.

Seek out an accountability partner who truly has your best interests at heart. In other words, choose someone who wants you to succeed, who loves you, and who will applaud your success and help you to overcome your failures. Choose a person who will keep anything you say confidential—this is especially important if you are admitting how out of shape you have been or if you divulge inner secrets about why you want to get into better shape. Choose someone you don't mind nagging you a little bit—a spouse is usually *not* the best accountability partner. Also choose someone who is not in a position of authority over you in another area of your life—for example, don't choose your boss or your pastor.

An ideal accountability partner is a person who wants to establish or continue the same habit that you want to establish or maintain. For example, if you are establishing the habit of walking at 6:30 each morning, find a person who is willing to walk *with* you. They may be able to walk two laps of the track while you are only walking one lap—so be it. Agree to meet at the end of your walk for a few minutes of conversation. Don't limit yourself, however, to having an exercise partner as an accountability partner. Sometimes it's better to report your change in habit to a nonexercise partner.

Check in with your accountability partner on a regular basis. Agree with your accountability partner how often this will be and CONT. NEXT PAGE>>>

²⁷Now when they had come and gathered the church together, they reported all that God had done with them, and that He had opened the door of faith to the Gentiles. ²⁸So they stayed there a long time with the disciples.

CONFLICT OVER CIRCUMCISION

15 And certain *men* came down from Judea and taught the brethren, "Unless you are circumcised according to the custom of Moses, you cannot be saved." ²Therefore, when Paul and Barnabas had no small dissension and dispute with them, they determined that Paul and Barnabas and certain others of them should go up to Jerusalem, to the apostles and elders, about this question.

³So, being sent on their way by the church, they passed through Phoenicia and Samaria, describing the conversion of the Gentiles; and they caused great joy to all the brethren. ⁴And when they had come to Jerusalem, they were received by the church and the apostles and the elders; and they reported all things that God had done with them. ⁵But some of the sect of the Pharisees who believed rose up, saying, "It is necessary to circumcise them, and to command *them* to keep the law of Moses."

THE JERUSALEM COUNCIL

⁶Now the apostles and elders came together to consider this matter. ⁷And when there had been much dispute, Peter rose up and said to them: "Men *and* brethren, you know that a good while ago God chose among us, that by my mouth the Gentiles should hear the word of the gospel and believe. ⁸So God, who knows the heart, acknowledged them by giving them the Holy Spirit, just as *He did* to us, ⁹and made no distinction between us and them, purifying their hearts by faith. ¹⁰Now therefore, why do you test God by putting a yoke on the neck of the disciples which neither our fathers nor we were able to bear? ¹¹But we believe that through the grace of the Lord Jesus Christ ᵃ we shall be saved in the same manner as they."

¹²Then all the multitude kept silent and listened to Barnabas and Paul declaring how many miracles and wonders God had worked through them among the Gentiles. ¹³And after they had become silent, James answered, saying, "Men *and* brethren, listen to me: ¹⁴Simon has declared how God at the first visited the Gentiles to take out of them a people for His name. ¹⁵And with this the words of the prophets agree, just as it is written:

¹⁶ 'After this I will return
   And will rebuild the tabernacle of David, which has fallen down;
   I will rebuild its ruins,
   And I will set it up;
¹⁷ So that the rest of mankind may seek the LORD,
   Even all the Gentiles who are called by My name,
   Says the LORD who does all these things.'ᵃ

¹⁸"Known to God from eternity are all His works."ᵃ ¹⁹Therefore I judge that we should not trouble those from among the Gentiles who are turning to God, ²⁰but that we write to them to abstain from things

---

15:11 ᵃNU-Text and M-Text omit *Christ.*   15:17 ᵃAmos 9:11, 12   15:18 ᵃNU-Text (combining with verse 17) reads *Says the Lord, who makes these things known from eternity (of old).*

polluted by idols, *from* sexual immorality,^a *from* things strangled, and *from* blood. ²¹For Moses has had throughout many generations those who preach him in every city, being read in the synagogues every Sabbath."

THE JERUSALEM DECREE

²²Then it pleased the apostles and elders, with the whole church, to send chosen men of their own company to Antioch with Paul and Barnabas, *namely,* Judas who was also named Barsabas,^a and Silas, leading men among the brethren.

²³They wrote this, *letter* by them:

The apostles, the elders, and the brethren,

To the brethren who are of the Gentiles in Antioch, Syria, and Cilicia:

Greetings.

²⁴Since we have heard that some who went out from us have troubled you with words, unsettling your souls, saying, *"You must* be circumcised and keep the law"*^a*—to whom we gave no *such* commandment—²⁵it seemed good to us, being assembled with one accord, to send chosen men to you with our beloved Barnabas and Paul, ²⁶men who have risked their lives for the name of our Lord Jesus Christ. ²⁷We have therefore sent Judas and Silas, who will also report the same things by word of mouth. ²⁸For it seemed good to the Holy Spirit, and to us, to lay upon you no greater burden than these necessary things: ²⁹that you abstain from things offered to idols, from blood, from things strangled, and from sexual immorality.^a If you keep yourselves from these, you will do well.

Farewell.

CONTINUING MINISTRY IN SYRIA

³⁰So when they were sent off, they came to Antioch; and when they had gathered the multitude together, they delivered the letter. ³¹When they had read it, they rejoiced over its encouragement. ³²Now Judas and Silas, themselves being prophets also, exhorted and strengthened the brethren with many words. ³³And after they had stayed *there* for a time, they were sent back with greetings from the brethren to the apostles.^a

³⁴However, it seemed good to Silas to remain there.^a ³⁵Paul and Barnabas also remained in Antioch, teaching and preaching the word of the Lord, with many others also.

DIVISION OVER JOHN MARK

³⁶Then after some days Paul said to Barnabas, "Let us now go back and visit our brethren in every city where we have preached the word of the Lord, *and see* how they are doing." ³⁷Now Barnabas was determined to take with them John called Mark. ³⁸But Paul insisted that they should not take with them the one who had departed from them in Pamphylia, and had not gone with them to the work. ³⁹Then the contention became so sharp that they parted from one another. And so Barnabas took Mark and sailed to Cyprus; ⁴⁰but Paul chose Silas and departed, being commended by the brethren to the grace of God. ⁴¹And he went through Syria and Cilicia, strengthening the churches.

TIMOTHY JOINS PAUL AND SILAS

16 Then he came to Derbe and Lystra. And behold, a certain disciple was there, named Timothy, *the* son of a certain Jewish woman who believed, but his father *was* Greek. ²He was well spoken of by the brethren who were at Lystra and Iconium. ³Paul wanted to have him go on with him. And he took *him* and circumcised him because of the Jews who were in that region, for they all knew that his father was Greek. ⁴And as they went through the cities, they delivered to them the decrees to keep, which were determined by the apostles and elders at Jerusalem. ⁵So the churches were strengthened in the faith, and increased in number daily.

"To preserve health is a moral and religious duty, for health is the basis of all social virtues. We can no longer be useful when not well." —*Samuel Johnson, English author (1708–1784)*

PREACHING HEALTH

THE MACEDONIAN CALL

⁶Now when they had gone through Phrygia and the region of Galatia, they were forbidden by the Holy Spirit to preach the word in Asia. ⁷After they had come to Mysia, they tried to go into Bithynia, but the Spirit^a did not permit them. ⁸So passing by Mysia, they came down to Troas. ⁹And a vision appeared to Paul in the night. A man of Macedonia stood and pleaded with him, saying, "Come over to Macedonia and help us." ¹⁰Now after he had seen the vision, immediately we sought to go to Macedonia, concluding that the Lord had called us to preach the gospel to them.

15:20 ^aOr *fornication*   15:22 ^aNU-Text and M-Text read *Barsabbas.*   15:24 ^aNU-Text omits *saying, "You must be circumcised and keep the law."*   15:29 ^aOr *fornication*   15:33 ^aNU-Text reads *to those who had sent them.*   15:34 ^aNU-Text and M-Text omit this verse.   16:7 ^aNU-Text adds *of Jesus.*

DIVINE HEALTH   **171**

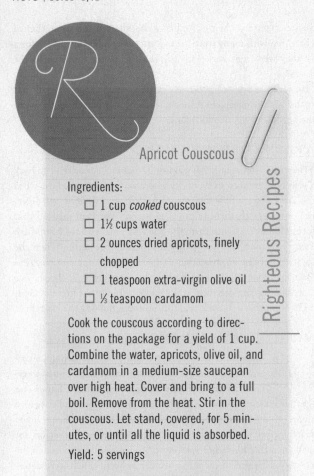

Apricot Couscous

Ingredients:

- ☐ 1 cup *cooked* couscous
- ☐ 1½ cups water
- ☐ 2 ounces dried apricots, finely chopped
- ☐ 1 teaspoon extra-virgin olive oil
- ☐ ⅓ teaspoon cardamom

Cook the couscous according to directions on the package for a yield of 1 cup. Combine the water, apricots, olive oil, and cardamom in a medium-size saucepan over high heat. Cover and bring to a full boil. Remove from the heat. Stir in the couscous. Let stand, covered, for 5 minutes, or until all the liquid is absorbed.

Yield: 5 servings

Righteous Recipes

LYDIA BAPTIZED AT PHILIPPI

¹¹Therefore, sailing from Troas, we ran a straight course to Samothrace, and the next *day* came to Neapolis, ¹²and from there to Philippi, which is the foremost city of that part of Macedonia, a colony. And we were staying in that city for some days. ¹³And on the Sabbath day we went out of the city to the riverside, where prayer was customarily made; and we sat down and spoke to the women who met *there.* ¹⁴Now a certain woman named Lydia heard *us.* She was a seller of purple from the city of Thyatira, who worshiped God. The Lord opened her heart to heed the things spoken by Paul. ¹⁵And when she and her household were baptized, she begged *us,* saying, "If you have judged me to be faithful to the Lord, come to my house and stay." So she persuaded us.

PAUL AND SILAS IMPRISONED

¹⁶Now it happened, as we went to prayer, that a certain slave girl possessed with a spirit of divination met us, who brought her masters much profit by fortune-telling. ¹⁷This girl followed Paul and us, and cried out, saying, "These men are the servants of the Most High God, who proclaim to us the way of salvation." ¹⁸And this she did for many days.

But Paul, greatly annoyed, turned and said to the spirit, "I command you in the name of Jesus Christ to come out of her." And he came out that very hour. ¹⁹But when her masters saw that their hope of profit was gone, they seized Paul and Silas and dragged *them* into the marketplace to the authorities.

²⁰And they brought them to the magistrates, and said, "These men, being Jews, exceedingly trouble our city; ²¹and they teach customs which are not lawful for us, being Romans, to receive or observe." ²²Then the multitude rose up together against them; and the magistrates tore off their clothes and commanded *them* to be beaten with rods. ²³And when they had laid many stripes on them, they threw *them* into prison, commanding the jailer to keep them securely. ²⁴Having received such a charge, he put them into the inner prison and fastened their feet in the stocks.

THE PHILIPPIAN JAILER SAVED

²⁵But at midnight Paul and Silas were praying and singing hymns to God, and the prisoners were listening to them. ²⁶Suddenly there was a great earthquake, so that the foundations of the prison were shaken; and immediately all the doors were opened and everyone's chains were loosed. ²⁷And the keeper of the prison, awaking from sleep and seeing the prison doors open, supposing the prisoners had fled, drew his sword and was about to kill himself. ²⁸But Paul called with a loud voice, saying, "Do yourself no harm, for we are all here."

²⁹Then he called for a light, ran in, and fell down trembling before Paul and Silas. ³⁰And he brought them out and said, "Sirs, what must I do to be saved?"

³¹So they said, "Believe on the Lord Jesus Christ, and you will be saved, you and your household." ³²Then they spoke the word of the Lord to him and to all who were in his house. ³³And he took them the same hour of the night and washed *their* stripes. And immediately he and all his *family* were baptized. ³⁴Now when he had brought them into his house, he set food before them; and he rejoiced, having believed in God with all his household.

PAUL REFUSES TO DEPART SECRETLY

³⁵And when it was day, the magistrates sent the officers, saying, "Let those men go."

³⁶So the keeper of the prison reported these words to Paul, saying, "The magistrates have sent to let you go. Now therefore depart, and go in peace."

³⁷But Paul said to them, "They have beaten us openly, uncondemned Romans, *and* have thrown *us* into prison. And now do they put us out secretly? No indeed! Let them come themselves and get us out."

³⁸And the officers told these words to the magistrates, and they were afraid when they heard that they were Romans. ³⁹Then they came and pleaded with them and brought *them* out, and asked *them* to depart from the city. ⁴⁰So they went out of the prison and entered *the house of* Lydia; and when they had seen the brethren, they encouraged them and departed.

PREACHING CHRIST AT THESSALONICA

17 Now when they had passed through Amphipolis and Apollonia, they came to Thessalonica, where there was a synagogue of the Jews. ²Then Paul, as his custom was, went in to them, and for three Sabbaths reasoned with them from the Scriptures, ³explaining and demonstrating that the Christ had to suffer and rise again from the dead, and *saying*, "This Jesus whom I preach to you is the Christ." ⁴And some of them were persuaded; and a great multitude of the devout Greeks, and not a few of the leading women, joined Paul and Silas.

ASSAULT ON JASON'S HOUSE

⁵But the Jews who were not persuaded, becoming envious,ᵃ took some of the evil men from the marketplace, and gathering a mob, set all the city in an uproar and attacked the house of Jason, and sought to bring them out to the people. ⁶But when they did not find them, they dragged Jason and some brethren to the rulers of the city, crying out, "These who have turned the world upside down have come here too. ⁷Jason has harbored them, and these are all acting contrary to the decrees of Caesar, saying there is another king—Jesus." ⁸And they troubled the crowd and the rulers of the city when they heard these things. ⁹So when they had taken security from Jason and the rest, they let them go.

MINISTERING AT BEREA

¹⁰Then the brethren immediately sent Paul and Silas away by night to Berea. When they arrived, they went into the synagogue of the Jews. ¹¹These were more fair-minded than those in Thessalonica, in that they received the word with all readiness, and searched the Scriptures daily *to find out* whether these things were so. ¹²Therefore many of them believed, and also not a few of the Greeks, prominent women as well as men. ¹³But when the Jews from Thessalonica learned that the word of God was preached by Paul at Berea, they came there also and stirred up the crowds. ¹⁴Then immediately the brethren sent Paul away, to go to the sea; but both Silas and Timothy remained there. ¹⁵So those who conducted Paul brought him to Athens; and receiving a command for Silas and Timothy to come to him with all speed, they departed.

THE PHILOSOPHERS AT ATHENS

¹⁶Now while Paul waited for them at Athens, his spirit was provoked within him when he saw that the city was given over to idols. ¹⁷Therefore he reasoned in the synagogue with the Jews and with the *Gentile* worshipers, and in the marketplace daily with those who happened to be there. ¹⁸Thenᵃ certain Epicurean and Stoic philosophers encountered him. And some said, "What does this babbler want to say?"

Others said, "He seems to be a proclaimer of foreign gods," because he preached to them Jesus and the resurrection.

¹⁹And they took him and brought him to the Areopagus, saying, "May we know what this new doctrine *is* of which you speak? ²⁰For you are bringing some strange things to our ears. Therefore we want to know what these things mean." ²¹For all the Athenians and the foreigners who were there spent their time in nothing else but either to tell or to hear some new thing.

PEACE LOVE JOY KINDNESS

The Healthy Soul
>Kindness

In the Bible the word for *kindness* usually has a much stronger meaning than most of us have for it in our society today. The word in Hebrew is *chesed*, which literally means "lovingkindness." It is unfailing kindness that flows from unconditional love and that has a winsome, "drawing" nature to it.

People who are kind are attractive. They manifest loyalty and consistency in the way they deal with other people, regardless of the person's rank, status, or position. They seek the best in others. They do nothing that they know will hurt another person's faith or diminish his or her reputation in the eyes of other people. They uphold, support, and nurture others in words and deeds. They deal with other people in a mannerly, courteous manner. They recognize that other people have free will, foibles and faults, and a "good side" that is worthy of encouragement.

Kindness is considered one of God's attributes, and is an attribute that God desires to see in us.

Even if you do not *feel* kind, you can show kindness. How? Intentionally choose to do something for another person every day of your life. Think "outward" and "others" more than you think "inward" and "me, myself, and I." Do something you know will bring a smile to the face or a feeling of inner pleasure to another person. What you give in kindness, you will soon experience back in your own soul.

ADDRESSING THE AREOPAGUS

²²Then Paul stood in the midst of the Areopagus and said, "Men of Athens, I perceive that in all things you are very religious; ²³for as I was passing through and considering the objects of your worship, I even found an altar with this inscription:

TO THE UNKNOWN GOD.

Therefore, the One whom you worship without knowing, Him I proclaim to you: ²⁴God, who made the world and everything in it, since He is Lord of heaven and earth, does not dwell in temples made with hands. ²⁵Nor is He worshiped with men's hands, as though He needed anything, since He gives to all life, breath, and all things. ²⁶And He has made from one bloodᵃ every nation of men to dwell on all the face of the earth, and has determined their preappointed times and the boundaries of their dwellings, ²⁷so that they should seek the Lord, in

17:5 ᵃNU-Text omits *who were not persuaded*; M-Text omits *becoming envious*.　17:18 ᵃNU-Text and M-Text add *also*.　17:26 ᵃNU-Text omits *blood*.

SCRIPTURE SOLUTIONS

[ASTHMA]

Since breath is so vital to life, an asthma attack is a very scary thing. Second Timothy 1:7 tells us that "God has not given us a spirit of fear," and in Acts 17:25 we read, "He gives to all life, breath, and all things." So, if God gives breath, why do we suffer from asthma?

Although there are many factors, indoors and outdoors, that contribute to asthma, the main outdoor culprit is polluted air. If you live in a highly polluted area, the only real help may come from moving to an area with cleaner air. Make sure you have good air filters for your home, and use air conditioning rather than expose yourself to pollutants.

Indoor allergens that can greatly impact asthma include dust mites, mold, animal dander, and cockroaches. Dust mites love to hang out in upholstery and drapes, as well as sheets, pillows, and mattresses. Here are a few things you can do to help eliminate these tiny but monstrous creatures:

☐ **Replace your carpet with hardwood, linoleum, or tile flooring.**

☐ **Wash all sheets, blankets, and bedcovers weekly in hot water of at least 130 degrees Fahrenheit.**

☐ **Eliminate clutter and items that normally collect dust.**

☐ **You might get a dehumidifier, since dust mites live in warm, humid places.**

☐ **Replace drapes with blinds, and upholstery with leather or vinyl.**

Have your home checked for mold. Mold can hide under baseboards and in any area that is exposed to frequent moisture. CONT. NEXT PAGE>>>

---

the hope that they might grope for Him and find Him, though He is not far from each one of us; [28]for in Him we live and move and have our being, as also some of your own poets have said, 'For we are also His offspring.' [29]Therefore, since we are the offspring of God, we ought not to think that the Divine Nature is like gold or silver or stone, something shaped by art and man's devising. [30]Truly, these times of ignorance God overlooked, but now commands all men everywhere to repent, [31]because He has appointed a day on which He will judge the world in righteousness by the Man whom He has ordained. He has given assurance of this to all by raising Him from the dead."

[32]And when they heard of the resurrection of the dead, some mocked, while others said, "We will hear you again on this *matter*." [33]So Paul departed from among them. [34]However, some men joined him and believed, among them Dionysius the Areopagite, a woman named Damaris, and others with them.

MINISTERING AT CORINTH

18 After these things Paul departed from Athens and went to Corinth. [2]And he found a certain Jew named Aquila, born in Pontus, who had recently come from Italy with his wife Priscilla (because Claudius had commanded all the Jews to depart from Rome); and he came to them. [3]So, because he was of the same trade, he stayed with them and worked; for by occupation they were tentmakers. [4]And he reasoned in the synagogue every Sabbath, and persuaded both Jews and Greeks.

[5]When Silas and Timothy had come from Macedonia, Paul was compelled by the Spirit, and testified to the Jews *that* Jesus *is* the Christ. [6]But when they opposed him and blasphemed, he shook *his* garments and said to them, "Your blood *be* upon your *own* heads; I *am* clean. From now on I will go to the Gentiles." [7]And he departed from there and entered the house of a certain *man* named Justus,ᵃ *one* who worshiped God, whose house was next door to the synagogue. [8]Then Crispus, the ruler of the synagogue, believed on the Lord with all his household. And many of the Corinthians, hearing, believed and were baptized.

[9]Now the Lord spoke to Paul in the night by a vision, "Do not be afraid, but speak, and do not keep silent; [10]for I am with you, and no one will attack you to hurt you; for I have many people in this city." [11]And he continued *there* a year and six months, teaching the word of God among them.

[12]When Gallio was proconsul of Achaia, the Jews with one accord rose up against Paul and brought him to the judgment seat, [13]saying, "This *fellow* persuades men to worship God contrary to the law."

[14]And when Paul was about to open *his* mouth, Gallio said to the Jews, "If it were a matter of wrongdoing or wicked crimes, O Jews, there would be reason why I should bear with you. [15]But if it is a question of words and names and your own law, look *to it* yourselves; for I do not want to be a judge of such *matters*." [16]And he drove them from the judgment seat. [17]Then all the Greeksᵃ took Sosthenes, the ruler of the synagogue, and beat *him* before the judgment seat. But Gallio took no notice of these things.

PAUL RETURNS TO ANTIOCH

[18]So Paul still remained a good while. Then he took leave of the brethren and sailed for Syria, and Priscilla and Aquila *were* with him.

18:7 ᵃNU-Text reads *Titius Justus*.   18:17 ᵃNU-Text reads *they all*.

Scripture Solutions Cont.>>>

Change the filters on your air conditioning or heating system regularly.

As much as you may love a pet, you may be wiser to refrain from having animals in your home.

When it comes to cockroaches, avoid pesticide sprays and use roach traps instead. The sprays can trigger asthma attacks, as well as headaches.

He had *his* hair cut off at Cenchrea, for he had taken a vow. [19]And he came to Ephesus, and left them there; but he himself entered the synagogue and reasoned with the Jews. [20]When they asked *him* to stay a longer time with them, he did not consent, [21]but took leave of them, saying, "I must by all means keep this coming feast in Jerusalem;[a] but I will return again to you, God willing." And he sailed from Ephesus.

[22]And when he had landed at Caesarea, and gone up and greeted the church, he went down to Antioch. [23]After he had spent some time *there*, he departed and went over the region of Galatia and Phrygia in order, strengthening all the disciples.

MINISTRY OF APOLLOS

[24]Now a certain Jew named Apollos, born at Alexandria, an eloquent man *and* mighty in the Scriptures, came to Ephesus. [25]This man had been instructed in the way of the Lord; and being fervent in spirit, he spoke and taught accurately the things of the Lord, though he knew only the baptism of John. [26]So he began to speak boldly in the synagogue. When Aquila and Priscilla heard him, they took him aside and explained to him the way of God more accurately. [27]And when he desired to cross to Achaia, the brethren wrote, exhorting the disciples to receive him; and when he arrived, he greatly helped those who had believed through grace; [28]for he vigorously refuted the Jews publicly, showing from the Scriptures that Jesus is the Christ.

PAUL AT EPHESUS

19 And it happened, while Apollos was at Corinth, that Paul, having passed through the upper regions, came to Ephesus. And finding some disciples [2]he said to them, "Did you receive the Holy Spirit when you believed?"

So they said to him, "We have not so much as heard whether there is a Holy Spirit."

[3]And he said to them, "Into what then were you baptized?"

So they said, "Into John's baptism."

[4]Then Paul said, "John indeed baptized with a baptism of repentance, saying to the people that they should believe on Him who would come after him, that is, on Christ Jesus."

[5]When they heard *this*, they were baptized in the name of the Lord Jesus. [6]And when Paul had laid hands on them, the Holy Spirit came upon them, and they spoke with tongues and prophesied. [7]Now the men were about twelve in all.

[8]And he went into the synagogue and spoke boldly for three months, reasoning and persuading concerning the things of the kingdom of God. [9]But when some were hardened and did not believe, but spoke evil of the Way before the multitude, he departed from them and withdrew the disciples, reasoning daily in the school of Tyrannus. [10]And this continued for two years, so that all who dwelt in Asia heard the word of the Lord Jesus, both Jews and Greeks.

MIRACLES GLORIFY CHRIST

[11]Now God worked unusual miracles by the hands of Paul, [12]so that even handkerchiefs or aprons were brought from his body to the sick, and the diseases left them and the evil spirits went out of them. [13]Then some of the itinerant Jewish exorcists took it upon themselves to call the name of the Lord Jesus over those who had evil spirits, saying, "We[a] exorcise you by the Jesus whom Paul preaches." [14]Also there were seven sons of Sceva, a Jewish chief priest, who did so.

[15]And the evil spirit answered and said, "Jesus I know, and Paul I know; but who are you?"

[16]Then the man in whom the evil spirit was leaped on them, overpowered[a] them, and prevailed against them,[b] so that they fled out of that house naked and wounded. [17]This became known both to all Jews and Greeks dwelling in Ephesus; and fear fell on them all, and the name of the Lord Jesus was magnified. [18]And many who had believed came confessing and telling their deeds. [19]Also, many of those who had practiced magic brought their books together and burned *them* in the sight of all. And they counted up the value of them, and *it* totaled fifty thousand *pieces* of silver. [20]So the word of the Lord grew mightily and prevailed.

THE RIOT AT EPHESUS

[21]When these things were accomplished, Paul purposed in the Spirit, when he had passed through Macedonia and Achaia, to go to Jerusalem, saying, "After I have been there, I must also see Rome." [22]So

Bible Health + Food Facts

Parched Corn

Some translations of the Bible refer to offerings of parched corn, or to people eating parched corn. (See Leviticus 23:14 and Ruth 2:14.) This refers to roasted heads of wheat, barley, millet, or other grains grown in the Middle East. It was *not* Indian corn or maize, which was unknown in that region during Bible times.

18:21 [a]NU-Text omits *I must* through *Jerusalem*.   19:13 [a]NU-Text reads *I*.   19:16 [a]M-Text reads *and they overpowered*. [b]NU-Text reads *both of them*.

he sent into Macedonia two of those who ministered to him, Timothy and Erastus, but he himself stayed in Asia for a time.

[23]And about that time there arose a great commotion about the Way. [24]For a certain man named Demetrius, a silversmith, who made silver shrines of Diana,ª brought no small profit to the craftsmen. [25]He called them together with the workers of similar occupation, and said: "Men, you know that we have our prosperity by this trade. [26]Moreover you see and hear that not only at Ephesus, but throughout almost all Asia, this Paul has persuaded and turned away many people, saying that they are not gods which are made with hands. [27]So not only is this trade of ours in danger of falling into disrepute, but also the temple of the great goddess Diana may be despised and her magnificence destroyed,ª whom all Asia and the world worship."

[28]Now when they heard *this*, they were full of wrath and cried out, saying, "Great *is* Diana of the Ephesians!" [29]So the whole city was filled with confusion, and rushed into the theater with one accord, having seized Gaius and Aristarchus, Macedonians, Paul's travel companions. [30]And when Paul wanted to go in to the people, the disciples would not allow him. [31]Then some of the officials of Asia, who were his friends, sent to him pleading that he would not venture into the theater. [32]Some therefore cried one thing and some another, for the assembly was confused, and most of them did not know why they had come together. [33]And they drew Alexander out of the multitude, the Jews putting him forward. And Alexander motioned with his hand, and wanted to make his defense to the people. [34]But when they found out that he was a Jew, all with one voice cried out for about two hours, "Great *is* Diana of the Ephesians!"

[35]And when the city clerk had quieted the crowd, he said: "Men of Ephesus, what man is there who does not know that the city of the Ephesians is temple guardian of the great goddess Diana, and of the *image* which fell down from Zeus? [36]Therefore, since these things cannot be denied, you ought to be quiet and do nothing rashly. [37]For you have brought these men here who are neither robbers of temples nor blasphemers of yourª goddess. [38]Therefore, if Demetrius and his fellow craftsmen have a case against anyone, the courts are open and there are proconsuls. Let them bring charges against one another. [39]But if you have any other inquiry to make, it shall be determined in the lawful assembly. [40]For we are in danger of being called in question for today's uproar, there being no reason which we may give to account for this disorderly gathering." [41]And when he had said these things, he dismissed the assembly.

Are the Bible's Food Laws for Today?

ULTIMATE HEALTH RESOURCE • ULTIMATE HEALTH RESOURCE • ULTIMATE HEALTH RESOURCE

Accepting Jesus as our Savior and Lord does not "free" us from keeping the Ten Commandments. Rather, we are empowered to *want* to keep them and to actually keep them! The same is true for the other laws in the Old Testament that are not directly related to our spiritual salvation, including laws related to morality and eating. Accepting Jesus empowers us to want to keep those laws and then to keep them.

The food laws were given to the Israelites for their *health* and *well-being*. God was not punishing His people by denying them certain foods. He was calling them to make choices that would give them the maximum quality of life for all the days of their lives.

The food laws of the Bible are found primarily in Leviticus 11 and Deuteronomy 14—fewer than 150 verses in all. The commandments called for the Israelites to limit their eating of animals, birds, fish, and other creatures to those that were designated as "clean." They were to eat animals that had been slaughtered specifically for consumption and had been drained of all blood. All fat was to be burned, not consumed. A young animal was not to be boiled in its mother's milk. These are not difficult dietary laws to keep!

Many Christians are eager to follow Jesus closely—to say what He said and do what He did. They don't seem very eager, however, to eat the way Jesus ate. The truth is that Jesus ate foods that were in keeping with the Levitical law, the law given to the Israelites from God through Moses.

People often say, "I don't live under the law. I live under grace!" My response as a physician is: God is giving you the grace today to learn about His law and to live according to it. The law that Jesus fulfilled completely in His own life and death had to do with spiritual atonement. We no longer need to sacrifice animals or shed blood in order to experience forgiveness for our sins. Jesus became the sacrifice for sin on the cross. When we accept His sacrifice, we are freed from the bondage of sin and are empowered by God to enter into a new relationship with Him and live a new life.

19:24 ªGreek *Artemis*   19:27 ªNU-Text reads *she be deposed from her magnificence.*   19:37 ªNU-Text reads *our.*

Simple Changes Can Make a Big Difference

We seem to have taken the concept of "make-over" to the extreme in our culture today! The truth is, some very basic, simple changes can make a huge difference in the lives of many people when it comes to better health and wholeness.

Researchers at Brigham Young University recently asked more than three hundred people to simply add more whole grains, fruits, and vegetables to their diets and to walk thirty minutes a day. They requested that the participants in this study make these basic changes for six weeks. The results were astounding: Those with high cholesterol experienced a 12 percent drop in cholesterol—for every 1 percent decline in cholesterol, heart disease risk drops 2 to 3 percent. Those with diabetes had 38 percent improvement in their need for insulin. Those with high blood pressure had a 60 percent drop in blood pressure readings. All from forty-two days of eating more of the right foods and walking thirty minutes a day!

☐ Intentionally doing one act of kindness a day can help you develop a more positive attitude, make more friends, and have greater success in the workplace.
☐ Reading the Bible and praying for fifteen minutes a day can do a great deal to help you become more loving, more faithful, and more hopeful, and to experience a growing relationship with God.
☐ Washing your hands for thirty seconds at a time, six times a day, can significantly reduce infections, colds, and the flu.
☐ Drinking eight to ten glasses of pure water a day can do more for your physical health than taking in any other food, beverage, or supplement.
☐ Writing a two-line note of thanks, encouragement, or apology can go a long way toward building a stronger relationship with someone.

Don't wait for the emotional, spiritual, or physical energy to undertake the massive overhaul you may feel you need in your life. Begin with baby steps—simple steps, basic steps.

WHOLENESS 101

JOURNEYS IN GREECE

20 After the uproar had ceased, Paul called the disciples to *himself,* embraced *them,* and departed to go to Macedonia. ²Now when he had gone over that region and encouraged them with many words, he came to Greece ³and stayed three months. And when the Jews plotted against him as he was about to sail to Syria, he decided to return through Macedonia. ⁴And Sopater of Berea accompanied him to Asia—also Aristarchus and Secundus of the Thessalonians, and Gaius of Derbe, and Timothy, and Tychicus and Trophimus of Asia. ⁵These men, going ahead, waited for us at Troas. ⁶But we sailed away from Philippi after the Days of Unleavened Bread, and in five days joined them at Troas, where we stayed seven days.

MINISTERING AT TROAS

⁷Now on the first *day* of the week, when the disciples came together to break bread, Paul, ready to depart the next day, spoke to them and continued his message until midnight. ⁸There were many lamps in the upper room where they* were gathered together. ⁹And in a window sat a certain young man named Eutychus, who was sinking into a deep sleep. He was overcome by sleep; and as Paul continued speaking, he fell down from the third story and was taken up dead. ¹⁰But Paul went down, fell on him, and embracing *him* said, "Do not trouble yourselves, for his life is in him." ¹¹Now when he had come up, had broken bread and eaten, and talked a long while, even till daybreak, he departed. ¹²And they brought the young man in alive, and they were not a little comforted.

FROM TROAS TO MILETUS

¹³Then we went ahead to the ship and sailed to Assos, there intending to take Paul on board; for so he had given orders, intending himself to go on foot. ¹⁴And when he met us at Assos, we took him on board and came to Mitylene. ¹⁵We sailed from there, and the next *day* came opposite Chios. The following *day* we arrived at Samos and stayed at Trogyllium. The next *day* we came to Miletus. ¹⁶For Paul had decided to sail past Ephesus, so that he would not have to spend time in Asia; for he was hurrying to be at Jerusalem, if possible, on the Day of Pentecost.

THE EPHESIAN ELDERS EXHORTED

¹⁷From Miletus he sent to Ephesus and called for the elders of the church. ¹⁸And when they had come to him, he said to them: "You know, from the first day that I came to Asia, in what manner I always lived among you, ¹⁹serving the Lord with all humility, with many tears and trials which happened to me by the plotting of the Jews; ²⁰how I kept back nothing that was helpful, but proclaimed it to you, and taught you publicly and from house to house, ²¹testifying to Jews, and also to Greeks, repentance toward God and faith toward our Lord Jesus Christ. ²²And see, now I go bound in the spirit to Jerusalem, not knowing the things that will happen to me there, ²³except that the

20:8 ªNU-Text and M-Text read *we.*

CONDIMENTS

☐ Honey

Honey was the main sweetener in Bible times. It also was used as a condiment to add a distinctive flavor to feta cheese, yogurt, or butter.

People in Bible times were not addicted to sugar or to sweets as we are today in the United States. Are you aware that the average American consumes about 150 pounds of sugar a year? That can result in more than 11,000 pounds of sugar during a person's lifetime, which is about half a truckload! Is it any wonder that we have an epidemic of diabetes in our nation?

We need to start saying "no, thank you" to sugary desserts and "yes" to fruits, nuts, and a small amount of honey.

Honey has medicinal uses. The ancient Egyptians had about nine hundred treatments for a wide variety of illnesses and injuries. More than five hundred of the treatments had honey as a primary ingredient. The Greeks and Romans knew that honey rubbed into wounds helped the healing process. Today, international travelers often take honey with them—it seems to work many times when nothing else does to put a stop to diarrhea. Honey may also be effective in combating pathogenic bacteria that can cause food poisoning.

A single serving of honey—about one tablespoon—has 64 calories and 17 carbohydrate grams. Even though honey is better for a person than refined sugar, honey is still high in calories.

Note: The Centers for Disease Control cautions parents of young children *not* to give honey to a child under the age of one year.

This dessert popular in the Middle East is among the simplest to make!

Honey Cream
¼ to ½ cup honey
2 cups plain yogurt, sour cream, or heavy cream

Place the honey and cream in separate bowls on the table, allowing guests to mix them together to taste. In the winter, the yogurt or cream may be served warm. In the summer months, serve it chilled. A couple of tablespoons of this dessert is a very satisfying end to a meal!

Holy Spirit testifies in every city, saying that chains and tribulations await me. [24]But none of these things move me; nor do I count my life dear to myself,[a] so that I may finish my race with joy, and the ministry which I received from the Lord Jesus, to testify to the gospel of the grace of God.

[25]"And indeed, now I know that you all, among whom I have gone preaching the kingdom of God, will see my face no more. [26]Therefore I testify to you this day that I *am* innocent of the blood of all *men.* [27]For I have not shunned to declare to you the whole counsel of God. [28]Therefore take heed to yourselves and to all the flock, among which the Holy Spirit has made you overseers, to shepherd the church of God[a] which He purchased with His own blood. [29]For I know this, that after my departure savage wolves will come in among you, not sparing the flock. [30]Also from among yourselves men will rise up, speaking perverse things, to draw away the disciples after themselves. [31]Therefore watch, and remember that for three years I did not cease to warn everyone night and day with tears.

[32]"So now, brethren, I commend you to God and to the word of His grace, which is able to build you up and give you an inheritance among all those who are sanctified. [33]I have coveted no one's silver or gold or apparel. [34]Yes,[a] you yourselves know that these hands have provided for my necessities, and for those who were with me. [35]I have shown you in every way, by laboring like this, that you must support the weak. And remember the words of the Lord Jesus, that He said, 'It is more blessed to give than to receive.' "

[36]And when he had said these things, he knelt down and prayed with them all. [37]Then they all wept freely, and fell on Paul's neck and kissed him, [38]sorrowing most of all for the words which he spoke, that they would see his face no more. And they accompanied him to the ship.

WARNINGS ON THE JOURNEY TO JERUSALEM

21 Now it came to pass, that when we had departed from them and set sail, running a straight course we came to Cos, the following *day* to Rhodes, and from there to Patara. [2]And finding a ship sailing over to Phoenicia, we went aboard and set sail. [3]When we had sighted Cyprus, we passed it on the left, sailed to Syria, and landed at Tyre; for there the ship was to unload her cargo. [4]And finding disciples,[a] we stayed there seven days. They told Paul through the Spirit not to go up to Jerusalem. [5]When we had come to the end of those days, we departed and went on our way; and they all accompanied us, with wives and children, till *we were* out of the city. And we knelt down on the shore and prayed. [6]When we had taken our leave of one another, we boarded the ship, and they returned home.

[7]And when we had finished *our* voyage from Tyre, we came to Ptolemais, greeted the brethren, and stayed with them one day. [8]On the next *day* we who were Paul's companions[a] departed and came to Caesarea, and entered the house of Philip the evangelist, who was *one of* the seven, and stayed with him. [9]Now this man had four virgin daughters who prophesied. [10]And as we stayed many days, a certain prophet named Agabus came down from Judea. [11]When he had come to us, he took Paul's belt, bound his *own* hands and feet, and said, "Thus says

the Holy Spirit, 'So shall the Jews at Jerusalem bind the man who owns this belt, and deliver *him* into the hands of the Gentiles.' "

¹²Now when we heard these things, both we and those from that place pleaded with him not to go up to Jerusalem. ¹³Then Paul answered, "What do you mean by weeping and breaking my heart? For I am ready not only to be bound, but also to die at Jerusalem for the name of the Lord Jesus."

¹⁴So when he would not be persuaded, we ceased, saying, "The will of the Lord be done."

PAUL URGED TO MAKE PEACE

¹⁵And after those days we packed and went up to Jerusalem. ¹⁶Also some of the disciples from Caesarea went with us and brought with them a certain Mnason of Cyprus, an early disciple, with whom we were to lodge.

¹⁷And when we had come to Jerusalem, the brethren received us gladly. ¹⁸On the following *day* Paul went in with us to James, and all the elders were present. ¹⁹When he had greeted them, he told in detail those things which God had done among the Gentiles through his ministry. ²⁰And when they heard *it,* they glorified the Lord. And they said to him, "You see, brother, how many myriads of Jews there are who have believed, and they are all zealous for the law; ²¹but they have been informed about you that you teach all the Jews who are among the Gentiles to forsake Moses, saying that they ought not to circumcise *their* children nor to walk according to the customs. ²²What then? The assembly must certainly meet, for they willᵃ hear that you have come. ²³Therefore do what we tell you: We have four men who have taken a vow. ²⁴Take them and be purified with them, and pay their expenses so that they may shave *their* heads, and that all may know that those things of which they were informed concerning you are nothing, but *that* you yourself also walk orderly and keep the law. ²⁵But concerning the Gentiles who believe, we have written *and* decided that they should observe no such thing, exceptᵃ that they should keep themselves from *things* offered to idols, from blood, from things strangled, and from sexual immorality."

ARRESTED IN THE TEMPLE

²⁶Then Paul took the men, and the next day, having been purified with them, entered the temple to announce the expiration of the days of purification, at which time an offering should be made for each one of them.

²⁷Now when the seven days were almost ended, the Jews from Asia, seeing him in the temple, stirred up the whole crowd and laid hands on him, ²⁸crying out, "Men of Israel, help! This is the man who teaches all *men* everywhere against the people, the law, and this place; and furthermore he also brought Greeks into the temple and has defiled this holy place." ²⁹(For they had previouslyᵃ seen Trophimus the Ephesian with him in the city, whom they supposed that Paul had brought into the temple.)

³⁰And all the city was disturbed; and the people ran together, seized Paul, and dragged him out of the temple; and immediately the doors were shut. ³¹Now as they were seeking to kill him, news came to the commander of the garrison that all Jerusalem was in an uproar. ³²He

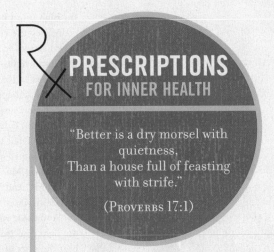

PRESCRIPTIONS
FOR INNER HEALTH

"Better is a dry morsel with quietness,
Than a house full of feasting with strife."

(Proverbs 17:1)

Feasting in this verse refers primarily to sacrificial meals that were a part of religious practices. The Bible is advising us that it's not the elegance of a meal or the gourmet nature of a dish that matters most, but rather, the emotional and spiritual atmosphere in which we are nourished. Make mealtimes at your house times of rest, with low-key conversation and an attitude of relaxation.

immediately took soldiers and centurions, and ran down to them. And when they saw the commander and the soldiers, they stopped beating Paul. ³³Then the commander came near and took him, and commanded *him* to be bound with two chains; and he asked who he was and what he had done. ³⁴And some among the multitude cried one thing and some another.

So when he could not ascertain the truth because of the tumult, he commanded him to be taken into the barracks. ³⁵When he reached the stairs, he had to be carried by the soldiers because of the violence of the mob. ³⁶For the multitude of the people followed after, crying out, "Away with him!"

ADDRESSING THE JERUSALEM MOB

³⁷Then as Paul was about to be led into the barracks, he said to the commander, "May I speak to you?"

He replied, "Can you speak Greek? ³⁸Are you not the Egyptian who some time ago stirred up a rebellion and led the four thousand assassins out into the wilderness?"

³⁹But Paul said, "I am a Jew from Tarsus, in Cilicia, a citizen of no mean city; and I implore you, permit me to speak to the people."

⁴⁰So when he had given him permission, Paul stood on the stairs and motioned with his hand to the people. And when there was a great silence, he spoke to *them* in the Hebrew language, saying,

---

21:22 ᵃNU-Text reads *What then is to be done? They will certainly.*   21:25 ᵃNU-Text omits *that they should observe no such thing, except.*   21:29 ᵃM-Text omits *previously.*

The LAW
AND THE
SCIENCE

[EATING LOCUSTS?]

>SCIENCE tells us that although we may find it repulsive to eat the four kinds of locusts that the LAW says are edible, these insects are rich sources of protein. People in many other cultures seem to enjoy them cooked almost to a crisp.

>THE LAW says: "All flying insects that creep on all fours shall be an abomination to you. Yet these you may eat of every flying insect that creeps on all fours; those which have jointed legs above their feet with which to leap on the earth. These you may eat: the locust after its kind, the destroying locust after its kind, the cricket after its kind, and the grasshopper after its kind. But all other flying insects which have four feet shall be an abomination to you" (Leviticus 11:20–23).

22 "Brethren and fathers, hear my defense before you now." ²And when they heard that he spoke to them in the Hebrew language, they kept all the more silent.

Then he said: ³"I am indeed a Jew, born in Tarsus of Cilicia, but brought up in this city at the feet of Gamaliel, taught according to the strictness of our fathers' law, and was zealous toward God as you all are today. ⁴I persecuted this Way to the death, binding and delivering into prisons both men and women, ⁵as also the high priest bears me witness, and all the council of the elders, from whom I also received letters to the brethren, and went to Damascus to bring in chains even those who were there to Jerusalem to be punished.

⁶"Now it happened, as I journeyed and came near Damascus at about noon, suddenly a great light from heaven shone around me. ⁷And I fell to the ground and heard a voice saying to me, 'Saul, Saul, why are you persecuting Me?' ⁸So I answered, 'Who are You, Lord?' And He said to me, 'I am Jesus of Nazareth, whom you are persecuting.'

⁹"And those who were with me indeed saw the light and were afraid,ᵃ but they did not hear the voice of Him who spoke to me. ¹⁰So I said, 'What shall I do, Lord?' And the Lord said to me, 'Arise and go into Damascus, and there you will be told all things which are appointed for you to do.' ¹¹And since I could not see for the glory of that light, being led by the hand of those who were with me, I came into Damascus.

¹²"Then a certain Ananias, a devout man according to the law, having a good testimony with all the Jews who dwelt there, ¹³came to me; and he stood and said to me, 'Brother Saul, receive your sight.' And at that same hour I looked up at him. ¹⁴Then he said, 'The God of our fathers has chosen you that you should know His will, and see the Just One, and hear the voice of His mouth. ¹⁵For you will be His witness to all men of what you have seen and heard. ¹⁶And now why are you waiting? Arise and be baptized, and wash away your sins, calling on the name of the Lord.'

¹⁷"Now it happened, when I returned to Jerusalem and was praying in the temple, that I was in a trance ¹⁸and saw Him saying to me, 'Make haste and get out of Jerusalem quickly, for they will not receive your testimony concerning Me.' ¹⁹So I said, 'Lord, they know that in every synagogue I imprisoned and beat those who believe on You. ²⁰And when the blood of Your martyr Stephen was shed, I also was standing by consenting to his death,ᵃ and guarding the clothes of those who were killing him.' ²¹Then He said to me, 'Depart, for I will send you far from here to the Gentiles.' "

PAUL'S ROMAN CITIZENSHIP

²²And they listened to him until this word, and *then* they raised their voices and said, "Away with such a *fellow* from the earth, for he is not fit to live!" ²³Then, as they cried out and tore off *their* clothes and threw dust into the air, ²⁴the commander ordered him to be brought into the barracks, and said that he should be examined under scourging, so that he might know why they shouted so against him. ²⁵And as they bound him with thongs, Paul said to the centurion who stood by, "Is it lawful for you to scourge a man who is a Roman, and uncondemned?"

²⁶When the centurion heard *that,* he went and told the commander, saying, "Take care what you do, for this man is a Roman."

²⁷Then the commander came and said to him, "Tell me, are you a Roman?"

He said, "Yes."

²⁸The commander answered, "With a large sum I obtained this citizenship."

And Paul said, "But I was born *a citizen.*"

²⁹Then immediately those who were about to examine him withdrew from him; and the commander was also afraid after he found out that he was a Roman, and because he had bound him.

THE SANHEDRIN DIVIDED

³⁰The next day, because he wanted to know for certain why he was accused by the Jews, he released him from *his* bonds, and commanded the chief priests and all their council to appear, and brought Paul down and set him before them.

23 Then Paul, looking earnestly at the council, said, "Men *and* brethren, I have lived in all good conscience before God until this day." ²And the high priest Ananias commanded those who stood by him to strike him on the mouth. ³Then Paul said to him, "God will strike you, *you* whitewashed wall! For you sit to judge me according to the law, and do you command me to be struck contrary to the law?"

22:9 ᵃNU-Text omits *and were afraid.*   22:20 ᵃNU-Text omits *to his death.*

[4]And those who stood by said, "Do you revile God's high priest?"

[5]Then Paul said, "I did not know, brethren, that he was the high priest; for it is written, 'You shall not speak evil of a ruler of your people.' "[a]

[6]But when Paul perceived that one part were Sadducees and the other Pharisees, he cried out in the council, "Men *and* brethren, I am a Pharisee, the son of a Pharisee; concerning the hope and resurrection of the dead I am being judged!"

[7]And when he had said this, a dissension arose between the Pharisees and the Sadducees; and the assembly was divided. [8]For Sadducees say that there is no resurrection—and no angel or spirit; but the Pharisees confess both. [9]Then there arose a loud outcry. And the scribes of the Pharisees' party arose and protested, saying, "We find no evil in this man; but if a spirit or an angel has spoken to him, let us not fight against God."[a]

[10]Now when there arose a great dissension, the commander, fearing lest Paul might be pulled to pieces by them, commanded the soldiers to go down and take him by force from among them, and bring him into the barracks.

THE PLOT AGAINST PAUL

[11]But the following night the Lord stood by him and said, "Be of good cheer, Paul; for as you have testified for Me in Jerusalem, so you must also bear witness at Rome."

[12]And when it was day, some of the Jews banded together and bound themselves under an oath, saying that they would neither eat nor drink till they had killed Paul. [13]Now there were more than forty who had formed this conspiracy. [14]They came to the chief priests and elders, and said, "We have bound ourselves under a great oath that we will eat nothing until we have killed Paul. [15]Now you, therefore, together with the council, suggest to the commander that he be brought down to you tomorrow,[a] as though you were going to make further inquiries concerning him; but we are ready to kill him before he comes near."

[16]So when Paul's sister's son heard of their ambush, he went and entered the barracks and told Paul. [17]Then Paul called one of the centurions to *him* and said, "Take this young man to the commander, for he has something to tell him." [18]So he took him and brought *him* to the commander and said, "Paul the prisoner called me to *him* and asked *me* to bring this young man to you. He has something to say to you."

[19]Then the commander took him by the hand, went aside, and asked privately, "What is it that you have to tell me?"

[20]And he said, "The Jews have agreed to ask that you bring Paul down to the council tomorrow, as though they were going to inquire more fully about him. [21]But do not yield to them, for more than forty of them lie in wait for him, men who have bound themselves by an oath that they will neither eat nor drink till they have killed him; and now they are ready, waiting for the promise from you."

[22]So the commander let the young man depart, and commanded *him*, "Tell no one that you have revealed these things to me."

SENT TO FELIX

[23]And he called for two centurions, saying, "Prepare two hundred soldiers, seventy horsemen, and two hundred spearmen to go to Cae-

sarea at the third hour of the night; [24]and provide mounts to set Paul on, and bring *him* safely to Felix the governor." [25]He wrote a letter in the following manner:

[26]Claudius Lysias,

To the most excellent governor Felix:

Greetings.

[27]This man was seized by the Jews and was about to be killed by them. Coming with the troops I rescued him, having learned that he was a Roman. [28]And when I wanted to know the reason they accused him, I brought him before their council. [29]I found out that he was accused concerning questions of their law, but had nothing charged against him deserving of death or chains. [30]And when it was told me that the Jews lay in wait for the man,[a] I sent him immediately to you, and also commanded his accusers to state before you the charges against him.

Farewell.

[31]Then the soldiers, as they were commanded, took Paul and brought *him* by night to Antipatris. [32]The next day they left the horsemen to go on with him, and returned to the barracks. [33]When they came to Caesarea and had delivered the letter to the governor, they also presented Paul to him. [34]And when the governor had read *it*, he asked what province he was from. And when he understood that *he was* from Cilicia, [35]he said, "I will hear you when your accusers also have come." And he commanded him to be kept in Herod's Praetorium.

ACCUSED OF SEDITION

24 Now after five days Ananias the high priest came down with the elders and a certain orator *named* Tertullus. These gave evidence to the governor against Paul.

[2]And when he was called upon, Tertullus began his accusation, saying: "Seeing that through you we enjoy great peace, and prosperity is being brought to this nation by your foresight, [3]we accept *it* always and in all places, most noble Felix, with all thankfulness. [4]Nevertheless, not to be tedious to you any further, I beg you to hear, by your cour-

23:5 [a]Exodus 22:28   23:9 [a]NU-Text omits last clause and reads *what if a spirit or an angel has spoken to him?*   23:15 [a]NU-Text omits *tomorrow.*   23:30 [a]NU-Text reads *there would be a plot against the man.*

DIVINE HEALTH   181

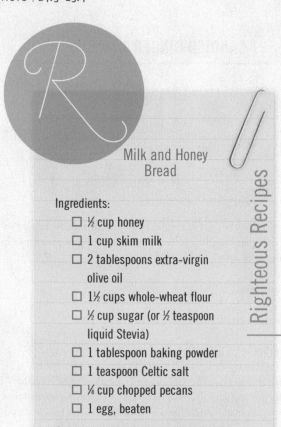

Righteous Recipes

Milk and Honey Bread

Ingredients:

- ☐ ½ cup honey
- ☐ 1 cup skim milk
- ☐ 2 tablespoons extra-virgin olive oil
- ☐ 1½ cups whole-wheat flour
- ☐ ½ cup sugar (or ½ teaspoon liquid Stevia)
- ☐ 1 tablespoon baking powder
- ☐ 1 teaspoon Celtic salt
- ☐ ¼ cup chopped pecans
- ☐ 1 egg, beaten

Combine the honey and milk in a medium saucepan over medium heat and cook, stirring constantly, until the honey dissolves. Stir in the olive oil. Remove from heat and let cool. Sift the flour, sugar, baking powder, and salt into a large mixing bowl. (If using liquid Stevia, wait to add this until later.) Add the pecans and toss to coat. Whisk the egg into the cooled milk mixture. (If using instead of sugar, add the liquid Stevia.) Add the egg mixture to the flour mixture. Beat just until blended.

Pour mixture into a lightly greased and floured loaf pan and smooth the top. Bake at 350 degrees for 65 to 75 minutes or until a wooden toothpick inserted into the center comes out clean. Cool in the pan on a wire rack for 10 minutes. Remove from the pan and cool completely on the rack.

Yield: 1 loaf

law. [7]But the commander Lysias came by and with great violence took *him* out of our hands, [8]commanding his accusers to come to you. By examining him yourself you may ascertain all these things of which we accuse him." [9]And the Jews also assented,ª maintaining that these things were so.

THE DEFENSE BEFORE FELIX

[10]Then Paul, after the governor had nodded to him to speak, answered: "Inasmuch as I know that you have been for many years a judge of this nation, I do the more cheerfully answer for myself, [11]because you may ascertain that it is no more than twelve days since I went up to Jerusalem to worship. [12]And they neither found me in the temple disputing with anyone nor inciting the crowd, either in the synagogues or in the city. [13]Nor can they prove the things of which they now accuse me. [14]But this I confess to you, that according to the Way which they call a sect, so I worship the God of my fathers, believing all things which are written in the Law and in the Prophets. [15]I have hope in God, which they themselves also accept, that there will be a resurrection of *the* dead,ª both of *the* just and *the* unjust. [16]This *being* so, I myself always strive to have a conscience without offense toward God and men.

[17]"Now after many years I came to bring alms and offerings to my nation, [18]in the midst of which some Jews from Asia found me purified in the temple, neither with a mob nor with tumult. [19]They ought to have been here before you to object if they had anything against me. [20]Or else let those who are *here* themselves say if they found any wrongdoingª in me while I stood before the council, [21]unless *it is* for this one statement which I cried out, standing among them, 'Concerning the resurrection of the dead I am being judged by you this day.' "

FELIX PROCRASTINATES

[22]But when Felix heard these things, having more accurate knowledge of *the* Way, he adjourned the proceedings and said, "When Lysias the commander comes down, I will make a decision on your case." [23]So he commanded the centurion to keep Paul and to let *him* have liberty, and told him not to forbid any of his friends to provide for or visit him.

[24]And after some days, when Felix came with his wife Drusilla, who was Jewish, he sent for Paul and heard him concerning the faith in Christ. [25]Now as he reasoned about righteousness, self-control, and the judgment to come, Felix was afraid and answered, "Go away for now; when I have a convenient time I will call for you." [26]Meanwhile he also hoped that money would be given him by Paul, that he might release him.ª Therefore he sent for him more often and conversed with him.

[27]But after two years Porcius Festus succeeded Felix; and Felix, wanting to do the Jews a favor, left Paul bound.

PAUL APPEALS TO CAESAR

25 Now when Festus had come to the province, after three days he went up from Caesarea to Jerusalem. [2]Then the high priestª and the chief men of the Jews informed him against Paul; and they petitioned him, [3]asking a favor against him, that he would summon him to Jerusalem—while *they* lay in ambush along the road to kill him. [4]But Festus answered that Paul should be kept at

tesy, a few words from us. [5]For we have found this man a plague, a creator of dissension among all the Jews throughout the world, and a ringleader of the sect of the Nazarenes. [6]He even tried to profane the temple, and we seized him,ª and wanted to judge him according to our

24:6 ªNU-Text ends the sentence here and omits the rest of verse 6, all of verse 7, and the first clause of verse 8.   24:9 ªNU-Text and M-Text read *joined the attack*.   24:15 ªNU-Text omits *of the dead*.   24:20 ªNU-Text and M-Text read *say what wrongdoing they found*.   24:26 ªNU-Text omits *that he might release him*.   25:2 ªNU-Text reads *chief priests*.

Caesarea, and that he himself was going *there* shortly. [5]"Therefore," he said, "let those who have authority among you go down with *me* and accuse this man, to see if there is any fault in him."

[6]And when he had remained among them more than ten days, he went down to Caesarea. And the next day, sitting on the judgment seat, he commanded Paul to be brought. [7]When he had come, the Jews who had come down from Jerusalem stood about and laid many serious complaints against Paul, which they could not prove, [8]while he answered for himself, "Neither against the law of the Jews, nor against the temple, nor against Caesar have I offended in anything at all."

[9]But Festus, wanting to do the Jews a favor, answered Paul and said, "Are you willing to go up to Jerusalem and there be judged before me concerning these things?"

[10]So Paul said, "I stand at Caesar's judgment seat, where I ought to be judged. To the Jews I have done no wrong, as you very well know. [11]For if I am an offender, or have committed anything deserving of death, I do not object to dying; but if there is nothing in these things of which these men accuse me, no one can deliver me to them. I appeal to Caesar."

[12]Then Festus, when he had conferred with the council, answered, "You have appealed to Caesar? To Caesar you shall go!"

PAUL BEFORE AGRIPPA

[13]And after some days King Agrippa and Bernice came to Caesarea to greet Festus. [14]When they had been there many days, Festus laid Paul's case before the king, saying: "There is a certain man left a prisoner by Felix, [15]about whom the chief priests and the elders of the Jews informed *me*, when I was in Jerusalem, asking for a judgment against him. [16]To them I answered, 'It is not the custom of the Romans to deliver any man to destruction[a] before the accused meets the accusers face to face, and has opportunity to answer for himself concerning the charge against him.' [17]Therefore when they had come together, without any delay, the next day I sat on the judgment seat and commanded the man to be brought in. [18]When the accusers stood up, they brought no accusation against him of such things as I supposed, [19]but had some questions against him about their own religion and about a certain Jesus, who had died, whom Paul affirmed to be alive. [20]And because I was uncertain of such questions, I asked whether he was willing to go to Jerusalem and there be judged concerning these matters. [21]But when Paul appealed to be reserved for the decision of Augustus, I commanded him to be kept till I could send him to Caesar."

[22]Then Agrippa said to Festus, "I also would like to hear the man myself."

"Tomorrow," he said, "you shall hear him."

[23]So the next day, when Agrippa and Bernice had come with great pomp, and had entered the auditorium with the commanders and the prominent men of the city, at Festus' command Paul was brought in. [24]And Festus said: "King Agrippa and all the men who are here present with us, you see this man about whom the whole assembly of the Jews petitioned me, both at Jerusalem and here, crying out that he was not fit to live any longer. [25]But when I found that he had committed nothing deserving of death, and that he himself had appealed to Augustus, I decided to send him. [26]I have nothing certain to write to my lord concerning him. Therefore I have brought him out before you, and especially before you, King Agrippa, so that after the examination has taken place I may have something to write. [27]For it seems to me unreasonable to send a prisoner and not to specify the charges against him."

PAUL'S EARLY LIFE

26 Then Agrippa said to Paul, "You are permitted to speak for yourself."

So Paul stretched out his hand and answered for himself: [2]"I think myself happy, King Agrippa, because today I shall answer for myself before you concerning all the things of which I am accused by the Jews, [3]especially because you are expert in all customs and questions which have to do with the Jews. Therefore I beg you to hear me patiently.

[4]"My manner of life from my youth, which was spent from the beginning among my own nation at Jerusalem, all the Jews know. [5]They knew me from the first, if they were willing to testify, that according to the strictest sect of our religion I lived a Pharisee. [6]And now I stand and am judged for the hope of the promise made by God to our fathers. [7]To this *promise* our twelve tribes, earnestly serving *God* night and day, hope to attain. For this hope's sake, King Agrippa, I am accused by the Jews. [8]Why should it be thought incredible by you that God raises the dead?

[9]"Indeed, I myself thought I must do many things contrary to the name of Jesus of Nazareth. [10]This I also did in Jerusalem, and many of the saints I shut up in prison, having received authority from the chief priests; and when they were put to death, I cast my vote against *them*. [11]And I punished them often in every synagogue and compelled *them* to blaspheme; and being exceedingly enraged against them, I persecuted *them* even to foreign cities.

PAUL RECOUNTS HIS CONVERSION

[12]"While thus occupied, as I journeyed to Damascus with authority and commission from the chief priests, [13]at midday, O king, along the

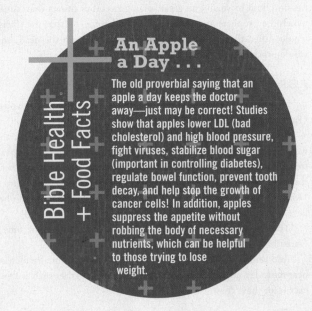

An Apple a Day . . .

Bible Health + Food Facts

The old proverbial saying that an apple a day keeps the doctor away—just may be correct! Studies show that apples lower LDL (bad cholesterol) and high blood pressure, fight viruses, stabilize blood sugar (important in controlling diabetes), regulate bowel function, prevent tooth decay, and help stop the growth of cancer cells! In addition, apples suppress the appetite without robbing the body of necessary nutrients, which can be helpful to those trying to lose weight.

25:16 [a]NU-Text omits *to destruction*, although it is implied.

road I saw a light from heaven, brighter than the sun, shining around me and those who journeyed with me. [14]And when we all had fallen to the ground, I heard a voice speaking to me and saying in the Hebrew language, 'Saul, Saul, why are you persecuting Me? *It is* hard for you to kick against the goads.' [15]So I said, 'Who are You, Lord?' And He said, 'I am Jesus, whom you are persecuting. [16]But rise and stand on your feet; for I have appeared to you for this purpose, to make you a minister and a witness both of the things which you have seen and of the things which I will yet reveal to you. [17]I will deliver you from the *Jewish* people, as well as *from* the Gentiles, to whom I now[a] send you, [18]to open their eyes, *in order* to turn *them* from darkness to light, and *from* the power of Satan to God, that they may receive forgiveness of sins and an inheritance among those who are sanctified by faith in Me.'

> **" . . . that the Christ would suffer, that He would be the first to rise from the dead, and would proclaim light to the Jewish people and to the Gentiles. "** — *Acts 26:23*

PAUL'S POST-CONVERSION LIFE

[19]"Therefore, King Agrippa, I was not disobedient to the heavenly vision, [20]but declared first to those in Damascus and in Jerusalem, and throughout all the region of Judea, and *then* to the Gentiles, that they should repent, turn to God, and do works befitting repentance. [21]For these reasons the Jews seized me in the temple and tried to kill *me*. [22]Therefore, having obtained help from God, to this day I stand, witnessing both to small and great, saying no other things than those which the prophets and Moses said would come— [23]that the Christ would suffer, that He would be the first to rise from the dead, and would proclaim light to the *Jewish* people and to the Gentiles."

AGRIPPA PARRIES PAUL'S CHALLENGE

[24]Now as he thus made his defense, Festus said with a loud voice, "Paul, you are beside yourself! Much learning is driving you mad!"

[25]But he said, "I am not mad, most noble Festus, but speak the words of truth and reason. [26]For the king, before whom I also speak freely, knows these things; for I am convinced that none of these things escapes his attention, since this thing was not done in a corner. [27]King Agrippa, do you believe the prophets? I know that you do believe."

[28]Then Agrippa said to Paul, "You almost persuade me to become a Christian."

[29]And Paul said, "I would to God that not only you, but also all who hear me today, might become both almost and altogether such as I am, except for these chains."

[30]When he had said these things, the king stood up, as well as the governor and Bernice and those who sat with them; [31]and when they had gone aside, they talked among themselves, saying, "This man is doing nothing deserving of death or chains."

[32]Then Agrippa said to Festus, "This man might have been set free if he had not appealed to Caesar."

THE VOYAGE TO ROME BEGINS

27 And when it was decided that we should sail to Italy, they delivered Paul and some other prisoners to *one* named Julius, a centurion of the Augustan Regiment. [2]So, entering a ship of Adramyttium, we put to sea, meaning to sail along the coasts of Asia. Aristarchus, a Macedonian of Thessalonica, was with us. [3]And the next *day* we landed at Sidon. And Julius treated Paul kindly and gave *him* liberty to go to his friends and receive care. [4]When we had put to sea from there, we sailed under *the shelter of* Cyprus, because the winds were contrary. [5]And when we had sailed over the sea which is off Cilicia and Pamphylia, we came to Myra, *a city* of Lycia. [6]There the centurion found an Alexandrian ship sailing to Italy, and he put us on board.

[7]When we had sailed slowly many days, and arrived with difficulty off Cnidus, the wind not permitting us to proceed, we sailed under *the shelter of* Crete off Salmone. [8]Passing it with difficulty, we came to a place called Fair Havens, near the city *of* Lasea.

PAUL'S WARNING IGNORED

[9]Now when much time had been spent, and sailing was now dangerous because the Fast was already over, Paul advised them, [10]saying, "Men, I perceive that this voyage will end with disaster and much loss, not only of the cargo and ship, but also our lives." [11]Nevertheless the centurion was more persuaded by the helmsman and the owner of the ship than by the things spoken by Paul. [12]And because the harbor was not suitable to winter in, the majority advised to set sail from there also, if by any means they could reach Phoenix, a harbor of Crete opening toward the southwest and northwest, *and* winter *there*.

IN THE TEMPEST

[13]When the south wind blew softly, supposing that they had obtained *their* desire, putting out to sea, they sailed close by Crete. [14]But not long after, a tempestuous head wind arose, called Euroclydon.[a] [15]So when the ship was caught, and could not head into the wind, we let *her* drive. [16]And running under *the shelter of* an island called Clauda,[a] we secured the skiff with difficulty. [17]When they had taken it on board, they used cables to undergird the ship; and fearing lest they should run aground on the Syrtis[a] *Sands*, they struck sail and so were driven. [18]And because we were exceedingly tempest-tossed, the next *day* they lightened the ship. [19]On the third *day* we threw the ship's tackle overboard with our own hands. [20]Now when neither sun nor stars appeared for many days, and no small tempest beat on *us*, all hope that we would be saved was finally given up.

[21]But after long abstinence from food, then Paul stood in the midst of them and said, "Men, you should have listened to me, and not have sailed from Crete and incurred this disaster and loss. [22]And now I urge

26:17 [a]NU-Text and M-Text omit *now.*   27:14 [a]NU-Text reads *Euraquilon.*   27:16 [a]NU-Text reads *Cauda.*   27:17 [a]M-Text reads *Syrtes.*

you to take heart, for there will be no loss of life among you, but only of the ship. ²³For there stood by me this night an angel of the God to whom I belong and whom I serve, ²⁴saying, 'Do not be afraid, Paul; you must be brought before Caesar; and indeed God has granted you all those who sail with you.' ²⁵Therefore take heart, men, for I believe God that it will be just as it was told me. ²⁶However, we must run aground on a certain island."

²⁷Now when the fourteenth night had come, as we were driven up and down in the Adriatic *Sea*, about midnight the sailors sensed that they were drawing near some land. ²⁸And they took soundings and found *it* to be twenty fathoms; and when they had gone a little farther, they took soundings again and found *it* to be fifteen fathoms. ²⁹Then, fearing lest we should run aground on the rocks, they dropped four anchors from the stern, and prayed for day to come. ³⁰And as the sailors were seeking to escape from the ship, when they had let down the skiff into the sea, under pretense of putting out anchors from the prow, ³¹Paul said to the centurion and the soldiers, "Unless these men stay in the ship, you cannot be saved." ³²Then the soldiers cut away the ropes of the skiff and let it fall off.

³³And as day was about to dawn, Paul implored *them* all to take food, saying, "Today is the fourteenth day you have waited and continued without food, and eaten nothing. ³⁴Therefore I urge you to take nourishment, for this is for your survival, since not a hair will fall from the head of any of you." ³⁵And when he had said these things, he took bread and gave thanks to God in the presence of them all; and when he had broken *it* he began to eat. ³⁶Then they were all encouraged, and also took food themselves. ³⁷And in all we were two hundred and seventy-six persons on the ship. ³⁸So when they had eaten enough, they lightened the ship and threw out the wheat into the sea.

SHIPWRECKED ON MALTA

³⁹When it was day, they did not recognize the land; but they observed a bay with a beach, onto which they planned to run the ship if possible. ⁴⁰And they let go the anchors and left *them* in the sea, meanwhile loosing the rudder ropes; and they hoisted the mainsail to the wind and made for shore. ⁴¹But striking a place where two seas met, they ran the ship aground; and the prow stuck fast and remained immovable, but the stern was being broken up by the violence of the waves.

⁴²And the soldiers' plan was to kill the prisoners, lest any of them should swim away and escape. ⁴³But the centurion, wanting to save Paul, kept them from *their* purpose, and commanded that those who could swim should jump *overboard* first and get to land, ⁴⁴and the rest, some on boards and some on *parts* of the ship. And so it was that they all escaped safely to land.

PAUL'S MINISTRY ON MALTA

28 Now when they had escaped, they then found out that the island was called Malta. ²And the natives showed us unusual kindness; for they kindled a fire and made us all welcome, because of the rain that was falling and because of the cold. ³But when Paul had gathered a bundle of sticks and laid *them* on the fire, a viper came out because of the heat, and fastened on his hand. ⁴So when the natives saw the creature hanging from his hand, they said to one another, "No doubt this man is a murderer, whom, though he has escaped the sea, yet justice does not allow to live." ⁵But he shook off the creature into the fire and suffered no harm. ⁶However, they were expecting that he would swell up or suddenly fall down dead. But after they had looked for a long time and saw no harm come to him, they changed their minds and said that he was a god.

⁷In that region there was an estate of the leading citizen of the island, whose name was Publius, who received us and entertained us courteously for three days. ⁸And it happened that the father of Publius lay sick of a fever and dysentery. Paul went in to him and prayed, and he laid his hands on him and healed him. ⁹So when this was done, the rest of those on the island who had diseases also came and were

---

> (Acts 27:43)

Swimming for Health. It's important you know how to swim and that you teach your children to swim. Thousands of people die each year because they do not know how to swim, float, or tread water. Swimming is one of the best ways to exercise for an aerobic workout and to improve flexibility. Swimming has a positive effect on insulin sensitivity, which leads to a lower risk of diabetes. It improves other health outcomes such as blood pressure.

If you don't know how to swim, look for an instructor with an American Red Cross Water Safety Instructor certification. A water aerobics class is a good way to get accustomed to being in a pool, and such classes often help people learn to swim. If you are just beginning a swimming program, start alternating swimming with rest—swim a length of the pool, then rest for 10 to 15 seconds, then swim another length. In a twenty-five-yard pool, a half mile is about thirty-six lengths. Make that your ultimate goal. Swim with various strokes—the crawl, backstroke, breaststroke, and so forth—for maximum flexibility in a swimming workout.

You may experience rip tides or dangerous currents while swimming in the ocean or a large lake. Swim parallel to the shore rather than try to fight the current. Eventually you will get to a place where the tides or currents allow you to get back to shore. And *always* swim with a buddy.

INSIGHTS | INTO THE WORD

PREACHING HEALTH

"Regularity in the hours of rising and retiring, perseverance in exercise, adaptation of dress to the variations of climate, simple and nutritious aliment, and temperance in all things are necessary branches of the regimen of health."
—Lydia H. Sigourney, American author (1791–1865)

healed. [10]They also honored us in many ways; and when we departed, they provided such things as were necessary.

ARRIVAL AT ROME

[11]After three months we sailed in an Alexandrian ship whose figurehead was the Twin Brothers, which had wintered at the island. [12]And landing at Syracuse, we stayed three days. [13]From there we circled round and reached Rhegium. And after one day the south wind blew; and the next day we came to Puteoli, [14]where we found brethren, and were invited to stay with them seven days. And so we went toward Rome. [15]And from there, when the brethren heard about us, they came to meet us as far as Appii Forum and Three Inns. When Paul saw them, he thanked God and took courage.

[16]Now when we came to Rome, the centurion delivered the prisoners to the captain of the guard; but Paul was permitted to dwell by himself with the soldier who guarded him.

PAUL'S MINISTRY AT ROME

[17]And it came to pass after three days that Paul called the leaders of the Jews together. So when they had come together, he said to them: "Men *and* brethren, though I have done nothing against our people or the customs of our fathers, yet I was delivered as a prisoner from Jerusalem into the hands of the Romans, [18]who, when they had examined me, wanted to let *me* go, because there was no cause for putting me to death. [19]But when the Jews[a] spoke against *it*, I was compelled to appeal to Caesar, not that I had anything of which to accuse my nation. [20]For this reason therefore I have called for you, to see *you* and speak with *you*, because for the hope of Israel I am bound with this chain."

[21]Then they said to him, "We neither received letters from Judea concerning you, nor have any of the brethren who came reported or spoken any evil of you. [22]But we desire to hear from you what you think; for concerning this sect, we know that it is spoken against everywhere."

[23]So when they had appointed him a day, many came to him at *his* lodging, to whom he explained and solemnly testified of the kingdom of God, persuading them concerning Jesus from both the Law of Moses and the Prophets, from morning till evening. [24]And some were persuaded by the things which were spoken, and some disbelieved. [25]So when they did not agree among themselves, they departed after Paul had said one word: "The Holy Spirit spoke rightly through Isaiah the prophet to our[a] fathers, [26]saying,

'Go to this people and say:
"Hearing you will hear, and shall not understand;
And seeing you will see, and not perceive;
[27] For the hearts of this people have grown dull.
Their ears are hard of hearing,
And their eyes they have closed,
Lest they should see with their eyes and hear with their ears,
Lest they should understand with their hearts and turn,
So that I should heal them." '[a]

[28]"Therefore let it be known to you that the salvation of God has been sent to the Gentiles, and they will hear it!" [29]And when he had said these words, the Jews departed and had a great dispute among themselves.[a]

[30]Then Paul dwelt two whole years in his own rented house, and received all who came to him, [31]preaching the kingdom of God and teaching the things which concern the Lord Jesus Christ with all confidence, no one forbidding him.

28:19 [a]That is, the ruling authorities   28:25 [a]NU-Text reads *your.*   28:27 [a]Isaiah 6:9, 10   28:29 [a]NU-Text omits this verse.

HEALTH NOTES

OMANS

This book was written by the apostle Paul to the Christians in Rome about 55–59 A.D. Paul had never met these people, but he hoped to visit them soon. His letter is something of an "advance summary" of what Paul believed about Jesus and the need for salvation. Some have called it a short-course in Christianity—perhaps even "Christianity 101." Paul's message is filled with the words grace, faith, mercy, peace, and freedom. He insists throughout that "All have sinned. Nobody is good enough to be made right with God according to their accomplishments, personality, or good deeds. Everybody needs to be made right by accepting Jesus Christ as Savior—and the good news is that God has made salvation through Jesus Christ a free gift available to all people."

Nothing is ever stronger than its foundation. That's true for a building. It's true for a life of integrity. It's true for health. The basic, sure, rock-solid principles of truth must be the foundation on which we build and grow. For a Christian, the rock-solid foundation is the grace of God—the gospel of Christ brings salvation to everyone who believes.

GREETING

1 Paul, a bondservant of Jesus Christ, called *to be* an apostle, separated to the gospel of God ²which He promised before through His prophets in the Holy Scriptures, ³concerning His Son Jesus Christ our Lord, who was born of the seed of David according to the flesh, ⁴*and* declared *to be* the Son of God with power according to the Spirit of holiness, by the resurrection from the dead. ⁵Through Him we have received grace and apostleship for obedience to the faith among all nations for His name, ⁶among whom you also are the called of Jesus Christ;

⁷To all who are in Rome, beloved of God, called *to be* saints:

Grace to you and peace from God our Father and the Lord Jesus Christ.

DESIRE TO VISIT ROME

⁸First, I thank my God through Jesus Christ for you all, that your faith is spoken of throughout the whole world. ⁹For God is my witness, whom I serve with my spirit in the gospel of His Son, that without ceasing I make mention of you always in my prayers, ¹⁰making request if, by some means, now at last I may find a way in the will of God to come to you. ¹¹For I long to see you, that I may impart to you some spiritual gift, so that you may be established— ¹²that is, that I may be encouraged together with you by the mutual faith both of you and me. ¹³Now I do not want you to be unaware, brethren, that I often planned to come to you (but was hindered until now), that I might have some fruit among you also, just as among the other Gentiles. ¹⁴I am a debtor both to Greeks and to barbarians, both to wise and to unwise. ¹⁵So, as much as is in me, *I am* ready to preach the gospel to you who are in Rome also.

THE JUST LIVE BY FAITH

¹⁶For I am not ashamed of the gospel of Christ,ᵃ for it is the power of God to salvation for everyone who believes, for the Jew first and also for the Greek. ¹⁷For in it the righteousness of God is revealed from faith to faith; as it is written, "The just shall live by faith."ᵃ

GOD'S WRATH ON UNRIGHTEOUSNESS

¹⁸For the wrath of God is revealed from heaven against all ungodliness and unrighteousness of men, who suppress the truth in unrighteousness, ¹⁹because what may be known of God is manifest in them, for God has shown *it* to them. ²⁰For since the creation of the world His invisible *attributes* are clearly seen, being understood by the things that are made, *even* His eternal power and Godhead, so that they are without excuse, ²¹because, although they knew God, they did not glorify *Him* as God, nor were thankful, but became futile in their thoughts, and their foolish hearts were darkened. ²²Professing to be wise, they became fools, ²³and changed the glory of the incorruptible God into an image made like corruptible man—and birds and four-footed animals and creeping things.

²⁴Therefore God also gave them up to uncleanness, in the lusts of their hearts, to dishonor their bodies among themselves, ²⁵who exchanged the truth of God for the lie, and worshiped and served the creature rather than the Creator, who is blessed forever. Amen.

²⁶For this reason God gave them up to vile passions. For even their

1:16 ᵃNU-Text omits *of Christ.*   1:17 ᵃHabakkuk 2:4

Stress Busters

Don't Be Type A!

Two San Francisco cardiologists, Meyer Friedman and Ray Rosenman, coined the phrase "type A personality." They used this term to identify a person who is impatient, extremely competitive, always in a hurry, and chronically angry and hostile. Type A personalities typically try to do more than one task at a time. They are highly aggressive, ambitious, hard-working, and easily irritated by delays and interruptions. Type A's usually have problems relaxing without feeling guilty, tend to finish other people's statements, and are easily frustrated. In essence, they suffer from "hurry sickness."

A number of medical research studies in the decades since this phrase was coined have found that the type A personality is associated with a higher incidence of coronary artery disease. Research has also revealed that type B personalities can be pushed into type A behavior if they are given too many responsibilities or feel too great a job-related pressure. The demands of urban life, deadlines, financial pressures, traffic problems, and the general busyness of schedules tend to press individuals into type A behavior, even if they don't already have a predisposition to that behavior style.

What can you do to keep from becoming a type A personality? One of the keys is to build "margin" into your life—a space between having enough energy and being exhausted. *Margin* means "having breathing room or reserve energy." Following are some of the things you can do to add margin:

☐ Get to the airport a half hour early.
☐ Plan to arrive at the concert, church service, or meeting fifteen minutes ahead of schedule so you have time to relax before the event begins, and perhaps even socialize or read through a printed program.
☐ Make a list of things to do in a given day and then eliminate a fourth of them.
☐ Put a nap or fifteen minute "mental vacation" on your daily appointment schedule and then keep that appointment!

women exchanged the natural use for what is against nature. [27]Likewise also the men, leaving the natural use of the woman, burned in their lust for one another, men with men committing what is shameful, and receiving in themselves the penalty of their error which was due.

[28]And even as they did not like to retain God in *their* knowledge, God gave them over to a debased mind, to do those things which are not fitting; [29]being filled with all unrighteousness, sexual immorality,[a] wickedness, covetousness, maliciousness; full of envy, murder, strife, deceit, evil-mindedness; *they are* whisperers, [30]backbiters, haters of God, violent, proud, boasters, inventors of evil things, disobedient to parents, [31]undiscerning, untrustworthy, unloving, unforgiving,[a] unmerciful; [32]who, knowing the righteous judgment of God, that those who practice such things are deserving of death, not only do the same but also approve of those who practice them.

GOD'S RIGHTEOUS JUDGMENT

2 Therefore you are inexcusable, O man, whoever you are who judge, for in whatever you judge another you condemn yourself; for you who judge practice the same things. [2]But we know that the judgment of God is according to truth against those who practice such things. [3]And do you think this, O man, you who judge those practicing such things, and doing the same, that you will escape the judgment of God? [4]Or do you despise the riches of His goodness, forbearance, and longsuffering, not knowing that the goodness of God leads you to repentance? [5]But in accordance with your hardness and your impenitent heart you are treasuring up for yourself wrath in the day of wrath and revelation of the righteous judgment of God, [6]who "will render to each one according to his deeds":[a] [7]eternal life to those who by patient continuance in doing good seek for glory, honor, and immortality; [8]but to those who are self-seeking and do not obey the truth, but obey unrighteousness—indignation and wrath, [9]tribulation and anguish, on every soul of man who does evil, of the Jew first and also of the Greek; [10]but glory, honor, and peace to everyone who works what is good, to the Jew first and also to the Greek. [11]For there is no partiality with God.

[12]For as many as have sinned without law will also perish without law, and as many as have sinned in the law will be judged by the law [13](for not the hearers of the law *are* just in the sight of God, but the doers of the law will be justified; [14]for when Gentiles, who do not have the law, by nature do the things in the law, these, although not having the law, are a law to themselves, [15]who show the work of the law written in their hearts, their conscience also bearing witness, and between themselves *their* thoughts accusing or else excusing *them*) [16]in the day when God will judge the secrets of men by Jesus Christ, according to my gospel.

THE JEWS GUILTY AS THE GENTILES

[17]Indeed[a] you are called a Jew, and rest on the law, and make your boast in God, [18]and know *His* will, and approve the things that are excellent, being instructed out of the law, [19]and are confident that you yourself are a guide to the blind, a light to those who are in darkness, [20]an instructor of the foolish, a teacher of babes, having the form of

1:29 [a]NU-Text omits *sexual immorality*.   1:31 [a]NU-Text omits *unforgiving*.   2:6 [a]Psalm 62:12; Proverbs 24:12   2:17 [a]NU-Text reads *But if*.

WEIGHING LESS & ENJOYING LIFE MORE!

[No Fudging When Calculating!]

A healthy meal is one that has only a few hundred calories, usually between 200 and 300 calories. In order to limit a meal to that amount, you are probably going to have to count calories diligently as you begin a weight-loss plan.

Know the calorie counts of the foods you generally eat, and also know the calorie counts for various portion sizes.

Don't fudge when it comes to the following:

Size of portion. A pat of butter has a hundred calories. Most people consider a "slab" of butter necessary to add to their piece of bread, which may actually be a muffin that is four times the size of the muffins your mother used to bake. A typical portion of food should be roughly equal to the size of a clenched fist or the palm of your hand.

Calling meat "lean." Make sure *all* the fat is trimmed away and if you are eating chopped meat such as hamburger meat, make it the leanest meat you can purchase at the market.

Estimating an "ounce." Use a scale. Scoops come in various sizes. Recipes that call for ounces of meat refer to ounces by *weight*. Recipes that call for ounces in baking refer to ounces by *volume* (that is, measured in a measuring cup). Most chicken breasts on the market today are six to eight ounces, not the two to three ounces that are more appropriate at any given meal.

knowledge and truth in the law. [21]You, therefore, who teach another, do you not teach yourself? You who preach that a man should not steal, do you steal? [22]You who say, "Do not commit adultery," do you commit adultery? You who abhor idols, do you rob temples? [23]You who make your boast in the law, do you dishonor God through breaking the law? [24]For "the name of God is blasphemed among the Gentiles because of you,"[a] as it is written.

CIRCUMCISION OF NO AVAIL

[25]For circumcision is indeed profitable if you keep the law; but if you are a breaker of the law, your circumcision has become uncircumcision. [26]Therefore, if an uncircumcised man keeps the righteous requirements of the law, will not his uncircumcision be counted as circumcision? [27]And will not the physically uncircumcised, if he fulfills the law, judge you who, *even* with *your* written *code* and circumcision, *are* a transgressor of the law? [28]For he is not a Jew who *is one* outwardly, nor *is* circumcision that which *is* outward in the flesh; [29]but *he is* a Jew who *is one* inwardly; and circumcision *is that* of the heart, in the Spirit, not in the letter; whose praise *is* not from men but from God.

GOD'S JUDGMENT DEFENDED

3 What advantage then has the Jew, or what *is* the profit of circumcision? [2]Much in every way! Chiefly because to them were committed the oracles of God. [3]For what if some did not believe? Will their unbelief make the faithfulness of God without effect? [4]Certainly not! Indeed, let God be true but every man a liar. As it is written:

"That You may be justified in Your words,
And may overcome when You are judged."[a]

[5]But if our unrighteousness demonstrates the righteousness of God, what shall we say? *Is* God unjust who inflicts wrath? (I speak as a man.) [6]Certainly not! For then how will God judge the world? [7]For if the truth of God has increased through my lie to His glory, why am I also still judged as a sinner? [8]And *why* not *say*, "Let us do evil that good may come"?—as we are slanderously reported and as some affirm that we say. Their condemnation is just.

ALL HAVE SINNED

[9]What then? Are we better *than they?* Not at all. For we have previously charged both Jews and Greeks that they are all under sin. [10]As it is written:

"There is none righteous, no, not one;
[11] There is none who understands;
There is none who seeks after God.
[12] They have all turned aside;
They have together become unprofitable;
There is none who does good, no, not one."[a]
[13] "Their throat is an open tomb;
With their tongues they have practiced deceit";[a]
"The poison of asps is under their lips";[b]
[14] "Whose mouth is full of cursing and bitterness."[a]
[15] "Their feet are swift to shed blood;

2:24 [a]Isaiah 52:5; Ezekiel 36:22   3:4 [a]Psalm 51:4   3:12 [a]Psalms 14:1–3; 53:1–3; Ecclesiastes 7:20   3:13 [a]Psalm 5:9 [b]Psalm 140:3   3:14 [a]Psalm 10:7

PEOPLE CALLED "BEAUTIFUL" IN THE BIBLE

Absalom

The Best Looking in the Land

The Bible says about Absalom: "In all Israel there was no one who was praised as much as Absalom for his good looks. From the sole of his foot to the crown of his head there was no blemish in him. And when he cut the hair of his head—at the end of every year he cut it because it was heavy on him—when he cut it, he weighed the hair of his head at two hundred shekels according to the king's standard" (2 Samuel 14:25, 26). The weight of hair described here is between four and five pounds. That's a lot of hair!

Absalom was not only good-looking, he was also David's son, so he was a prince, well-connected socially and politically, with every opportunity ahead of him. He had three sons and a beautiful daughter. If ever there was a man with potential, Absalom was that man.

Absalom, however, suffered from highly negative emotions that arose from feeling rejected—unloved and unjustly treated—by his father, King David. After Absalom had killed Amnon—another of David's sons who had raped Absalom's sister—Absalom went two years without seeing David. He became angry at this rejection and burned the field of Joab, David's close advisor, in an effort to gain attention. It worked.

Joab arranged for David and Absalom to meet and the meeting appeared to go well—David kissed his son and Absalom bowed before his father. The relationship between David and Absalom, however, was not fully made right. Absalom continued to feel deep inner hurt and he eventually led a rebellion against his father and overthrew him. David literally had to run for his life from Jerusalem.

Just because a person may seem to have life "together" on the outside—in physical appearance, in status, in relationships, in career success—doesn't mean that a person is "together" on the inside. Absalom had all the potential a person could have, but no ability to turn that potential into real success. He allowed himself to be ruled by highly negative emotions associated with rejection and lack of expressed love. He became an angry, bitter, resentful man who displayed his anger and bitterness in ways that were ultimately hurtful to others.

Absalom's crowning glory, his thick hair, became his downfall. In battle, his hair became caught in the branches of a terebinth tree as he and his mule tried to escape those who were pursuing him. Absalom was pulled from his mule and left dangling helplessly in the tree's branches until he was killed there. His body was taken down and cast into a large pit in the woods with a heap of stones laid over him. We can learn two great lessons from Absalom's life:

1. Never trust in your appearance to win success for you.
2. Don't allow inner hurts to keep you from becoming all that God desires for you to be.

---

[16] Destruction and misery are in their ways;
[17] And the way of peace they have not known."[a]
[18] "There is no fear of God before their eyes."[a]

[19] Now we know that whatever the law says, it says to those who are under the law, that every mouth may be stopped, and all the world may become guilty before God. [20] Therefore by the deeds of the law no flesh will be justified in His sight, for by the law *is* the knowledge of sin.

GOD'S RIGHTEOUSNESS THROUGH FAITH

[21] But now the righteousness of God apart from the law is revealed, being witnessed by the Law and the Prophets, [22] even the righteousness of God, through faith in Jesus Christ, to all and on all[a] who believe. For there is no difference; [23] for all have sinned and fall short of the glory of God, [24] being justified freely by His grace through the redemption that is in Christ Jesus, [25] whom God set forth *as* a propitiation by His blood, through faith, to demonstrate His righteousness, because in His forbearance God had passed over the sins that were previously committed, [26] to demonstrate at the present time His righteousness, that He might be just and the justifier of the one who has faith in Jesus.

BOASTING EXCLUDED

[27] Where *is* boasting then? It is excluded. By what law? Of works? No, but by the law of faith. [28] Therefore we conclude that a man is justified by faith apart from the deeds of the law. [29] Or *is He* the God of the Jews only? *Is He* not also the God of the Gentiles? Yes, of the Gentiles also, [30] since *there is* one God who will justify the circumcised by faith and the uncircumcised through faith. [31] Do we then make void the law through faith? Certainly not! On the contrary, we establish the law.

3:17 [a]Isaiah 59:7, 8   3:18 [a]Psalm 36:1   3:22 [a]NU-Text omits *and on all.*

ABRAHAM JUSTIFIED BY FAITH

4 What then shall we say that Abraham our father has found according to the flesh?[a] 2For if Abraham was justified by works, he has *something* to boast about, but not before God. 3For what does the Scripture say? "Abraham believed God, and it was accounted to him for righteousness."[a] 4Now to him who works, the wages are not counted as grace but as debt.

DAVID CELEBRATES THE SAME TRUTH

5But to him who does not work but believes on Him who justifies the ungodly, his faith is accounted for righteousness, 6just as David also describes the blessedness of the man to whom God imputes righteousness apart from works:

7 "Blessed are those whose lawless deeds are forgiven,
And whose sins are covered;
8 Blessed is the man to whom the LORD shall not impute
sin."[a]

ABRAHAM JUSTIFIED BEFORE CIRCUMCISION

9*Does* this blessedness then *come* upon the circumcised *only*, or upon the uncircumcised also? For we say that faith was accounted to Abraham for righteousness. 10How then was it accounted? While he was circumcised, or uncircumcised? Not while circumcised, but while uncircumcised. 11And he received the sign of circumcision, a seal of the righteousness of the faith which *he had while still* uncircumcised, that he might be the father of all those who believe, though they are uncircumcised, that righteousness might be imputed to them also, 12and the father of circumcision to those who not only *are* of the circumcision, but who also walk in the steps of the faith which our father Abraham *had while still* uncircumcised.

THE PROMISE GRANTED THROUGH FAITH

13For the promise that he would be the heir of the world *was* not to Abraham or to his seed through the law, but through the righteousness of faith. 14For if those who are of the law *are* heirs, faith is made void and the promise made of no effect, 15because the law brings about wrath; for where there is no law *there is* no transgression.

16Therefore *it is* of faith that *it might be* according to grace, so that the promise might be sure to all the seed, not only to those who are of the law, but also to those who are of the faith of Abraham, who is the father of us all 17(as it is written, "I have made you a father of many nations"[a]) in the presence of Him whom he believed—God, who gives life to the dead and calls those things which do not exist as though they did; 18who, contrary to hope, in hope believed, so that he became the father of many nations, according to what was spoken, "So shall your descendants be."[a] 19And not being weak in faith, he did not consider his own body, already dead (since he was about a hundred years old), and the deadness of Sarah's womb. 20He did not waver at the promise of God through unbelief, but was strengthened in faith, giving glory to God, 21and being fully convinced that what He had promised He was also able to perform. 22And therefore "it was accounted to him for righteousness."[a]

23Now it was not written for his sake alone that it was imputed to him, 24but also for us. It shall be imputed to us who believe in Him who raised up Jesus our Lord from the dead, 25who was delivered up because of our offenses, and was raised because of our justification.

 Bible Beverages
Tea

A number of tea recipes date back to Bible times, many of them based on a combination of herbs intended for medicinal purposes more than as a mealtime beverage. Mint tea was certainly common in the first century, as it is today. It can be enjoyed hot or on ice. Fresh mint is usually one of the easiest herbs to grow in a family garden, flower bed, or garden container. A couple of sprigs can add good flavor to an entire pitcher of iced tea.

Herbal teas today include those made with a wide variety of herbs as well as fruits, especially raspberry and lemon. Herbal teas generally do not have caffeine. Some herbal teas are recommended as agents to stimulate sleep, especially tea made with chamomile.

Contrary to what many people seem to think, green tea is not necessarily herbal tea. It is simply tea made with leaves that have been steamed to preserve the natural color. Black tea leaves have been crushed, then fermented before being dried. Green tea can contain just as much stimulant as black tea.

Note: Orange pekoe tea is *not* herbal. *Pekoe* refers to a grade of leaf size—small. The original tea was flavored with orange blossoms, but today the flavor can vary widely.

4:1 [a]Or *Abraham our (fore)father according to the flesh has found?*   4:3 [a]Genesis 15:6   4:8 [a]Psalm 32:1, 2   4:17 [a]Genesis 17:5   4:18 [a]Genesis 15:5   4:22 [a]Genesis 15:6

WISE CHOICES

Choose range-fed meat and poultry products.
Range-fed meats are from animals grazed in open pastures that have not been treated with an overabundance of pesticides. The animals have not been treated with the antibiotics, steroids, or growth hormones common in animals that are not labeled *range-fed.*

FAITH TRIUMPHS IN TROUBLE

5 Therefore, having been justified by faith, we have[a] peace with God through our Lord Jesus Christ, [2]through whom also we have access by faith into this grace in which we stand, and rejoice in hope of the glory of God. [3]And not only *that,* but we also glory in tribulations, knowing that tribulation produces perseverance; [4]and perseverance, character; and character, hope. [5]Now hope does not disappoint, because the love of God has been poured out in our hearts by the Holy Spirit who was given to us.

CHRIST IN OUR PLACE

[6]For when we were still without strength, in due time Christ died for the ungodly. [7]For scarcely for a righteous man will one die; yet perhaps for a good man someone would even dare to die. [8]But God demonstrates His own love toward us, in that while we were still sinners, Christ died for us. [9]Much more then, having now been justified by His blood, we shall be saved from wrath through Him. [10]For if when we were enemies we were reconciled to God through the death of His Son, much more, having been reconciled, we shall be saved by His life. [11]And not only *that,* but we also rejoice in God through our Lord Jesus Christ, through whom we have now received the reconciliation.

DEATH IN ADAM, LIFE IN CHRIST

[12]Therefore, just as through one man sin entered the world, and death through sin, and thus death spread to all men, because all sinned— [13](For until the law sin was in the world, but sin is not imputed when there is no law. [14]Nevertheless death reigned from Adam to Moses, even over those who had not sinned according to the likeness of the transgression of Adam, who is a type of Him who was to come. [15]But the free gift *is* not like the offense. For if by the one man's offense many died, much more the grace of God and the gift by the grace of the one Man, Jesus Christ, abounded to many. [16]And the gift *is* not like *that which came* through the one who sinned. For the judgment *which came* from one *offense resulted* in condemnation, but the free gift *which came* from many offenses *resulted* in justification. [17]For if by the one man's offense death reigned through the one, much more those who receive abundance of grace and of the gift of righteousness will reign in life through the One, Jesus Christ.)

[18]Therefore, as through one man's offense *judgment came* to all men, resulting in condemnation, even so through one Man's righteous act *the free gift came* to all men, resulting in justification of life. [19]For as by one man's disobedience many were made sinners, so also by one Man's obedience many will be made righteous.

[20]Moreover the law entered that the offense might abound. But where sin abounded, grace abounded much more, [21]so that as sin reigned in death, even so grace might reign through righteousness to eternal life through Jesus Christ our Lord.

DEAD TO SIN, ALIVE TO GOD

6 What shall we say then? Shall we continue in sin that grace may abound? [2]Certainly not! How shall we who died to sin live any longer in it? [3]Or do you not know that as many of us as were baptized into Christ Jesus were baptized into His death? [4]Therefore we were buried with Him through baptism into death, that just as Christ was raised from the dead by the glory of the Father, even so we also should walk in newness of life.

[5]For if we have been united together in the likeness of His death, certainly we also shall be *in the likeness* of *His* resurrection, [6]knowing this, that our old man was crucified with *Him,* that the body of sin might be done away with, that we should no longer be slaves of sin. [7]For he who has died has been freed from sin. [8]Now if we died with Christ, we believe that we shall also live with Him, [9]knowing that Christ, having been raised from the dead, dies no more. Death no longer has dominion over Him. [10]For *the death* that He died, He died to sin once for all; but *the life* that He lives, He lives to God. [11]Likewise you also, reckon yourselves to be dead indeed to sin, but alive to God in Christ Jesus our Lord.

[12]Therefore do not let sin reign in your mortal body, that you should obey it in its lusts. [13]And do not present your members *as* instruments of unrighteousness to sin, but present yourselves to God as being alive from the dead, and your members *as* instruments of righteousness to God. [14]For sin shall not have dominion over you, for you are not under law but under grace.

FROM SLAVES OF SIN TO SLAVES OF GOD

[15]What then? Shall we sin because we are not under law but under grace? Certainly not! [16]Do you not know that to whom you present yourselves slaves to obey, you are that one's slaves whom you obey, whether of sin *leading* to death, or of obedience *leading* to righteousness? [17]But God be thanked that *though* you were slaves of sin, yet you obeyed from the heart that form of doctrine to which you were delivered. [18]And having been set free from sin, you became slaves of righteousness. [19]I speak in human *terms* because of the weakness of your flesh. For just as you presented your members *as* slaves of uncleanness, and of lawlessness *leading* to *more* lawlessness, so now present your members *as* slaves of righteousness for holiness.

[20]For when you were slaves of sin, you were free in regard to righteousness. [21]What fruit did you have then in the things of which you are now ashamed? For the end of those things *is* death. [22]But now hav-

---

5:1 [a]Another ancient reading is, *let us have peace.*

June

| 1 | 2 | 3 | 4 | 5 | 6 | 7 |

Now Is the Time To...

☐ Sign up for pool and tennis clubs. ☐ Explore farmers' markets and co-ops for the freshest summer produce. ☐ Leave room in your refrigerator for small bottles of water so that you'll always have a cool bottle to take as you run errands. ☐ Check the filters of your air-conditioning system.

Seasonal Tips

| 8 | 9 | 10 | 11 | 12 | 13 | 14 |

☐ Make sure that you store foods in the refrigerator immediately after a meal. Don't let any items made with mayonnaise, meat, fish, eggs, or dairy products sit out for more than an hour in a cool area, or more than ten minutes after a meal in a warm area—bacteria breeds and oils go rancid quickly. ☐ If you are going on a long walk in the woods, be sure to take insect repellant with you. Take along a whistle too—it is one of the best items to have should you get lost or injured. ☐ If you are going out on the water on a Jet Ski or water skis, or in a boat or other water craft, wear a life jacket!

| 15 | 16 | 17 | 18 | 19 | 20 | 21 |

In the Garden

☐ Plant tomatoes for summer-long ripening. The growing time for tomato plants varies from fifty to eighty days—know what you are planting and when you can expect tomatoes. Late-maturing varieties can provide not only late-season slicing tomatoes, but also an abundance of small green tomatoes for making relishes. ☐ Protect your emerging produce and flowers from deer, rabbits, raccoons, ducks, and other creatures that enjoy fresh veggies, fruits, and blossoms as much as you do!

| 22 | 23 | 24 | 25 | 26 | 27 | 28 |

Let's Celebrate

☐ **Midsummer Day** is June 24. Although this occurs near the summer solstice, the farmer traditionally considered this day to be the midpoint of the growing season, halfway between planting and harvest. It was the occasion of major festivals in England in centuries past. This also marks the day the liturgical church celebrates the life and ministry of John the Baptist.

| 29 | 30 |

Table Fresh

☐ Enjoy fresh corn on the cob—grilled! Remove the silks and husks from ears of corn. Wash the corn and let it soak in cool water for 15 minutes. Brush grill racks with olive oil and grill the corn over hot coals for about 15 minutes or until tender, turning frequently. ☐ Make your own trail mix by combining dried fruits and nuts. ☐ Keep ice cube trays filled with freshly squeezed fruit juices in the freezer.

Women's Issues
Menstruation

Although menstruation was considered a normal part of womanhood, and a divine blessing in that it made childbearing possible, women who were menstruating were considered "unclean" under the Law of Moses. A woman who was menstruating was to be "set apart seven days." Whoever touched her was considered unclean until evening. Everything that she might lie upon or sit upon was considered unclean. Everything she touched needed to be washed in water and a menstruating woman was not to have sexual relations with a man. (See Leviticus 15:19–24.) These same rules applied to a woman who might have an abnormal discharge from her body, such as bleeding as the result of endometriosis. As long as a woman was bleeding, she was considered unclean.

As the Israelites wandered in the wilderness, the women who were menstruating were usually sent out of the camp to a compound at the edge of the camp. There, they sat on the ground so that the discharge from their bodies could go directly into the earth, which was considered the only thing that did not become "unclean" or defiled when blood touched it. The women did no work, other than handwork and things they could do while seated.

For many of the women this was a time of "retreat." The women enjoyed being together with their friends for a week of talking and sharing news from the various tribes. Many Jewish traditions—especially CONT. NEXT PAGE>>>

ing been set free from sin, and having become slaves of God, you have your fruit to holiness, and the end, everlasting life. ²³For the wages of sin *is* death, but the gift of God *is* eternal life in Christ Jesus our Lord.

FREED FROM THE LAW

7 Or do you not know, brethren (for I speak to those who know the law), that the law has dominion over a man as long as he lives? ²For the woman who has a husband is bound by the law to *her* husband as long as he lives. But if the husband dies, she is released from the law of *her* husband. ³So then if, while *her* husband lives, she marries another man, she will be called an adulteress; but if her husband dies, she is free from that law, so that she is no adulteress, though she has married another man. ⁴Therefore, my brethren, you also have become dead to the law through the body of Christ, that you may be married to another—to Him who was raised from the dead, that we should bear fruit to God. ⁵For when we were in the flesh, the sinful passions which were aroused by the law were at work in our members to bear fruit to death. ⁶But now we have been delivered from the law, having died to what we were held by, so that we should serve in the newness of the Spirit and not *in* the oldness of the letter.

SIN'S ADVANTAGE IN THE LAW

⁷What shall we say then? *Is* the law sin? Certainly not! On the contrary, I would not have known sin except through the law. For I would not have known covetousness unless the law had said, "You shall not covet." ᵃ ⁸But sin, taking opportunity by the commandment, produced in me all *manner of* evil desire. For apart from the law sin *was* dead. ⁹I was alive once without the law, but when the commandment came, sin revived and I died. ¹⁰And the commandment, which *was* to *bring* life, I found to *bring* death. ¹¹For sin, taking occasion by the commandment, deceived me, and by it killed *me*. ¹²Therefore the law *is* holy, and the commandment holy and just and good.

LAW CANNOT SAVE FROM SIN

¹³Has then what is good become death to me? Certainly not! But sin, that it might appear sin, was producing death in me through what is good, so that sin through the commandment might become exceedingly sinful. ¹⁴For we know that the law is spiritual, but I am carnal, sold under sin. ¹⁵For what I am doing, I do not understand. For what I will to do, that I do not practice; but what I hate, that I do. ¹⁶If, then, I do what I will not to do, I agree with the law that *it is* good. ¹⁷But now, *it is* no longer I who do it, but sin that dwells in me. ¹⁸For I know that in me (that is, in my flesh) nothing good dwells; for to will is present with me, but *how* to perform what is good I do not find. ¹⁹For the good that I will *to do,* I do not do; but the evil I will not *to do,* that I practice. ²⁰Now if I do what I will not *to do,* it is no longer I who do it, but sin that dwells in me.

²¹I find then a law, that evil is present with me, the one who wills to do good. ²²For I delight in the law of God according to the inward man. ²³But I see another law in my members, warring against the law of my mind, and bringing me into captivity to the law of sin which is in my members. ²⁴O wretched man that I am! Who will deliver me from this body of death? ²⁵I thank God—through Jesus Christ our Lord!

So then, with the mind I myself serve the law of God, but with the flesh the law of sin.

7:7 ᵃExodus 20:17; Deuteronomy 5:21

those that were not written in the Mosaic Law and were handed down by word of mouth through the women—arose out of these "girl talks" outside the camp. Jewish women who were fertile tended to spend much of their childbearing years pregnant or nursing babies, so the times set apart during a menstrual period were somewhat rare and highly prized by the women. This was a time of rest and rejuvenation for them, a tremendous time for socializing and learning about how to become better wives and mothers.

For irregular periods, try the herb chasteberry (also called vitex). It comes as an extract or tea.

For cyclic breast tenderness, try GLA, which is found in evening primrose oil, borage oil, and black currant oil.

For excessive bleeding, first rule out the possibility of large uterine fibroids with a pelvic ultrasound. A woman may benefit from a progesterone cream. If excessive bleeding lasts a long time, a woman may need an iron supplement.

For cramps, consider taking the herb dong quai, which comes in capsules, tablets, tinctures, or teas.

FREE FROM INDWELLING SIN

8 *There* is therefore now no condemnation to those who are in Christ Jesus,ª who do not walk according to the flesh, but according to the Spirit. ²For the law of the Spirit of life in Christ Jesus has made me free from the law of sin and death. ³For what the law could not do in that it was weak through the flesh, God *did* by sending His own Son in the likeness of sinful flesh, on account of sin: He condemned sin in the flesh, ⁴that the righteous requirement of the law might be fulfilled in us who do not walk according to the flesh but according to the Spirit. ⁵For those who live according to the flesh set their minds on the things of the flesh, but those *who live* according to the Spirit, the things of the Spirit. ⁶For to be carnally minded *is* death, but to be spiritually minded *is* life and peace. ⁷Because the carnal mind *is* enmity against God; for it is not subject to the law of God, nor indeed can be. ⁸So then, those who are in the flesh cannot please God.

⁹But you are not in the flesh but in the Spirit, if indeed the Spirit of God dwells in you. Now if anyone does not have the Spirit of Christ, he is not His. ¹⁰And if Christ *is* in you, the body *is* dead because of sin, but the Spirit *is* life because of righteousness. ¹¹But if the Spirit of Him who raised Jesus from the dead dwells in you, He who raised Christ from the dead will also give life to your mortal bodies through His Spirit who dwells in you.

SONSHIP THROUGH THE SPIRIT

¹²Therefore, brethren, we are debtors—not to the flesh, to live according to the flesh. ¹³For if you live according to the flesh you will die; but if by the Spirit you put to death the deeds of the body, you will live. ¹⁴For as many as are led by the Spirit of God, these are sons of God. ¹⁵For you did not receive the spirit of bondage again to fear, but you received the Spirit of adoption by whom we cry out, "Abba, Father." ¹⁶The Spirit Himself bears witness with our spirit that we are children of God, ¹⁷and if children, then heirs—heirs of God and joint heirs with Christ, if indeed we suffer with *Him*, that we may also be glorified together.

FROM SUFFERING TO GLORY

¹⁸For I consider that the sufferings of this present time are not worthy *to be compared* with the glory which shall be revealed in us. ¹⁹For the earnest expectation of the creation eagerly waits for the revealing of the sons of God. ²⁰For the creation was subjected to futility, not willingly, but because of Him who subjected *it* in hope; ²¹because the creation itself also will be delivered from the bondage of corruption into the glorious liberty of the children of God. ²²For we know that the whole creation groans and labors with birth pangs together until now. ²³Not only *that*, but we also who have the firstfruits of the Spirit, even we ourselves groan within ourselves, eagerly waiting for the adoption, the redemption of our body. ²⁴For we were saved in this hope, but hope that is *seen* is not hope; for why does one still hope for what he sees? ²⁵But if we hope for what we do not see, we eagerly wait for *it* with perseverance.

²⁶Likewise the Spirit also helps in our weaknesses. For we do not know what we should pray for as we ought, but the Spirit Himself makes intercession for usª with groanings which cannot be uttered. ²⁷Now He who searches the hearts knows what the mind of the Spirit *is*, because He makes intercession for the saints according to *the will of* God.

²⁸And we know that all things work together for good to those who love God, to those who are the called according to *His* purpose. ²⁹For whom He foreknew, He also predestined *to be* conformed to the image of His Son, that He might be the firstborn among many brethren. ³⁰Moreover whom He predestined, these He also called; whom He called, these He also justified; and whom He justified, these He also glorified.

GOD'S EVERLASTING LOVE

³¹What then shall we say to these things? If God *is* for us, who *can be* against us? ³²He who did not spare His own Son, but delivered Him up for us all, how shall He not with Him also freely give us all things? ³³Who shall bring a charge against God's elect? *It is* God who justifies. ³⁴Who *is* he who condemns? *It is* Christ who died, and furthermore is

FACT MORSELS

[SPIRULINA]

Spirulina helps suppress the appetite in a natural way, while adding good nutrients to the body.

OVERCOMING OBSTINATE OBSTACLES • OVERCOMING OBSTINATE OBSTACLES • OVERCOMING OBSTINATE OBSTACLES • OVERCOMING OBSTINATE OBSTACLES •

Throughout the Bible we find these two words often repeated: *Fear not!* God knew as He sent His angels and His Son into various situations that people would likely respond with fear of the supernatural. Fear is one of the most potent emotions built in to human beings.

Fear of the unknown is just as forceful as fear of the well known. And all types of fear can be deadly. Fear has been associated with a wide variety of diseases, including cardiovascular diseases and hypertension; digestive-tract diseases such as colitis, Crohn's disease, irritable bowel syndrome, and ulcers; headaches; and skin disorders such as psoriasis, eczema, and stress acne. Fear can cause a decreased immune response, which may lead to frequent infections or the development of deadly disease. It is a powerful emotion that produces a very potent psychological response, which in turn, creates a powerful physical consequence!

Get to the root cause of your fears so you can address them and begin to work through them. The root cause of fear often lies in the answer to one of these three questions:

1. Are you "overcaring"—caring beyond a normal point where you can "let go and let God," or caring to the point of stressing yourself or the person you care about? Overcaring leads to abiding fears of abandonment, rejection, and loss.
2. Are you hanging on to or pursuing things that aren't necessary or aren't part of God's plan for your life—fearful that if you don't reach certain goals or maintain a level of accomplishment that you will be a failure? A fear of failure leads to a fear that you won't be worth as much to God or to others.
3. Do you truly trust God to provide for you *all* that you need, in His timing and according to His methods?

The ultimate cure for fear is *faith*. Always remember: God wants you to care, but He also wants you to cast *all* your cares upon Him (1 Peter 5:7). He alone can fully care for the person you love. God's love for you, in turn, is never dependent upon what you earn, win, or accomplish. He loves you because He created you and desires a relationship with you. God desires to provide for you everything that is for your eternal benefit. Trust Him to have your best interests always at the forefront of His plan, and to work things out for you in just the right timing. Romans 8:28 tells us, "All things work together for good to those who love God, to those who are the called according to His purpose."

---

also risen, who is even at the right hand of God, who also makes intercession for us. ³⁵Who shall separate us from the love of Christ? *Shall* tribulation, or distress, or persecution, or famine, or nakedness, or peril, or sword? ³⁶As it is written:

"For Your sake we are killed all day long;
We are accounted as sheep for the slaughter."ᵃ

³⁷Yet in all these things we are more than conquerors through Him who loved us. ³⁸For I am persuaded that neither death nor life, nor angels nor principalities nor powers, nor things present nor things to come, ³⁹nor height nor depth, nor any other created thing, shall be able to separate us from the love of God which is in Christ Jesus our Lord.

ISRAEL'S REJECTION OF CHRIST

9 I tell the truth in Christ, I am not lying, my conscience also bearing me witness in the Holy Spirit, ²that I have great sorrow and continual grief in my heart. ³For I could wish that I myself were accursed from Christ for my brethren, my countrymenᵃ according to the flesh, ⁴who are Israelites, to whom *pertain* the adoption, the glory, the covenants, the giving of the law, the service *of God,* and the promises; ⁵of whom *are* the fathers and from whom, according to the flesh, Christ *came,* who is over all, *the* eternally blessed God. Amen.

ISRAEL'S REJECTION AND GOD'S PURPOSE

⁶But it is not that the word of God has taken no effect. For they *are* not all Israel who *are* of Israel, ⁷nor *are they* all children because they are the seed of Abraham; but, "In Isaac your seed shall be called."ᵃ ⁸That is, those who *are* the children of the flesh, these *are* not the children of God; but the children of the promise are counted as the seed. ⁹For this *is* the word of promise: "At this time I will come and Sarah shall have a son."ᵃ

¹⁰And not only *this,* but when Rebecca also had conceived by one man, *even* by our father Isaac ¹¹(for *the children* not yet being born, nor having done any good or evil, that the purpose of God according to

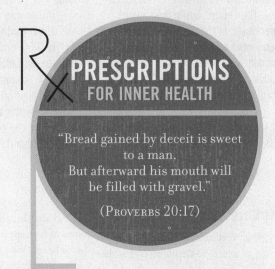

You're an Omnivore!

Bible Health + Food Facts

From the time of Creation, human beings have been omnivores, which means we are capable of living on both plant and animal foods. Initially, mankind ate only plant foods. After the Flood, God also authorized man to eat animal foods. Our physical anatomy has been engineered, however, so that we are better suited for consuming *more* plant products than animal products.

election might stand, not of works but of Him who calls), [12]it was said to her, "The older shall serve the younger."[a] [13]As it is written, "Jacob I have loved, but Esau I have hated."[a]

ISRAEL'S REJECTION AND GOD'S JUSTICE

[14]What shall we say then? *Is there* unrighteousness with God? Certainly not! [15]For He says to Moses, "I will have mercy on whomever I will have mercy, and I will have compassion on whomever I will have compassion."[a] [16]So then *it is* not of him who wills, nor of him who runs, but of God who shows mercy. [17]For the Scripture says to the Pharaoh, "For this very purpose I have raised you up, that I may show My power in you, and that My name may be declared in all the earth."[a] [18]Therefore He has mercy on whom He wills, and whom He wills He hardens.

[19]You will say to me then, "Why does He still find fault? For who has resisted His will?" [20]But indeed, O man, who are you to reply against God? Will the thing formed say to him who formed *it*, "Why have you made me like this?" [21]Does not the potter have power over the clay, from the same lump to make one vessel for honor and another for dishonor?

[22]*What* if God, wanting to show *His* wrath and to make His power known, endured with much longsuffering the vessels of wrath prepared for destruction, [23]and that He might make known the riches of His glory on the vessels of mercy, which He had prepared beforehand for glory, [24]even us whom He called, not of the Jews only, but also of the Gentiles?

[25]As He says also in Hosea:

"I will call them My people, who were not My people,
  And her beloved, who was not beloved."[a]
[26] "And it shall come to pass in the place where it was said to them,
  'You are not My people,'
  There they shall be called sons of the living God."[a]

[27]Isaiah also cries out concerning Israel:[a]

"Though the number of the children of Israel be as the sand of the
  sea,
  The remnant will be saved.
[28] For He will finish the work and cut it short in righteousness,
  Because the LORD will make a short work upon the earth."[a]

[29]And as Isaiah said before:

"Unless the LORD of Sabaoth[a] had left us a seed,
  We would have become like Sodom,
  And we would have been made like Gomorrah."[b]

PRESENT CONDITION OF ISRAEL

[30]What shall we say then? That Gentiles, who did not pursue righteousness, have attained to righteousness, even the righteousness of faith; [31]but Israel, pursuing the law of righteousness, has not attained to the law of righteousness.[a] [32]Why? Because *they did* not *seek it* by faith, but as it were, by the works of the law.[a] For they stumbled at that stumbling stone. [33]As it is written:

"Behold, I lay in Zion a stumbling stone and rock of offense,
  And whoever believes on Him will not be put to shame."[a]

PRESCRIPTIONS FOR INNER HEALTH

"Bread gained by deceit is sweet to a man,
But afterward his mouth will be filled with gravel."

(PROVERBS 20:17)

People often feel very smug and self-satisfied if they think they have pulled a "fast one" or have "pulled the wool" over another person's eyes in order to get something they desire. However, anything tainted by cheating, dishonesty, or less than pure motives will eventually become disgusting or dissatisfying.

9:12 [a]Genesis 25:23   9:13 [a]Malachi 1:2, 3   9:15 [a]Exodus 33:19   9:17 [a]Exodus 9:16   9:25 [a]Hosea 2:23   9:26 [a]Hosea 1:10   9:27 [a]Isaiah 10:22, 23   9:28 [a]NU-Text reads *For the LORD will finish the work and cut it short upon the earth.*   9:29 [a]Literally, in Hebrew, *Hosts* [b]Isaiah 1:9   9:31 [a]NU-Text omits *of righteousness.*   9:32 [a]NU-Text reads *by works.*   9:33 [a]Isaiah 8:14; 28:16

WWJE?

[WHAT WOULD JESUS EAT]

[BUTTER AND CHEESE]

Herb Yogurt-Cheese

Bible Health + Food Facts

To a half pound of farmer's cheese, cream cheese, or yogurt cheese, add: four cloves of garlic, two tablespoons of olive oil, and a tablespoon each of fresh dill, fresh thyme, and fresh parsley. (If you don't have fresh herbs, use only one teaspoon each of these three herbs dried.) Add a little Celtic salt to taste. This mixture is excellent on whole-grain "nutty" breads.

Whole milk could not be stored in biblical times, so milk products were "fermented" to keep them from spoiling. The cheese, butter, and yogurt mentioned in the Bible were made from fermented milk from cows, goats, camels, and sheep. One or more of the following were often added to cheese: garlic, parsley, thyme, dill, and olive oil.

A cup of milk has 250 mg calcium, 8.4 g protein, 406 mg potassium, and 126 mg sodium. Milk, butter, and cheese, however, are high in saturated fats, which raises LDL (bad) cholesterol.

Butter was a rare commodity in Jesus' time. For the most part, the "butter" in Bible times was olive oil, not our milk-based butter. If you choose to eat butter, I recommend that you mix equal parts of olive oil with butter. To do this, melt the butter and then add the olive oil. Return the mixture to the refrigerator to harden it. Use it sparingly.

ISRAEL NEEDS THE GOSPEL

10 Brethren, my heart's desire and prayer to God for Israel[a] is that they may be saved. [2]For I bear them witness that they have a zeal for God, but not according to knowledge. [3]For they being ignorant of God's righteousness, and seeking to establish their own righteousness, have not submitted to the righteousness of God. [4]For Christ is the end of the law for righteousness to everyone who believes.

[5]For Moses writes about the righteousness which is of the law, "The man who does those things shall live by them."[a] [6]But the righteousness of faith speaks in this way, "Do not say in your heart, 'Who will ascend into heaven?' "[a] (that is, to bring Christ down from above) [7]or, " 'Who will descend into the abyss?' "[a] (that is, to bring Christ up from the dead). [8]But what does it say? "The word is near you, in your mouth and in your heart"[a] (that is, the word of faith which we preach): [9]that if you confess with your mouth the Lord Jesus and believe in your heart that God has raised Him from the dead, you will be saved. [10]For with the heart one believes unto righteousness, and with the mouth confession is made unto sal-

vation. [11]For the Scripture says, "Whoever believes on Him will not be put to shame."[a] [12]For there is no distinction between Jew and Greek, for the same Lord over all is rich to all who call upon Him. [13]For "whoever calls on the name of the LORD shall be saved."[a]

ISRAEL REJECTS THE GOSPEL

[14]How then shall they call on Him in whom they have not believed? And how shall they believe in Him of whom they have not heard? And how shall they hear without a preacher? [15]And how shall they preach unless they are sent? As it is written:

"How beautiful are the feet of those who
preach the gospel of peace,[a]
Who bring glad tidings of good things!"[b]

[16]But they have not all obeyed the gospel. For Isaiah says, "LORD, who has believed our report?"[a] [17]So then faith comes by hearing, and hearing by the word of God.

[18]But I say, have they not heard? Yes indeed:

"Their sound has gone out to all the earth,
And their words to the ends of the
world."[a]

[19]But I say, did Israel not know? First Moses says:

"I will provoke you to jealousy by those
who are not a nation,

10:1 [a]NU-Text reads them.   10:5 [a]Leviticus 18:5   10:6 [a]Deuteronomy 30:12   10:7 [a]Deuteronomy 30:13   10:8 [a]Deuteronomy 30:14   10:11 [a]Isaiah 28:16   10:13 [a]Joel 2:32   10:15 [a]NU-Text omits preach the gospel of peace, Who. [b]Isaiah 52:7; Nahum 1:15   10:16 [a]Isaiah 53:1   10:18 [a]Psalm 19:4

QUIZ 3

ARE YOU GROWING?

None of us will ever arrive at perfect health—we are finite creatures living in a fallen world! We can, however, seek to grow continually to the fullness of our potential. We can seek to become more whole day by day, month by month, and year by year. The questions below are designed to help you evaluate your own growth toward wholeness.

	Are things BETTER than they were a year ago?	Are things WORSE than they were a year ago?
1. Overall physical health		
2. Amount of debt owed		
3. Relationship with spouse		
4. Relationship with child or children		
5. Satisfaction with work or career		
6. Optimal weight and body mass index		
7. Management of time		
8. Sense of purpose and fulfillment		
9. Hope about the future		
10. Feelings of accomplishment or progress		
11. Level of stress		
12. Healthy friendships		
13. Level of frustration or anxiety		
14. Management of material goods and resources (house, car, and so forth)		
15. Level of outreach to other people		
16. Personal spiritual disciplines (such as prayer, reading the Bible, attending church)		
17. Balance of work and play		
18. Learning new information or acquiring new skills		
19. Character traits of love, peace, joy, patience, kindness, mercy, self-control, and faithfulness		
20. Insight into who God created you to be and why you are on the earth		

Go back and circle those areas in which you believe you need to concentrate your efforts and your prayers! Ask God to show you what you must do to grow more into the likeness of Jesus Christ. Especially look for ways in which items you have marked as "worse" might be related—such as an increasing level of stress with more financial indebtedness, or negative relationships associated with an imbalance in work and play.

The Dangers of Too Much Wine

Some people argue in favor of the consumption of "a little wine." (See 1 Timothy 5:23.) Others argue strongly against the drinking of any alcoholic beverages. (See Proverbs 20:1.) The Bible presents a very balanced picture when all verses related to alcohol are considered. Wine was readily consumed in Bible times. The health benefits of the antioxidants in red wine are well documented by science. But, both the Bible and science agree on this point: too much wine is *not* good.

For some people, one alcoholic drink is too much. There are certain people who should *never* drink. The Bible also commands that priests on duty should not drink "wine or intoxicating drink" (Leviticus 10:9). The Bible advises kings not to drink wine or intoxicating beverages so they might retain clarity of mind, memory, and judgment (Proverbs 31:4, 5).

Several people in the Bible, including Noah and Lot, had very negative experiences directly related to excessive alcohol consumption. Not only were their personal lives impacted, but also the lives of their descendants. (See Genesis 9:20–27 and Genesis 19:30–38.)

The Bible gives a simple protocol for determining if you have a problem with alcohol. It is found in Proverbs 23:29–35:

Who has woe?
Who has sorrow?
Who has contentions?
Who has complaints?
Who has wounds without cause?
Who has redness of eyes?
Those who linger long at the wine,
Those who go in search of mixed wine.
Do not look on the wine when it is red,
When it sparkles in the cup,
When it swirls around smoothly;
At the last it bites like a serpent,
And stings like a viper.
Your eyes will see strange things,
And your heart will utter perverse things.
Yes, you will be like one who lies down in the midst of the sea,
Or like one who lies at the top of the mast, saying:
They have struck me, but I was not hurt;
They have beaten me, but I did not feel it.
When shall I awake, that I may seek another drink?

This brief passage gives seven benchmarks for determining if alcohol is a problem in your life or the life of someone you love.

1. Do you love to linger over drinks—having drink after drink, each drink enticing you to have "just one more"?
2. Do you seek out places that serve alcoholic beverages?
3. Do you awaken in the morning thinking about when you can have a drink?
4. Has anybody ever told you that your personality has changed since you started drinking more?
5. Have you found yourself regretting things you said or did after consuming alcohol?
6. Do you crave the feelings you have after several drinks—feeling more confident, or feeling impervious to the insults or rejection from other people?
7. Have you experienced any loss that has been attributed to your drinking—such as the loss of a relationship, the loss of a job, or the loss of a major client's account?

If the answer is yes to any one of these questions, you are drinking too much! Address your alcohol problem. If you feel incapable of cutting back or stopping your consumption of alcohol, get professional help.

I will move you to anger by a foolish nation."[a]

[20]But Isaiah is very bold and says:

"I was found by those who did not seek Me;

I was made manifest to those who did not ask for Me."[a]

[21]But to Israel he says:

"All day long I have stretched out My hands
To a disobedient and contrary people."[a]

ISRAEL'S REJECTION NOT TOTAL

11 I say then, has God cast away His people? Certainly not! For I also am an Israelite, of the seed of Abraham, of the tribe of Benjamin. [2]God has not cast away His people whom He

10:19 [a]Deuteronomy 32:21   10:20 [a]Isaiah 65:1   10:21 [a]Isaiah 65:2

foreknew. Or do you not know what the Scripture says of Elijah, how he pleads with God against Israel, saying, [3]"LORD, they have killed Your prophets and torn down Your altars, and I alone am left, and they seek my life"?[a] [4]But what does the divine response say to him? "I have reserved for Myself seven thousand men who have not bowed the knee to Baal."[a] [5]Even so then, at this present time there is a remnant according to the election of grace. [6]And if by grace, then it is no longer of works; otherwise grace is no longer grace.[a] But if it is of works, it is no longer grace; otherwise work is no longer work.

[7]What then? Israel has not obtained what it seeks; but the elect have obtained it, and the rest were blinded. [8]Just as it is written:

> "God has given them a spirit of stupor,
>   Eyes that they should not see
>   And ears that they should not hear,
>   To this very day."[a]

[9]And David says:

> "Let their table become a snare and a trap,
>   A stumbling block and a recompense to them.
> [10] Let their eyes be darkened, so that they do not see,
>   And bow down their back always."[a]

ISRAEL'S REJECTION NOT FINAL

[11]I say then, have they stumbled that they should fall? Certainly not! But through their fall, to provoke them to jealousy, salvation has come to the Gentiles. [12]Now if their fall is riches for the world, and their failure riches for the Gentiles, how much more their fullness!

[13]For I speak to you Gentiles; inasmuch as I am an apostle to the Gentiles, I magnify my ministry, [14]if by any means I may provoke to jealousy those who are my flesh and save some of them. [15]For if their being cast away is the reconciling of the world, what will their acceptance be but life from the dead?

[16]For if the firstfruit is holy, the lump is also holy; and if the root is holy, so are the branches. [17]And if some of the branches were broken off, and you, being a wild olive tree, were grafted in among them, and with them became a partaker of the root and fatness of the olive tree, [18]do not boast against the branches. But if you do boast, remember that you do not support the root, but the root supports you.

[19]You will say then, "Branches were broken off that I might be grafted in." [20]Well said. Because of unbelief they were broken off, and you stand by faith. Do not be haughty, but fear. [21]For if God did not spare the natural branches, He may not spare you either. [22]Therefore consider the goodness and severity of God: on those who fell, severity; but toward you, goodness,[a] if you continue in His goodness. Otherwise you also will be cut off. [23]And they also, if they do not continue in unbelief, will be grafted in, for God is able to graft them in again. [24]For if you were cut out of the olive tree which is wild by nature, and were grafted contrary to nature into a cultivated olive tree, how much more will these, who are natural branches, be grafted into their own olive tree?

[25]For I do not desire, brethren, that you should be ignorant of this mystery, lest you should be wise in your own opinion, that blindness in part has happened to Israel until the fullness of the Gentiles has come in. [26]And so all Israel will be saved,[a] as it is written:

> "The Deliverer will come out of Zion,
>   And He will turn away ungodliness from Jacob;
> [27] For this is My covenant with them,
>   When I take away their sins."[a]

[28]Concerning the gospel they are enemies for your sake, but concerning the election they are beloved for the sake of the fathers. [29]For the gifts and the calling of God are irrevocable. [30]For as you were once disobedient to God, yet have now obtained mercy through their disobedience, [31]even so these also have now been disobedient, that through the mercy shown you they also may obtain mercy. [32]For God has committed them all to disobedience, that He might have mercy on all.

[33]Oh, the depth of the riches both of the wisdom and knowledge of God! How unsearchable are His judgments and His ways past finding out!

> [34] "For who has known the mind of the LORD?
>   Or who has become
>   His counselor?"[a]
> [35] "Or who has first given
>   to Him
>   And it shall be repaid
>   to him?"[a]

[36]For of Him and through Him and to Him are all things, to whom be glory forever. Amen.

LIVING SACRIFICES TO GOD

12 I beseech you therefore, brethren, by the mercies of God, that you present your bodies a living sacrifice, holy, acceptable to God, which is your reasonable service. [2]And do not be conformed to this world, but be transformed by the renewing of your mind, that you may prove what is that good and acceptable and perfect will of God.

SERVE GOD WITH SPIRITUAL GIFTS

[3]For I say, through the grace given to me, to everyone who is among you, not to think of himself more highly than he ought to

WISE CHOICES

Choose cooked fish over raw fish.

Avoid eating raw fish. It is important to cook fish adequately to destroy any parasites that may be in the flesh of the fish.

11:3 [a]1 Kings 19:10, 14   11:4 [a]1 Kings 19:18   11:6 [a]NU-Text omits the rest of this verse.   11:8 [a]Deuteronomy 29:4; Isaiah 29:10   11:10 [a]Psalm 69:22, 23   11:22 [a]NU-Text adds of God.   11:26 [a]Or delivered   11:27 [a]Isaiah 59:20, 21   11:34 [a]Isaiah 40:13; Jeremiah 23:18   11:35 [a]Job 41:11

think, but to think soberly, as God has dealt to each one a measure of faith. [4]For as we have many members in one body, but all the members do not have the same function, [5]so we, *being* many, are one body in Christ, and individually members of one another. [6]Having then gifts differing according to the grace that is given to us, *let us use them:* if prophecy, *let us prophesy* in proportion to our faith; [7]or ministry, *let us use it* in *our* ministering; he who teaches, in teaching; [8]he who exhorts, in exhortation; he who gives, with liberality; he who leads, with diligence; he who shows mercy, with cheerfulness.

BEHAVE LIKE A CHRISTIAN

[9]*Let* love *be* without hypocrisy. Abhor what is evil. Cling to what is good. [10]*Be* kindly affectionate to one another with brotherly love, in honor giving preference to one another; [11]not lagging in diligence, fervent in spirit, serving the Lord; [12]rejoicing in hope, patient in tribulation, continuing steadfastly in prayer; [13]distributing to the needs of the saints, given to hospitality.

[14]Bless those who persecute you; bless and do not curse. [15]Rejoice with those who rejoice, and weep with those who weep. [16]Be of the same mind toward one another. Do not set your mind on high things, but associate with the humble. Do not be wise in your own opinion.

[17]Repay no one evil for evil. Have regard for good things in the sight of all men. [18]If it is possible, as much as depends on you, live peaceably with all men. [19]Beloved, do not avenge yourselves, but *rather* give place to wrath; for it is written, "Vengeance is Mine, I will repay,"[a] says the Lord. [20]Therefore

> "If your enemy is hungry, feed him;
> If he is thirsty, give him a drink;
> For in so doing you will heap coals of fire on his
>   head."[a]

[21]Do not be overcome by evil, but overcome evil with good.

SUBMIT TO GOVERNMENT

13 Let every soul be subject to the governing authorities. For there is no authority except from God, and the authorities that exist are appointed by God. [2]Therefore whoever resists the authority resists the ordinance of God, and those who resist will bring judgment on themselves. [3]For rulers are not a terror to good works, but to evil. Do you want to be unafraid of the authority? Do what is good, and you will have praise from the same. [4]For he is God's minister to you for good. But if you do evil, be afraid; for he does not bear the sword in vain; for he is God's minister, an avenger to *execute* wrath on him who practices evil. [5]Therefore *you* must be subject, not only because of wrath but also for conscience' sake. [6]For because of this you also pay taxes, for they are God's ministers attending continually to this very thing. [7]Render therefore to all their due: taxes to whom taxes *are due*, customs to whom customs, fear to whom fear, honor to whom honor.

LOVE YOUR NEIGHBOR

[8]Owe no one anything except to love one another, for he who loves another has fulfilled the law. [9]For the commandments, "You shall not commit adultery," "You shall not murder," "You shall not steal," "You shall not bear false witness,"[a] "You shall not covet,"[b] and if *there is* any other commandment, are *all* summed up in this saying, namely, "You shall love your neighbor as yourself."[c] [10]Love does no harm to a neighbor; therefore love *is* the fulfillment of the law.

PUT ON CHRIST

[11]And *do* this, knowing the time, that now *it is* high time to awake out of sleep; for now our salvation *is* nearer than when we *first* believed. [12]The night is far spent, the day is at hand. Therefore let us cast off the works of darkness, and let us put on the armor of light. [13]Let us walk properly, as in the day, not in revelry and drunkenness, not in lewdness and lust, not in strife and envy. [14]But put on the Lord Jesus Christ, and make no provision for the flesh, to *fulfill its* lusts.

INSIGHTS INTO THE WORD

> (Romans 12:20, 21)

Nourish Your Enemy. Our first impulse when someone hurts us is to retaliate or seek revenge. God's Word calls us to show kindness—if an enemy is hungry, to give him bread to eat; if he is thirsty, to give him water to drink (Proverbs 25:21). The act of kindness may very well defuse the person from doing you further harm. It certainly will turn your own attitude toward *good* instead of *evil*—and thus, your actions bring God's reward on your life.

"Coals of fire" may refer to feelings of guilt and shame, which may cause your "enemy" to change his or her ways—better a little guilt than negative consequences for either the person inflicting harm or the person receiving it. "Coals of fire," however, may also refer to a time in the Old Testament when the people sinned and a plague erupted in the camp of the Israelites. Aaron ran into the midst of the congregation with a censer filled with coals from the altar of the tabernacle, and the plague stopped. (See Numbers 16:44–48.) Acts of kindness can put a definitive stop to an endless cycle of revenge and retaliation that may have become a "plague" in a family, community, church, or between ethnic groups.

12:19 [a]Deuteronomy 32:35   12:20 [a]Proverbs 25:21, 22   13:9 [a]NU-Text omits *"You shall not bear false witness."* [b]Exodus 20:13–15, 17; Deuteronomy 5:17–19, 21 [c]Leviticus 19:18

204   DIVINE HEALTH

THE LAW OF LIBERTY

14 Receive one who is weak in the faith, *but* not to disputes over doubtful things. ²For one believes he may eat all things, but he who is weak eats *only* vegetables. ³Let not him who eats despise him who does not eat, and let not him who does not eat judge him who eats; for God has received him. ⁴Who are you to judge another's servant? To his own master he stands or falls. Indeed, he will be made to stand, for God is able to make him stand.

⁵One person esteems *one* day above another; another esteems every day *alike.* Let each be fully convinced in his own mind. ⁶He who observes the day, observes *it* to the Lord;ᵃ and he who does not observe the day, to the Lord he does not observe *it.* He who eats, eats to the Lord, for he gives God thanks; and he who does not eat, to the Lord he does not eat, and gives God thanks. ⁷For none of us lives to himself, and no one dies to himself. ⁸For if we live, we live to the Lord; and if we die, we die to the Lord. Therefore, whether we live or die, we are the Lord's. ⁹For to this end Christ died and roseᵃ and lived again, that He might be Lord of both the dead and the living. ¹⁰But why do you judge your brother? Or why do you show contempt for your brother? For we shall all stand before the judgment seat of Christ.ᵃ ¹¹For it is written:

"As I live, says the LORD,
 Every knee shall bow to Me,
 And every tongue shall confess to
  God."ᵃ

¹²So then each of us shall give account of himself to God. ¹³Therefore let us not judge one another anymore, but rather resolve this, not to put a stumbling block or a cause to fall in *our* brother's way.

THE LAW OF LOVE

¹⁴I know and am convinced by the Lord Jesus that *there is* nothing unclean of itself; but to him who considers anything to be unclean, to him *it is* unclean. ¹⁵Yet if your brother is grieved because of *your* food, you are no longer walking in love. Do not destroy with your food the one for whom Christ died. ¹⁶Therefore do not let your good be spoken of as evil; ¹⁷for the kingdom of God is not eating and drinking, but righteousness and peace and joy in the Holy Spirit. ¹⁸For he who serves Christ in these thingsᵃ *is* acceptable to God and approved by men.

¹⁹Therefore let us pursue the things *which make* for peace and the things by which one may edify another. ²⁰Do not destroy the work of God for the sake of food. All things indeed *are* pure, but *it is* evil for the man who eats with offense. ²¹*It is* good neither to eat meat nor drink wine nor *do anything* by which your brother stumbles or is offended or is made weak.ᵃ ²²Do you have faith?ᵃ Have *it* to yourself before God. Happy *is* he who does not condemn himself in what he approves. ²³But he who doubts is condemned if he eats, because *he does* not *eat* from faith; for whatever *is* not from faith is sin.ᵃ

BEARING OTHERS' BURDENS

15 We then who are strong ought to bear with the scruples of the weak, and not to please ourselves. ²Let each of us please *his* neighbor for *his* good, leading to edification. ³For even Christ did not please Himself; but as it is written, "The reproaches of those who reproached You fell on Me."ᵃ ⁴For whatever things were written before were written for our learning, that we through the patience and comfort of the Scriptures might have hope. ⁵Now may the God of patience and comfort grant you to be like-minded toward one another, according to Christ Jesus, ⁶that you may with one mind *and* one mouth glorify the God and Father of our Lord Jesus Christ.

GLORIFY GOD TOGETHER

⁷Therefore receive one another, just as Christ also received us,ᵃ to the glory of God.

GODLY & GOODLOOKIN'

Get Your Beauty Rest

Most Americans don't get enough rest. Insufficient amounts can result in stress, sickness, and over time, can shave years off your life.

To look fresh, alive, and beautiful, follow these steps to ensure you are getting the proper amount of rest:

☐ *Go to bed early.* Many of us either don't hear the alarm, or we are hitting the snooze (again and again). Try going to bed earlier so you are waking up on your own without the assistance of an alarm.

☐ *Nap.* If you get sleepy during the day, take a fifteen-minute cat-nap to revitalize you.

☐ *Watch the caffeine.* A good cut-off time for drinking caffeine is 3 P.M.

☐ *Are you comfortable?* Check your bed, pillows, and the thermostat.

In addition, healthy eating, drinking plenty of water, and breathing will greatly improve your rest.

14:6 ᵃNU-Text omits the rest of this sentence.   14:9 ᵃNU-Text omits *and rose.*   14:10 ᵃNU-Text reads *of God.*   14:11 ᵃIsaiah 45:23   14:18 ᵃNU-Text reads *this.*   14:21 ᵃNU-Text omits *or is offended or is made weak.*   14:22 ᵃNU-Text reads *The faith which you have—have.*   14:23 ᵃM-Text puts Romans 16:25–27 here.   15:3 ᵃPsalm 69:9   15:7 ᵃNU-Text and M-Text read *you.*

SCRIPTURE SOLUTIONS

[HEADACHES]

Many experts believe nearly 50 percent of all migraines are triggered by stress, which can be drastically reduced by walking and exercise. Stretching and a wide variety of relaxation techniques can help as well. The following are four things you can put into your life on a regular basis to help prevent headaches:

☐ Do aerobic exercise, such as brisk walking, swimming, or cycling, twenty to thirty minutes at least three to four times per week. Regular aerobic exercise over time can dramatically reduce the number of tension headaches a person experiences, as well as the severity of them. This exercise also improves the overall cardiovascular system, which includes improved blood flow to the brain, neck, and head.

☐ Do slow gentle stretches to help relieve tension and stress. Try to stretch for a few minutes wherever you are, even at the office.

☐ Take advantage of these wonderful methods of relaxation: a long warm shower, deep breathing, massage, or acupressure. Good posture also can help a person relax.

☐ Eat a healthy, balanced diet and take a good multivitamin daily.

[8]Now I say that Jesus Christ has become a servant to the circumcision for the truth of God, to confirm the promises *made* to the fathers, [9]and that the Gentiles might glorify God for *His* mercy, as it is written:

"For this reason I will confess to You among the Gentiles,
And sing to Your name."[a]

[10] And again he says:

"Rejoice, O Gentiles, with His people!"[a]

[11]And again:

"Praise the LORD, all you Gentiles!
Laud Him, all you peoples!"[a]

[12] And again, Isaiah says:

"There shall be a root of Jesse;
And He who shall rise to reign over the Gentiles,
In Him the Gentiles shall hope."[a]

[13]Now may the God of hope fill you with all joy and peace in believing, that you may abound in hope by the power of the Holy Spirit.

FROM JERUSALEM TO ILLYRICUM

[14]Now I myself am confident concerning you, my brethren, that you also are full of goodness, filled with all knowledge, able also to admonish one another.[a] [15]Nevertheless, brethren, I have written more boldly to you on *some* points, as reminding you, because of the grace given to me by God, [16]that I might be a minister of Jesus Christ to the Gentiles, ministering the gospel of God, that the offering of the Gentiles might be acceptable, sanctified by the Holy Spirit. [17]Therefore I have reason to glory in Christ Jesus in the things *which pertain* to God. [18]For I will not dare to speak of any of those things which Christ has not accomplished through me, in word and deed, to make the Gentiles obedient— [19]in mighty signs and wonders, by the power of the Spirit of God, so that from Jerusalem and round about to Illyricum I have fully preached the gospel of Christ. [20]And so I have made it my aim to preach the gospel, not where Christ was named, lest I should build on another man's foundation, [21]but as it is written:

"To whom He was not announced, they shall see;
And those who have not heard shall understand."[a]

PLAN TO VISIT ROME

[22]For this reason I also have been much hindered from coming to you. [23]But now no longer having a place in these parts, and having a great desire these many years to come to you, [24]whenever I journey to Spain, I shall come to you.[a] For I hope to see you on my journey, and to be helped on my way there by you, if first I may enjoy your *company* for a while. [25]But now I am going to Jerusalem to minister to the saints. [26]For it pleased those from Macedonia and Achaia to make a certain contribution for the poor among the saints who are in Jerusalem. [27]It pleased them indeed, and they are their debtors. For if the Gentiles have been partakers of their spiritual things, their duty is also to minister to them in material things. [28]Therefore, when I have performed this and have sealed to them this fruit, I shall go by way of you to Spain. [29]But I know that when I come to you, I shall come in the fullness of the blessing of the gospel[a] of Christ.

[30]Now I beg you, brethren, through the Lord Jesus Christ, and through the love of the Spirit, that you strive together with me in

---

15:9 [a]2 Samuel 22:50; Psalm 18:49   15:10 [a]Deuteronomy 32:43   15:11 [a]Psalm 117:1   15:12 [a]Isaiah 11:10   15:14 [a]M-Text reads *others.*   15:21 [a]Isaiah 52:15   15:24 [a]NU-Text omits *I shall come to you*
(and joins *Spain* with the next sentence).   15:29 [a]NU-Text omits *of the gospel.*

prayers to God for me, [31]that I may be delivered from those in Judea who do not believe, and that my service for Jerusalem may be acceptable to the saints, [32]that I may come to you with joy by the will of God, and may be refreshed together with you. [33]Now the God of peace *be* with you all. Amen.

SISTER PHOEBE COMMENDED

16 I commend to you Phoebe our sister, who is a servant of the church in Cenchrea, [2]that you may receive her in the Lord in a manner worthy of the saints, and assist her in whatever business she has need of you; for indeed she has been a helper of many and of myself also.

GREETING ROMAN SAINTS

[3]Greet Priscilla and Aquila, my fellow workers in Christ Jesus, [4]who risked their own necks for my life, to whom not only I give thanks, but also all the churches of the Gentiles. [5]Likewise *greet* the church that is in their house.

Greet my beloved Epaenetus, who is the firstfruits of Achaia[a] to Christ. [6]Greet Mary, who labored much for us. [7]Greet Andronicus and Junia, my countrymen and my fellow prisoners, who are of note among the apostles, who also were in Christ before me.

[8]Greet Amplias, my beloved in the Lord. [9]Greet Urbanus, our fellow worker in Christ, and Stachys, my beloved. [10]Greet Apelles, approved in Christ. Greet those who are of the *household* of Aristobulus. [11]Greet Herodion, my countryman.[a] Greet those who are of the *household* of Narcissus who are in the Lord.

[12]Greet Tryphena and Tryphosa, who have labored in the Lord. Greet the beloved Persis, who labored much in the Lord. [13]Greet Rufus, chosen in the Lord, and his mother and mine. [14]Greet Asyncritus, Phlegon, Hermas, Patrobas, Hermes, and the brethren who are with them. [15]Greet Philologus and Julia, Nereus and his sister, and Olympas, and all the saints who are with them.

[16]Greet one another with a holy kiss. The[a] churches of Christ greet you.

AVOID DIVISIVE PERSONS

[17]Now I urge you, brethren, note those who cause divisions and offenses, contrary to the doctrine which you learned, and avoid them. [18]For those who are such do not serve our Lord Jesus[a] Christ, but their own belly, and by smooth words and flattering speech deceive the hearts of the simple. [19]For your obedience has become known to all. Therefore I am glad on your behalf; but I want you to be wise in what is good, and simple concerning evil. [20]And the God of peace will crush Satan under your feet shortly.

The grace of our Lord Jesus Christ *be* with you. Amen.

GREETINGS FROM PAUL'S FRIENDS

[21]Timothy, my fellow worker, and Lucius, Jason, and Sosipater, my countrymen, greet you.

[22]I, Tertius, who wrote *this* epistle, greet you in the Lord.

[23]Gaius, my host and *the host* of the whole church, greets you. Erastus, the treasurer of the city, greets you, and Quartus, a brother. [24]The grace of our Lord Jesus Christ *be* with you all. Amen.[a]

BENEDICTION

[25]Now to Him who is able to establish you according to my gospel and the preaching of Jesus Christ, according to the revelation of the mystery kept secret since the world began [26]but now made manifest, and by the prophetic Scriptures made known to all nations, according to the commandment of the everlasting God, for obedience to the faith— [27]to God, alone wise, *be* glory through Jesus Christ forever. Amen.[a]

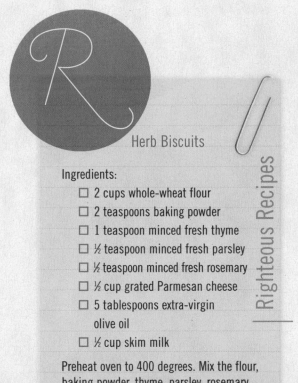

Righteous Recipes

Herb Biscuits

Ingredients:

- ☐ 2 cups whole-wheat flour
- ☐ 2 teaspoons baking powder
- ☐ 1 teaspoon minced fresh thyme
- ☐ ½ teaspoon minced fresh parsley
- ☐ ½ teaspoon minced fresh rosemary
- ☐ ½ cup grated Parmesan cheese
- ☐ 5 tablespoons extra-virgin olive oil
- ☐ ½ cup skim milk

Preheat oven to 400 degrees. Mix the flour, baking powder, thyme, parsley, rosemary, and Parmesan cheese in a large bowl, using a fork to combine the ingredients. Slowly stir in the olive oil—the mixture will be crumbly. Add the milk and stir until the dough holds together. You may add more milk if necessary. Drop by large spoonfuls about 1 inch apart onto a greased baking sheet. Bake 10–12 minutes.

Yield: 10–12 biscuits

16:5 [a]NU-Text reads *Asia*.   16:11 [a]Or *relative*   16:16 [a]NU-Text reads *All the churches*.   16:18 [a]NU-Text and M-Text omit *Jesus*.   16:24 [a]NU-Text omits this verse.   16:27 [a]M-Text puts Romans 16:25–27 after Romans 14:23.

CORINTHIANS

Talk about dysfunctional and scandalous! This book is a letter from the apostle Paul to a church that was filled with disorderly behavior, corruption, sexual sin, hypocrisy, and error. The people were divided, their thinking had strayed off course, their behavior was undisciplined. Paul doesn't back down from the trouble. He confronts the difficult issues head-on and answers the questions of the Corinthians clearly and with boldness. He cuts to the heart of the various issues and proclaims with great authority and power: "There's a better way to live!" He calls the people to glorify God in body and spirit and to flee immorality and idolatry. When it comes to healing the division they are experiencing in their midst, Paul says with great eloquence: "Love is the answer"—not a weak, sentimental love, but a strong and godly love that endures.

What heals like nothing else? A huge dose of what is good for a person—often, a simple statement of God's truth—wrapped up in tender expressions of genuine love.

GREETING

1 Paul, called *to be* an apostle of Jesus Christ through the will of God, and Sosthenes *our* brother,

2 To the church of God which is at Corinth, to those who are sanctified in Christ Jesus, called *to be* saints, with all who in every place call on the name of Jesus Christ our Lord, both theirs and ours:

3 Grace to you and peace from God our Father and the Lord Jesus Christ.

SPIRITUAL GIFTS AT CORINTH

4 I thank my God always concerning you for the grace of God which was given to you by Christ Jesus, 5 that you were enriched in everything by Him in all utterance and all knowledge, 6 even as the testimony of Christ was confirmed in you, 7 so that you come short in no gift, eagerly waiting for the revelation of our Lord Jesus Christ, 8 who will also confirm you to the end, *that you may be* blameless in the day of our Lord Jesus Christ. 9 God *is* faithful, by whom you were called into the fellowship of His Son, Jesus Christ our Lord.

SECTARIANISM IS SIN

10 Now I plead with you, brethren, by the name of our Lord Jesus Christ, that you all speak the same thing, and *that* there be no divisions among you, but *that* you be perfectly joined together in the same mind and in the same judgment. 11 For it has been declared to me concerning you, my brethren, by those of Chloe's *household*, that there are contentions among you. 12 Now I say this, that each of you says, "I am

of Paul," or "I am of Apollos," or "I am of Cephas," or "I am of Christ." 13 Is Christ divided? Was Paul crucified for you? Or were you baptized in the name of Paul?

14 I thank God that I baptized none of you except Crispus and Gaius, 15 lest anyone should say that I had baptized in my own name. 16 Yes, I also baptized the household of Stephanas. Besides, I do not know whether I baptized any other. 17 For Christ did not send me to baptize, but to preach the gospel, not with wisdom of words, lest the cross of Christ should be made of no effect.

CHRIST THE POWER AND WISDOM OF GOD

18 For the message of the cross is foolishness to those who are perishing, but to us who are being saved it is the power of God. 19 For it is written:

"I will destroy the wisdom of the wise,
And bring to nothing the understanding of the prudent."[a]

20 Where *is* the wise? Where *is* the scribe? Where *is* the disputer of this age? Has not God made foolish the wisdom of this world? 21 For since, in the wisdom of God, the world through wisdom did not know God, it pleased God through the foolishness of the message preached to save those who believe. 22 For Jews request a sign, and Greeks seek after wisdom; 23 but we preach Christ crucified, to the Jews a stumbling block and to the Greeks[a] foolishness, 24 but to those who are called, both Jews and Greeks, Christ the power of God and the wisdom of God. 25 Because the foolishness of God is wiser than men, and the weakness of God is stronger than men.

1:19 [a]Isaiah 29:14   1:23 [a]NU-Text reads *Gentiles.*

GLORY ONLY IN THE LORD

²⁶For you see your calling, brethren, that not many wise according to the flesh, not many mighty, not many noble, *are called.* ²⁷But God has chosen the foolish things of the world to put to shame the wise, and God has chosen the weak things of the world to put to shame the things which are mighty; ²⁸and the base things of the world and the things which are despised God has chosen, and the things which are not, to bring to nothing the things that are, ²⁹that no flesh should glory in His presence. ³⁰But of Him you are in Christ Jesus, who became for us wisdom from God—and righteousness and sanctification and redemption— ³¹that, as it is written, "He who glories, let him glory in the LORD."ᵃ

CHRIST CRUCIFIED

2 And I, brethren, when I came to you, did not come with excellence of speech or of wisdom declaring to you the testimonyᵃ of God. ²For I determined not to know anything among you except Jesus Christ and Him crucified. ³I was with you in weakness, in fear, and in much trembling. ⁴And my speech and my preaching *were* not with persuasive words of humanᵃ wisdom, but in demonstration of the Spirit and of power, ⁵that your faith should not be in the wisdom of men but in the power of God.

SPIRITUAL WISDOM

⁶However, we speak wisdom among those who are mature, yet not the wisdom of this age, nor of the rulers of this age, who are coming to nothing. ⁷But we speak the wisdom of God in a mystery, the hidden *wisdom* which God ordained before the ages for our glory, ⁸which none of the rulers of this age knew; for had they known, they would not have crucified the Lord of glory.

⁹But as it is written:

PEACE LOVE JOY KINDNESS

Nightshades

Bible Health + Food Facts

Certain foods called *nightshades* seem to inflame the joints of some arthritis patients. If you suffer from arthritis, avoid eggplant, tomatoes, potatoes, and bell peppers.

The Healthy Soul
>Mercy

To be merciful is to do whatever a person might be able to do to promote compassion, forgiveness, and a love for God in other people. Mercy flows from a desire to see other people do the right thing in any situation, and to establish or maintain a right relationship with God and other people.

Forgiveness and mercy are closely related—in some ways, they are like the two sides of a coin. To forgive is to release or let go. To forgive another person is to "let go" of that person, placing him or her squarely into God's hands. It is to let go of painful memories, trusting God to remember all things. It is to let go of feelings of vengeance, trusting God to be a wise and fair judge. To be forgiven by God is to know that your sins have been removed and you are set free from their gripping bondage and any eternal consequences.

To be merciful, in contrast, is to "hang on." It is to continue to believe for the best, hope for the best, and encourage the best in others. It is to "hang on" to the good image or the good nature that we believe others have, choosing to overlook faults, failures, and infractions. To be merciful is to hang on to the hope that a person will be saved from his sins, or if the person has made a mistake, to hang on to the hope that he will come to his senses and seek to remedy a bad situation or right a wrong that has been done. To be merciful is to refuse to say that a person is beyond God's redemption, or that a person should be abandoned or rejected as being unworthy.

Those who are merciful are usually quick to forgive. They are quick to defend the innocent and to seek justice for those who have been wronged. In many ways, mercy is the opposite of bitterness and resentment. Mercy focuses on the good, not on the bad.

"Eye has not seen, nor ear heard,
Nor have entered into the heart of man
The things which God has prepared for those who love Him."ᵃ

¹⁰But God has revealed *them* to us through His Spirit. For the Spirit searches all things, yes, the deep things of God. ¹¹For what man knows the things of a man except the spirit of the man which is in him? Even so no one knows the things of God except the Spirit of God. ¹²Now we

1:31 ªJeremiah 9:24   2:1 ªNU-Text reads *mystery.*   2:4 ªNU-Text omits *human.*   2:9 ªIsaiah 64:4

have received, not the spirit of the world, but the Spirit who is from God, that we might know the things that have been freely given to us by God.

[13]These things we also speak, not in words which man's wisdom teaches but which the Holy[a] Spirit teaches, comparing spiritual things with spiritual. [14]But the natural man does not receive the things of the Spirit of God, for they are foolishness to him; nor can he know *them*, because they are spiritually discerned. [15]But he who is spiritual judges all things, yet he himself is *rightly* judged by no one. [16]For "who has known the mind of the LORD that he may instruct Him?"[a] But we have the mind of Christ.

SECTARIANISM IS CARNAL

3 And I, brethren, could not speak to you as to spiritual *people* but as to carnal, as to babes in Christ. [2]I fed you with milk and not with solid food; for until now you were not able *to receive it,* and even now you are still not able; [3]for you are still carnal. For where *there are* envy, strife, and divisions among you, are you not carnal and behaving like *mere* men? [4]For when one says, "I am of Paul," and another, "I *am* of Apollos," are you not carnal?

WATERING, WORKING, WARNING

[5]Who then is Paul, and who *is* Apollos, but ministers through whom you believed, as the Lord gave to each one? [6]I planted, Apollos watered, but God gave the increase. [7]So then neither he who plants is anything, nor he who waters, but God who gives the increase. [8]Now he who plants and he who waters are one, and each one will receive his own reward according to his own labor.

[9]For we are God's fellow workers; you are God's field, *you are* God's building. [10]According to the grace of God which was given to me, as a wise master builder I have laid the foundation, and another builds on it. But let each one take heed how he builds on it. [11]For no other foundation can anyone lay than that which is laid, which is Jesus Christ. [12]Now if anyone builds on this foundation *with* gold, silver, precious stones, wood, hay, straw, [13]each one's work will become clear; for the Day will declare it, because it will be revealed by fire; and the fire will test each one's work, of what sort it is. [14]If anyone's work which he has built on *it* endures, he will receive a reward. [15]If anyone's work is burned, he will suffer loss; but he himself will be saved, yet so as through fire.

[16]Do you not know that you are the temple of God and *that* the Spirit of God dwells in you? [17]If anyone defiles the temple of God, God will destroy him. For the temple of God is holy, which *temple* you are.

AVOID WORLDLY WISDOM

[18]Let no one deceive himself. If anyone among you seems to be wise in this age, let him become a fool that he may become wise. [19]For the wisdom of this world is foolishness with God. For it is written, "He catches the wise in their *own* craftiness";[a] [20]and again, "The LORD knows the thoughts of the wise, that they are futile."[a] [21]Therefore let no one boast in men. For all things are yours: [22]whether Paul or Apollos or Cephas, or the world or life or death, or things present or things to come—all are yours. [23]And you *are* Christ's, and Christ *is* God's.

STEWARDS OF THE MYSTERIES OF GOD

4 Let a man so consider us, as servants of Christ and stewards of the mysteries of God. [2]Moreover it is required in stewards that one be found faithful. [3]But with me it is a very small thing that I should be judged by you or by a human court.[a] In fact, I do not even judge myself. [4]For I know of nothing against myself, yet I am not justified by this; but He who judges me is the Lord. [5]Therefore judge nothing before the time, until the Lord comes, who will both bring to light the hidden things of darkness and reveal the counsels of the hearts. Then each one's praise will come from God.

CONDIMENTS

☐ Mint

The taste of mint is very pleasing to most people, but mint is listed among the "bitter herbs" in Exodus 12:8 and Numbers 9:11. For that matter, so are many of the items we would consider "salad greens"

Mint added to a fruit salad can be a welcome addition. Mint gives a unique taste to a green salad as well.

The two most common species of mint grown in the Middle East are spearmint and peppermint.

The Romans and Greeks used mint to keep milk from spoiling. They routinely offered mint after meals as a digestive aid. Modern herbalists recommend peppermint for menstrual cramps, morning sickness, colds, flu, motion sickness, heartburn, fever, headache, and insomnia.

Mint is also an antispasmodic. Mint soothes the muscles of the digestive tract and uterus. It is helpful in treating nausea. Women who have a history of miscarriages, however, should avoid peppermint as a treatment for morning sickness.

2:13 [a]NU-Text omits *Holy.*   2:16 [a]Isaiah 40:13   3:19 [a]Job 5:13   3:20 [a]Psalm 94:11   4:3 [a]Literally *day*

FOOLS FOR CHRIST'S SAKE

⁶Now these things, brethren, I have figuratively transferred to myself and Apollos for your sakes, that you may learn in us not to think beyond what is written, that none of you may be puffed up on behalf of one against the other. ⁷For who makes you differ *from another*? And what do you have that you did not receive? Now if you did indeed receive *it,* why do you boast as if you had not received *it*?

⁸You are already full! You are already rich! You have reigned as kings without us—and indeed I could wish you did reign, that we also might reign with you! ⁹For I think that God has displayed us, the apostles, last, as men condemned to death; for we have been made a spectacle to the world, both to angels and to men. ¹⁰We *are* fools for Christ's sake, but you *are* wise in Christ! We *are* weak, but you *are* strong! You *are* distinguished, but we *are* dishonored! ¹¹To the present hour we both hunger and thirst, and we are poorly clothed, and beaten, and homeless. ¹²And we labor, working with our own hands. Being reviled, we bless; being persecuted, we endure; ¹³being defamed, we entreat. We have been made as the filth of the world, the offscouring of all things until now.

PAUL'S PATERNAL CARE

¹⁴I do not write these things to shame you, but as my beloved children I warn *you.* ¹⁵For though you might have ten thousand instructors in Christ, yet *you do* not *have* many fathers; for in Christ Jesus I have begotten you through the gospel. ¹⁶Therefore I urge you, imitate me. ¹⁷For this reason I have sent Timothy to you, who is my beloved and

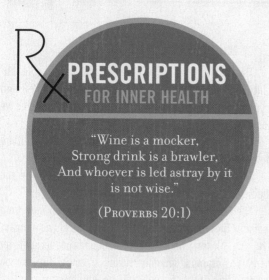

PRESCRIPTIONS
FOR INNER HEALTH

"Wine is a mocker,
Strong drink is a brawler,
And whoever is led astray by it
is not wise."

(PROVERBS 20:1)

People who are drunk often become loud, aggressive, and do abusive and foolish things. Excessive use of any form of intoxicating drink was expressly forbidden for God's people. The Bible warns repeatedly about how quickly too much alcohol can become a snare and destroyer.

[SMOKING]

FACT MORSELS

Smoking and Wrinkles. Early wrinkling occurs because the skin does not have sufficient oxygen. Smoking is a prime source of oxygen deprivation of the skin. Don't smoke!

---

faithful son in the Lord, who will remind you of my ways in Christ, as I teach everywhere in every church.

¹⁸Now some are puffed up, as though I were not coming to you. ¹⁹But I will come to you shortly, if the Lord wills, and I will know, not the word of those who are puffed up, but the power. ²⁰For the kingdom of God *is* not in word but in power. ²¹What do you want? Shall I come to you with a rod, or in love and a spirit of gentleness?

IMMORALITY DEFILES THE CHURCH

5 It is actually reported *that there is* sexual immorality among you, and such sexual immorality as is not even named^a among the Gentiles—that a man has his father's wife! ²And you are puffed up, and have not rather mourned, that he who has done this deed might be taken away from among you. ³For I indeed, as absent in body but present in spirit, have already judged (as though I were present) him who has so done this deed. ⁴In the name of our Lord Jesus Christ, when you are gathered together, along with my spirit, with the power of our Lord Jesus Christ, ⁵deliver such a one to Satan for the destruction of the flesh, that his spirit may be saved in the day of the Lord Jesus.^a

⁶Your glorying *is* not good. Do you not know that a little leaven leavens the whole lump? ⁷Therefore purge out the old leaven, that you may be a new lump, since you truly are unleavened. For indeed Christ, our Passover, was sacrificed for us.^a ⁸Therefore let us keep the feast, not with old leaven, nor with the leaven of malice and wickedness, but with the unleavened *bread* of sincerity and truth.

IMMORALITY MUST BE JUDGED

⁹I wrote to you in my epistle not to keep company with sexually immoral people. ¹⁰Yet *I* certainly *did* not *mean* with the sexually immoral people of this world, or with the covetous, or extortioners, or idolaters, since then you would need to go out of the world. ¹¹But now I have written to you not to keep company with anyone named a brother, who is sexually immoral, or covetous, or an idolater, or a reviler, or a drunkard, or an extortioner—not even to eat with such a person.

¹²For what *have I to do* with judging those also who are outside? Do you not judge those who are inside? ¹³But those who are outside God judges. Therefore "put away from yourselves the evil person."^a

---

5:1 ^aNU-Text omits *named.*   5:5 ^aNU-Text omits *Jesus.*   5:7 ^aNU-Text omits *for us.*   5:13 ^aDeuteronomy 17:7; 19:19; 22:21, 24; 24:7

DO NOT SUE THE BRETHREN

6 Dare any of you, having a matter against another, go to law before the unrighteous, and not before the saints? ²Do you not know that the saints will judge the world? And if the world will be judged by you, are you unworthy to judge the smallest matters? ³Do you not know that we shall judge angels? How much more, things that pertain to this life? ⁴If then you have judgments concerning things pertaining to this life, do you appoint those who are least esteemed by the church to judge? ⁵I say this to your shame. Is it so, that there is not a wise man among you, not even one, who will be able to judge between his brethren? ⁶But brother goes to law against brother, and that before unbelievers!

⁷Now therefore, it is already an utter failure for you that you go to law against one another. Why do you not rather accept wrong? Why do you not rather *let yourselves* be cheated? ⁸No, you yourselves do wrong and cheat, and *you do* these things *to your* brethren! ⁹Do you not know that the unrighteous will not inherit the kingdom of God? Do not be deceived. Neither fornicators, nor idolaters, nor adulterers, nor homosexuals,ᵃ nor sodomites, ¹⁰nor thieves, nor covetous, nor drunkards, nor revilers, nor extortioners will inherit the kingdom of God. ¹¹And such were some of you. But you were washed, but you were sanctified, but you were justified in the name of the Lord Jesus and by the Spirit of our God.

GLORIFY GOD IN BODY AND SPIRIT

¹²All things are lawful for me, but all things are not helpful. All things are lawful for me, but I will not be brought under the power of any. ¹³Foods for the stomach and the stomach for foods, but God will destroy both it and them. Now the body *is* not for sexual immorality but for the Lord, and the Lord for the body. ¹⁴And God both raised up the Lord and will also raise us up by His power.

¹⁵Do you not know that your bodies are members of Christ? Shall I then take the members of Christ and make *them* members of a harlot? Certainly not! ¹⁶Or do you not know that he who is joined to a harlot is one body *with her*? For "the two," He says, "shall become one flesh."ᵃ ¹⁷But he who is joined to the Lord is one spirit *with Him*.

¹⁸Flee sexual immorality. Every sin that a man does is outside the body, but he who commits sexual immorality sins against his own body. ¹⁹Or do you not know that your body is the temple of the Holy Spirit *who is* in you, whom you have from God, and you are not your own? ²⁰For you were bought at a price; therefore glorify God in your bodyᵃ and in your spirit, which are God's.

PRINCIPLES OF MARRIAGE

7 Now concerning the things of which you wrote to me:

It is good for a man not to touch a woman. ²Nevertheless, because of sexual immorality, let each man have his own wife, and let each woman have her own husband. ³Let the husband render to his wife the affection due her, and likewise also the wife to her husband. ⁴The wife does not have authority over her own body, but the husband *does*. And likewise the husband does not have authority over his own body, but the wife *does*. ⁵Do not deprive one another except with consent for a time, that you may give yourselves to fasting and prayer; and come together again so that Satan does not tempt you because of your lack of self-control. ⁶But I say this as a concession, not as a commandment. ⁷For I wish that all

WISE CHOICES

Choose plain yogurt over fruit yogurt.
Plain yogurt has only about 144 calories per cup. Fruit yogurt can have 225 or more calories per cup. To flavor your yogurt, add your own fresh fruit! If you need your plain yogurt to be a little sweeter, add a drop of Stevia.

> (1 Corinthians 6:12)

Lawful vs. Beneficial. The Corinthians, once pagans or Jews living under the Law and now Christians taught they were "free in Christ Jesus," had developed the "theological" slogan: "All things are lawful for me!" They used this to justify all sorts of behavior. They ate whatever they wanted, and did whatever they wanted to sexually. What they didn't understand, and what many people today do not understand, is that the freedom to do whatever you like really isn't freedom at all. It's the most insidious form of bondage.

The Law was intended for man's benefit, and ultimately, laws and rules have value only if they are in the context of what is helpful or beneficial. We need to ask, *Is this truly beneficial?* about what we choose to do—including what we choose to put into our bodies. Does it produce physical or emotional health? Does it make me more whole? Does it enhance my relationship with God, my witness for Jesus Christ, or my sensitivity to the guidance of the Holy Spirit? Does it truly lead me toward the full potential that God desires for me? Just because we *can* do something doesn't mean that we are wise to do it!

INSIGHTS | **INTO THE WORD**

6:9 ᵃThat is, catamites   6:16 ᵃGenesis 2:24   6:20 ᵃNU-Text ends the verse at *body*.

The LAW AND THE SCIENCE

[AVOID THE CREEPY CRAWLERS]

>SCIENCE tells us that reptiles and rodents are among the creatures that eat dead, dying, or sick animals. As such, they are prone to carrying diseases that can be very dangerous to human beings. Avoid eating that rattlesnake offered to you at a cowboy barbecue!

>THE LAW says: "These also shall be unclean to you among the creeping things that creep on the earth: the mole, the mouse, and the large lizard after its kind; the gecko, the monitor lizard, the sand reptile, the sand lizard, and the chameleon. These are unclean to you among all that creep. Whoever touches them when they are dead shall be unclean until evening" (Leviticus 11:29–31).

men were even as I myself. But each one has his own gift from God, one in this manner and another in that.

⁸But I say to the unmarried and to the widows: It is good for them if they remain even as I am; ⁹but if they cannot exercise self-control, let them marry. For it is better to marry than to burn *with passion.*

KEEP YOUR MARRIAGE VOWS

¹⁰Now to the married I command, *yet* not I but the Lord: A wife is not to depart from *her* husband. ¹¹But even if she does depart, let her remain unmarried or be reconciled to *her* husband. And a husband is not to divorce *his* wife.

¹²But to the rest I, not the Lord, say: If any brother has a wife who does not believe, and she is willing to live with him, let him not divorce her. ¹³And a woman who has a husband who does not believe, if he is willing to live with her, let her not divorce him. ¹⁴For the unbelieving husband is sanctified by the wife, and the unbelieving wife is sanctified by the husband; otherwise your children would be unclean, but now they are holy. ¹⁵But if the unbeliever departs, let him depart; a brother or a sister is not under bondage in such *cases.* But God has called us to peace. ¹⁶For how do you know, O wife, whether you will save *your* husband? Or how do you know, O husband, whether you will save *your* wife?

LIVE AS YOU ARE CALLED

¹⁷But as God has distributed to each one, as the Lord has called each one, so let him walk. And so I ordain in all the churches. ¹⁸Was anyone called while circumcised? Let him not become uncircumcised. Was anyone called while uncircumcised? Let him not be circumcised. ¹⁹Circumcision is nothing and uncircumcision is nothing, but keeping the commandments of God *is what matters.* ²⁰Let each one remain in the same calling in which he was called. ²¹Were you called *while* a slave? Do not be concerned about it; but if you can be made free, rather use *it.* ²²For he who is called in the Lord *while* a slave is the Lord's freedman. Likewise he who is called *while* free is Christ's slave. ²³You were bought at a price; do not become slaves of men. ²⁴Brethren, let each one remain with God in that *state* in which he was called.

TO THE UNMARRIED AND WIDOWS

²⁵Now concerning virgins: I have no commandment from the Lord; yet I give judgment as one whom the Lord in His mercy has made trustworthy. ²⁶I suppose therefore that this is good because of the present distress—that *it is* good for a man to remain as he is: ²⁷Are you bound to a wife? Do not seek to be loosed. Are you loosed from a wife? Do not seek a wife. ²⁸But even if you do marry, you have not sinned; and if a virgin marries, she has not sinned. Nevertheless such will have trouble in the flesh, but I would spare you.

²⁹But this I say, brethren, the time *is* short, so that from now on even those who have wives should be as though they had none, ³⁰those who weep as though they did not weep, those who rejoice as though they did not rejoice, those who buy as though they did not possess, ³¹and those who use this world as not misusing *it.* For the form of this world is passing away.

³²But I want you to be without care. He who is unmarried cares for the things of the Lord—how he may please the Lord. ³³But he who is married cares about the things of the world—how he may please *his* wife. ³⁴There is^a a difference between a wife and a virgin. The unmarried woman cares about the things of the Lord, that she may be holy both in body and in spirit. But she who is married cares about the things of the world—how she may please *her* husband. ³⁵And this I say for your own profit, not that I may put a leash on you, but for what is proper, and that you may serve the Lord without distraction.

³⁶But if any man thinks he is behaving improperly toward his virgin, if she is past the flower of youth, and thus it must be, let him do what he wishes. He does not sin; let them marry. ³⁷Nevertheless he who stands steadfast in his heart, having no necessity, but has power over his own will, and has so determined in his heart that he will keep his virgin,^{a} does well. ³⁸So then he who gives *her*^{a} in marriage does well, but he who does not give *her* in marriage does better.

³⁹A wife is bound by law as long as her husband lives; but if her husband dies, she is at liberty to be married to whom she wishes, only in the Lord. ⁴⁰But she is happier if she remains as she is, according to my judgment— and I think I also have the Spirit of God.

BE SENSITIVE TO CONSCIENCE

8 Now concerning things offered to idols: We know that we all have knowledge. Knowledge puffs up, but love edifies. ²And if anyone thinks that he knows anything, he knows nothing yet as he ought to know. ³But if anyone loves God, this one is known by Him.

⁴Therefore concerning the eating of things offered to idols, we know that an idol *is* nothing in the world, and that *there is* no other God but one. ⁵For even if there are so-called gods, whether in heaven or on earth (as there are many gods and many lords), ⁶yet for us *there is* one God, the Father, of whom *are* all things, and we for Him; and one Lord Jesus Christ, through whom *are* all things, and through whom we *live*.

⁷However, *there is* not in everyone that knowledge; for some, with consciousness of the idol, until now eat *it* as a thing offered to an idol; and their conscience, being weak, is defiled. ⁸But food does not commend us to God; for neither if we eat are we the better, nor if we do not eat are we the worse.

⁹But beware lest somehow this liberty of yours become a stumbling block to those who are weak. ¹⁰For if anyone sees you who have knowledge eating in an idol's temple, will not the conscience of him who is weak be emboldened to eat those things offered to idols? ¹¹And because of your knowledge shall the weak brother perish, for whom Christ died? ¹²But when you thus sin against the brethren, and wound their weak conscience, you sin against Christ. ¹³Therefore, if food makes my brother stumble, I will never again eat meat, lest I make my brother stumble.

Melons and Cucumbers

Bible Health + Food Facts

Although some varieties of melons are common in Egypt, including watermelon, the melons the Israelites craved may have been cucumbers. If you peel and scoop the seeds out of a cucumber, you'll find that the remaining part of the cucumber tastes like melon!

A PATTERN OF SELF-DENIAL

9 Am I not an apostle? Am I not free? Have I not seen Jesus Christ our Lord? Are you not my work in the Lord? ²If I am not an apostle to others, yet doubtless I am to you. For you are the seal of my apostleship in the Lord.

> (1 Corinthians 8:4, 7–9)

Foods Offered to Idols. The pagans who worshiped Greek and Roman gods gave offerings of food and drink to their gods. The Jews gave offerings of meat, birds, grain, oil, and wine to their God. What was the difference? The pagans gave their offerings in an effort to appease the gods and gain their favor. They saw their role as providing what the gods needed in order to remain happy. (To anger a pagan god meant surefire retribution, usually in the form of drought, crop failure, infertility, injury, sickness, personal calamity, or widespread catastrophe.) Furthermore, when a pagan purchased meat that had been offered to a Roman god and from a temple market, he believed that he was fully identifying with the god by partaking of his "leftovers."

The Jewish perspective was vastly different. The Jew brought periodic sacrifices to the temple in Jerusalem in obedience to specific commands God gave for atonement, resolution of conflict, and thanksgiving. The Jew believed that God was the One who blessed mankind—God alone was the ultimate Caregiver and Provider of all that man needed for life and happiness. The Jews gave to God in humility and with thanksgiving, trusting God to deal justly with His creation. Any portion of meat returned to a Jewish family after the offering of a sacrifice was to be eaten with joy and appreciation—with a full awareness that God is God and man is man.

The apostle Paul taught the former pagans, now Christians in the church at Corinth, that the meat in temple markets was no different than meat in "secular" markets since the gods worshiped by the pagans didn't really exist. Paul added, however, that other people might see a Christian purchase such meat and conclude that the Christian was attempting to bribe or identify with a pagan god. Paul advised that Christians should refrain from purchasing meat in the temple market if there was any chance that their behavior might be misinterpreted and cause others to draw false conclusions. After all, there was plenty of other meat that could be purchased and consumed!

INSIGHTS | INTO THE WORD

[3]My defense to those who examine me is this: [4]Do we have no right to eat and drink? [5]Do we have no right to take along a believing wife, as do also the other apostles, the brothers of the Lord, and Cephas? [6]Or is it only Barnabas and I who have no right to refrain from working? [7]Who ever goes to war at his own expense? Who plants a vineyard and does not eat of its fruit? Or who tends a flock and does not drink of the milk of the flock?

[8]Do I say these things as a mere man? Or does not the law say the same also? [9]For it is written in the law of Moses, "You shall not muzzle an ox while it treads out the grain."[a] Is it oxen God is concerned about? [10]Or does He say it altogether for our sakes? For our sakes, no doubt, this is written, that he who plows should plow in hope, and he who threshes in hope should be partaker of his hope. [11]If we have sown spiritual things for you, is it a great thing if we reap your material things? [12]If others are partakers of this right over you, are we not even more?

Nevertheless we have not used this right, but endure all things lest we hinder the gospel of Christ. [13]Do you not know that those who minister the holy things eat of the things of the temple, and those who serve at the altar partake of the offerings of the altar? [14]Even so the Lord has commanded that those who preach the gospel should live from the gospel.

[15]But I have used none of these things, nor have I written these things that it should be done so to me; for it would be better for me to die than that anyone should make my boasting void. [16]For if I preach the gospel, I have nothing to boast of, for necessity is laid upon me; yes, woe is me if I do not preach the gospel! [17]For if I do this willingly, I have a reward; but if against my will, I have been entrusted with a stewardship. [18]What is my reward then? That when I preach the gospel, I may present the gospel of Christ[a] without charge, that I may not abuse my authority in the gospel.

SERVING ALL MEN

[19]For though I am free from all men, I have made myself a servant to all, that I might win the more; [20]and to the Jews I became as a Jew, that I might win Jews; to those who are under the law, as under the law,[a] that I might win those who are under the law; [21]to those who are without law, as without law (not being without law toward God,[a] but under law toward Christ[b]), that I might win those who are without law; [22]to the weak I became as[a] weak, that I might win the weak. I have become all things to all men, that I might by all means save some. [23]Now this I do for the gospel's sake, that I may be partaker of it with you.

STRIVING FOR A CROWN

[24]Do you not know that those who run in a race all run, but one receives the prize? Run in

---

Breaking Bread—with Caution ▲

ULTIMATE HEALTH RESOURCE • ULTIMATE HEALTH RESOURCE

In the Bible to "break bread" with another person was very serious business. Since bread was considered to be the staple of life, eating bread together was considered an act of binding people together to face life's circumstances. This was especially true among nomadic people where food was scarce and a single meal could mean the difference between death and survival. A host who served a meal to a wandering visitor became responsible for that visitor as long as he was in his home.

The Bible cautions about sharing a meal with two types of people: a person who has power over you or seeks to exert power over you, and a miser. Proverbs 23:1–3 says:

When you sit down to eat with a ruler,
Consider carefully what is before you;
And put a knife to your throat

If you are a man given to appetite.
Do not desire his delicacies,
For they are deceptive food.

Beware of eating with people who try to entice you with fine food—you will find yourself under obligation to them, and usually to the degree to which you have eaten at their table! The saying is true: There's no such thing as a free lunch. Proverbs 23:6–8 warns:

Do not eat the bread of a miser,
Nor desire his delicacies;
For as he thinks in his heart, so is he.
"Eat and drink!" he says to you,
But his heart is not with you.
The morsel you have eaten, you will vomit up,
And waste your pleasant words.

A miserly person will resent what you eat at his table. He will see you as "stealing" from him even though he may not say so openly. No matter what you say during the course of the meal, he will twist your words to ill intent. In the end, the meal will be totally unsatisfying to you both—the time together will result in bad feelings, not good rapport.

9:9 [a]Deuteronomy 25:4   9:18 [a]NU-Text omits of Christ.   9:20 [a]NU-Text adds though not being myself under the law.   9:21 [a]NU-Text reads God's law. [b]NU-Text reads Christ's law.   9:22 [a]NU-Text omits as.

PEOPLE CALLED "BEAUTIFUL" IN THE BIBLE

Tamar

A Tragic Tale

Tamar was the sister of the most handsome man in Israel, Absalom. It is little wonder that the Bible says she was "lovely" (2 Samuel 13:1). A princess, Tamar had little reason to fear for her personal safety. She wore richly colored robes and no doubt lived a secluded, pampered life. Her half brother Amnon, however, became filled with lust at her beauty. With the help of a crafty friend and cousin, he enticed Tamar to his chambers. Pretending to be sick, he requested that Tamar be the one who prepared food for him and fed him during his illness. Tamar willingly obliged. Once she arrived in Amnon's chambers, he raped her and then filled with hatred for her that matched his former lust, he sent Tamar away. She remained "desolate in her brother Absalom's house" (2 Samuel 13:20).

It appears from what the Bible tells us that Tamar suffered lifelong emotional trauma. Although Absalom avenged her rape by having Amnon murdered, there is no mention that this brought about any peace to Tamar's heart, or that it helped her overcome the shame she felt.

Sometimes people falsely conclude that the rich, the privileged, or the "beautiful people" never suffer from emotional trauma or great tragedy. This may not be as prevalent a misconception now as it was in decades past when people were not so quick to talk about their innermost pain on prime-time talk shows. Nevertheless, the assumption is still often made that people of certain status or appearance are immune from real hurt. That simply is not true. Feelings of shame haunt many people.

Shame is the opposite of self-esteem. It is the feeling of having no value, and of being hopelessly defective, inferior, and unlovable. Shame may begin with an external sin or abusive experience, but it becomes internalized until "shameful" becomes a person's core identity. Both men and women can experience shame, although women seem more often to be the victims of abusive behavior that result in feelings of shame.

Healing from shame begins when a person identifies and confesses the lies that he or she has come to believe about himself or herself. Those lies must be replaced with biblical truth about who God is and who the person is as His beloved child—a person of immeasurable worth, righteous and uncondemned. (See Romans 8:1, 31–39 and 2 Corinthians 5:17, 21.)

Only Jesus, through the power of His Holy Spirit, can bring full emotional cleansing and freedom from shame. Ask Him to be the Healer!

such a way that you may obtain *it*. [25]And everyone who competes *for the prize* is temperate in all things. Now they *do it* to obtain a perishable crown, but we *for* an imperishable *crown*. [26]Therefore I run thus: not with uncertainty. Thus I fight: not as *one who* beats the air. [27]But I discipline my body and bring *it* into subjection, lest, when I have preached to others, I myself should become disqualified.

OLD TESTAMENT EXAMPLES

10 Moreover, brethren, I do not want you to be unaware that all our fathers were under the cloud, all passed through the sea, [2]all were baptized into Moses in the cloud and in the sea, [3]all ate the same spiritual food, [4]and all drank the same spiritual drink. For they drank of that spiritual Rock that followed them, and that Rock was Christ. [5]But with most of them God was not well pleased, for *their bodies* were scattered in the wilderness.

[6]Now these things became our examples, to the intent that we should not lust after evil things as they also lusted. [7]And do not become idolaters as *were* some of them. As it is written, "The people sat down to eat and drink, and rose up to play."[a] [8]Nor let us commit sexual immorality, as some of them did, and in one day twenty-three

thousand fell; [9]nor let us tempt Christ, as some of them also tempted, and were destroyed by serpents; [10]nor complain, as some of them also complained, and were destroyed by the destroyer. [11]Now all[a] these things happened to them as examples, and they were written for our admonition, upon whom the ends of the ages have come.

[12]Therefore let him who thinks he stands take heed lest he fall. [13]No temptation has overtaken you except such as is common to man; but God *is* faithful, who will not allow you to be tempted beyond what you are able, but with the temptation will also make the way of escape, that you may be able to bear *it*.

Q Who is the first man in the Bible described as being drunk?

A Noah *(Genesis 9:21).*

10:7 [a]Exodus 32:6   10:11 [a]NU-Text omits *all.*

walking the walk

[WALK 'N' DO]

Ever used the excuse "I just don't have time to exercise"? Ever used the excuse that "exercise seems like a waste of time"? Double-tasking addresses both of these excuses!

Double-tasking refers simply to the idea of doing two things simultaneously. There are dozens of things you can do to make the most of your exercise time—most are likely things you enjoy doing more than you enjoy the physical exertion.

During your morning walk you can also do the following:

☐ Pray for your family members and friends.
☐ Pray for your unsaved neighbors—especially as you walk past their homes.
☐ Pick up bits of trash—beautify your neighborhood as an act of community service. (Wear plastic gloves and take a plastic bag with you.)
☐ Sing praises to the Lord—take along some music and a set of earphones.
☐ Listen to tapes—educational or inspirational.
☐ Learn a new language—practice a foreign language using tapes or CDs.
☐ Catch up on the news if you have a portable news source.
☐ Listen to Bible tapes.

Use time on a treadmill to do the following:

☐ Catch up on the morning news on television.
☐ Watch a movie or video.
☐ Read a magazine.
☐ Read a book—fiction or nonfiction.
☐ Read the Bible.

CONT. NEXT PAGE>>>

FLEE FROM IDOLATRY

[14]Therefore, my beloved, flee from idolatry. [15]I speak as to wise men; judge for yourselves what I say. [16]The cup of blessing which we bless, is it not the communion of the blood of Christ? The bread which we break, is it not the communion of the body of Christ? [17]For we, *though* many, are one bread *and* one body; for we all partake of that one bread.

[18]Observe Israel after the flesh: Are not those who eat of the sacrifices partakers of the altar? [19]What am I saying then? That an idol is anything, or what is offered to idols is anything? [20]Rather, that the things which the Gentiles sacrifice they sacrifice to demons and not to God, and I do not want you to have fellowship with demons. [21]You cannot drink the cup of the Lord and the cup of demons; you cannot partake of the Lord's table and of the table of demons. [22]Or do we provoke the Lord to jealousy? Are we stronger than He?

ALL TO THE GLORY OF GOD

[23]All things are lawful for me,[a] but not all things are helpful; all things are lawful for me,[b] but not all things edify. [24]Let no one seek his own, but each one the other's *well-being*.

[25]Eat whatever is sold in the meat market, asking no questions for conscience' sake; [26]for "the earth is the LORD'S, and all its fullness."[a]

[27]If any of those who do not believe invites you *to dinner*, and you desire to go, eat whatever is set before you, asking no question for conscience' sake. [28]But if anyone says to you, "This was offered to idols," do not eat it for the sake of the one who told you, and for conscience' sake;[a] for "the earth is the LORD'S, and all its fullness."[b] [29]"Conscience," I say, not your own, but that of the other. For why is my liberty judged by another *man's* conscience? [30]But if I partake with thanks, why am I evil spoken of for *the food* over which I give thanks?

[31]Therefore, whether you eat or drink, or whatever you do, do all to the glory of God. [32]Give no offense, either to the Jews or to the Greeks or to the church of God, [33]just as I also please all *men* in all *things*, not seeking my own profit, but the *profit* of many, that they may be saved.

11

Imitate me, just as I also *imitate* Christ.

HEAD COVERINGS

[2]Now I praise you, brethren, that you remember me in all things and keep the traditions just as I delivered *them* to you. [3]But I want you to know that the head of every man is Christ, the head of woman *is* man, and the head of Christ *is* God. [4]Every man praying or prophesying, having *his* head covered, dishonors his head. [5]But every woman who prays or prophesies with *her* head uncovered dishonors her head, for that is one and the same as if her head were shaved. [6]For if a woman is not covered, let her also be shorn. But if it is shameful for a woman to be shorn or shaved, let her be covered. [7]For a man indeed ought not to cover *his* head, since he is the image and glory of God; but woman is the glory of man. [8]For man is not from woman, but woman from man. [9]Nor was man created for the woman, but woman for the man. [10]For this reason the woman ought to have *a symbol of* authority on *her* head, because of the angels. [11]Nevertheless, neither *is* man independent of woman, nor woman independent of man, in the Lord. [12]For as

---

10:23 [a]NU-Text omits *for me*. [b]NU-Text omits *for me*. 10:26 [a]Psalm 24:1 10:28 [a]NU-Text omits the rest of this verse. [b]Psalm 24:1

woman *came* from man, even so man also *comes* through woman; but all things are from God.

¹³Judge among yourselves. Is it proper for a woman to pray to God with her head uncovered? ¹⁴Does not even nature itself teach you that if a man has long hair, it is a dishonor to him? ¹⁵But if a woman has long hair, it is a glory to her; for *her* hair is given to her*ᵃ* for a covering. ¹⁶But if anyone seems to be contentious, we have no such custom, nor *do* the churches of God.

CONDUCT AT THE LORD'S SUPPER

¹⁷Now in giving these instructions I do not praise *you,* since you come together not for the better but for the worse. ¹⁸For first of all, when you come together as a church, I hear that there are divisions among you, and in part I believe it. ¹⁹For there must also be factions among you, that those who are approved may be recognized among you. ²⁰Therefore when you come together in one place, it is not to eat the Lord's Supper. ²¹For in eating, each one takes his own supper ahead of *others;* and one is hungry and another is drunk. ²²What! Do you not have houses to eat and drink in? Or do you despise the church of God and shame those who have nothing? What shall I say to you? Shall I praise you in this? I do not praise *you.*

INSTITUTION OF THE LORD'S SUPPER

²³For I received from the Lord that which I also delivered to you: that the Lord Jesus on the *same* night in which He was betrayed took bread; ²⁴and when He had given thanks, He broke *it* and said, "Take, eat;*ᵃ* this is My body which is broken*ᵇ* for you; do this in remembrance of Me." ²⁵In the same manner He also *took* the cup after supper, saying, "This cup is the new covenant in My blood. This do, as often as you drink *it,* in remembrance of Me."

²⁶For as often as you eat this bread and drink this cup, you proclaim the Lord's death till He comes.

EXAMINE YOURSELF

²⁷Therefore whoever eats this bread or drinks *this* cup of the Lord in an unworthy manner will be guilty of the body and blood*ᵃ* of the Lord. ²⁸But let a man examine himself, and so let him eat of the bread and drink of the cup. ²⁹For he who eats and drinks in an unworthy manner*ᵃ* eats and drinks judgment to himself, not discerning the Lord's*ᵇ* body. ³⁰For this reason many *are* weak and sick among you, and many sleep. ³¹For if we would judge ourselves, we would not be judged. ³²But when we are judged, we are chastened by the Lord, that we may not be condemned with the world.

³³Therefore, my brethren, when you come together to eat, wait for one another. ³⁴But if anyone is hungry, let him eat at home, lest you come together for judgment. And the rest I will set in order when I come.

SPIRITUAL GIFTS: UNITY IN DIVERSITY

12 Now concerning spiritual *gifts,* brethren, I do not want you to be ignorant: ²You know that*ᵃ* you were Gentiles, carried away to these dumb idols, however you were led. ³Therefore I make known to you that no one speaking by the Spirit of God calls Jesus accursed, and no one can say that Jesus is Lord except by the Holy Spirit.

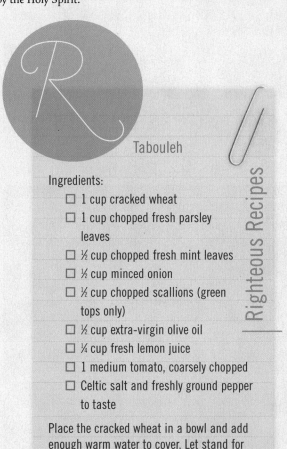

Righteous Recipes

Tabouleh

Ingredients:
☐ 1 cup cracked wheat
☐ 1 cup chopped fresh parsley leaves
☐ ½ cup chopped fresh mint leaves
☐ ½ cup minced onion
☐ ½ cup chopped scallions (green tops only)
☐ ½ cup extra-virgin olive oil
☐ ¼ cup fresh lemon juice
☐ 1 medium tomato, coarsely chopped
☐ Celtic salt and freshly ground pepper to taste

Place the cracked wheat in a bowl and add enough warm water to cover. Let stand for 1 hour (it will expand greatly). Drain and press out the excess water. Place the soaked wheat, parsley, mint, onion, scallions, olive oil, lemon juice, tomato, salt, and pepper in a bowl and toss to combine. Cover and chill for at least one hour.

Yield: 6 servings

Note: Tabouleh in the Middle East has a much higher percentage of Italian parsley than this recipe, and also more tomatoes. Middle-Eastern tabouleh has very little grain.

11:15 ᵃM-Text omits *to her.*   **11:24** ᵃNU-Text omits *Take, eat.*   ᵇNU-Text omits *broken.*   **11:27** ᵃNU-Text and M-Text read *the blood.*   **11:29** ᵃNU-Text omits *in an unworthy manner.*   ᵇNU-Text omits *Lord's.*   **12:2** ᵃNU-Text and M-Text add *when.*

Stress Busters

Get Off the Do-More, Have-More Treadmill

Countless people today are on a "do-more so I can have-more" treadmill. The more some people have, the more they want, and therefore, the more they "do" so they can have their desires. It's a no-win uphill climb because people who are afflicted with this type of greed *never* have enough, and therefore, they *never* feel they are doing enough.

God's Word tells us, "Do not love the world or the things in the world. If anyone loves the world, the love of the Father is not in him" (1 John 2:15). We need to recognize that everything we "own" really owns us. The more things we own, the more time and energy they consume. Everything we own needs maintenance of some kind. The same is true for relationships. Every good relationship needs time and nurture to maintain a flow of friendship and love. Make wise and thoughtful decisions about what you choose to purchase, and which relationships you seek to add to your life.

Also recognize that you can never truly own anything apart from your integrity and beliefs. We are guests on this earth, and stewards of it while we are here. The only thing we take from this life is our relationship with God. If we don't have a relationship with Him, we have nothing to take with us as we leave this life! Choose to invest your time in influencing and loving people.

There's an old adage that continues to ring true: Love people and use things. Never allow yourself to fall into a pattern of loving things and using people!

⁴There are diversities of gifts, but the same Spirit. ⁵There are differences of ministries, but the same Lord. ⁶And there are diversities of activities, but it is the same God who works all in all. ⁷But the manifestation of the Spirit is given to each one for the profit *of all:* ⁸for to one is given the word of wisdom through the Spirit, to another the word of knowledge through the same Spirit, ⁹to another faith by the same Spirit, to another gifts of healings by the same" Spirit, ¹⁰to another the working of miracles, to another prophecy, to another discerning of spirits, to another *different* kinds of tongues, to another the interpretation of tongues. ¹¹But one and the same Spirit works all these things, distributing to each one individually as He wills.

UNITY AND DIVERSITY IN ONE BODY

¹²For as the body is one and has many members, but all the members of that one body, being many, are one body, so also *is* Christ. ¹³For by one Spirit we were all baptized into one body—whether Jews or Greeks, whether slaves or free—and have all been made to drink into" one Spirit. ¹⁴For in fact the body is not one member but many.

¹⁵If the foot should say, "Because I am not a hand, I am not of the body," is it therefore not of the body? ¹⁶And if the ear should say, "Because I am not an eye, I am not of the body," is it therefore not of the body? ¹⁷If the whole body *were* an eye, where *would be* the hearing? If the whole *were* hearing, where *would be* the smelling? ¹⁸But now God has set the members, each one of them, in the body just as He pleased. ¹⁹And if they were all one member, where *would* the body *be?*

²⁰But now indeed *there are* many members, yet one body. ²¹And the eye cannot say to the hand, "I have no need of you"; nor again the head to the feet, "I have no need of you." ²²No, much rather, those members of the body which seem to be weaker are necessary. ²³And those *members* of the body which we think to be less honorable, on these we bestow greater honor; and our unpresentable *parts* have greater modesty, ²⁴but our presentable *parts* have no need. But God composed the body, having given greater honor to that *part* which lacks it, ²⁵that there should be no schism in the body, but *that* the members should have the same care for one another. ²⁶And if one member suffers, all the members suffer with *it;* or if one member is honored, all the members rejoice with *it.*

²⁷Now you are the body of Christ, and members individually. ²⁸And God has appointed these in the church: first apostles, second prophets, third teachers, after that miracles, then gifts of healings, helps, administrations, varieties of tongues. ²⁹*Are* all apostles? *Are* all prophets? *Are* all teachers? *Are* all workers of miracles? ³⁰Do all have gifts of healings? Do all speak with tongues? Do all interpret? ³¹But earnestly desire the best" gifts. And yet I show you a more excellent way.

THE GREATEST GIFT

13 Though I speak with the tongues of men and of angels, but have not love, I have become sounding brass or a clanging cymbal. ²And though I have *the gift of* prophecy, and understand all mysteries and all knowledge, and though I have all faith, so that I could remove mountains, but have not love, I am nothing. ³And though I bestow all my goods to feed *the poor,* and though I give my body to be burned," but have not love, it profits me nothing.

12:9 "NU-Text reads *one.*   12:13 "NU-Text omits *into.*   12:31 "NU-Text reads *greater.*   13:3 "NU-Text reads *so I may boast.*

July

| 1 | 2 | 3 | 4 | 5 | 6 | 7 |

Let's Celebrate

☐ **The Fourth of July**—the "birthday" of the United States. Celebrate the freedoms advocated by the Founding Fathers, especially the freedom to choose a religious affiliation, to assemble together with other believers, and to speak openly about one's faith.

Seasonal Tips

| 8 | 9 | 10 | 11 | 12 | 13 | 14 |

☐ Guard against mosquito and tick bites. Both can carry dangerous diseases—mosquitoes are carriers of the West Nile virus and ticks carry Rocky Mountain spotted fever and Lyme disease. ☐ If a sign or lifeguard says "no swimming"—heed the warning! Never dive into waters where you cannot see the bottom clearly. Never leave children unattended around any body of water, no matter how shallow. ☐ Do not allow young children to have access to firecrackers or other fireworks! Even sparklers have the potential to badly burn a child.

In the Garden

| 15 | 16 | 17 | 18 | 19 | 20 | 21 |

☐ Keep dead blossoms plucked from annuals such as petunias to keep the plants blooming all summer. ☐ Pick produce as it ripens—don't let vegetables or fruit rot on the vine or fall from the tree. Decaying produce attracts undesirable rodents and insects. ☐ Pick and replant—a number of vegetables can have more than one "season" of growth in a garden. Lettuce is a good example. Continue to plant lettuce so you might enjoy a continual harvest of lettuce. Plant a variety of greens.

Table Fresh

| 22 | 23 | 24 | 25 | 26 | 27 | 28 |

☐ Peaches should be in abundance. Slice them over bran cereal for breakfast, serve them with a salad for lunch, grill them as a side dish for dinner, and enjoy them fresh as a snack at any time. ☐ It's melon season! Enjoy a wide variety of melons, especially vine-ripened watermelon. A scoop of fat-free frozen vanilla yogurt in half of a cantaloupe is a great summer dessert—so is a small chunk of feta cheese served with a slice of cantaloupe.

| 29 | 30 | 31 |

Now Is the Time To...

☐ Guard against sunburn. Sunburned skin has been correlated to skin cancer later in life, including deadly melanomas. Use a sunscreen designated as SPF 30 or higher and continue to apply sunscreen every hour or so when you are at the beach, by the pool, or working outside. ☐ Wear sunglasses that do not allow ultraviolet (UV) rays to pass through and burn the eyes.

WWJE?

[BREAD]

[WHAT WOULD JESUS EAT]

Bread is universally considered to be the staple of life. It certainly was the cornerstone of life for the Israelites and for Jesus in His day. A loaf of bread in Jesus' time, however, was not the baker's loaf we find in our grocery stores. Bread was baked on large, flat rocks—the dough was stretched and twirled in a circular fashion to make a large, flat circle. The resulting loaf was larger than a pancake but thin, like paper. The pita bread of today is a modern version of these loaves. Each person ate one to three loaves of bread at each meal during Bible times.

Bread in Bible times was made with barley or wheat. Wheat was considered the "king of grains" and was used as a measure of wealth. A family that had wheat bread was considered to be a fairly high-class family.

Wheat flour, of course, was *whole-wheat* flour in Jesus' day. Wheat germ is high in B vitamins, iron, magnesium, zinc, chromium, manganese, and vitamin E. Just a quarter of a cup of wheat germ has five grams of fiber.

Wheat bran's high-fiber content is one of the best-known dietary sources of insoluble fiber. It helps protect against and cure constipation, intestinal infections, hemorrhoids, varicose veins, and helps guard against colon cancer. A healthy amount of wheat bran is one to two heaping tablespoons per day.

Jesus referred to bread in a number of His teachings and regarded bread as a good gift. (See Matthew 7:7–11 and John 6:48–51.)

Bread was usually made with a leavening agent. The Feast of Unleavened Bread which lasted for seven days—also known as Passover—was a feast marked by the consumption of lamb, bitter herbs, and unleavened bread. (See Exodus 12.) When the Israelites left Egypt they took batches of unleavened dough with them, "having their kneading bowls bound up in their clothes on their shoulders" (Exodus 12:34). Their provision as they traveled to and through the Red Sea included unleavened bread baked from these batches of dough.

In the Bible, leaven is referred to in both good and bad ways. Jesus warned His followers to beware of the "leaven," or teachings, of the Pharisees and Sadducees (religious leaders in Jesus' day). On another occasion, however, Jesus said, "The kingdom of heaven is like leaven" (Matthew 13:33). Jesus didn't have anything against yeast bread—most of the bread Jesus consumed had leavening. After Jesus rose from the dead, He joined His disciples by the Sea of Galilee for a breakfast of bread and fish (John 21:9–13).

4Love suffers long *and* is kind; love does not envy; love does not parade itself, is not puffed up; 5does not behave rudely, does not seek its own, is not provoked, thinks no evil; 6does not rejoice in iniquity, but rejoices in the truth; 7bears all things, believes all things, hopes all things, endures all things.

8Love never fails. But whether *there are* prophecies, they will fail; whether *there are* tongues, they will cease; whether *there is* knowledge, it will vanish away. 9For we know in part and we prophesy in part. 10But when that which is perfect has come, then that which is in part will be done away.

11When I was a child, I spoke as a child, I understood as a child, I thought as a child; but when I became a man, I put away childish things. 12For now we see in a mirror, dimly, but then face to face. Now I know in part, but then I shall know just as I also am known.

13And now abide faith, hope, love, these three; but the greatest of these *is* love.

PROPHECY AND TONGUES

14 Pursue love, and desire spiritual *gifts*, but especially that you may prophesy. 2For he who speaks in a tongue does not speak to men but to God, for no one understands *him;* however, in the spirit he speaks mysteries. 3But he who prophesies speaks edification and exhortation and comfort to men. 4He who speaks in a tongue edifies himself, but he who prophesies edifies the church. 5I wish you all spoke with tongues, but even more that you prophesied; fora he who prophesies *is* greater than

14:5 aNU-Text reads *and.*

he who speaks with tongues, unless indeed he interprets, that the church may receive edification.

TONGUES MUST BE INTERPRETED

6But now, brethren, if I come to you speaking with tongues, what shall I profit you unless I speak to you either by revelation, by knowledge, by prophesying, or by teaching? 7Even things without life, whether flute or harp, when they make a sound, unless they make a distinction in the sounds, how will it be known what is piped or played? 8For if the trumpet makes an uncertain sound, who will prepare for battle? 9So likewise you, unless you utter by the tongue words easy to understand, how will it be known what is spoken? For you will be speaking into the air. 10There are, it may be, so many kinds of languages in the world, and none of them *is* without significance. 11Therefore, if I do not know the meaning of the language, I shall be a foreigner to him who speaks, and he who speaks *will be* a foreigner to me. 12Even so you, since you are zealous for spiritual *gifts, let it be* for the edification of the church *that* you seek to excel.

13Therefore let him who speaks in a tongue pray that he may interpret. 14For if I pray in a tongue, my spirit prays, but my understanding is unfruitful. 15What is *the conclusion* then? I will pray with the spirit, and I will also pray with the understanding. I will sing with the spirit, and I will also sing with the understanding. 16Otherwise, if you bless with the spirit, how will he who occupies the place of the uninformed say "Amen" at your giving of thanks, since he does not understand what you say? 17For you indeed give thanks well, but the other is not edified.

18I thank my God I speak with tongues more than you all; 19yet in the church I would rather speak five words with my understanding, that I may teach others also, than ten thousand words in a tongue.

TONGUES A SIGN TO UNBELIEVERS

20Brethren, do not be children in understanding; however, in malice be babes, but in understanding be mature.

21In the law it is written:

"With *men* of other tongues and other lips
I will speak to this people;
And yet, for all that, they will not hear Me,"ᵃ

says the Lord.

22Therefore tongues are for a sign, not to those who believe but to unbelievers; but prophesying is not for unbelievers but for those who believe. 23Therefore if the whole church comes together in one place, and all speak with tongues, and there come in *those who are* uninformed or unbelievers, will they not say that you are out of your mind? 24But if all prophesy, and an unbeliever or an uninformed person comes in, he is convinced by all, he is convicted by all. 25And thusᵃ the secrets of his heart are revealed; and so, falling down on *his* face, he will worship God and report that God is truly among you.

The Healthy Soul
>Love

In the Bible, *love* is an action verb! In Hebrew, *ahab*, and in Greek, *agape*, *love* means going beyond mere emotion to an *expression* or an act of giving. It is to say and do what the *other* person perceives to be beneficial. True love is characterized as patient, slow to anger, kind, gentle, unselfish, truthful, honest, hopeful, encouraging, and enduring. It has no taint of envy, pride, self-centeredness, rudeness, boastfulness, arrogance, jealousy, or provocation. Love is a permanent, unconditional concern for others. It leads us to think the best of others, to rejoice in the truth, to bear all things, and to believe and hope for all the promises of God to be fulfilled in our lives.

Only the Holy Spirit can compel such godly love in a human being. It is our natural human tendency to put ourselves first and to "look out for number one." It is the Holy Spirit's work to transform us into people who put others first.

The apostle Paul taught the Corinthians that the three supreme traits in a Christian are faith, hope, and love, but that the greatest of these is love. Why? One reason is that only love extends into eternity. In heaven we will have no need for hope or faith. All that we ever hoped for will be ours, and all that we trusted God to do will be what He is fully doing for us!

Love is the character quality that will govern how we relate to others in eternity. To show godly love for other people now is a "dress rehearsal" for the way we will be living forever and ever. So, when it comes to showing God's love to other people, keep practicing!

PEACE LOVE JOY KINDNESS

ORDER IN CHURCH MEETINGS

26How is it then, brethren? Whenever you come together, each of you has a psalm, has a teaching, has a tongue, has a revelation, has an interpretation. Let all things be done for edification. 27If anyone speaks in a tongue, *let there be* two or at the most three, *each* in turn, and let one interpret. 28But if there is no interpreter, let him keep silent in church, and let him speak to himself and to God. 29Let two or three prophets speak, and let the others judge. 30But if *anything* is revealed to another who sits by, let the first keep silent. 31For you can all prophesy one by one, that all may learn and all may be encouraged. 32And the spirits of the prophets are subject to the prophets. 33For God is not *the author* of confusion but of peace, as in all the churches of the saints.

34Let yourᵃ women keep silent in the churches, for they are not

14:21 ᵃIsaiah 28:11, 12   14:25 ᵃNU-Text omits *And thus.*   14:34 ᵃNU-Text omits *your.*

GODLY & GOODLOOKIN'

How Did You Get That Great Hair?

Do you frequently have a bad hair day? Readjusting the fats in your life can help!

Seek to increase your omega-3s (good fats) and lower your omega-6s (bad fats). Avoid fats such as corn oil and margarine. Incorporate more good fats into your diet by eating the following:

☐ Salmon, tuna, mackerel, halibut, and cod
☐ Nuts
☐ Olives and olive oil
☐ Leafy green vegetables
☐ Flaxseed

Flaxseed is beneficial not only to your hair, but also to your entire body. Research studies have shown flaxseed to reduce and help prevent certain cancers. Optimal supplementation: one tablespoon of flaxseed oil twice a day, plus five teaspoons of ground flaxseed. You can grind flaxseed in a coffee grinder and add it to your protein drink or cereal. Avoid cooking flaxseed, as it will oxidize, forming a very dangerous fat.

permitted to speak; but *they are* to be submissive, as the law also says. ³⁵And if they want to learn something, let them ask their own husbands at home; for it is shameful for women to speak in church.

³⁶Or did the word of God come *originally* from you? Or *was it* you only that it reached? ³⁷If anyone thinks himself to be a prophet or spiritual, let him acknowledge that the things which I write to you are the commandments of the Lord. ³⁸But if anyone is ignorant, let him be ignorant.ᵃ

³⁹Therefore, brethren, desire earnestly to prophesy, and do not forbid to speak with tongues. ⁴⁰Let all things be done decently and in order.

THE RISEN CHRIST, FAITH'S REALITY

15 Moreover, brethren, I declare to you the gospel which I preached to you, which also you received

and in which you stand, ²by which also you are saved, if you hold fast that word which I preached to you—unless you believed in vain.

³For I delivered to you first of all that which I also received: that Christ died for our sins according to the Scriptures, ⁴and that He was buried, and that He rose again the third day according to the Scriptures, ⁵and that He was seen by Cephas, then by the twelve. ⁶After that He was seen by over five hundred brethren at once, of whom the greater part remain to the present, but some have fallen asleep. ⁷After that He was seen by James, then by all the apostles. ⁸Then last of all He was seen by me also, as by one born out of due time.

⁹For I am the least of the apostles, who am not worthy to be called an apostle, because I persecuted the church of God. ¹⁰But by the grace of God I am what I am, and His grace toward me was not in vain; but I labored more abundantly than they all, yet not I, but the grace of God *which was* with me. ¹¹There-

fore, whether *it was* I or they, so we preach and so you believed.

THE RISEN CHRIST, OUR HOPE

¹²Now if Christ is preached that He has been raised from the dead, how do some among you say that there is no resurrection of the dead? ¹³But if there is no resurrection of the dead, then Christ is not risen. ¹⁴And if Christ is not risen, then our preaching *is* empty and your faith *is* also empty. ¹⁵Yes, and we are found false witnesses of God, because we have testified of God that He raised up Christ, whom He did not raise up—if in fact the dead do not rise. ¹⁶For if *the* dead do not rise, then Christ is not risen. ¹⁷And if Christ is not risen, your faith *is* futile; you are still in your sins! ¹⁸Then also those who have fallen asleep in Christ have perished. ¹⁹If in this life only we have hope in Christ, we are of all men the most pitiable.

THE LAST ENEMY DESTROYED

²⁰But now Christ is risen from the dead, *and* has become the firstfruits of those who have fallen asleep. ²¹For since by man *came* death, by Man also *came* the resurrection of the dead. ²²For as in Adam all die, even so in Christ all shall be made alive. ²³But each one in his own order: Christ the firstfruits, afterward those *who are* Christ's at His coming. ²⁴Then *comes* the end, when He delivers the kingdom to God the Father, when He puts an end to all rule and all authority and power. ²⁵For He must reign till He has put all enemies under His feet. ²⁶The last enemy *that* will be destroyed *is* death. ²⁷For "He has put all things under His feet."ᵃ But when He says "all things are put under *Him,*" *it is* evident that He who put all things under Him is excepted. ²⁸Now when all things are made subject to Him, then the Son Himself will also be subject to Him who put all things under Him, that God may be all in all.

EFFECTS OF DENYING THE RESURRECTION

²⁹Otherwise, what will they do who are baptized for the dead, if the dead do not rise

14:38 ᵃNU-Text reads *if anyone does not recognize this, he is not recognized.* 15:27 ᵃPsalm 8:6

at all? Why then are they baptized for the dead? ³⁰And why do we stand in jeopardy every hour? ³¹I affirm, by the boasting in you which I have in Christ Jesus our Lord, I die daily. ³²If, in the manner of men, I have fought with beasts at Ephesus, what advantage *is it* to me? If *the* dead do not rise, "Let us eat and drink, for tomorrow we die!"ᵃ

³³Do not be deceived: "Evil company corrupts good habits." ³⁴Awake to righteousness, and do not sin; for some do not have the knowledge of God. I speak *this* to your shame.

A GLORIOUS BODY

³⁵But someone will say, "How are the dead raised up? And with what body do they come?" ³⁶Foolish one, what you sow is not made alive unless it dies. ³⁷And what you sow, you do not sow that body that shall be, but mere grain—perhaps wheat or some other *grain.* ³⁸But God gives it a body as He pleases, and to each seed its own body.

³⁹All flesh *is* not the same flesh, but *there is* one *kind of* fleshᵃ of men, another flesh of animals, another of fish, *and* another of birds.

⁴⁰*There are* also celestial bodies and terrestrial bodies; but the glory of the celestial *is* one, and the *glory* of the terrestrial *is* another. ⁴¹*There is* one glory of the sun, another glory of the moon, and another glory of the stars; for *one* star differs from *another* star in glory.

⁴²So also *is* the resurrection of the dead. *The body* is sown in corruption, it is raised in incorruption. ⁴³It is sown in dishonor, it is raised in glory. It is sown in weakness, it is raised in power. ⁴⁴It is sown a natural body, it is raised a spiritual body. There is a natural body, and there is a spiritual body. ⁴⁵And so it is written, "The first man Adam became a living being."ᵃ The last Adam *became* a life-giving spirit.

⁴⁶However, the spiritual is not first, but the natural, and afterward the spiritual. ⁴⁷The first man *was* of the earth, *made* of dust; the second Man *is* the Lordᵃ from heaven. ⁴⁸As *was* the *man* of dust, so also *are* those *who are made* of dust; and as *is* the heavenly *Man,* so also *are* those *who are* heavenly. ⁴⁹And as we have borne the image of the *man* of dust, we shall also bearᵃ the image of the heavenly *Man.*

OUR FINAL VICTORY

⁵⁰Now this I say, brethren, that flesh and blood cannot inherit the kingdom of God; nor does corruption inherit incorruption. ⁵¹Behold, I tell you a mystery: We shall not all sleep, but we shall all be changed— ⁵²in a moment, in the twinkling of an eye, at the last trumpet. For the trumpet will sound, and the dead will be raised incorruptible, and we shall be changed. ⁵³For this corruptible must put on incorruption, and this mortal *must* put on immortality. ⁵⁴So when this corruptible has put on incorruption, and this mortal has put on immortality, then shall be brought to pass the saying that is written: "Death is swallowed up in victory."ᵃ

⁵⁵ "O Death, where is your sting?ᵃ
   O Hades, where is your victory?"ᵇ

⁵⁶The sting of death *is* sin, and the strength of sin *is* the law. ⁵⁷But thanks *be* to God, who gives us the victory through our Lord Jesus Christ.

⁵⁸Therefore, my beloved brethren, be steadfast, immovable, always abounding in the work of the Lord, knowing that your labor is not in vain in the Lord.

COLLECTION FOR THE SAINTS

16 Now concerning the collection for the saints, as I have given orders to the churches of Galatia, so you must do also: ²On the first *day* of the week let

---

WEIGHING Less & ENJOYING LIFE MORE!

[Try a Step-Down Approach]

If you have a lot of weight to lose—such as forty or more pounds—you are going to find it difficult to move from your current calorie consumption to what would be the ideal calorie consumption for your ideal weight. You likely will become discouraged and feel so hungry that you'll be prone to binging.

Try a step-down approach.

First, determine how many calories you are currently consuming. A simple way to do this is to multiply your weight by ten. If you weigh three hundred pounds, you need 3,000 calories a day to maintain that weight.

Next, determine how many calories you will need at your desired weight. If you desire to weigh two hundred pounds, you will need only 2,000 calories a day to maintain that weight.

Rather than immediately drop your daily calorie count by a thousand calories, drop it by 200. Drop an additional 200 calories every two weeks. By the seventh week of your diet, you'll be eating 1,400 fewer calories. Also by that time, you likely will have lost at least fifteen pounds, so you'll feel as if your lower calorie count is really working for you! You'll be more motivated to continue your weight-loss plan.

15:32 ᵃIsaiah 22:13   **15:39** ᵃNU-Text and M-Text omit *of flesh.*   **15:45** ᵃGenesis 2:7   **15:47** ᵃNU-Text omits *the Lord.*   **15:49** ᵃM-Text reads *let us also bear.*   **15:54** ᵃIsaiah 25:8   **15:55** ᵃHosea 13:14
ᵇNU-Text reads *O Death, where is your victory? O Death, where is your sting?*

each one of you lay something aside, storing up as he may prosper, that there be no collections when I come. [3]And when I come, whomever you approve by *your* letters I will send to bear your gift to Jerusalem. [4]But if it is fitting that I go also, they will go with me.

PERSONAL PLANS

[5]Now I will come to you when I pass through Macedonia (for I am passing through Macedonia). [6]And it may be that I will remain, or even spend the winter with you, that you may send me on my journey, wherever I go. [7]For I do not wish to see you now on the way; but I hope to stay a while with you, if the Lord permits.

[8]But I will tarry in Ephesus until Pentecost. [9]For a great and effective door has opened to me, and *there are* many adversaries.

[10]And if Timothy comes, see that he may be with you without fear; for he does the work of the Lord, as I also *do.* [11]Therefore let no one despise him. But send him on his journey in peace, that he may come to me; for I am waiting for him with the brethren.

[12]Now concerning *our* brother Apollos, I strongly urged him to come to you with the brethren, but he was quite unwilling to come at this time; however, he will come when he has a convenient time.

FINAL EXHORTATIONS

[13]Watch, stand fast in the faith, be brave, be strong. [14]Let all *that* you do be done with love.

[15]I urge you, brethren—you know the household of Stephanas, that it is the firstfruits of Achaia, and *that* they have devoted themselves to the ministry of the saints— [16]that you also submit to such, and to everyone who works and labors with *us.*

[17]I am glad about the coming of Stephanas, Fortunatus, and Achaicus, for what was lacking on your part they supplied. [18]For they refreshed my spirit and yours. Therefore acknowledge such men.

GREETINGS AND A SOLEMN FAREWELL

[19]The churches of Asia greet you. Aquila and Priscilla greet you heartily in the Lord, with the church that is in their house. [20]All the brethren greet you.

Greet one another with a holy kiss.

[21]The salutation with my own hand— Paul's.

[22]If anyone does not love the Lord Jesus Christ, let him be accursed.[a] O Lord, come![b]

[23]The grace of our Lord Jesus Christ *be* with you. [24]My love *be* with you all in Christ Jesus. Amen.

PREACHING HEALTH

"Some people think that doctors and nurses can put scrambled eggs back into the shell."
—*Dorothy Canfield, American author (1879–1958)*

16:22 [a]Greek *anathema* [b]Aramaic *Maranatha*

HEALTH NOTES

CORINTHIANS

Between the time Paul wrote the first letter to the Corinthians and this letter to the church at Corinth, he had visited Corinth personally, and may have written another letter to the Corinthians that we do not have. The problems in the Corinthians church were deep and Paul was not seeing the results he desired! Even so, instead of becoming more strident in tone, Paul becomes more gentle. He reveals more of His personal testimony, sharing about the troubles in his life and the ways in which God had helped him to overcome difficulties and continue steadfast in the faith. He conveys from firsthand experience that repentance and reconciliation are possible.

People often don't care what you know—about any subject or topic—until they know that you care. That may have been the case in Corinth. Paul assures the Corinthians that he loves them and that he desires for them the immeasurable rewards associated with a godly life.

Do you desire for someone you love to give up a bad health habit? First let the person know how much you love him and want the highest and best for him.

GREETING

 Paul, an apostle of Jesus Christ by the will of God, and Timothy *our* brother,

To the church of God which is at Corinth, with all the saints who are in all Achaia:

²Grace to you and peace from God our Father and the Lord Jesus Christ.

COMFORT IN SUFFERING

³Blessed *be* the God and Father of our Lord Jesus Christ, the Father of mercies and God of all comfort, ⁴who comforts us in all our tribulation, that we may be able to comfort those who are in any trouble, with the comfort with which we ourselves are comforted by God. ⁵For as the sufferings of Christ abound in us, so our consolation also abounds through Christ. ⁶Now if we are afflicted, *it is* for your consolation and salvation, which is effective for enduring the same sufferings which we also suffer. Or if we are comforted, *it is* for your consolation and salvation. ⁷And our hope for you *is* steadfast, because we know that as you are partakers of the sufferings, so also *you will partake* of the consolation.

DELIVERED FROM SUFFERING

⁸For we do not want you to be ignorant, brethren, of our trouble which came to us in Asia: that we were burdened beyond measure, above strength, so that we despaired even of life. ⁹Yes, we had the sentence of death in ourselves, that we should not trust in ourselves but in God who raises the dead, ¹⁰who delivered us from so great a death, and does⁰ deliver us; in whom we trust that He will still deliver *us*, ¹¹you also helping together in prayer for us, that thanks may be given by many persons on our⁰ behalf for the gift *granted* to us through many.

PAUL'S SINCERITY

¹²For our boasting is this: the testimony of our conscience that we conducted ourselves in the world in simplicity and godly sincerity, not with fleshly wisdom but by the grace of God, and more abundantly toward you. ¹³For we are not writing any other things to you than what you read or understand. Now I trust you will understand, even to the end ¹⁴(as also you have understood us in part), that we are your boast as you also *are* ours, in the day of the Lord Jesus.

SPARING THE CHURCH

¹⁵And in this confidence I intended to come to you before, that you might have a second benefit— ¹⁶to pass by way of you to Macedonia, to come again from Macedonia to you, and be helped by you on my way to Judea. ¹⁷Therefore, when I was planning this, did I do it lightly? Or the things I plan, do I plan according to the flesh, that with me there should be Yes, Yes, and No, No? ¹⁸But *as* God *is* faithful, our word to you was not Yes and No. ¹⁹For the Son of God, Jesus Christ, who was preached among you by us—by me, Silvanus, and Timothy—was not Yes and No, but in Him was Yes. ²⁰For all the promises of God in Him *are* Yes, and in Him Amen, to the glory of God through us. ²¹Now He who establishes us with you in Christ and has anointed us *is* God, ²²who also has sealed us and given us the Spirit in our hearts as a guarantee.

1:10 ⁰NU-Text reads *shall.* 1:11 ⁰M-Text reads *your behalf.*

[23]Moreover I call God as witness against my soul, that to spare you I came no more to Corinth. [24]Not that we have dominion over your faith, but are fellow workers for your joy; for by faith you stand.

2 But I determined this within myself, that I would not come again to you in sorrow. [2]For if I make you sorrowful, then who is he who makes me glad but the one who is made sorrowful by me?

FORGIVE THE OFFENDER

[3]And I wrote this very thing to you, lest, when I came, I should have sorrow over those from whom I ought to have joy, having confidence in you all that my joy is *the joy* of you all. [4]For out of much affliction and anguish of heart I wrote to you, with many tears, not that you should be grieved, but that you might know the love which I have so abundantly for you.

[5]But if anyone has caused grief, he has not grieved me, but all of you to some extent—not to be too severe. [6]This punishment which *was inflicted* by the majority *is* sufficient for such a man, [7]so that, on the contrary, you *ought* rather to forgive and comfort *him,* lest perhaps such a one be swallowed up with too much sorrow. [8]Therefore I urge you to reaffirm *your* love to him. [9]For to this end I also wrote, that I might put you to the test, whether you are obedient in all things. [10]Now whom you forgive anything, I also *forgive.* For if indeed I have forgiven anything, I have forgiven that one[a] for your sakes in the presence of Christ, [11]lest Satan should take advantage of us; for we are not ignorant of his devices.

TRIUMPH IN CHRIST

[12]Furthermore, when I came to Troas to *preach* Christ's gospel, and a door was opened to me by the Lord, [13]I had no rest in my spirit, because I did not find Titus my brother; but taking my leave of them, I departed for Macedonia.

[14]Now thanks *be* to God who always leads us in triumph in Christ, and through us diffuses the fragrance of His knowledge in every place. [15]For we are to God the fragrance of Christ among those who are being saved and among those who are perishing. [16]To the one *we are* the aroma of death *leading* to death, and to the other the aroma of life lead-

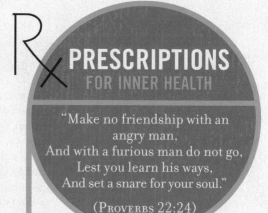

R PRESCRIPTIONS
FOR INNER HEALTH

"Make no friendship with an angry man,
And with a furious man do not go,
Lest you learn his ways,
And set a snare for your soul."
(PROVERBS 22:24)

Anger is one of the most damaging emotions a person can experience—not only in the context of relationships with other people, but also physically. Anger causes dangerous stress hormones to be released into the bloodstream, and over time, a steady release of these hormones can do great damage to the human body.

ing to life. And who *is* sufficient for these things? [17]For we are not, as so many,[a] peddling the word of God; but as of sincerity, but as from God, we speak in the sight of God in Christ.

CHRIST'S EPISTLE

3 Do we begin again to commend ourselves? Or do we need, as some *others,* epistles of commendation to you or *letters* of commendation from you? [2]You are our epistle written in our

INSIGHTS INTO THE WORD

> (2 Corinthians 2:7, 8, 10)

An End to Revenge. In just a few sentences, the apostle Paul gave the cure for revenge to the Corinthians: forgive, comfort, reaffirm love—and don't take on the unforgiving attitudes of others! So many family, community, and even national and international conflicts could be resolved if people would only choose to forgive; to refuse to take on the vengeful thinking and attitude of others they admire or with whom they are affiliated. An endless cycle of unforgiveness, hatred, bitterness, and revenge is what leads to family feuds, tribal warfare, international conflicts, and many acts of terrorism.

Instead of agreeing with those who are unforgiving, helping them to justify their attitude, or approving of their behavior, we need to be encouraging other people to forgive—to let go of their pain and trust God to deal with the offender rather than trying to engineer personal justice for an offense. If the offender is truly repentant, we certainly need to reach out to the person with godly comfort and love—in an appropriate manner.

2:10 [a]NU-Text reads *For indeed, what I have forgiven, if I have forgiven anything, I did it.*   2:17 [a]M-Text reads *the rest.*

OVERCOMING OBSTINATE OBSTACLES • OVERCOMING OBSTINATE OBSTACLES • OVERCOMING OBSTINATE OBSTACLES •

Overcoming Resentment and Bitterness

Resentment and bitterness are strongly linked to anger. They are the smoldering, lingering ashes of rage and hostility. Medical research is showing that a number of diseases seem to correlate with high levels of resentment and bitterness, including rheumatoid arthritis, multiple sclerosis, Hashimoto thyroiditis, psoriasis, and type 1 diabetes, and perhaps even lupus, ulcerative colitis, and Crohn's disease. That does not mean that people with these diseases are filled with resentment and bitterness—it means that people filled with resentment and bitterness may be at higher risk for these diseases.

Resentment and bitterness begin when a person holds a grievance and refuses to let it go. A grievance is any circumstance or complaint that a person considers to be unjust or hurtful. It can be real or imagined. The person may be taking a grievance too personally, blaming an offender for how he or she feels, or creating a "grievance story" that he or she tells repeatedly. The endless loop of grievance stories can actually cause a depressed immune response in the body, which increases the risk of a person for autoimmune diseases.

If you are harboring resentment and bitterness, consider the following:

☐ Move into *forgiveness*. Quit playing the "blame game"—stop blaming other people and stop blaming God. Begin to trust God even in your pain and start taking life as it is, not as you wish it could be or think it ought to be.

☐ Stop comparing yourself to others or dwelling on what you think *you* deserve. Resentment is linked many times to jealousy. Keep your eyes on your own abilities, the development of your own talents, and the blessings God has given you. Trust God to meet *your* needs.

☐ Take a positive step by reaching out to someone who has a genuine need or is hurting. Give to that person in helpful ways without bringing up your own needs or hurts.

hearts, known and read by all men; ³clearly you are an epistle of Christ, ministered by us, written not with ink but by the Spirit of the living God, not on tablets of stone but on tablets of flesh, *that is,* of the heart.

THE SPIRIT, NOT THE LETTER

⁴And we have such trust through Christ toward God. ⁵Not that we are sufficient of ourselves to think of anything as *being* from ourselves, but our sufficiency *is* from God, ⁶who also made us sufficient as ministers of the new covenant, not of the letter but of the Spirit;ᵃ for the letter kills, but the Spirit gives life.

GLORY OF THE NEW COVENANT

⁷But if the ministry of death, written *and* engraved on stones, was glorious, so that the children of Israel could not look steadily at the face of Moses because of the glory of his countenance, which *glory* was passing away, ⁸how will the ministry of the Spirit not be more glorious? ⁹For if the ministry of condemnation *had* glory, the ministry of righteousness exceeds much more in glory. ¹⁰For even what was made glorious had no glory in this respect, because of the glory that excels. ¹¹For if what is passing away *was* glorious, what remains *is* much more glorious.

¹²Therefore, since we have such hope, we use great boldness of speech— ¹³unlike Moses, *who* put a veil over his face so that the children of Israel could not look steadily at the end of what was passing away. ¹⁴But their minds were blinded. For until this day the same veil remains unlifted in the reading of the Old Testament, because the *veil* is taken away in Christ. ¹⁵But even to this day, when Moses is read, a veil lies on their heart. ¹⁶Nevertheless when one turns to the Lord, the veil is taken away. ¹⁷Now the Lord is the Spirit; and where the Spirit of the Lord *is,* there *is* liberty. ¹⁸But we all, with unveiled face, beholding as in a mirror the glory of the Lord, are being transformed into the same image from glory to glory, just as by the Spirit of the Lord.

FACT MORSELS

[ALLERGIES AND CHEMICALS]

Question: Which of these have been linked in scientific research studies to allergies? Artificial coloring, artificial flavoring, artificial sweeteners, MSG, preservatives, sulfites.
Answer: All of them.

WHOLENESS 101

Salting the Earth

Jesus told His followers that they were the "salt of the earth" (Matthew 5:13). The properties of salt have a direct spiritual analogy.

☐ *Salt flavors.* Salt enhances or "brings out" the flavor in many foods, especially as they are cooked. As the "salt of the earth," Christians can help others discover and then share with the world their innermost God-given traits.

☐ *Salt cleanses and heals.* It especially guards wounds against infection. Jesus called His followers to promote the physical, mental, and spiritual healing of those who were hurting. Just as salt sometimes stings when it gets into a cut, so the truth sometimes stings those who need to hear it, even when the truth is spoken from a motive of love and genuine concern.

☐ *Salt nourishes the body.* It is one of many nutrients required by our bodies to stay healthy.

Too much salt, of course, can damage health. Just the right amount is required. The followers of Jesus were admonished to bring balance and equilibrium to a world in need of love, compassion, and spiritual nourishment.

☐ *Salt preserves.* In ancient times, many foods were wrapped in cakes of salt to preserve them in the desert climate of Israel. Jesus called His followers to preserve and safeguard the truths of God.

Most people in the United States consume too much salt (sodium) and far too little potassium. Salt needs to be taken in small quantities, and balanced with other nutrients. Too much salt can make a dish inedible! The spiritual analogy should not be overlooked. We sometimes need to properly balance our "saltiness" with compassion before we try to influence others.

There's an old saying that Christians are meant to be the "salt lick in the pasture of life." They are to make others thirsty to experience the "living water" offered by Jesus Christ.

THE LIGHT OF CHRIST'S GOSPEL

4 Therefore, since we have this ministry, as we have received mercy, we do not lose heart. [2]But we have renounced the hidden things of shame, not walking in craftiness nor handling the word of God deceitfully, but by manifestation of the truth commending ourselves to every man's conscience in the sight of God. [3]But even if our gospel is veiled, it is veiled to those who are perishing, [4]whose minds the god of this age has blinded, who do not believe, lest the light of the gospel of the glory of Christ, who is the image of God, should shine on them. [5]For we do not preach ourselves, but Christ Jesus the Lord, and ourselves your bondservants for Jesus' sake. [6]For it is the God who commanded light to shine out of darkness, who has shone in our hearts to *give* the light of the knowledge of the glory of God in the face of Jesus Christ.

Q Who in the Bible was so tired that he sold his birthright for a bowl of lentil stew?

A Esau, firstborn son of Isaac and Rebekah *(Genesis 25:29–34).*

CAST DOWN BUT UNCONQUERED

[7]But we have this treasure in earthen vessels, that the excellence of the power may be of God and not of us. [8]*We are* hard-pressed on every side, yet not crushed; *we are* perplexed, but not in despair; [9]persecuted, but not forsaken; struck down, but not destroyed— [10]always carrying about in the body the dying of the Lord Jesus, that the life of Jesus also may be manifested in our body. [11]For we who live are always delivered to death for Jesus' sake, that the life of Jesus also may be manifested in our mortal flesh. [12]So then death is working in us, but life in you.

[13]And since we have the same spirit of faith, according to what is written, "I believed and therefore I spoke," [a] we also believe and therefore speak, [14]knowing that He who raised up the Lord Jesus will also raise us up with Jesus, and will present *us* with you. [15]For all things *are* for your sakes, that grace, having spread through the many, may cause thanksgiving to abound to the glory of God.

SEEING THE INVISIBLE

[16]Therefore we do not lose heart. Even though our outward man is perishing, yet the inward *man* is being renewed day by day. [17]For our light affliction, which is but for a moment, is working for us a far more exceeding *and* eternal weight of glory, [18]while we do not look at the things which are seen, but at the things which are not seen. For the things which are seen *are* temporary, but the things which are not seen *are* eternal.

4:13 [a]Psalm 116:10

ASSURANCE OF THE RESURRECTION

5 For we know that if our earthly house, *this* tent, is destroyed, we have a building from God, a house not made with hands, eternal in the heavens. ²For in this we groan, earnestly desiring to be clothed with our habitation which is from heaven, ³if indeed, having been clothed, we shall not be found naked. ⁴For we who are in *this* tent groan, being burdened, not because we want to be unclothed, but further clothed, that mortality may be swallowed up by life. ⁵Now He who has prepared us for this very thing *is* God, who also has given us the Spirit as a guarantee.

⁶So *we are* always confident, knowing that while we are at home in the body we are absent from the Lord. ⁷For we walk by faith, not by sight. ⁸We are confident, yes, well pleased rather to be absent from the body and to be present with the Lord.

THE JUDGMENT SEAT OF CHRIST

⁹Therefore we make it our aim, whether present or absent, to be well pleasing to Him. ¹⁰For we must all appear before the judgment seat of Christ, that each one may receive the things *done* in the body, according to what he has done, whether good or bad. ¹¹Knowing, therefore, the terror of the Lord, we persuade men; but we are well known to God, and I also trust are well known in your consciences.

BE RECONCILED TO GOD

¹²For we do not commend ourselves again to you, but give you opportunity to boast on our behalf, that you may have *an answer* for those who boast in appearance and not in heart. ¹³For if we are beside ourselves, *it is* for God; or if we are of sound mind, *it is* for you. ¹⁴For the love of Christ compels us, because we judge thus: that if One died for all, then all died; ¹⁵and He died for all, that those who live should live no longer for themselves, but for Him who died for them and rose again.

¹⁶Therefore, from now on, we regard no one according to the flesh. Even though we have known Christ according to the flesh, yet now we know *Him thus* no longer. ¹⁷Therefore, if anyone *is* in Christ, *he is* a new creation; old things have passed away; behold, all things have become new. ¹⁸Now all things *are* of God, who has reconciled us to Himself through Jesus Christ, and has given us the ministry of reconciliation, ¹⁹that is, that God was in Christ reconciling the world to Himself, not imputing their trespasses to them, and has committed to us the word of reconciliation.

²⁰Now then, we are ambassadors for Christ, as though God were pleading through us: we implore *you* on Christ's behalf, be reconciled to God. ²¹For He made Him who knew no sin *to be* sin for us, that we might become the righteousness of God in Him.

MARKS OF THE MINISTRY

6 We then, *as* workers together *with Him* also plead with *you* not to receive the grace of God in vain. ²For He says:

"In an acceptable time I have heard you,
And in the day of salvation I have helped you."ᵃ

SCRIPTURE SOLUTIONS

[DIABETES]

More than fifteen million people in the United States now have diabetes, which is the fourth major cause of death by illness in our nation. Millions more likely have the disease and are unaware of it.

Type 1 diabetes usually strikes in childhood and accounts for 10 to 20 percent of all patients. It requires regular insulin by injection or insulin pump. Type 2 diabetes is noninsulin dependent and it normally strikes adults. It occurs when the pancreas makes enough insulin but the body cannot use it. Type 2 diabetes can often be corrected and managed with a proper diet and nutrition.

If you have type 2 diabetes, you can greatly assist your recovery by decreasing the amounts of high-glycemic starches in your diet. These starches are found in bread, potatoes, corn, and white rice. Lower your intake of fats, including saturated fats and fried foods. At the same time, increase your fiber intake, especially water-soluble fibers.

In addition to making these nutritional changes, a good walking program can help greatly. Try to walk thirty to forty minutes a day.

Behold, now *is* the accepted time; behold, now *is* the day of salvation. ³We give no offense in anything, that our ministry may not be blamed. ⁴But in all *things* we commend ourselves as ministers of God: in much patience, in tribulations, in needs, in distresses, ⁵in stripes, in imprisonments, in tumults, in labors, in sleeplessness, in fastings; ⁶by purity, by knowledge, by longsuffering, by kindness, by the Holy Spirit, by sincere love, ⁷by the word of truth, by the power of God, by the armor of righteousness on the right hand and on the left, ⁸by honor and dishonor, by evil report and good report; as deceivers, and *yet* true; ⁹as unknown, and *yet* well known; as dying, and behold we live; as chastened, and *yet* not killed; ¹⁰as sorrowful, yet always rejoicing; as poor, yet

6:2 ᵃIsaiah 49:8

ULTIMATE HEALTH RESOURCE • ULTIMATE HEALTH RESOURCE • ULTIMATE HEALTH RESOURCE

Gluttony is usually associated with excessive eating and drinking, or with a ravenous, nearly unstoppable appetite. It involves a "greediness" for food—there's never enough to satisfy. However, gluttony from a biblical standpoint is not simply a matter of quantity. It also involves eating the *wrong* foods. Specifically, gluttony for the Israelites was associated with eating forbidden foods. Some of those forbidden foods were the meat and delicacies called "deceptive food." (See Proverbs 23:1–3, 20, 21.) These were foods rich in fat, including fatty meat.

Gluttony was associated with being undisciplined—being disobedient, stubborn, and rebellious. Those who were called gluttons were associated with being lazy, out of control, and without generosity toward others. They were said to bring poverty to themselves and shame to others. (See Proverbs 28:7.)

It is amazing that gluttony seems to be smiled on in our culture today! We love the supersizing of portions at fast-food restaurants that serve fat-laden foods. We love the "platters" of food served as individual portions in many restaurants. We love huge muffins and extra-rich donuts. We choose coffee beverages loaded with cream or ice cream. Sadly, we are a culture of people "given to appetite," as Solomon said in the Book of Proverbs (Proverbs 23:2).

The Bible calls upon God's people to use their bodies to bring glory to God. It calls upon believers to live disciplined lives. Gluttony may be one of the most difficult challenges we face in our society today. But it's a challenge we must face if we are to live long and healthy lives.

making many rich; as having nothing, and *yet* possessing all things.

BE HOLY

[11]O Corinthians! We have spoken openly to you, our heart is wide open. [12]You are not restricted by us, but you are restricted by your *own* affections. [13]Now in return for the same (I speak as to children), you also be open.

[14]Do not be unequally yoked together with unbelievers. For what fellowship has righteousness with lawlessness? And what communion has light with darkness? [15]And what accord has Christ with Belial? Or what part has a believer with an unbeliever? [16]And what agreement has the temple of God with idols? For you[a] are the temple of the living God. As God has said:

"I will dwell in them
And walk among *them.*
I will be their God,
And they shall be My people."[b]

[17]Therefore

"Come out from among them
And be separate, says the Lord.
Do not touch what is unclean,
And I will receive you."[a]
[18] "I will be a Father to you,
And you shall be My sons and daughters,
Says the LORD Almighty."[a]

7 Therefore, having these promises, beloved, let us cleanse ourselves from all filthiness of the flesh and spirit, perfecting holiness in the fear of God.

THE CORINTHIANS' REPENTANCE

[2]Open *your hearts* to us. We have wronged no one, we have corrupted no one, we have cheated no one. [3]I do not say *this* to condemn; for I have said before that you are in our hearts, to die together and to live together. [4]Great *is* my boldness of speech toward you, great *is* my boasting on your behalf. I am filled with comfort. I am exceedingly joyful in all our tribulation.

[5]For indeed, when we came to Macedonia, our bodies had no rest, but we were troubled on every side. Outside *were* conflicts, inside *were* fears. [6]Nevertheless God, who comforts the downcast, comforted us by the coming of Titus, [7]and not only by his coming, but also by the consolation with which he was comforted in you, when he told us of your earnest desire, your mourning, your zeal for me, so that I rejoiced even more.

[8]For even if I made you sorry with my letter, I do not regret it; though I did regret it. For I perceive that the same epistle made you sorry, though only for a while. [9]Now I rejoice, not that you were made sorry, but that your sorrow led to repentance. For you were made sorry in a godly manner, that you might suffer loss from us in nothing. [10]For godly sorrow produces repentance *leading* to salvation, not to be regretted; but the sorrow of the world produces death. [11]For observe this very thing, that you sorrowed in a godly manner: What diligence it produced in you, *what* clearing *of yourselves, what* indignation, *what* fear, *what* vehement desire, *what* zeal, *what* vindication! In all *things* you proved yourselves to be clear in this matter. [12]Therefore, although I wrote to you, *I did* not *do it* for the sake of him who

6:16 [a]NU-Text reads *we.* [b]Leviticus 26:12; Jeremiah 32:38; Ezekiel 37:27   6:17 [a]Isaiah 52:11; Ezekiel 20:34, 41   6:18 [a]2 Samuel 7:14

had done the wrong, nor for the sake of him who suffered wrong, but that our care for you in the sight of God might appear to you.

THE JOY OF TITUS

[13]Therefore we have been comforted in your comfort. And we rejoiced exceedingly more for the joy of Titus, because his spirit has been refreshed by you all. [14]For if in anything I have boasted to him about you, I am not ashamed. But as we spoke all things to you in truth, even so our boasting to Titus was found true. [15]And his affections are greater for you as he remembers the obedience of you all, how with fear and trembling you received him. [16]Therefore I rejoice that I have confidence in you in everything.

EXCEL IN GIVING

8 Moreover, brethren, we make known to you the grace of God bestowed on the churches of Macedonia: [2]that in a great trial of affliction the abundance of their joy and their deep poverty abounded in the riches of their liberality. [3]For I bear witness that according to *their* ability, yes, and beyond *their* ability, *they were* freely willing, [4]imploring us with much urgency that we would receive[a] the gift and the fellowship of the ministering to the saints. [5]And not *only* as we had hoped, but they first gave themselves to the Lord, and *then* to us by the will of God. [6]So we urged Titus, that as he had begun, so he would also complete this grace in you as well. [7]But as you abound in everything—in faith, in speech, in knowledge, in all diligence, and in your love for us—*see* that you abound in this grace also.

CHRIST OUR PATTERN

[8]I speak not by commandment, but I am testing the sincerity of your love by

WISE CHOICES

Choose locally grown organic produce.
In choosing locally grown organic produce whenever possible, you will not only avoid pesticides and fungicides, but you will probably find the produce more flavorful. Why? There's a greater likelihood the produce was picked when it was ripe. Aim for the shortest possible time between the time ripe produce is picked and the time you eat it!

The Healthy Soul
>Faithfulness

To be faithful is to "do the right thing" and "believe the right things" with tenacity. It is to keep on being faithful to God—*no matter what!*

Faithfulness is closely linked to commitment. Those who are faithful stand by the vows they have made. They choose to remain in the relationships, earthly or heavenly, in which a covenant has been established. They have a heart that is "bonded" with permanency.

Faithfulness, like all of the soul fruit, is rooted in a choice. A person must *choose* to be faithful to follow Jesus in good times and bad, easy times and not-so-easy times, in the presence of wonderful saints and horrible sinners.

There is also an element of exclusivity to faithfulness. A person cannot be faithful to God and to the world at the same time. A person cannot be faithful to a spouse and entertain romantic notions about other people. A person cannot be faithful to Jesus and openly embrace all other religions as equal pathways of salvation. To be faithful is to be unwavering in loyalty.

Faithfulness is the ongoing choice to remain in a committed relationship.

Faithfulness is a highly desirable quality, but the Bible gives a strong warning about choosing carefully those to whom we make vows and commitments, and those to whom we are faithful. We are *not* to be yoked with unbelievers (2 Corinthians 6:14).

The more you are faithful in your walk with the Lord, the more your faith is built up and your character becomes more Christlike. Faithfulness requires time, work, and determination. It is not just a matter of being faithful today, but being faithful in all the tomorrows of a lifetime.

the diligence of others. [9]For you know the grace of our Lord Jesus Christ, that though He was rich, yet for your sakes He became poor, that you through His poverty might become rich.

[10]And in this I give advice: It is to your advantage not only to be doing what you began and were desiring to do a year ago; [11]but now you also must complete the doing *of it;* that as *there was* a readiness to desire *it,* so *there* also *may be* a completion out of what *you* have. [12]For if there is first a willing mind, *it is* accepted according to what one has, *and* not according to what he does not have.

8:4 [a]NU-Text and M-Text omit *that we would receive,* thus changing text to *urgency for the favor and fellowship....*

Gardening for Health

Refuse to Create a Toxic Dump

As much as people don't like to think of their food being drenched in pesticides or the idea of moving close to a toxic dump, people also tend to create their own toxic dumps with their use of pesticides, fungicides, and herbicides in their gardens, yards, and homes!

Much of the increase in asthma among children appears to be linked to pesticide exposure during the first year of a child's life.

The smartest way to avoid pesticide use is to caulk foundation cracks, clean cluttered floors, keep food tightly sealed, and cover trash cans. These methods send a "not welcome" signal to pests.

In your yard, use safe alternatives to potentially toxic chemicals:

- ☐ To fight crabgrass, sprinkle corn gluten meal on lawns in the spring.
- ☐ Learn to like dandelions. The leaves taste like endive in a salad. The plants attract ladybugs that eat aphid (plant lice).
- ☐ To fight weeds in flower beds, spread plastic sheets and cover them with bark mulch.
- ☐ To kill lawn grubs, use "milky spore," a safe and naturally occurring bacteria (found at eco-friendly lawn and garden centers).
- ☐ Kill aphids with a less toxic insecticidal soap, such as Concern Insecticidal Soap.
- ☐ Fight termites with Bora-Care, a boric acid product that has low toxicity.
- ☐ You can make effective traps for cockroaches by placing a piece of banana inside a glass jar and lining the inside rim of the jar with petroleum jelly. The roaches crawl in to feast, but can't crawl out because of the slippery surface. Place the "traps" under sinks and near where pipes enter the house. When you've pinpointed where the roaches seem to congregate, use a hand applicator to inject boric

CONT. NEXT PAGE>>>

[13]For *I do* not *mean* that others should be eased and you burdened; [14]but by an equality, *that* now at this time your abundance *may supply* their lack, that their abundance also may *supply* your lack—that there may be equality. [15]As it is written, "He who *gathered* much had nothing left over, and he who *gathered* little had no lack."[a]

COLLECTION FOR THE JUDEAN SAINTS

[16]But thanks *be* to God who puts[a] the same earnest care for you into the heart of Titus. [17]For he not only accepted the exhortation, but being more diligent, he went to you of his own accord. [18]And we have sent with him the brother whose praise *is* in the gospel throughout all the churches, [19]and not only *that,* but who was also chosen by the churches to travel with us with this gift, which is administered by us to the glory of the Lord Himself and *to show* your ready mind, [20]avoiding this: that anyone should blame us in this lavish gift which is administered by us— [21]providing honorable things, not only in the sight of the Lord, but also in the sight of men.

[22]And we have sent with them our brother whom we have often proved diligent in many things, but now much more diligent, because of the great confidence which *we have* in you. [23]If *anyone inquires* about Titus, *he is* my partner and fellow worker concerning you. Or if our brethren *are inquired about, they are* messengers of the churches, the glory of Christ. [24]Therefore show to them, and[a] before the churches, the proof of your love and of our boasting on your behalf.

ADMINISTERING THE GIFT

9 Now concerning the ministering to the saints, it is superfluous for me to write to you; [2]for I know your willingness, about which I boast of you to the Macedonians, that Achaia was ready a year ago; and your zeal has stirred up the majority. [3]Yet I have sent the brethren, lest our boasting of you should be in vain in this respect, that, as I said, you may be ready; [4]lest if *some* Macedonians come with me and find you unprepared, we (not to mention you!) should be ashamed of this confident boasting.[a] [5]Therefore I thought it necessary to exhort the brethren to go to you ahead of time, and prepare your generous gift beforehand, which *you had* previously promised, that it may be ready as *a matter of* generosity and not as a grudging obligation.

THE CHEERFUL GIVER

[6]But this *I say:* He who sows sparingly will also reap sparingly, and he who sows bountifully will also reap bountifully. [7]*So let* each one *give* as he purposes in his heart, not grudgingly or of necessity; for God loves a cheerful giver. [8]And God *is* able to make all grace abound toward you, that you, always having all sufficiency in all *things,* may have an abundance for every good work. [9]As it is written:

"He has dispersed abroad,
    He has given to the poor;
    His righteousness endures forever."[a]

[10]Now may[a] He who supplies seed to the sower, and bread for food, supply and multiply the seed you have *sown* and increase the fruits of

8:15 [a]Exodus 16:18   8:16 [a]NU-Text reads *has put.*   8:24 [a]NU-Text and M-Text omit *and.*   9:4 [a]NU-Text reads *this confidence.*   9:9 [a]Psalm 112:9   9:10 [a]NU-Text reads *Now He who supplies . . . will supply. . . .*

236   DIVINE HEALTH

Gardening for Health Cont.>>>

acid, a low-toxicity mineral available at home centers, into nearby cracks and crevices.

☐ Fight moths by freezing woolen clothes for a few days at the beginning and ending of the moth season—the sudden change of temperature kills larvae. Or, send your woolen garments to a dry cleaner.

your righteousness, ¹¹while *you are* enriched in everything for all liberality, which causes thanksgiving through us to God. ¹²For the administration of this service not only supplies the needs of the saints, but also is abounding through many thanksgivings to God, ¹³while, through the proof of this ministry, they glorify God for the obedience of your confession to the gospel of Christ, and for *your* liberal sharing with them and all *men,* ¹⁴and by their prayer for you, who long for you because of the exceeding grace of God in you. ¹⁵Thanks *be* to God for His indescribable gift!

THE SPIRITUAL WAR

10 Now I, Paul, myself am pleading with you by the meekness and gentleness of Christ—who in presence *am* lowly among you, but being absent am bold toward you. ²But I beg *you* that when I am present I may not be bold with that confidence by which I intend to be bold against some, who think of us as if we walked according to the flesh. ³For though we walk in the flesh, we do not war according to the flesh. ⁴For the weapons of our warfare *are* not carnal but mighty in God for pulling down strongholds, ⁵casting down arguments and every high thing that exalts itself against the knowledge of God, bringing every thought into captivity to the obedience of Christ, ⁶and being ready to punish all disobedience when your obedience is fulfilled.

REALITY OF PAUL'S AUTHORITY

⁷Do you look at things according to the outward appearance? If anyone is convinced in himself that he is Christ's, let him again consider this in himself, that just as he *is* Christ's, even so we *are* Christ's.ᵃ ⁸For even if I should boast somewhat more about our authority, which the Lord gave usᵃ for edification and not for your destruction, I shall not be ashamed— ⁹lest I seem to terrify you by letters. ¹⁰"For *his* letters," they say, "*are* weighty and powerful, but *his* bodily presence *is* weak, and *his* speech contemptible." ¹¹Let such a person consider this, that what we are in word by letters when we are absent, such *we will* also *be* in deed when we are present.

LIMITS OF PAUL'S AUTHORITY

¹²For we dare not class ourselves or compare ourselves with those who commend themselves. But they, measuring themselves by themselves, and comparing themselves among themselves, are not wise. ¹³We, however, will not boast beyond measure, but within the limits of the sphere which God appointed us—a sphere which especially includes you. ¹⁴For we are not overextending ourselves (as though *our authority* did not extend to you), for it was to you that we came with the gospel of Christ; ¹⁵not boasting of things beyond measure, *that is,* in other men's labors, but having hope, *that* as your faith is increased, we shall be greatly enlarged by you in our sphere, ¹⁶to preach the gospel in the *regions* beyond you, *and* not to boast in another man's sphere of accomplishment.

CONDIMENTS

☐ Saffron

The most expensive spice in the world is saffron. Although it is not mentioned specifically in the Bible, it is a spice common in Greece, Turkey, Morocco, and other nations bordering the Mediterranean Sea.

Saffron filaments, or threads, are actually the dried stigmas of the saffron flower, *Crocus Sativus Linneaus.* Each flower contains only three stigmas. These threads must be picked from each flower by hand. More than seventy-five thousand of these flowers are needed to produce just one pound of saffron filaments—making it the world's most precious spice.

Fortunately, saffron has very strong coloring and flavoring power, so it can be used sparingly. It gives a bright yellow-orange color to foods. Essential oils in saffron also give it therapeutic properties. Most people who use saffron prefer the filaments rather than powder because it is easier for suppliers to mix fillers with pure saffron powder and detract from the value of the spice as well as the potency of the taste, aroma, and color.

Rice dishes are among the most popular dishes in which saffron is used.

10:7 ᵃNU-Text reads *even as we are.*   10:8 ᵃNU-Text omits *us.*

PEOPLE CALLED "BEAUTIFUL" IN THE BIBLE

Rachel

Enticing and Scheming

Rachel, the younger daughter of Laban, is described in the Bible as being "beautiful of form and appearance" (Genesis 29:17). In other words, she had a beautiful face and a great figure! The moment Jacob arrived at his Uncle Laban's fields, it appears that he saw Rachel and fell in love with her. He had an immediate desire to marry her. Customs being what they were in those days, Jacob had to pay a "bride price" for Rachel and since he had arrived with no money in hand, Jacob agreed to work for seven years for Laban to earn the right to marry his daughter.

When the time for the wedding arrived, Laban tricked Jacob into marrying his older daughter, Leah. According to traditional customs at that time, the elder daughter was supposed to marry before any younger daughters. Jacob was appalled and angry at what had happened when the morning after the wedding ceremony he discovered the trickery. He agreed, nevertheless, to fulfill the obligation to Leah, and he also agreed to work seven additional years for Rachel. He married Rachel a week after he married Leah, but remained in service to Laban. Rachel and Leah shared Jacob in a polygamous relationship.

Many people assume that beautiful women are never jealous of other women since they have no reason to be jealous. This just isn't so. It certainly wasn't true for Rachel. She was intensely jealous of her older sister Leah. Although Leah was not physically attractive, she was quick to conceive children. Rachel had a very difficult time conceiving and that fact was at the core of their rivalry. Rachel had Jacob's affection, but that wasn't enough. She was desperate to have children and did everything she knew to conceive. Eventually she had two sons, but died giving birth to the second one.

Rachel not only wanted sons, but she also wanted her sons to have their grandfather Laban's inheritance in the future. When Jacob secretly left Laban's household and took his family with him, Rachel stole the family idols. Laban was not a worshiper of Yahweh. He was an idol worshiper and these idols, called "teraphim," were small household figurines that may have been used for divination. They also connected ownership of property to the person who possessed them. Rachel was, in effect, stealing the title deed to her father's land and properties. Laban came looking for Jacob, his daughters, and grandchildren. He also came looking for his "gods."

Jacob invited Laban to search the camp for the idols. When Laban went to search Rachel's tent he found Rachel sitting on the ground. She actually was sitting on a camel's saddle in which she had placed the idols. Laban searched the remainder of the tent and didn't find the idols. Rachel said to her father, "Let it not displease my lord that I cannot rise before you, for the manner of women is with me" (Genesis 31:35). What did she mean?

In those days, women who were menstruating spent much of their period sitting over a hole that they dug in the ground so that the discharge of their body went directly into the earth. Rachel was pretending that she was having a menstrual period and therefore, her father did not require that she stand up. He took her words at face value. Thus, Rachel kept the idols out of sight and she made it all the way to Canaan with the idols in her possession. In addition to being a jealous woman, she was a woman willing to resort to lies and schemes to get what she wanted.

Rachel may have been beautiful in appearance, but her inner character was not beautiful. The old saying, "beauty is as beauty does" certainly may be applied to her.

---

[17]But "he who glories, let him glory in the LORD."[a] [18]For not he who commends himself is approved, but whom the Lord commends.

CONCERN FOR THEIR FAITHFULNESS

11 Oh, that you would bear with me in a little folly—and indeed you do bear with me. [2]For I am jealous for you with godly jealousy. For I have betrothed you to one husband, that I may present you as a chaste virgin to Christ. [3]But I fear, lest somehow, as the serpent deceived Eve by his craftiness, so your minds may be corrupted from the simplicity[a] that is in Christ. [4]For if he who comes preaches another Jesus whom we have not preached, or if you receive a different spirit which you have not received, or a different gospel which you have not accepted—you may well put up with it!

PAUL AND FALSE APOSTLES

[5]For I consider that I am not at all inferior to the most eminent apostles. [6]Even though I am untrained in speech, yet I am not in knowledge. But we have been thoroughly manifested[a] among you in all things.

[7]Did I commit sin in humbling myself that you might be exalted, be-

---

10:17 [a]Jeremiah 9:24   11:3 [a]NU-Text adds *and purity.*   11:6 [a]NU-Text omits *been.*

cause I preached the gospel of God to you free of charge? [8]I robbed other churches, taking wages *from them* to minister to you. [9]And when I was present with you, and in need, I was a burden to no one, for what I lacked the brethren who came from Macedonia supplied. And in everything I kept myself from being burdensome to you, and so I will keep *myself.* [10]As the truth of Christ is in me, no one shall stop me from this boasting in the regions of Achaia. [11]Why? Because I do not love you? God knows!

[12]But what I do, I will also continue to do, that I may cut off the opportunity from those who desire an opportunity to be regarded just as we are in the things of which they boast. [13]For such *are* false apostles, deceitful workers, transforming themselves into apostles of Christ. [14]And no wonder! For Satan himself transforms himself into an angel of light. [15]Therefore *it is* no great thing if his ministers also transform themselves into ministers of righteousness, whose end will be according to their works.

RELUCTANT BOASTING

[16]I say again, let no one think me a fool. If otherwise, at least receive me as a fool, that I also may boast a little. [17]What I speak, I speak not according to the Lord, but as it were, foolishly, in this confidence of boasting. [18]Seeing that many boast according to the flesh, I also will boast. [19]For you put up with fools gladly, since you *yourselves* are wise! [20]For you put up with it if one brings you into bondage, if one devours *you,* if one takes *from you,* if one exalts himself, if one strikes you on the face. [21]To *our* shame I say that we were too weak for that! But in whatever anyone is bold—I speak foolishly—I am bold also.

SUFFERING FOR CHRIST

[22]Are they Hebrews? So *am* I. Are they Israelites? So *am* I. Are they the seed of Abraham? So *am* I. [23]Are they ministers of Christ?—I speak as a fool—I *am* more: in labors more abundant, in stripes above measure, in prisons more frequently, in deaths often. [24]From the Jews five times I received forty *stripes* minus one. [25]Three times I was beaten with rods; once I was stoned; three times I was shipwrecked; a night and a day I have been in the deep; [26]*in* journeys often, *in* perils of waters, *in* perils of robbers, *in* perils of *my own* countrymen, *in* perils of the Gentiles, *in* perils in the city, *in* perils in the wilderness, *in* perils in the sea, *in* perils among false brethren; [27]in weariness and toil, in sleeplessness often, in hunger and thirst, in fastings often, in cold and nakedness— [28]besides the other things, what comes upon me daily: my deep concern for all the churches. [29]Who is weak, and I am not weak? Who is made to stumble, and I do not burn *with indignation?*

[30]If I must boast, I will boast in the things which concern my infirmity. [31]The God and Father of our Lord Jesus Christ, who is blessed forever, knows that I am not lying. [32]In Damascus the governor, under Aretas the king, was guarding the city of the Damascenes with a garrison, desiring to arrest me; [33]but I was let down in a basket through a window in the wall, and escaped from his hands.

THE VISION OF PARADISE

12 It is doubtless[a] not profitable for me to boast. I will come to visions and revelations of the Lord: [2]I know a man in Christ who fourteen years ago—whether in the

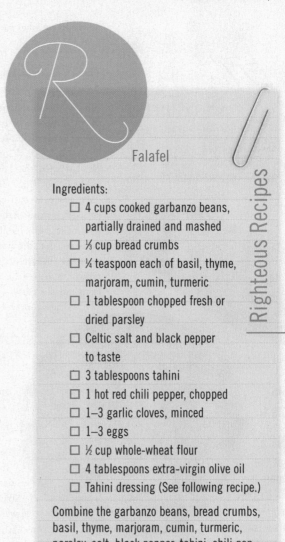

Falafel

Ingredients:

- ☐ 4 cups cooked garbanzo beans, partially drained and mashed
- ☐ ⅓ cup bread crumbs
- ☐ ¼ teaspoon each of basil, thyme, marjoram, cumin, turmeric
- ☐ 1 tablespoon chopped fresh or dried parsley
- ☐ Celtic salt and black pepper to taste
- ☐ 3 tablespoons tahini
- ☐ 1 hot red chili pepper, chopped
- ☐ 1–3 garlic cloves, minced
- ☐ 1–3 eggs
- ☐ ½ cup whole-wheat flour
- ☐ 4 tablespoons extra-virgin olive oil
- ☐ Tahini dressing (See following recipe.)

Combine the garbanzo beans, bread crumbs, basil, thyme, marjoram, cumin, turmeric, parsley, salt, black pepper, tahini, chili pepper, and garlic in a large bowl. Mix lightly. Mix in the eggs, one at a time. The mixture will have a semisoft consistency. Shape garbanzo mixture into 1-inch balls or small patties and roll them in flour to coat. Brown in olive oil in a heavy skillet over medium heat. Drain on paper towels.

Add tahini dressing, or Italian dressing, to taste.

Serve in pita bread halves with yogurt, chopped tomatoes, lettuce or sprouts, and shredded cheese.

Yield: 8–10 servings

Righteous Recipes

12:1 [a]NU-Text reads *necessary, though not profitable,* to boast.

The LAW
AND THE
SCIENCE

[ALL FAT IS THE LORD'S]

>SCIENCE tells us that the most dangerous natural fats for the human cardiovascular system are saturated fats—the fats from red meat. Eating excess animal fat can lead to high cholesterol, high triglycerides, and eventually to clogged arteries. Trim all excess fat away from red meat before you eat it!

>THE LAW says: "All the fat is the LORD's. This shall be a perpetual statute throughout your generations in all your dwellings: you shall eat neither fat nor blood" (Leviticus 3:16, 17). This LAW refers primarily to the excess fat of animals, especially that surrounding the kidneys and intestines, otherwise known as "midriff fat." It does not refer to fat that has been "marbled" into meat.

of me above what he sees me *to be* or hears from me.

THE THORN IN THE FLESH

⁷And lest I should be exalted above measure by the abundance of the revelations, a thorn in the flesh was given to me, a messenger of Satan to buffet me, lest I be exalted above measure. ⁸Concerning this thing I pleaded with the Lord three times that it might depart from me. ⁹And He said to me, "My grace is sufficient for you, for My strength is made perfect in weakness." Therefore most gladly I will rather boast in my infirmities, that the power of Christ may rest upon me. ¹⁰Therefore I take pleasure in infirmities, in reproaches, in needs, in persecutions, in distresses, for Christ's sake. For when I am weak, then I am strong.

SIGNS OF AN APOSTLE

¹¹I have become a fool in boasting;ᵃ you have compelled me. For I ought to have been commended by you; for in nothing was I behind the most eminent apostles, though I am nothing. ¹²Truly the signs of an apostle were accomplished among you with all perseverance, in signs and wonders and mighty deeds. ¹³For what is it in which you were inferior to

other churches, except that I myself was not burdensome to you? Forgive me this wrong!

LOVE FOR THE CHURCH

¹⁴Now *for* the third time I am ready to come to you. And I will not be burdensome to you; for I do not seek yours, but you. For the children ought not to lay up for the parents, but the parents for the children. ¹⁵And I will very gladly spend and be spent for your souls; though the more abundantly I love you, the less I am loved.

¹⁶But be that *as it may*, I did not burden you. Nevertheless, being crafty, I caught you by cunning! ¹⁷Did I take advantage of you by any of those whom I sent to you? ¹⁸I urged Titus, and sent our brother with *him*. Did Titus take advantage of you? Did we not walk in the same spirit? Did *we* not *walk* in the same steps?

¹⁹Again, do you thinkᵃ that we excuse ourselves to you? We speak before God in Christ. But *we do* all things, beloved, for your edification. ²⁰For I fear lest, when I come, I shall not find you such as I wish, and *that* I shall be found by you such as you do not wish; lest *there be* contentions, jealousies, outbursts of wrath, selfish ambitions, backbitings, whisperings, conceits, tumults; ²¹lest, when I come again, my God will humble me among you, and I shall mourn for many who have sinned before and have not repented of the uncleanness, fornication, and lewdness which they have practiced.

body I do not know, or whether out of the body I do not know, God knows—such a one was caught up to the third heaven. ³And I know such a man—whether in the body or out of the body I do not know, God knows—⁴how he was caught up into Paradise and heard inexpressible words, which it is not lawful for a man to utter. ⁵Of such a one I will boast; yet of myself I will not boast, except in my infirmities. ⁶For though I might desire to boast, I will not be a fool; for I will speak the truth. But I refrain, lest anyone should think

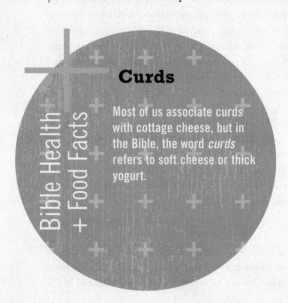

Bible Health + Food Facts

Curds

Most of us associate curds with cottage cheese, but in the Bible, the word *curds* refers to soft cheese or thick yogurt.

12:11 ᵃNU-Text omits *in boasting*.   **12:19** ᵃNU-Text reads *You have been thinking for a long time.* . . .

COMING WITH AUTHORITY

13 This *will be* the third *time* I am coming to you. "By the mouth of two or three witnesses every word shall be established."[a] [2]I have told you before, and foretell as if I were present the second time, and now being absent I write[c] to those who have sinned before, and to all the rest, that if I come again I will not spare— [3]since you seek a proof of Christ speaking in me, who is not weak toward you, but mighty in you. [4]For though He was crucified in weakness, yet He lives by the power of God. For we also are weak in Him, but we shall live with Him by the power of God toward you.

[5]Examine yourselves *as to* whether you are in the faith. Test yourselves. Do you not know yourselves, that Jesus Christ is in you?—unless indeed you are disqualified. [6]But I trust that you will know that we are not disqualified.

PAUL PREFERS GENTLENESS

[7]Now I[a] pray to God that you do no evil, not that we should appear approved, but that you should do what is honorable, though we may seem disqualified. [8]For we can do nothing against the truth, but for the truth. [9]For we are glad when we are weak and you are strong. And this also we pray, that you may be made complete. [10]Therefore I write these things being absent, lest being present I should use sharpness, according to the authority which the Lord has given me for edification and not for destruction.

GREETINGS AND BENEDICTION

[11]Finally, brethren, farewell. Become complete. Be of good comfort, be of one mind, live in peace; and the God of love and peace will be with you.

[12]Greet one another with a holy kiss.

[13]All the saints greet you.

[14]The grace of the Lord Jesus Christ, and the love of God, and the communion of the Holy Spirit *be* with you all. Amen.

WHOLENESS 101

Detoxify Your Liver

The body's main detoxifier is the liver, but what happens when the liver needs detoxification? Yeast, food allergies, and various chemical toxins can do great damage to the liver over time. It is important, therefore, to take herbs and supplements that support and improve liver detoxification.

Detoxification of the liver takes place in two phases:

Phase 1: Take a comprehensive antioxidant formula to release toxins from tissues. Such a formula contains plenty of vitamin E, vitamin C, lipoic acid, coenzyme Q10, grape seed and pine bark extract, beta carotene, and the minerals copper, zinc, manganese, selenium, and sulfur.

Phase 2: Take amino acids that render the toxic compounds harmless. Also eat foods that contain sulfur. These elements bind to the toxins in a harmless way so they can be fully released from the body through normal elimination channels (urine and bowel movements). The most important amino acids are cysteine, taurine, and methionine. Good food sources for these amino acids are eggs, garlic, onions, cruciferous vegetables (cabbage, broccoli, cauliflower, Brussels sprouts), fish, poultry, and meats.

To restore life to the liver, consider supplementation with milk thistle, glutathione, and lipoic acid.

13:1 [a]Deuteronomy 19:15 13:2 [c]NU-Text omits *I write*. 13:7 [a]NU-Text reads *we*.

ALATIANS

If Paul was writing this letter today, he probably would have used words such as peer pressure or "media mindedness." The Galatians were becoming influenced by people who had come into their midst with teachings that were not the pure Gospel that Paul had taught them. They were starting to backtrack, returning to their "old ways" of striving to keep the law and all its rituals, and placing less importance upon faith. Paul states clearly that the Christian life is not bound up in legalistic "don'ts." Rather, the Christian life is filled with love that compels a Christian to "do" those things that reveals the nature of God—in other words, to do what is loving, joyful, peaceable, longsuffering, kind, good, faithful, gentle, and measured out in moderation.

Paul makes it very clear that to "walk in the Spirit" does not mean a person is free to live any way he chooses—rather, it means a person is free to experience a life that is not bound by sin, guilt, or shame.

The "works of the flesh" produce disease and death—emotional as well as physical. The "fruit of the Spirit" produces health and life.

GREETING

1 Paul, an apostle (not from men nor through man, but through Jesus Christ and God the Father who raised Him from the dead), ²and all the brethren who are with me,

To the churches of Galatia:

³Grace to you and peace from God the Father and our Lord Jesus Christ, ⁴who gave Himself for our sins, that He might deliver us from this present evil age, according to the will of our God and Father, ⁵to whom *be* glory forever and ever. Amen.

ONLY ONE GOSPEL

⁶I marvel that you are turning away so soon from Him who called you in the grace of Christ, to a different gospel, ⁷which is not another; but there are some who trouble you and want to pervert the gospel of Christ. ⁸But even if we, or an angel from heaven, preach any other gospel to you than what we have preached to you, let him be accursed. ⁹As we have said before, so now I say again, if anyone preaches any other gospel to you than what you have received, let him be accursed.

¹⁰For do I now persuade men, or God? Or do I seek to please men? For if I still pleased men, I would not be a bondservant of Christ.

CALL TO APOSTLESHIP

¹¹But I make known to you, brethren, that the gospel which was preached by me is not according to man. ¹²For I neither received it from man, nor was I taught *it,* but *it came* through the revelation of Jesus Christ.

¹³For you have heard of my former conduct in Judaism, how I persecuted the church of God beyond measure and *tried to* destroy it. ¹⁴And I advanced in Judaism beyond many of my contemporaries in my own nation, being more exceedingly zealous for the traditions of my fathers.

¹⁵But when it pleased God, who separated me from my mother's womb and called *me* through His grace, ¹⁶to reveal His Son in me, that I might preach Him among the Gentiles, I did not immediately confer with flesh and blood, ¹⁷nor did I go up to Jerusalem to those *who were* apostles before me; but I went to Arabia, and returned again to Damascus.

CONTACTS AT JERUSALEM

¹⁸Then after three years I went up to Jerusalem to see Peter,ᵃ and remained with him fifteen days. ¹⁹But I saw none of the other apostles except James, the Lord's brother. ²⁰(Now *concerning* the things which I write to you, indeed, before God, I do not lie.)

²¹Afterward I went into the regions of Syria and Cilicia. ²²And I was unknown by face to the churches of Judea which *were* in Christ. ²³But they were hearing only, "He who formerly persecuted us now preaches the faith which he once *tried to* destroy." ²⁴And they glorified God in me.

DEFENDING THE GOSPEL

2 Then after fourteen years I went up again to Jerusalem with Barnabas, and also took Titus with *me.* ²And I went up by revelation, and communicated to them that gospel which I preach among the Gentiles, but privately to those who were of reputation, lest

1:18 ᵃNU-Text reads *Cephas.*

WWJE?

[WHAT WOULD JESUS EAT]

[WHOLE GRAINS]

In addition to using grains for flour, grains in Bible times were roasted, boiled, parched, or even eaten green from the stalk. Grains were ground, crushed, pounded, and dried to make soups, grain-based salads, casseroles, and even desserts.

Bulgur wheat is a special preparation of the wheat grain commonly found in the Middle East today. In bulgur wheat, the wheat kernels are washed, scrubbed, cracked, and then dried. The smaller grains can then be cooked or soaked in water—as they soak or cook, they swell. The grain is commonly used in making tabouleh.

Another form of cracked wheat that is smaller than bulgur wheat is called couscous. This grain can also be used in making tabouleh but it is usually used as a main dish or in casseroles. Couscous is easily prepared by pouring boiling water over the cracked wheat.

Look for the term *unpearled* on a box of barley grain or flour. This means that the barley is unprocessed and high in fiber. It is available at most health-food stores. In contrast, barley that is labeled *Scotch* or *pearled* has been processed and does not have nearly the health benefit. Barley grain is rarely eaten by itself—it is usually used as an ingredient in soup.

In addition to whole wheat and whole barley, there are many other whole grains that are beneficial. In all, worldwide, more than eight thousand species of plants supply grain! Other grains mentioned in the Bible are millet and rye. Millet has a high protein content (between 10 and 12 percent), is high in minerals, and is easily digested. Rye is high in fiber, has approximately 20 percent protein, and also has a lower gluten rate than wheat. It is high in B vitamins and other minerals. Pure rye bread is difficult to find—it is nearly black in color but is very nourishing and flavorful. Most rye breads are made with refined rye flour mixed with processed wheat flour.

Try experimenting with various whole grains available in your health-food store. They can provide a delicious alternative to potatoes or rice. Plus, nongluten grains of millet, buckwheat, amaranth, and quinoa are usually good for people with wheat allergies. If you'd rather "drink" your whole grains, wheat grass and barley grass products are available in juice form. These products are usually rich in chlorophyll and flavonoids, which are phytonutrients. They are often packaged with chlorella, spirulina, and blue-green algae as "green foods" or "superfoods."

Whole Grain for Weight Loss

A medical research study recently found that women who consumed more high-fiber, whole-grain foods were 49 percent less likely to gain weight, and on average, were nine pounds lighter than their nongrain-eating counterparts. (Note that this study referred only to *whole*-grain products, not *refined*-grain products.)

by any means I might run, or had run, in vain. ³Yet not even Titus who *was* with me, being a Greek, was compelled to be circumcised. ⁴And *this occurred* because of false brethren secretly brought in (who came in by stealth to spy out our liberty which we have in Christ Jesus, that they might bring us into bondage), ⁵to whom we did not yield submission even for an hour, that the truth of the gospel might continue with you.

⁶But from those who seemed to be something—whatever they were, it makes no difference to me; God shows personal favoritism to no man—for those who seemed *to be something* added nothing to me. ⁷But on the contrary, when they saw that the gospel for the uncircumcised had been committed to me, as *the gospel* for the circumcised *was* to Peter ⁸(for He who worked effectively in Peter for the apostleship to the circumcised also worked effectively in me toward the Gentiles), ⁹and when James, Cephas, and John, who seemed to be pillars, perceived the grace that had been given to me, they gave me and Barnabas the right hand of fellowship, that we *should go* to the Gentiles and they to the circumcised. ¹⁰*They desired* only that we should remember the poor, the very thing which I also was eager to do.

NO RETURN TO THE LAW

¹¹Now when Peter[a] had come to Antioch, I withstood him to his face, because he was to be blamed; ¹²for before certain men came from James, he would eat with the Gentiles; but when they came, he withdrew and separated himself, fearing those who were of the circumcision. ¹³And the rest of the Jews also played the hypocrite with him, so that even Barnabas was carried away with their hypocrisy.

¹⁴But when I saw that they were not straightforward about the truth of the gospel, I said to Peter before *them* all, "If you, being a Jew, live in the manner of Gentiles and not as the Jews, why do you[a] compel Gentiles to live as Jews?[b] ¹⁵We *who are* Jews by nature, and not sinners of the Gentiles, ¹⁶knowing that a man is not justified by the works of the law but by faith in Jesus Christ, even we have believed in Christ Jesus, that we might be justified by faith in Christ and not by the works of the law; for by the works of the law no flesh shall be justified.

2:11 [a]NU-Text reads *Cephas*.   2:14 [a]NU-Text reads *how can you.* [b]Some interpreters stop the quotation here.

August

1   2   3   4   5   6   7

Let's Celebrate

☐ **Family!** For many families, the main celebration in August is a family reunion or family vacation. Reconnect with your loved ones this month.   ☐ **Lammas Day** is August 1. Lammas comes from the Old English half maesse, which means "loaf mass." Lammas Day traditionally marked the beginning of the harvest. Loaves of bread were baked from the first-ripened grain and brought to the churches to be consecrated.   ☐ "Dog days" of summer are considered to be the period between early July and early September. These are traditionally considered the hottest and most unhealthy days of the year. The name comes from the rising of the Dog Star, Sirius.

8   9   10   11   12   13   14

Seasonal Tips

☐ Keep your garbage can clean and emptied of rainwater that may collect there.   ☐ Hold a bottle of frozen water between your wrists for 30 seconds. Then hold that same bottle of frozen water along the side of your neck—extending from your jaw to behind your ear—for 30 seconds on each side. Repeat. This can reduce your body temperature by several degrees in just a few minutes!   ☐ Make certain that you never leave a child unattended by a swimming pool of any size.

In the Garden

15   16   17   18

☐ Reposition potted plants that are sun sensitive near trees or shrubs so that they receive some late-day shade.   ☐ Raise your lawn mower blade height a half-inch. This will encourage turf grass to root deeper and will shade the soil to protect the grass crowns—where stem and root meet—against heat stress.

19   20   21

22   23   24   25

Table Fresh

☐ Enjoy sorbets made from fresh fruit.   ☐ Try grilling veggies—such as bell peppers, zucchini and yellow summer squash, onions, eggplant, and new potatoes. Experiment with vegetable "kabobs" on skewers.   ☐ Avoid drinking caffeinated beverages, even iced tea. They can be dehydrating.

26   27   28

29   30   31

Now Is the Time To...

☐ Watch out for poison ivy and poison oak. Learn what these plants look like and teach your children to avoid them.   ☐ Remember to wear a hat or visor to protect against the summer sun. Consider choosing a summer hat that you can soak with water.   ☐ Wear light-colored, loose-fitting cotton clothing for maximum comfort in the summer heat.   ☐ Can, dehydrate, or freeze extra produce.

◀ Victory in a Bean Field ▶

ULTIMATE HEALTH RESOURCE • ULTIMATE HEALTH RESOURCE • ULTIMATE HEALTH RESOURCE

Some people seem to believe that their value as human beings is directly associated with outward circumstances and associations that are in some way "noble" or "prestigious."

One of the men described as a "mighty man" of King David—in fact, one of the three greatest "mighty men"—was Shammah, the son of Agee the Hararite. The Bible says this about Shammah: "The Philistines had gathered together into a troop where there was a piece of ground full of lentils. So the people fled from the Philistines. But he stationed himself in the middle of the field, defended it, and killed the Philistines. So the LORD brought about a great victory" (2 Samuel 23:11, 12).

Shammah thought a bean field was worth defending with his life! His great claim to fame was single-handedly winning a battle against the enemy in a field filled with lentils.

This story is valuable to us today for two great reasons. First, the bean field Shammah defended was worth defending because it was part of God's property that had been invaded by an enemy that had no regard for God or His people. Second, the bean field Shammah defended was the place where God had placed him. Shammah knew that God had put him in this place to do what he was skilled to do—it didn't matter that the battlefield was unusual, awkward perhaps, or unlike other battlefields.

A great deal of our emotional health—and resulting physical health—is related to following Shammah's example. We must fight *only* those battles that are truly worth the fight. Our battle is against things that are evil and offensive to God, not against things that are a nuisance, inconvenience, or that stem from a petty gripe or injustice.

Second, we must be content with the place where God has put us. No matter the position or outward circumstance, if we are in the position where God has put us, we can take tremendous satisfaction in knowing that God has a plan and purpose for us that can *only* be fulfilled if we will hold our present ground and be a witness for God there.

loved me and gave Himself for me. ²¹I do not set aside the grace of God; for if righteousness *comes* through the law, then Christ died in vain."

JUSTIFICATION BY FAITH

3 O foolish Galatians! Who has bewitched you that you should not obey the truth,[a] before whose eyes Jesus Christ was clearly portrayed among you[b] as crucified? ²This only I want to learn from you: Did you receive the Spirit by the works of the law, or by the hearing of faith? ³Are you so foolish? Having begun in the Spirit, are you now being made perfect by the flesh? ⁴Have you suffered so many things in vain—if indeed *it was* in vain?

⁵Therefore He who supplies the Spirit to you and works miracles among you, *does He do it* by the works of the law, or by the hearing of faith?— ⁶just as Abraham "believed God, and it was accounted to him for righteousness."[a] ⁷Therefore know that *only* those who are of faith are sons of Abraham. ⁸And the Scripture, foreseeing that God would justify the Gentiles by faith, preached the gospel to Abraham beforehand, *saying,* "In you all the nations shall be blessed."[a] ⁹So then those who *are* of faith are blessed with believing Abraham.

THE LAW BRINGS A CURSE

¹⁰For as many as are of the works of the law are under the curse; for it is written, "Cursed is everyone who does not continue in all things which are written in the book of the law, to do them."[a] ¹¹But that no one is justified by the law in the sight of God *is* evident, for "the just shall live by faith."[a] ¹²Yet the law is not of faith, but "the man who does them shall live by them."[a]

¹³Christ has redeemed us from the curse of the law, having become a curse for us (for it is written, "Cursed is everyone who hangs on a tree"[a]), ¹⁴that the blessing of Abraham might come upon the Gentiles in Christ Jesus, that we might receive the promise of the Spirit through faith.

THE CHANGELESS PROMISE

¹⁵Brethren, I speak in the manner of men: Though *it is* only a man's covenant, yet *if it is* confirmed, no one annuls or adds to it. ¹⁶Now

¹⁷"But if, while we seek to be justified by Christ, we ourselves also are found sinners, *is* Christ therefore a minister of sin? Certainly not! ¹⁸For if I build again those things which I destroyed, I make myself a transgressor.

¹⁹For I through the law died to the law that I might live to God. ²⁰I have been crucified with Christ; it is no longer I who live, but Christ lives in me; and the *life* which I now live in the flesh I live by faith in the Son of God, who

3:1 [a]NU-Text omits *that you should not obey the truth.* [b]NU-Text omits *among you.* **3:6** [a]Genesis 15:6 **3:8** [a]Genesis 12:3; 18:18; 22:18; 26:4; 28:14 **3:10** [a]Deuteronomy 27:26 **3:11** [a]Habakkuk 2:4 **3:12** [a]Leviticus 18:5 **3:13** [a]Deuteronomy 21:23

246   DIVINE HEALTH

is neither Jew nor Greek, there is neither slave nor free, there is neither male nor female; for you are all one in Christ Jesus. ²⁹And if you *are* Christ's, then you are Abraham's seed, and heirs according to the promise.

4 Now I say *that* the heir, as long as he is a child, does not differ at all from a slave, though he is master of all, ²but is under guardians and stewards until the time appointed by the father. ³Even so we, when we were children, were in bondage under the

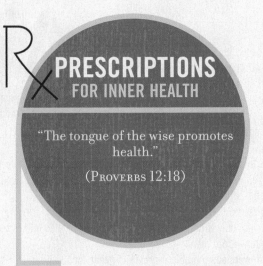

PRESCRIPTIONS
FOR INNER HEALTH

"The tongue of the wise promotes health."

(PROVERBS 12:18)

Watch what you say! Your words promote health and a sense of well-being in other people, or they promote disharmony and discord. The words you speak are heard first and foremost by your own ears, so what you speak also can promote well-being and health in your own spirit, mind, and body.

to Abraham and his Seed were the promises made. He does not say, "And to seeds," as of many, but as of one, "And to your Seed,"ᵃ who is Christ. ¹⁷And this I say, *that* the law, which was four hundred and thirty years later, cannot annul the covenant that was confirmed before by God in Christ,ᵃ that it should make the promise of no effect. ¹⁸For if the inheritance *is* of the law, *it is* no longer of promise; but God gave *it* to Abraham by promise.

PURPOSE OF THE LAW

¹⁹What purpose then *does* the law *serve?* It was added because of transgressions, till the Seed should come to whom the promise was made; *and it was* appointed through angels by the hand of a mediator. ²⁰Now a mediator does not *mediate* for one *only,* but God is one.

²¹*Is* the law then against the promises of God? Certainly not! For if there had been a law given which could have given life, truly righteousness would have been by the law. ²²But the Scripture has confined all under sin, that the promise by faith in Jesus Christ might be given to those who believe. ²³But before faith came, we were kept under guard by the law, kept for the faith which would afterward be revealed. ²⁴Therefore the law was our tutor *to bring us* to Christ, that we might be justified by faith. ²⁵But after faith has come, we are no longer under a tutor.

SONS AND HEIRS

²⁶For you are all sons of God through faith in Christ Jesus. ²⁷For as many of you as were baptized into Christ have put on Christ. ²⁸There

Bible Beverages
Fruit Juice and Fruit Punch

Berries, including pomegranates, were often mashed into juice in Bible times. Mulberries were also crushed to make a refreshing beverage in the first century. Although there is no specific reference to Jesus drinking fruit juices, He may have since there is no food law restricting the eating of fruits and vegetables. Spiced fruit-based wines were also common in Bible times.

The danger of drinking too much fruit juice is that juice is loaded with sugar, especially the commercial fruit-juice drinks—some of which have *no* real fruit juice in them at all! Don't drink more than a glass of juice a day. Even apple juice is high in sugar.

If you want the taste of fruit juice without the harmful sugar overload, try adding a couple of tablespoons of freshly squeezed juice to a glass of sparkling water. A good party punch can be made with equal parts of mango juice, tonic water, and club soda—consume sparingly.

3:16 ªGenesis 12:7; 13:15; 24:7   3:17 ªNU-Text omits *in Christ.*

WEIGHING LESS &
ENJOYING LIFE MORE!

[Avoid Becoming "Flabby"]

Many people who are on strict weight-loss plans become discouraged when they see their bodies becoming flabby. There's a way to avoid this!

First, make sure you eat a good balance of fresh vegetables and fresh fruits, along with moderate amounts of lean protein. You need protein for muscle.

Second, eat your healthy meals about thirty minutes *after* exercising. For up to two hours after intense exercise, the body works to restore glycogen directly to the muscles, bypassing the liver and other storage sites, including fat cells.

Third, after you exercise, be sure to rehydrate your muscle cells by drinking sufficient pure water. The water not only is beneficial for your muscles, it also makes you feel less hungry before you sit down to a meal.

Fourth, do a variety of exercises. Aerobic exercise is great for the heart but it does little for your muscles. Weight-training exercises—also called resistance training—is good for the muscles. Calisthenics and flexibility exercises can also help tone your body.

Lose fat, but gain muscle! Muscle burns more calories than other tissues, so the greater the percentage of muscle in your body, the easier it will be for you to maintain weight loss.

---

elements of the world. ⁴But when the fullness of the time had come, God sent forth His Son, born[a] of a woman, born under the law, ⁵to redeem those who were under the law, that we might receive the adoption as sons.

Q Who is the first person in the Bible described as a shepherd— "a keeper of sheep"?

A Abel *(Genesis 4:2).*

⁶And because you are sons, God has sent forth the Spirit of His Son into your hearts, crying out, "Abba, Father!" ⁷Therefore you are no longer a slave but a son, and if a son, then an heir of[b] God through Christ.

FEARS FOR THE CHURCH

⁸But then, indeed, when you did not know God, you served those which by nature are not gods. ⁹But now after you have known God, or rather are known by God, how *is it that* you turn again to the weak and beggarly elements, to which you desire again to be in bondage? ¹⁰You observe days and months and seasons and years. ¹¹I am afraid for you, lest I have labored for you in vain.

¹²Brethren, I urge you to become like me, for I *became* like you. You have not injured me at all. ¹³You know that because of physical infirmity I preached the gospel to you at the first. ¹⁴And my trial which was in my flesh you did not despise or reject, but you received me as an angel of God, *even* as Christ Jesus. ¹⁵What[a] then was the blessing you *enjoyed?* For I bear you witness that, if possible, you would have plucked out your own eyes and given them to me. ¹⁶Have I therefore become your enemy because I tell you the truth?

¹⁷They zealously court you, *but* for no good; yes, they want to exclude you, that you may be zealous for them. ¹⁸But it is good to be zealous in a good thing always, and not only when I am present with you. ¹⁹My little children, for whom I labor in birth again until Christ is formed in you, ²⁰I would like to be present with you now and to change my tone; for I have doubts about you.

TWO COVENANTS

²¹Tell me, you who desire to be under the law, do you not hear the law? ²²For it is written that Abraham had two sons: the one by a bondwoman, the other by a freewoman. ²³But he *who was* of the bondwoman was born according to the flesh, and he of the freewoman through promise, ²⁴which things are symbolic. For these are the[a] two covenants: the one from Mount Sinai which gives birth to bondage, which is Hagar— ²⁵for this Hagar is Mount Sinai in Arabia, and corresponds to Jerusalem which now is, and is in bondage with her children— ²⁶but the Jerusalem above is free, which is the mother of us all. ²⁷For it is written:

"Rejoice, O barren,
  You who do not bear!
Break forth and shout,
You who are not in labor!

4:4 [a]*Or made* 4:7 [a]NU-Text reads *through God* and omits *through Christ.* 4:15 [a]NU-Text reads *Where.* 4:24 [a]NU-Text and M-Text omit *the.*

For the desolate has many more children
Than she who has a husband."ᵃ

²⁸Now we, brethren, as Isaac *was,* are children of promise. ²⁹But, as he who was born according to the flesh then persecuted him *who was born* according to the Spirit, even so *it is* now. ³⁰Nevertheless what does the Scripture say? "Cast out the bondwoman and her son, for the son of the bondwoman shall not be heir with the son of the freewoman."ᵃ ³¹So then, brethren, we are not children of the bondwoman but of the free.

CHRISTIAN LIBERTY

5 Stand fast therefore in the liberty by which Christ has made us free,ᵃ and do not be entangled again with a yoke of bondage. ²Indeed I, Paul, say to you that if you become circumcised, Christ will profit you nothing. ³And I testify again to every man who becomes circumcised that he is a debtor to keep the whole law. ⁴You have become estranged from Christ, you who *attempt to* be justified by law; you have fallen from grace. ⁵For we through the Spirit eagerly wait for the hope of righteousness by faith. ⁶For in Christ Jesus neither circumcision nor uncircumcision avails anything, but faith working through love.

LOVE FULFILLS THE LAW

⁷You ran well. Who hindered you from obeying the truth? ⁸This persuasion does not *come* from Him who calls you. ⁹A little leaven leavens the whole lump. ¹⁰I have confidence in you, in the Lord, that you will have no other mind; but he who troubles you shall bear his judgment, whoever he is.

¹¹And I, brethren, if I still preach circumcision, why do I still suffer persecution? Then the offense of the cross has ceased. ¹²I could wish that those who trouble you would even cut themselves off!

¹³For you, brethren, have been called to liberty; only do not *use* liberty as an opportunity for the flesh, but through love serve one another. ¹⁴For all the law is fulfilled in one word, *even* in this: "You shall love your neighbor as yourself."ᵃ ¹⁵But if you bite and devour one another, beware lest you be consumed by one another!

WALKING IN THE SPIRIT

¹⁶I say then: Walk in the Spirit, and you shall not fulfill the lust of the flesh. ¹⁷For the flesh lusts against the Spirit, and the Spirit against the flesh; and these are contrary to one another, so that you do not do the things that you wish. ¹⁸But if you are led by the Spirit, you are not under the law.

> " Walk in the Spirit, and you shall not fulfill the lust of the flesh. For the flesh lusts against the Spirit, and the Spirit against the flesh; and these are contrary to one another, so that you do not do the things that you wish. " — *Galatians 5:16–17*

¹⁹Now the works of the flesh are evident, which are: adultery,ᵃ fornication, uncleanness, lewdness, ²⁰idolatry, sorcery, hatred, contentions, jealousies, outbursts of wrath, selfish ambitions, dissensions, heresies, ²¹envy, murders,ᵃ drunkenness, revelries, and the like; of which I tell you beforehand, just as I also told *you* in time past, that those who practice such things will not inherit the kingdom of God.

²²But the fruit of the Spirit is love, joy, peace, longsuffering, kindness, goodness, faithfulness, ²³gentleness, self-control. Against such there is no law. ²⁴And those *who are* Christ's have crucified the flesh with its passions and desires. ²⁵If we live in the Spirit, let us also walk in the Spirit. ²⁶Let us not become conceited, provoking one another, envying one another.

> (Galatians 5:19–21)

Sin Is Stressful. One thing many people tend to overlook is that sin is *stressful.* That's one reason that death can be called the "wages" of sin (Romans 3:23). Sin that causes deep internal stress—usually in the form of unresolved and ongoing guilt and shame—can be directly related to increased adrenaline and cortisone levels in the body, which given time can cause life-threatening diseases.

Paul identified several deadly emotions in this brief passage—hatred, jealousy and envy, wrath (anger), a striving for perfection and success, and arguments. He also identified behaviors that are a direct assault on health—drunkenness, murder, and overindulgence at "revelries" (parties and likely, orgies). There's nothing about sinful behavior that contributes to health or wholeness. In fact, one of the definitions of sin is that it detracts from our being whole. That's why forgiveness is so important in dealing with all forms of stress. We must not only seek God's forgiveness, but we must forgive others and forgive ourselves.

INSIGHTS INTO THE WORD

4:27 ᵃIsaiah 54:1   4:30 ᵃGenesis 21:10   5:1 ᵃNU-Text reads *For freedom Christ has made us free; stand fast therefore.*   5:14 ᵃLeviticus 19:18   5:19 ᵃNU-Text omits *adultery.* 5:21 ᵃNU-Text omits *murders.*

BEAR AND SHARE THE BURDENS

6 Brethren, if a man is overtaken in any trespass, you who *are* spiritual restore such a one in a spirit of gentleness, considering yourself lest you also be tempted. ²Bear one another's burdens, and so fulfill the law of Christ. ³For if anyone thinks himself to be something, when he is nothing, he deceives himself. ⁴But let each one examine his own work, and then he will have rejoicing in himself alone, and not in another. ⁵For each one shall bear his own load.

BE GENEROUS AND DO GOOD

⁶Let him who is taught the word share in all good things with him who teaches.

⁷Do not be deceived, God is not mocked; for whatever a man sows, that he will also reap. ⁸For he who sows to his flesh will of the flesh reap corruption, but he who sows to the Spirit will of the Spirit reap everlasting life. ⁹And let us not grow weary while doing good, for in due season we shall reap if we do not lose heart. ¹⁰Therefore, as we have opportunity, let us do good to all, especially to those who are of the household of faith.

GLORY ONLY IN THE CROSS

¹¹See with what large letters I have written to you with my own hand! ¹²As many as desire to make a good showing in the flesh, these *would* compel you to be circumcised, only that they may not suffer persecution for the cross of Christ. ¹³For not even those who are circumcised keep the law, but they desire to have you circumcised that they may boast in your flesh. ¹⁴But God forbid that I should boast except in the cross of our Lord Jesus Christ, by whom^a the world has been crucified to me, and I to the world. ¹⁵For in Christ Jesus neither circumcision nor uncircumcision avails anything, but a new creation.

BLESSING AND A PLEA

¹⁶And as many as walk according to this rule, peace and mercy *be* upon them, and upon the Israel of God.

¹⁷From now on let no one trouble me, for I bear in my body the marks of the Lord Jesus.

¹⁸Brethren, the grace of our Lord Jesus Christ *be* with your spirit. Amen.

PREACHING HEALTH

"To become a thoroughly good man is the best prescription for keeping a sound mind in a sound body."
—*Francis Bowen, American philosopher (1811–1890)*

6:14 ᵃOr *by which* (the cross)

HEALTH NOTES

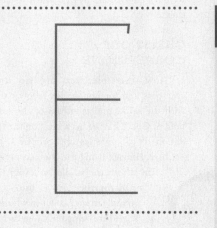

PHESIANS

This letter from the apostle Paul to the church at Ephesus is all about relationships—and about how to "walk in unity" with other believers, not only in the church but in marriages, families, and working relationships. Paul continually calls believers to recognize that they each have the same redemption and forgiveness made possible by Christ, the same access to God's grace and God's wisdom, and the same set of spiritual gifts that are intended to produce a strong church. We each face the same three challenges: to think and act as new creatures, to put on the character likeness of Christ, and to walk in love with one another. With those principles as a backdrop, Paul then defines specifics about the lines of authority and responsibility in husband-wife, parent-child, and servant-master relationships. In the end, Paul says, we must recognize that "disunity" is the evil scheme of the devil—we must become unified in our assault on spiritual evil and put on the whole armor of God, the nature of Christ, to stand against the "rulers of darkness."

Wholeness, by its very definition, requires agreement and cooperation.

GREETING

1 Paul, an apostle of Jesus Christ by the will of God,

To the saints who are in Ephesus, and faithful in Christ Jesus:

²Grace to you and peace from God our Father and the Lord Jesus Christ.

REDEMPTION IN CHRIST

³Blessed *be* the God and Father of our Lord Jesus Christ, who has blessed us with every spiritual blessing in the heavenly *places* in Christ, ⁴just as He chose us in Him before the foundation of the world, that we should be holy and without blame before Him in love, ⁵having predestined us to adoption as sons by Jesus Christ to Himself, according to the good pleasure of His will, ⁶to the praise of the glory of His grace, by which He made us accepted in the Beloved.

⁷In Him we have redemption through His blood, the forgiveness of sins, according to the riches of His grace ⁸which He made to abound toward us in all wisdom and prudence, ⁹having made known to us the mystery of His will, according to His good pleasure which He purposed in Himself, ¹⁰that in the dispensation of the fullness of the times He might gather together in one all things in Christ, both*ᵃ* which are in heaven and which are on earth—in Him. ¹¹In Him also we have obtained an inheritance, being predestined according to the purpose of Him who works all things according to the counsel of His will, ¹²that we who first trusted in Christ should be to the praise of His glory.

¹³In Him you also *trusted*, after you heard the word of truth, the gospel of your salvation; in whom also, having believed, you were sealed with the Holy Spirit of promise, ¹⁴"who" is the guarantee of our inheritance until the redemption of the purchased possession, to the praise of His glory.

PRAYER FOR SPIRITUAL WISDOM

¹⁵Therefore I also, after I heard of your faith in the Lord Jesus and your love for all the saints, ¹⁶do not cease to give thanks for you, making mention of you in my prayers: ¹⁷that the God of our Lord Jesus Christ, the Father of glory, may give to you the spirit of wisdom and revelation in the knowledge of Him, ¹⁸the eyes of your understanding*ᵃ* being enlightened; that you may know what is the hope of His calling, what are the riches of the glory of His inheritance in the saints, ¹⁹and what *is* the exceeding greatness of His power toward us who believe, according to the working of His mighty power ²⁰which He worked in Christ when He raised Him from the dead and seated *Him* at His right hand in the heavenly *places*, ²¹far above all principality and power and might and dominion, and every name that is named, not only in this age but also in that which is to come.

²²And He put all *things* under His feet, and gave Him *to be* head over all *things* to the church, ²³which is His body, the fullness of Him who fills all in all.

BY GRACE THROUGH FAITH

2 And you *He made alive*, who were dead in trespasses and sins, ²in which you once walked according to the course of this world, according to the prince of the power of the air, the spirit who now works in the sons of disobedience, ³among whom also we all once conducted ourselves in the lusts of our flesh, fulfilling the desires

---

1:10 ªNU-Text and M-Text omit *both*.   1:14 ªNU-Text reads *which*.   1:18 ªNU-Text and M-Text read *hearts*.

GODLY & GOODLOOKIN'

Smile!

Those who smile are automatically perceived as more attractive. Surely that's why most of us want to take photos of people who are smiling, as well as have photos taken of us that show us wearing our best smile or laugh. A recent study reported that people who smile are perceived to be as many as five to ten years younger than they actually are. Another study showed that children think adults who smile are both smarter and kinder. (In truth, most adults probably think the same.)

A smile is generally associated with "feeling good"—about life in general, current circumstances, one's health and well-being, one's relationships with God and other people, and the future. Take a closer look at most before-and-after photos for commercials related to aging or weight-loss products. The "after" photo nearly always shows the person smiling!

From a health standpoint, those who smile *on purpose* become more likely to smile *spontaneously*. A smile has an impact on a person's soul and attitude. Proverbs 15:30 links a cheerful countenance with a merry heart.

preached peace to you who were afar off and to those who were near. [18]For through Him we both have access by one Spirit to the Father.

CHRIST OUR CORNERSTONE

[19]Now, therefore, you are no longer strangers and foreigners, but fellow citizens with the saints and members of the household of God, [20]having been built on the foundation of the apostles and prophets, Jesus Christ Himself being the chief corner*stone*, [21]in whom the whole building, being fitted together, grows into a holy temple in the Lord, [22]in whom you also are being built together for a dwelling place of God in the Spirit.

WISE CHOICES

Choose fruit and nuts for dessert.
Rather than pie, cake, or ice cream for dessert, choose fresh or frozen fruit. Perhaps add a little yogurt, honey, or a few nuts. You *can* train your taste buds to be satisfied with a dessert that isn't syrupy sweet!

of the flesh and of the mind, and were by nature children of wrath, just as the others.

[4]But God, who is rich in mercy, because of His great love with which He loved us, [5]even when we were dead in trespasses, made us alive together with Christ (by grace you have been saved), [6]and raised *us* up together, and made *us* sit together in the heavenly *places* in Christ Jesus, [7]that in the ages to come He might show the exceeding riches of His grace in *His* kindness toward us in Christ Jesus. [8]For by grace you have been saved through faith, and that not of yourselves; *it is* the gift of God, [9]not of works, lest anyone should boast. [10]For we are His workmanship, created in Christ Jesus for good works, which God prepared beforehand that we should walk in them.

BROUGHT NEAR BY HIS BLOOD

[11]Therefore remember that you, once Gentiles in the flesh—who are called Uncircum-

cision by what is called the Circumcision made in the flesh by hands— [12]that at that time you were without Christ, being aliens from the commonwealth of Israel and strangers from the covenants of promise, having no hope and without God in the world. [13]But now in Christ Jesus you who once were far off have been brought near by the blood of Christ.

CHRIST OUR PEACE

[14]For He Himself is our peace, who has made both one, and has broken down the middle wall of separation, [15]having abolished in His flesh the enmity, *that is*, the law of commandments *contained* in ordinances, so as to create in Himself one new man *from* the two, *thus* making peace, [16]and that He might reconcile them both to God in one body through the cross, thereby putting to death the enmity. [17]And He came and

THE MYSTERY REVEALED

3 For this reason I, Paul, the prisoner of Christ Jesus for you Gentiles— ²if indeed you have heard of the dispensation of the grace of God which was given to me for you, ³how that by revelation He made known to me the mystery (as I have briefly written already, ⁴by which, when you read, you may understand my knowledge in the mystery of Christ), ⁵which in other ages was not made known to the sons of men, as it has now been revealed by the Spirit to His holy apostles and prophets: ⁶that the Gentiles should be fellow heirs, of the same body, and partakers of His promise in Christ through the gospel, ⁷of which I became a minister according to the gift of the grace of God given to me by the effective working of His power.

PURPOSE OF THE MYSTERY

⁸To me, who am less than the least of all the saints, this grace was given, that I should preach among the Gentiles the unsearchable riches of Christ, ⁹and to make all see what *is* the fellowship^a of the mystery, which from the beginning of the ages has been hidden in God who created all things through Jesus Christ;^b ¹⁰to the intent that now the manifold wisdom of God might be made known by the church to the principalities and powers in the heavenly *places,* ¹¹according to the eternal purpose which He accomplished in Christ Jesus our Lord, ¹²in whom we have boldness and access with confidence through faith in Him. ¹³Therefore I ask that you do not lose heart at my tribulations for you, which is your glory.

APPRECIATION OF THE MYSTERY

¹⁴For this reason I bow my knees to the Father of our Lord Jesus Christ,^a ¹⁵from whom the whole family in heaven and earth is named, ¹⁶that He would grant you, according to the riches of His glory, to be strengthened with might through His Spirit in the inner man, ¹⁷that Christ may dwell in your hearts through faith; that you, being rooted and grounded in love, ¹⁸may be able to comprehend with all the saints what *is* the width and length and depth and height— ¹⁹to know the love of Christ which passes knowledge; that you may be filled with all the fullness of God.

²⁰Now to Him who is able to do exceed-

Stress Busters
Change Your Distortional Thinking

We each have "distortional thinking" at some time, to some degree. This is thinking according to the way we personally perceive things to be, when in reality they are different. We each face the ongoing challenge of addressing our distortional thought processes—they are a major source of stress! Here are five types of distortional thinking common to millions of people:

1. *All or nothing thinking.* People who think this way see everything in black-and-white. There are no shades of gray. These people are often perfectionists and see their work as either perfect or worthless. Healthy thinkers, in contrast, recognize that absolute perfection is impossible to achieve and that most things in life have some element of flaw or failure.

2. *Overgeneralization.* This is the tendency to draw sweeping conclusions from very little evidence. People who overgeneralize think that if one thing goes wrong, nothing will ever go right. Healthy thinkers, on the other hand, draw conclusions only after taking in a great deal of evidence.

3. *A negative mental filter.* These people filter out any bit of information that is positive or good, and hear only criticism. They cannot "hear" compliments or words of affirmation or praise. They focuses on negative details. Healthy thinkers remember both successes and failures, and choose to focus on strengths that might lead to future success rather than focus on weaknesses.

4. *Disqualifying the positive.* These people hear the compliment but discount it. They explain away words of affirmation or praise. Healthy thinkers receive compliments and praise, and use them to validate their own self-esteem. They aren't blind to their weaknesses, but see them as areas in which to improve or gain strength, rather than as fatal flaws.

5. *Jumping to conclusions.* These people believe that they know what other people are thinking about them even when they say nothing. Those who jump to conclusions make negative assessments without having any facts to support their conclusions. They are prone to mind reading, fortune-telling, or predicting the future. Typically they anticipate the worst possible outcome for their own futures, or predict that circumstances will be negative. Healthy thinkers wait before drawing a final conclusion about any encounter, experience, or event. They weigh all facts and ask follow-up questions.

3:9 ^aNU-Text and M-Text read *stewardship* (*dispensation*). ^bNU-Text omits *through Jesus Christ.* **3:14** ^aNU-Text omits *of our Lord Jesus Christ.*

ingly abundantly above all that we ask or think, according to the power that works in us, ²¹to Him *be* glory in the church by Christ Jesus to all generations, forever and ever. Amen.

WALK IN UNITY

4 I, therefore, the prisoner of the Lord, beseech you to walk worthy of the calling with which you were called, ²with all lowliness and gentleness, with longsuffering, bearing with one another in love, ³endeavoring to keep the unity of the Spirit in the bond of peace. ⁴*There is* one body and one Spirit, just as you were called in one hope of your calling; ⁵one Lord, one faith, one baptism; ⁶one God and Father of all, who *is* above all, and through all, and in you* all.

SPIRITUAL GIFTS

⁷But to each one of us grace was given according to the measure of Christ's gift. ⁸Therefore He says:

"When He ascended on high,
   He led captivity captive,
   And gave gifts to men."*

⁹(Now this, *"He ascended"*—what does it mean but that He also first* descended into the lower parts of the earth? ¹⁰He who descended is also the One who ascended far above all the heavens, that He might fill all things.)

¹¹And He Himself gave some *to be* apostles, some prophets, some evangelists, and some pastors and teachers, ¹²for the equipping of the saints for the work of ministry, for the edifying of the body of Christ, ¹³till we all come to the unity of the faith and of the knowledge of the Son of God, to a perfect man, to the measure of the stature of the fullness of Christ; ¹⁴that we should no longer be children, tossed to and fro and carried about with every wind of doctrine, by the trickery of men, in the cunning craftiness of deceitful plotting, ¹⁵but, speaking the

---

℞ PRESCRIPTIONS FOR INNER HEALTH

"Anxiety in the heart of man causes depression,
But a good word makes it glad."

(PROVERBS 12:25)

The Bible had it right long before psychology became a behavioral science! People who are anxious and worried become fearful, and ever-present fears and the stress hormones that result are directly linked to depression. Choose to speak words of faith, hope, and love. Choose to praise God frequently every day. You will be blessing your mind, emotions, and body!

---

truth in love, may grow up in all things into Him who is the head— Christ— ¹⁶from whom the whole body, joined and knit together by what every joint supplies, according to the effective working by which every part does its share, causes growth of the body for the edifying of itself in love.

THE NEW MAN

¹⁷This I say, therefore, and testify in the Lord, that you should no longer walk as the rest of* the Gentiles walk, in the futility of their mind, ¹⁸having their understanding darkened, being alienated from the life of God, because of the ignorance that is in them, because of the blindness of their heart; ¹⁹who, being past feeling, have given themselves over to lewdness, to work all uncleanness with greediness.

²⁰But you have not so learned Christ, ²¹if indeed you have heard Him and have been taught by Him, as the truth is in Jesus: ²²that you put off, concerning your former conduct, the old man which grows corrupt according to the deceitful lusts, ²³and be renewed in the spirit of

---

INSIGHTS INTO THE WORD

> (Ephesians 4:1–6)

The Extension of Wholeness. We often think of healing and wholeness as pertaining only to our own physical, emotional, and spiritual selves. From God's perspective, personal wholeness is one factor involved in an even greater wholeness—the wholeness of His body, the church. God desires for believers to get along with one another and to be "whole" as communities of the faithful—to live together in mutual support and peace, with a prevailing atmosphere of humility, love, and patience.

We are to keep our eyes on our commonalities, among them: the fact that we each have been saved by the shed blood of Jesus Christ, our ongoing devotion to follow the Lord, and our pursuit of godly disciplines and faith. We have a responsibility before God not only to become whole as individuals, but also to contribute to the greater wholeness of the churches to which we belong.

4:6 ªNU-Text omits *you;* M-Text reads *us.*   4:8 ªPsalm 68:18   4:9 ªNU-Text omits *first.*   4:17 ªNU-Text omits *the rest of.*

PEACE LOVE JOY KINDNESS

The Healthy Soul
>Gentleness

Gentleness is virtually synonymous with *tenderness* and *humility*. It is an expression toward others that causes them to feel valued, worthy, loved, cherished, and comforted. Those who are gentle are not proud or self-seeking. They desire to see others do their best and to become all they can be.

In some Bible translations, the soul fruit of *gentleness* is translated *meekness*. Unfortunately, many people in our world today equate meekness or gentleness with being wimpy or weak. Nothing is further from the truth! *Meekness*, which in the Greek is the word *prautes*, refers to the quality of the heart that is completely submitted to, or "given" to seeing the best in others.

One of the Greek meanings for the word *prautes* has to do with the putting of a bit in a horse's mouth. The horse that has been "meeked" is a horse that does the bidding of its rider—it goes where the rider directs, and stops and starts at the discretion of the rider. In a very similar way, the person who has been filled with God's Spirit is "meeked" by the Spirit. That person treats other people as Jesus would treat them, says to others what Jesus would say, and goes where the Spirit directs. He or she starts and stops doing various behaviors or tasks under the convicting guidance of the Spirit.

There's nothing weak about yielding to the Holy Spirit! The Holy Spirit uses precisely such a person to manifest great miracles and acts of power, all of which are to be done with a huge coating of love and compassion. The gentle person—the meek person—lives to serve others. That's what Jesus did.

your mind, ²⁴and that you put on the new man which was created according to God, in true righteousness and holiness.

DO NOT GRIEVE THE SPIRIT

²⁵Therefore, putting away lying, "Let each one *of you* speak truth with his neighbor,"ᵃ for we are members of one another. ²⁶"Be angry, and do not sin":ᵃ do not let the sun go down on your wrath, ²⁷nor give place to the devil. ²⁸Let him who stole steal no longer, but rather let him labor, working with *his* hands what is good, that he may have something to give him who has need. ²⁹Let no corrupt word proceed out of your mouth, but what is good for necessary edification, that it may impart grace to the hearers. ³⁰And do not grieve the Holy Spirit of God, by whom you were sealed for the day of redemption. ³¹Let all bitterness, wrath, anger, clamor, and evil speaking be put away from you, with all malice. ³²And be kind to one another, tenderhearted, forgiving one another, even as God in Christ forgave you.

WALK IN LOVE

5 Therefore be imitators of God as dear children. ²And walk in love, as Christ also has loved us and given Himself for us, an offering and a sacrifice to God for a sweet-smelling aroma.

³But fornication and all uncleanness or covetousness, let it not even be named among you, as is fitting for saints; ⁴neither filthiness, nor foolish talking, nor coarse jesting, which are not fitting, but rather giving of thanks. ⁵For this you know,ᵃ that no fornicator, unclean person, nor covetous man, who is an idolater, has any inheritance in the kingdom of Christ and God. ⁶Let no one deceive you with empty words, for because of these things the wrath of God comes upon the sons of disobedience. ⁷Therefore do not be partakers with them.

WALK IN LIGHT

⁸For you were once darkness, but now *you are* light in the Lord. Walk as children of light ⁹(for the fruit of the Spiritᵃ *is* in all goodness, righteousness, and truth), ¹⁰finding out what is acceptable to the Lord. ¹¹And have no fellowship with the unfruitful works of darkness, but rather expose *them*. ¹²For it is shameful even to speak of those things

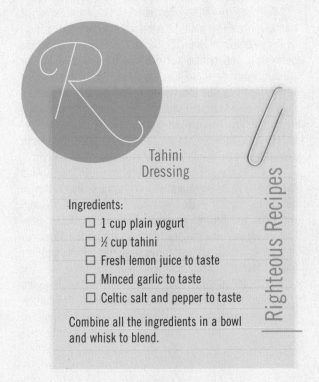

Tahini Dressing

Ingredients:
☐ 1 cup plain yogurt
☐ ½ cup tahini
☐ Fresh lemon juice to taste
☐ Minced garlic to taste
☐ Celtic salt and pepper to taste

Combine all the ingredients in a bowl and whisk to blend.

Righteous Recipes

4:25 ᵃZechariah 8:16   4:26 ᵃPsalm 4:4   5:5 ᵃNU-Text reads *For know this*.   5:9 ᵃNU-Text reads *light*.

Women's Issues
Rape and Incest

Social science surveys have revealed repeatedly in the last several decades that as many as one in four adult women in our society have been abused sexually. That number is staggering! Many eating disorders and other psychological disorders have a very high correlation with sexual abuse. The impact of incest and rape upon a woman is devastating.

Although the Bible does not use the word *incest*, it strongly advocates purity of relationships in the inner family circle (Leviticus 18:6–18). Sexual intimacy was forbidden between closely related persons and the punishments for persons violating these laws were death, childlessness, or being cursed by God (Deuteronomy 28:20–23). God's desire is the wholeness of individuals—emotional, physical, spiritual, and psychological. Laws about family fidelity set believers apart from the heathen, and also guarded the Jewish people against unhealthy genetic mutation.

Perhaps the foremost example of incest in the Bible is the case of Lot's daughters, who encouraged their father to get drunk so that each might have a sexual relationship with him and become pregnant. The sons produced from this incest became the heads of two tribes, the Moabites and the Ammonites. These tribes struggled bitterly and frequently with the Israelites for hundreds of years.

Rape and incest victims may suffer for years from the psychological trauma they have experienced. They often have nightmares, severe and lingering fears, and feelings of CONT. NEXT PAGE>>>

which are done by them in secret. [13]But all things that are exposed are made manifest by the light, for whatever makes manifest is light. [14]Therefore He says:

> "Awake, you who sleep,
>   Arise from the dead,
>   And Christ will give you light."

WALK IN WISDOM

[15]See then that you walk circumspectly, not as fools but as wise, [16]redeeming the time, because the days are evil. [17]Therefore do not be unwise, but understand what the will of the Lord *is.* [18]And do not be drunk with wine, in which is dissipation; but be filled with the Spirit, [19]speaking to one another in psalms and hymns and spiritual songs, singing and making melody in your heart to the Lord, [20]giving thanks always for all things to God the Father in the name of our Lord Jesus Christ, [21]submitting to one another in the fear of God.[a]

MARRIAGE—CHRIST AND THE CHURCH

[22]Wives, submit to your own husbands, as to the Lord. [23]For the husband is head of the wife, as also Christ is head of the church; and He is the Savior of the body. [24]Therefore, just as the church is subject to Christ, so *let* the wives *be* to their own husbands in everything.

[25]Husbands, love your wives, just as Christ also loved the church and gave Himself for her, [26]that He might sanctify and cleanse her with the washing of water by the word, [27]that He might present her to Himself a glorious church, not having spot or wrinkle or any such thing, but that she should be holy and without blemish. [28]So husbands ought to love their own wives as their own bodies; he who loves his wife loves himself. [29]For no one ever hated his own flesh, but nourishes and cherishes it, just as the Lord *does* the church. [30]For we are members of His body,[a] of His flesh and of His bones. [31]"For this reason a man shall leave his father and mother and be joined to his wife, and the two shall become one flesh."[a] [32]This is a great mystery, but I speak concerning Christ and the church. [33]Nevertheless let each one of you in particular so love his own wife as himself, and let the wife *see* that she respects *her* husband.

CHILDREN AND PARENTS

6 Children, obey your parents in the Lord, for this is right. [2]"Honor your father and mother," which is the first commandment with promise: [3]"that it may be well with you and you may live long on the earth."[a]

[4]And you, fathers, do not provoke your children to wrath, but bring them up in the training and admonition of the Lord.

BONDSERVANTS AND MASTERS

[5]Bondservants, be obedient to those who are your masters according to the flesh, with fear and trembling, in sincerity of heart, as to Christ; [6]not with eyeservice, as men-pleasers, but as bondservants of Christ, doing the will of God from the heart, [7]with goodwill doing service, as to the Lord, and not to men, [8]knowing that whatever good anyone does, he will receive the same from the Lord, whether *he is* a slave or free.

5:21 [a]NU-Text reads *Christ.*   5:30 [a]NU-Text omits the rest of this verse.   5:31 [a]Genesis 2:24   6:3 [a]Deuteronomy 5:16

low self-worth. Those who experience date rape often register strong emotions of shock, denial, shame, anger, and depression, as well as a degree of guilt. Each woman who has experienced a sexual violation should be encouraged to seek God's healing help and to find a way of releasing the negative feelings and any desire for revenge she may feel. To harbor these emotions gives even more power to the rapist—indeed, the loss of health is an ongoing act of violation.

[9]And you, masters, do the same things to them, giving up threatening, knowing that your own Master also[a] is in heaven, and there is no partiality with Him.

THE WHOLE ARMOR OF GOD

[10]Finally, my brethren, be strong in the Lord and in the power of His might. [11]Put on the whole armor of God, that you may be able to stand against the wiles of the devil. [12]For we do not wrestle against flesh and blood, but against principalities, against powers, against the rulers of the darkness of this age,[a] against spiritual *hosts* of wickedness in the heavenly *places*. [13]Therefore take up the whole armor of God, that you may be able to withstand in the evil day, and having done all, to stand.

[14]Stand therefore, having girded your waist with truth, having put on the breastplate of righteousness, [15]and having shod your feet with the preparation of the gospel of peace; [16]above all, taking the shield of faith with which you will be able to quench all the fiery darts of the wicked one. [17]And take the helmet of salvation, and the sword of the Spirit, which is the word of God; [18]praying always with all prayer and supplication in the Spirit, being watchful to this end with all perseverance and supplication for all the saints— [19]and for me, that utterance may be given to me, that I may open my mouth boldly to make known the mystery of the gospel, [20]for which I am an ambassador in chains; that in it I may speak boldly, as I ought to speak.

A GRACIOUS GREETING

[21]But that you also may know my affairs *and* how I am doing, Tychicus, a beloved brother and faithful minister in the Lord, will make all things known to you; [22]whom I have sent to you for this very purpose, that you may know our affairs, and *that* he may comfort your hearts.

[23]Peace to the brethren, and love with faith, from God the Father and the Lord Jesus Christ. [24]Grace *be* with all those who love our Lord Jesus Christ in sincerity. Amen.

Q Who is the first person in the Bible described as the planter of a vineyard?

A Noah *(Genesis 9:20).*

walking the walk

[NO PAIN, NO GAIN?]

The proverbial exercise statement "No pain, no gain" has become common. Is it really true?

It may be true for body builders—those individuals who are trying to bulk up muscles. Muscles need to be exercised to the "burning" point for sufficient tear down and rebuilding. It is *not* true, however, for most other forms of exercise.

Pain is generally a signal that something is being injured and a person is wise to stop the exercise at the point pain begins. Enduring pain or stress injuries on a regular basis serves no good purpose for either the body or the soul.

Physicians who treat pain distinguish between nociceptic pain, which is pain caused by injury or trauma to the body's tissues, and pain that does not have a bodily origin. In some cases, pain is *psychosomatic*—it has its origins in the emotions and mind rather than an organic condition. In most cases people are not disabled by nociceptic pain, which generally can be treated and if the origin discovered, remedied fairly quickly. People tend to be disabled by chronic, long-term pain that is much more difficult to isolate and diagnose.

We also need to recognize that people experience pain in different ways according to their genetic differences in enzymes and *opioid* receptors. There are also people who have CIPA, congenital insensitivity to pain with *anhidrosis*—a condition that affects nerve endings. These people do not have the ability to sense pain and are therefore extremely vulnerable to serious cuts, fractures, and burns.

The concept of "no pain, no gain" is advocated in some religions in which the endurance of pain is regarded as a pathway to greater spirituality. Pain, however, is *not* advocated as a path to spiritual growth in Christianity. The Bible calls on believers to endure pain associated with persecution, but it does not advocate the self-infliction of pain!

6:9 [a]NU-Text reads *He who is both their Master and yours.*   6:12 [a]NU-Text reads *rulers of this darkness.*

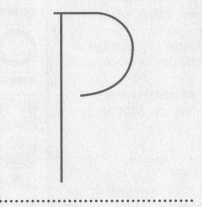

PHILIPPIANS

Philippians has been called the "feel good" book of the New Testament. Although the apostle Paul is often perceived as being angry or scolding in tone, this letter is all about joy, elation, delight, happiness, and hope. The positive tone of Philippians is especially interesting given the fact that one of Paul's main purposes in writing is to take up an offering!

Physicians today know the great value of a positive attitude toward recovery from illness and surgery, as well as the value of hope and optimism in avoiding illness. In contrast, fear, worry, and other negative attitudes can greatly damage one's health. In these matters of health-related wisdom, Paul was way ahead of his time! It is to the Philippians that Paul wrote, "be anxious for nothing"—rather, we are to pray with thanksgiving and rejoice in the Lord always! He also instructed the Philippians to do all things without complaining and disputing. He commanded the Philippians to think about good things, knowing that what we think about creates our attitudes and perspective, which in turn impacts our behavior—and in the end, how and what we think about are directly related to our health and well-being.

GREETING

1 Paul and Timothy, bondservants of Jesus Christ,

To all the saints in Christ Jesus who are in Philippi, with the bishops^a and deacons:

[2]Grace to you and peace from God our Father and the Lord Jesus Christ.

THANKFULNESS AND PRAYER

[3]I thank my God upon every remembrance of you, [4]always in every prayer of mine making request for you all with joy, [5]for your fellowship in the gospel from the first day until now, [6]being confident of this very thing, that He who has begun a good work in you will complete *it* until the day of Jesus Christ; [7]just as it is right for me to think this of you all, because I have you in my heart, inasmuch as both in my chains and in the defense and confirmation of the gospel, you all are partakers with me of grace. [8]For God is my witness, how greatly I long for you all with the affection of Jesus Christ.

[9]And this I pray, that your love may abound still more and more in knowledge and all discernment, [10]that you may approve the things that are excellent, that you may be sincere and without offense till the day of Christ, [11]being filled with the fruits of righteousness which *are* by Jesus Christ, to the glory and praise of God.

CHRIST IS PREACHED

[12]But I want you to know, brethren, that the things *which happened* to me have actually turned out for the furtherance of the gospel, [13]so that it has become evident to the whole palace guard, and to all the rest, that my chains are in Christ; [14]and most of the brethren in the Lord, having become confident by my chains, are much more bold to speak the word without fear.

[15]Some indeed preach Christ even from envy and strife, and some also from goodwill: [16]The former^a preach Christ from selfish ambition, not sincerely, supposing to add affliction to my chains; [17]but the latter out of love, knowing that I am appointed for the defense of the gospel. [18]What then? Only *that* in every way, whether in pretense or in truth, Christ is preached; and in this I rejoice, yes, and will rejoice.

TO LIVE IS CHRIST

[19]For I know that this will turn out for my deliverance through your prayer and the supply of the Spirit of Jesus Christ, [20]according to my earnest expectation and hope that in nothing I shall be ashamed, but with all boldness, as always, so now also Christ will be magnified in my body, whether by life or by death. [21]For to me, to live *is* Christ, and to die *is* gain. [22]But if *I* live on in the flesh, this *will mean* fruit from *my* labor; yet what I shall choose I cannot tell. [23]For^a I am hard-pressed between the two, having a desire to depart and be with Christ, *which is* far better. [24]Nevertheless to remain in the flesh *is* more needful for you. [25]And being confident of this, I know that I shall remain and continue with you all for your progress and joy of faith, [26]that your rejoicing for me may be more abundant in Jesus Christ by my coming to you again.

STRIVING AND SUFFERING FOR CHRIST

[27]Only let your conduct be worthy of the gospel of Christ, so that whether I come and see you or am absent, I may hear of your affairs,

1:1 ^aLiterally *overseers*   1:16 ^aNU-Text reverses the contents of verses 16 and 17.   1:23 ^aNU-Text and M-Text read *But.*

WHOLENESS 101

The Decision for Purity

A number of young people these days are wearing "purity rings" on their wedding-ring fingers. These rings are often a gift from a father to a daughter or from a mother to a son. The ring is intended to be a reminder to the wearer—and to send a signal to everybody else—that the young person has made a decision to remain a virgin until marriage.

Making a decision for purity is a decision that every Christian is called to make! Certainly sexual purity is required. Unmarried Christians are to live celibate lives; married Christians are to be faithful to one spouse of the opposite sex.

Purity in other areas of life is also essential. And it is always a *choice*—an intentional, conscious decision to pursue what God considers pure, not necessarily what man defines as pure.

When it comes to the natural world, choose to breathe pure air, drink pure water, and to eat foods that are free of pesticides, herbicides, antibiotics, or genetic engineering. Also choose to eat foods that are not loaded with sugar, fats, or hydrogenated or partially hydrogenated oils.

When it comes to what you put into your mind, choose to expose your thinking to books, magazines, movies, and television programs that are informative, inspirational, and edifying. Violent images, vulgar language, and explicit sexual references and behavior are so commonplace in our media that you may be amazed at just how widespread they are once you make a decision for purity.

When it comes to the way you order your material life and make decisions about relationships and various procedures, ask yourself frequently:

☐ *Does this complicate or simplify my life?*
☐ *Does this streamline or add clutter to my world?*
☐ *Does this pollute or clean up my environment or the greater environment around me?*
☐ *Does this make things clearer or more obtuse?*
☐ *Does this make things easier or more difficult?*

While the questions above are not directly aimed at purity, very often purity and simplicity go hand in hand!

Above all, ask yourself, *Is this the way God originally intended men and women to live?* God's original design for creation was pure, simple, and good.

---

that you stand fast in one spirit, with one mind striving together for the faith of the gospel, [28]and not in any way terrified by your adversaries, which is to them a proof of perdition, but to you of salvation,[a] and that from God. [29]For to you it has been granted on behalf of Christ, not only to believe in Him, but also to suffer for His sake, [30]having the same conflict which you saw in me and now hear *is* in me.

UNITY THROUGH HUMILITY

2 Therefore if *there is* any consolation in Christ, if any comfort of love, if any fellowship of the Spirit, if any affection and mercy, [2]fulfill my joy by being like-minded, having the same love, *being* of one accord, of one mind. [3]*Let* nothing *be done* through selfish ambition or conceit, but in lowliness of mind let each esteem others better than himself. [4]Let each of you look out not only for his own interests, but also for the interests of others.

THE HUMBLED AND EXALTED CHRIST

[5]Let this mind be in you which was also in Christ Jesus, [6]who, being in the form of God, did not consider it robbery to be equal with God, [7]but made Himself of no reputation, taking the form of a bondservant, *and* coming in the likeness of men. [8]And being found in appearance as a man, He humbled Himself and became obedient to *the point of* death, even the death of the cross. [9]Therefore God also has highly exalted Him and given Him the name which is above every name, [10]that at the name of Jesus every knee should bow, of those in heaven, and of those on earth, and of those under the earth, [11]and *that* every tongue should confess that Jesus Christ *is* Lord, to the glory of God the Father.

LIGHT BEARERS

[12]Therefore, my beloved, as you have always obeyed, not as in my presence only, but now much more in my absence, work out your own salvation with fear and trembling; [13]for it is God who works in you both to will and to do for *His* good pleasure.

[14]Do all things without complaining and disputing, [15]that you may

---

Q What is better to be chosen than great riches? Than silver and gold?

A "A good name . . . rather than great riches. Loving favor rather than silver and gold" *(Proverbs 22:1).*

1:28 [a]NU-Text reads *of your salvation.*

become blameless and harmless, children of God without fault in the midst of a crooked and perverse generation, among whom you shine as lights in the world, ¹⁶holding fast the word of life, so that I may rejoice in the day of Christ that I have not run in vain or labored in vain.

¹⁷Yes, and if I am being poured out *as a drink offering* on the sacrifice and service of your faith, I am glad and rejoice with you all. ¹⁸For the same reason you also be glad and rejoice with me.

TIMOTHY COMMENDED

¹⁹But I trust in the Lord Jesus to send Timothy to you shortly, that I also may be encouraged when I know your state. ²⁰For I have no one like-minded, who will sincerely care for your state. ²¹For all seek their own, not the things which are of Christ Jesus. ²²But you know his proven character, that as a son with *his* father he served with me in the gospel. ²³Therefore I hope to send him at once, as soon as I see how it goes with me. ²⁴But I trust in the Lord that I myself shall also come shortly.

EPAPHRODITUS PRAISED

²⁵Yet I considered it necessary to send to you Epaphroditus, my brother, fellow worker, and fellow soldier, but your messenger and the one who ministered to my need; ²⁶since he was longing for you all, and was distressed because you had heard that he was sick. ²⁷For indeed he was sick almost unto death; but God had mercy on him, and not only on him but on me also, lest I should have sorrow upon sorrow. ²⁸Therefore I sent him the more eagerly, that when you see him again you may rejoice, and I may be less sorrowful. ²⁹Receive him therefore in the Lord with all gladness, and hold such men in esteem; ³⁰because for the work of Christ he came close to death, not regarding his life, to supply what was lacking in your service toward me.

ALL FOR CHRIST

3 Finally, my brethren, rejoice in the Lord. For me to write the same things to you *is* not tedious, but for you *it is* safe.
²Beware of dogs, beware of evil workers, beware of the mutilation! ³For we are the circumcision, who worship God in the Spirit,ᵃ

> " **Let nothing be done through selfish ambition or conceit, but in lowliness of mind let each esteem others better than himself. Let each of you look out not only for his own interests, but also for the interests of others.** " — *Philippians 2:3–4*

The Healthy Soul
>Peace

Peace in the Old and New Testaments has one main definition: being in right relationship with God and other people. The Greek word for *peace, eirene*, has a similar meaning to *shalom*, the Hebrew word for *peace*. Both words depict a spiritual peace that includes a sense of well-being and fulfillment that comes from God alone and is dependent on His presence.

From a biblical point of view, peace is not the absence of conflict. Rather, it is the ability to maintain one's inner quiet confidence regardless of conflict. The true peace of God protects a person from worry, fear, and anxiety. It transcends rationality and logic. Why? Because when a person knows he has been forgiven of sin and is in right relationship with God, and his conscience is clear of any ill motive or past trespass against other people, that person experiences a wonderful contentment that all is right—now and for all eternity.

Peace is more than a "feeling." It is a "knowing," a firm believing that according to God's Word, all has been done that needs to be done in order to qualify for a home in heaven and a life of abundant blessing on this earth. Peace is living continually, every hour of every day, fully prepared for that hour to be your last on this earth—and knowing that if it is, all is well with your soul.

A person usually finds that he feels much greater peace if he spends a portion of each day in quiet prayer, reflection on God's goodness, and contemplation of the Scriptures. Time alone with God helps a person to experience God's abiding and loving presence. A focus on God's nature and His promises in the Bible helps a person turn from the worrisome aspects of the world.

When we truly see God as being bigger than our biggest problem, we are better able to trust Him. When we see God as being more loving than our worst behavior, we are better able to receive His love. When we see God as being in control of all things at all times and for good purposes, we have hope. This blend of faith, hope, and love is truly what produces peace in us.

PEACE LOVE JOY KINDNESS

rejoice in Christ Jesus, and have no confidence in the flesh, ⁴though I also might have confidence in the flesh. If anyone else thinks he may have confidence in the flesh, I more so: ⁵circumcised the eighth day, of the stock of Israel, *of* the tribe of Benjamin, a Hebrew of the Hebrews; concerning the law, a Pharisee; ⁶concerning zeal, persecuting the

3:3 ᵃNU-Text and M-Text read *who worship in the Spirit of God.*

The LAW AND THE SCIENCE

[REFUSE TO EAT BLOOD]

>SCIENCE tells us that if an animal or bird—wild or domesticated—is harboring harmful bacteria, that bacteria is most concentrated in the blood of the animal or bird. Also, if an animal, such as a deer, is killed in the wild and the blood is not drained from it immediately, the blood will be the first part of the animal subject to contamination and infection. Although this Law was probably established to keep people respectful of all living creatures and to keep people from eating creatures that are still living, we have learned through medical, sociological, and anthropological research studies that the drinking of blood and eating of live animal tissue can be very harmful to human beings—not only physically but also psychologically. A lack of respect for animal life is directly linked to a lack of respect for human life.

> **>THE LAW** says: "You may slaughter and eat meat within all your gates . . . Only you shall not eat the blood . . . You may slaughter from your herd and from your flock which the LORD has given you, just as I have commanded you, and you may eat within your gates as much as your heart desires. Just as the gazelle and the deer are eaten, so you may eat them . . . Only be sure that you do not eat the blood, for the blood is the life; you may not eat the life with the meat" (Deuteronomy 12:15, 16, 21–23).

church; concerning the righteousness which is in the law, blameless.

7But what things were gain to me, these I have counted loss for Christ. 8Yet indeed I also count all things loss for the excellence of the knowledge of Christ Jesus my Lord, for whom I have suffered the loss of all things, and count them as rubbish, that I may gain Christ 9and be found in Him, not having my own righteousness, which *is* from the law, but that which *is* through faith in Christ, the righteousness which is from God by faith; 10that I may know Him and the power of His resurrection, and the fellowship of His sufferings, being conformed to His death, 11if, by any means, I may attain to the resurrection from the dead.

PRESSING TOWARD THE GOAL

12Not that I have already attained, or am already perfected; but I press on, that I may lay hold of that for which Christ Jesus has also laid hold of me. 13Brethren, I do not count myself to have apprehended; but one thing *I do,* forgetting those things which are behind and reaching forward to those things which are ahead, 14I press toward the goal for the prize of the upward call of God in Christ Jesus.

15Therefore let us, as many as are mature, have this mind; and if in anything you think otherwise, God will reveal even this to you. 16Nevertheless, to *the degree* that we have already attained, let us walk by the same rule,ᵃ let us be of the same mind.

OUR CITIZENSHIP IN HEAVEN

17Brethren, join in following my example, and note those who so walk, as you have us for a pattern. 18For many walk, of whom I have told you often, and now tell you even weeping, *that they are* the enemies of the cross of Christ: 19whose end *is* destruction, whose god *is their* belly, and *whose* glory *is* in their shame—who set their mind on earthly things. 20For our citizenship is in heaven, from which we also eagerly wait for the Savior, the Lord Jesus Christ, 21who will transform our lowly body that it may be conformed to His glorious body, according to the working by which He is able even to subdue all things to Himself.

4 Therefore, my beloved and longed-for brethren, my joy and crown, so stand fast in the Lord, beloved.

BE UNITED, JOYFUL, AND IN PRAYER

2I implore Euodia and I implore Syntyche to be of the same mind in the Lord. 3Andᵃ I urge you also, true companion, help these women who labored with me in the gospel, with Clement also, and the rest of my fellow workers, whose names *are* in the Book of Life.

4Rejoice in the Lord always. Again I will say, rejoice!

5Let your gentleness be known to all men. The Lord *is* at hand.

6Be anxious for nothing, but in everything by prayer and supplication, with thanksgiving, let your requests be made known to God; 7and the peace of God, which surpasses all understanding, will guard your hearts and minds through Christ Jesus.

MEDITATE ON THESE THINGS

8Finally, brethren, whatever things are true, whatever things *are* noble, whatever things *are* just, whatever things *are* pure, whatever things *are* lovely, whatever things *are* of good report, if *there is* any virtue and if *there is* anything praiseworthy—meditate on these things. 9The things which you learned and received and heard and saw in me, these do, and the God of peace will be with you.

PHILIPPIAN GENEROSITY

10But I rejoiced in the Lord greatly that now at last your care for me has flourished again; though you surely did care, but you lacked opportunity. 11Not that I speak in regard to need, for I have learned in whatever state I am, to be content: 12I know how to be abased, and I know how to abound. Everywhere and in all things I have learned both to be full and to be hungry, both to abound and to suffer need. 13I can do all things through Christᵃ who strengthens me.

14Nevertheless you have done well that you shared in my distress. 15Now you Philippians know also that in the beginning of the gospel, when I departed from Macedonia, no church shared with me concerning giving and receiving but you only. 16For even in Thessalonica you sent *aid* once and again for my necessities. 17Not that I seek the gift, but I seek the fruit that abounds to your account.

3:16 ᵃNU-Text omits *rule* and the rest of the verse.   4:3 ᵃNU-Text and M-Text read *Yes.*   4:13 ᵃNU-Text reads *Him who.*

INSIGHTS | INTO THE WORD

> (Philippians 4:8, 9)

You Are What You Think. There's an old saying that "you are what you eat." That's literally true. Food provides the building blocks for physical strength and vitality, and a lack of proper nutrients results in physical weakness and lower immunity. When it comes to emotional health, there's an equally true saying: "You are what you think" ! If you focus on the negative side of life, you will quickly become frustrated, anxious, fearful, confused, discouraged, depressed, and you may even become despondent and give in to despair.

If you want to stay emotionally healthy, guard what you think about! Be intentional in *choosing* to think on the bright side of life. Focus your attention and your times of contemplation on those things that are uplifting, or as Paul says, things that are true (not rumor or speculation), pure (not lewd or crude), lovely (not seamy), of good report (not malicious or damaging gossip), virtuous (not scandalous), and praiseworthy (not rooted in cynicism, criticism, or ridicule).

¹⁸Indeed I have all and abound. I am full, having received from Epaphroditus the things *sent* from you, a sweet-smelling aroma, an acceptable sacrifice, well pleasing to God. ¹⁹And my God shall supply all your need according to His riches in glory by Christ Jesus. ²⁰Now to our God and Father *be* glory forever and ever. Amen.

GREETING AND BLESSING

²¹Greet every saint in Christ Jesus. The brethren who are with me greet you. ²²All the saints greet you, but especially those who are of Caesar's household.

²³The grace of our Lord Jesus Christ be with you all.ᵃ Amen.

4:23 ᵃNU-Text reads *your spirit.*

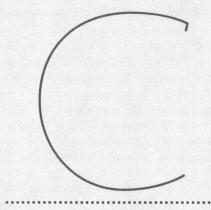

COLOSSIANS

There's a common belief today that aspects of various religions can be mixed with Christianity without harmful effect. Paul addresses this very issue in writing to the Colossians, who had started mingling heresies into their faith. Paul states clearly that Jesus Christ is the Savior, the divine Creator and Sustainer, and that Christ is preeminent over all and the divine Reconciler to God the Father. Paul has no tolerance for the teachings of philosophy, legalism, or acceptance of carnal behavior in the church at Colosse. He calls for the believers there to be holy and to reflect the attributes of tender mercies, kindness, humility, meekness, and patience as they bear with one another and forgive one another.

No dilution or pollution of the truth. That's Paul's message. It's one that is good for health and wholeness as well. Don't pollute your mind, your body, or your environment. To do so is to dilute your levels of energy and health, and in turn, dilute the degree to which you might accomplish great things for Christ in this world.

GREETING

1 Paul, an apostle of Jesus Christ by the will of God, and Timothy our brother,

²To the saints and faithful brethren in Christ *who are* in Colosse:

Grace to you and peace from God our Father and the Lord Jesus Christ.ᵃ

THEIR FAITH IN CHRIST

³We give thanks to the God and Father of our Lord Jesus Christ, praying always for you, ⁴since we heard of your faith in Christ Jesus and of your love for all the saints; ⁵because of the hope which is laid up for you in heaven, of which you heard before in the word of the truth of the gospel, ⁶which has come to you, as *it has* also in all the world, and is bringing forth fruit,ᵃ as *it is* also among you since the day you heard and knew the grace of God in truth; ⁷as you also learned from Epaphras, our dear fellow servant, who is a faithful minister of Christ on your behalf, ⁸who also declared to us your love in the Spirit.

PREEMINENCE OF CHRIST

⁹For this reason we also, since the day we heard it, do not cease to pray for you, and to ask that you may be filled with the knowledge of His will in all wisdom and spiritual understanding; ¹⁰that you may walk worthy of the Lord, fully pleasing *Him*, being fruitful in every good work and increasing in the knowledge of God; ¹¹strengthened with all might, according to His glorious power, for all patience and longsuffering with joy; ¹²giving thanks to the Father who has qualified us to be partakers of the inheritance of the saints in the light. ¹³He has delivered us from the power of darkness and conveyed *us* into the kingdom of the Son of His love, ¹⁴in whom we have redemption through His blood,ᵃ the forgiveness of sins.

¹⁵He is the image of the invisible God, the firstborn over all creation. ¹⁶For by Him all things were created that are in heaven and that are on earth, visible and invisible, whether thrones or dominions or principalities or powers. All things were created through Him and for Him. ¹⁷And He is before all things, and in Him all things consist. ¹⁸And He is the head of the body, the church, who is the beginning, the firstborn from the dead, that in all things He may have the preeminence.

RECONCILED IN CHRIST

¹⁹For it pleased *the Father that* in Him all the fullness should dwell, ²⁰and by Him to reconcile all things to Himself, by Him, whether things on earth or things in heaven, having made peace through the blood of His cross.

²¹And you, who once were alienated and enemies in your mind by wicked works, yet now He has reconciled ²²in the body of His flesh through death, to present you holy, and blameless, and above reproach in His sight— ²³if indeed you continue in the faith, grounded and steadfast, and are not moved away from the hope of the gospel which you heard, which was preached to every creature under heaven, of which I, Paul, became a minister.

1:2 ᵃNU-Text omits *and the Lord Jesus Christ.*   1:6 ᵃNU-Text and M-Text add *and growing.*   1:14 ᵃNU-Text and M-Text omit *through His blood.*

> (Colossians 1:9–12)

A Lesson in What to Pray. Have you ever been asked to pray for someone and not known what to say? This is often the case when we are called upon to pray for someone who is sick or facing a major loss in his or her life. A very positive and encouraging approach is to open your Bible and pray what Paul prayed for the Colossians:

☐ "Be filled with the knowledge of His will in all wisdom and spiritual understanding." (That the person might truly understand what God is seeking to accomplish through his or her life and witness.)

☐ "Walk worthy of the Lord, fully pleasing Him." (That he or she might keep the commandments and abstain from all evil.)

☐ "Be fruitful in every good work." (That his or her prayers, words, and deeds might be filled with productivity, purpose, and satisfaction.)

☐ "Increase in the knowledge of God." (That he or she might draw closer and closer to God with each passing day, and have a genuine friendship with God.)

☐ "Be strengthened with all might according to His glorious power." (That he or she might receive the grace and power of the Holy Spirit to endure whatever comes his or her way.)

☐ "Experience patience and longsuffering with joy." (That he or she might "keep his or her cool" and stay calmly joyful regardless of circumstances.)

☐ "Give thanks to the Father who has qualified us to be partakers of the inheritance of the saints in the light." (That he or she might always be mindful and thankful for his or her salvation.)

What a wonderful thing to have someone pray for you in this way! What a blessing it is to pray for others in this way! Such a prayer is filled with encouragement, hope, faith, and love—the best healing agents for anyone's soul.

PRESCRIPTIONS FOR INNER HEALTH

"Hope deferred makes the heart sick,
But when the desire comes,
it is a tree of life."

(PROVERBS 13:12)

Discouragement and disappointment often cause a person to become depressed, and even dismayed to the point that life seems meaningless and without purpose. Keep your hopes and dreams alive no matter what circumstances you face. Hopes and desires that are turned into plans and action usually produce "good fruit" that benefits not only you, but also others. In many ways, hope is the seed of future success.

SACRIFICIAL SERVICE FOR CHRIST

24 I now rejoice in my sufferings for you, and fill up in my flesh what is lacking in the afflictions of Christ, for the sake of His body, which is the church, 25 of which I became a minister according to the stewardship from God which was given to me for you, to fulfill the word of God, 26 the mystery which has been hidden from ages and from generations, but now has been revealed to His saints. 27 To them God willed to make known what are the riches of the glory of this mystery among the Gentiles: which[a] is Christ in you, the hope of glory. 28 Him we preach, warning every man and teaching every man in all wisdom, that we may present every man perfect in Christ Jesus. 29 To this *end* I also labor, striving according to His working which works in me mightily.

NOT PHILOSOPHY BUT CHRIST

2 For I want you to know what a great conflict I have for you and those in Laodicea, and *for* as many as have not seen my face in the flesh, 2 that their hearts may be encouraged, being knit together in love, and *attaining* to all riches of the full assurance of understanding, to the knowledge of the mystery of God, both of the Father and[a] of Christ, 3 in whom are hidden all the treasures of wisdom and knowledge.

4 Now this I say lest anyone should deceive you with persuasive words. 5 For though I am absent in the flesh, yet I am with you in spirit, rejoicing to see your *good* order and the steadfastness of your faith in Christ.

6 As you therefore have received Christ Jesus the Lord, so walk in Him, 7 rooted and built up in Him and established in the faith, as you have been taught, abounding in it[a] with thanksgiving.

1:27 [a]M-Text reads *who*.   2:2 [a]NU-Text omits *both of the Father and*.   2:7 [a]NU-Text omits *in it*.

[8]Beware lest anyone cheat you through philosophy and empty deceit, according to the tradition of men, according to the basic principles of the world, and not according to Christ. [9]For in Him dwells all the fullness of the Godhead bodily; [10]and you are complete in Him, who is the head of all principality and power.

NOT LEGALISM BUT CHRIST

[11]In Him you were also circumcised with the circumcision made without hands, by putting off the body of the sins[a] of the flesh, by the circumcision of Christ, [12]buried with Him in baptism, in which you also were raised with *Him* through faith in the working of God, who raised Him from the dead. [13]And you, being dead in your trespasses and the uncircumcision of your flesh, He has made alive together with Him, having forgiven you all trespasses, [14]having wiped out the handwriting of requirements that was against us, which was contrary to us. And He has taken it out of the way, having nailed it to the cross. [15]Having disarmed principalities and powers, He made a public spectacle of them, triumphing over them in it.

[16]So let no one judge you in food or in drink, or regarding a festival or a new moon or sabbaths, [17]which are a shadow of things to come, but the substance is of Christ. [18]Let no one cheat you of your reward, taking delight in *false* humility and worship of angels, intruding into those things which he has not[a] seen, vainly puffed up by his fleshly mind, [19]and not holding fast to the Head, from whom all the body, nourished and knit together by joints and ligaments, grows with the increase *that is* from God.

[20]Therefore,[a] if you died with Christ from the basic principles of the

[OILY SKIN]

FACT MORSELS

Don't Decry Oily Skin. People with oily skin will generally retain a more youthful appearance than those with dry skin.

PEOPLE CALLED "BEAUTIFUL" IN THE BIBLE

Rebekah

A Brave, Beautiful Manipulator

Rebekah, the wife chosen for Isaac, is described in the Bible as "very beautiful to behold" (Genesis 24:16). Her story in the Bible also reveals that she was a courageous woman who was not unwilling to work hard. When the servant of Abraham arrived in her area to search out a bride for Abraham's son Isaac, he planted himself at the town well. That was the ideal place to survey all the young women showing up to draw water—and sure enough, Rebekah showed up. When the servant asked for a drink, she not only gave him a drink, but also offered to draw water for all his camels. Since each camel might hold several gallons of water in its body, Rebekah likely was drawing water from the well for some time!

It was when all the camels had finished drinking that the man discovered that this beautiful young virgin girl was Isaac's cousin and qualified to be Isaac's wife. After fairly quick negotiations with a fairly large dowry, Rebekah willingly agreed to go with the servant to become Isaac's wife. Her decision meant leaving her family and home and traveling a couple of hundred miles, a long and difficult journey in those days, to become the bride of a man she had never met who likely was twice her age. That took courage!

The good news for Rebekah was that when Isaac looked up and saw her coming he instantly claimed her as his wife. The Bible tells us simply that "he loved her" (Genesis 24:67).

Although she seemed to be infertile, Rebekah eventually was able to conceive twins, Esau and Jacob. In later years Re-

bekah found it difficult to trust God with her sons' futures. In a rash act of manipulation intended to gain both inheritance and blessing for her more beloved son Jacob, she lost the immediate presence of Jacob. Her beloved Jacob had to run for his life and it appears she never saw him again. Esau married women Rebekah didn't like and these daughters-in-law proved to be difficult people in her life. Rebekah paid a bitter price for her deceitful actions.

Rebekah is an example for many young women today that those who are beautiful are not given a "privileged" status that precludes them from working or from doing menial tasks. All of the major heroines of the Bible times were women of courage and fortitude, women willing to take on household and shepherding chores as part of their commitment to their families.

ULTIMATE HEALTH RESOURCE • ULTIMATE HEALTH RESOURCE • ULTIMATE HEALTH RESOURCE

More and more people today are fishing for relaxation and companionship (68 percent in 2000 compared to only 33 percent in 1980). Only about 5 percent of all people fishing today are fishing for *food*. That wasn't the case in Jesus' day.

Fishing in New Testament times was a major profession—the Sea of Galilee had hundreds of commercial fishing boats on it during the first century. Jesus called several fishermen to be among His closest followers—Peter, James, John, and Andrew. He told numerous parables about fishing and provided miraculous catches of fish on at least three occasions. One of the most famous lines in the New Testament is the call of Jesus to "Follow Me, and I will make you become fishers of men" (Mark 1:17).

There are several tips we can learn from professional fishermen when it comes to our *continuing* to follow Jesus and fish for lost souls to be saved. Consider these basics about fishing:

☐ *Use bait that works the best for a specific species of fish.* Different fish respond to different insects and lures—and different people respond to different presentations of the gospel. Be sensitive to the person you are trying to reach. Don't assume that one method of soul winning works for all people.

☐ *Don't worry about the one that got away.* If a person rejects your message, don't stop giving the message—simply move on to another person!

☐ *Timing is important.* Fishing is better at certain times of year and under certain weather conditions. Timing is also important in soul winning. Ask the Lord to help you be sensitive as to *when* to share the gospel with a person, especially if that person is a close friend or relative.

☐ *Practice your technique.* Nobody becomes a good fly fisherman in five minutes—it takes practice to learn to fly-fish or cast a net. The same for soul winning! Practice, practice, practice—but always with the intent of succeeding!

☐ *Mash down the barbs on your hooks.* One fishing manual claims that this "makes a smaller hole in the fish's mouth, and you won't lose the fish as long as you keep pressure on the line when you're bringing the fish in." Don't wound a person emotionally as you share the gospel! Preserve a person's dignity. A ramrod, overbearing approach can turn a person off.

☐ *Go where the fish are.* Fish hide under banks, obstructions, and in front of and beside rocks. Fish from downstream to upstream to avoid stirring up debris. In the spiritual realm, go where the sinners are. Don't stir up things unnecessarily—simply "cast the gospel" and see who bites.

☐ *Wear polarized sunglasses to see fish better.* Wear "spiritual insight" to see sinners better.

☐ *Don't let your shadow fall on the water while you are fishing.* It scares the fish away. Focus on presenting what Jesus did and who Jesus was. Get yourself out of the way when you are witnessing.

☐ *Have patience.* Have patience with yourself, with other people, and with God. We share the gospel. It is the Spirit that draws people to Christ. It is the Father who saves souls.

Fish bite best at night. If you play a guitar at night, the fish will come near to the surface of the water because they love the music!

Butter

Bible Health
+ Food Facts

In the Middle East, "butter" for bread is often olive oil! Individuals dip pieces of bread in a shallow dish of olive oil that has been flavored with herbs or pepper.

CONDIMENTS

world, why, as *though* living in the world, do you subject yourselves to regulations— ²¹"Do not touch, do not taste, do not handle," ²²which all concern things which perish with the using—according to the commandments and doctrines of men? ²³These things indeed have an appearance of wisdom in self-imposed religion, *false* humility, and neglect of the body, *but are* of no value against the indulgence of the flesh.

NOT CARNALITY BUT CHRIST

3 If then you were raised with Christ, seek those things which are above, where Christ is, sitting at the right hand of God. ²Set your mind on things above, not on things on the earth. ³For you died, and your life is hidden with Christ in God. ⁴When Christ *who is* our life appears, then you also will appear with Him in glory.

⁵Therefore put to death your members which are on the earth: fornication, uncleanness, passion, evil desire, and covetousness, which is idolatry. ⁶Because of these things the wrath of God is coming upon the sons of disobedience, ⁷in which you yourselves once walked when you lived in them.

⁸But now you yourselves are to put off all these: anger, wrath, malice, blasphemy, filthy language out of your mouth. ⁹Do not lie to one another, since you have put off the old man with his deeds, ¹⁰and have put on the new *man* who is renewed in knowledge according to the image of Him who created him, ¹¹where there is neither Greek nor Jew, circumcised nor uncircumcised, barbarian, Scythian, slave *nor* free, but Christ *is* all and in all.

CHARACTER OF THE NEW MAN

¹²Therefore, as *the* elect of God, holy and beloved, put on tender mercies, kindness, humility, meekness, longsuffering; ¹³bearing with one another, and forgiving one another, if anyone has a complaint against another; even as Christ forgave you, so you also *must do.* ¹⁴But above all these things put on love, which is the bond of perfection. ¹⁵And let the peace of God rule in your hearts, to which also you were

☐ Hyssop

Hyssop is the Bible name for a spice we commonly call marjoram. It is part of the mint family. Hyssop grew abundantly in Israel and in the Sinai Peninsula during Bible times, and it is still used extensively in the Middle East for flavoring and in medicinal teas.

Hyssop is known to help prevent blood from coagulating and it is an age-old decongestant. Modern experiments show that hyssop halts the growth of the herpes simplex virus, which causes cold sores and genital herpes. Some nutritionists believe hyssop to be very powerful in expelling mucus from the respiratory tract, thus relieving congestion. Others advocate hyssop as a good spice for regulating blood pressure.

Q Who was the fastest runner in the Bible?

A It may have been Elijah—he outran King Ahab's chariot in getting back to Jezreel when a rainstorm began *(1 Kings 18:46).*

♂ ## Men's Issues
Prostate Disorders

The prostate is a walnut-shaped gland in men that lies directly under the bladder and surrounds the upper portion of the urethra—a tube through which urine flows out of the body. It is about one and a half inches long and looks a little like a small doughnut with a straw (the urethra) extending from the center of the doughnut. The prostate gland produces most of the fluid that makes up semen, which is the fluid essential to reproduction.

Three major prostate disorders are prostate cancer, an enlarged prostate (actually called "benign prostatic hypertrophy" or BPH), and prostatitis.

Prostate cancer. A medical test called the PSA test is usually used to detect prostate cancer.

Enlarged prostate. An enlarged prostate has symptoms that include a weak urinary stream, problems starting and stopping urination, excessive nighttime urination, and an urgent need to urinate.

Prostatitis. Prostatitis usually occurs in men between twenty-five and forty-five years of age. Its symptoms include frequent urination, burning while urinating, painful ejaculation, excessive nighttime urination, and problems starting and stopping urination.

Studies have shown that men who eat more than 100 grams of fat a day increase their risk of prostate cancer by as much as 50 percent! To help protect against prostate cancer,
CONT. NEXT PAGE>>>

called in one body; and be thankful. ¹⁶Let the word of Christ dwell in you richly in all wisdom, teaching and admonishing one another in psalms and hymns and spiritual songs, singing with grace in your hearts to the Lord. ¹⁷And whatever you do in word or deed, *do* all in the name of the Lord Jesus, giving thanks to God the Father through Him.

THE CHRISTIAN HOME

¹⁸Wives, submit to your own husbands, as is fitting in the Lord. ¹⁹Husbands, love your wives and do not be bitter toward them. ²⁰Children, obey your parents in all things, for this is well pleasing to the Lord. ²¹Fathers, do not provoke your children, lest they become discouraged. ²²Bondservants, obey in all things your masters according to the flesh, not with eyeservice, as men-pleasers, but in sincerity of heart, fearing God. ²³And whatever you do, do it heartily, as to the Lord and not to men, ²⁴knowing that from the Lord you will receive the reward of the inheritance; for[a] you serve the Lord Christ. ²⁵But he who does wrong will be repaid for what he has done, and there is no partiality.

4 Masters, give your bondservants what is just and fair, knowing that you also have a Master in heaven.

CHRISTIAN GRACES

²Continue earnestly in prayer, being vigilant in it with thanksgiving; ³meanwhile praying also for us, that God would open to us a door for the word, to speak the mystery of Christ, for which I am also in chains, ⁴that I may make it manifest, as I ought to speak.

⁵Walk in wisdom toward those *who are* outside, redeeming the time. ⁶*Let* your speech always *be* with grace, seasoned with salt, that you may know how you ought to answer each one.

FINAL GREETINGS

⁷Tychicus, a beloved brother, faithful minister, and fellow servant in the Lord, will tell you all the news about me. ⁸I am sending him to you for this very purpose, that he[a] may know your circumstances and comfort your hearts, ⁹with Onesimus, a faithful and beloved brother, who

wise choices

Choose pure water over other beverages.
Pure water has no calories! No caffeine! No harmful chemicals, such as those found in diet beverages that have aspartame or saccharine! Pure water has loads of health benefits for every cell of the body.

Men's Issues Cont.>>>

therefore, cut out fat. Avoid saturated fats in meat, poultry skin, cheese, butter, whole milk, ice cream, fried foods, mayonnaise, and polyunsaturated fats found in most plant oils, including soy bean, safflower, and sunflower oil.

Those interested in improving prostate health should also take in plenty of antioxidants, such as green tea; increase their intake of fiber; and consider adding more soy products to their diets. Chinese and Japanese men have 90 percent less risk of prostate cancer than men in the United States. Their diets are filled with soy products, little red meat, and few bad fats.

These supplements are recommended: vitamin E, selenium, vitamin D, coenzyme Q10, and lipoic acid. Supplements helpful for those with enlarged prostate are saw palmetto, beta-sitosterol, pygeum Africanum, nettle root, and zinc. Avoid taking all supplemental hormones, such as testosterone, androstenedione, and DHEA.

is *one* of you. They will make known to you all things which *are happening* here.

[10]Aristarchus my fellow prisoner greets you, with Mark the cousin of Barnabas (about whom you received instructions: if he comes to you, welcome him), [11]and Jesus who is called Justus. These *are my* only fellow workers for the kingdom of God who are of the circumcision; they have proved to be a comfort to me.

[12]Epaphras, who is *one* of you, a bondservant of Christ, greets you, always laboring fervently for you in prayers, that you may stand perfect and complete[a] in all the will of God. [13]For I bear him witness that he has a great zeal[a] for you, and those who are in Laodicea, and those in Hierapolis. [14]Luke the beloved physician and Demas greet you. [15]Greet the brethren who are in Laodicea, and Nymphas and the church that *is* in his[a] house.

CLOSING EXHORTATIONS AND BLESSING

[16]Now when this epistle is read among you, see that it is read also in the church of the Laodiceans, and that you likewise read the *epistle* from Laodicea. [17]And say to Archippus, "Take heed to the ministry which you have received in the Lord, that you may fulfill it."

[18]This salutation by my own hand—Paul. Remember my chains. Grace *be* with you. Amen.

4:12 [a]NU-Text reads *fully assured.* 4:13 [a]NU-Text reads *concern.* 4:15 [a]NU-Text reads *Nympha . . . her house.*

1

THESSALONIANS

The church in Thessalonica was a mission church—barely established by Paul before he was run out of town on trumped-up charges. Between the time Paul left and this letter arrived, the church had faced heavy persecution and some had even lost their lives for the cause of Christ. Paul sent this short letter to instruct the Thessalonians and give them hope for those times when life feels out of control, or when frustration, disillusionment, pain, and loss seem overwhelming. In difficult times, Paul says, "Keep your eyes on the Lord. God is still on the throne and Jesus is coming again!" Paul commands the young converts to abstain from sexual immorality, lead quiet and productive lives, show brotherly love to one another, rejoice always, pray without ceasing, abstain from every form of evil, hold fast to everything that is good, and do nothing that might quench the Holy Spirit's work in their midst. What a good prescription this is for us today!

GREETING

1 Paul, Silvanus, and Timothy,

To the church of the Thessalonians in God the Father and the Lord Jesus Christ:

Grace to you and peace from God our Father and the Lord Jesus Christ.[a]

THEIR GOOD EXAMPLE

²We give thanks to God always for you all, making mention of you in our prayers, ³remembering without ceasing your work of faith, labor of love, and patience of hope in our Lord Jesus Christ in the sight of our God and Father, ⁴knowing, beloved brethren, your election by God. ⁵For our gospel did not come to you in word only, but also in power, and in the Holy Spirit and in much assurance, as you know what kind of men we were among you for your sake.

⁶And you became followers of us and of the Lord, having received the word in much affliction, with joy of the Holy Spirit, ⁷so that you became examples to all in Macedonia and Achaia who believe. ⁸For from you the word of the Lord has sounded forth, not only in Macedonia and Achaia, but also in every place. Your faith toward God has gone out, so that we do not need to say anything. ⁹For they themselves declare concerning us what manner of entry we had to you, and how you turned to God from idols to serve the living and true God, ¹⁰and to wait for His Son from heaven, whom He raised from the dead, *even Je*sus who delivers us from the wrath to come.

PAUL'S CONDUCT

2 For you yourselves know, brethren, that our coming to you was not in vain. ²But even[a] after we had suffered before and were spitefully treated at Philippi, as you know, we were bold in our God to speak to you the gospel of God in much conflict. ³For our exhortation *did* not *come* from error or uncleanness, nor *was it* in deceit.

⁴But as we have been approved by God to be entrusted with the gospel, even so we speak, not as pleasing men, but God who tests our hearts. ⁵For neither at any time did we use flattering words, as you know, nor a cloak for covetousness—God *is* witness. ⁶Nor did we seek glory from men, either from you or from others, when we might have made demands as apostles of Christ. ⁷But we were gentle among you, just as a nursing *mother* cherishes her own children. ⁸So, affectionately longing for you, we were well pleased to impart to you not only the gospel of God, but also our own lives, because you had become dear to us. ⁹For you remember, brethren, our labor and toil; for laboring night and day, that we might not be a burden to any of you, we preached to you the gospel of God.

¹⁰You *are* witnesses, and God *also*, how devoutly and justly and blamelessly we behaved ourselves among you who believe; ¹¹as you know how we exhorted, and comforted, and charged[a] every one of you, as a father *does* his own children, ¹²that you would walk worthy of God who calls you into His own kingdom and glory.

THEIR CONVERSION

¹³For this reason we also thank God without ceasing, because when you received the word of God which you heard from us, you welcomed *it* not *as* the word of men, but as it is in truth, the word of God, which

1:1 ᵃNU-Text omits *from God our Father and the Lord Jesus Christ.*   2:2 ᵃNU-Text and M-Text omit *even.*   2:11 ᵃNU-Text and M-Text read *implored.*

WWJE?

[WHAT WOULD JESUS EAT]

[OLIVES AND OLIVE OIL]

The olive tree is one of the longest living and most resilient trees—many live more than a thousand years. Some trees in Israel may have been alive two thousand years ago when Jesus walked the earth.

During Jesus' day, olives were eaten both raw and cooked, but most olives were pressed into oil. Olive oil was extracted from olives using large wooden presses. In Old Testament times, some olive oil was extracted by the treading of olives by feet, or by pressing the fruit with a round millstone. (See Micah 6:15.) Olive oil was used for cooking, in the making of bread, and also as an ointment for making medicines, cosmetics, and soap. Castile soap today is made of pure olive oil. Olive oil was also considered an important ingredient in food recipes.

All olive oil is not equal. It comes in different grades depending on the pressing from which the oil is derived. Whole, undamaged olives are pressed mechanically several times without heat. The temperature for extraction ranges from 58 to 110 degrees Fahrenheit—"cold-processed" oil.

Extra-virgin olive oil is oil from the first pressing—the oil is extracted, filtered, and undergoes no further refining. It is the highest quality oil. Virgin olive oil is from the end of the first pressing or from a second pressing. These two grades of olive oil are the ones you want to consume! After the second pressing, the oil is often heated above 300 degrees Fahrenheit, which chemically changes the oil and causes it to lose many of its positive health effects. The later pressings are acceptable, however, for cosmetics and soap.

Studies show that olive oil helps decrease LDL (bad) cholesterol levels and increase HDL (good) cholesterol levels. Olive oil also helps decrease the stickiness of platelets, thus helping to prevent blood clots and coronary thrombosis. Olive oil stimulates the gallbladder to help prevent gallstones and eliminate biliary sludge. Consult a physician, however, before using olive oil for this purpose. It also helps relieve constipation.

Olive oil is high in vitamin E, beta carotene, lecithin, chlorophyll, and squalenes, which help deliver oxygen to bodily tissue. Many other phytonutrients are found in whole olives, all of which have health-promoting effects.

Research studies show that even the leaf of the olive tree has health benefits. Olive leaf extract is useful in treating sore throats, sinusitis, skin diseases, and fungal and bacterial infections.

Use olive oil on salads as a dressing and as a condiment for bread instead of butter. Also use it in cooking (at low temperatures). Add olive oil to your overall eating plan slowly—it can have a laxative effect if you use too much too soon.

also effectively works in you who believe. [14]For you, brethren, became imitators of the churches of God which are in Judea in Christ Jesus. For you also suffered the same things from your own countrymen, just as they *did* from the Judeans, [15]who killed both the Lord Jesus and their own prophets, and have persecuted us; and they do not please God and are contrary to all men, [16]forbidding us to speak to the Gentiles that they may be saved, so as always to fill up *the measure of* their sins; but wrath has come upon them to the uttermost.

LONGING TO SEE THEM

[17]But we, brethren, having been taken away from you for a short time in presence, not in heart, endeavored more eagerly to see your face with great desire. [18]Therefore we wanted to come to you—even I, Paul, time and again—but Satan hindered us. [19]For what *is* our hope, or joy, or crown of rejoicing? *Is it* not even you in the presence of our Lord Jesus Christ at His coming? [20]For you are our glory and joy.

CONCERN FOR THEIR FAITH

3 Therefore, when we could no longer endure it, we thought it good to be left in Athens alone, [2]and sent Timothy, our brother and minister of God, and our fellow laborer in the gospel of Christ, to establish you and encourage you concerning your faith, [3]that no one should be shaken by these afflictions; for you yourselves know that we are appointed to this. [4]For, in fact, we told you before when we were with you that we would suffer tribulation, just as it happened, and you know. [5]For this reason, when I could no longer endure it, I sent to know your faith, lest by some means the tempter had tempted you, and our labor might be in vain.

ENCOURAGED BY TIMOTHY

[6]But now that Timothy has come to us from you, and brought us good news of your faith and love, and that you always have good remembrance of us, greatly desiring to see us, as we also *to see* you— [7]therefore, brethren, in all our affliction and distress we were comforted concerning you by your faith. [8]For now we live, if you stand fast in the Lord. [9]For what thanks can we render to God for

September

1   2   3   4   5   6   7

Now Is the Time To...

☐ Clear garden plots of vegetable plants that have finished producing. Consider establishing a compost area where you can discard this foliage along with grass clippings. ☐ Guard against fall allergens. Wear a surgical-style mask when raking dusty leaves. ☐ Take a bicycle trip as the weather begins to get cooler and the trees begin to take on color.

Let's Celebrate

8   9   10   11   12   13   14

☐ **The Feast of Tabernacles**—also called Sukkoth. This feast in the Bible marked the wandering of the Israelites in the wilderness. Jews today celebrate the weeklong feast by eating their meals and sleeping outside in temporary shelters. ☐ **Harvest Home.** In Europe and in some areas of the United States—particularly among the Pennsylvania Dutch—the conclusion of a harvest season was marked by festivals of fun, feasting, and thanksgiving known as "Harvest Home." This was considered a time to pay workers, collect rents, and hold elections.

Seasonal Tips

15   16   17   18   19   20   21

☐ This is a great time of year to visit roadside stands for fresh fall produce, or to visit farms where you can pick your own pumpkins for carving, decorating, or cooking. ☐ Think salsa! Make good use of your extra produce. Don't limit yourself to tomato-based recipes. Many vegetables and fruits can become tasty accompaniments for meats, grains, veggies, and whole-grain chips. ☐ Bring out stored sweaters, blankets, and coats and send them to the cleaners or air them out in anticipation of their use during the coming weeks.

In the Garden

22   23   24   25   26   27   28

☐ Chrysanthemums should be in full bloom in many varieties. Enjoy bouquets rich in gold, yellow, orange, and deep maroon colors. These flowers produce an abundance of blooms and endure cold weather well. ☐ Grapes should be in abundance. Consider using them in all your salads, including chicken salad.

29   30

Table Fresh

☐ Find new and creative ways to prepare squash, which usually is in abundance in many varieties! ☐ Apples are plentiful. The pectin in the skin of an apple is especially beneficial to the heart, so choose to eat your apples fresh, rather than in juice form. There's much truth in the old saying, "An apple a day keeps the doctor away."

SCRIPTURE SOLUTIONS

[SLEEP DISORDERS]

Sleep is God's once-a-day natural healing therapy designed for every person to experience! Sleep benefits every aspect of a human being.

The Mind. Sleep allows your mind to be recharged and refreshed for the next day. While you sleep your mind actually takes a break. In addition, sleep helps restore and preserve memory.

The Body. As you sleep your body is producing hormones that indicate where it may need repairs of various organs and tissues. As you sleep, cells are rebuilt, toxins removed, and strength and energy renewed.

The Emotions. Although some people may have difficulty in retrieving dreams, most people do dream. Dreams help the mind sort out and deal with emotional conflict. If you remain asleep through the "dream stage," you will awaken more refreshed. If you consistently do not enjoy restful sleep, here are several suggestions:

☐ **Try to limit the use of your bedroom primarily to sleep. Make sure the room is very dark, and the temperature and noise level of the house are *low*.**

☐ **If reading helps you relax and fall asleep, then read. But, if you find yourself reading a book that you just can't put down—or one that stimulates you to think and create—save that book for daytime reading!**

☐ **Your bed is perhaps the most important piece of furniture in your house. Check the firmness and the overall comfort level of your bed, pillow, and covers to ensure the best sleep possible.**

☐ **Don't drink liquids more than an hour before going to bed.**   CONT. NEXT PAGE>>>

Righteous Recipes

Middle Eastern Cabbage Rolls

Ingredients:
☐ 1 cup dry whole-grain rice, cooked
☐ 1 pound coarsely ground free-range beef
☐ 2 cups canned tomatoes, or one 6-ounce can tomato paste
☐ 2 teaspoons Celtic salt
☐ ½ teaspoon pepper
☐ ½ teaspoon allspice
☐ 1 head cabbage
☐ 3 garlic cloves
☐ Juice of 2 limes

Place the rice, ground beef, and half the tomatoes or half the tomato paste in a bowl. Add 1½ teaspoons salt, pepper, and allspice. Mix well. Place several cups of water and a pinch of Celtic salt in a saucepan and bring it to a boil. Separate the cabbage leaves. Drop several leaves at a time into the boiling salted water. Cook for about 5 minutes or until limp. Drain well. Trim off the heavy stems of the cabbage leaves. Arrange the stems in the bottom of a heavy saucepan or Dutch oven.

Place one heaping tablespoon of the ground beef mixture in the center of each cabbage leaf until all the beef mixture is used. Roll each cabbage leaf firmly. Arrange the cabbage rolls in neat rows on the stems in a heavy saucepan or Dutch oven. You may have several layers. Place garlic cloves among the rolls.

Add the remaining tomatoes or tomato paste and enough hot water to cover the rolls. Sprinkle ½ teaspoon salt over the top. Simmer, covered, for 45 minutes to 1 hour or until the beef is well cooked. Add the lime juice during the last 15 minutes of cooking.

Yield: 8–10 servings

Scripture Solutions Cont.>>>

☐ Eat a small portion of protein about an hour before going to bed. It will help sustain your blood sugar levels through the night.

☐ Avoid arguments or heavy-duty conversations before going to bed. Apologize and make peace with your spouse long in advance of bedtime. The Bible has it right: "Do not let the sun go down on your wrath" (Ephesians 4:26).

☐ Avoid spicy foods or foods that create bloating. Eat your last meal each day at least three hours before bedtime.

you, for all the joy with which we rejoice for your sake before our God, ¹⁰night and day praying exceedingly that we may see your face and perfect what is lacking in your faith?

PRAYER FOR THE CHURCH

¹¹Now may our God and Father Himself, and our Lord Jesus Christ, direct our way to you. ¹²And may the Lord make you increase and abound in love to one another and to all, just as we *do* to you, ¹³so that He may establish your hearts blameless in holiness before our God and Father at the coming of our Lord Jesus Christ with all His saints.

PLEA FOR PURITY

4 Finally then, brethren, we urge and exhort in the Lord Jesus that you should abound more and more, just as you received from us how you ought to walk and to please God; ²for you know what commandments we gave you through the Lord Jesus.

³For this is the will of God, your sanctification: that you should abstain from sexual immorality; ⁴that each of you should know how to possess his own vessel in sanctification and honor, ⁵not in passion of lust, like the Gentiles who do not know God; ⁶that no one should take advantage of and defraud his brother in this matter, because the Lord *is* the avenger of all such, as we also forewarned you and testified. ⁷For God did not call us to uncleanness, but in holiness. ⁸Therefore he who rejects *this* does not reject man, but God, who has also given[a] us His Holy Spirit.

A BROTHERLY AND ORDERLY LIFE

⁹But concerning brotherly love you have no need that I should write to you, for you yourselves are taught by God to love one another; ¹⁰and indeed you do so toward all the brethren who are in all Macedonia. But we urge you, brethren, that you increase more and more; ¹¹that you also aspire to lead a quiet life, to mind your own business, and to work with your own hands, as we commanded

WEIGHING
Less &
ENJOYING LIFE MORE!

[Focus on Fat Loss and Fat-Burners]

When people start an exercise program to enhance their chances of losing weight, they often become discouraged because they see a slight *increase* in their weight. That's because muscle tissue is denser and heavier than body fat. You will start gaining muscle weight at the same time you start burning body fat.

Make *fat loss* your goal, not *weight loss.*

Exercise is not only beneficial in helping build muscle, but it will help you greatly down the line in keeping excess weight off. Exercise also helps to tone the body so your clothes fit better and your body shape becomes more pleasing, even with the loss of just fifteen to twenty pounds.

Focus on fat-burning foods. Those are foods that take more calories to *digest* than they have in them! Other foods help boost the body's metabolism naturally. Among the foods that are excellent fat-burners are these: alfalfa sprouts, asparagus, broccoli, cabbage, cauliflower, celery, cucumbers, eggplant, greens (such as beet, collard, dandelion, mustard, turnip), lettuce, okra, pea pods, peppers (green, red, chiles), pickles (dill), radishes, sauerkraut, soy beans, spinach, string beans, summer squash, tomatoes, and zucchini. A number of these foods also have beneficial effects in lowering insulin secretions after a meal.

Hot red pepper (capsaicin) is considered a fat-burner food that helps the body burn more calories. Try it—cautiously—in place of salt. Cayenne pepper and dried red pepper flakes are convenient sources of capsaicin.

4:8 ªNU-Text reads *who also gives.*

GODLY & GOODLOOKIN'

Hydrate Your Skin

Your skin is the largest organ of your body when it comes to square inches. All cells and organs of the body need a continual flushing of water from the *inside out*, but especially the skin because it is exposed to the greatest likelihood for evaporation as well as sun damage, scarring, and callus formation. Soft, supple skin also needs moisture from the outside in!

One of the ways to enhance water's skin moisturizing effect is to allow your skin to air dry after a bath or shower. Apply moisturizers to your skin while it is still damp. Various moisturizing lotions and creams do their best work if they cause water to be retained in the skin. Dry skin and wrinkles go hand in hand. To stay good lookin' avoid overexposure to the sun and keep your skin well hydrated.

From a health standpoint, well-hydrated skin is less likely to crack or peel, which reduces a person's likelihood of developing skin-related infections.

[18]Therefore comfort one another with these words.

THE DAY OF THE LORD

5 But concerning the times and the seasons, brethren, you have no need that I should write to you. [2]For you yourselves know perfectly that the day of the Lord so comes as a thief in the night. [3]For when they say, "Peace and safety!" then sudden destruction comes upon them, as labor pains upon a pregnant woman. And they shall not escape. [4]But you, brethren, are not in darkness, so that this Day should overtake you as a thief. [5]You are all sons of light and sons of the day. We are not of the night nor of darkness. [6]Therefore let us not sleep, as others *do*, but let us watch and be sober. [7]For those who sleep, sleep at night, and those who get drunk are drunk at night. [8]But let us who are of the day be sober, putting on the breastplate of faith and love, and *as* a helmet the hope of salvation. [9]For God did not appoint us to wrath, but to obtain salvation through our Lord Jesus Christ,

you, [12]that you may walk properly toward those who are outside, and *that* you may lack nothing.

THE COMFORT OF CHRIST'S COMING

[13]But I do not want you to be ignorant, brethren, concerning those who have fallen asleep, lest you sorrow as others who have no hope. [14]For if we believe that Jesus died and rose again, even so God will bring with Him those who sleep in Jesus.[a]

[15]For this we say to you by the word of the Lord, that we who are alive *and* remain until the coming of the Lord will by no means precede those who are asleep. [16]For the Lord Himself will descend from heaven with a shout, with the voice of an archangel, and with the trumpet of God. And the dead in Christ will rise first. [17]Then we who are alive *and* remain shall be caught up together with them in the clouds to meet the Lord in the air. And thus we shall always be with the Lord.

Q Who was the oldest man in the Bible?

A Methuselah—he lived 969 years *(Genesis 5:27)*. Before the Flood, the patriarchs had an average lifespan of about 900 years. After the Flood, the ages of the patriarchs dropped rapidly and gradually leveled off. The Flood may have brought about major environmental changes to the earth, including a change in the overall barometric pressure of the earth's atmosphere. (Plants grown in experimental barometric pressure chambers grow much larger and live much longer than plants grown in the earth's normal atmosphere.)

4:14 [a]Or those who through Jesus sleep

[10]who died for us, that whether we wake or sleep, we should live together with Him.

[11]Therefore comfort each other and edify one another, just as you also are doing.

VARIOUS EXHORTATIONS

[12]And we urge you, brethren, to recognize those who labor among you, and are over you in the Lord and admonish you, [13]and to esteem them very highly in love for their work's sake. Be at peace among yourselves.

[14]Now we exhort you, brethren, warn those who are unruly, comfort the fainthearted, uphold the weak, be patient with all. [15]See that no one renders evil for evil to anyone, but always pursue what is good both for yourselves and for all.

[16]Rejoice always, [17]pray without ceasing, [18]in everything give thanks; for this is the will of God in Christ Jesus for you.

[19]Do not quench the Spirit. [20]Do not despise prophecies. [21]Test all things; hold fast what is good. [22]Abstain from every form of evil.

BLESSING AND ADMONITION

[23]Now may the God of peace Himself sanctify you completely; and may your whole spirit, soul, and body be preserved blameless at the coming of our Lord Jesus Christ. [24]He who calls you *is* faithful, who also will do *it*.

[25]Brethren, pray for us.

[26]Greet all the brethren with a holy kiss.

[27]I charge you by the Lord that this epistle be read to all the holy[a] brethren.

[28]The grace of our Lord Jesus Christ *be* with you. Amen.

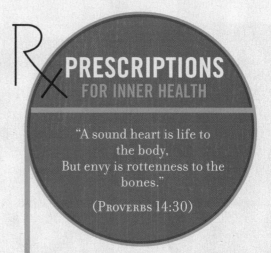

PRESCRIPTIONS
FOR INNER HEALTH

"A sound heart is life to the body,
But envy is rottenness to the bones."

(PROVERBS 14:30)

A "sound heart" may also be translated as a "healthy, tranquil mind." The heart to the Jews was a concept that included the will and attitude of a person. When your attitude toward others is generous, loving, kind, and respectful, then your mental and emotional health is better—and so is your physical health. Envy and jealousy cause you to become brittle both emotionally and physically.

5:27 [a]NU-Text omits *holy*.

THESSALONIANS

Have you ever been misunderstood or had your words twisted into a message that bears a wrong emphasis? That may have been what happened to Paul at Thessalonica. The believers there appear to have taken Paul's words about the soon coming of Jesus so to heart that they had stopped working and stopped witnessing to the lost. Some were about to go on welfare while they waited for the Second Coming. Others were becoming discouraged in their faith that Jesus had not arrived yet. Paul wrote clearly that they were to continue working and witnessing, and to continue steadfast in their faith. God alone knows the timing of Christ's return! Until that moment, we are to remain productive in our work, hopeful in our outlook, and diligent in our ministry to others. Paul's words are an admonition to us, too, when we become discouraged that things in this life aren't producing the results we desire or that God's timetable may not be our timetable for healing, blessings, or reward: "Do not grow weary in doing good."

GREETING

1 Paul, Silvanus, and Timothy,

To the church of the Thessalonians in God our Father and the Lord Jesus Christ:

²Grace to you and peace from God our Father and the Lord Jesus Christ.

GOD'S FINAL JUDGMENT AND GLORY

³We are bound to thank God always for you, brethren, as it is fitting, because your faith grows exceedingly, and the love of every one of you all abounds toward each other, ⁴so that we ourselves boast of you among the churches of God for your patience and faith in all your persecutions and tribulations that you endure, ⁵*which is* manifest evidence of the righteous judgment of God, that you may be counted worthy of the kingdom of God, for which you also suffer; ⁶since *it is* a righteous thing with God to repay with tribulation those who trouble you, ⁷and to *give* you who are troubled rest with us when the Lord Jesus is revealed from heaven with His mighty angels, ⁸in flaming fire taking vengeance on those who do not know God, and on those who do not obey the gospel of our Lord Jesus Christ. ⁹These shall be punished with everlasting destruction from the presence of the Lord and from the glory of His power, ¹⁰when He

comes, in that Day, to be glorified in His saints and to be admired among all those who believe,ᵃ because our testimony among you was believed.

¹¹Therefore we also pray always for you that our God would count you worthy of *this* calling, and fulfill all the good pleasure of *His* goodness and the work of faith with power, ¹²that the name of our Lord Jesus Christ may be glorified in you, and you in Him, according to the grace of our God and the Lord Jesus Christ.

Q What was Nehemiah's job in the court of King Artaxerxes?

A Cupbearer *(Nehemiah 1:11).* The cupbearer was responsible for drinking a sip of the wine that was about to be served. If the wine was poisoned, the cupbearer died instead of the king. The cupbearer was a person the king trusted completely.

1:10 ᵃNU-Text and M-Text read *have believed.*

OVERCOMING OBSTINATE OBSTACLES • OVERCOMING OBSTINATE OBSTACLES • OVERCOMING OBSTINATE OBSTACLES

Those who feel helpless nearly always feel hopeless as well. To overcome feelings of helplessness, a person needs to confront their errant thinking and to recapture a sense of hope.

Many people learn helplessness, sometimes as the direct consequence of a parent being depressed and unable to instill confidence in the child. The good news is that if helplessness is *learned*, it can be unlearned! How can you tell if you have learned the habit of feeling helpless? You are likely to say such things as:

"Nothing good ever happens to me."

"If anything can go wrong, it will."

"It's always been this way and it'll always be this way in my life."

A person who perpetually feels helpless thinks that bad events are likely to *persist*. The cure for that type of wrong thinking is to *choose* to be optimistic. He needs to begin to think and speak what Annie, the curly-topped red-headed orphan, sings in the musical named for her: "The sun will come out tomorrow!"

A person who perpetually feels helpless tends to overgeneralize, falsely concluding that if he fails in one area of life, he will fail in all areas and is, therefore, a "failure." The cure for this wrong thinking is to recognize the pattern of all-or-nothing thinking and begin to compartmentalize failures. A failure in one area of life does not predict ongoing failure in all areas of life.

A person who perpetually feels helpless also tends to believe that somebody or some institution is out to do him in—personally. Sometimes he believes this about God. The cure for this wrong thinking is to begin to see external events as being totally independent of personal blame.

Above all, a person who perpetually feels helpless needs to confront his own feelings of being worthless or undeserving. He needs to begin to believe what God says about every person in His Word: *each* human being is valuable, beloved, and worthy of forgiveness and blessing in God's eyes. God has a plan and purpose for every person He has created, and He desires the eternal best for every person.

When a person begins to believe what God says about the worth of every human being, hope takes root and begins to grow. As long as a person has *hope*, there's far less likelihood that he will fall into the despondency of feeling *helpless*.

Bible Health + Food Facts

A Complete Meal

In Old Testament times, a complete meal was considered to consist of bread, a beverage, and stew—generally made with beans or vegetables and sometimes seasoned with meat. (See Genesis 25:29–34 and 2 Kings 4:38–41.)

THE GREAT APOSTASY

2 Now, brethren, concerning the coming of our Lord Jesus Christ and our gathering together to Him, we ask you, [2]not to be soon shaken in mind or troubled, either by spirit or by word or by letter, as if from us, as though the day of Christ[a] had come. [3]Let no one deceive you by any means; for *that Day will not come* unless the falling away comes first, and the man of sin[a] is revealed, the son of perdition, [4]who opposes and exalts himself above all that is called God or that is worshiped, so that he sits as God[a] in the temple of God, showing himself that he is God.

[5]Do you not remember that when I was still with you I told you these things? [6]And now you know what is restraining, that he may be revealed in his own time. [7]For the mystery of lawlessness is already at work; only He[a] who now restrains *will do so* until He[b] is taken out of the way. [8]And then the lawless one will be revealed, whom the Lord will consume with the breath of His mouth and destroy with the brightness of His coming. [9]The coming of the *lawless one* is according to the working of Satan, with all power, signs, and lying wonders, [10]and with all

---

2:2 [a]NU-Text reads *the Lord.*   2:3 [a]NU-Text reads *lawlessness.*   2:4 [a]NU-Text omits *as God.*   2:7 [a]Or *he* [b]Or *he*

unrighteous deception among those who perish, because they did not receive the love of the truth, that they might be saved. [11]And for this reason God will send them strong delusion, that they should believe the lie, [12]that they all may be condemned who did not believe the truth but had pleasure in unrighteousness.

STAND FAST

[13]But we are bound to give thanks to God always for you, brethren beloved by the Lord, because God from the beginningchose you for salvation through sanctification by the Spirit and belief in the truth, [14]to which He called you by our gospel, for the obtaining of the glory of our Lord Jesus Christ. [15]Therefore, brethren, stand fast and hold the traditions which you were taught, whether by word or our epistle.

[16]Now may our Lord Jesus Christ Himself, and our God and Father, who has loved us and given *us* everlasting consolation and good hope by grace, [17]comfort your hearts and establish you in every good word and work.

WISE CHOICES

Choose olive oil over saturated fats.
Monosaturated oils such as olive oil have a health benefit. Saturated fats are associated with animals and animal products, including milk fats, butter, and sour cream—saturated fats can be very damaging sources of cholesterol.

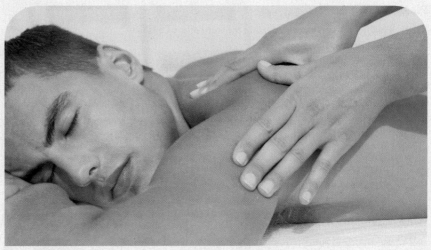

 Stress Busters

Stroking the Tension Away—
Have a Massage!

Several types of therapeutic massage are commonly practiced in the United States. Getting a massage on a regular basis is a wonderful way to relieve stress. Make sure you go to a skilled and licensed massage therapist.

When using massage at home, perhaps with a spouse, there are a number of good books and videos with easy-to-follow directions. The most important thing to be aware of is the direction of the strokes. Here are the basic strokes:

☐ Clockwise motion—releases tension, calms the body, decreases physiological activity.
☐ Counterclockwise motion—activates energy and stimulates physiological response. (Follow with clockwise motion.)
☐ Gliding movements with palms and thumbs are used for relaxation.
☐ Friction movements are small circular movements made with the heel of the hand, fingertips, or thumb. These movement break up and release fibrous areas, adhesions, and connective tissue.
☐ Kneading and squeezing strokes with hands and fingers use rhythmic, gentle pressure to relax major muscles and improve circulation.
☐ Percussionlike movements use tapping, clapping, cupping, and light slapping to stimulate deep muscles, nerves, and tendons. These movements aid circulation and metabolism. The movements can be relaxing or stimulating depending on the tempo used.
☐ Swinglike movements that shake or vibrate the body can be used to either stimulate or relax.

Make sure that you are on a firm surface if you are receiving a massage. A bed isn't firm enough. A large bath or beach towel covered with a cotton bed sheet works well for either the floor or a futon.

Massage increases lymphatic and blood circulation. It has been used in controlling cardiovascular and neurological ailments, relieving headaches, jaw problems, muscle spasms, and swelling from fractures and injuries. It has long-term benefits in improving muscular and skeletal endurance, skin texture, immune response, elimination of toxins, and increasing the flow of life-giving oxygen to the tissues of the body.

PRAY FOR US

3 Finally, brethren, pray for us, that the word of the Lord may run *swiftly* and be glorified, just as *it is* with you, ²and that we may be delivered from unreasonable and wicked men; for not all have faith.

³But the Lord is faithful, who will establish you and guard *you* from the evil one. ⁴And we have confidence in the Lord concerning you, both that you do and will do the things we command you.

⁵Now may the Lord direct your hearts into the love of God and into the patience of Christ.

WARNING AGAINST IDLENESS

⁶But we command you, brethren, in the name of our Lord Jesus Christ, that you withdraw from every brother who walks disorderly and not according to the tradition which heª received from us. ⁷For you yourselves know how you ought to follow us, for we were not disorderly among you; ⁸nor did we eat anyone's bread free of charge, but worked with labor and toil night and day, that we might not be a burden to any of you, ⁹not because we do not have authority, but to make ourselves an example of how you should follow us.

¹⁰For even when we were with you, we commanded you this: If anyone will not work, neither shall he eat. ¹¹For we hear that there are some who walk among you in a disorderly manner, not working at all, but are busybodies. ¹²Now those who are such we command and exhort through our Lord Jesus Christ that they work in quietness and eat their own bread.

¹³But *as for* you, brethren, do not grow weary *in* doing good. ¹⁴And if anyone does not obey our word in this epistle, note that person and do not keep company with him, that he may be ashamed. ¹⁵Yet do not count *him* as an enemy, but admonish *him* as a brother.

BENEDICTION

¹⁶Now may the Lord of peace Himself give you peace always in every way. The Lord *be* with you all.

¹⁷The salutation of Paul with my own hand, which is a sign in every epistle; so I write.

¹⁸The grace of our Lord Jesus Christ *be* with you all. Amen.

PEACE LOVE JOY KINDNESS

The Healthy Soul
>Self-Control

It may seem a little ironic that when we yield full control of our lives to the Holy Spirit, He gives back to us the ability to take control! What precisely does the Holy Spirit give us control over? Over all things related to our earthly, sensual desires. He gives us the ability to say "no" to temptation and "yes" to obeying God. He gives us the ability to make good choices for wholeness and then to follow through on them. He links up His power to our will to give us genuine "will power."

Another word for *self-control* is *discipline*. If a person is going to develop the habits that lead to the best possible health—both physical and emotional—that person is going to have to be disciplined when it comes to the way he or she eats, exercises, orders his or her daily life, relates to other people, and relates to God. To be disciplined means to make consistently good choices until good habits are formed, and to continue to engage in good habits until good character is formed. To live with self-control is to make a *daily* decision to be guided by the Spirit, to pursue all things that are healthful and beneficial, and to place one's relationship with God above all other relationships.

To have self under control is to say every morning, "This is the day the Lord has made. I will follow Him today. I will do what He leads me to do, say what He prompts me to say, and go where He directs me to go. I will yield all aspects of my life to Him and seek to bring Him honor and glory in all things. I will make choices that are good for today, good for the future, and good for eternity. I will *choose* to be as much like Jesus as I can possibly be."

In making such an intentional decision each day, a person is automatically turning away from flailing about in this life, giving in to every passing whim or temptation. A person who is disciplined is a person who does not fall easily for the lies and tricks of the devil, nor the lies and deceitful behavior of other people. A person who is disciplined stays the course and walks sure-footed on the path of right living.

3:6 ªNU-Text and M-Text read *they*.

HEALTH NOTES

TIMOTHY

Sometimes encouragement from our dearest friends and family is just what we need to keep going. The book was written to Timothy as a letter from his close friend and mentor, Paul.

The letter specifically addresses the tasks and responsibilities that a young man like Timothy faced in being the pastor of a new church. Even today, this letter continues to provide direction and give assistance for pastors, church leaders, missionaries, and ministers.

This book also has great benefit for our personal lives. Do you rule your own body? To whom does your flesh belong? This letter tells how to exert leadership and authority over your own flesh.

In addition, Paul warned Timothy about idle babblings and contradictions. Paul urged young Timothy to seek out and stay focused on the truth and to honor the church elders.

Real leadership is displayed when we honor ourselves and God, and stay focused on the task at hand. Timothy served the church with diligence and gentleness. We can do the same no matter what career we may have.

GREETING

1 Paul, an apostle of Jesus Christ, by the commandment of God our Savior and the Lord Jesus Christ, our hope,

²To Timothy, a true son in the faith:

Grace, mercy, *and* peace from God our Father and Jesus Christ our Lord.

NO OTHER DOCTRINE

³As I urged you when I went into Macedonia—remain in Ephesus that you may charge some that they teach no other doctrine, ⁴nor give heed to fables and endless genealogies, which cause disputes rather than godly edification which is in faith. ⁵Now the purpose of the commandment is love from a pure heart, *from* a good conscience, and *from* sincere faith, ⁶from which some, having strayed, have turned aside to idle talk, ⁷desiring to be teachers of the law, understanding neither what they say nor the things which they affirm.

⁸But we know that the law *is* good if one uses it lawfully, ⁹knowing this: that the law is not made for a righteous person, but for *the* lawless and insubordinate, for *the* ungodly and for sinners, for *the* unholy and profane, for murderers of fathers and murderers of mothers, for manslayers, ¹⁰for fornicators, for sodomites, for kidnappers, for liars, for perjurers, and if there is any other thing that is contrary to sound doctrine, ¹¹according to the glorious gospel of the blessed God which was committed to my trust.

GLORY TO GOD FOR HIS GRACE

¹²And I thank Christ Jesus our Lord who has enabled me, because He counted me faithful, putting *me* into the ministry, ¹³although I was formerly a blasphemer, a persecutor, and an insolent man; but I obtained mercy because I did *it* ignorantly in unbelief. ¹⁴And the grace of our Lord was exceedingly abundant, with faith and love which are in Christ Jesus. ¹⁵This *is* a faithful saying and worthy of all acceptance, that Christ Jesus came into the world to save sinners, of whom I am chief. ¹⁶However, for this reason I obtained mercy, that in me first Jesus Christ might show all longsuffering, as a pattern to those who are going to believe on Him for everlasting life. ¹⁷Now to the King eternal, immortal, invisible, to God who alone is wise,ᵃ *be* honor and glory forever and ever. Amen.

FIGHT THE GOOD FIGHT

¹⁸This charge I commit to you, son Timothy, according to the prophecies previously made concerning you, that by them you may wage the good warfare, ¹⁹having faith and a good conscience, which some having rejected, concerning the faith have suffered shipwreck, ²⁰of whom are Hymenaeus and Alexander, whom I delivered to Satan that they may learn not to blaspheme.

PRAY FOR ALL MEN

2 Therefore I exhort first of all that supplications, prayers, intercessions, *and* giving of thanks be made for all men, ²for kings and all who are in authority, that we may lead a quiet and peaceable life in all godliness and reverence. ³For this *is* good and acceptable in the sight of God our Savior, ⁴who desires all men to be

1:17 ᵃNU-Text reads *to the only God.*

WEIGHING Less & ENJOYING LIFE MORE!

[Six Simple Rules]

There are six simple rules of thumb that can help a person lose weight and maintain weight loss without engaging in any formal diet.

1. Reserve special foods for special occasions. You don't need to feel as if you are depriving yourself forever of a favorite dessert or calorie-laden casserole. Just reserve that food for a once- or twice-a-year occasion that you consider to be a celebration.

2. Eat your main meal—one with protein and grains—at noon instead of at night. This will give your body longer to work off the calories and to digest and absorb the protein.

3. Avoid eating after seven o'clock in the evening. Give yourself at least two or three hours between your last meal and your bedtime.

4. Do something active *before* you eat. Wait at least thirty minutes between exercise and eating. That way your exercise will burn off calories from fat reserves in your body, rather than the calories of a snack or meal. Do, however, drink water after you exercise to keep your body hydrated.

5. Drink a large glass of pure water about twenty minutes before you eat. It will help give you a "full" feeling that translates into a desire to eat less.

6. Start leaving a few bites of food on your plate rather than "cleaning" your plate. If you add up all the uneaten bites over the course of a month, you are likely to have several meals worth of food!

---

saved and to come to the knowledge of the truth. ⁵For *there is* one God and one Mediator between God and men, *the* Man Christ Jesus, ⁶who gave Himself a ransom for all, to be testified in due time, ⁷for which I was appointed a preacher and an apostle—I am speaking the truth in Christ[a] *and* not lying—a teacher of the Gentiles in faith and truth.

INSIGHTS INTO THE WORD

> (1 Timothy 2:9, 10)

Hair Sends a Message. For thousands of years, women have been concerned with hairstyles, clothing, and jewelry. The apostle Paul warned, however, of sending a "wrong message" when it comes to personal style. Marble sculptures of women in the first century show a hairstyle known as the *nodus* (knot or knob). The style involved a topknot or roll above the forehead, connected by a central braid to a bun at the back of the head.

This hairstyle was made popular by Livia Druscilla, Caesar Augustus's wife, as a contrasting style to the long flowing tresses of Cleopatra (Marc Antony's lover). Those who adopted Livia's style sent a political message of alignment with the "republican virtues" of Rome at the time. Paul admonished Christian women in the Roman empire to dress modestly in a way that would put the focus on what a woman *did* in expressing her faith in Jesus, not on what she wore.

MEN AND WOMEN IN THE CHURCH

⁸I desire therefore that the men pray everywhere, lifting up holy hands, without wrath and doubting; ⁹in like manner also, that the women adorn themselves in modest apparel, with propriety and moderation, not with braided hair or gold or pearls or costly clothing, ¹⁰but, which is proper for women professing godliness, with good works. ¹¹Let a woman learn in silence with all submission. ¹²And I do not permit a woman to teach or to have authority over a man, but to be in silence. ¹³For Adam was formed first, then Eve. ¹⁴And Adam was not deceived, but the woman being deceived, fell into transgression. ¹⁵Nevertheless she will be saved in childbearing if they continue in faith, love, and holiness, with self-control.

QUALIFICATIONS OF OVERSEERS

3 This *is* a faithful saying: If a man desires the position of a bishop,[a] he desires a good work. ²A bishop then must be blameless, the husband of one wife, temperate, sober-minded, of good behavior, hospitable, able to teach;

2:7 ªNU-Text omits *in Christ.*   3:1 ªLiterally *overseer*

Food combining and nutrient sequencing have a powerful effect on digestion. Here are the five basics:

Better Digestion—Not Just for the Body!

1. Meats and proteins should not be eaten with high-starch foods.
2. Meats and proteins may be eaten with low-starch vegetables, such as green beans, broccoli, cauliflower, asparagus, zucchini squash, and lettuce-based salads.
3. Low-starch vegetables may be eaten with starchy vegetables, such as potatoes, and with whole grains.
4. Fruits should be eaten approximately thirty minutes before a meal and should be eaten alone.
5. Liquid should be consumed half an hour before a meal, with no more than four ounces taken with a meal.

How does this relate to the emotional, mental, or spiritual aspects of what you take in to your being? The key is in understanding the process of digestion.

Digestion is the "breaking down of food so that it can be absorbed effectively." Sometimes the breaking-down process involves eating or drinking some things before others. Sometimes the process involves eating the right combination of foods.

In many ways, the processes of "breaking down" and "combining" are directly related to mental growth or education. We need to break down and sequence information in order to learn it better, remember it more accurately, and apply it more effectively. A child must learn basic math before moving on to calculus. As you try to learn a new skill, don't try to learn everything at once. Learn bit by bit. Take in information that is linked to things you already know. Combine your study, even your study of the Scripture, so that you are learning things that seem by nature to be linked together.

Emotionally speaking, don't try to be everything to everybody. Some people are mentors, others are people you are mentoring. Some people are friends, others are acquaintances. One of the fine arts of entertaining is to know how to invite people to social gatherings who have something in common or who will find one another interesting. Learn how to relate to people one on one, and how to deal with small groups. Sometimes it is important to meet with one or two people before a meeting or conference in order to help them prepare for the meeting or to deal with potential problems prior to a decision-making or task-assigning session.

In the spiritual realm God has designed us for relationship with Him. The primary ways in which we experience God are prayer, reading the Scriptures, and being in fellowship with other Christians who are willing to use their spiritual gifts in helpful, wholesome ways as well as to receive the ministry of others' spiritual gifts. Pray before you read your Bible. Allow your mind and heart to become quiet in the Lord's presence so that you truly can hear from God as you read His Word. Pray before ministry activities.

Ask the Lord to lead and guide you in being sensitive to others and providing what they truly need from you. Ministry is always more effective if two or three like-minded believers are focused on the same task or prayer request. Pray after a time of Bible study or ministry that God will help you remember and build on what you have learned or experienced.

In every area of our lives, we are wise to be sensitive to the importance of sequencing information and encounters, and of combining elements in the most helpful and healthful ways. We need to be able to "digest" life if we truly are going to get the most out of life!

WHOLENESS 101

[3]not given to wine, not violent, not greedy for money,[a] but gentle, not quarrelsome, not covetous; [4]one who rules his own house well, having *his* children in submission with all reverence [5](for if a man does not know how to rule his own house, how will he take care of the church of God?); [6]not a novice, lest being puffed up with pride he fall into the *same* condemnation as the devil. [7]Moreover he must have a good testimony among those who are outside, lest he fall into reproach and the snare of the devil.

QUALIFICATIONS OF DEACONS

[8]Likewise deacons *must be* reverent, not double-tongued, not given to much wine, not greedy for money, [9]holding the mystery of the faith with a pure conscience. [10]But let these also first be tested; then let them serve as deacons, being *found* blameless. [11]Likewise, *their* wives *must be* reverent, not slanderers, temperate, faithful in all things. [12]Let deacons be the husbands of one wife, ruling *their* children and their own houses well. [13]For those who have served well as deacons obtain for themselves a good standing and great boldness in the faith which is in Christ Jesus.

THE GREAT MYSTERY

[14]These things I write to you, though I hope to come to you shortly; [15]but if I am delayed, *I write* so that you may know how you ought to conduct yourself in the house of God, which is the church of the living

3:3 [a]NU-Text omits *not greedy for money.*

> (1 Timothy 4:7, 8)

Is Exercise Profitable? Yes! How profitable? The answer from the Bible is, at least "a little"! Paul did not dismiss the benefit of physical exercise. Rather, he pointed out that in the infinite context of eternity, the physical disciplines we develop and employ now are only for a temporary period of time. The benefits are not eternal but for this life. Certainly physical exercise helps a person to have a stronger and more flexible body—to have more energy, greater endurance, and better health. Other forms of exercise are also for the here-and-now of this world.

In the long run, however, the exercise of spiritual disciplines—of learning how to live a godly life and then practicing the principles of godly living—not only helps us live to the maximum of our potential *now*, but also prepares us for eternity. As we seek to become physically fit, we need to seek even more to become spiritually fit.

conscience seared with a hot iron, ³forbidding to marry, *and commanding* to abstain from foods which God created to be received with thanksgiving by those who believe and know the truth. ⁴For every creature of God *is* good, and nothing is to be refused if it is received with thanksgiving; ⁵for it is sanctified by the word of God and prayer.

A GOOD SERVANT OF JESUS CHRIST

⁶If you instruct the brethren in these things, you will be a good minister of Jesus Christ, nourished in the words of faith and of the good doctrine which you have carefully followed. ⁷But reject profane and old wives' fables, and exercise yourself toward godliness. ⁸For bodily exercise profits a little, but godliness is profitable for all things, having promise of the life that now is and of that which is to come. ⁹This *is* a faithful saying and worthy of all acceptance. ¹⁰For to this *end* we both labor and suffer reproach,ᵃ because we trust in the living God, who is *the* Savior of all men, especially of those who believe. ¹¹These things command and teach.

God, the pillar and ground of the truth. ¹⁶And without controversy great is the mystery of godliness:

Godᵃ was manifested in the flesh,
Justified in the Spirit,
Seen by angels,
Preached among the Gentiles,
Believed on in the world,
Received up in glory.

THE GREAT APOSTASY

Now the Spirit expressly says that in latter times some will depart from the faith, giving heed to deceiving spirits and doctrines of demons, ²speaking lies in hypocrisy, having their own

TAKE HEED TO YOUR MINISTRY

¹²Let no one despise your youth, but be an example to the believers in word, in conduct, in love, in spirit,ᵃ in faith, in purity. ¹³Till I come, give attention to reading, to exhortation, to doctrine. ¹⁴Do not neglect the gift that is in you, which was given to you by prophecy with the laying on of the hands of the eldership. ¹⁵Meditate on these things; give yourself entirely to them, that your progress may be evident to all. ¹⁶Take heed to yourself and to the doctrine. Continue in them, for in

> (1 Timothy 4:15)

Godly Meditation. Meditation is one of the best stress busters you can adopt as a daily habit. For the Christian to meditate is to spend some time in quiet contemplation on the things of God. Rather than adopt certain postures or repeat senseless words, Christ-centered meditation is a time to pray or to repeat memorized Scriptures, and to spend time in contemplation on what you have spoken. To prepare for effective and calming meditation times, discipline yourself to memorize fifteen to twenty verses that you find especially comforting or inspiring. Commit these words from the Lord to long-term memory.

If you include a time of meditation after reading a passage of Scripture as part of a daily devotional time, choose a phrase or sentence from that passage to repeat to the Lord, pausing to contemplate on what it means to you and how you might apply its truth to your life. Speak sentences of praise or the names and attributes that the Bible gives for God the Father, Jesus the Son, or the Holy Spirit. Invite the Lord to reveal Himself to you in new ways as you reflect quietly and focus on His nature and the relationship He desires to have with you. As you meditate, relax your body and open yourself up to God's presence. You will likely find that you are holding on to much less stress if you will do this every day!

3:16 ᵃNU-Text reads *Who.* 4:10 ᵃNU-Text reads *we labor and strive.* 4:12 ᵃNU-Text omits *in spirit.*

doing this you will save both yourself and those who hear you.

TREATMENT OF CHURCH MEMBERS

5 Do not rebuke an older man, but exhort *him* as a father, younger men as brothers, ²older women as mothers, younger women as sisters, with all purity.

HONOR TRUE WIDOWS

³Honor widows who are really widows. ⁴But if any widow has children or grandchildren, let them first learn to show piety at home and to repay their parents; for this is good and*ᵃ* acceptable before God. ⁵Now she who is really a widow, and left alone, trusts in God and continues in supplications and prayers night and day. ⁶But she who lives in pleasure is dead while she lives. ⁷And these things command, that they may be blameless. ⁸But if anyone does not provide for his own, and especially for those of his household, he has denied the faith and is worse than an unbeliever.

⁹Do not let a widow under sixty years old be taken into the number, *and not unless* she has been the wife of one man, ¹⁰well reported for good works: if she has brought up children, if she has lodged strangers, if she has washed the saints' feet, if she has relieved the afflicted, if she has diligently followed every good work.

¹¹But refuse *the* younger widows; for when they have begun to grow wanton against Christ, they desire to marry, ¹²having condemnation because they have cast off their first faith. ¹³And besides they learn *to be* idle, wandering about from house to house, and not only idle but also gossips and busybodies, saying things which they ought not. ¹⁴Therefore I desire that *the* younger *widows* marry, bear children, manage the house, give no opportunity to the adversary to speak reproachfully. ¹⁵For some have already turned aside after Satan. ¹⁶If any believing man or*ᵃ* woman has widows, let them relieve them, and do not let the church be burdened, that it may relieve those who are really widows.

HONOR THE ELDERS

¹⁷Let the elders who rule well be counted worthy of double honor, especially those who

▲ Roman Orgies and Sacrifices ▲

ULTIMATE HEALTH RESOURCE • ULTIMATE HEALTH RESOURCE

We tend to associate the word *orgy* today with drunkenness, gluttony, and debauchery. While the Roman orgies may have included an overdose of wine, food, and sensual behavior—the *purpose* of an orgy was not simply to overindulge the body and senses.

Orgies were originally secret rites or customs that were connected with the worship of some of the pagan deities, such as the secret worship of Demeter or the festival of Dionysus. These ritualistic feasts were accompanied with mystic symbolism, and at times sexual behavior intended to appease the fertility gods. The food and wine consumed at the orgies was food and wine that was first sacrificed to Roman gods. Because of this, the men and women believed they were identifying completely with the god and were in some mystical way forming a relationship with the god.

Archaeologists in Israel uncovered a number of altars in the major Romanized cities of the first century. These altars were used for daily sacrifice to the Roman gods. Cattle were sacrificed to the "gods above"—the various

gods associated with the heavens and the earth. Pigs were sacrificed to the "gods below" or to the "gods of the netherworld." The pagan gods were not only linked to the physical earth, sky, and water, but also to the symbolic realms of good (above) and evil (below).

An orgy feast almost always was required to make both beef and pork available, just to make sure the complete gamut of deities would be covered. The more food that could be consumed, the better—gluttony was an act of showing more complete association with the god. Hence, the practice of binging and purging became commonplace at orgies.

In many ways, the Roman orgies were in direct contrast to the celebration of Jewish feast days—intended to be days of quiet reflection, joyful relaxation with family and friends, and days of simplicity in eating and drinking. The Jews never believed that the food they ate or the wine they drank intertwined them with Yahweh—they believed food and drink were gifts from God and were thankful for His provision. Their worship of God was manifested primarily in obedience to God's commandments. Worship was regarded as for the pleasure of God, not the pleasure of man.

Something to consider: the parties you give, and the party food you serve, send a signal to others about your relationship with God.

5:4 ªNU-Text and M-Text omit *good and.*   5:16 ªNU-Text omits *man or.*

labor in the word and doctrine. [18]For the Scripture says, "You shall not muzzle an ox while it treads out the grain,"[a] and, "The laborer is worthy of his wages."[b] [19]Do not receive an accusation against an elder except from two or three witnesses. [20]Those who are sinning rebuke in the presence of all, that the rest also may fear.

[21]I charge you before God and the Lord Jesus Christ and the elect angels that you observe these things without prejudice, doing nothing with partiality. [22]Do not lay hands on anyone hastily, nor share in other people's sins; keep yourself pure.

[23]No longer drink only water, but use a little wine for your stomach's sake and your frequent infirmities.

[24]Some men's sins are clearly evident, preceding them to judgment, but those of some men follow later. [25]Likewise, the good works of some are clearly evident, and those that are otherwise cannot be hidden.

HONOR MASTERS

6 Let as many bondservants as are under the yoke count their own masters worthy of all honor, so that the name of God and His doctrine may not be blasphemed. [2]And those who have believing masters, let them not despise them because they are brethren, but rather serve them because those who are benefited are believers and beloved. Teach and exhort these things.

CONDIMENTS

☐ Parsley

Parsley is believed to be one of the "scented herbs" in the Bible (Song of Solomon 5:13). It grows profusely in Israel and is one of the first herbs to appear in the spring. That may be one of the reasons it is part of a traditional Passover meal.

Many salads in the Middle East include parsley greens. The parsley used in the Middle East has larger leaves than most parsley in the United States.

Parsley is a rich source of vitamins C and A. Two of the chemicals in parsley, myristicin and apiol, act as a mild laxative and a strong diuretic. This diuretic action may help control high blood pressure. In Germany, parsley tea is often prescribed for that purpose.

Research has also shown that parsley blocks the formation of histamines, the chemical that triggers allergy attacks. It may help those who suffer from hay fever or have an outbreak of hives. Other nutritional researchers have concluded that parsley is helpful for a wide variety of ailments: digestive problems and gas, bed-wetting, hypertension, edema, bad breath, and kidney disease. It is believed to be helpful in restoring bladder, kidney, liver, lung, stomach, and thyroid function.

Don't leave that sprig of parsley on your plate thinking it was placed there just for color or appearance. Eating parsley can be just as effective as sucking on a breath mint!

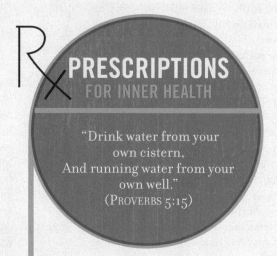

℞ PRESCRIPTIONS
FOR INNER HEALTH

"Drink water from your
own cistern,
And running water from your
own well."
(PROVERBS 5:15)

Although this may sound like good advice about drinking pure water—which is always a good idea—this proverb actually has to do with abstaining from adultery and fornication. God's Word contains numerous commands for husbands to be faithful to their wives and to "rejoice with the wife of your youth" (Proverbs 5:18). Those who practice infidelity are prone to countless sexually transmitted diseases, very few of which are found in people who are celibate or faithful to one spouse.

5:18 [a]Deuteronomy 25:4 [b]Luke 10:7

ERROR AND GREED

³If anyone teaches otherwise and does not consent to wholesome words, *even* the words of our Lord Jesus Christ, and to the doctrine which accords with godliness, ⁴he is proud, knowing nothing, but is obsessed with disputes and arguments over words, from which come envy, strife, reviling, evil suspicions, ⁵useless wranglingsᵃ of men of corrupt minds and destitute of the truth, who suppose that godliness is a *means of* gain. From such withdraw yourself.ᵇ

⁶Now godliness with contentment is great gain. ⁷For we brought nothing into *this* world, *and it is* certainᵃ we can carry nothing out. ⁸And having food and clothing, with these we shall be content. ⁹But those who desire to be rich fall into temptation and a snare, and *into* many foolish and harmful lusts which drown men in destruction and perdition. ¹⁰For the love of money is a root of all *kinds of* evil, for which some have strayed from the faith in their greediness, and pierced themselves through with many sorrows.

THE GOOD CONFESSION

¹¹But you, O man of God, flee these things and pursue righteousness, godliness, faith, love, patience, gentleness. ¹²Fight the good fight of faith, lay hold on eternal life, to which you were also called and have confessed the good confession in the presence of many witnesses. ¹³I urge you in the sight of God who gives life to all things, and *before* Christ Jesus who witnessed the good confession before Pontius Pilate, ¹⁴that you keep *this* commandment without spot, blameless until our Lord Jesus Christ's appearing, ¹⁵which He will manifest in His own time, *He who is* the blessed and only Potentate, the King of kings and Lord of lords, ¹⁶who alone has immortality, dwelling in unapproachable light, whom no man has seen or can see, to whom *be* honor and everlasting power. Amen.

INSTRUCTIONS TO THE RICH

¹⁷Command those who are rich in this present age not to be haughty, nor to trust in uncertain riches but in the living God, who gives us richly all things to enjoy. ¹⁸*Let them* do good, that they be rich in good works, ready to give, willing to share, ¹⁹storing up for themselves a good foundation for the time to come, that they may lay hold on eternal life.

GUARD THE FAITH

²⁰O Timothy! Guard what was committed to your trust, avoiding the profane *and* idle babblings and contradictions of what is falsely called knowledge— ²¹by professing it some have strayed concerning the faith.

Grace *be* with you. Amen.

Lamb Stew

Righteous Recipes

Ingredients:
- ☐ 4 tablespoons extra-virgin olive oil
- ☐ 1 garlic clove, halved
- ☐ ½ onion, thinly sliced
- ☐ 3 pounds lean free-range lamb, cut into 1-inch cubes
- ☐ ⅓ cup flour
- ☐ 1½ teaspoons Celtic salt
- ☐ ¼ teaspoon pepper
- ☐ 4 medium carrots, sliced
- ☐ 3 cups low-sodium beef or chicken broth
- ☐ ½ teaspoon thyme
- ☐ 10–15 fresh mushrooms, halved

Heat the olive oil in a heavy skillet. Sauté the garlic and onion in the hot oil for 5 minutes. Remove garlic and onion and place them in a small bowl. Coat the lamb with a mixture of the flour, salt, and pepper. Brown well in the hot oil, adding more oil if necessary. Return the onion and garlic to the skillet. Add the carrots, broth, and thyme. Simmer, covered, for 1½ hours or until tender. Sauté the mushrooms in olive oil for 5 minutes. Add the mushrooms to the lamb mixture and mix gently. Simmer for 10 more minutes over very low heat.

Yield: 8–10 servings

Note: You can also prepare this stew in a slow cooker on high for about 6 hours. Add the mushrooms the last 15 minutes of cooking time.

6:5 ᵃNU-Text and M-Text read *constant friction.* ᵇNU-Text omits this sentence. 6:7 ᵃNU-Text omits *and it is certain.*

TIMOTHY

What do you hope to win? What is the race you are running or the fight you are fighting? Where is your finish line? Is it at the end of one-mile walk, a 5k race, or a marathon? In 2 Timothy, Paul reminds us to stir up the gifts (2 Timothy 1:6), and he relays to us that God has not given us a spirit of fear (2 Timothy 1:7).

Timothy's goal, like Paul's, was to see the church mature in strength, unity, grace, and gentleness. Regardless of situations, both men had both pressed on with diligence. In this letter Paul encourages Timothy to be faithful and to persevere in the face of future difficulties and hardship.

In 2 Timothy 4:7 Paul writes, "I have fought the good fight, I have finished the race, I have kept the faith." I have fought...I have finished...I have kept. That is the pattern we need to win our race.

Establish your goals, set your plan, stay focused, and regardless how difficult it is, endure—keep pressing forward to the finish line.

GREETING

1 Paul, an apostle of Jesus Christ[a] by the will of God, according to the promise of life which is in Christ Jesus,

[2] To Timothy, a beloved son:

Grace, mercy, *and* peace from God the Father and Christ Jesus our Lord.

TIMOTHY'S FAITH AND HERITAGE

[3] I thank God, whom I serve with a pure conscience, as *my* forefathers *did,* as without ceasing I remember you in my prayers night and day, [4] greatly desiring to see you, being mindful of your tears, that I may be filled with joy, [5] when I call to remembrance the genuine faith that is in you, which dwelt first in your grandmother Lois and your mother Eunice, and I am persuaded is in you also. [6] Therefore I remind you to stir up the gift of God which is in you through the laying on of my hands. [7] For God has not given us a spirit of fear, but of power and of love and of a sound mind.

NOT ASHAMED OF THE GOSPEL

[8] Therefore do not be ashamed of the testimony of our Lord, nor of me His prisoner, but share with me in the sufferings for the gospel according to the power of God, [9] who has saved us and called *us* with a holy calling, not according to our works, but according to His own purpose and grace which was given to us in Christ Jesus before time began, [10] but has now been revealed by the appearing of our Savior Jesus Christ, *who* has abolished death and brought life and immortality to light through the gospel, [11] to which I was appointed a preacher, an apostle, and a teacher of the Gentiles.[a] [12] For this reason I also suffer these things; nevertheless I am not ashamed, for I know whom I have believed and am persuaded that He is able to keep what I have committed to Him until that Day.

BE LOYAL TO THE FAITH

[13] Hold fast the pattern of sound words which you have heard from me, in faith and love which are in Christ Jesus. [14] That good thing which was committed to you, keep by the Holy Spirit who dwells in us.

[15] This you know, that all those in Asia have turned away from me, among whom are Phygellus and Hermogenes. [16] The Lord grant mercy to the household of Onesiphorus, for he often refreshed me, and was not ashamed of my chain; [17] but when he arrived in Rome, he sought me out very zealously and found *me.* [18] The Lord grant to him that he may find mercy from the Lord in that Day—and you know very well how many ways he ministered *to me*[a] at Ephesus.

BE STRONG IN GRACE

2 You therefore, my son, be strong in the grace that is in Christ Jesus. [2] And the things that you have heard from me among many witnesses, commit these to faithful men who will be able

---

1:1 [a]NU-Text and M-Text read *Christ Jesus.*   1:11 [a]NU-Text omits *of the Gentiles.*   1:18 [a]*To me* is from the Vulgate and a few Greek manuscripts.

> (2 Timothy 1:7)

The Hallmarks of Emotional Wellness.

The apostle Paul gave Timothy the hallmarks of emotional wellness. First, there's no fear. This refers to fear that is spiritual or emotional in nature, not a fear of fire, falling, dying, and so forth. Spiritual and emotional fears can cripple and paralyze a person, keeping the person from moving forward with faith to fulfill all that God has created him to be, become, and do. The person who is truly free of fear, and thus, filled with confidence born of trust in God, is a person who will have the power to act and accomplish good deeds, engage in good works, and have the confidence to speak up with good words that encourage, enrich, inform, edify, and bring conviction.

The person who is truly free of fear will be willing to take the risk of entering into loving relationships. The person will be generous toward others, giving what is appropriate and beneficial, without expecting servitude or gratitude. The person who is free of fear will have a sound mind, which is a mind free of confusion, doubt, or constant struggling with temptations. A sound mind is focused on what can be done now and in the future, rather than what has been done in the past. Faith and forgiveness free a person from spiritual fear. Faith and forgiveness also give a person the ability to walk in confidence, love others, and make the best possible decisions and choices. That's emotional health!

---

to teach others also. ³You therefore must endure° hardship as a good soldier of Jesus Christ. ⁴No one engaged in warfare entangles himself with the affairs of *this* life, that he may please him who enlisted him as a soldier. ⁵And also if anyone competes in athletics, he is not crowned unless he competes according to the rules. ⁶The hardworking farmer must be first to partake of the crops. ⁷Consider what I say, and may° the Lord give you understanding in all things.

⁸Remember that Jesus Christ, of the seed of David, was raised from the dead according to my gospel, ⁹for which I suffer trouble as an evildoer, *even* to the point of chains; but the word of God is not chained. ¹⁰Therefore I endure all things for the sake of the elect, that they also may obtain the salvation which is in Christ Jesus with eternal glory.

¹¹*This is* a faithful saying:

For if we died with *Him,*
We shall also live with *Him.*
¹² If we endure,
We shall also reign with *Him.*
If we deny *Him,*
He also will deny us.
¹³ If we are faithless,
He remains faithful;
He cannot deny Himself.

APPROVED AND DISAPPROVED WORKERS

¹⁴Remind *them* of these things, charging *them* before the Lord not to strive about words to no profit, to the ruin of the hearers. ¹⁵Be diligent to present yourself approved to God, a worker who does not need to be ashamed, rightly dividing the word of truth. ¹⁶But shun profane *and* idle babblings, for they will increase to more ungodliness. ¹⁷And their message will spread like cancer. Hymenaeus and Philetus are of this sort, ¹⁸who have strayed concerning the truth, saying that the resurrection is already past; and

GODLY & GOODLOOKIN'

Lose Weight

We live in a society that values "thin" over "fat," so the general perception is usually that thin people are better looking. An interesting poll was reported recently. It revealed that people, on average, thought overweight people were an average of *nine years older* than they actually were. This had nothing to do with whether the people being polled thought excess weight was a bad or good thing. In reality, the overweight people likely walked more slowly with greater signs of discomfort, had difficulty getting up from chairs, and had more difficulty maneuvering in and out of vehicles—all of which are frequently signs of aging associated with older adults.

2:3 °NU-Text reads *You must share.*   2:7 °NU-Text reads *the Lord will give you.*

they overthrow the faith of some. ¹⁹Nevertheless the solid foundation of God stands, having this seal: "The Lord knows those who are His," and, "Let everyone who names the name of Christ* depart from iniquity."

²⁰But in a great house there are not only vessels of gold and silver, but also of wood and clay, some for honor and some for dishonor. ²¹Therefore if anyone cleanses himself from the latter, he will be a vessel for honor, sanctified and useful for the Master, prepared for every good work. ²²Flee also youthful lusts; but pursue righteousness, faith, love, peace with those who call on the Lord out of a pure heart. ²³But avoid foolish and ignorant disputes, knowing that they generate strife. ²⁴And a servant of the Lord must not quarrel but be gentle to all, able to teach, patient, ²⁵in humility correcting those who are in opposition, if God perhaps will grant them repentance, so that they may know the truth, ²⁶and *that* they may come to their senses *and escape* the snare of the devil, having been taken captive by him to *do* his will.

PERILOUS TIMES AND PERILOUS MEN

3 But know this, that in the last days perilous times will come: ²For men will be lovers of themselves, lovers of money, boasters, proud, blasphemers, disobedient to parents, unthankful,

Q What did John the Baptist eat according to the Gospel of Matthew?

A Locusts and wild honey *(Matthew 3:4).* Although locusts are insects and not considered desirable as food by many people today, they are a good source of protein. John may have been eating carob pods, which are similar in taste to chocolate and from a distance appear similar in shape and color to locusts. Either way, the food was enough to sustain John in his wilderness life.

▲ Overcoming Self-Hatred ▲

OVERCOMING OBSTINATE OBSTACLES • OVERCOMING OBSTINATE OBSTACLES • OVERCOMING OBSTINATE OBSTACLES

You are valuable to God beyond measure no matter what you have done or what has been done to you! *Knowing* that and *feeling* that, however, are often two different things. The person who doesn't feel valuable or lovable to God and others is a person who is likely experiencing self-hatred.

How can you tell if you are troubled with self-hatred? The symptoms are usually feelings of guilt or shame. Guilt is a state of having done something wrong or having committed an offense, legal or ethical. It is a painful feeling of self-reproach for having done something that you recognize as being immoral, wrong, a crime, or sin. Shame generally arises from what *another* person has done, something that society widely recognizes as immoral, wrong, a crime, or sin. Shame is the reflection onto the victim of an abuser's bad behavior.

Guilt and shame often create feelings of deep sorrow and sadness in a person, as well as an abiding feeling of being unworthy or unlovable. These feelings of low self-worth are at the core of self-hatred.

Both guilt and shame create an endless circle of negative thinking. They *never* lead to emotional freedom, strength, or health, either emotionally or physically.

Very often the first step in overcoming guilt and shame is to identify whether the guilt is true or false guilt. If you are experiencing true guilt for a wrong committed, you need to ask forgiveness of God and forgiveness of the person you wronged. Then you need to forgive yourself. With false guilt—guilt that is rooted in something another person did—you need to recognize that you didn't sin, ask God to help you walk freely from the person who did sin, and to forgive the offender. Always remember that forgiveness means to release, not to exonerate.

Ask God to heal your heart. You can know the truth about guilt and shame mentally, and even forgive mentally, and still have low self-worth. That's because feelings of self-worth are deeply emotional. Ask God to reveal to your heart how much He loves you and how much He values you. Find a way to release the emotions associated with your pain—and then do so in a way that will bring healing to your heart without wounding another person.

Gardening for Health

Your Garden: Filling and Subduing the Earth

God's command to Adam and Eve was to "Be fruitful and multiply; fill the earth and subdue it; have dominion over the fish of the sea, over the birds of the air, and over every living thing that moves on the earth" (Genesis 1:28). For many people through the ages, this command has been used as a strong rationale for man's *use* of the environment—such as using animals in laborsaving ways, catching fish and raising birds and using these creatures as well as animals for food.

For some it meant controlling species and if necessary, eliminating their ability to reproduce (such as in the case of mosquitoes or disease-bearing rodents). In more recent years, this command has been perceived as a strong admonition for people to become good stewards of the environment—to restore natural habitats and preserve wilderness areas and endangered species.

What does it really mean to "fill the earth and subdue it"? God intended for Adam and Eve to be fruitful and multiply until the earth was filled with people who were just like them—people who were blessed by God, loved God, enjoyed close fellowship with Him, and obeyed His commands. They were to expand the beauty and orderliness of the Garden of Eden until the entire earth was a productive, pleasing, balanced, harmonious gardenlike atmosphere in which God and man might walk together in close fellowship.

The earth was to be "tamed" by them—put in order, domesticated, made useful, so that all who lived on the earth would be blessed by the earth. To fulfill this command meant that Adam and Eve needed to become consummate biologists, botanists, and geologists! They needed to understand the interrelationships between plants and animals, the propagation of plants, good gardening techniques, and the different types of plants suited to different types of soil. Most of all, they needed to be people who sought to welcome God into their world at every hour of every day.

What did it mean to "have dominion" over the fish, birds, and living creatures? It meant to rule over these creatures, and a significant aspect of ruling CONT. NEXT PAGE>>>

unholy, [3]unloving, unforgiving, slanderers, without self-control, brutal, despisers of good, [4]traitors, headstrong, haughty, lovers of pleasure rather than lovers of God, [5]having a form of godliness but denying its power. And from such people turn away! [6]For of this sort are those who creep into households and make captives of gullible women loaded down with sins, led away by various lusts, [7]always learning and never able to come to the knowledge of the truth. [8]Now as Jannes and Jambres resisted Moses, so do these also resist the truth: men of corrupt minds, disapproved concerning the faith; [9]but they will progress no further, for their folly will be manifest to all, as theirs also was.

THE MAN OF GOD AND THE WORD OF GOD

[10]But you have carefully followed my doctrine, manner of life, purpose, faith, longsuffering, love, perseverance, [11]persecutions, afflictions, which happened to me at Antioch, at Iconium, at Lystra—what persecutions I endured. And out of *them* all the Lord delivered me. [12]Yes, and all who desire to live godly in Christ Jesus will suffer persecution. [13]But evil men and impostors will grow worse and worse, deceiving and being deceived. [14]But you must continue in the things which you have learned and been assured of, knowing from whom you have learned *them,* [15]and that from childhood you have known the Holy Scriptures, which are able to make you wise for salvation through faith which is in Christ Jesus.

[SOY PROTEIN]

FACT MORSELS

Soy—Queen of the Plant Proteins. One of the most beneficial plants God created is the soybean. Native to China, the soybean has been cultivated for thousands of years. It is the most widely grown and used bean in the world. In the United States, the soybean is used mainly for its oil and for animal feed. However, the soybean has an amino acid profile that makes it a rich source of protein for humans as well!

Soybeans are packed with phytonutrients that are powerful protectors against cancer. The Japanese consume thirty to fifty times more soy products than Americans and they have approximately a quarter of the incidences of breast and prostate cancer that we have in the United States.

Gardening for Health Cont.>>>

involved naming the creatures. To name was to identify the nature of a creature and to understand its features, habits, and purpose. To fulfill this command meant that Adam and Eve needed to become consummate zoologists!

What is the challenge that we face as individuals today? Each of us has a piece of the earth in which we dwell. It may be an apartment with a balcony or two, a house or condominium with a yard, a multi-acre estate, or a thousand-acre ranch. God has entrusted us with a portion of the earth to subdue, and if we have animals or pets occupying our land allotment, He has entrusted us to have dominion over these creatures. We need to do our best to turn our portion of the earth into a garden that is beautiful and productive. We need to do our best to treat our animals in a way that is in keeping with their God-given purpose on the earth. Most of all, we need to create an atmosphere that is filled with praise and worship of God—a place where good flourishes and evil is banished.

Inch by inch, square yard by square yard, we are to carve out a space in a sin-filled world in which God and man can walk together in close fellowship day in and day out. And inch by inch, square yard by square yard, we are to *expand* that space until the entire earth has been reclaimed.

[16]All Scripture *is* given by inspiration of God, and *is* profitable for doctrine, for reproof, for correction, for instruction in righteousness, [17]that the man of God may be complete, thoroughly equipped for every good work.

PREACH THE WORD

4 I charge *you* therefore before God and the Lord Jesus Christ, who will judge the living and the dead at[a] His appearing and His kingdom: [2]Preach the word! Be ready in season *and* out of season. Convince, rebuke, exhort, with all longsuffering and teaching. [3]For the time will come when they will not endure sound doctrine, but according to their own desires, *because* they have itching ears, they will heap up for themselves teachers; [4]and they will turn *their* ears away from the truth, and be turned aside to fables. [5]But you be watchful in all things, endure afflictions, do the work of an evangelist, fulfill your ministry.

PAUL'S VALEDICTORY

[6]For I am already being poured out as a drink offering, and the time of my departure is at hand. [7]I have fought the good fight, I have finished the race, I have kept the faith. [8]Finally, there is laid up for me the crown of righteousness, which the Lord, the righteous Judge, will give to me on that Day, and not to me only but also to all who have loved His appearing.

WALKING THE WALK

[JESUS WAS A WALKER!]

When Jesus was a child, perhaps as young as four or five years old, He traveled with His family from Egypt to Nazareth, a distance of more than four hundred miles. Jesus likely walked a number of those miles, if not all of them. A devout Jew, Jesus' earthly father, Joseph, would have attended the three annual feasts celebrated in Jerusalem each year. Jesus certainly made these trips with His family and during His earthly ministry. The trip from the Galilee region to Jerusalem was a distance of about 120 miles—much of this in mountainous or desert regions. Making this trip three times a year from the age of five until the age of thirty meant that Jesus likely walked at least 18,000 miles just on these annual pilgrimages.

A man once calculated the total miles Jesus walked during the three years of His public ministry as 3,125 miles, not counting the trips from the Galilee to Jerusalem for feast days. In all, counting the childhood trek from Egypt, Jesus may have walked close to 22,000 miles during His earthly life!

It appears Jesus walked between ten and twenty miles on many days. We have no idea how many miles He may have walked during His forty-day stay in the wilderness.

The distance around the world at the equator is 24,901.55 miles. It is not difficult to assume that Jesus walked almost the distance around the world in His lifetime!

4:1 [a]NU-Text omits *therefore* and reads *and by* for *at*.

DIVINE HEALTH 301

Stress Busters
Become Mindful of the Moment

Mindfulness involves focusing your attention on the present moment. So many people do not live in the present moment—they are wishing for a different moment—either past or future. They live in an "I wish I could—" or "I wish I had—" world. Mindfulness means letting go of any thought that is unrelated to the present moment, and finding something to enjoy in the present moment.

Mindfulness is not something you do once or twice. It must be practiced on a regular basis until it becomes habitual. It takes time for the habit of worry and fretting to develop, and it takes time to change these habits—the process involves both the dropping of an old habit and the adopting of a new one.

There are a number of ways in which you and your family can work on developing mindfulness. You might make it a game, helping one another to identify when thoughts go astray to the future or past—purposefully and intentionally calling one another back to the present.

Here are three ways to become more mindful of the present moment:

☐ Look closely at the world around you. When you walk with a spouse, friend, or child, focus on the beautiful scenery, the chirping of the birds and crickets, and the feel of the warm sunshine or the chill in the air. Focus on the way your body feels as you move your muscles during a brisk twenty-minute walk.

☐ If a stressful thought comes to mind, choose to move on to a thought that is related to what you are presently seeing, hearing, smelling, or feeling. *Will* yourself to think about something else!

☐ Consciously look for things around you—what you see, smell, hear, or can touch—for which you can say, "Thank You, God!" or "I praise You, heavenly Father!"

As people practice mindfulness, their muscles generally begin to relax. Mindfulness is the foundation on which other muscle-relaxation techniques should be based.

THE ABANDONED APOSTLE

[9]Be diligent to come to me quickly; [10]for Demas has forsaken me, having loved this present world, and has departed for Thessalonica—Crescens for Galatia, Titus for Dalmatia. [11]Only Luke is with me. Get Mark and bring him with you, for he is useful to me for ministry. [12]And Tychicus I have sent to Ephesus. [13]Bring the cloak that I left with Carpus at Troas when you come—and the books, especially the parchments.

[14]Alexander the coppersmith did me much harm. May the Lord repay him according to his works. [15]You also must beware of him, for he has greatly resisted our words.

[16]At my first defense no one stood with me, but all forsook me. May it not be charged against them.

THE LORD IS FAITHFUL

[17]But the Lord stood with me and strengthened me, so that the message might be preached fully through me, and *that* all the Gentiles might hear. Also I was delivered out of the mouth of the lion. [18]And the Lord will deliver me from every evil work and preserve *me* for His heavenly kingdom. To Him *be* glory forever and ever. Amen!

COME BEFORE WINTER

[19]Greet Prisca and Aquila, and the household of Onesiphorus. [20]Erastus stayed in Corinth, but Trophimus I have left in Miletus sick.

[21]Do your utmost to come before winter. Eubulus greets you, as well as Pudens, Linus, Claudia, and all the brethren.

FAREWELL

[22]The Lord Jesus Christ[a] be with your spirit. Grace be with you. Amen.

4:22 [a]NU-Text omits *Jesus Christ.*

HEALTH NOTES

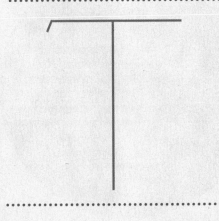

ITUS

Under Paul's mentoring, Titus was appointed as pastor in the city of Crete, not an easy place for a young man in ministry. Paul's letter to Titus has truths and directives similar to those Paul wrote to Timothy. His letter deals with basic issues of Christian behavior and leadership.

Crete was known to be a place where the people were lazy and pirates and sailors enjoyed getting drunk. In Titus 1:12, one of their own actually describes Cretans as "always liars, evil beasts, and lazy gluttons." It is no wonder that moral character and holy living were the top priorities in Titus' teaching and preaching.

There may be times when we each have a desire to act in an unholy or unrighteous way—our rebellion may be displayed by getting drunk or eating an entire box of donuts in one sitting. In Titus 3:1–7 Paul reminds us that it is only by the blood of Christ and the power of the Holy Spirit that we can have full dominion over our flesh.

GREETING

1 Paul, a bondservant of God and an apostle of Jesus Christ, according to the faith of God's elect and the acknowledgment of the truth which accords with godliness, ²in hope of eternal life which God, who cannot lie, promised before time began, ³but has in due time manifested His word through preaching, which was committed to me according to the commandment of God our Savior;

⁴To Titus, a true son in *our* common faith:

Grace, mercy, *and* peace from God the Father and the Lord Jesus Christᵃ our Savior.

QUALIFIED ELDERS

⁵For this reason I left you in Crete, that you should set in order the things that are lacking, and appoint elders in every city as I commanded you— ⁶if a man is blameless, the husband of one wife, having faithful children not accused of dissipation or insubordination. ⁷For a bishopᵃ must be blameless, as a steward of God, not self-willed, not quick-tempered, not given to wine, not violent, not greedy for money, ⁸but hospitable, a lover of what is good, sober-minded, just, holy, self-controlled, ⁹holding fast the faithful word as he has been taught, that he may be able, by sound doctrine, both to exhort and convict those who contradict.

THE ELDERS' TASK

¹⁰For there are many insubordinate, both idle talkers and deceivers, especially those of the circumcision, ¹¹whose mouths must be stopped, who subvert whole households, teaching things which they ought not, for the sake of dishonest gain. ¹²One of them, a prophet of their own, said, "Cretans *are* always liars, evil beasts, lazy gluttons." ¹³This testimony is true. Therefore rebuke them sharply, that they may be sound in the faith, ¹⁴not giving heed to Jewish fables and commandments of men who turn from the truth. ¹⁵To the pure all things are pure, but to those who are defiled and unbelieving nothing is pure; but even their mind and conscience are defiled. ¹⁶They profess to know God, but in works they deny Him, being abominable, disobedient, and disqualified for every good work.

QUALITIES OF A SOUND CHURCH

2 But as for you, speak the things which are proper for sound doctrine: ²that the older men be sober, reverent, temperate, sound in faith, in love, in patience; ³the older women likewise, that they be reverent in behavior, not slanderers, not given to much wine, teachers of good things— ⁴that they admonish the young women to love their husbands, to love their children, ⁵to be discreet, chaste, homemakers, good, obedient to their own husbands, that the word of God may not be blasphemed.

⁶Likewise, exhort the young men to be sober-minded, ⁷in all things showing yourself *to be* a pattern of good works; in doctrine *showing* integrity, reverence, incorruptibility,ᵃ ⁸sound speech that cannot be condemned, that one who is an opponent may be ashamed, having nothing evil to say of you.ᵃ

⁹*Exhort* bondservants to be obedient to their own masters, to be well pleasing in all *things*, not answering back, ¹⁰not pilfering, but showing all good fidelity, that they may adorn the doctrine of God our Savior in all things.

1:4 ᵃNU-Text reads *and Christ Jesus.*   1:7 ᵃLiterally *overseer*   2:7 ᵃNU-Text omits *incorruptibility.*   2:8 ᵃNU-Text and M-Text read *us.*

WWJE?

[WHAT WOULD JESUS EAT]

[POULTRY]

Bible Health + Food Facts

More Fiber!

Just five grams of fiber a day—about the amount in a single serving of many bran cereals—may cut your risk of heart disease by as much as one third. Aim for 25 grams of fiber a day for women and 38 grams a day for men. Men and women over fifty need fewer (21 for women, 30 for men).

Twenty-four types of birds are identified in the Book of Leviticus, many of them birds of prey that were forbidden as food for the Israelites. Deuteronomy 14:20 states, however, that the Israelites could eat "all clean birds." These birds included chicken, geese, turkeys, ducks, and doves.

During Jesus' time, Jews consumed domestic fowl and in addition to the above birds, they ate pigeons, partridges, and quail. The laws related to the slaughter of red meat also applied to the slaughter of fowl. Poultry is made kosher by boiling, soaking, and salting the meat.

The problem with many chicken products today is that chickens, like beef, are often given steroids, growth hormones, and antibiotics. In addition, chickens that are routinely housed in overcrowded conditions get very little exercise and the result is a rise in the fat content of chicken meat. Organic, free-range chickens and kosher chickens are raised primarily on grain and grasses, and are kept free of hormones, antibiotics, and pesticides. They are significantly lower in fat.

Chickens and eggs are carriers of drug-resistant strains of salmonella, staphylococcus, and campylobacter bacteria. These are pathogenic bacteria commonly associated with food poisoning. Always make sure that you wash and cook poultry thoroughly, and that you use separate knives and cutting boards for the preparation of poultry. Wash your hands thoroughly, as well, between the handling of poultry and other foods, especially veggies and lettuce that you may be serving raw.

Remove all fat and skin from poultry before cooking it, or if you must leave the skin on during cooking, remove the skin before eating the meat. You'll take in far fewer fat grams! Bake, grill, or roast chicken rather than frying or deep-frying it.

A proper portion of poultry is four ounces. Choose white meat over dark meat if you are counting calories.

TRAINED BY SAVING GRACE

[11]For the grace of God that brings salvation has appeared to all men, [12]teaching us that, denying ungodliness and worldly lusts, we should live soberly, righteously, and godly in the present age, [13]looking for the blessed hope and glorious appearing of our great God and Savior Jesus Christ, [14]who gave Himself for us, that He might redeem us from every lawless deed and purify for Himself *His* own special people, zealous for good works.

[15]Speak these things, exhort, and rebuke with all authority. Let no one despise you.

GRACES OF THE HEIRS OF GRACE

3 Remind them to be subject to rulers and authorities, to obey, to be ready for every good work, [2]to speak evil of no one, to be peaceable, gentle, showing all humility to all men. [3]For we ourselves were also once foolish, disobedient, deceived, serving various lusts and pleasures, living in malice and envy, hateful and hating one another. [4]But when the kindness and the love of God our Savior toward man appeared, [5]not by works of righteousness which we have done, but according to His mercy He saved us, through the washing of regeneration and renewing of the Holy Spirit, [6]whom He poured out on us abundantly through Jesus Christ our Savior, [7]that having been justified by His grace we should become heirs according to the hope of eternal life.

[8]This is a faithful saying, and these things

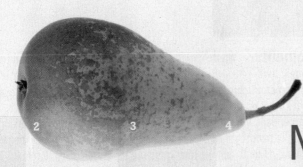

October

1   2   3   4   5   6   7

Now Is the Time To...

☐ **Celebrate a senior.** As the holidays are approaching and the weather turns cooler, the senior community can sometimes feel left out. Those who stay within the confines of their house or apartment are especially prone to depression and loneliness. The death rate among older people is always higher in the winter. Invite a senior citizen to lunch or to go with you for a day of holiday shopping this month. You may never know how much you have brightened his or her day! ☐ Plan a weekend getaway with your family. Hotel rates tend to be cheaper, places are less crowded, and the weather is likely to be pleasant. You don't need a reason for the excursion—just have fun together!

8   9   10   11   12   13   14

Seasonal Tips

☐ October is the best month to lime, fertilize, and seed your lawn.
☐ Bring indoors any houseplants that were enjoying the outdoors.
☐ Drain your garden hoses and store them on reels or hooks if you live in an area prone to early "hard freezes."

In the Garden

15   16   17   18   19   20   21

☐ Get ready to plant! The fall season is a wonderful time to plant trees, shrubs, bulbs, and perennials. The cooler temperatures are helpful both to the plants and those who plant them. After planting remember to water and fertilize the plants. ☐ Just before the first frost hits, pick the largest, not-yet-ripe green tomatoes. Place them in a paper bag with some apples. They will ripen just as sweet as if they were still on the vine.

Table Fresh

22   23   24   25   26   27   28

☐ Roast the seeds from fresh pumpkins you may have carved or decorated. Add a little cooking oil and salt to the scooped-out fresh seeds. Spread them out on a wax-paper-covered cookie sheet. Allow them to dry for 24 to 48 hours. Then, remove the wax paper and bake for 40 minutes at 325 degrees. The roasted seeds will be a wonderful snack for the entire family. In addition, package them in small cellophane bags tied with ribbons to include in holiday gift baskets. ☐ Add fresh apple slices, pear slices, and raspberries to a bed of mixed greens for a delightful salad. Top your salad with walnuts and squeeze on a little fresh lemon juice.

29   30   31

Let's Celebrate

☐ As an alternative to Halloween, suggest that your children get involved in a harvest party or festival at church, school, or in the community. ☐ Bypass the crowds and start your gift shopping early. ☐ Buy and address Thanksgiving cards for mailing in early November. Your friends will be thankful that you are thankful for them! ☐ **St. Luke's little summer.** This is a name used for the spell of warm weather that often occurs·about the time of the saint's feast day, October 18. This period is also called Indian summer.

INSIGHTS INTO THE WORD

> (Titus 3:9–11)

At the Root of "Arguments." What causes a person to become argumentative—always looking for a fight, seemingly with a perpetual chip on his or her shoulder? That person is very likely harboring hate and anger related to a hurtful experience in his or her past. Negative emotions do nothing to contribute to health and wholeness. The Bible encourages us to confront those who are continually critical, argumentative, or contentious. We are to challenge them to seek healing for the inner pain they are carrying, and to forgive those who have hurt or offended them. If they refuse our wise counsel, we are to refrain from an ongoing association with them. Why?

The purpose is not to hurt the person who is argumentative, but rather, to keep their negative emotions from infecting us. It's difficult to remain positive if you are around a person who is continually negative and critical. Don't adopt another person's negative attitude!

I want you to affirm constantly, that those who have believed in God should be careful to maintain good works. These things are good and profitable to men.

AVOID DISSENSION

⁹But avoid foolish disputes, genealogies, contentions, and strivings about the law; for they are unprofitable and useless. ¹⁰Reject a divisive man after the first and second admonition, ¹¹knowing that such a person is warped and sinning, being self-condemned.

FINAL MESSAGES

¹²When I send Artemas to you, or Tychicus, be diligent to come to me at Nicopolis, for I have decided to spend the winter there. ¹³Send Zenas the lawyer and Apollos on their journey with haste, that they may lack nothing. ¹⁴And let our *people* also learn to maintain good works, to *meet* urgent needs, that they may not be unfruitful.

FAREWELL

¹⁵All who *are* with me greet you. Greet those who love us in the faith.

Grace *be* with you all. Amen.

HEALTH NOTES

HILEMON

In this brief letter Paul urges Philemon to have mercy upon his runaway slave Onesimus, and to receive him back into his home as a beloved brother. This likely would be difficult for Philemon since Onesimus had stolen money from him before fleeing to Rome. In Rome, however, Onesimus had met Paul and received Jesus Christ as his Savior. Paul came to consider Onesimus a brother in the faith, but would Philemon see him that same way? Paul hopes so.

Has someone betrayed you? Stolen from you? Maybe you need to extend mercy and forgiveness to yourself? Have you ever felt guilty that you have contracted a disease, or failed in a relationship, or have not always been consistent in controlling personal habits related to your weight or fitness?

Paul urged Philemon to see Onesimus as "profitable" to him. Seeing a seed of benefit in a personal failure may be the first step toward turning a negative into a positive in your life. What you have learned in a time of trouble or failure may be the very lesson you needed to learn to move forward to success or to help others in a similar situation.

GREETING

Paul, a prisoner of Christ Jesus, and Timothy *our* brother,

To Philemon our beloved *friend* and fellow laborer, [2]to the beloved[a] Apphia, Archippus our fellow soldier, and to the church in your house:

[3]Grace to you and peace from God our Father and the Lord Jesus Christ.

PHILEMON'S LOVE AND FAITH

[4]I thank my God, making mention of you always in my prayers, [5]hearing of your love and faith which you have toward the Lord Jesus and toward all the saints, [6]that the sharing of your faith may become effective by the acknowledgment of every good thing which is in you[a] in Christ Jesus. [7]For we have[a] great joy[b] and consolation in your love, because the hearts of the saints have been refreshed by you, brother.

THE PLEA FOR ONESIMUS

[8]Therefore, though I might be very bold in Christ to command you what is fitting, [9]*yet* for love's sake I rather appeal *to you*—being such a one as Paul, the aged, and now also a prisoner of Jesus Christ— [10]I appeal to you for my son Onesimus, whom I have begotten *while* in my chains, [11]who once was unprofitable to you, but now is profitable to you and to me.

[12]I am sending him back.[a] You therefore receive him, that is, my own heart, [13]whom I wished to keep with me, that on your behalf he might minister to me in my chains for the gospel. [14]But without your consent I wanted

℞ PRESCRIPTIONS FOR INNER HEALTH

"All the days of the afflicted are evil,
But he who is of a merry heart has a continual feast."

(PROVERBS 15:15)

Those who are "afflicted" are people who continually see the negative side of life. They are always looking for what might go wrong or what has gone wrong. They see nothing good for their future and indeed, they attract the bad things they anticipate! The person who is joyful, optimistic, and cheerful is a person who sees all of life as a playground to be explored and a feast to enjoy. You can *choose* how you will perceive life and the attitudes you will hold.

2 [a]NU-Text reads *to our sister Apphia.*   6 [a]NU-Text and M-Text read *us.*   7 [a]NU-Text reads *had.*   [b]M-Text reads *thanksgiving.*   12 [a]NU-Text reads *back to you in person, that is, my own heart.*

Chicken Barese

Righteous Recipes

Ingredients:

- ☐ 3–4 potatoes, peeled
- ☐ 1 free-range chicken (3 pounds), cut up
- ☐ 3 cans (8-ounces each) of tomatoes, drained
- ☐ Garlic and parsley to taste
- ☐ Celtic salt and freshly ground pepper to taste
- ☐ ½ cup freshly grated Parmesan cheese
- ☐ 2 tablespoons extra-virgin olive oil
- ☐ ½ cup water

Cut the potatoes into the shapes of French fries about ¾-inch thick. Combine the potatoes and chicken in a 9" x 13" baking pan. Break up the tomatoes and layer them over the chicken mixture. Season with garlic, parsley, salt, and pepper. Sprinkle with Parmesan cheese. Drizzle the olive oil and water over the top. Bake at 350 degrees for about 1 hour or until the chicken is cooked through and the potatoes are tender.

Yield: 4–8 servings

Note: Barese is the region in Italy that arguably produces the finest olive oils. You can use 6 lamb chops—fat trimmed—instead of chicken for this recipe. The dish then becomes Lamb Barese!

to do nothing, that your good deed might not be by compulsion, as it were, but voluntary.

[15]For perhaps he departed for a while for this *purpose*, that you might receive him forever, [16]no longer as a slave but more than a slave—a beloved brother, especially to me but how much more to you, both in the flesh and in the Lord.

PHILEMON'S OBEDIENCE ENCOURAGED

[17]If then you count me as a partner, receive him as *you would* me. [18]But if he has wronged you or owes anything, put that on my account. [19]I, Paul, am writing with my own hand. I will repay—not to mention to you that you owe me even your own self besides. [20]Yes, brother, let me have joy from you in the Lord; refresh my heart in the Lord.

[21]Having confidence in your obedience, I write to you, knowing that you will do even more than I say. [22]But, meanwhile, also prepare a guest room for me, for I trust that through your prayers I shall be granted to you.

FAREWELL

[23]Epaphras, my fellow prisoner in Christ Jesus, greets you, [24]*as do* Mark, Aristarchus, Demas, Luke, my fellow laborers.

[25]The grace of our Lord Jesus Christ *be* with your spirit. Amen.

WISE CHOICES

Choose to steam your vegetables rather than boil them.
Steaming leaves the nutrients in the vegetables rather than leeching the nutrients out into the water. Don't overcook your vegetables—you'll get more health value and flavor from them.

HEALTH NOTES

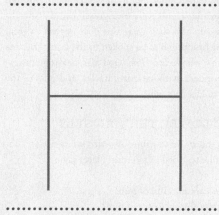

EBREWS

As the Jewish Christians were expecting Christ's return yet not seeing it, they were tempted to turn back to their old beliefs. The book of Hebrews was written to encourage these Christians to continue in the faith until the end.

We, too, can find comfort and encouragement from the writings of this unknown author. What is it you are anticipating or hoping to see? A new weight on the scale? A new size in your clothes? A healing in your body? More energy or greater muscle tone? Hebrews 11:1 tells us, "Now faith is the substance of things hoped for, the evidence of things not seen." See in your spirit what it is that you desire and know to be God's best, and then continue to believe that you will one day experience this blessing.

Hebrews 10:36 says, "For you have need of endurance, so that after you have done the will of God, you may receive the promise." As difficult as it may seem, continue to press on. The path toward your goal may be tough—indeed, it may seem impossible—but your day is coming! Keep believing, and never give up!

GOD'S SUPREME REVELATION

1 God, who at various times and in various ways spoke in time past to the fathers by the prophets, ²has in these last days spoken to us by *His* Son, whom He has appointed heir of all things, through whom also He made the worlds; ³who being the brightness of *His* glory and the express image of His person, and upholding all things by the word of His power, when He had by Himself^a purged our^b sins, sat down at the right hand of the Majesty on high, ⁴having become so much better than the angels, as He has by inheritance obtained a more excellent name than they.

THE SON EXALTED ABOVE ANGELS

⁵For to which of the angels did He ever say:

"You are My Son,
Today I have begotten You"?^a

And again:

"I will be to Him a Father,
And He shall be to Me a Son"?^b

⁶But when He again brings the firstborn into the world, He says:

"Let all the angels of God worship Him."^a

⁷And of the angels He says:

"Who makes His angels spirits
And His ministers a flame of fire."^a

⁸But to the Son *He says:*

"Your throne, O God, is forever and ever;
A scepter of righteousness is the scepter of Your kingdom.
⁹ You have loved righteousness and hated lawlessness;
Therefore God, Your God, has anointed You
With the oil of gladness more than Your companions."^a

¹⁰And:

"You, LORD, in the beginning laid the foundation of the earth,
And the heavens are the work of Your hands.
¹¹ They will perish, but You remain;
And they will all grow old like a garment;
¹² Like a cloak You will fold them up,
And they will be changed.
But You are the same,
And Your years will not fail."^a

¹³But to which of the angels has He ever said:

"Sit at My right hand,
Till I make Your enemies Your footstool"?^a

¹⁴Are they not all ministering spirits sent forth to minister for those who will inherit salvation?

1:3 ^aNU-Text omits *by Himself.* ^bNU-Text omits *our.*   1:5 ^aPsalm 2:7 ^b2 Samuel 7:14   1:6 ^aDeuteronomy 32:43 (Septuagint, Dead Sea Scrolls); Psalm 97:7   1:7 ^aPsalm 104:4   1:9 ^aPsalm 45:6, 7   1:12 ^aPsalm 102:25–27   1:13 ^aPsalm 110:1

⚥ Women's Issues
Abortion

Although the Bible does not specifically address the subject of abortion, it does clearly regard the unborn child as valuable—as a full and unique expression of human life. Jesus affirmed the value of the unborn child in the womb through His Incarnation, coming as a baby rather than arriving on earth as an adult. The psalmist speaks of God's care for a baby in the womb (Psalms 139:13–16). The Law of Moses required that those who committed violent acts against an unborn child be punished in the same way as if the violent act had been inflicted on a full-grown adult (Exodus 21:22–25).

The Bible teaches that the existence and personality of a person is established at conception (Jeremiah 1:4, 5; Psalms 22:10). While John the Baptist was still in the womb his mother felt him "leap" in the presence of Jesus (Luke 1:41–45). The unborn child is considered an *actual* human being, not just a *potential* human being. In Amos 1:13, God expressed anger over the killing of unborn children.

A woman who has had an abortion—for whatever reason—needs to know that Jesus still loves her and stands ready to forgive her just as He freely forgave people who erred against His law in other ways. (See John 8:1–11 as an example.)

The real antidote for abortion is love—a willingness to embrace the gift of life God has given, regardless of the timing or circumstances associated with the conception.

DO NOT NEGLECT SALVATION

2 Therefore we must give the more earnest heed to the things we have heard, lest we drift away. ²For if the word spoken through angels proved steadfast, and every transgression and disobedience received a just reward, ³how shall we escape if we neglect so great a salvation, which at the first began to be spoken by the Lord, and was confirmed to us by those who heard *Him*, ⁴God also bearing witness both with signs and wonders, with various miracles, and gifts of the Holy Spirit, according to His own will?

THE SON MADE LOWER THAN ANGELS

⁵For He has not put the world to come, of which we speak, in subjection to angels. ⁶But one testified in a certain place, saying:

"What is man that You are mindful of him,
Or the son of man that You take care of him?
⁷ You have made him a little lower than the angels;
You have crowned him with glory and honor,ᵃ
And set him over the works of Your hands.
⁸ You have put all things in subjection under his feet."ᵃ

For in that He put all in subjection under him, He left nothing *that is* not put under him. But now we do not yet see all things put under him. ⁹But we see Jesus, who was made a little lower than the angels, for the suffering of death crowned with glory and honor, that He, by the grace of God, might taste death for everyone.

BRINGING MANY SONS TO GLORY

¹⁰For it was fitting for Him, for whom *are* all things and by whom *are* all things, in bringing many sons to glory, to make the captain of their salvation perfect through sufferings. ¹¹For both He who sanctifies and those who are being sanctified *are* all of one, for which reason He is not ashamed to call them brethren, ¹²saying:

"I will declare Your name to My brethren;
In the midst of the assembly I will sing praise to You."ᵃ

¹³And again:

"I will put My trust in Him."ᵃ

And again:

"Here am I and the children whom God has given Me."ᵇ

¹⁴Inasmuch then as the children have partaken of flesh and blood, He Himself likewise shared in the same, that through death He might destroy him who had the power of death, that is, the devil, ¹⁵and release those who through fear of death were all their lifetime subject to bondage. ¹⁶For indeed He does not give aid to angels, but He does give aid to the seed of Abraham. ¹⁷Therefore, in all things He had to be made like *His* brethren, that He might be a merciful and faithful High Priest in things *pertaining* to God, to make propitiation for the sins of

2:7 ᵃNU-Text and M-Text omit the rest of verse 7.   2:8 ᵃPsalm 8:4–6   2:12 ᵃPsalm 22:22   2:13 ᵃ2 Samuel 22:3; Isaiah 8:17   ᵇIsaiah 8:18

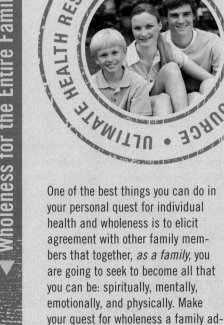

One of the best things you can do in your personal quest for individual health and wholeness is to elicit agreement with other family members that together, *as a family*, you are going to seek to become all that you can be: spiritually, mentally, emotionally, and physically. Make your quest for wholeness a family adventure!

All of the ideals associated with living in *divine health* can be summed up in one word: *wholeness*.

Jesus repeatedly said to people, "Be made whole."

Wholeness is at the very heart of the gospel because to be whole means the following:

☐ *Life is in balance.* Body, soul, and spirit—relationships, emotions, finances, material goods, and everything associated with one's inner and outer life—are in right proportion according to God's design.

☐ *Life is productive.* When the wheels of an automobile are balanced, the car drives more smoothly, without veering. So it is, also, in our lives. When all aspects of our lives are in right balance, we become more productive in reaching our full potential, our goals, our purposes in life, and all other things that we might consider to be the best and highest rewards of this life and in eternity. We accomplish more, without a continual veering into temptations.

☐ *Life has maximum quality.* Those who are whole enjoy their lives. They have a deep sense of contentment and an abiding enthusiasm for living.

Wholeness is far more than a lack of disease or ailment or trouble. It is living life with zest—with the greatest possible amount of delight in God and in other people. It is living with strong self-esteem and emotional health, trusting God to complete His perfecting process in us even as we work to develop and use in positive ways all that God gives to us.

One of the most important aspects of wholeness is that we model who we are to other people. When our children see us pursuing wholeness and becoming more whole, they, too, will want to pursue wholeness and to become whole. When people with whom we work, worship, or live in relationship with as friends and neighbors see us in pursuit of the good things of God, they will also want to pursue a relationship with Him and seek out all the things He desires to give them.

Wholeness is the best witness possible for the gospel. Wholeness is the expression of a godly life—a life that is holy, pure, in right relationship with God, with the maximum amount of character, integrity, and generosity.

From the beginning, God called people of faith to be "blessed, and be a blessing." God said to Abraham, "I will bless you and make your name great; and you shall be a blessing" (Genesis 12:2). That's the main reason to seek to become whole today.

Health is a blessing. Everything that makes us whole and keeps us whole—spirit, soul, and body—is a blessing. And what we experience from God as a blessing, we are to give away to others.

Never apologize for your efforts to help another person become healthier or more whole—which means, of course, that you deliver your "efforts" in a loving, kind, and respectful way. You are doing them a tremendous favor. They will look on you as a blessing, perhaps not today or tomorrow—but one day.

Be whole. Give from your wholeness to help others become whole. That's the life that Jesus calls us to experience!

---

the people. [18]For in that He Himself has suffered, being tempted, He is able to aid those who are tempted.

THE SON WAS FAITHFUL

3 Therefore, holy brethren, partakers of the heavenly calling, consider the Apostle and High Priest of our confession, Christ Jesus, [2]who was faithful to Him who appointed Him, as Moses also *was faithful* in all His house. [3]For this One has been counted worthy of more glory than Moses, inasmuch as He who built the house has more honor than the house. [4]For every house is built by someone, but He who built all things *is* God. [5]And Moses indeed *was* faithful in all His house as a servant, for a testimony of those things which would be spoken *afterward*, [6]but Christ as a Son over His own house, whose house we are if we hold fast the confidence and the rejoicing of the hope firm to the end.[a]

3:6 [a]NU-Text omits *firm to the end.*

SCRIPTURE SOLUTIONS

[STRONG BONES]

All my bones shall say,
"Lord, who is like You,
Delivering the poor from
him
who is too strong for him,
Yes, the poor and the
needy
from him who plunders
him?"

(Psalms 35:10)

Although it seems logical that after we become adults that our bone structure would remain the same, it simply isn't the case. Men as well as women can suffer from osteoporosis and increased fractures.

Here are a few warning signs.

Fractures. Your bones will reach their peak in bone mass by the time you are thirty-five. However, between the ages of fifty-five and seventy, you will probably lose about one-third of your bone mass. Although the slow degeneration of the bones is silent, a fractured rib, hip, or part of the spine can be a major alarm that the bones are losing mass.

Loss of Height. You should have your height checked every year by a physician to see if you are losing a substantial amount of height. That's a sign that the bones are losing mass.

The Hump. Osteoporosis is often characterized by the downward hump of the upper back and neck. Watch yourself in the mirror to see if you are naturally bending and slumping, even if you think you are standing up straight.

If you recognize any of the above signs, you may want to consult with your physician. Proper nutrition and exercise are vital keys in maintaining bone mass. Eat foods high in calcium and vitamin D to rebuild or maintain of strong bones. Weight-bearing exercises are the best stimulant for bone growth.

BE FAITHFUL

⁷Therefore, as the Holy Spirit says:

"Today, if you will hear His voice,
⁸ Do not harden your hearts as in the rebellion,
In the day of trial in the wilderness,
⁹ Where your fathers tested Me, tried Me,
And saw My works forty years.
¹⁰ Therefore I was angry with that generation,
And said, 'They always go astray in their heart,
And they have not known My ways.'
¹¹ So I swore in My wrath,
'They shall not enter My rest.' "ᵃ

¹²Beware, brethren, lest there be in any of you an evil heart of unbelief in departing from the living God; ¹³but exhort one another daily, while it is called *"Today,"* lest any of you be hardened through the deceitfulness of sin. ¹⁴For we have become partakers of Christ if we hold the beginning of our confidence steadfast to the end, ¹⁵while it is said:

"Today, if you will hear His voice,
Do not harden your hearts as in the rebellion."ᵃ

FAILURE OF THE WILDERNESS WANDERERS

¹⁶For who, having heard, rebelled? Indeed, *was it* not all who came out of Egypt, *led* by Moses? ¹⁷Now with whom was He angry forty years? *Was it* not with those who sinned, whose corpses fell in the wilderness? ¹⁸And to whom did He swear that they would not enter His rest, but to those who did not obey? ¹⁹So we see that they could not enter in because of unbelief.

THE PROMISE OF REST

4 Therefore, since a promise remains of entering His rest, let us fear lest any of you seem to have come short of it. ²For indeed the gospel was preached to us as well as to them; but the word which they heard did not profit them,ᵃ not being mixed with faith in those who heard *it.* ³For we who have believed do enter that rest, as He has said:

"So I swore in My wrath,
'They shall not enter My rest,' "ᵃ

although the works were finished from the foundation of the world. ⁴For He has spoken in a certain place of the seventh *day* in this way: "And God rested on the seventh day from all His works";ᵃ ⁵and again in this *place:* "They shall not enter My rest."ᵃ

⁶Since therefore it remains that some *must* enter it, and those to whom it was first preached did not enter because of disobedience, ⁷again He designates a certain day, saying in David, "Today," after such a long time, as it has been said:

"Today, if you will hear His voice,
Do not harden your hearts."ᵃ

3:11 ᵃPsalm 95:7–11   3:15 ᵃPsalm 95:7, 8   4:2 ᵃNU-Text and M-Text read *profit them,* since they were not united by faith with those who heeded it.   4:3 ᵃPsalm 95:11   4:4 ᵃGenesis 2:2
4:5 ᵃPsalm 95:11   4:7 ᵃPsalm 95:7, 8

[8]For if Joshua had given them rest, then He would not afterward have spoken of another day. [9]There remains therefore a rest for the people of God. [10]For he who has entered His rest has himself also ceased from his works as God *did* from His.

THE WORD DISCOVERS OUR CONDITION

[11]Let us therefore be diligent to enter that rest, lest anyone fall according to the same example of disobedience. [12]For the word of God *is* living and powerful, and sharper than any two-edged sword, piercing even to the division of soul and spirit, and of joints and marrow, and is a discerner of the thoughts and intents of the heart. [13]And there is no creature hidden from His sight, but all things *are* naked and open to the eyes of Him to whom we *must give* account.

OUR COMPASSIONATE HIGH PRIEST

[14]Seeing then that we have a great High Priest who has passed through the heavens, Jesus the Son of God, let us hold fast *our* confession. [15]For we do not have a High Priest who cannot sympathize with our weaknesses, but was in all *points* tempted as *we are, yet* without sin. [16]Let us therefore come boldly to the throne of grace, that we may obtain mercy and find grace to help in time of need.

QUALIFICATIONS FOR HIGH PRIESTHOOD

5 For every high priest taken from among men is appointed for men in things *pertaining* to God, that he may offer both gifts and sacrifices for sins. [2]He can have compassion on those who are ignorant and going astray, since he himself is also subject to weakness. [3]Because of this he is required as for the people, so also for himself, to offer *sacrifices* for sins. [4]And no man takes this honor to himself, but he who is called by God, just as Aaron *was*.

A PRIEST FOREVER

[5]So also Christ did not glorify Himself to become High Priest, but *it was* He who said to Him:

"You are My Son,
Today I have begotten You."[a]

[6]As *He* also says in another *place*:

"You are a priest forever
According to the order of Melchizedek";[a]

[7]who, in the days of His flesh, when He had offered up prayers and supplications, with vehement cries and tears to Him who was able to save Him from death, and was heard because of His godly fear, [8]though He was a Son, *yet* He learned obedience by the things which He suffered. [9]And having been perfected, He became the author of eternal salvation to all who obey Him, [10]called by God as High Priest "according to the order of Melchizedek," [11]of whom we have much to say, and hard to explain, since you have become dull of hearing.

Bible Beverages
Vegetable Juice

Although there is no mention of vegetable juice in the Bible, a number of vegetables known to Bible people can be used in juices. Vegetable juices often contain carrots and beets. The hidden danger of vegetable juice is that it *seems* to be a totally healthful source of carbohydrates, but in reality, many vegetables are high on the glycemic index. Carrots, for example, have a great deal of sugar, so carrot juice has a high sugar content. In addition, people who would eat only one carrot and consider that a major vegetable portion are likely to consume four or five carrots in juiced form. Broccoli juice would probably be the most healthful vegetable juice, but who wants to drink a class of broccoli for breakfast?

The tomato is technically a fruit and not a vegetable, but most people think of tomatoes in terms of vegetables. Tomato juice in small quantities can be healthful, especially if the juice is made from fresh, vine-ripened tomatoes. You might try adding a dash of Worcestershire sauce to a small glass of tomato juice over ice—or a dash of sauerkraut juice or a very small amount of prepared horseradish sauce (not the creamed variety). For many people, these additions make tomato juice spicier and more satisfying in small quantities.

Be sure to check the sodium content on canned vegetable juices, such as tomato juice or the mixed-vegetable varieties. Many of these juice products are loaded with salt!

5:5 [a]Psalm 2:7   5:6 [a]Psalm 110:4

QUIZ 4

ARE YOU GETTING ALL THE NUTRIENTS YOU NEED?

God designed the human body to have a basic need for a wide variety of nutrients, but the exact amount of each nutrient varies from individual to individual. Recommended Daily Allowances guidelines are just that—guidelines. The RDA numbers are amounts of various vitamins and minerals that are deemed appropriate for the average-size adult with normal health at the median age of the nation.

"Appropriate," of course, means that this amount will do no harm to an individual, and may do some good.

"Average-size" varies—you may need more or less.

"Normal" health has never been defined, and every person's individual health needs vary. If you are not in your late thirties, you are not at the median age. Older people often need more of certain nutrients.

Where does this leave us? It means that you need to work with a physician to determine—on the basis of blood, saliva, family history, and other tests—the amount of basic nutrients that you need for optimal health. It is likely that you need supplementation in pill, granule, capsule, or other form. Below is a basic chart for you to begin this process of analysis. Note that only a few of the many benefits of these nutrients are provided, and the food sources listed for these nutrients only identify the foremost foods.

VITAMINS

Nutrient	Sources	Benefits	I Get Enough	I Don't Get Enough
Vitamin A	Fish oils, liver, eggs	Helps with vision, tissue structure, & immunity		
Vitamin B *Should be taken in a balanced complex form.*	Whole grains, dried yeast, green leafy vegetables, organ meats	Digestion of proteins, fats, and carbohydrates; good brain function; cell division & reproduction; resistance to infection		
Vitamin C	Citrus fruits, berries, raw vegetables	Antioxidant protection of cells and organs; essential for production of collagen; helps the heart, muscles, bones, and cardiovascular system; enhances immunity		
Vitamin D	Sunshine, fish oils	Helps the body use calcium & phosphorus for strong bones		
Vitamin E *Supplements need to be d-tocopherol, not dl-tocopherol.*	Wheat germ oil, whole grains, leafy vegetables	Powerful antioxidant protects heart, promotes slow aging, & protects skin		
Vitamin K	Yogurt, spinach	Helps proper blood clotting & bone mineralization		
Bioflavonoids (Vitamin P)	Pulp of citrus fruits	Relieves pain & swelling; protects capillaries		

MINERALS

Note: Many other minerals & trace minerals are necessary for optimal health. A high-potency mineral tablet may be the best way to ensure a balance of minerals & trace minerals.

Nutrient	Sources	Benefits	I Get Enough	I Don't Get Enough
Calcium *Needs to be in balance with phosphorus.*	Milk, egg yolks	Necessary for strong bones & teeth; protects against heart palpitations; & aids digestion		
Chromium	Brewer's yeast, molasses	Makes release of insulin more effective; helps synthesize fatty acids & cholesterol		
Iron	Liver, other organ meats	Needed for red blood cells		
Magnesium	All green vegetables	Necessary for good nerve function, release of blood sugar, formation of new cells		
Potassium *Needs to be in proper balance with sodium*	Bananas, apricots	Maintains balance of water in body; helps prevent heart attacks; needed for removal of toxins from cells		
Selenium	Organ meats, tuna, garlic, brewer's yeast	Strong protective effect against cancer; helpful to heart health		
Sodium *Needs to be in proper balance with potassium*	Meat, poultry, milk, cheese	Regulates water balance in the body		
Zinc	Wheat germ, fresh oysters	Needed for production of testosterone		

OTHER NUTRIENTS

Nutrient	Sources	Benefits	I Get Enough	I Don't Get Enough
Carotenoids	Carrots, leafy vegetables, tomatoes, apricots, watermelon	Protects vision; helps prevent heart disease & prostate, colorectal, lung, & breast cancers		
Flavonoids	Tea, coffee, citrus fruits	Cuts risk of mouth, throat, & stomach cancers; defends against heart disease		
Saponins	Beans, other legumes	Lowers cholesterol		
Diallyl	Onions, leeks	Helps fight heart disease		
Disulfides	Garlic, chives	Prostate cancer		
Terpenes	Cherries, citrus fruit zest, rosemary	Protects against skin cancer		
Polyphenols	Green tea, grapes, wine	Reduces risk of heart disease, stroke, & some cancers		
Isoflavones	Soybeans, tofu, soy milk	Defends against prostate cancer; reduces hot flashes		
Indoles	Broccoli, cauliflower, cabbage, Brussels sprouts	Wards off breast cancer; preserves memory; lowers heart disease risk		

Store the Dinner Plates

Bible Health + Food Facts

Get out your salad or bread-and-butter plates and serve dinner on them to keep portions smaller and more sensible.

SPIRITUAL IMMATURITY

[12]For though by this time you ought to be teachers, you need *someone* to teach you again the first principles of the oracles of God; and you have come to need milk and not solid food. [13]For everyone who partakes *only* of milk *is* unskilled in the word of righteousness, for he is a babe. [14]But solid food belongs to those who are of full age, *that is,* those who by reason of use have their senses exercised to discern both good and evil.

THE PERIL OF NOT PROGRESSING

6 Therefore, leaving the discussion of the elementary *principles* of Christ, let us go on to perfection, not laying again the foundation of repentance from dead works and of faith toward God, [2]of the doctrine of baptisms, of laying on of hands, of resurrection of the dead, and of eternal judgment. [3]And this we will[a] do if God permits.

[4]For *it is* impossible for those who were once enlightened, and have tasted the heavenly gift, and have become partakers of the Holy Spirit, [5]and have tasted the good word of God and the powers of the age to come, [6]if they fall away,[a] to renew them again to repentance, since they crucify again for themselves the Son of God, and put *Him* to an open shame.

[7]For the earth which drinks in the rain that often comes upon it, and bears herbs useful for those by whom it is cultivated, receives blessing from God; [8]but if it bears thorns and briers, *it is* rejected and near to being cursed, whose end *is* to be burned.

A BETTER ESTIMATE

[9]But, beloved, we are confident of better things concerning you, yes, things that accompany salvation, though we speak in this manner. [10]For God *is* not unjust to forget your work and labor of[a] love which you have shown toward His name, *in that* you have ministered to the saints, and do minister. [11]And we desire that each one of you show the same diligence to the full assurance of hope until the end, [12]that you do not become sluggish, but imitate those who through faith and patience inherit the promises.

GOD'S INFALLIBLE PURPOSE IN CHRIST

[13]For when God made a promise to Abraham, because He could swear by no one greater, He swore by Himself, [14]saying, "Surely blessing I will bless you, and multiplying I will multiply you."[a] [15]And so, after he had patiently endured, he obtained the promise. [16]For men indeed swear by the greater, and an oath for confirmation *is* for them an end of all dispute. [17]Thus God, determining to show more abundantly to the heirs of promise the immutability of His counsel, confirmed *it* by an oath, [18]that by two immutable things, in which it *is* impossible for God to lie, we might[a] have strong consolation, who have fled for refuge to lay hold of the hope set before *us.*

[19]This *hope* we have as an anchor of the soul, both sure and steadfast, and which enters the *Presence* behind the veil, [20]where the forerunner has entered for us, *even* Jesus, having become High Priest forever according to the order of Melchizedek.

THE KING OF RIGHTEOUSNESS

7 For this Melchizedek, king of Salem, priest of the Most High God, who met Abraham returning from the slaughter of the kings and blessed him, [2]to whom also Abraham gave a tenth part of all, first being translated "king of righteousness," and then also king of Salem, meaning "king of peace," [3]without father, without mother, without genealogy, having neither beginning of days nor end of life, but made like the Son of God, remains a priest continually.

[4]Now consider how great this man *was,* to whom even the patriarch Abraham gave a tenth of the spoils. [5]And indeed those who are of the sons of Levi, who receive the priesthood, have a commandment to receive tithes from the people according to the law, that is, from their brethren, though they have come from the loins of Abraham; [6]but he whose genealogy is not derived from them received tithes from Abraham and blessed him who had the promises. [7]Now beyond all contradiction the lesser is blessed by the better. [8]Here mortal men receive tithes, but there he *receives them,* of whom it is witnessed that he lives. [9]Even Levi, who receives tithes, paid tithes through Abraham, so to speak, [10]for he was still in the loins of his father when Melchizedek met him.

Q When you fast, who should know about it?

A Only God the Father. Jesus said, "When you fast, anoint your head and wash your face, so that you do not appear to men to be fasting, but to your Father who is in the secret place; and your Father who sees in secret will reward you openly" *(Matthew 6:17, 18).*

6:3 [a]M-Text reads *let us do.*   6:6 [a]Or *and have fallen away*   6:10 [a]NU-Text omits *labor of.*   6:14 [a]Genesis 22:17   6:18 [a]M-Text omits *might.*

NEED FOR A NEW PRIESTHOOD

[11]Therefore, if perfection were through the Levitical priesthood (for under it the people received the law), what further need *was there* that another priest should rise according to the order of Melchizedek, and not be called according to the order of Aaron? [12]For the priesthood being changed, of necessity there is also a change of the law. [13]For He of whom these things are spoken belongs to another tribe, from which no man has officiated at the altar.

[14]For *it is* evident that our Lord arose from Judah, of which tribe Moses spoke nothing concerning priesthood.[a] [15]And it is yet far more evident if, in the likeness of Melchizedek, there arises another priest [16]who has come, not according to the law of a fleshly commandment, but according to the power of an endless life. [17]For He testifies:[a]

"You are a priest forever
According to the order of Melchizedek."[b]

[18]For on the one hand there is an annulling of the former commandment because of its weakness and unprofitableness, [19]for the law made nothing perfect; on the other hand, *there is the* bringing in of a better hope, through which we draw near to God.

GREATNESS OF THE NEW PRIEST

[20]And inasmuch as *He was* not *made priest* without an oath [21](for they have become priests without an oath, but He with an oath by Him who said to Him:

"The LORD has sworn
And will not relent,
'You are a priest forever[a]
According to the order of Melchizedek' "),[b]

[22]by so much more Jesus has become a surety of a better covenant.

[23]Also there were many priests, because they were prevented by death from continuing. [24]But He, because He continues forever, has an unchangeable priesthood. [25]Therefore He is also able to save to the uttermost those who come to God through Him, since He always lives to make intercession for them.

[26]For such a High Priest was fitting for us, *who is* holy, harmless, undefiled, separate from sinners, and has become higher than the heavens; [27]who does not need daily, as those high priests, to offer up sacrifices, first for His own sins and then for the people's, for this He did once for all when He offered up Himself. [28]For the law appoints as high priests men who have weakness, but the word of the oath, which came after the law, *appoints* the Son who has been perfected forever.

THE NEW PRIESTLY SERVICE

8 Now *this is* the main point of the things we are saying: We have such a High Priest, who is seated at the right hand of the throne of the Majesty in the heavens, [2]a Minister of the sanctuary and of the true tabernacle which the Lord erected, and not man. [3]For every high priest is appointed to offer both gifts and sacrifices. Therefore *it is* necessary that this One also have something to offer. [4]For

if He were on earth, He would not be a priest, since there are priests who offer the gifts according to the law; [5]who serve the copy and shadow of the heavenly things, as Moses was divinely instructed when he was about to make the tabernacle. For He said, "See that you make all things according to the pattern shown you on the mountain."[a] [6]But now He has obtained a more excellent ministry, inasmuch as He is also Mediator of a better covenant, which was established on better promises.

walking the walk

[WALKING GEAR]

Apart from an excellent pair of walking shoes and appropriate clothing, you may want to consider taking along the following "gear" as you walk for exercise:

☐ *Sunglasses.* Regardless of the season, if the sun is bright, remember to wear sunglasses.

☐ *Hat.* You will feel cooler if you wear a hat or visor.

☐ *Pedometer.* If you want to check the distance you are walking, strap on a pedometer.

☐ *Heart rate monitor.* This can help you stay within a good "heart rate zone" as you walk.

☐ *Wristwatch.* Many training programs call for you to know the start and stop times of your walk. A watch is also helpful in knowing how long you have walked before you stop to stretch. (Your cell phone may double as a watch.)

☐ *Accessory or pocket for ID, etc.* Remember to wear clothing that has a pocket of some type for your car keys and ID.

☐ *Cell phone.* It's always good to carry a cell phone in case of an emergency.

☐ *Map.* If you are walking while on a business trip or vacation, it's always good to have a map along with you.

☐ *Whistle.* If you are walking on wilderness trails, take along a whistle. It can help alert others if you get lost.

7:14 [a]NU-Text reads *priests.*   7:17 [a]NU-Text reads *it is testified.*   [b]Psalm 110:4   7:21 [a]NU-Text ends the quotation here.   [b]Psalm 110:4   8:5 [a]Exodus 25:40

GODLY & GOODLOOKIN'

Grunge Isn't Gorgeous

The "grunge" look may be fashionable in some circles—including jeans with holes in them, unkempt beards, and scraggly hair. Most people, however, do *not* think grunge is beautiful. To the contrary, polls have revealed that a grungy, dirty, or unkempt appearance is usually associated with laziness, a lack of consideration for others, and low-paying jobs. People as a whole find cleanliness an absolute "must" factor for a person to be considered good-looking. This doesn't mean you can't get dirty occasionally—just choose to clean up after exercising, doing physical labor, playing rigorous sports, or camping out.

One of the best health practices a person can adopt is to wash his or her hands frequently and bathe daily. Bacteria thrive on skin that is unclean.

A NEW COVENANT

⁷For if that first *covenant* had been faultless, then no place would have been sought for a second. ⁸Because finding fault with them, He says: "Behold, the days are coming, says the LORD, when I will make a new covenant with the house of Israel and with the house of Judah— ⁹not according to the covenant that I made with their fathers in the day when I took them by the hand to lead them out of the land of Egypt; because they did not continue in My covenant, and I disregarded them, says the LORD. ¹⁰For this is the covenant that I will make with the house of Israel after those days, says the LORD: I will put My laws in their mind and write them on their hearts; and I will be their God, and they shall be My people. ¹¹None of them shall teach his neighbor, and none his brother, saying, 'Know the LORD,' for all shall know Me, from the least of them to the greatest of them. ¹²For I will be merciful to their unrighteousness, and their sins and their lawless deeds[a] I will remember no more."[b]

¹³In that He says, "A new covenant," He has made the first obsolete. Now what is becoming obsolete and growing old is ready to vanish away.

THE EARTHLY SANCTUARY

9 Then indeed, even the first *covenant* had ordinances of divine service and the earthly sanctuary. ²For a tabernacle was prepared: the first *part,* in which *was* the lampstand, the table, and the showbread, which is called the sanctuary; ³and behind the second veil, the part of the tabernacle which is called the Holiest of All, ⁴which had the golden censer and the ark of the covenant overlaid on all sides with gold, in which *were* the golden pot that had the manna, Aaron's rod that budded, and the tablets of the covenant; ⁵and above it were the cherubim of glory overshadowing the mercy seat. Of these things we cannot now speak in detail.

LIMITATIONS OF THE EARTHLY SERVICE

⁶Now when these things had been thus prepared, the priests always went into the first part of the tabernacle, performing *the services.* ⁷But into the second part the high priest *went* alone once a year, not without blood, which he offered for himself and *for* the people's sins *committed* in ignorance; ⁸the Holy Spirit indicating this, that the way into the Holiest of All was not yet made manifest while the first tabernacle was still standing. ⁹It *was* symbolic for the present time in which both gifts and sacrifices are offered which cannot make him who performed the service perfect in regard to the conscience— ¹⁰*concerned* only with foods and drinks, various washings, and fleshly ordinances imposed until the time of reformation.

THE HEAVENLY SANCTUARY

¹¹But Christ came *as* High Priest of the good things to come,[a] with the greater

W

WISE CHOICES

Choose items without hydrogenated oils.
Check all labels for the phrases "hydrogenated" and "partially hydrogenated" oils. They are a major source of free radicals in the body—they not only clog the arteries, but also cause an oxidizing effect. Think about how a cut apple turns brown and mushy when exposed to air—that's what these oils do to the cells inside your body!

8:12 [a]NU-Text omits *and their lawless deeds.* [b]Jeremiah 31:31–34   9:11 [a]NU-Text reads *that have come.*

and more perfect tabernacle not made with hands, that is, not of this creation. [12]Not with the blood of goats and calves, but with His own blood He entered the Most Holy Place once for all, having obtained eternal redemption. [13]For if the blood of bulls and goats and the ashes of a heifer, sprinkling the unclean, sanctifies for the purifying of the flesh, [14]how much more shall the blood of Christ, who through the eternal Spirit offered Himself without spot to God, cleanse your conscience from dead works to serve the living God? [15]And for this reason He is the Mediator of the new covenant, by means of death, for the redemption of the transgressions under the first covenant, that those who are called may receive the promise of the eternal inheritance.

THE MEDIATOR'S DEATH NECESSARY

[16]For where there *is* a testament, there must also of necessity be the death of the testator. [17]For a testament *is* in force after men are dead, since it has no power at all while the testator lives. [18]Therefore not even the first *covenant* was dedicated without blood. [19]For when Moses had spoken every precept to all the people according to the law, he took the blood of calves and goats, with water, scarlet wool, and hyssop, and sprinkled both the book itself and all the people, [20]saying, "This is the blood of the covenant which God has commanded you."[a] [21]Then likewise he sprinkled with blood both the tabernacle and all the vessels of the ministry. [22]And according to the law almost all things are purified with blood, and without shedding of blood there is no remission.

GREATNESS OF CHRIST'S SACRIFICE

[23]Therefore *it was* necessary that the copies of the things in the heavens should be purified with these, but the heavenly things themselves with better sacrifices than these. [24]For Christ has not entered the holy places made with hands, *which are* copies of the true, but into heaven itself, now to appear in the presence of God for us; [25]not that He should offer Himself often, as the high priest enters the Most Holy Place every year with blood of another— [26]He then would have had to suffer often since the foundation of the world; but now, once at the end of the ages, He has appeared to put away sin by the sacrifice of Himself. [27]And as it is appointed for men to die once, but after this the judgment, [28]so Christ was offered once to bear the sins of many. To those who eagerly wait for Him He will appear a second time, apart from sin, for salvation.

ANIMAL SACRIFICES INSUFFICIENT

10 For the law, having a shadow of the good things to come, *and* not the very image of the things, can never with these same sacrifices, which they offer continually year by year, make those who approach perfect. [2]For then would they not have ceased to be offered? For the worshipers, once purified, would have had no more consciousness of sins. [3]But in those *sacrifices there is* a reminder of sins every year. [4]For *it is* not possible that the blood of bulls and goats could take away sins.

CHRIST'S DEATH FULFILLS GOD'S WILL

[5]Therefore, when He came into the world, He said:

CONDIMENTS

☐ Throw Out the Sugar Bowl

Sugar, flour, and coffee. These were once considered the basics for any kitchen canister set! Sugar is still a staple condiment in many homes. A healthier approach is to throw out all white sugar that may be lurking in your cupboards. Learn to drink tea and coffee without sugar. (Eliminating sugar may also help you overcome a caffeine addiction!)

The consumption of white sugar causes blood sugar levels to increase rapidly in the body. White sugar is quickly absorbed into the bloodstream, especially when it is consumed in the form of sugar-laced beverages. This sudden rise in blood sugar triggers the pancreas to produce more insulin, a hormone that regulates blood sugar. The more sugar a person consumes, the harder the pancreas has to work. Depending on genetics, lifestyle, and weight, the body can become resistant and may not be able to keep up the demand for insulin production. This is called "insulin resistance" and it leads to type 2 diabetes. Type 2 diabetes is now appearing at alarming rates in our society, not only among adults, but also among children.

"Sacrifice and offering You did not desire,
But a body You have prepared for Me.
[6] In burnt offerings and sacrifices for sin
You had no pleasure.
[7] Then I said, 'Behold, I have come—
In the volume of the book it is written of Me—
To do Your will, O God.' "[a]

[8]Previously saying, "Sacrifice and offering, burnt offerings, and offerings for sin You did not desire, nor had pleasure in them" (which are

The LAW AND THE SCIENCE

[ENJOY MEALTIMES]

>SCIENCE tells us that when we eat in a relaxed way, with a joyful and thankful attitude, we digest our food much better.

>THE LAW says: "You shall rejoice before the Lord your God in all to which you put your hands" (Deuteronomy 12:18). Some people believe this verse refers to the *work* we do with our hands, but it actually appears in the Bible in the context of the *food* we prepare and eat with our hands!

offered according to the law), [9]then He said, "Behold, I have come to do Your will, O God."[a] He takes away the first that He may establish the second. [10]By that will we have been sanctified through the offering of the body of Jesus Christ once *for all*.

CHRIST'S DEATH PERFECTS THE SANCTIFIED

[11]And every priest stands ministering daily and offering repeatedly the same sacrifices, which can never take away sins. [12]But this Man, after He had offered one sacrifice for sins forever, sat down at the right hand of God, [13]from that time waiting till His enemies are made His footstool. [14]For by one offering He has perfected forever those who are being sanctified.

[15]But the Holy Spirit also witnesses to us; for after He had said before,

[16]"This is the covenant that I will make with them after those days, says the Lord: I will put My laws into their hearts, and in their minds I will write them,"[a] [17]then He adds, "Their sins and their lawless deeds I

will remember no more."[a] [18]Now where there is remission of these, *there is* no longer an offering for sin.

HOLD FAST YOUR CONFESSION

[19]Therefore, brethren, having boldness to enter the Holiest by the blood of Jesus, [20]by a new and living way which He consecrated for us, through the veil, that is, His flesh, [21]and *having* a High Priest over the house of God, [22]let us draw near with a true heart in full assurance of faith, having our hearts sprinkled from an evil conscience and our bodies washed with pure water. [23]Let us hold fast the confession of *our* hope without wavering, for He who promised *is* faithful. [24]And let us consider one another in order to stir up love and good works, [25]not forsaking the assembling of ourselves together, as *is* the manner of some, but exhorting *one another,* and so much the more as you see the Day approaching.

THE JUST LIVE BY FAITH

[26]For if we sin willfully after we have received the knowledge of the truth, there no longer remains a sacrifice for sins, [27]but a certain fearful expectation of judgment, and fiery indignation which will devour the adversaries. [28]Anyone who has rejected Moses' law dies without mercy on the testimony of two or three witnesses. [29]Of how much worse punishment, do you suppose, will he be thought worthy who has trampled the Son of God underfoot, counted the blood of the covenant by which he was sanctified a common thing, and insulted the Spirit of grace? [30]For we know Him who said, "Vengeance is Mine, I will repay,"[a] says the Lord.[b] And again, "The Lord will judge His people."[c] [31]It is a fearful thing to fall into the hands of the living God.

[32]But recall the former days in which, after you were illuminated, you endured a great struggle with sufferings: [33]partly while you were made a spectacle both by reproaches and tribulations, and partly while you became

companions of those who were so treated; [34]for you had compassion on me[a] in my chains, and joyfully accepted the plundering of your goods, knowing that you have a better and an enduring possession for yourselves in heaven.[b] [35]Therefore do not cast away your confidence, which has great reward. [36]For you have need of endurance, so that after you have done the will of God, you may receive the promise:

[37]"For yet a little while,
    And He[a] who is coming will come and
        will not tarry.
[38]Now the[a] just shall live by faith;
    But if anyone draws back,
    My soul has no pleasure in him."[b]

[39]But we are not of those who draw back to perdition, but of those who believe to the saving of the soul.

WISE CHOICES

Choose tea over coffee. Three good reasons to choose tea: Tea has caffeine, but less than coffee. Tea does not have the tannic acid that coffee has. Tea has antioxidants that coffee does not have.

10:9 [a]NU-Text and M-Text omit *O God.*   10:16 [a]Jeremiah 31:33   10:17 [a]Jeremiah 31:34   10:30 [a]Deuteronomy 32:35   [b]NU-Text omits *says the Lord.*   [c]Deuteronomy 32:36   10:34 [a]NU-Text reads *the prisoners* instead of *me in my chains.*   [b]NU-Text omits *in heaven.*   10:37 [a]Or *that which*   10:38 [a]NU-Text reads *My just one.*   [b]Habakkuk 2:3, 4

BY FAITH WE UNDERSTAND

11 Now faith is the substance of things hoped for, the evidence of things not seen. ²For by it the elders obtained a *good* testimony.

³By faith we understand that the worlds were framed by the word of God, so that the things which are seen were not made of things which are visible.

FAITH AT THE DAWN OF HISTORY

⁴By faith Abel offered to God a more excellent sacrifice than Cain, through which he obtained witness that he was righteous, God testifying of his gifts; and through it he being dead still speaks.

⁵By faith Enoch was taken away so that he did not see death, "and was not found, because God had taken him";ᵃ for before he was taken he had this testimony, that he pleased God. ⁶But without faith *it is* impossible to please *Him,* for he who comes to God must believe that He is, and *that* He is a rewarder of those who diligently seek Him.

⁷By faith Noah, being divinely warned of things not yet seen, moved with godly fear, prepared an ark for the saving of his household, by which he condemned the world and became heir of the righteousness which is according to faith.

FAITHFUL ABRAHAM

⁸By faith Abraham obeyed when he was called to go out to the place which he would receive as an inheritance. And he went out, not knowing where he was going. ⁹By faith he dwelt in the land of promise as *in* a foreign country, dwelling in tents with Isaac and Jacob, the heirs with him of the same promise; ¹⁰for he waited for the city which has foundations, whose builder and maker *is* God.

¹¹By faith Sarah herself also received strength to conceive seed, and she bore a childᵃ when she was past the age, because she judged Him faithful who had promised. ¹²Therefore from one man, and him as good as dead, were born *as many* as the stars of the sky in multitude—innumerable as the sand which is by the seashore.

THE HEAVENLY HOPE

¹³These all died in faith, not having received the promises, but having seen them afar off were assured of them,ᵃ embraced *them* and confessed that they were strangers and pilgrims on the earth. ¹⁴For those who say such things declare plainly that they seek a homeland. ¹⁵And truly if they had called to mind that *country* from which they had come out, they would have had opportunity to return. ¹⁶But now they desire a better, that is, a heavenly *country.* Therefore God is not ashamed to be called their God, for He has prepared a city for them.

THE FAITH OF THE PATRIARCHS

¹⁷By faith Abraham, when he was tested, offered up Isaac, and he who had received the promises offered up his only begotten *son,* ¹⁸of whom it was said, "In Isaac your seed shall be called,"ᵃ ¹⁹concluding that God *was* able to raise *him* up, even from the dead, from which he also received him in a figurative sense.

²⁰By faith Isaac blessed Jacob and Esau concerning things to come.

²¹By faith Jacob, when he was dying, blessed each of the sons of Joseph, and worshiped, *leaning* on the top of his staff.

²²By faith Joseph, when he was dying, made mention of the departure of the children of Israel, and gave instructions concerning his bones.

THE FAITH OF MOSES

²³By faith Moses, when he was born, was hidden three months by his parents, because they saw *he was* a beautiful child; and they were not afraid of the king's command.

²⁴By faith Moses, when he became of age, refused to be called the son of Pharaoh's daughter, ²⁵choosing rather to suffer affliction with the people of God than to enjoy the passing pleasures of sin, ²⁶esteeming

---

> (Hebrews 11:6)

Diligently Seeking. The Bible assures us that God is a "rewarder." He desires good things in our lives, not only those things that reap eternal benefit, but also material, physical, emotional, and spiritual blessings on this earth. God gives eternal life and an abundant life (John 10:10). The key to receiving God's rewards is to *diligently* seek Him. This means to study the Scriptures, to learn God's ways, and to seek greater understanding of God's principles.

This is certainly true in areas related to health and wholeness! If we want to be healthier, we need to study *how* to be healthier. Diligence has to do with the way we use our time. Are you focused, intentional, and specific in the way you order the hours of any given day? Do you seek to manage your time, rather than allow circumstances to detour you continually away from the priorities you consider to be most important?

Those who are *diligent* are those who learn to say "no" to any activity that draws them away from their God-given goals and purpose. If you truly want to experience God's rewards of better health, you need to be diligent in your pursuit of knowledge and truth about health, and then be diligent in the way you budget your time so you can do the things that produce a healthy life!

INSIGHTS INTO THE WORD

11:5 ᵃGenesis 5:24   11:11 ᵃNU-Text omits *she bore a child.*   11:13 ᵃNU-Text and M-Text omit *were assured of them.*   11:18 ᵃGenesis 21:12

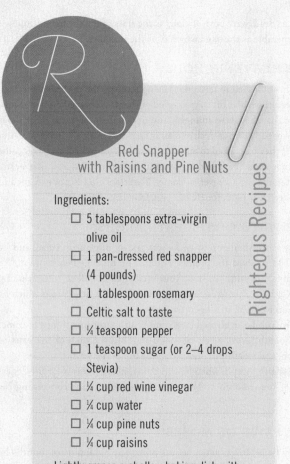

Red Snapper with Raisins and Pine Nuts

Righteous Recipes

Ingredients:

- ☐ 5 tablespoons extra-virgin olive oil
- ☐ 1 pan-dressed red snapper (4 pounds)
- ☐ 1 tablespoon rosemary
- ☐ Celtic salt to taste
- ☐ ¼ teaspoon pepper
- ☐ 1 teaspoon sugar (or 2–4 drops Stevia)
- ☐ ¼ cup red wine vinegar
- ☐ ¼ cup water
- ☐ ¼ cup pine nuts
- ☐ ¼ cup raisins

Lightly grease a shallow baking dish with 1 tablespoon olive oil. Center the fish in the baking dish. Sprinkle it with rosemary, salt, and pepper. Combine the sugar, vinegar, and water in a small bowl; whisk until sugar is dissolved. Then whisk in the remaining 4 tablespoons olive oil. Drizzle the vinegar mixture evenly over the fish and sprinkle with pine nuts and raisins over the top. Bake, covered, at 400 degrees for 20 minutes. Uncover and bake 30 minutes longer, basting with the pan juices. Remove from the oven. Spoon the raisins, pine nuts, and pan juices over the fish after it has been placed on a platter or on plates as individual servings.

Yield: 8 servings

the reproach of Christ greater riches than the treasures in[ª] Egypt; for he looked to the reward.

²⁷By faith he forsook Egypt, not fearing the wrath of the king; for he endured as seeing Him who is invisible. ²⁸By faith he kept the Passover and the sprinkling of blood, lest he who destroyed the firstborn should touch them.

²⁹By faith they passed through the Red Sea as by dry *land, whereas* the Egyptians, attempting to do so, were drowned.

BY FAITH THEY OVERCAME

³⁰By faith the walls of Jericho fell down after they were encircled for seven days. ³¹By faith the harlot Rahab did not perish with those who did not believe, when she had received the spies with peace.

³²And what more shall I say? For the time would fail me to tell of Gideon and Barak and Samson and Jephthah, also *of* David and Samuel and the prophets: ³³who through faith subdued kingdoms, worked righteousness, obtained promises, stopped the mouths of lions, ³⁴quenched the violence of fire, escaped the edge of the sword, out of weakness were made strong, became valiant in battle, turned to flight the armies of the aliens. ³⁵Women received their dead raised to life again.

Others were tortured, not accepting deliverance, that they might obtain a better resurrection. ³⁶Still others had trial of mockings and scourgings, yes, and of chains and imprisonment. ³⁷They were stoned, they were sawn in two, were tempted,[ª] were slain with the sword. They wandered about in sheepskins and goatskins, being destitute, afflicted, tormented— ³⁸of whom the world was not worthy. They wandered in deserts and mountains, *in* dens and caves of the earth.

³⁹And all these, having obtained a good testimony through faith, did not receive the promise, ⁴⁰God having provided something better for us, that they should not be made perfect apart from us.

THE RACE OF FAITH

12 Therefore we also, since we are surrounded by so great a cloud of witnesses, let us lay aside every weight, and the sin which so easily ensnares *us,* and let us run with endurance the race that is set before us, ²looking unto Jesus, the author and finisher of *our* faith, who for the joy that was set before Him endured the cross, despising the shame, and has sat down at the right hand of the throne of God.

THE DISCIPLINE OF GOD

³For consider Him who endured such hostility from sinners against Himself, lest you become weary and discouraged in your souls. ⁴You have not yet resisted to bloodshed, striving against sin. ⁵And you have forgotten the exhortation which speaks to you as to sons:

"My son, do not despise the chastening of the LORD,
Nor be discouraged when you are rebuked by Him;
⁶ For whom the LORD loves He chastens,
And scourges every son whom He receives."[ª]

⁷If[ª] you endure chastening, God deals with you as with sons; for what son is there whom a father does not chasten? ⁸But if you are without chastening, of which all have become partakers, then you are illegitimate and not sons. ⁹Furthermore, we have had human fathers who corrected *us,* and we paid *them* respect. Shall we not much more readily be in subjection to the Father of spirits and live? ¹⁰For they indeed for a few days chastened *us* as seemed *best* to them, but He for *our*

11:26 ªNU-Text and M-Text read *of.* 11:37 ªNU-Text omits *were tempted.* 12:6 ªProverbs 3:11, 12 12:7 ªNU-Text and M-Text read *It is for discipline that you endure; God . . . .*

328 DIVINE HEALTH

profit, that *we* may be partakers of His holiness. ¹¹Now no chastening seems to be joyful for the present, but painful; nevertheless, afterward it yields the peaceable fruit of righteousness to those who have been trained by it.

RENEW YOUR SPIRITUAL VITALITY

¹²Therefore strengthen the hands which hang down, and the feeble knees, ¹³and make straight paths for your feet, so that what is lame may not be dislocated, but rather be healed.

¹⁴Pursue peace with all *people,* and holiness, without which no one will see the Lord: ¹⁵looking carefully lest anyone fall short of the grace of God; lest any root of bitterness springing up cause trouble, and by this many become defiled; ¹⁶lest there *be* any fornicator or profane person like Esau, who for one morsel of food sold his birthright. ¹⁷For you know that afterward, when he wanted to inherit the blessing, he was rejected, for he found no place for repentance, though he sought it diligently with tears.

THE GLORIOUS COMPANY

¹⁸For you have not come to the mountain that^{*a*} may be touched and that burned with fire, and to blackness and darkness^{*b*} and tempest, ¹⁹and the sound of a trumpet and the voice of words, so that those who heard *it* begged that the word should not be spoken to them anymore. ²⁰(For they could not endure what was commanded: "And if so much as a beast touches the mountain, it shall be stoned^{*a*} or shot with an arrow."^{*b*} ²¹And so terrifying was the sight *that* Moses said, "I am exceedingly afraid and trembling."^{*a*})

²²But you have come to Mount Zion and to the city of the living God, the heavenly Jerusalem, to an innumerable company of angels, ²³to the general assembly and church of the firstborn *who are* registered in heaven, to God the Judge of all, to the spirits of just men made perfect, ²⁴to Jesus the Mediator of the new covenant, and to the blood of sprinkling that speaks better things than *that of* Abel.

HEAR THE HEAVENLY VOICE

²⁵See that you do not refuse Him who speaks. For if they did not escape who refused Him who spoke on earth, much more *shall we not escape* if we turn away from Him who *speaks* from heaven, ²⁶whose voice then shook the earth; but now He has promised, saying, "Yet once more I shake^{*a*} not only the earth, but also heaven."^{*b*} ²⁷Now this, "Yet once more," indicates the removal of those things that are being shaken, as of things that are made, that the things which cannot be shaken may remain.

²⁸Therefore, since we are receiving a kingdom which cannot be shaken, let us have grace, by which we may^{*a*} serve God acceptably with reverence and godly fear. ²⁹For our God *is* a consuming fire.

CONCLUDING MORAL DIRECTIONS

13 Let brotherly love continue. ²Do not forget to entertain strangers, for by so *doing* some have unwittingly entertained angels. ³Remember the prisoners as if chained with them—those who are mistreated—since you yourselves are in the body also.

⁴Marriage *is* honorable among all, and the bed undefiled; but fornicators and adulterers God will judge.

⁵*Let your* conduct *be* without covetousness; *be* content with such things as you have. For He Himself has said, "I will never leave you nor forsake you."^{*a*} ⁶So we may boldly say:

"The LORD is my helper;
  I will not fear.
  What can man do to me?"^{*a*}

CONCLUDING RELIGIOUS DIRECTIONS

⁷Remember those who rule over you, who have spoken the word of God to you, whose faith follow, considering the outcome of *their* conduct. ⁸Jesus Christ *is* the same yesterday, today, and forever. ⁹Do not be carried about^{*a*} with various and strange doctrines. For *it is* good that the heart be established by grace, not with foods which have not profited those who have been occupied with them.

¹⁰We have an altar from which those who serve the tabernacle have no right to eat. ¹¹For the bodies of those animals, whose blood is brought into the sanctuary by the high priest for sin, are burned outside the camp. ¹²Therefore Jesus also, that He might sanctify the people with His own blood, suffered outside the gate. ¹³Therefore let us go forth to Him, outside the camp, bearing His reproach. ¹⁴For here we

> **> (Hebrews 12:14, 15)**

Pursue Peace—and Don't Become Bitter.

If bitterness, which arises from intense animosity and resentment, takes *root* in a person's life, it can't help but produce the *fruit* of bitterness. The nature of a root is reflected in the nature of that plant's fruit! This is true for all aspects of creation. The fruit of bitterness erupts in acts of ill will, anger, jealousy, dissension, and immorality.

Just as a plant may grow slowly, with fruit not appearing for weeks, months, or in some cases, years, so bitterness deep within a person may not produce fruit for some time. Eventually, however, that fruit will appear—and unfortunately, it sometimes appears in the form of disease or symptoms of disease. Bitterness within a marriage, family, or church, can have effects beyond one individual's "bad fruit." It can destroy the peace that God desires to be the hallmark of all relationships.

INSIGHTS | **INTO THE WORD**

12:18 ^aNU-Text reads *to that which.* ^bNU-Text reads *gloom.*   **12:20** ^aNU-Text and M-Text omit the rest of this verse. ^bExodus 19:12, 13   **12:21** ^aDeuteronomy 9:19   **12:26** ^aNU-Text reads *will shake.* ^bHaggai 2:6   **12:28** ^aM-Text omits *may.*   **13:5** ^aDeuteronomy 31:6, 8; Joshua 1:5   **13:6** ^aPsalm 118:6   **13:9** ^aNU-Text and M-Text read *away.*

weighing Less &
enjoying Life more!

[Become "Supermarket Savvy"]

Part of the secret to successful weight-loss and weight-loss maintenance is keeping all junk food, processed food, and tempting foods out of your grocery cart and out of your house. Here are seven tips to help you become "supermarket savvy."

1. Plan your meals in advance and then make a list of items that you need. Stick to your list!
2. Don't go to the supermarket when you are hungry. You'll be easy prey for on-shelf advertising of the most delicious and most calorie-laden foods in the market.
3. Don't go to the supermarket when you are in a rush to get home to fix dinner. You'll succumb to fast-food and deli items, which are likely to be frozen, or prepared foods that are high in fat content, sodium, or calories. Especially stay away from the fried foods and mayonnaise-dripping salads in the deli.
4. Shop the perimeter of the grocery store. In most grocery stores, that's where you are going to find fruits and vegetables, meat and fish, and dairy products.
5. Avoid going to the bakery in the supermarket.
6. Don't go down the aisles that you know have chips, cookies, or other tempting foods that are unhealthy.
7. Walk through the store as quickly as you can while picking up the things on your list. The brisk walk may not count technically as "exercise," but you'll be less likely to become tempted by foods not on your grocery list if you are moving by those foods at a quick pace!

have no continuing city, but we seek the one to come. [15]Therefore by Him let us continually offer the sacrifice of praise to God, that is, the fruit of *our* lips, giving thanks to His name. [16]But do not forget to do good and to share, for with such sacrifices God is well pleased.

[17]Obey those who rule over you, and be submissive, for they watch out for your souls, as those who must give account. Let them do so with joy and not with grief, for that would be unprofitable for you.

PRAYER REQUESTED

[18]Pray for us; for we are confident that we have a good conscience, in all things desiring to live honorably. [19]But I especially urge *you* to do this, that I may be restored to you the sooner.

BENEDICTION, FINAL EXHORTATION, FAREWELL

[20]Now may the God of peace who brought up our Lord Jesus from the dead, that great Shepherd of the sheep, through the blood of the everlasting covenant, [21]make you complete in every good work to do His will, working in you[a] what is well pleasing in His sight, through Jesus Christ, to whom *be* glory forever and ever. Amen.

[22]And I appeal to you, brethren, bear with the word of exhortation, for I have written to you in few words. [23]Know that *our* brother Timothy has been set free, with whom I shall see you if he comes shortly.

[24]Greet all those who rule over you, and all the saints. Those from Italy greet you.

[25]Grace *be* with you all. Amen.

13:21 [a]NU-Text and M-Text read *us*.

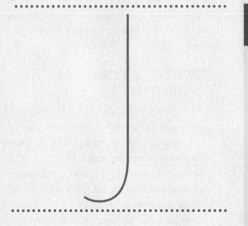

AMES

Bridle my tongue? For some of us that can be hard, James says. So, too, is the battle against many areas of the flesh. James is very direct in his writings, giving 54 commands in only 108 verses. He doesn't let religious theories or viewpoints come into play. With James, issues are black and white, sometimes cut and dried.

James seeks to inspire his readers to pursue a "pure and undefiled religion" that is marked by personal growth, a faith that is active in producing good works, and a spiritual life that works successfully in a variety of social settings. He compels his readers to be dedicated, disciplined, determined, and focused. These are the very attributes required if a person is going to pursue the goals of wholeness and to exercise, eat right, and overcome disease.

James 3:3 says "We put bits in horses' mouths that they may obey us, and we turn their whole body." How are you bridling your own speech and behavior as you move toward greater wholeness? Are you saying and doing what truly promotes physical and emotional well-being?

GREETING TO THE TWELVE TRIBES

1 James, a bondservant of God and of the Lord Jesus Christ,

To the twelve tribes which are scattered abroad:

Greetings.

PROFITING FROM TRIALS

²My brethren, count it all joy when you fall into various trials, ³knowing that the testing of your faith produces patience. ⁴But let patience have *its* perfect work, that you may be perfect and complete, lacking nothing. ⁵If any of you lacks wisdom, let him ask of God, who gives to all liberally and without reproach, and it will be given to him. ⁶But let him ask in faith, with no doubting, for he who doubts is like a wave of the sea driven and tossed by the wind. ⁷For let not that man suppose that he will receive anything from the Lord; ⁸*he is* a double-minded man, unstable in all his ways.

THE PERSPECTIVE OF RICH AND POOR

⁹Let the lowly brother glory in his exaltation, ¹⁰but the rich in his humiliation, because as a flower of the field he will pass away. ¹¹For no sooner has the sun risen with a burning heat than it withers the grass; its flower falls, and its beautiful appearance perishes. So the rich man also will fade away in his pursuits.

LOVING GOD UNDER TRIALS

¹²Blessed *is* the man who endures temptation; for when he has been approved, he will receive the crown of life which the Lord has promised to those who love Him. ¹³Let no one say when he is tempted, "I am tempted by God"; for God cannot be tempted by evil, nor does He Himself tempt anyone. ¹⁴But each one is tempted when he is drawn away by his own desires and enticed. ¹⁵Then, when desire has conceived, it gives birth to sin; and sin, when it is full-grown, brings forth death.

¹⁶Do not be deceived, my beloved brethren. ¹⁷Every good gift and every perfect gift is from above, and comes down from the Father of lights, with whom there is no variation or shadow of turning. ¹⁸Of His own will He brought us forth by the word of truth, that we might be a kind of firstfruits of His creatures.

QUALITIES NEEDED IN TRIALS

¹⁹So then,ᵃ my beloved brethren, let every man be swift to hear, slow to speak, slow to wrath; ²⁰for the wrath of man does not produce the righteousness of God.

DOERS—NOT HEARERS ONLY

²¹Therefore lay aside all filthiness and overflow of wickedness, and receive with meekness the implanted word, which is able to save your souls.

²²But be doers of the word, and not hearers only, deceiving yourselves. ²³For if anyone is a hearer of the word and not a doer, he is like a man observing his natural face in a mirror; ²⁴for he observes himself, goes away, and immediately forgets what kind of man he was. ²⁵But he who looks into the perfect law of liberty and continues *in it,* and is not a forgetful hearer but a doer of the work, this one will be blessed in what he does.

²⁶If anyone among youᵃ thinks he is religious, and does not bridle

1:19 ᵃNU-Text reads *Know this* or *This you know.*   1:26 ᵃNU-Text omits *among you.*

WWJE?

[FRUIT]

[WHAT WOULD JESUS EAT]

Fruit was a staple food in Jesus' time, as it had been for the Israelites for thousands of years. Grapes, figs, and pomegranates are three fruits mentioned frequently in the Bible. Other fruits include apples, apricots, berries, melons, dates, and raisins.

Grapes are a very rich source of nutrients. Purple grapes and red grapes are rich in anthocyanin, a form of flavonoid that functions as an antioxidant. Grapes have been shown to fight tooth decay and to stop viruses. They are high in caffeic acid, a substance shown to be a strong cancer-fighting agent. They are also high in resveratrol, an antioxidant that helps protect the heart and blood vessels in several ways. One of the most important benefits of resveratrol is that it acts as a Cox-2 inhibitor. When the Cox-2 enzyme is inhibited, cancer activity is reduced, as is inflammation. Grapes are high in a number of minerals and vitamins A, B, and C. They are low in calories and have virtually no fat.

Figs were also abundant in Bible times. They have numerous health benefits and are high in fiber, magnesium, potassium, calcium, manganese, copper, iron, and vitamins C and B_6. They have been used around the world for centuries to help fight countless diseases, including skin cancers, constipation, scurvy, gangrene, boils, and liver ailments. In Bible times, figs were usually eaten as a dried fruit or pressed into cakes. Dried figs are high in sugar and can have a laxative effect—don't eat too many at one time! If you are buying dried figs check to make sure what may have been added to them—some people are allergic to sulfites, often used to dry figs and other fruits.

Pomegranates have been grown in Israel for thousands of years. According to

Jewish tradition, they have 613 seeds when fully mature—the same number as the number of laws God gave to Israel. The juice of pomegranates, called grenadine, is also popular in the Middle East. It is usually mixed with carbonated mineral water. Pomegranates are high in potassium and vitamins B and C, copper, magnesium, and fiber. It is very likely that the "apples" of the Bible were actually pomegranates or bitter oranges.

A number of citrus fruits are also popular in the Middle East, as are berries, apples, and apricots. Apricots are actually known as "golden apples." Dried apricots are a rich source of vitamin A, as well as other carotenes and minerals.

Apples have been shown to have numerous health benefits—but most of these apply only to eating fresh apples that have been organically grown and packaged without pesticides, chemicals, or waxes. Eating two or three apples a day can greatly boost the body's protection against heart disease.

Try Making Grape Honey

Wash four cups of grapes, removing all stems. Place the grapes in a pan with half a cup of water and boil the mixture about twenty minutes or until it thickens. Strain out the grape seeds. Store the mixture in sterilized jars and refrigerate. The natural sugars in the grapes become concentrated—the sweeter the grapes to begin with, the sweeter the grape "honey" will be. Try this on whole-grain bread. Delicious!

Try a Pluot!

This new fruit is a cross between a plum (75 percent) and an apricot (25 percent). It has the tang and juiciness of a plum and the sweetness of an apricot. It is available in grocery stores in midsummer.

his tongue but deceives his own heart, this one's religion *is* useless. ²⁷Pure and undefiled religion before God and the Father is this: to visit orphans and widows in their trouble, *and* to keep oneself unspotted from the world.

BEWARE OF PERSONAL FAVORITISM

2 My brethren, do not hold the faith of our Lord Jesus Christ, *the Lord* of glory, with partiality. ²For if there should come into your assembly a man with gold rings, in fine apparel, and there should also come in a poor man in filthy clothes, ³and you pay attention to the one wearing the fine clothes and say to him, "You sit here in a good place," and say to the poor man, "You stand there," or, "Sit here at my footstool," ⁴have you not shown partiality among yourselves, and become judges with evil thoughts?

⁵Listen, my beloved brethren: Has God not chosen the poor of this world *to be* rich in faith and heirs of the kingdom which He promised to those who love Him? ⁶But you have dishonored the poor man. Do not the rich oppress you and drag you into the courts? ⁷Do they not blaspheme that noble name by which you are called?

⁸If you really fulfill *the* royal law according to the Scripture, "You shall love your neighbor as yourself,"ᵃ you do well; ⁹but if you show partiality, you commit sin, and are convicted by the law as transgressors. ¹⁰For whoever shall keep the whole law, and yet stumble in one *point*, he is guilty of all. ¹¹For He who said, "Do not commit adultery,"ᵃ also said, "Do not murder."ᵇ Now if you do not commit adultery, but you do murder, you have become a transgressor of the law. ¹²So speak and so do as those who will be judged by the law of liberty. ¹³For judgment is without mercy to the one who has shown no mercy. Mercy triumphs over judgment.

FAITH WITHOUT WORKS IS DEAD

¹⁴What *does it* profit, my brethren, if someone says he has faith but does not have works? Can faith save him? ¹⁵If a brother or sister is naked and destitute of daily food, ¹⁶and one of you says to them, "Depart in peace, be warmed and filled," but you do not

November

1   2   3   4   5   6   7

Now Is the Time To...

☐ Send out your Thanksgiving dinner invitations as early in the month as possible. Always allow room at your table for a few unexpected guests. Consider inviting college students who may not be able to travel home for the holiday. ☐ Get out and walk. Don't let the holidays interrupt your exercise schedule. ☐ Reduce the holiday pressure by signing and addressing Christmas cards this month so they will be ready to mail in early December. ☐ Check your "gift closet" or "gift drawer" for gifts you may have tucked away earlier in the year. You may be surprised at what you already have, but had forgotten.

8   9   10   11   12   13   14

Table Fresh

☐ Add fresh cranberries and walnuts to your dressing or stuffing recipe. ☐ Put fresh lemons—cut up in quarters—into the cavity of a turkey before baking. ☐ Try baking fresh sweet potatoes for your holiday meal. They have far fewer calories than regular mashed potatoes and gravy, or candied yams.

15   16   17   18   19   20   21

In the Garden

☐ As the pine trees drop their cones, grab a grocery sack and gather some cones for holiday decorating. Thoroughly rinse off the cones you have collected and then place the wet cones on a wax-paper-covered cookie sheet to dry them in a warm oven for a few minutes. You'll fill your house with a wonderful pine fragrance. Once the cones are cool, set them aside. They can be painted or decorated in creative ways to use as part of wreaths or evergreen ropes to place on mantels or over doorways. They can also become tree ornaments.

Let's Celebrate

22   23   24   25   26   27   28

☐ Are you hosting Thanksgiving dinner? This year ask family members and friends to each bring a dish and a dessert. Those who cannot cook might bring bottles of sparkling juice. With everyone helping out, you'll feel less stress in preparing the main dishes and enjoy more the opportunity to decorate your house and tables for the grand event. ☐ Who said Thanksgiving dinner had to be eaten at noon? Why not plan Thanksgiving as a dinner party that begins at 5 or 6 P.M.? By eating light during the day, you won't be as likely to overeat at dinner. Purchase "to go" boxes so everyone can take home some leftovers and you'll have fewer calories lurking in your refrigerator the next day! Light some candles and enjoy a quiet evening of conversation about all the things you are thankful for.

29   30

Seasonal Tips

☐ Rake all the leaves from your yard before the first snow. Some leaves might be raked into flower beds to protect young plants from freezing during the winter. ☐ After your final lawn cutting, clean your lawn mower thoroughly and drain the gasoline from the tank before storing the mower for the winter. ☐ Polish silver well in advance of parties or holiday feasts. Here are a few tips: 1) Before you polish, rinse the silver in hot water and dry each piece with a cool towel. 2) While the silver is still warm, spread on polish with a sponge. 3) Rub and polish each piece with a dry towel until it sparkles. 4) Rinse the polished piece in soapy and then clean water and hand dry it. ☐ Untangle and test your Christmas lights. Turn the lights on for half an hour and make certain that none of the wires or bulbs get hot. If they do, throw them away and purchase new ones.

WEIGHING Less &
ENJOYING LIFE MORE!

[Nutrients That Help with Weight Loss]

Several nutrients that can be taken in supplemental form are helpful in a fat-loss program. They include:

Chromium picolinate—reduces sugar cravings and stabilizes the metabolism of simple carbohydrates

Lecithin—a fat emulsifier—in other words, it breaks down fat for better removal from the body

Zinc gluconate—enhances the effectiveness of insulin

Magnesium—keeps energy high while losing weight

Bromelain, papain, and pancreatin—supplements that can aid in the digestion of proteins, carbohydrates, and fats

Spirulina (blue-green algae)—a natural food supplement that has substantial amounts of protein, essential fatty acids, vitamins, and minerals. It is very low in calories and helps curb the appetite. This is also true for other "green" foods that can be taken as supplements.

Some weight-loss nutritionists recommend a "bedtime" formula that includes L-arginine, L-ornithine and L-Lysine, plus vitamins B_6 and C, as a potion to help the body burn fat all night long.

---

give them the things which are needed for the body, what *does it* profit? [17]Thus also faith by itself, if it does not have works, is dead.

[18]But someone will say, "You have faith, and I have works." Show me your faith without your[a] works, and I will show you my faith by my[b] works. [19]You believe that there is one God. You do well. Even the demons believe—and tremble! [20]But do you want to know, O foolish man, that faith without works is dead?[a] [21]Was not Abraham our father justified by works when he offered Isaac his son on the altar? [22]Do you see that faith was working together with his works, and by works faith was made perfect? [23]And the Scripture was fulfilled which says, "Abraham believed God, and it was accounted to him for righteousness."[a] And he was called the friend of God. [24]You see then that a man is justified by works, and not by faith only.

[25]Likewise, was not Rahab the harlot also justified by works when she received the messengers and sent *them* out another way?

[26]For as the body without the spirit is dead, so faith without works is dead also.

THE UNTAMABLE TONGUE

3 My brethren, let not many of you become teachers, knowing that we shall receive a stricter judgment. [2]For we all stumble in many things. If anyone does not stumble in word, he *is* a perfect man, able also to bridle the whole body. [3]Indeed,[a] we put bits in horses' mouths that they may obey us, and we turn their whole body. [4]Look also at ships: although they are so large and are driven by fierce winds, they are turned by a very small rudder wherever the pilot desires. [5]Even so the tongue is a little member and boasts great things.

See how great a forest a little fire kindles! [6]And the tongue *is* a fire, a world of iniquity. The tongue is so set among our members that it defiles the whole body, and sets on fire the course of nature; and it is set on fire by hell. [7]For every kind of beast and bird, of reptile and creature of the sea, is tamed and has been tamed by mankind. [8]But no man can tame the tongue. *It is* an unruly evil, full of deadly poison. [9]With it we bless our God and Father, and with it we curse men, who have been

Their Fat Didn't Help

Bible Health + Food Facts

Two men for whom obesity definitely contributed to their demise: King Eglon (Judges 3:14–30) and the high priest Eli (1 Samuel 4:18). Their stories may inspire you to shed those unnecessary pounds!

2:18 [a]NU-Text omits *your*. [b]NU-Text omits *my*. 2:20 [a]NU-Text reads *useless*. 2:23 [a]Genesis 15:6 3:3 [a]NU-Text reads *Now if*.

earthly, sensual, demonic. [16]For where envy and self-seeking *exist*, confusion and every evil thing *are* there. [17]But the wisdom that is from above is first pure, then peaceable, gentle, willing to yield, full of mercy and good fruits, without partiality and without hypocrisy. [18]Now the fruit of righteousness is sown in peace by those who make peace.

PRIDE PROMOTES STRIFE

4 Where do wars and fights *come* from among you? Do *they* not *come* from your *desires for* pleasure that war in your members? [2]You lust and do not have. You murder and covet and cannot

The Healthy Soul
>Patience

PEACE LOVE JOY KINDNESS

The word *longsuffering* is sometimes translated as *patient* but the word *longsuffering* actually means more than being patient with other people. To be longsuffering is not the absence of anger, but being slow to anger (Psalms 145:8). It means showing an extra measure of mercy and love, being willing to tolerate insults, rejection, and indifference without jumping to conclusions, quickly retaliating, or seeking "quick justice." The main reason for being patient or longsuffering with other people, even those who are tremendously trying and irritating to us, is a hope that the person might recognize his or her own flaws and failures and turn to God for help in becoming more emotionally whole and mature.

God's tremendous compassion is linked to His longsuffering nature, and for us as well, compassion and patience are to be linked. We are to have so much compassion to see other people accept Jesus as their Savior and be freed from their sins that we are patient with them, hoping to encourage them to move one step closer to Christ, rather than to become impatient with them and hinder their spiritual development.

James encouraged Christians to be patient for the Lord to return. They were to have an inner strength and determination to persevere and endure whatever came their way. No matter how much they might be oppressed or persecuted, they were to hold on to their hope that eventually Christ would make certain that any injustice was righted, any lack of respect was reversed, and any mean-spirited behavior from others was punished. (See James 5:7–11.)

made in the similitude of God. [9]Out of the same mouth proceed blessing and cursing. My brethren, these things ought not to be so. [11]Does a spring send forth fresh *water* and bitter from the same opening? [12]Can a fig tree, my brethren, bear olives, or a grapevine bear figs? Thus no spring yields both salt water and fresh.[a]

HEAVENLY VERSUS DEMONIC WISDOM

[13]Who *is* wise and understanding among you? Let him show by good conduct *that* his works *are done* in the meekness of wisdom. [14]But if you have bitter envy and self-seeking in your hearts, do not boast and lie against the truth. [15]This wisdom does not descend from above, but *is*

Righteous Recipes

Chicken and Goat Cheese in Grape Leaves

Ingredients:
- [ ] 4 boneless skinless free-range chicken breasts
- [ ] ½ teaspoon Celtic salt
- [ ] ⅓ teaspoon pepper
- [ ] 6 ounces fresh goat cheese
- [ ] 4 fresh basil leaves
- [ ] 4 fresh sage leaves
- [ ] 8–12 grape leaves in brine
- [ ] 1 garlic clove
- [ ] Sprig of rosemary

Season the chicken breasts with salt and pepper. Spread ¼ of the goat cheese over the top of each piece of chicken. Place 1 basil leaf and 1 sage leaf over each piece of chicken and then wrap each piece with 2–3 grape leaves. Place about 1 inch of water in a large saucepan with a steaming rack. Arrange the wrapped chicken on the steaming rack. Add garlic and rosemary to the water and bring to a boil. Cover and cook over high heat for about 20 minutes, making sure the water doesn't completely evaporate from the pan. Serve with brown rice or another whole grain.

Yield: 4 servings

3:12 [a]NU-Text reads *Neither can a salty spring produce fresh water.*

SCRIPTURE SOLUTIONS

[BACK PAIN]

Back pain is no laughing matter. But, laughing just may do some good for the person who is suffering from back pain! Proverbs 17:22 tells us that "a merry heart does good like medicine, but a broken spirit dries the bones."

Back pain may be triggered by a variety of things, such as a herniated disk; strains, sprains, fractures, and trauma to the spine; and osteoarthritis. If one of these conditions is the cause of your back pain, work with a physician and physical therapist to restore the nerves, muscles, and tendons along your neck and spine.

Spinal pain can be also linked to repressed negative emotion. Here are some emotional conditions that have been directly linked to the severity and longevity of neck and spine pain:

- ☐ Anger or rage
- ☐ Bitterness
- ☐ Disappointment
- ☐ Unforgiveness
- ☐ Humiliation
- ☐ Anxiety
- ☐ Fear
- ☐ Frustration
- ☐ Any other repressed toxic emotion

Although incidents may have happened many years ago, they never go away until they are dealt with in a positive manner. They do not just "disappear" because they are repressed or suppressed. Negative emotions can produce negative physical conditions. The body must find a way of releasing tension and emotional pain. Sometimes that pathway is through pain in the body.

Ask God to help you release emotional pain and forgive others and yourself. It may be the key to major physical relief from tension-related pain in your neck and back.

obtain. You fight and war. Yet[a] you do not have because you do not ask. [3]You ask and do not receive, because you ask amiss, that you may spend *it* on your pleasures. [4]Adulterers and[a] adulteresses! Do you not know that friendship with the world is enmity with God? Whoever therefore wants to be a friend of the world makes himself an enemy of God. [5]Or do you think that the Scripture says in vain, "The Spirit who dwells in us yearns jealously"?

[6]But He gives more grace. Therefore He says:

"God resists the proud,
But gives grace to the humble."[a]

HUMILITY CURES WORLDLINESS

[7]Therefore submit to God. Resist the devil and he will flee from you. [8]Draw near to God and He will draw near to you. Cleanse *your* hands, *you* sinners; and purify *your* hearts, *you* double-minded. [9]Lament and mourn and weep! Let your laughter be turned to mourning and *your* joy to gloom. [10]Humble yourselves in the sight of the Lord, and He will lift you up.

DO NOT JUDGE A BROTHER

[11]Do not speak evil of one another, brethren. He who speaks evil of a brother and judges his brother, speaks evil of the law and judges the law. But if you judge the law, you are not a doer of the law but a judge. [12]There is one Lawgiver,[a] who is able to save and to destroy. Who[b] are you to judge another?[c]

DO NOT BOAST ABOUT TOMORROW

[13]Come now, you who say, "Today or tomorrow we will[a] go to such and such a city, spend a year there, buy and sell, and make a profit"; [14]whereas you do not know what *will happen* tomorrow. For what *is* your life? It is even a vapor that appears for a little time and then vanishes away. [15]Instead you *ought* to say, "If the Lord wills, we shall live and do this or that." [16]But now you boast in your arrogance. All such boasting is evil.

[17]Therefore, to him who knows to do good and does not do *it*, to him it is sin.

RICH OPPRESSORS WILL BE JUDGED

5 Come now, *you* rich, weep and howl for your miseries that are coming upon *you!* [2]Your riches are corrupted, and your garments are moth-eaten. [3]Your gold and silver are corroded, and their corrosion will be a witness against you and will eat your flesh like fire. You have heaped up treasure in the last days. [4]Indeed the wages of the laborers who mowed your fields, which you kept back by fraud, cry out; and the cries of the reapers have reached the ears of the Lord of Sabaoth.[a] [5]You have lived on the earth in pleasure and luxury; you have fattened your hearts as[a] in a day of slaughter. [6]You have condemned, you have murdered the just; he does not resist you.

BE PATIENT AND PERSEVERING

[7]Therefore be patient, brethren, until the coming of the Lord. See *how* the farmer waits for the precious fruit of the earth, waiting pa-

---

4:2 [a]NU-Text and M-Text omit *Yet.*   4:4 [a]NU-Text omits *Adulterers and.*   4:6 [a]Proverbs 3:34   4:12 [a]NU-Text adds *and Judge.*   [b]NU-Text and M-Text read *But who.*   [c]NU-Text reads *a neighbor.*
4:13 [a]M-Text reads *let us.*   5:4 [a]Literally, in Hebrew, *Hosts*   5:5 [a]NU-Text omits *as.*

> (James 5:14, 15)

When You Are Sick. No matter what the source of your sickness—physical, emotional, or spiritual—we are wise to call on those in spiritual authority over us to pray for us. These Bible verses provide a "snapshot" of a major Bible principle—we simply cannot compartmentalize the physical, emotional, and spiritual aspects of our lives. We are intricately bound together body, soul, and spirit. What impacts one area of our lives impacts all other areas. We see this, of course, when finances impact emotions or when a person's spiritual relationship with God impacts his or her choices about behavior.

Since our spiritual natures are at the core of our identities as human beings, the Bible calls on us to seek out *spiritual* help as a first resort—not as a last resort. We must be sure we call on people who will pray for us in the name of Jesus and will pray for us with faith. If there is any root of sin associated with our sickness, including the sin of neglecting to do what is *healthful*, we should be quick to seek God's forgiveness for our sin. Forgiveness frees us up spiritually and emotionally to receive a flow of healing in our bodies.

---

tiently for it until it receives the early and latter rain. ⁸You also be patient. Establish your hearts, for the coming of the Lord is at hand.

⁹Do not grumble against one another, brethren, lest you be condemned.ᵃ Behold, the Judge is standing at the door! ¹⁰My brethren, take the prophets, who spoke in the name of the Lord, as an example of suffering and patience. ¹¹Indeed we count them blessed who endure. You have heard of the perseverance of Job and seen the end *intended by* the Lord—that the Lord is very compassionate and merciful.

¹²But above all, my brethren, do not swear, either by heaven or by earth or with any other oath. But let your "Yes" be "Yes," and *your* "No," "No," lest you fall into judgment.ᵃ

MEETING SPECIFIC NEEDS

¹³Is anyone among you suffering? Let him pray. Is anyone cheerful? Let him sing psalms. ¹⁴Is anyone among you sick? Let him call for the elders of the church, and let them pray over him, anointing him with oil in the name of the Lord. ¹⁵And the prayer of faith will save the sick, and the Lord will raise him up. And if he has committed sins, he will be forgiven. ¹⁶Confess *your* trespassesᵃ to one another, and pray for one another, that you may be healed. The effective, fervent prayer of a righteous man avails much. ¹⁷Elijah was a man with a nature like ours, and he prayed earnestly that it would not rain; and it did not rain on the land for three years and six months. ¹⁸And he prayed again, and the heaven gave rain, and the earth produced its fruit.

BRING BACK THE ERRING ONE

¹⁹Brethren, if anyone among you wanders from the truth, and someone turns him back, ²⁰let him know that he who turns a sinner from the error of his way will save a soulᵃ from death and cover a multitude of sins.

> (James 5:16)

Confession, Healing, and Prayer. This Bible verse presents a critically important biblical principle: first you must *know* that you are sick and in some way must take responsibility for your sickness. You may not have done anything directly to bring a disease upon your body, but you do bear full responsibility for how you behave once you are sick and what you choose to do to get well. You must be willing to take charge of your own health. At times taking charge of your health means that you are willing to visit a doctor!

Second, you must openly acknowledge any aspect of your sickness that may be related to a flaw or failure in your relationships with other people. If you are physically sick because you are harboring negative emotions related to a particular person or group of people, you need to address those emotions. You must seek to deal with the problem at its *root*. When you do, you put yourself into the best possible position for healing.

And third, you must be willing to pray with and to be prayed for by those who truly believe God heals and restores. The person who is in right standing with God and trusts God completely is a person who will pray fervently, and thus, effectively. He *believes* for miracles. When confession, forgiveness, prayer, and faith in God flow freely in a marriage, family, or church, the relationships are stronger. They become "whole." Never underestimate the power of confession, forgiveness, prayer, and faith in God to heal your relationship with your spouse, your children, or those with whom you worship.

5:9 ᵃNU-Text and M-Text read *judged*.   **5:12** ᵃM-Text reads *hypocrisy*.   **5:16** ᵃNU-Text reads *Therefore confess your sins*.   **5:20** ᵃNU-Text reads *his soul*.

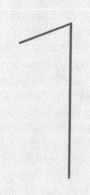

PETER

Peter was writing to a church that was facing imminent persecution. Nobody likes that possibility, then or now. Fear and dread were rampant. Peter believed that the degree of suffering might be limited if believers would do these things: First, put their hope in Jesus Christ and take joy in their salvation; second, take control over their fear and at the same time, recognize that life on earth is temporary; third, submit themselves completely to God even as they yielded to human authorities, and fourth, make sure that they were suffering for doing good, not evil.

Peter gave important principles for submission—in truth, everybody has to submit to somebody! He also pointed out that suffering is part of life— even Christ suffered.

Too often we have expectations that are far too high, not only for ourselves, but for others around us. Perfectionism, fighting against "the system," and allowing fear to run rampant are all major contributors to stress. Don't fall into those traps.

Only Jesus can make us whole. Only Jesus was perfect. Only faith in Jesus can free us from fear. If you are facing a difficult time, work first and foremost on your relationship with Jesus.

GREETING TO THE ELECT PILGRIMS

1 Peter, an apostle of Jesus Christ,

To the pilgrims of the Dispersion in Pontus, Galatia, Cappadocia, Asia, and Bithynia, [2]elect according to the foreknowledge of God the Father, in sanctification of the Spirit, for obedience and sprinkling of the blood of Jesus Christ:

Grace to you and peace be multiplied.

A HEAVENLY INHERITANCE

[3]Blessed *be* the God and Father of our Lord Jesus Christ, who according to His abundant mercy has begotten us again to a living hope through the resurrection of Jesus Christ from the dead, [4]to an inheritance incorruptible and undefiled and that does not fade away, reserved in heaven for you, [5]who are kept by the power of God through faith for salvation ready to be revealed in the last time.

[6]In this you greatly rejoice, though now for a little while, if need be, you have been grieved by various trials, [7]that the genuineness of your faith, *being* much more precious than gold that perishes, though it is tested by fire, may be found to praise, honor, and glory at the revelation of Jesus Christ, [8]whom having not seen[a] you love. Though now you do not see *Him,* yet believing, you rejoice with joy inexpressible and full of glory, [9]receiving the end of your faith—the salvation of *your* souls.

[10]Of this salvation the prophets have inquired and searched carefully, who prophesied of the grace *that would come* to you, [11]searching what, or what manner of time, the Spirit of Christ who was in them was indicating when He testified beforehand the sufferings of Christ and the glories that would follow. [12]To them it was revealed that, not to themselves, but to us[a] they were ministering the things which now have been reported to you through those who have preached the gospel to you by the Holy Spirit sent from heaven—things which angels desire to look into.

LIVING BEFORE GOD OUR FATHER

[13]Therefore gird up the loins of your mind, be sober, and rest *your* hope fully upon the grace that is to be brought to you at the revelation of Jesus Christ; [14]as obedient children, not conforming yourselves to the former lusts, *as* in your ignorance; [15]but as He who called you *is* holy, you also be holy in all *your* conduct, [16]because it is written, "Be holy, for I am holy."[a]

[17]And if you call on the Father, who without partiality judges according to each one's work, conduct yourselves throughout the time of your stay *here* in fear; [18]knowing that you were not redeemed with corruptible things, *like* silver or gold, from your aimless conduct *received* by tradition from your fathers, [19]but with the precious blood of Christ, as of a lamb without blemish and without spot. [20]He indeed was foreordained before the foundation of the world, but was manifest in these last times for you [21]who through Him believe in God, who raised Him from the dead and gave Him glory, so that your faith and hope are in God.

THE ENDURING WORD

[22]Since you have purified your souls in obeying the truth through the Spirit[a] in sincere love of the brethren, love one another fervently with a pure heart, [23]having been born again, not of corruptible seed but incorruptible, through the word of God which lives and abides forever,[a] [24]because

1:8 [a]M-Text reads *known.*   1:12 [a]NU-Text and M-Text read *you.*   1:16 [a]Leviticus 11:44, 45; 19:2; 20:7   1:22 [a]NU-Text omits *through the Spirit.*   1:23 [a]NU-Text omits *forever.*

Get Off the Blood-Sugar Roller Coaster

ULTIMATE HEALTH RESOURCE

The phrases "sugar high" and "sugar low" have become commonplace in our society. Most people, however, don't realize that this roller coaster of highs and lows can have a very negative impact over time.

A "sugar high" generally occurs twenty to thirty minutes after a person eats foods high in sucrose—candy, soda pop, juice drinks, ice cream, cookies, cake, pie, sugared cereals, and other sugar-rich foods. When sucrose hits the liver, the liver releases hormones that cause the pancreas to release a dose of insulin in sufficient quantity to deal with the amount of sucrose in the body. The insulin breaks the sucrose down into chemicals that give energy to the body, and then the remainder of the sucrose is stored in fat cells.

After this surge of chemicals—mainly adrenaline and cortisol—the body goes into a lull so the liver and various endocrine glands might recover. The person experiencing a "sugar low" is likely to feel tired, lethargic, and even shaky. To remedy these feelings, the person is likely to reach for yet another sugar-rich food, which starts the process over again.

Over time, this pattern creates a general depletion of insulin and a resistance to the hormones released by the liver. The entire body begins to suffer at that point. Type 2 diabetes may result, along with increased damage to the heart, cardiovascular system, and the cells throughout the body.

How can a person get off this roller coaster?

First, replace sucrose-laden foods with fresh fruit. Have some *whole* fruits first thing in the morning, such as pineapple, grapefruit, berries, melon, or banana. If you are craving something sweet later in the day, reach for an apple or have a small bowl of fruit salad (made from cut-up whole fruits).

Second, have a portion of protein every three hours you are awake, beginning with breakfast. A protein portion might be an egg; a half cup of nonfat yogurt or a half cup of nonfat cottage cheese; a small protein-powder drink; three to four ounces of poultry, meat, or fish; or a cup of beans (*not* baked with sugar).

Third, eat lots of whole grains and vegetables. These complex carbohydrates release themselves more slowly into the bloodstream.

Fourth, drink sufficient pure water to flush toxins from the body—a minimum of eight to ten glasses a day.

By cutting out sugar and eating five to six small protein-rich meals a day, a person almost always finds that he or she has greater sustained energy throughout the day, is able to think more clearly, and over time, has fewer cravings for sweets. It may take a few months to see major health changes, but if you will stick with this plan, those changes nearly always become evident.

God created Adam and Eve to "graze" through the Garden of Eden, eating whole fruits, vegetables, nuts, and seeds as they found them. They "harvested" Eden's produce and lived in divine health, eating whole, fresh foods grown in an unpolluted environment. We would be wise to come as close to their Eden lifestyle as possible.

"All flesh is as grass,
And all the glory of man[a] as the flower of the grass.
The grass withers,
And its flower falls away,
25 But the word of the LORD endures forever."[a]

Now this is the word which by the gospel was preached to you.

2 Therefore, laying aside all malice, all deceit, hypocrisy, envy, and all evil speaking, [2]as newborn babes, desire the pure milk of the word, that you may grow thereby,[a] [3]if indeed you have tasted that the Lord *is* gracious.

THE CHOSEN STONE AND HIS CHOSEN PEOPLE

[4]Coming to Him *as to* a living stone, rejected indeed by men, but chosen by God *and* precious, [5]you also, as living stones, are being built up a spiritual house, a holy priesthood, to offer up spiritual sacrifices acceptable to God through Jesus Christ. [6]Therefore it is also contained in the Scripture,

"Behold, I lay in Zion
A chief cornerstone, elect, precious,
And he who believes on Him will by no means be put to shame."[a]

1:24 [a]NU-Text reads *all its glory.*   1:25 [a]Isaiah 40:6–8   2:2 [a]NU-Text adds *up to salvation.*   2:6 [a]Isaiah 28:16

⁷Therefore, to you who believe, *He is* precious; but to those who are disobedient,ᵃ

"The stone which the builders rejected
Has become the chief cornerstone,"ᵇ

⁸and

"A stone of stumbling
And a rock of offense."ᵃ

They stumble, being disobedient to the word, to which they also were appointed.
⁹But you *are* a chosen generation, a royal priesthood, a holy nation, His own special people, that you may proclaim the praises of Him who called you out of darkness into His marvelous light; ¹⁰who once *were* not a people but *are* now the people of God, who had not obtained mercy but now have obtained mercy.

LIVING BEFORE THE WORLD

¹¹Beloved, I beg *you* as sojourners and pilgrims, abstain from fleshly lusts which war against the soul, ¹²having your conduct honorable among the Gentiles, that when they speak against you as evildoers, they may, by *your* good works which they observe, glorify God in the day of visitation.

SUBMISSION TO GOVERNMENT

¹³Therefore submit yourselves to every ordinance of man for the Lord's sake, whether to the king as supreme, ¹⁴or to governors, as to those who are sent by him for the punishment of evildoers and *for the* praise of those who do good. ¹⁵For this is the will of God, that by doing good you may put to silence the ignorance of foolish men— ¹⁶as free, yet not using liberty as a cloak for vice, but as bondservants of

R̶x PRESCRIPTIONS
FOR INNER HEALTH

"Pleasant words are like a honeycomb,
Sweetness to the soul and health to the bones."

(PROVERBS 16:24)

You are the main recipient of your own tone of voice! If you speak words that are true and wise, and in a tone of voice that is pleasant and cheerful, you will begin to have an *attitude* of joyful serenity. Those who live in peace and joy enjoy not only greater emotional health, but also better physical health.

God. ¹⁷Honor all *people.* Love the brotherhood. Fear God. Honor the king.

SUBMISSION TO MASTERS

¹⁸Servants, *be* submissive to *your* masters with all fear, not only to the good and gentle, but also to the harsh. ¹⁹For this *is* commendable, if because of conscience toward God one endures grief, suffering

> (1 Peter 2:17)

Less-Stress Relationships. The apostle Paul gave a simple four-point formula for getting along with other people in a way that greatly reduces stress.

1. Honor all people—respect the dignity of other people and value them as beloved creations of God. Even if others hurt you, forgive them and release them to God for His chastisement and love.
2. Love the brotherhood. Be generous in your giving to fellow Christians—go beyond respect to help them carry their emotional burdens. Be forgiving and kind, helping others through your practical assistance as well as the administration of your spiritual gifts.

3. Fear God. Honor and worship God as your supreme King. Continually offer thanksgiving and praise because you have great awe, appreciation, and respect for God as your loving heavenly Father, not because you live in fear (dread) of His judgment.
4. Honor the king. Obey the laws of the land.

So much stress would be eliminated in our world if we each would do these four things! So many negative emotions are linked to the way we respond to fellow believers, authority figures in our lives, other people, and God. To live with less stress, try the New Testament way of relating to other people.

INSIGHTS INTO THE WORD

walking the walk

[DON'T FORGET TO STRETCH]

Stretching is essential for injury-free walking and exercise.

☐ Walk for about five minutes before stretching. This warms up the body and muscles. It is easier to stretch a warm rubber band than a cold one, so, too, with muscles.

☐ Always stretch lightly and gently, especially at the beginning, to avoid pulling or harming the muscle.

☐ Always breathe while you're stretching, as it provides oxygen to the muscles.

Following are some key stretches for walkers. Do these stretches at the beginning of your walk, and also at the end.

1. *Calf Stretch*
Stand at arm's length from the wall.
Lean into the wall, bracing yourself with your arms.
Place one leg forward, bent at the knee.
Extend the other leg back for the stretch, with knee straight and heel down.
Keep your back straight and move your hips toward the wall until you feel a stretch.
Hold 30 seconds.
Relax.
Repeat with other leg.

2. *Hip Stretch*
Stand up and take a half step back with your right foot.
Bend your left knee as you shift your weight back to your right hip.
While keeping your right leg straight, bend your body forward more and reach with your arms down your right leg.
Hold 20–30 seconds.
Relax.
Repeat with other leg. CONT. NEXT PAGE>>>

---

wrongfully. [20]For what credit *is it* if, when you are beaten for your faults, you take it patiently? But when you do good and suffer, if you take it patiently, this *is* commendable before God. [21]For to this you were called, because Christ also suffered for us,[a] leaving us[b] an example, that you should follow His steps:

[22] "Who committed no sin,
Nor was deceit found in His mouth";[a]

[23]who, when He was reviled, did not revile in return; when He suffered, He did not threaten, but committed *Himself* to Him who judges righteously; [24]who Himself bore our sins in His own body on the tree, that we, having died to sins, might live for righteousness—by whose stripes you were healed. [25]For you were like sheep going astray, but have now returned to the Shepherd and Overseer[a] of your souls.

SUBMISSION TO HUSBANDS

3 Wives, likewise, *be* submissive to your own husbands, that even if some do not obey the word, they, without a word, may be won by the conduct of their wives, [2]when they observe your chaste conduct *accompanied* by fear. [3]Do not let your adornment be *merely* outward—arranging the hair, wearing gold, or putting on *fine* apparel—[4]rather *let it be* the hidden person of the heart, with the incorruptible *beauty* of a gentle and quiet spirit, which is very precious in the sight of God. [5]For in this manner, in former times, the holy women who trusted in God also adorned themselves, being submissive to their own husbands, [6]as Sarah obeyed Abraham, calling him lord, whose daughters you are if you do good and are not afraid with any terror.

A WORD TO HUSBANDS

[7]Husbands, likewise, dwell with *them* with understanding, giving honor to the wife, as to the weaker vessel, and as *being* heirs together of the grace of life, that your prayers may not be hindered.

CALLED TO BLESSING

[8]Finally, all *of you be* of one mind, having compassion for one another; love as brothers, *be* tenderhearted, *be* courteous;[a] [9]not returning evil for evil or reviling for reviling, but on the contrary blessing, knowing that you were called to this, that you may inherit a blessing. [10]For

"He who would love life
And see good days,
Let him refrain his tongue from evil,
And his lips from speaking deceit.
[11] Let him turn away from evil and do good;
Let him seek peace and pursue it.
[12] For the eyes of the LORD are on the righteous,
And His ears are open to their prayers;
But the face of the LORD is against those who do evil."[a]

SUFFERING FOR RIGHT AND WRONG

[13]And who *is* he who will harm you if you become followers of what is good? [14]But even if you should suffer for righteousness' sake, *you are*

2:21 [a]NU-Text reads *you.* [b]NU-Text and M-Text read *you.*   **2:22** [a]Isaiah 53:9   **2:25** [a]Greek *Episkopos*   **3:8** [a]NU-Text reads *humble.*   **3:12** [a]Psalm 34:12–16

344   DIVINE HEALTH

3. *Quadriceps Stretch*

Stand up straight, holding on to a wall for support if necessary.

Standing on your right leg, bend your left knee behind your right leg and grasp your left foot with your hand, gently pulling the heel toward your buttocks.

Stand up straight pushing your knee gently back as far as you can. (*Note:* Your hand is only there to hold the heel in proper position.)

It may be easier to hold this stretch using the hand from the opposite side.

Hold 20–30 seconds.

Relax.

Repeat with other leg.

In addition, even if you are not walking or working out, stretching is excellent for relaxation, flexibility, and good health. Try spending thirty minutes to an hour just stretching.

☐ Move through your whole body, stretching all muscle groups.

☐ Hold each stretch for 30 seconds.

☐ Relax and breathe while you're stretching.

blessed. "And do not be afraid of their threats, nor be troubled."[a] [15]But sanctify the Lord God[a] in your hearts, and always *be* ready to *give* a defense to everyone who asks you a reason for the hope that is in you, with meekness and fear; [16]having a good conscience, that when they defame you as evildoers, those who revile your good conduct in Christ may be ashamed. [17]For *it is* better, if it is the will of God, to suffer for doing good than for doing evil.

CHRIST'S SUFFERING AND OURS

[18]For Christ also suffered once for sins, the just for the unjust, that He might bring us[a] to God, being put to death in the flesh but made alive by the Spirit, [19]by whom also He went and preached to the spirits in prison, [20]who formerly were disobedient, when once the Divine longsuffering waited[a] in the days of Noah, while *the* ark was being prepared, in which a few, that is, eight souls, were saved through water. [21]There is also an antitype which now saves us—baptism (not the removal of the filth of the flesh, but the answer of a good conscience toward God), through the resurrection of Jesus Christ, [22]who has gone into heaven and is at the right hand of God, angels and authorities and powers having been made subject to Him.

SCRIPTURE SOLUTIONS

[HIGH BLOOD PRESSURE]

A poor lifestyle—including improper nutrition, lack of exercise, and stress—is the main contributor to high blood pressure for most people. Many people, however, do not know that they have high blood pressure until it is in an advanced stage. At that point, it can be much more difficult to treat. Normal blood pressure is considered to be 120/80. Any blood pressure reading that is 140 or higher for the "top" number and 90 or higher for the bottom number is considered high blood pressure.

Take a look over the following risk factors to see if you are a possible candidate for high blood pressure.

Genetics. What does your family tree indicate? Do you know if your parents or grandparents had high blood pressure? You have a great chance of developing hypertension if either of your parents had hypertension. If only one parent had it, your chances are 25 percent. If both suffered from high blood pressure, your risk is 60 percent.

Sex and Age. Men and women are different in this. Men have the greatest risk of developing hypertension before the age of fifty, and women after the age of fifty. Regardless of their specific sex or age, all people have a greater chance of developing hypertension as they get older.

Race. African Americans will develop hypertension two to one over Caucasians. Mexicans, Cubans, and Puerto Ricans have an elevated chance as well.

Gender, age, and race cannot be changed but other factors that contribute to hypertension can! The conditions below are directly related to increased risk for high blood pressure:

☐ Obesity   ☐ Poor nutrition

☐ General inactivity   ☐ Excessive use of alcohol

☐ Smoking   ☐ Lack of exercise

The sooner you discover hypertension and get it under control, the better.

3:14 [a]Isaiah 8:12   3:15 [a]NU-Text reads *Christ as Lord.*   3:18 [a]NU-Text and M-Text read *you.*   3:20 [a]NU-Text and M-Text read *when the longsuffering of God waited patiently.*

GODLY & GOODLOOKIN'

A Sight to Behold

A mirror is a wonderful tool, but in order to fix what might need fixing in your appearance, you need to be able to see into that mirror with good eyesight! There are several things you can do to increase the health of your eyes and improve your eyesight:

- ☐ Avoid foods with monosodium glutamate (MSG). This additive has been proven to cause glaucoma.
- ☐ Eat foods high in vitamin C, E, and bioflavonoids to have healthier blood vessels and to prevent their breakage. Fatty fish and omega-3 fats are vital for healthy blood vessels, including the blood vessels in the eye.
- ☐ Beta-carotene is an important nutrient for eye health. Vitamin E will help the body absorb and use beta-carotene more effectively.
- ☐ Eat more greens—for example, spinach, kale, and collard greens. (Don't take beta-carotene supplements, however, at the same time you eat these foods. They don't mix well in the body when consumed at the same time.)
- ☐ Protect your eyes from the sun. The eyeball can become sunburned in the same way skin becomes sunburned, and too many ultraviolet rays can cause damage to the inner eye.

Make a quick adjustment in your nutrients for the sake of your eyes, and you'll be able to take maximum advantage of a good mirror!

4 Therefore, since Christ suffered for
us[a] in the flesh, arm yourselves also
with the same mind, for he who has
suffered in the flesh has ceased from sin, [2]that
he no longer should live the rest of *his* time in
the flesh for the lusts of men, but for the will
of God. [3]For we *have spent* enough of our past
lifetime[a] in doing the will of the Gentiles—
when we walked in lewdness, lusts, drunkenness, revelries, drinking parties, and abominable idolatries. [4]In regard to these, they
think it strange that you do not run with *them*
in the same flood of dissipation, speaking evil
of *you.* [5]They will give an account to Him who
is ready to judge the living and the dead. [6]For
this reason the gospel was preached also to
those who are dead, that they might be judged according to men in the flesh, but live according to God in the spirit.

SERVING FOR GOD'S GLORY

[7]But the end of all things is at hand; therefore be serious and watchful in your prayers.
[8]And above all things have fervent love for
one another, for "love will cover a multitude of
sins."[a] [9]*Be* hospitable to one another without
grumbling. [10]As each one has received a gift,
minister it to one another, as good stewards
of the manifold grace of God. [11]If anyone
speaks, *let him speak* as the oracles of God. If
anyone ministers, *let him do it* as with the ability which God supplies, that in all things God may be glorified through Jesus Christ, to whom belong the glory and the dominion forever and ever. Amen.

SUFFERING FOR GOD'S GLORY

[12]Beloved, do not think it strange concerning the fiery trial which is to try you, as though some strange thing happened to you;
[13]but rejoice to the extent that you partake of Christ's sufferings, that when His glory is revealed, you may also be glad with exceeding joy. [14]If
you are reproached for the name of Christ, blessed *are you,* for the Spirit of glory and of God rests upon you.[a] On their part He is blasphemed, but on your part He is glorified. [15]But let none
of you suffer as a murderer, a thief, an evildoer, or as a busybody in other people's matters. [16]Yet if *anyone suffers* as
a Christian, let him not be ashamed, but let him glorify God in this matter.[a]
[17]For the time *has come* for judgment to be-

WISE CHOICES

Choose activity over inactivity.
Even minor activity burns calories and adds to general strength and vitality. Take the stairs instead of the elevator. Park a little farther from the front door of an office building, church, mall, or store. Get up and change the channel instead of using the remote!

4:1 [a]NU-Text omits *for us.* 4:3 [a]NU-Text reads *time.* 4:8 [a]Proverbs 10:12 4:14 [a]NU-Text omits the rest of this verse. 4:16 [a]NU-Text reads *name.*

gin at the house of God; and if *it begins* with us first, what will *be* the end of those who do not obey the gospel of God? [18]Now

> "If the righteous one is scarcely saved,
> Where will the ungodly and the sinner appear?"[a]

[19]Therefore let those who suffer according to the will of God commit their souls *to Him* in doing good, as to a faithful Creator.

SHEPHERD THE FLOCK

5 The elders who are among you I exhort, I who am a fellow elder and a witness of the sufferings of Christ, and also a partaker of the glory that will be revealed: [2]Shepherd the flock of God which is among you, serving as overseers, not by compulsion but willingly,[a] not for dishonest gain but eagerly; [3]nor as being lords over those entrusted to you, but being examples to the flock; [4]and when the Chief Shepherd appears, you will receive the crown of glory that does not fade away.

SUBMIT TO GOD, RESIST THE DEVIL

[5]Likewise you younger people, submit yourselves to *your* elders. Yes, all of *you* be submissive to one another, and be clothed with humility, for

> "God resists the proud,
> But gives grace to the humble."[a]

[6]Therefore humble yourselves under the mighty hand of God, that He may exalt you in due time, [7]casting all your care upon Him, for He cares for you.

[8]Be sober, be vigilant; because[a] your adversary the devil walks about like a roaring lion, seeking whom he may devour. [9]Resist him, steadfast in the faith, knowing that the same sufferings are experienced by your brotherhood in the world. [10]But may[a] the God of all grace, who called us[b] to His eternal glory by Christ Jesus, after you have suffered a while, perfect, establish, strengthen, and settle *you.* [11]To Him *be* the glory and the dominion forever and ever. Amen.

FAREWELL AND PEACE

[12]By Silvanus, our faithful brother as I consider him, I have written to you briefly, exhorting and testifying that this is the true grace of God in which you stand.

[13]She who is in Babylon, elect together with *you,* greets you; and *so does* Mark my son. [14]Greet one another with a kiss of love.

Peace to you all who are in Christ Jesus. Amen.

4:18 [a]Proverbs 11:31   5:2 [a]NU-Text adds *according to God.*   5:5 [a]Proverbs 3:34   5:8 [a]NU-Text and M-Text omit *because.*   5:10 [a]NU-Text reads *But the God of all grace . . . will perfect, establish, strengthen, and settle you.*   [b]NU-Text and M-Text read *you.*

PETER

Peter in his second letter addressed a major principle that is as important for us today as it was for those facing Roman persecution. He said, in essence, forces from within can be just as dangerous in destroying you as forces from without. He warned the believers of "false prophets amongst the people," "false teachers among you," and that "many will follow these destructive ways." He admonished the church to stir up pure minds that were steeped in the words of holy prophets, and to be on the lookout for "scoffers" who would come to use the church for their personal ambitions of fame, power, and wealth.

We know in the health world that the majority of people who die in the United States each year die primarily of longstanding bad health habits, including overeating, smoking, the intake of toxins, and a failure to give our bodies the nutrients they need. We die more from "forces within" than from epidemics that are viral or bacterial, or from accidents. Be mindful of what you are doing to harm yourself, even as you are mindful of the potentially harmful forces and people around you.

GREETING THE FAITHFUL

1 Simon Peter, a bondservant and apostle of Jesus Christ,

To those who have obtained like precious faith with us by the righteousness of our God and Savior Jesus Christ:

²Grace and peace be multiplied to you in the knowledge of God and of Jesus our Lord, ³as His divine power has given to us all things that *pertain* to life and godliness, through the knowledge of Him who called us by glory and virtue, ⁴by which have been given to us exceedingly great and precious promises, that through these you may be partakers of the divine nature, having escaped the corruption *that is* in the world through lust.

FRUITFUL GROWTH IN THE FAITH

⁵But also for this very reason, giving all diligence, add to your faith virtue, to virtue knowledge, ⁶to knowledge self-control, to self-control perseverance, to perseverance godliness, ⁷to godliness brotherly kindness, and to brotherly kindness love. ⁸For if these things are yours and abound, *you* *will be* neither barren nor unfruitful in the knowledge of our Lord Jesus Christ. ⁹For he who lacks these things is shortsighted, even to blindness, and has forgotten that he was cleansed from his old sins.

¹⁰Therefore, brethren, be even more diligent to make your call and election sure, for if you do these things you will never stumble; ¹¹for so an entrance will be supplied to you abundantly into the everlasting kingdom of our Lord and Savior Jesus Christ.

> (2 Peter 1:5–7)

More and More Whole. The New Testament repeatedly assures us that God desires us to become more and more whole. There's an upward progression to our becoming more Christlike. God does not want us to be without faith, which is the most important attribute of our inner life. But He wants us to add good works and good character to our faith.

He also desires that we understand His ways and principles and that we seek to apply them to our lives in a way that produces self-control. We are to endure in our pursuit of wholeness and to continually seek to do the godly thing, always with an attitude of kindness and deep brotherly love. If you want a definition of emotional and spiritual wholeness, these few verses in 2 Peter provide them! The "whole" person has faith, virtue (good character), knowledge, self-control, a persevering spirit, godly motives, kind behavior, unselfish generosity, and love.

INSIGHTS | **INTO THE WORD**

OVERCOMING OBSTINATE OBSTACLES • OVERCOMING OBSTINATE OBSTACLES • OVERCOMING OBSTINATE OBSTACLES

At the core of most people with a wounded spirit are deep hurts that are usually the result of feeling rejected, abandoned, or abused. It's normal to feel emotionally wounded when others openly exclude us, mistreat us, or leave us. A wounded spirit becomes chronic when we continue to dwell on our pain and to rehearse repeatedly what a person said or did that was so hurtful to us. These rehearsals of the past bring back the emotions felt at the time of the wounding. When we continue to dwell mentally on what was done to us, we develop a habit of pricking our heart again and again with a painful memory.

A person who repeatedly inflicts harm on himself or herself physically, needs psychological help. If you are repeatedly inflicting harm on yourself emotionally by replaying hurtful memories, you also need help! Seek out someone who can counsel you, pray with you, or help you begin to heal from your emotional wounds.

One of the things that many have found helpful in the healing process is to write down as fully as possible exactly what happened and the resulting feelings. Then, seal up this statement and put it in a safety deposit box. There's release for the emotions in knowing that the "truth has been told," even if that statement is never read again.

Other people find it very helpful is to take symbolic action that "separates" them from the person. For example, write the person's name and what he or she did, put the paper in a bottle, cork the bottle, and cast it off a bridge into the ocean. Or, carve the person's name onto a stick and bury the stick at the end of a walk in a forest. As you perform this "separating act," you might say aloud: "I am removing you and all the bad memories associated with you from my life." Even if you must have contact from time to time with an abuser or someone who has hurt or rejected you, you perform a symbolic action of separation for the wrong committed against you.

Finally, make a conscious decision that you will *not* continue to rehearse the hurtful memories of the past. A very simple way to help with this is to wear a rubber band around your wrist and intentionally choose to snap that rubber band each time you bring up the offender's name in conversation or even as his or her name or image comes to your mind. This is not a form of punishing or hurting yourself—it is a means of gaining self-awareness about how many times you are rehearsing a painful memory. Each time you snap the rubber band, say: "I will *not* think about this again." Then, immediately change the focus of your thinking or the topic of your conversation. Focus on a new idea that takes your full concentration.

PETER'S APPROACHING DEATH

[12]For this reason I will not be negligent to remind you always of these things, though you know and are established in the present truth. [13]Yes, I think it is right, as long as I am in this tent, to stir you up by reminding *you*, [14]knowing that shortly I *must* put off my tent, just as our Lord Jesus Christ showed me. [15]Moreover I will be careful to ensure that you always have a reminder of these things after my decease.

THE TRUSTWORTHY PROPHETIC WORD

[16]For we did not follow cunningly devised fables when we made known to you the power and coming of our Lord Jesus Christ, but were eyewitnesses of His majesty. [17]For He received from God the Father honor and glory when such a voice came to Him from the Excellent Glory: "This is My beloved Son, in whom I am well pleased." [18]And we heard this voice which came from heaven when we were with Him on the holy mountain.

[19]And so we have the prophetic word confirmed,ᵃ which you do well to heed as a light that shines in a dark place, until the day dawns and the morning star rises in your hearts; [20]knowing this first, that no prophecy of Scripture is of any private interpretation,ᵃ [21]for prophecy never came by the will of man, but holy men of Godᵃ spoke *as they were* moved by the Holy Spirit.

> **Q** According to Jesus, what kept His disciples from being able to cast out the demons from an epileptic boy—a boy who often fell into the fire and the water?
>
> **A** Their unbelief *(Matthew 17:20).*

1:19 ᵃOr *We also have the more sure prophetic word.*   1:20 ᵃOr *origin*   1:21 ᵃNU-Text reads *but men spoke from God.*

Righteous Recipes

Mediterranean Stuffed Eggplant

Ingredients:

- ☐ 1 eggplant, halved lengthwise
- ☐ 4 tablespoons extra-virgin olive oil
- ☐ ½ cup chopped onion
- ☐ 1 garlic clove, minced
- ☐ 1 can (16 ounces) diced tomatoes, drained, liquid reserved
- ☐ 2 tablespoons whole-wheat flour
- ☐ ½ teaspoon oregano or marjoram
- ☐ ⅓ teaspoon freshly ground pepper
- ☐ ⅛ teaspoon Celtic salt
- ☐ ½ cup feta cheese or drained cottage cheese

Scoop the pulp from the eggplant, leaving ½-inch shells; chop the pulp and set aside. Place the shells in a microwave-safe dish; microwave on high for 8 minutes or until tender. Heat the olive oil in a skillet over medium heat. Sauté the eggplant pulp, onion, and garlic in the hot oil for 5 to 10 minutes or until tender. Remove from heat. Add enough water to the tomato liquid to make 1 cup and place in a saucepan over medium heat; add the flour and whisk to combine. Cook for 5 minutes or until thickened, whisking frequently. Add the flour mixture and drained tomatoes to the eggplant mixture; mix well. Stir in the oregano, pepper, and salt. Place the eggplant shells cut side up on a baking sheet. Fill with the eggplant mixture. Top with feta cheese. Bake at 350 degrees for 30 minutes or until lightly browned and bubbly.

Yield: 4 servings

WALKING THE WALK

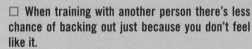

[TRAINING WITH OTHERS]

Do you usually walk alone or with another person or a team? Have you ever considered participating in a 5K, 10K, or half- or full marathon? That's a good time to begin training with other people.

Training with someone else for a purpose or goal will help keep you on a committed training schedule and you'll be less likely to slack off. Here are some reasons:

- ☐ When training with another person there's less chance of backing out just because you don't feel like it.
- ☐ If you train for an event or race, then you have a goal that keeps you motivated.
- ☐ Walking with others provides emotional support. If one is weak, then another is strong—that's teamwork!

DESTRUCTIVE DOCTRINES

2 But there were also false prophets among the people, even as there will be false teachers among you, who will secretly bring in destructive heresies, even denying the Lord who bought them, *and* bring on themselves swift destruction. ²And many will follow their destructive ways, because of whom the way of truth will be blasphemed. ³By covetousness they will exploit you with deceptive words; for a long time their judgment has not been idle, and their destruction does[a] not slumber.

DOOM OF FALSE TEACHERS

⁴For if God did not spare the angels who sinned, but cast *them* down to hell and delivered *them* into chains of darkness, to be reserved for judgment; ⁵and did not spare the ancient world, but saved Noah, *one of eight people,* a preacher of righteousness, bringing in the flood on the world of the ungodly; ⁶and turning the cities of Sodom and Gomorrah

2:3 [a]M-Text reads *will not.*

WEIGHING Less & ENJOYING LIFE More!

[Two Basic Questions to Ask]

Many people find that when they are overweight, they engage in what might be called "mindless eating." They eat without really *thinking* about what they are putting into their bodies. One chip after another—and pretty soon, the bag is empty. One cookie after another—and pretty soon, the cookie jar is empty.

Ask yourself two basic questions about what you eat and drink:

1. *Why do I eat (or drink) this?* Most of what we eat flows from ill-founded, unwise, and mostly unconscious food choices. In some cases, we are the victims of bad habits we learned in childhood. In other cases, we have "good memories" associated with foods we might call "comfort foods"—most of which are loaded with fat or are based on white-flour pastas, white-sugar desserts, or white-cream sauces.
2. *Would Jesus eat this?* Most of what we eat in a given day may *not* be what Jesus would have eaten if He were walking in our shoes.

The more you become conscious of what you eat, and the more you seek to eat the kinds of foods Jesus ate, the more you will find yourself making good food choices that can lead to your enjoying better health and having more energy!

---

into ashes, condemned *them* to destruction, making *them* an example to those who afterward would live ungodly; [7]and delivered righteous Lot, *who was* oppressed by the filthy conduct of the wicked [8](for that righteous man, dwelling among them, tormented *his* righteous soul from day to day by seeing and hearing *their* lawless deeds)— [9]then the Lord knows how to deliver the godly out of temptations and to reserve the unjust under punishment for the day of judgment, [10]and especially those who walk according to the flesh in the lust of uncleanness and despise authority. *They are* presumptuous, self-willed. They are not afraid to speak evil of dignitaries, [11]whereas angels, who are greater in power and might, do not bring a reviling accusation against them before the Lord.

DEPRAVITY OF FALSE TEACHERS

[12]But these, like natural brute beasts made to be caught and destroyed, speak evil of the things they do not understand, and will utterly perish in their own corruption, [13]*and* will receive the wages of unrighteousness, *as* those who count it pleasure to carouse in the daytime. *They are* spots and blemishes, carousing in their own deceptions while they feast with you, [14]having eyes full of adultery and that cannot cease from sin, enticing unstable souls. *They have* a heart trained in covetous practices, *and are* accursed children. [15]They have forsaken the right way and gone astray, following the way of Balaam the *son of* Beor, who loved the wages of unrighteousness; [16]but he was rebuked for his iniquity: a dumb donkey speaking with a man's voice restrained the madness of the prophet.

[17]These are wells without water, clouds[a] carried by a tempest, for whom is reserved the blackness of darkness forever.[b]

DECEPTIONS OF FALSE TEACHERS

[18]For when they speak great swelling *words* of emptiness, they allure through the lusts of the flesh, through lewdness, the ones who have actually escaped[a] from those who live in error. [19]While they promise them liberty, they themselves are slaves of corruption; for by whom a person is overcome, by him also he is brought into bondage. [20]For if, after they have escaped the pollutions of the world through the knowledge of the Lord and Savior Jesus Christ, they are again entangled in them and overcome, the latter end is worse for them than the beginning. [21]For it would have been better for them not to have known the way of righteousness, than having known *it,* to turn from the holy commandment delivered to them. [22]But it has happened to them according to the true proverb: "A dog returns to his own vomit,"[a] and, "a sow, having washed, to her wallowing in the mire."

GOD'S PROMISE IS NOT SLACK

3 Beloved, I now write to you this second epistle (in *both of* which I stir up your pure minds by way of reminder), [2]that you may be mindful of the words which were spoken before by the holy prophets, and of the commandment of us,[a] the apostles of the Lord and Savior, [3]knowing this first: that scoffers will come in the last days, walking according to their own lusts, [4]and saying, "Where is the promise of His coming? For since the fathers fell asleep, all things continue as *they were* from the beginning of creation." [5]For this they willfully forget: that by the word of God the heavens were of old, and the earth standing out of water and in the water, [6]by which the world *that* then existed perished, being flooded with water. [7]But the heavens and the earth *which* are now preserved by the same word, are reserved for fire until the day of judgment and perdition of ungodly men.

2:17 [a]NU-Text reads *and mists.* [b]NU-Text omits *forever.* 2:18 [a]NU-Text reads *are barely escaping.* 2:22 [a]Proverbs 26:11 3:2 [a]NU-Text and M-Text read *commandment of the apostles of your Lord and Savior* or *commandment of your apostles of the Lord and Savior.*

[8]But, beloved, do not forget this one thing, that with the Lord one day *is* as a thousand years, and a thousand years as one day. [9]The Lord is not slack concerning *His* promise, as some count slackness, but is longsuffering toward us,[a] not willing that any should perish but that all should come to repentance.

THE DAY OF THE LORD

[10]But the day of the Lord will come as a thief in the night, in which the heavens will pass away with a great noise, and the elements will melt with fervent heat; both the earth and the works that are in it will be burned up.[a] [11]Therefore, since all these things will be dissolved, what

Stress Busters
Exhale Your Stress!

Most people take breathing for granted. They rarely think about breathing. The practice of deep breathing is an intentional process—it is breathing with a mental focus and discipline. The good news is that deep breathing is one of the easiest to learn, simplest, and best ways to decrease muscle tension and relieve stress.

There are two main types of breathing: chest breathing (or thoracic breathing), and abdominal breathing (diaphragmatic breathing). As infants, we are abdominal breathers. Our abdominal muscles force air out of our lungs and contract to allow air to enter our lungs. This is the normal pattern for both babies and sleeping adults. As we grow up, however, most of us become chest breathers. We begin to use our shoulder and upper chest muscles to contract and expand our lungs.

In times of stress, a person typically breathes faster and shallower. An extremely anxious person may have a habit of rapid shallow chest breathing, which can make a person prone to both holding his breath and hyperventilating. The result is that an insignificant amount of air enters the lungs and the blood does not become adequately oxygenated. Blood vessels constrict. The brain, therefore, does not get enough oxygen and heart rate increases. Muscles begin to tense and the individual generally feels shaky, light-headed, and may even feel a little nauseated. The condition may turn into a full-blown panic attack or headache. Very often people who develop this breathing habit in their lives are prone to greater generalized anxiety, phobias, fatigue, and depression.

While chest breathing is associated with stress, abdominal breathing is associated with relaxation. To find out if you are a chest or abdominal breather, simply lie on your back and place your right hand on your abdomen at your waistline (or on your belly button). Then place your left hand on the center of your chest. Now simply breathe normally and notice which hand rises more when you inhale. For most people, the hand on their chest will rise more. This means you are a chest breather. If the hand on your abdomen rises more, you are an abdominal breather.

To become an abdominal breather you need to learn how to control your diaphragm. The diaphragm is a dome-shaped muscle that separates the chest cavity from the abdominal cavity. As you inhale, the diaphragm flattens downward, allowing the lungs more space to fill. By intentionally flattening this muscle, a person allows more oxygen into the body and more carbon dioxide out of the body. To do this, lie on your back on a bed, carpet, or futon. Put your legs straight out and mildly apart, with your toes pointed outward. Place one hand on your abdomen over the belly button and the other hand at the center of your chest. Slowly inhale through your nose and make sure the hand on the abdomen rises—intentionally push out the diaphragm muscle—and the hand on the chest moves only a little. As you inhale through your nose, count, "One thousand one, one thousand two, one thousand three." As you exhale through your mouth, count, "One thousand one, one thousand two, one thousand three." You should feel your abdomen falling as you exhale.

Continue breathing this way for five minutes. Eventually you may want to work up to ten to twenty minutes, one to two times a day. With practice, you will be able to inhale and exhale using abdominal breathing standing or sitting.

Begin to breathe in this way every time you sense your muscles are becoming tense or you are feeling stressed.

3:9 [a]NU-Text reads *you*.   3:10 [a]NU-Text reads *laid bare* (literally *found*).

Whole-Person Exercise

Bible Health + Food Facts

Exercise, purely defined, means to put something into effect—to use something in order to develop it or experience benefit from it. We use our muscles, hearts, and lungs to produce fitness. We use our minds to grow in knowledge, understanding, and wisdom. We use our emotions to address and resolve problems and produce personal and community justice. We use our spiritual strength to prepare ourselves for eternal life. Every aspect of our beings can and should be exercised to its maximum potential!

manner *of persons* ought you to be in holy conduct and godliness, [12]looking for and hastening the coming of the day of God, because of which the heavens will be dissolved, being on fire, and the elements will melt with fervent heat? [13]Nevertheless we, according to His promise, look for new heavens and a new earth in which righteousness dwells.

BE STEADFAST

[14]Therefore, beloved, looking forward to these things, be diligent to be found by Him in peace, without spot and blameless; [15]and consider *that* the longsuffering of our Lord *is* salvation—as also our beloved brother Paul, according to the wisdom given to him, has written to you, [16]as also in all his epistles, speaking in them of these things, in which are some things hard to understand, which untaught and unstable *people* twist to their own destruction, as *they do* also the rest of the Scriptures.

[17]You therefore, beloved, since you know *this* beforehand, beware lest you also fall from your own steadfastness, being led away with the error of the wicked; [18]but grow in the grace and knowledge of our Lord and Savior Jesus Christ.

To Him *be* the glory both now and forever. Amen.

HEALTH NOTES

JOHN

In this letter, John has three main concerns: don't listen to liars, don't pursue the same things the world pursues, and don't fail to love people around you. What great wisdom!

False information, speculation, innuendo, rumor, and "false teaching" are rampant in our world. Choose to stick to the basic principles of your faith, and when it comes to health, stick to the basic principles for good health. Don't get caught up in fad diets, fad remedies, or fad procedures. At the same time, don't allow yourself to be swept up by your own lusts for immoral sex, food, pleasure, possessions, fame, or power. Pursue things that contribute to emotional health, not emotional demise.

When it comes to love, put God first. Then, love others generously and with a pure heart. If you have trouble loving someone, ask God to impart a little bit of His love for them to your own heart. See other people as God's beloved children.

If you want a definition for a stress-free living, John gives a good one: Steer clear of lies and choose to love the truth and to love people. That's the secret to a clear conscience and peaceful heart.

WHAT WAS HEARD, SEEN, AND TOUCHED

1 That which was from the beginning, which we have heard, which we have seen with our eyes, which we have looked upon, and our hands have handled, concerning the Word of life— ²the life was manifested, and we have seen, and bear witness, and declare to you that eternal life which was with the Father and was manifested to us— ³that which we have seen and heard we declare to you, that you also may have fellowship with us; and truly our fellowship *is* with the Father and with His Son Jesus Christ. ⁴And these things we write to you that your^a joy may be full.

FELLOWSHIP WITH HIM AND ONE ANOTHER

⁵This is the message which we have heard from Him and declare to you, that God is light and in Him is no darkness at all. ⁶If we say that we have fellowship with Him, and walk in darkness, we lie and do not practice the truth. ⁷But if we walk in the light as He is in the light, we have fellowship with one another, and the blood of Jesus Christ His Son cleanses us from all sin.

⁸If we say that we have no sin, we deceive ourselves, and the truth is not in us. ⁹If we confess our sins, He is faithful and just to forgive us *our* sins and to cleanse us from all unrighteousness. ¹⁰If we say that we have not sinned, we make Him a liar, and His word is not in us.

2 My little children, these things I write to you, so that you may not sin. And if anyone sins, we have an Advocate with the Father, Jesus Christ the righteous. ²And He Himself is the propitiation for our sins, and not for ours only but also for the whole world.

THE TEST OF KNOWING HIM

³Now by this we know that we know Him, if we keep His commandments. ⁴He who says, "I know Him," and does not keep His commandments, is a liar, and the truth is not in him. ⁵But whoever keeps His word, truly the love of God is perfected in him. By this we know that we are in Him. ⁶He who says he abides in Him ought himself also to walk just as He walked.

⁷Brethren,^a I write no new commandment to you, but an old commandment which you have had from the beginning. The old commandment is the word which you heard from the beginning.^b ⁸Again, a new commandment I write to you, which thing is true in Him and in you, because the darkness is passing away, and the true light is already shining.

⁹He who says he is in the light, and hates his brother, is in darkness until now. ¹⁰He who loves his brother abides in the light, and there is no cause for stumbling in him. ¹¹But he who hates his brother is in darkness and walks in darkness, and does not know where he is going, because the darkness has blinded his eyes.

THEIR SPIRITUAL STATE

¹² I write to you, little children,
    Because your sins are forgiven you for His name's sake.
¹³ I write to you, fathers,

1:4 ^aNU-Text and M-Text read *our*.   2:7 ^aNU-Text reads *Beloved*. ^bNU-Text omits *from the beginning*.

ULTIMATE HEALTH RESOURCE • ULTIMATE HEALTH RESOURCE • ULTIMATE HEALTH RESOURCE

Throughout the Bible, a long and healthy life is considered to be a tremendous blessing from God. The Bible writers clearly believed that the *length* of a person's life was to be determined by God alone—the commandments against the taking of innocent life are very strong. Hebrews 9:27 tells us that "it is *appointed* for men to die once." Physical death is inevitable. Even those who experience the "rapture" of the saints, as described in 1 Thessalonians 4:16, 17, will experience some type of physical change. For the Christian, death is just that—a change, a moment of transition from this current physical body and natural world to a spiritual body and heavenly world.

Can a person prolong his God-appointed length of days? Probably not, although the example of King Hezekiah seems to present the possibility that a person may ask God for an extension of life and have such an extension granted. (See 2 Kings 20:1–7.)

The more important question to ask is: Can a person impact the quality of his or her life up to the moment of death? Absolutely! The vast majority of diseases that debilitate, weaken, and cause human suffering in our society are a result of *lifestyle choices.* They are caused by or are made more severe by the following:

☐ Poor nutrition—often decades of eating the wrong foods or overeating, or both
☐ Lack of exercise—often decades of a mostly sedentary lifestyle
☐ Use of tobacco in any form
☐ Overuse of alcohol
☐ Excessive or prolonged stress—from physical, natural, or emotional sources
☐ Sexual immorality—resulting in sexually transmitted diseases that may include some forms of cancer
☐ Use of drugs—including overuse of prescription medications
☐ Exposure to pollutants—in the air, in the water, and in foods (as the result of pesticides, herbicides, fungicides, antibiotic use in animals, genetic engineering in animals and plants, and harmful chemical additives or preservatives)
☐ Unhealthful food manufacturing—scientists are discovering more and more harmful consequences of the many processes we employ in food production, including the hydrogenation of oils, the refinement of flour, and the pasteurization of milk.

For the most part, we have a *choice* when it comes to these factors. In addition to making wise lifestyle choices, a person can greatly enhance the quality of life by making an intentional choice to do the following:

☐ **Trust God**
☐ **Love other people**
☐ **Hope for a better tomorrow**
☐ **Remain thankful**
☐ **Be joyful**
☐ **Continue to learn, grow, and change**
☐ **Express personal creativity**
☐ **Pray and praise continually**

Finally, a Christian bears a responsibility for living with as much strength, energy, and vitality as possible, so he might fulfill all that God has placed him on Earth to do, say, and "be" in relationship with others.

Because you have known Him *who is* from the beginning.
I write to you, young men,
    Because you have overcome the wicked one.
I write to you, little children,
    Because you have known the Father.
¹⁴ I have written to you, fathers,
    Because you have known Him *who is* from the beginning.
I have written to you, young men,
    Because you are strong, and the word of God abides in you,
    And you have overcome the wicked one.

DO NOT LOVE THE WORLD

¹⁵Do not love the world or the things in the world. If anyone loves the world, the love of the Father is not in him. ¹⁶For all that *is* in the world—the lust of the flesh, the lust of the eyes, and the pride of life—is not of the Father but is of the world. ¹⁷And the world is passing away, and the lust of it; but he who does the will of God abides forever.

DECEPTIONS OF THE LAST HOUR

¹⁸Little children, it is the last hour; and as you have heard that the ͣ Antichrist is coming, even now many antichrists have come, by which

2:18 ͣNU-Text omits *the.*

QUIZ 5

ARE YOU FULLFILLING YOUR PURPOSE FOR LIVING?

The age-old question of philosophy is Why am I here? The Bible gives a very clear, direct answer. You are living on this earth as God's beloved creation for three reasons: 1) to be in fellowship with God, 2) to live out the fullness of the talents, gifts, & attributes that He has placed in you from birth, & 3) to help other people around you in every way you can. Below is a set of questions related to these three purposes. Use them as a starting point for your own reflection, decision making, & setting priorities in your life. These questions are in no way intended to bring feelings of guilt or condemnation to you. They are offered as a means of identifying how you might live a more fulfilled, whole, & balanced life.

	YES	NO

Fellowship with God

1. Do I have a personal relationship with God through Jesus Christ?
2. Do I spend time in prayer daily?
3. Do I acknowledge God as the source of everything good & beneficial in my life?
4. Do I thank & praise God often?
5. Do I read God's Word daily?
6. Do I obey God's Word?
7. Am I relying daily on the Holy Spirit to guide my decisions & choices?

Using My Talents to the Fullest

1. Do I have a good understanding of my God-given talents, abilities, & traits?
2. Am I developing or improving skills that are related to my basic talents?
3. Am I using my talents, practicing them or employing them in useful & beneficial ways?
4. Am I seeking to change or develop habits for greater wholeness?
5. Am I seeking to become more emotionally whole?
6. Am I learning new things?
7. Am I applying what I am learning?

Helping Others

1. Am I using my talents & skills to help other people?
2. Am I sensitive to the needs of others around me?
3. Do I seek ways to bring greater justice or effective solutions to those I encounter who cannot defend or help themselves?
4. Am I respectful of the dignity of others?
5. Do I generously applaud, encourage, or mentor others?
6. Am I seeking to leave something of value to the next generation?

Go back & circle those areas in which you believe you need to concentrate your efforts & your prayers! Ask God to show you what you must do to grow more into the likeness of Jesus Christ. Especially look for ways in which items you have marked as "worse" might be related—such as an increasing level of stress with more financial indebtedness, or negative relationships associated with an imbalance in work & play.

Women's Issues
Menopause

Menopause occurs when a woman no longer has any eggs left in her ovaries. She then stops menstruating. For a majority of women menopause occurs at about fifty years of age, although some women go through it as early as age thirty-five and as late as age sixty.

Some of the symptoms that women experience during menopause include hot flashes and vaginal dryness, which are the most common symptoms, as well as mood swings, frequent vaginal infections, cold hands and feet, night sweats, fatigue, headaches, a decreased sex drive, breast tenderness, palpitations of the heart, insomnia, drying of the skin, vaginal itching, bladder infections, dizziness, and an inability to concentrate. During a hot flash, blood vessels dilate and skin temperature rises and flushes the skin. This usually occurs about the neck and head and only lasts from a few seconds to a minute.

Many of the symptoms associated with menopause are related to a lower production of estrogen in the body. Synthetic hormones, especially the drugs Premarin and Provera, are often prescribed to premenopausal and menopausal women to provide estrogen and progesterone to the body. A number of highly negative side effects are associated with these drugs.

A *natural* approach is to add plant-derived phytoestrogens to the body, especially the natural progesterones found in soybeans or tropical wild CONT. NEXT PAGE>>>

we know that it is the last hour. ¹⁹They went out from us, but they were not of us; for if they had been of us, they would have continued with us; but *they went out* that they might be made manifest, that none of them were of us.

²⁰But you have an anointing from the Holy One, and you know all things.ᵃ ²¹I have not written to you because you do not know the truth, but because you know it, and that no lie is of the truth.

²²Who is a liar but he who denies that Jesus is the Christ? He is antichrist who denies the Father and the Son. ²³Whoever denies the Son does not have the Father either; he who acknowledges the Son has the Father also.

LET TRUTH ABIDE IN YOU

²⁴Therefore let that abide in you which you heard from the beginning. If what you heard from the beginning abides in you, you also will abide in the Son and in the Father. ²⁵And this is the promise that He has promised us—eternal life.

²⁶These things I have written to you concerning those who *try to* deceive you. ²⁷But the anointing which you have received from Him abides in you, and you do not need that anyone teach you; but as the same anointing teaches you concerning all things, and is true, and is not a lie, and just as it has taught you, you willᵃ abide in Him.

THE CHILDREN OF GOD

²⁸And now, little children, abide in Him, that whenᵃ He appears, we may have confidence and not be ashamed before Him at His coming. ²⁹If you know that He is righteous, you know that everyone who practices righteousness is born of Him.

3 Behold what manner of love the Father has bestowed on us, that we should be called children of God!ᵃ Therefore the world does not know us,ᵇ because it did not know Him. ²Beloved, now we are children of God; and it has not yet been revealed what we shall be, but we know that when He is revealed, we shall be like Him, for we shall see Him as He is. ³And everyone who has this hope in Him purifies himself, just as He is pure.

SIN AND THE CHILD OF GOD

⁴Whoever commits sin also commits lawlessness, and sin is lawlessness. ⁵And you know that He was manifested to take away our sins, and in Him there is no sin. ⁶Whoever abides in Him does not sin. Whoever sins has neither seen Him nor known Him.

⁷Little children, let no one deceive you. He who practices righteousness is righteous, just as He is righteous. ⁸He who sins is of the devil, for the devil has sinned from the beginning. For this purpose the Son of God was manifested, that He might destroy the works of the devil. ⁹Whoever has been born of God does not sin, for His seed remains in him; and he cannot sin, because he has been born of God.

THE IMPERATIVE OF LOVE

¹⁰In this the children of God and the children of the devil are manifest: Whoever does not practice righteousness is not of God, nor *is* he

---

2:20 ªNU-Text reads *you all know.*   2:27 ªNU-Text reads *you abide.*   2:28 ªNU-Text reads *if.*   3:1 ªNU-Text adds *And we are.*   ᵇM-Text reads *you.*

Women's Issues Cont.>>>

yams. Progesterone and estrogen levels can be monitored by blood or saliva testing and exact formulas can be prepared at a natural-medicine pharmacy to fit a woman's specific needs. Natural progesterone cream can help decrease hot flashes and a natural estriol cream can help with thinning and dryness of the vaginal lining.

Foods that are highest in plant estrogens are soy, flaxseed oil, alfalfa, fennel seeds, flaxseed, whole grains, parsley, and celery. Studies have shown that one cup of soy is equivalent to a regular dose of Premarin. Soy flour or whole soy products rather than soy proteins are the most efficient way for a woman to get phytoestrogens from soy.

Since hormones such as estrogen and progesterone are made from cholesterol it is important that a woman not go on a no-cholesterol or no-fat diet. A woman should, however, avoid hydrogenated, polyunsaturated and saturated fats, and unsaturated vegetable oils. On the other hand, olive and fish oils and flaxseed oil are important to include in a daily diet.

Some of the herbs helpful in controlling menopausal symptoms are black cohosh, dong quai, chasteberry, licorice root, ginkgo biloba, and genistein. Promensil is an isoflavone supplement made from red clover that may also be helpful.

Bible Health + Food Facts

No Word for "Hot Flash"

Did you know that there isn't a word in Japanese for "hot flash"? Why? Because in Asian nations where women eat a lot of soy foods, only about 16 percent claim any problem with menopausal discomfort. In nations where soy foods are used less often, 75 percent of menopausal women complain of hot flashes.

---

who does not love his brother. ¹¹For this is the message that you heard from the beginning, that we should love one another, ¹²not as Cain *who* was of the wicked one and murdered his brother. And why did he murder him? Because his works were evil and his brother's righteous.

¹³Do not marvel, my brethren, if the world hates you. ¹⁴We know that we have passed from death to life, because we love the brethren. He who does not love *his* brother[a] abides in death. ¹⁵Whoever hates his brother is a murderer, and you know that no murderer has eternal life abiding in him.

THE OUTWORKING OF LOVE

¹⁶By this we know love, because He laid down His life for us. And we also ought to lay down *our* lives for the brethren. ¹⁷But whoever has this world's goods, and sees his brother in need, and shuts up his heart from him, how does the love of God abide in him?

¹⁸My little children, let us not love in word or in tongue, but in deed and in truth. ¹⁹And by this we know[a] that we are of the truth, and shall assure our hearts before Him. ²⁰For if our heart condemns us, God is greater than our heart, and knows all things. ²¹Beloved, if our heart does not condemn us, we have confidence toward God. ²²And whatever we ask we receive from Him, because we keep His commandments and do those things that are pleasing in His sight. ²³And this is His commandment: that we should believe on the name of His Son Jesus Christ and love one another, as He gave us[a] commandment.

> (1 John 3:22)

Answers to Prayers. If you are discouraged that God does not seem to be answering your prayers, check two things in your life—are you obeying the commands of God to forgive, love, and live a godly life? Are you doing the things that God has gifted you to do, and with a joy in your heart as you administer your talents and skills to the benefit of others?

God's Word tells us that we will receive what we ask of God if we are doing these two things. In part, we will "receive from Him" because if we are obeying Him and seeking to serve Him in all things, we will ask things that are in complete harmony with what God desires. His will becomes our will, and our requests become what He already desires to do. The privilege of prayer is like a trigger—we "activate" on this earth what God has already authorized in heaven. If we request things with a wrong attitude, a spirit of rebellion, or a lack of compassion for others—or if we request things that are not in keeping with God's Word—our prayers have the same effect as firing blanks. We make noise but to no effect.

INSIGHTS | INTO THE WORD

3:14 [a]NU-Text omits *his brother*.   3:19 [a]NU-Text reads *we shall know*.   3:23 [a]M-Text omits *us*.

♂ Men's Issues
A Man's Need for Sex

Men and women are radically different physically, emotionally, and spiritually. Even so, they have been designed by God to *complement* each other and to become "one flesh" (Genesis 2:24). Men and women both have a need for sexual expression.

Sex in the Bible is not solely for the purpose of procreation, but is also for the mutual meeting of physical and emotional needs. It is presented in the Bible as a means for gaining greater understanding in how to relate to other people and to God. In the act of sexual intercourse, when the act is loving and mutually agreed upon, both men and women are expected to find tremendous benefit and pleasure! (See Matthew 19:5; Mark 10:8; 1 Corinthians 6:16; and Ephesians 5:31.)

The Bible has very specific commandments and rules related to sexual intimacy. Sexual intercourse is to be between one man and one woman who are in a covenant (marriage) relationship. Fornication, which is sex between unmarried people, and adultery, which is sex between a married person and a person other than the spouse, are strictly forbidden (Exodus 20:14; Deuteronomy 22:22; 1 Corinthians 6:9, 10). Sexual union is not to be used as a weapon or a reward, but is to be regarded as a rightful need and expectation of each marriage partner (1 Corinthians 7:3–5).

Deviant sexual behavior is prohibited, including homosexuality (Leviticus 18:22; Romans 1:26, 27; 1 Corinthians 6:9, 10), bestiality (Exodus 22:19; Leviticus 19:23), and rape (Deuteronomy 22:23–29). CONT. NEXT PAGE>>>

THE SPIRIT OF TRUTH AND THE SPIRIT OF ERROR

²⁴Now he who keeps His commandments abides in Him, and He in him. And by this we know that He abides in us, by the Spirit whom He has given us.

4 Beloved, do not believe every spirit, but test the spirits, whether they are of God; because many false prophets have gone out into the world. ²By this you know the Spirit of God: Every spirit that confesses that Jesus Christ has come in the flesh is of God, ³and every spirit that does not confess that[a] Jesus Christ has come in the flesh is not of God. And this is the *spirit* of the Antichrist, which you have heard was coming, and is now already in the world.

⁴You are of God, little children, and have overcome them, because He who is in you is greater than he who is in the world. ⁵They are of the world. Therefore they speak *as* of the world, and the world hears them. ⁶We are of God. He who knows God hears us; he who is not of God does not hear us. By this we know the spirit of truth and the spirit of error.

KNOWING GOD THROUGH LOVE

⁷Beloved, let us love one another, for love is of God; and everyone who loves is born of God and knows God. ⁸He who does not love does not know God, for God is love. ⁹In this the love of God was manifested toward us, that God has sent His only begotten Son into the world, that we might live through Him. ¹⁰In this is love, not that we loved God, but that He loved us and sent His Son *to be* the propitiation for our sins. ¹¹Beloved, if God so loved us, we also ought to love one another.

SEEING GOD THROUGH LOVE

¹²No one has seen God at any time. If we love one another, God abides in us, and His love has been perfected in us. ¹³By this we know that we abide in Him, and He in us, because He has given us of His Spirit. ¹⁴And we have seen and testify that the

WISE CHOICES

Choose a Chinese take-out or restaurant that does not use MSG.
MSG has been shown to have harmful health side effects for many people, especially severe headaches. MSG is especially used in Chinese restaurants. Call ahead to find out if a Chinese restaurant uses MSG. If so, go elsewhere!

4:3 ᵃNU-Text omits *that* and *Christ has come in the flesh.*

Men's Issues Cont.>>>

Masturbation is not expressly prohibited, but is considered dangerous if it is behavior that fuels lust. Seductive behavior is denounced because it is rooted in a desire to manipulate and control another person.

Sexual intercourse is intended to give a man satisfaction and joy when it is within the God-ordained boundaries of marriage (Proverbs 5:19; Ecclesiastes 9:9). The Bible encourages husbands to be concerned with meeting a wife's unique needs (Deuteronomy 24:5; 1 Peter 3:7). A wife is held responsible for being available to her husband, preparing and planning for sex, maintaining interest in sex, and being sensitive to a man's unique masculine needs (1 Corinthians 7:3–5; Song of Solomon 4:9; 5:2; Genesis 24:67).

A healthy sexual relationship contributes to overall health. Unhealthy sexual behavior can be emotionally damaging and physically deadly.

---

5 Whoever believes that Jesus is the Christ is born of God, and everyone who loves Him who begot also loves him who is begotten of Him. [2]By this we know that we love the children of God, when we love God and keep His commandments. [3]For this is the love of God, that we keep His commandments. And His commandments are not burdensome. [4]For whatever is born of God overcomes the world. And this is the victory that has overcome the world—our[a] faith. [5]Who is he who overcomes the world, but he who believes that Jesus is the Son of God?

THE CERTAINTY OF GOD'S WITNESS

[6]This is He who came by water and blood—Jesus Christ; not only by water, but by water and blood. And it is the Spirit who bears witness, because the Spirit is truth. [7]For there are three that bear witness in heaven: the Father, the Word, and the Holy Spirit; and these three are one. [8]And there are three that bear witness on earth:[a] the Spirit, the water, and the blood; and these three agree as one.

[9]If we receive the witness of men, the witness of God is greater; for this is the witness of God which[a] He has testified of His Son.

Father has sent the Son *as* Savior of the world. [15]Whoever confesses that Jesus is the Son of God, God abides in him, and he in God. [16]And we have known and believed the love that God has for us. God is love, and he who abides in love abides in God, and God in him.

THE CONSUMMATION OF LOVE

[17]Love has been perfected among us in this: that we may have boldness in the day of judgment; because as He is, so are we in this world. [18]There is no fear in love; but perfect love casts out fear, because fear involves torment. But he who fears has not been made perfect in love. [19]We love Him[a] because He first loved us.

OBEDIENCE BY FAITH

[20]If someone says, "I love God," and hates his brother, he is a liar; for he who does not love his brother whom he has seen, how can[a] he love God whom he has not seen? [21]And this commandment we have from Him: that he who loves God *must* love his brother also.

> " If someone says, "I love God,"
> and hates his brother, he is a liar;
> for he who does not love his brother
> whom he has seen, how can
> he love God whom he has
> not seen? " — *1 John 4:20*

PRESCRIPTIONS
FOR INNER HEALTH

"It is honorable for a man to stop striving,
Since any fool can start a quarrel."

(Proverbs 20:3)

If you think you are always right and others are always wrong—you are wrong! If you think others are right all the time and you are always wrong—you are also wrong! But if you think that sometimes you are right and sometimes others are right—you are *right!* Those who continually debate, contend, criticize, and argue usually believe that they must control everything and every one around them in order to have personal validity or worth. Choose instead to yield control to God and to accept the truth that God loves you and counts you as valuable and worthy in spite of your foibles, weaknesses, and flaws.

4:19 [a]NU-Text omits *Him*.   4:20 [a]NU-Text reads *he cannot*.   5:4 [a]M-Text reads *your*.   5:8 [a]NU-Text and M-Text omit the words from *in heaven* (verse 7) through *on earth* (verse 8). Only four or five very late manuscripts contain these words in Greek.   5:9 [a]NU-Text reads *God, that*.

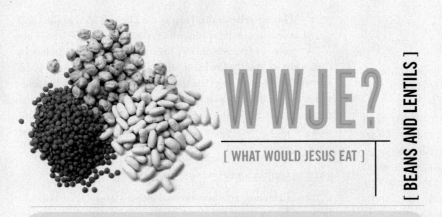

WWJE?

[WHAT WOULD JESUS EAT]

[BEANS AND LENTILS]

Beans, peas, and lentils were easily cultivated in Bible times and used to make purees, pottages, and when mixed with millet, a coarse bread. They were easily dried and stored. Beans are packed with vitamin C and have virtually no fat. They are loaded with soluble fiber, which helps lower LDL (bad) cholesterol and reduces blood pressure. The fiber in beans also helps keep blood sugar levels stable and helps to reduce the insulin requirements of diabetics. Beans help prevent constipation and other bowel-related problems. Beans and garlic have historically been boiled together to produce a primitive version of cough medicine.

Lentils were commonly consumed in Bible times—in fact, lentils are one of the oldest cultivated plants. They are high in protein, but are deficient in amino acids methionine and cysteine. They are low in fat and high in soluble fiber. They are great in combination with other vegetables in soups, stews, and casseroles.

Garbanzo beans are very popular in the Middle East, especially when combined with tahina, garlic, and cumin to make hummus. Hummus has been called the "peanut butter of the Middle East." Many people eat only hummus and pita bread with a few olives for lunch. Garbanzo beans, also called chickpeas, are used to make falafel (Middle Eastern meatballs).

Other beans that are highly nutritious are lima beans, green peas, black-eyed peas, white beans, navy beans, black beans, and kidney beans.

Add Fiber Slowly

If you are not used to eating large quantities of fiber-rich beans, lentils, fresh fruits, vegetables, or whole grains, add fiber slowly to your eating plan to avoid excessive bloating, gas, and cramps. It may take a month or longer to introduce sufficient high-fiber foods into your diet. Start by choosing whole-grain bread over white bread, whole fruits over juices, and a baked potato with the skin over potato chips or mashed potatoes. Gradually introduce more beans and whole grains into your diet. Always take in sufficient water when increasing your intake of fiber. If you are choosing a fiber supplement as a way of adding fiber to your diet, be sure to take it at a different time than you take vitamin and mineral supplements.

[10] He who believes in the Son of God has the witness in himself; he who does not believe God has made Him a liar, because he has not believed the testimony that God has given of His Son. [11] And this is the testimony: that God has given us eternal life, and this life is in His Son. [12] He who has the Son has life; he who does not have the Son of God does not have life. [13] These things I have written to you who believe in the name of the Son of God, that you may know that you have eternal life,[a] and that you may *continue to* believe in the name of the Son of God.

CONFIDENCE AND COMPASSION IN PRAYER

[14] Now this is the confidence that we have in Him, that if we ask anything according to His will, He hears us. [15] And if we know that He hears us, whatever we ask, we know that we have the petitions that we have asked of Him.

[16] If anyone sees his brother sinning a sin *which does* not *lead* to death, he will ask, and He will give him life for those who commit sin not *leading* to death. There is sin *leading* to death. I do not say that he should pray about that. [17] All unrighteousness is sin, and there is sin not *leading* to death.

KNOWING THE TRUE— REJECTING THE FALSE

[18] We know that whoever is born of God does not sin; but he who has been born of God keeps himself,[a] and the wicked one does not touch him.

[19] We know that we are of God, and the whole world lies *under the sway of* the wicked one.

[20] And we know that the Son of God has come and has given us an understanding, that we may know Him who is true; and we are in Him who is true, in His Son Jesus Christ. This is the true God and eternal life.

[21] Little children, keep yourselves from idols. Amen.

HEALTH NOTES

JOHN This short, sweet love letter from John was written either to a specific woman and her children, or to a church and its members. Either way, it is a letter that is aimed at reminding its readers of two major truths: Follow Jesus and love other people. John also warned that if someone came with any other teaching, that person should be sent on his way. To entertain or host such a false teacher makes a person just as guilty as the false teacher.

In other words, watch what you entertain in your thought life! Guard what you hear and what you see, just as you watch what you eat. Don't get away from the basics, and never stop loving. If anybody tries to tell you that Jesus is anything other than the divine Son of God, a full member of the Trinity—Father, Son, and Holy Spirit—tune out that person completely. Entertaining their opinion can only cause you harm.

GREETING THE ELECT LADY

The Elder,

To the elect lady and her children, whom I love in truth, and not only I, but also all those who have known the truth, ²because of the truth which abides in us and will be with us forever:

³Grace, mercy, *and* peace will be with you^a from God the Father and from the Lord Jesus Christ, the Son of the Father, in truth and love.

WALK IN CHRIST'S COMMANDMENTS

⁴I rejoiced greatly that I have found *some* of your children walking in truth, as we received commandment from the Father. ⁵And now I plead with you, lady, not as though I wrote a new commandment to you, but that which we have had from the beginning: that we love one another. ⁶This is love, that we walk according to His commandments. This is the commandment, that as you have heard from the beginning, you should walk in it.

BEWARE OF ANTICHRIST DECEIVERS

⁷For many deceivers have gone out into the world who do not confess Jesus Christ *as* coming in the flesh. This is a deceiver and an antichrist. ⁸Look to yourselves, that we^a do not lose those things we worked for, but *that* we^b may receive a full reward. ⁹Whoever transgresses^a and does not abide in the doctrine of Christ does not have God. He who abides in the doctrine of Christ has both the Father and the Son. ¹⁰If anyone comes to you and does not bring this doctrine, do not receive him into your house nor greet him; ¹¹for he who greets him shares in his evil deeds.

The LAW AND THE SCIENCE

[PRACTICE WHAT PROMOTES LIFE]

>SCIENCE especially the historical and anthropological sciences—tells us that it was a common practice among the Canaanites' fertility cult to cook a young goat in its mother's milk. The Israelites were told to avoid this practice not only because it was part of a pagan ritual, but also because the practice was profaning the very reason for the mother goat's milk. Milk was intended to sustain the life of a young goat, not be the medium of its death! The Bible takes a strong stance against using anything God intended for *life* as a practice or means of promoting *death*.

>THE LAW says: "You shall not boil a young goat in its mother's milk" (Deuteronomy 14:21).

---

3 ^aNU-Text and M-Text read *us.*   8 ^aNU-Text reads *you.* ^bNU-Text reads *you.*   9 ^aNU-Text reads *goes ahead.*

Zucchini Casserole

Righteous Recipes

Ingredients:

- ☐ 2 cups small curd creamed cottage cheese
- ☐ 1½ teaspoons basil
- ☐ 1 teaspoon oregano
- ☐ 1 garlic clove, minced
- ☐ 1½ cups coarsely chopped pitted black olives
- ☐ 2 tablespoons extra-virgin olive oil
- ☐ 2 pounds zucchini, diagonally sliced ¼-inch thick (should yield about 7 cups)
- ☐ 1 medium onion, cut into wedges
- ☐ ½ teaspoon Celtic salt
- ☐ ¼ cup whole-wheat flour
- ☐ 2 tablespoons freshly grated Parmesan cheese

Combine the cottage cheese, basil, oregano, garlic, and olives in a bowl. Mix well. Heat the olive oil in a heavy skillet over high heat. Sauté the zucchini and onion in hot oil for about 5 minutes or until tender-crisp. Remove from heat. Sprinkle with salt and flour, and mix well. Layer half the zucchini mixture, the cottage cheese mixture, and the remaining zucchini mixture in a shallow 2-quart baking dish. Sprinkle with Parmesan cheese. Bake, uncovered, at 350 degrees for 30 minutes or until hot and bubbly. Garnish with olives and serve.

Yield: 10–12 servings

> **" Grace, mercy, and peace will be with you from God the Father and from the Lord Jesus Christ, the Son of the Father, in truth and love. "**
>
> — *2 John 3*

JOHN'S FAREWELL GREETING

[12] Having many things to write to you, I did not wish *to do so* with paper and ink; but I hope to come to you and speak face to face, that our joy may be full.

[13] The children of your elect sister greet you. Amen.

HEALTH NOTES

JOHN

"My dear friend, do not follow what is bad; follow what is good. The one who does good belongs to God." (3 John 11) People long to follow good leaders who will produce good results. But how can we tell? John tells us: Look at the fruit of their lives! Do they live what they teach or preach? If they are promoting health, for example, are they healthy? If they are advocating for a product, do they use it? If so, what are the results? Look for solid evidence. Those things that produce good fruit and lead to wholeness are the things we should focus on doing. Everything else is a detour that can lead to a downfall.

GREETING TO GAIUS

The Elder,

To the beloved Gaius, whom I love in truth:

²Beloved, I pray that you may prosper in all things and be in health, just as your soul prospers. ³For I rejoiced greatly when brethren came and testified of the truth *that is* in you, just as you walk in the truth. ⁴I have no greater joy than to hear that my children walk in truth.ᵃ

GAIUS COMMENDED FOR GENEROSITY

⁵Beloved, you do faithfully whatever you do for the brethren andᵃ for strangers, ⁶who have borne witness of your love before the church. *If* you send them forward on their journey in a manner worthy of God, you will do well, ⁷because they went forth for His name's sake, taking nothing from the Gentiles. ⁸We therefore ought to receiveᵃ such, that we may become fellow workers for the truth.

DIOTREPHES AND DEMETRIUS

⁹I wrote to the church, but Diotrephes, who loves to have the preeminence among them, does not receive us. ¹⁰Therefore, if I come, I will call to mind his deeds which he does, prating against us with malicious words. And not content with that, he himself does not receive the brethren, and forbids those who wish to, putting *them* out of the church.

> ## > (3 John 2)

Whole-Person Prayer. In one sentence, John gave us a model for a "wholeness" prayer. In his letter to a beloved fellow believer named Gaius, John said he was praying that Gaius would prosper in *all* areas of his life and be in health. In other words, John was praying that he would be *whole*. Then John said, "just as your soul prospers." The health of the body is linked to the prospering of the soul, which is the way a person thinks, believes, and activates his will.

One of the most powerful prayers you can pray for a person is that God will heal them and make them *whole*. This prayer is appropriate for emotional, spiritual, and physical disorders because there is no way any one person can know the full extent of what may be causing a disease or ailment in another person's life.

INSIGHTS INTO THE WORD

4 ᵃNU-Text reads *the truth*.   5 ᵃNU-Text adds *especially*.   8 ᵃNU-Text reads *support*.

Overcoming Fatigue

Overcoming Obstinate Obstacles

People who feel tired all the time may have a chronic disease or ailment of some type. Consult a physician. On the other hand, regular fatigue can be the result of the following:

Eating the wrong foods. Too much sugar in a person's diet can send blood sugar levels soaring, only to have those same blood sugar levels "crash" into exhaustion. Keep in mind that milk products produce lactose (milk sugar) and most processed foods, such as breads and pastas, have a significant amount of sucrose (sugar). Try replacing sugary foods with fresh vegetables and fruits, whole grains, and protein sources such as meat, poultry, fish, or beans. If you need to replenish your energy at the cellular level, you may need supplements. Allow several weeks for supplements and a new eating plan to work—it takes time to replenish nutrients for ongoing energy.

Failure to exercise. Contrary to what many people believe, exercise does not make a person more tired in the long run. Exercise energizes a person and also helps a person to sleep better. You don't need to overdo the exercise—thirty minutes of walking a day, even in three ten-minute sessions, will provide great benefits to the average person.

Failure to get sufficient sleep. The average adult needs between seven and nine hours of sleep a night. The vast majority of Americans are sleep deprived—the result is lack of productivity, lack of quality and more accidents on the job, shorter tempers and more strain on relationships, and general health problems. Get the sleep you need!

---

¹¹Beloved, do not imitate what is evil, but what is good. He who does good is of God, butᵃ he who does evil has not seen God.

¹²Demetrius has a *good* testimony from all, and from the truth itself. And we also bear witness, and you know that our testimony is true.

FAREWELL GREETING

¹³I had many things to write, but I do not wish to write to you with pen and ink; ¹⁴but I hope to see you shortly, and we shall speak face to face. Peace to you. Our friends greet you. Greet the friends by name.

---

11 ᵃNU-Text and M-Text omit *but.*

HEALTH NOTES

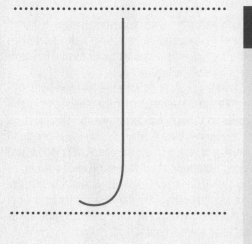

UDE

The Book of Jude was written to people who were being fed a pack of lies about sexual behavior and the uniqueness of Jesus Christ. False teachers were saying that it was acceptable to have sex outside the bonds of marriage between one man and one woman. They were also saying that Jesus was just a good man, not God. John says clearly, "Don't listen to them!" What they are saying will destroy you physically and spiritually.

The author of Jude also points out that the people who are giving these false teachings were ruled solely by their own whims and desires—they did not believe in the Word of God and relied rather on flattery and a play on emotions to convince others that their opinions were right.

It's easy to follow someone who only tells you what you want to hear. Wake up! Listen to those who tell you what God wants you to hear. What God says is for your eternal benefit, not merely for temporary pleasure.

GREETING TO THE CALLED

Jude, a bondservant of Jesus Christ, and brother of James,

To those who are called, sanctified[a] by God the Father, and preserved in Jesus Christ:

[2]Mercy, peace, and love be multiplied to you.

CONTEND FOR THE FAITH

[3]Beloved, while I was very diligent to write to you concerning our common salvation, I found it necessary to write to you exhorting you to contend earnestly for the faith which was once for all delivered to the saints. [4]For certain men have crept in unnoticed, who long ago were marked out for this condemnation, ungodly men, who turn the grace of our God into lewdness and deny the only Lord God[a] and our Lord Jesus Christ.

OLD AND NEW APOSTATES

[5]But I want to remind you, though you once knew this, that the Lord, having saved the people out of the land of Egypt, afterward destroyed those who did not believe. [6]And the angels who did not keep their proper domain, but left their own abode, He has reserved in everlasting chains under darkness for the judgment of the great day; [7]as Sodom and Gomorrah, and the cities around them in a similar manner to these, having given themselves over to sexual immorality and gone after strange flesh, are set forth as an example, suffering the vengeance of eternal fire.

[8]Likewise also these dreamers defile the flesh, reject authority, and speak evil of dignitaries. [9]Yet Michael the archangel, in contending with the devil, when he disputed about the body of Moses, dared not bring against him a reviling accusation, but said, "The Lord rebuke you!" [10]But these speak evil of whatever they do not know; and whatever they know naturally, like brute beasts, in these things they corrupt themselves. [11]Woe to them! For they have gone in the way of Cain, have run greedily in the error of Balaam for profit, and perished in the rebellion of Korah.

> **PREACHING HEALTH**
>
> "The first sure symptoms of a mind in health are rest of heart and pleasure found at home."
> —*Edward Young, English poet (1683–1765)*

1 [a]NU-Text reads *beloved*.   4 [a]NU-Text omits *God*.

> (Jude 5–11)

What About Suffering? The Bible presents a number of causes for suffering. The one-chapter Book of Jude covers several of them, including sexual sins, those who defile the flesh, reject authority, and speak evil of dignitaries, as well as those who openly try to insight vengeance against those who have persecuted them. In the political, material, and social worlds in which we live, it is easy to see how persecution and suffering can result from these actions.

The harboring of negative emotions and continued pursuit of bad health practices can produce in us physical and emotional conditions that cause us to suffer. Because everybody suffers in some way at some time, we must be clear that there is nothing about suffering that automatically makes a person stronger or better. It's how we *respond* to suffering that determines whether our suffering makes us better human beings or bitter, miserable human beings.

So what are we to do when we find ourselves suffering? We are to forgive God, forgive others, and forgive ourselves as the very *first* things we do! We need to let go of any sins we have been holding on to as "pet sins." We must give up ideas of vengeance, retaliation, and speaking negatively about others. We must yield to the authority that God has placed over us and choose to live a pure and godly life *no matter how others treat us or what they may say about us!* Only then can suffering be turned to an eternal good.

APOSTATES DEPRAVED AND DOOMED

[12]These are spots in your love feasts, while they feast with you without fear, serving *only* themselves. *They are* clouds without water, carried about[a] by the winds; late autumn trees without fruit, twice dead, pulled up by the roots; [13]raging waves of the sea, foaming up their own shame; wandering stars for whom is reserved the blackness of darkness forever.

[14]Now Enoch, the seventh from Adam, prophesied about these men also, saying, "Behold, the Lord comes with ten thousands of His saints, [15]to execute judgment on all, to convict all who are ungodly among them of all their ungodly deeds which they have committed in an ungodly way, and of all the harsh things which ungodly sinners have spoken against Him."

A number of the healing miracles of Jesus involved people who were blind or deaf. Jesus seemed equally concerned with those who suffered from spiritual blindness and spiritual deafness.

What does it mean to be spiritually blind? It means to fail to see the needs of others, as well as to fail to recognize the sovereignty and goodness of God.

What does it mean to be spiritually deaf? It means that a person intentionally chooses to ignore the spoken word of the Lord—the teaching of the commandments (the Torah, the Law) and the admonitions of the prophets. Very few people had access to written scrolls of the Old Testament in Jesus' day. Nearly all instruction was oral. The spiritually deaf included those who did not go to the synagogues to hear the Word of God read aloud and preached, did not engage in the study of the Old Testament with a rabbi or teacher, and also those who put themselves in the presence of a reader, rabbi, teacher, or prophet but came with their minds closed to the message.

☐ How sensitive are you to the needs of others?
☐ How aware are you of God's goodness displayed all around you?
☐ How willing are you to be taught?
☐ How willing are you to be impacted and changed by the Word of God and those who teach it and preach it accurately?

12 [a]NU-Text and M-Text read *along.*

APOSTATES PREDICTED

[16]These are grumblers, complainers, walking according to their own lusts; and they mouth great swelling *words*, flattering people to gain advantage. [17]But you, beloved, remember the words which were spoken before by the apostles of our Lord Jesus Christ: [18]how they told you that there would be mockers in the last time who would walk according to their own ungodly lusts. [19]These are sensual persons, who cause divisions, not having the Spirit.

MAINTAIN YOUR LIFE WITH GOD

[20]But you, beloved, building yourselves up on your most holy faith, praying in the Holy Spirit, [21]keep yourselves in the love of God, looking for the mercy of our Lord Jesus Christ unto eternal life.

[22]And on some have compassion, making a distinction;[a] [23]but others save with fear, pulling *them* out of the fire,[a] hating even the garment defiled by the flesh.

GLORY TO GOD

[24] Now to Him who is able to keep you[a] from stumbling,
And to present *you* faultless
Before the presence of His glory with exceeding joy,
[25] To God our Savior,[a]
Who alone is wise,[b]
Be glory and majesty,
Dominion and power,[c]
Both now and forever.
Amen.

SCRIPTURE SOLUTIONS

[HEART DISEASE]

Heart attacks claimed a half-million lives this year, but yours does not need to be one of them! Even if you have neglected your nutrition and fitness level for years, it's never too late to adopt good eating and exercise habits. Good nutrition can help with a number of heart ailments, including heart disease.

Antioxidants are some of the most important nutrients you can supply to your heart. Antioxidants have the ability to repair or block free-radical reactions in the body, as well as help prevent oxidation. Since the heart is the hardest working muscle in the body, it needs a good supply of antioxidants to stay in repair. The same goes for the arteries and veins, especially artery walls. The repair work on torn or damaged arteries requires adequate consumption of antioxidants. Some antioxidants even help prevent damage.

Following is a list of antioxidants recommended for a healthy heart, arteries, and blood vessels:

- ☐ **Vitamin C (1,000–3,000 mg daily)**
- ☐ **Vitamin E (400–800 IU daily)**
- ☐ **Grape seed extract (50–200 mg daily)**
- ☐ **Pine bark extract (50–200 mg daily)**
- ☐ **Beta-carotene (25,000 IU daily)**
- ☐ **Selenium (200 mcg daily)**

Although heart problems may seem overwhelming, always remember that God is the ultimate source of all strength! (See Hebrews 12:1, 2.)

22 [a]NU-Text reads *who are doubting* (or *making distinctions*).   **23** [a]NU-Text adds *and on some have mercy with fear* and omits *with fear* in first clause.   **24** [a]M-Text reads *them.*   **25** [a]NU-Text reads *To the only God our Savior.* [b]NU-Text omits *Who . . . is wise* and adds *Through Jesus Christ our Lord.* [c]NU-Text adds *Before all time.*

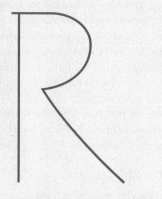

REVELATION

The Book of Revelation has numerous interpretations but it is clear that the writer of this book strongly believed two things: If the good things associated with Jesus and His teachings are carried to their full and logical conclusion, paradise is the result! If the things that are opposite what Jesus taught are carried to their full and logical conclusion, pain, suffering, sorrow, and eternal separation from God are the results.

Make wise choices today about every aspect of your life. What you pursue today will influence who you are tomorrow. The decision you make about Jesus determines where you will live in eternity. The choices you make about how you will serve Christ have an impact on how you will live in eternity.

The person who lives only for the pleasures and gratification of today is a person who is very shortsighted. Life on this earth cannot be compared with eternity either in terms of time or quality of a person's existence. Only what honors Christ Jesus truly lasts and truly produces the highest quality of life, now and forever.

INTRODUCTION AND BENEDICTION

1 The Revelation of Jesus Christ, which God gave Him to show His servants—things which must shortly take place. And He sent and signified it by His angel to His servant John, ²who bore witness to the word of God, and to the testimony of Jesus Christ, to all things that he saw. ³Blessed is he who reads and those who hear the words of this prophecy, and keep those things which are written in it; for the time is near.

GREETING THE SEVEN CHURCHES

⁴John, to the seven churches which are in Asia:

Grace to you and peace from Him who is and who was and who is to come, and from the seven Spirits who are before His throne, ⁵and from Jesus Christ, the faithful witness, the firstborn from the dead, and the ruler over the kings of the earth.

To Him who loved us and washed ᵃ us from our sins in His own blood, ⁶and has made us kings ᵃ and priests to His God and Father, to Him be glory and dominion forever and ever. Amen.

⁷Behold, He is coming with clouds, and every eye will see Him, even they who pierced Him. And all the tribes of the earth will mourn because of Him. Even so, Amen.

⁸"I am the Alpha and the Omega, the Beginning and the End," ᵃ says the Lord, ᵇ "who is and who was and who is to come, the Almighty."

VISION OF THE SON OF MAN

⁹I, John, both ᵃ your brother and companion in the tribulation and kingdom and patience of Jesus Christ, was on the island that is called Patmos for the word of God and for the testimony of Jesus Christ. ¹⁰I was in the Spirit on the Lord's Day, and I heard behind me a loud voice, as of a trumpet, ¹¹saying, "I am the Alpha and the Omega, the First and the Last," ᵃ and, "What you see, write in a book and send it to the seven churches which are in Asia: ᵇ to Ephesus, to Smyrna, to Pergamos, to Thyatira, to Sardis, to Philadelphia, and to Laodicea."

¹²Then I turned to see the voice that spoke with me. And having turned I saw seven golden lampstands, ¹³and in the midst of the seven lampstands One like the Son of Man, clothed with a garment down to the feet and girded about the chest with a golden band. ¹⁴His head and hair were white like wool, as white as snow, and His eyes like a flame of fire; ¹⁵His feet were like fine brass, as if refined in a furnace, and His voice as the sound of many waters; ¹⁶He had in His right hand seven stars, out of His mouth went a sharp two-edged sword, and His countenance was like the sun shining in its strength. ¹⁷And when I saw Him, I fell at His feet as dead. But He laid His right hand on me, saying to me, ᵃ "Do not be afraid; I am the First and the Last. ¹⁸I am He who lives, and was dead, and behold, I am alive forevermore. Amen. And I have the keys of Hades and of Death. ¹⁹Write ᵃ the things which you have seen, and the things which are, and the things which will take place after this. ²⁰The mystery of the seven stars which you saw in My right hand, and the seven golden lampstands: The seven stars are the angels of the seven churches, and the seven lampstands which you saw ᵃ are the seven churches.

THE LOVELESS CHURCH

2 "To the angel of the church of Ephesus write,
'These things says He who holds the seven stars in His right hand, who walks in the midst of the seven golden lampstands:

1:5 ᵃNU-Text reads loves us and freed; M-Text reads loves us and washed. 1:6 ᵃNU-Text and M-Text read a kingdom. 1:8 ᵃNU-Text and M-Text omit the Beginning and the End. ᵇNU-Text and M-Text add God. 1:9 ᵃNU-Text and M-Text omit both. 1:11 ᵃNU-Text and M-Text omit I am through third and. ᵇNU-Text and M-Text omit which are in Asia. 1:17 ᵃNU-Text and M-Text omit to me. 1:19 ᵃNU-Text and M-Text read Therefore, write. 1:20 ᵃNU-Text and M-Text omit which you saw.

Women's Issues

PMS and Mood Swings

A woman's body is a delicate balance of hormones! A number of nutritional and fitness factors can help keep a body in balance. It is especially important that a woman not have *excess* estrogen in her system. Here are some basics to check:

☐ Avoid exposure to xeno-hormones or xeno-estrogens, which are man-made chemicals in the environment that fool your body into believing they are natural estrogen. These chemicals are found in alcohol, fingernail polish and fingernail polish remover, varnishes, degreasers, dry-cleaning fluids, herbicides, emulsifiers in cosmetics and soaps, paints, industrial cleaners, glues, pesticides, plastics, and PCBs.

☐ Avoid over-consumption of alcohol. It can contribute to a poorly functioning liver, which impacts estrogen levels.

☐ Avoid excessive use of prescription medications and over-the-counter medications such as Tylenol that can place strain on the liver.

☐ Avoid xeno-estrogens in fatty beef, whole milk, butter, cheese, pork, and other fatty cuts of meat. Choose meats that are lean, free-range meats, organic foods, and fat-free or low-fat dairy products.

☐ Add soy to your diet—in the form of soy flour, soy milk, or tofu.

☐ Curb your intake of caffeine and salt.

CONT. NEXT PAGE>>>

[2] "I know your works, your labor, your patience, and that you cannot bear those who are evil. And you have tested those who say they are apostles and are not, and have found them liars; [3] and you have persevered and have patience, and have labored for My name's sake and have not become weary. [4] Nevertheless I have *this* against you, that you have left your first love. [5] Remember therefore from where you have fallen; repent and do the first works, or else I will come to you quickly and remove your lampstand from its place—unless you repent. [6] But this you have, that you hate the deeds of the Nicolaitans, which I also hate.

[7] "He who has an ear, let him hear what the Spirit says to the churches. To him who overcomes I will give to eat from the tree of life, which is in the midst of the Paradise of God." '

THE PERSECUTED CHURCH

[8] "And to the angel of the church in Smyrna write,

'These things says the First and the Last, who was dead, and came to life: [9] "I know your works, tribulation, and poverty (but you are rich); and *I know* the blasphemy of those who say they are Jews and are not, but *are* a synagogue of Satan. [10] Do not fear any of those things which you are about to suffer. Indeed, the devil is about to throw *some* of you into prison, that you may be tested, and you will have tribulation ten days. Be faithful until death, and I will give you the crown of life.

[11] "He who has an ear, let him hear what the Spirit says to the churches. He who overcomes shall not be hurt by the second death." '

THE COMPROMISING CHURCH

[12] "And to the angel of the church in Pergamos write,

'These things says He who has the sharp two-edged sword: [13] "I know your works, and where you dwell, where Satan's throne *is*. And you hold fast to My name, and did not deny My faith even in the days in which Antipas *was* My faithful martyr, who was killed among you, where Satan dwells. [14] But I have a few things against you, because you have there those who hold the doctrine of Balaam, who taught Balak to put a stumbling block before the children of Israel, to eat things sacrificed to idols, and to commit sexual immorality. [15] Thus you also have those who hold the doctrine of the Nicolaitans, which thing I hate.[a] [16] Repent, or else I will come to you quickly and will fight against them with the sword of My mouth.

[17] "He who has an ear, let him hear what the Spirit says to the churches. To him who overcomes I will give some of the hidden manna to eat. And I will give him a white stone, and on the stone a new name written which no one knows except him who receives *it*." '

THE CORRUPT CHURCH

[18] "And to the angel of the church in Thyatira write,

'These things says the Son of God, who has eyes like a flame of fire, and His feet like fine brass: [19] "I know your works, love, service, faith,[a] and your patience; and *as for* your works, the last *are* more than the first. [20] Nevertheless I have a few things against you, because you allow[a] that woman[b] Jezebel, who calls herself a prophetess, to teach and seduce[c] My servants to commit sexual immorality and eat things sacrificed to idols. [21] And I gave her time to repent of her sexual im-

---

2:15 [a]NU-Text and M-Text read *likewise* for *which thing I hate.*　　**2:19** [a]NU-Text and M-Text read *faith, service.*　　**2:20** [a]NU-Text and M-Text read *I have against you that you tolerate.*　　[b]M-Text reads *your wife Jezebel.*　　[c]NU-Text and M-Text read *and teaches and seduces.*

blot out his name from the Book of Life; but I will confess his name before My Father and before His angels.

⁶"He who has an ear, let him hear what the Spirit says to the churches." '

THE FAITHFUL CHURCH

⁷"And to the angel of the church in Philadelphia write,

'These things says He who is holy, He who is true, "He who has the key of David, He who opens and no one shuts, and shuts and no one opens":ᵃ ⁸"I know your works. See, I have set before you an open door, and no one can shut it;ᵃ for you have a little strength, have kept My word, and have not denied My name. ⁹Indeed I will make *those* of the synagogue of Satan, who say they are Jews and are not, but lie—indeed I will make them come and worship before your feet, and to know that I have loved you. ¹⁰Because you have kept My command to persevere, I also will keep you from the hour of trial which shall come upon the whole world, to test those who dwell on the earth. ¹¹Behold,ᵃ I am coming quickly! Hold fast what you have, that no one may take your crown. ¹²He who overcomes, I will make him a pillar in the temple of My God, and he shall go out no more. I will write on him the name of

morality, and she did not repent.ᵃ ²²Indeed I will cast her into a sickbed, and those who commit adultery with her into great tribulation, unless they repent of theirᵃ deeds. ²³I will kill her children with death, and all the churches shall know that I am He who searches the minds and hearts. And I will give to each one of you according to your works.

²⁴"Now to you I say, andᵃ to the rest in Thyatira, as many as do not have this doctrine, who have not known the depths of Satan, as they say, I willᵇ put on you no other burden. ²⁵But hold fast what you have till I come. ²⁶And he who overcomes, and keeps My works until the end, to him I will give power over the nations—

²⁷ 'He shall rule them with a rod of iron;
They shall be dashed to pieces like the potter's vessels'ᵃ—

as I also have received from My Father; ²⁸and I will give him the morning star.

²⁹"He who has an ear, let him hear what the Spirit says to the churches." '

THE DEAD CHURCH

3 "And to the angel of the church in Sardis write,

'These things says He who has the seven Spirits of God and the seven stars: "I know your works, that you have a name that you are alive, but you are dead. ²Be watchful, and strengthen the things which remain, that are ready to die, for I have not found your works perfect before God.ᵃ ³Remember therefore how you have received and heard; hold fast and repent. Therefore if you will not watch, I will come upon you as a thief, and you will not know what hour I will come upon you. ⁴Youᵃ have a few names even in Sardis who have not defiled their garments; and they shall walk with Me in white, for they are worthy. ⁵He who overcomes shall be clothed in white garments, and I will not

PRESCRIPTIONS FOR INNER HEALTH

"Do not let your heart envy sinners,
But be zealous for the fear of the LORD all the day;
For surely there is a hereafter,
And your hope will not be cut off."

(PROVERBS 23:17, 18)

Envy and jealousy are truly "green-eyed monsters" that can eat away at a person's joy—and in turn, a person's emotional and physical heath. Envy and jealousy certainly can cause a person to become distracted from what is truly important and eternal. Rather than turn your desire to what sinful people have, do, and are, turn your desire toward gaining what God desires for you to have, do, and be! All of the treasures and status that you can ever desire will be yours one day in eternity if you will keep your priorities in order now.

2:21 ᵃNU-Text and M-Text read *time to repent, and she does not want to repent of her sexual immorality.* 2:22 ᵃNU-Text and M-Text read *her.* 2:24 ᵃNU-Text and M-Text omit *and.* ᵇNU-Text and M-Text omit *will.* 2:27 ᵃPsalm 2:9 3:2 ᵃNU-Text and M-Text read *My God.* 3:4 ᵃNU-Text and M-Text read *Nevertheless you have a few names in Sardis.* 3:7 ᵃIsaiah 22:22 3:8 ᵃNU-Text and M-Text read *which no one can shut.* 3:11 ᵃNU-Text and M-Text omit *Behold.*

DIVINE HEALTH 381

CONDIMENTS

☐ Experiment with Flavor

Common spices in Middle Eastern cooking include dill, cumin, turmeric, cinnamon, and mustard. Not all of these are mentioned in the Bible, but they are all great flavor enhancers. Experiment with them! Dill added to yogurt can make an excellent dip or sauce for fish. Cinnamon is great added to ground beef, along with onions and garlic. Mustard goes great with freshly steamed greens (such as collard greens) and a dash of vinegar. Dill mixed with a small amount of no-fat mayonnaise can be great with tuna and tomatoes in a pita bread sandwich with lots of fresh, finely chopped lettuce.

The more you cleanse your body of toxins and cut down on fatty and sugary foods, the more your taste buds will become sensitive to small nuances of flavor. A little spice can go a long way! As your palate becomes cleansed, you will probably enjoy the flavors of fresh food more, and you'll find that you no longer need to load your foods with salt, hot sauce, or heavy salad dressings and sauces.

If you don't know how a spice tastes, try a very small amount on your finger first. The intensity of some spices and herbs is enhanced by heat. Perhaps try a little in boiling water before you add a new spice or herb to a bowl of steamed vegetables or whole grains.

My God and the name of the city of My God, the New Jerusalem, which comes down out of heaven from My God. And *I will write on him* My new name.

¹³"He who has an ear, let him hear what the Spirit says to the churches." '

THE LUKEWARM CHURCH

¹⁴"And to the angel of the church of the Laodiceans" write,

'These things says the Amen, the Faithful and True Witness, the Beginning of the creation of God: ¹⁵"I know your works, that you are neither cold nor hot. I could wish you were cold or hot. ¹⁶So then, because you are lukewarm, and neither cold nor hot," I will vomit you out of My mouth. ¹⁷Because you say, 'I am rich, have become wealthy, and have need of nothing'—and do not know that you are wretched, miserable, poor, blind, and naked— ¹⁸I counsel you to buy from Me gold refined in the fire, that you may be rich; and white garments, that you may be clothed, *that* the shame of your nakedness may not be revealed; and anoint your eyes with eye salve, that you may see. ¹⁹As many as I love, I rebuke and chasten. Therefore be zealous and repent. ²⁰Behold, I stand at the door and knock. If anyone hears My voice and opens the door, I will come in to him and dine with him, and he with Me. ²¹To him who overcomes I will grant to sit with Me on My throne, as I also overcame and sat down with My Father on His throne.

²²"He who has an ear, let him hear what the Spirit says to the churches." ' "

THE THRONE ROOM OF HEAVEN

4 After these things I looked, and behold, a door *standing* open in heaven. And the first voice which I heard *was* like a trumpet speaking with me, saying, "Come up here, and I will show you things which must take place after this."

²Immediately I was in the Spirit; and behold, a throne set in heaven, and *One* sat on the throne. ³And He who sat there was" like a jasper and a sardius stone in appearance; and *there was* a rainbow around the throne, in appearance like an emerald. ⁴Around the throne *were* twenty-four thrones, and on the thrones I saw twenty-four elders sitting, clothed in white robes; and they had crowns" of gold on their heads. ⁵And from the throne proceeded lightnings, thunderings, and voices." Seven lamps of fire *were* burning before the throne, which are theᵇ seven Spirits of God.

⁶Before the throne *there was*" a sea of glass, like crystal. And in the midst of the throne, and around the throne, *were* four living creatures full of eyes in front and in back. ⁷The first living creature *was* like a lion, the second living creature like a calf, the third living creature had a face like a man, and the fourth living creature *was* like a flying eagle.

Q What amount of faith did Jesus ask His disciples to have?

A **"Faith as a mustard seed"** *(Matthew 17:20)*. **A mustard seed in the Middle East is about the size of a single grain of cayenne pepper.**

3:14 "NU-Text and M-Text read *in Laodicea*. 3:16 "NU-Text and M-Text read *hot nor cold*. 4:3 "M-Text omits *And He who sat there was* (which makes the description in verse 3 modify the throne rather than God). 4:4 "NU-Text and M-Text read *robes, with crowns*. 4:5 "NU-Text and M-Text read *voices, and thunderings*. ᵇM-Text omits *the*. 4:6 "NU-Text and M-Text add *something like*.

December

1   2   3   4   5   6   7

Now Is the Time To...

☐ Prepare your tree to last. If you have chopped down your own tree, wash it thoroughly before bringing it into the house. Soak it using the water hose outside and remove the dead needles and any bugs that may be lurking in the inside growth area of the tree. Bring the tree inside and place it in a tree stand that has a watering bowl. Check the water supply every day. Water will evaporate faster in the heat and dryness of indoor air. Make certain you are not placing your tree too close to a heating vent. ☐ Make an extra effort to get to the gym. Exercise can help relieve added holiday stress! ☐ Make a checklist. You'll be less likely to forget something important and more likely to accomplish more in less time.

Seasonal Tips

8   9   10   11   12   13   14

☐ Remember to unplug your tree lights when you leave the house. ☐ Make plans to recycle your Christmas tree by delivering it to a place that mulches evergreens. ☐ Get the most from your Christmas gift plants by remembering these tips: 1) Water plants less than you would in the summer months, and refrain from using fertilizers. If water collects in a drain dish, empty it after one hour. 2) Place flowering plants where they will receive the most sunlight. 3) Winter plants prefer cooler temperatures, and do much better away from heat ducts or in areas where the temperature may fluctuate, such as close to a door or a single-paned window.

In the Garden

15   16   17   18   19

☐ Check all outdoor faucets to make sure they are protected from freezing weather.
☐ If you live where walks and driveways are likely to freeze, make sure you have de-icer. Choose a de-icer that is calcium-chloride based to avoid salt damage to your car. You can also use sand, or clay kitty litter.

22   23   24   25   26

Table Fresh

☐ Make a few large pots of hearty soup early in December and freeze the soup in dinner-sized portions. Soup, served with a little cheese, bread, and a salad, can be a quick, easy, nutritious, and satisfying meal on days when you have lots of shopping or decorating to do. ☐ Freeze orange slices and cranberries after they have been thoroughly washed. Add them to water glasses at holiday meals and parties. They will add festive color to your table, add a slight flavor to the water, and replace the need for ice.

29   30   31

Let's Celebrate

☐ Do you still have holiday shopping to do? Many malls and stores extend their hours. Try to arrive when the store opens. The store will be less crowded and you will be able to make your selections faster and easier. If you are planning to shop in a mall, strap on a pedometer to count the steps you take. You may find that you can skip going to the gym that evening! ☐ Take time out to enjoy the lights . . . candles . . . music . . . and aromas of the holiday season. Live in the moment! ☐ If you are planning to travel during the holiday season, here are some tips: 1) Plan to leave home rested. Start packing and preparing so you can get a good night's sleep the night before your trip. 2) Begin packing early and use a checklist. You'll be more likely to take everything you need. 3) Pack light. Heavy luggage can make a trip feel more burdensome—literally! ☐ **Advent.** The days leading up to Christmas are intended to be solemn days for reflection on the coming of Christ—both His First Coming and His coming again. Add some quiet devotional times to your holiday calendar.

Stress Busters
The Anxiety-Prone Personality

Do any of these behaviors describe you?

☐ Black-and-white thinking
☐ Keeping secrets
☐ Perfectionist expectations
☐ Suppressing feelings
☐ Taking things personally
☐ Jumping to conclusion
☐ Avoiding preparation or frequently lacking in preparation (winging it)

If any of these behaviors apply, you may have an anxiety-prone personality.

[8]*The* four living creatures, each having six wings, were full of eyes around and within. And they do not rest day or night, saying:

"Holy, holy, holy,[a]
Lord God Almighty,
Who was and is and is to come!"

[9]Whenever the living creatures give glory and honor and thanks to Him who sits on the throne, who lives forever and ever, [10]the twenty-four elders fall down before Him who sits on the throne and worship Him who lives forever and ever, and cast their crowns before the throne, saying:

[11]"You are worthy, O Lord,[a]
To receive glory and honor and power;
For You created all things,
And by Your will they exist[b] and were created."

THE LAMB TAKES THE SCROLL

5 And I saw in the right *hand* of Him who sat on the throne a scroll written inside and on the back, sealed with seven seals. [2]Then I saw a strong angel proclaiming with a loud voice, "Who is worthy to open the scroll and to loose its seals?" [3]And no one in heaven or on the earth or under the earth was able to open the scroll, or to look at it.

[4]So I wept much, because no one was found worthy to open and read[a] the scroll, or to look at it. [5]But one of the elders said to me, "Do not weep. Behold, the Lion of the tribe of Judah, the Root of David, has prevailed to open the scroll and to loose[a] its seven seals."

[6]And I looked, and behold,[a] in the midst of the throne and of the four living creatures, and in the midst of the elders, stood a Lamb as though it had been slain, having seven horns and seven eyes, which are the seven Spirits of God sent out into all the earth. [7]Then He came and took the scroll out of the right hand of Him who sat on the throne.

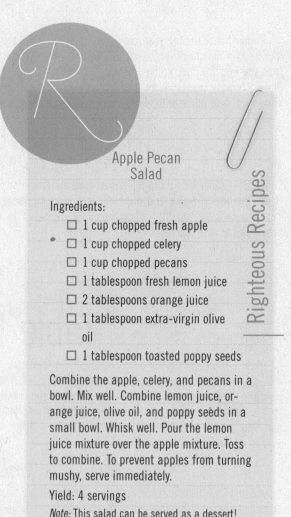

Righteous Recipes

Apple Pecan Salad

Ingredients:
☐ 1 cup chopped fresh apple
☐ 1 cup chopped celery
☐ 1 cup chopped pecans
☐ 1 tablespoon fresh lemon juice
☐ 2 tablespoons orange juice
☐ 1 tablespoon extra-virgin olive oil
☐ 1 tablespoon toasted poppy seeds

Combine the apple, celery, and pecans in a bowl. Mix well. Combine lemon juice, orange juice, olive oil, and poppy seeds in a small bowl. Whisk well. Pour the lemon juice mixture over the apple mixture. Toss to combine. To prevent apples from turning mushy, serve immediately.

Yield: 4 servings
Note: This salad can be served as a dessert!

4:8 [a]M-Text has *holy* nine times.   4:11 [a]NU-Text and M-Text read *our Lord and God.* [b]NU-Text and M-Text read *existed.*   5:4 [a]NU-Text and M-Text omit *and read.*   5:5 [a]NU-Text and M-Text omit *to loose.*   5:6 [a]NU-Text and M-Text read *I saw in the midst . . . a Lamb standing.*

weighing Less &
enjoying life more!

[Smoothies—the Ultimate Fast Food]

One of the best things you can have for breakfast, or as a mid-afternoon mini-meal is a smoothie made with foods that are *good* for you, and not as fattening as many breakfast and snack foods!

A fruit smoothie is easy to make. Put 10 ounces of fresh berries in a blender—such as blueberries, raspberries, or strawberries. You can use frozen fruit, but it's best to thaw it to room temperature first. Then add a 15-ounce can of peaches or pears in natural syrup. Add 2 tablespoons honey and blend until smooth. Serve immediately. (This amount makes 2 servings.)

Or try a refreshing fruit shake. I like a shake made with melons. Put 1 cup cubed watermelon, 1 cup cubed cantaloupe, and 1 cup cubed honeydew melon in a blender. Process until smooth. Then mix together 1 cup low-fat or nonfat yogurt, 2 tablespoons lemon juice, a half teaspoon vanilla extract, and a half cup of crushed ice in a bowl. Slowly blend in this mixture to the melon. Process until smooth and serve immediately. (This recipe makes 4–6 servings.)

Protein powder—such as whey powder—can be added to fruit and nonfat milk for a good protein shake.

To any of these shakes you can usually add a few crystals of vitamin C to keep the shake from oxidizing (turning brown). You might want to split the portions, drinking one as breakfast and the second portion a couple of hours later as a mid-morning snack.

WORTHY IS THE LAMB

[8]Now when He had taken the scroll, the four living creatures and the twenty-four elders fell down before the Lamb, each having a harp, and golden bowls full of incense, which are the prayers of the saints. [9]And they sang a new song, saying:

"You are worthy to take the scroll,
And to open its seals;
For You were slain,
And have redeemed us to God by Your blood
Out of every tribe and tongue and people and nation,
[10] And have made us[a] kings[b] and priests to our God;
And we[c] shall reign on the earth."

[11]Then I looked, and I heard the voice of many angels around the throne, the living creatures, and the elders; and the number of them was ten thousand times ten thousand, and thousands of thousands, [12]saying with a loud voice:

"Worthy is the Lamb who was slain
To receive power and riches and wisdom,
And strength and honor and glory and blessing!"

[13]And every creature which is in heaven and on the earth and under the earth and such as are in the sea, and all that are in them, I heard saying:

"Blessing and honor and glory and power
Be to Him who sits on the throne,
And to the Lamb, forever and ever!"[a]

[14]Then the four living creatures said, "Amen!" And the twenty-four[a] elders fell down and worshiped Him who lives forever and ever.[b]

FIRST SEAL: THE CONQUEROR

6 Now I saw when the Lamb opened one of the seals;[a] and I heard one of the four living creatures saying with a voice like thunder, "Come and see." [2]And I looked, and behold, a white horse. He who sat on it had a bow; and a crown was given to him, and he went out conquering and to conquer.

"Joy, temperance, and repose, slam the door on the doctor's nose." —*Henry Wadsworth Longfellow, American poet (1807–1882)*

PREACHING HEALTH

5:10 [a]NU-Text and M-Text read *them.* [b]NU-Text reads *a kingdom.* [c]NU-Text and M-Text read *they.*   5:13 [a]M-Text adds *Amen.*   5:14 [a]NU-Text and M-Text omit *twenty-four.* [b]NU-Text and M-Text omit *Him who lives forever and ever.*   6:1 [a]NU-Text and M-Text read *seven seals.*

walking the walk

[PUTTING YOUR BEST FOOT FORWARD]

As natural as walking is for most people, you might think it's impossible to walk incorrectly. Mistakes, however, do occur while walking as exercise, and some of them can have serious consequences. Do the following to put your "best foot forward":

Buy the Right Shoes for You. To get the best walking shoes for your feet, visit a reputable sports shoe retailer who will measure your feet and analyze your walking technique. This information is important if you want the optimal shoes. Good walking or running shoes may cost a little more, but you will likely experience fewer injuries and the shoes will probably last longer!

Replace Worn-Out Shoes. Walking shoes should be replaced every 250 miles.

Use the Right Posture. Poor posture in walking can lead to sore muscles and injuries, and deny you the best workout. When picking up speed, rather than expand your stride, lean slightly into the walk. This does not mean to lean at the hips, but rather, lean your entire body. Your body should still be in a straight line yet at a slight forward angle. You may lean or thrust more when walking up steep hills.

Use Your Arms. By pumping your arms as you walk, you will help trim your waistline and improve your overall time. Pump your arms in a firm yet flexible forward motion to aid in moving you forward.

Don't "Stomp." Keep your feet in a *rolling* or *curved* motion while in step. If you are hitting the ground hard, are stiff from the ankles down, or walk in a stomping fashion you may be setting yourself up for injury or pains in your shins. Let your feet propel you forward. CONT. NEXT PAGE>>>

SECOND SEAL: CONFLICT ON EARTH

³When He opened the second seal, I heard the second living creature saying, "Come and see."ᵃ ⁴Another horse, fiery red, went out. And it was granted to the one who sat on it to take peace from the earth, and that *people* should kill one another; and there was given to him a great sword.

THIRD SEAL: SCARCITY ON EARTH

⁵When He opened the third seal, I heard the third living creature say, "Come and see." So I looked, and behold, a black horse, and he who sat on it had a pair of scales in his hand. ⁶And I heard a voice in the midst of the four living creatures saying, "A quartᵃ of wheat for a denarius,ᵇ and three quarts of barley for a denarius; and do not harm the oil and the wine."

FOURTH SEAL: WIDESPREAD DEATH ON EARTH

⁷When He opened the fourth seal, I heard the voice of the fourth living creature saying, "Come and see." ⁸So I looked, and behold, a pale horse. And the name of him who sat on it was Death, and Hades followed with him. And power was given to them over a fourth of the earth, to kill with sword, with hunger, with death, and by the beasts of the earth.

FIFTH SEAL: THE CRY OF THE MARTYRS

⁹When He opened the fifth seal, I saw under the altar the souls of those who had been slain for the word of God and for the testimony which they held. ¹⁰And they cried with a loud voice, saying, "How long, O Lord, holy and true, until You judge and avenge our blood on those who dwell on the earth?" ¹¹Then a white robe was given to each of them; and it was said to them that they should rest a little while longer, until both *the number of* their fellow servants and their brethren, who would be killed as they *were,* was completed.

SIXTH SEAL: COSMIC DISTURBANCES

¹²I looked when He opened the sixth seal, and behold,ᵃ there was a great earthquake; and the sun became black as sackcloth of hair, and the moonᵇ became like blood. ¹³And the stars of heaven fell to the earth, as a fig tree drops its late figs when it is shaken by a mighty wind. ¹⁴Then the sky receded as a scroll when it is rolled up, and every mountain and island was moved out of its place. ¹⁵And the kings of the earth, the great men, the rich men, the commanders,ᵃ the mighty men, every slave and every free man, hid themselves in the caves and in the rocks of the mountains, ¹⁶and said to the mountains and rocks, "Fall on us and hide us from the face of Him who sits on the throne and from the wrath of the Lamb! ¹⁷For the great day of His wrath has come, and who is able to stand?"

THE SEALED OF ISRAEL

7 After these things I saw four angels standing at the four corners of the earth, holding the four winds of the earth, that the wind should not blow on the earth, on the sea, or on any tree. ²Then I saw another angel ascending from the east, having the seal of the living God. And he cried with a loud voice to the four angels to

6:3 ᵃNU-Text and M-Text omit *and see.* 6:6 ᵃGreek *choinix;* that is, approximately one quart ᵇThis was approximately one day's wage for a worker. 6:12 ᵃNU-Text and M-Text omit *behold.* ᵇNU-Text and M-Text read *the whole moon.* 6:15 ᵃNU-Text and M-Text read *the commanders, the rich men.*

Walking the Walk Cont.>>>

Look Ahead. Look up and watch where you're going. This helps to keep the neck and spine straight and aligned.

Take Along Food and Water. When walking outdoors, you should always carry water. Your body requires water to function properly. When you are walking briskly or hiking for more than two hours, you should be drinking an electrolyte-replacement sports drink. Food is also essential if you are planning to walk for more than ninety minutes. Take along an energy bar, a small baggie of nuts or pretzels, or a sports food gel in your pocket.

whom it was granted to harm the earth and the sea, ³saying, "Do not harm the earth, the sea, or the trees till we have sealed the servants of our God on their foreheads." ⁴And I heard the number of those who were sealed. One hundred *and* forty-four thousand of all the tribes of the children of Israel *were* sealed:

⁵ of the tribe of Judah twelve thousand *were* sealed;ᵃ
   of the tribe of Reuben twelve thousand *were* sealed;
   of the tribe of Gad twelve thousand *were* sealed;
⁶ of the tribe of Asher twelve thousand *were* sealed;
   of the tribe of Naphtali twelve thousand *were* sealed;
   of the tribe of Manasseh twelve thousand *were* sealed;
⁷ of the tribe of Simeon twelve thousand *were* sealed;
   of the tribe of Levi twelve thousand *were* sealed;
   of the tribe of Issachar twelve thousand *were* sealed;
⁸ of the tribe of Zebulun twelve thousand *were* sealed;
   of the tribe of Joseph twelve thousand *were* sealed;
   of the tribe of Benjamin twelve thousand *were* sealed.

A MULTITUDE FROM THE GREAT TRIBULATION

⁹After these things I looked, and behold, a great multitude which no one could number, of all nations, tribes, peoples, and tongues, standing before the throne and before the Lamb, clothed with white robes, with palm branches in their hands, ¹⁰and crying out with a loud voice, saying, "Salvation *belongs* to our God who sits on the throne, and to the Lamb!" ¹¹All the angels stood around the throne and the elders and the four living creatures, and fell on their faces before the throne and worshiped God, ¹²saying:

"Amen! Blessing and glory and wisdom,
   Thanksgiving and honor and power and might,
   Be to our God forever and ever.
   Amen."

The Brain–Body Connection in Heart Attacks

Scientists are learning more and more about how the brain and body are connected. Consider this simple sequence:

1. Stress impacts the level of neurotransmitters (hormones and chemicals) in the brain. Various psychological factors, including chronic anxiety and fear, cause lower production of neurotransmitters.

2. The neurotransmitters, in turn, send signals about the formation of T-cells and other immune-related systems. If the neurotransmitters are weakened, damaged, or partially destroyed, fewer T-cells are formed or activated, and other immune functions become depressed.

3. When immunity is down, infection can more readily take hold. Infection not only impacts the tissues of the body, weakening them and causing general lethargy and fatigue, but infection also can invade the lining of the blood vessels.

4. When infection in the lining of the blood vessels "erupts," cholesterol trapped by plaque build-up along the vessel walls is released as "clots" into the bloodstream. These clots are often the cause of sudden and fatal heart attacks and strokes.

This is just one way in which psychological factors of stress have very real physical consequences. There are many others.

The Bible says about our human nature: "As he thinks in his heart, so is he" (Proverbs 23:7). Stress we feel emotionally *does* translate into the way we feel physically.

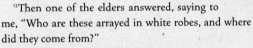

¹³Then one of the elders answered, saying to me, "Who are these arrayed in white robes, and where did they come from?"

¹⁴And I said to him, "Sir,ᵃ you know."

So he said to me, "These are the ones who come out of the great tribulation, and washed their robes and made them white in the blood of the Lamb. ¹⁵Therefore they are before the throne of God, and serve Him day

7:5 ᵃIn NU-Text and M-Text *were sealed* is stated only in verses 5a and 8c; the words are understood in the remainder of the passage.   7:14 ᵃNU-Text and M-Text read *My lord.*

ULTIMATE HEALTH RESOURCE • ULTIMATE HEALTH RESOURCE • ULTIMATE HEALTH RESOURCE

Our Creator designed every aspect of our lives to be in a balance of input and output. Consider the balance God has designed in these areas:

Input	Output	God's Plan for Balance and Health
Breathe in	Breathe out	Oxygenate the blood; deep breathing can relieve stress
Food in	Food out	Energy, strength, renewal of cells in the body—all enhanced when a person eats the right foods in the right quantity and with great digestion, absorption, and elimination
Water in	Water out	Hydration of all cells; removal of toxins; better blood flow and maintenance of water-based bodily fluids
Hearing the Word of God	Stronger faith; greater trust in God	Emotional stability and inner confidence,higher self-esteem, greater humility
Receiving from godly people	Giving to others in a godly way	Education, edification, strong friendships, mutual sharing of spiritual gifts, meeting of practical needs
Forgiveness received from God and others	Forgiveness given to others and self	Emotional health, less stress, greater feelings of peace and freedom, stronger relationships
Peaceful sleep and adequate relaxation	Productive and enjoyable work and activity	Feelings of well-being, strength, and satisfaction
Education, the development of talents, the acquisition of skills	Creative productivity and accomplishments at work	Feelings of fulfillment and enhanced feelings of purpose for living
Wise counsel from mentors, friends, and God's Word	A moral and ethical life	Feelings of success, eternal relationships, reputation of godliness and integrity, greater wisdom and understanding
Earning what you can	Spending only what you earn	Faithfulness in tithes and offerings, good stewardship of resources, balanced budgets,meeting of practical needs, improved sense of self-worth, sufficient savings for emergencies
Reaping	Sowing, cultivating, and replenishing	Good stewardship of the environment, furthering life cycles, renewing the earth
Time spent in prayer, praise, and meditation	Ministry to the church and witnessing to the lost	Salvation of lost souls, discipleship of God's people

and night in His temple. And He who sits on the throne will dwell among them. [16]They shall neither hunger anymore nor thirst anymore; the sun shall not strike them, nor any heat; [17]for the Lamb who is in the midst of the throne will shepherd them and lead them to living fountains of waters.[a] And God will wipe away every tear from their eyes."

SEVENTH SEAL: PRELUDE TO THE SEVEN TRUMPETS

8 When He opened the seventh seal, there was silence in heaven for about half an hour. [2]And I saw the seven angels who stand before God, and to them were given seven trumpets. [3]Then another angel, having a golden censer, came and stood at the altar. He was given much incense, that he should offer *it* with the prayers of all the saints upon the golden altar which was before the throne. [4]And the smoke of the incense, with the prayers of the saints, ascended before God from the angel's hand. [5]Then the angel took the censer, filled it with fire from the altar, and threw *it* to the earth. And there were noises, thunderings, lightnings, and an earthquake.

[6]So the seven angels who had the seven trumpets prepared themselves to sound.

FIRST TRUMPET: VEGETATION STRUCK

[7]The first angel sounded: And hail and fire followed, mingled with blood, and were thrown to the earth.[a] And a third of the trees were burned up, and all green grass was burned up.

SECOND TRUMPET: THE SEAS STRUCK

[8]Then the second angel sounded: And *something* like a great mountain burning with fire was thrown into the sea, and a third of the sea became blood. [9]And a third of the living creatures in the sea died, and a third of the ships were destroyed.

THIRD TRUMPET: THE WATERS STRUCK

[10]Then the third angel sounded: And a great star fell from heaven, burning like a torch, and it fell on a third of the rivers and on the springs of water. [11]The name of the star is Wormwood. A third of the waters became wormwood, and many men died from the water, because it was made bitter.

FOURTH TRUMPET: THE HEAVENS STRUCK

[12]Then the fourth angel sounded: And a third of the sun was struck, a third of the moon, and a third of the stars, so that a third of them were darkened. A third of the day did not shine, and likewise the night.

[13]And I looked, and I heard an angel[a] flying through the midst of heaven, saying with a loud voice, "Woe, woe, woe to the inhabitants of the earth, because of the remaining blasts of the trumpet of the three angels who are about to sound!"

FIFTH TRUMPET: THE LOCUSTS FROM THE BOTTOMLESS PIT

9 Then the fifth angel sounded: And I saw a star fallen from heaven to the earth. To him was given the key to the bottomless pit. [2]And he opened the bottomless pit, and smoke arose

SCRIPTURE SOLUTIONS

[HIGH CHOLESTEROL]

Cholesterol is essential to our bodies functioning properly, but *elevated* cholesterol levels are unhealthy. Cholesterol is a soft, waxy, white substance we consume through animal-related foods such as eggs, red meat, poultry, and dairy products. Our cell membranes and certain hormones—estrogen, progesterone, and testosterone among them—are all formed through cholesterol.

Surprisingly enough, our bodies would do just fine with the cholesterol they produce on their own without any additional consumption of cholesterol. A healthy liver manufactures about 1,000 mg of cholesterol per day, which is really all a person needs. We Americans, however, get in trouble with cholesterol because we consume another 400 to 500 mg in our average daily diet.

Answer the questions below. These questions contain some of the factors that put a person at a higher threat level for high cholesterol.

☐ **Are you a man over the age of forty-five?**
☐ **Are you a woman over the age of fifty-five?**
☐ **Do you smoke cigarettes?**
☐ **Is there a history of premature coronary disease in your family?**
☐ **Do you have hypertension with a blood pressure reading of 140/90 or above?**
☐ **Do you have HDL cholesterol levels of 40 mg/dl or below?**

If you have high cholesterol and answered yes to two or more of the questions above, you may want to talk to your physician and seek out the best approach for reducing your cholesterol.

7:17 [a]NU-Text and M-Text read *to fountains of the waters of life.*   **8:7** [a]NU-Text and M-Text add *and a third of the earth was burned up.*   **8:13** [a]NU-Text and M-Text read *eagle.*

GODLY & GOODLOOKIN'

Firmin' the Fanny

Do your buttocks need a little toning? Regardless if you think your rear is too big or too small, these exercises can give your backside better muscle tone:

Squats. Stand with your feet hip-width apart, and imagine that the wall has a built-in chair directly behind you. As you keep your chest upright and as straight as possible against the wall, sit "down" as far as you can, sliding your body against the wall. Do not let your knees extend past your toes—in other words, maintain as close to a ninety-degree angle for your knees as possible with your feet directly under your knees. Lock in your abs, plant your weight on your heels, and hold this position for ten seconds. Do 2 sets of 15 repetitions each as part of your overall workout.

Lunges. With one knee bent and in front of you, take the other leg back into a lunge position. Then, stand upright. Keep your abs tight as you raise and lower your torso to and from the lunge position. Do 2 sets of 15 repetitions as part of your workout. You should feel the muscles in your buttocks as you do this exercise.

Walking. For maximum benefit to the buttocks, walk hills. Running and hiking on mountain trails can burn even more calories and firm the buttocks faster.

out of the pit like the smoke of a great furnace. So the sun and the air were darkened because of the smoke of the pit. [7]Then out of the smoke locusts came upon the earth. And to them was given power, as the scorpions of the earth have power. [4]They were commanded not to harm the grass of the earth, or any green thing, or any tree, but only those men who do not have the seal of God on their foreheads. [5]And they were not given *authority* to kill them, but to torment them *for* five months. Their torment *was* like the torment of a scorpion when it strikes a man. [6]In those days men will seek death and will not find it; they will desire to die, and death will flee from them.

[7]The shape of the locusts was like horses prepared for battle. On their heads were crowns of something like gold, and their faces *were* like the faces of men. [8]They had hair like women's hair, and their teeth were like lions' *teeth.* [9]And they had breastplates like breastplates of iron, and the sound of their wings *was* like the sound of chariots with many horses running into battle. [10]They had tails like scorpions, and there were stings in their tails. Their power *was* to hurt men five months. [11]And they had as king over them the angel of the bottomless pit, whose name in Hebrew *is* Abaddon, but in Greek he has the name Apollyon.

[12]One woe is past. Behold, still two more woes are coming after these things.

SIXTH TRUMPET: THE ANGELS FROM THE EUPHRATES

[13]Then the sixth angel sounded: And I heard a voice from the four horns of the golden altar which is before God, [14]saying to the sixth angel who had the trumpet, "Release the four angels who are bound at the great river Euphrates." [15]So the four angels, who had been prepared for the hour and day and month and year, were released to kill a third of mankind. [16]Now the number of the army of the horsemen *was* two hundred million; I heard the number of them. [17]And thus I saw the horses in the vision: those who sat on them had breastplates of fiery red, hyacinth blue, and sulfur yellow; and the heads of the horses *were* like the heads of lions; and out of their mouths came fire, smoke, and brimstone. [18]By these three *plagues* a third of mankind was killed—by the fire and the smoke and the brimstone which came out of their mouths. [19]For their power[a] is in their mouth and in their tails; for their tails *are* like serpents, having heads; and with them they do harm.

[20]But the rest of mankind,

WISE CHOICES

Choose good character over good appearance. Good moral character is genuine and lasting—it doesn't disappoint. Appearances can be deceiving and disappointing. Always evaluate appearance against the criterion of character.

9:19 [a]NU-Text and M-Text read *the power of the horses.*

who were not killed by these plagues, did not repent of the works of their hands, that they should not worship demons, and idols of gold, silver, brass, stone, and wood, which can neither see nor hear nor walk. ²¹And they did not repent of their murders or their sorceries*a* or their sexual immorality or their thefts.

THE MIGHTY ANGEL WITH THE LITTLE BOOK

10 I saw still another mighty angel coming down from heaven, clothed with a cloud. And a rainbow *was* on his head, his face *was* like the sun, and his feet like pillars of fire. ²He had a little book open in his hand. And he set his right foot on the sea and *his* left *foot* on the land, ³and cried with a loud voice, as *when* a lion roars. When he cried out, seven thunders uttered their voices. ⁴Now when the seven thunders uttered their voices,*a* I was about to write; but I heard a voice from heaven saying to me,*b* "Seal up the things which the seven thunders uttered, and do not write them."

⁵The angel whom I saw standing on the sea and on the land raised up his hand*a* to heaven ⁶and swore by Him who lives forever and ever, who created heaven and the things that are in it, the earth and the things that are in it, and the sea and the things that are in it, that there should be delay no longer, ⁷but in the days of the sounding of the seventh angel, when he is about to sound, the mys-

R℞ PRESCRIPTIONS
FOR INNER HEALTH

"Like one who takes away a garment
in cold weather,
And like vinegar on soda,
Is one who sings songs to a
heavy heart."

(PROVERBS 25:20)

In spite of our good intentions of cheering up those who may be grieving or in deep sorrow, we are wiser just to be quietly present. We must never say to a person, "It didn't matter," "It's all for the best," "You'll get over it," or "You'll survive." Those words ring hollow to a person in deep emotional distress. Sitting quietly with a person, perhaps crying with them or touching them gently, is more soothing—it allows the person to vent their sorrow and for the Lord to begin the healing process from the inside out.

The Healthy Soul
>Joy

PEACE LOVE JOY KINDNESS

A healthy soul is marked by joy. The question many of us need to ask is, How can I increase my level of joy?

First, recognize that happiness and joy are two different things. Happiness is a feeling of pleasure, contentment, or well-being that is directly connected to a person's environment or to an event or circumstance. It is dependent on external factors.

Joy, in contrast, is abiding or enduring. It comes from an internal feeling of contentment deep inside a person. Joy is related to an inner sense of value, purpose, fulfillment, and satisfaction.

If your goal is to find happiness through pleasure, you will never be fully satisfied because you will need to pursue pleasure nonstop. In the end, you will be more prone to addictions related to pleasure-producing substances. Happiness also tends to be related to immediate gratification or results. In truth, the things that give us genuine joy tend to be those things that we have trusted God to help us accomplish or receive over time and with the full use of our talents and skills.

Second, recognize that joy is directly related to thanksgiving and praise. The more you thank God and praise Him, the more joy you will feel welling up inside you. Thanksgiving and praise take a person's attention away from life's problems and heartaches and put the focus on God's ability to produce, sustain, nurture, and provide all things that are good for life and beneficial for eternity. Praise turns a person's heart away from the negatives in the immediate external world and toward the promise of *all* the positives that God embodies and might create!

Third, recognize that the more you allow yourself to be filled to overflowing with God's Spirit, the more genuine joy you will have. God is not sorrowful or somber. The true picture of God in the Bible is that He *delights* in His creation and *takes joy* in human beings who trust in Him. God imparts His joy to His people—His joy is infectious!

tery of God would be finished, as He declared to His servants the prophets.

JOHN EATS THE LITTLE BOOK

⁸Then the voice which I heard from heaven spoke to me again and said, "Go, take the little book which is open in the hand of the angel who stands on the sea and on the earth."

9:21 *a*NU-Text and M-Text read *drugs.* 10:4 *a*NU-Text and M-Text read *sounded.* *b*NU-Text and M-Text omit *to me.* 10:5 *a*NU-Text and M-Text read *right hand.*

walking the walk

[WALK FOR A CAUSE]

Walking is a wonderful sport and there are multiple benefits to walking as exercise. When you decide to walk to help save lives, however, the rewards of walking are even greater.

Consider walking to raise funds for your favorite charity.

When you participate in a walk or a run for a charity, you are basically asking people to give money to sponsor you in the event. They may be giving you dollars per mile, or per minute, or they may just be giving to be listed as one of your sponsors in a program, brochure, or published report. Sometimes the person who raises the most money for an event is honored for their fund-raising efforts at an organization's annual banquet or in their annual report. The money often goes for medical research.

Some organizations offer free training with certified coaches as part of their commitment to you, while others allow you to form teams so you might train together. Here are four organizations that provide training help:

☐ *Team in Training* assigns you a coach and team to train with as you seek to raise money for the Leukemia and Lymphoma Society.
☐ *Team MS* supports the Multiple Sclerosis Society.
☐ *Walk America* is nationally known for raising money for the March of Dimes.
☐ *Joints in Motion* is the training program for the Arthritis Foundation.

Other foundations and charities you can walk for are: the American Diabetes Association, the American Stroke Association, the Susan G. Komen Breast Cancer Foundation, the American Heart Association, CONT. NEXT PAGE>>>

---

⁹So I went to the angel and said to him, "Give me the little book." And he said to me, "Take and eat it; and it will make your stomach bitter, but it will be as sweet as honey in your mouth." ¹⁰Then I took the little book out of the angel's hand and ate it, and it was as sweet as honey in my mouth. But when I had eaten it, my stomach became bitter. ¹¹And heᵃ said to me, "You must prophesy again about many peoples, nations, tongues, and kings."

THE TWO WITNESSES

11 Then I was given a reed like a measuring rod. And the angel stood,ᵃ saying, "Rise and measure the temple of God, the altar, and those who worship there. ²But leave out the court which is outside the temple, and do not measure it, for it has been given to the Gentiles. And they will tread the holy city underfoot *for* forty-two months. ³And I will give *power* to my two witnesses, and they will prophesy one thousand two hundred and sixty days, clothed in sackcloth."

⁴These are the two olive trees and the two lampstands standing before the Godᵃ of the earth. ⁵And if anyone wants to harm them, fire proceeds from their mouth and devours their enemies. And if anyone wants to harm them, he must be killed in this manner. ⁶These have power to shut heaven, so that no rain falls in the days of their prophecy; and they have power over waters to turn them to blood, and to strike the earth with all plagues, as often as they desire.

THE WITNESSES KILLED

⁷When they finish their testimony, the beast that ascends out of the bottomless pit will make war against them, overcome them, and kill them. ⁸And their dead bodies *will lie* in the street of the great city which spiritually is called Sodom and Egypt, where also ourᵃ Lord was crucified. ⁹Then *those* from the peoples, tribes, tongues, and nations will see their dead bodies three-and-a-half days, and not allowᵃ their dead bodies to be put into graves. ¹⁰And those who dwell on the earth will rejoice over them, make merry, and send gifts to one another, because these two prophets tormented those who dwell on the earth.

THE WITNESSES RESURRECTED

¹¹Now after the three-and-a-half days the breath of life from God entered them, and they stood on their feet, and great fear fell on those who saw them. ¹²And theyᵃ heard a loud voice from heaven saying to them, "Come up here." And they ascended to heaven in a cloud, and their enemies saw them. ¹³In the same hour there was a great earthquake, and a tenth of the city fell. In the earthquake seven thousand people were killed, and the rest were afraid and gave glory to the God of heaven.

¹⁴The second woe is past. Behold, the third woe is coming quickly.

SEVENTH TRUMPET: THE KINGDOM PROCLAIMED

¹⁵Then the seventh angel sounded: And there were loud voices in heaven, saying, "The kingdomsᵃ of this world have become *the kingdoms* of our Lord and of His Christ, and He shall reign forever and ever!" ¹⁶And the twenty-four elders who sat before God on their thrones fell on their faces and worshiped God, ¹⁷saying:

10:11 ᵃNU-Text and M-Text read *they.*   **11:1** ᵃNU-Text and M-Text omit *And the angel stood.*   **11:4** ᵃNU-Text and M-Text read *Lord.*   **11:8** ᵃNU-Text and M-Text read *their.*   **11:9** ᵃNU-Text and M-Text read *nations see . . . and will not allow.*   **11:12** ᵃM-Text reads *I.*   **11:15** ᵃNU-Text and M-Text read *kingdom . . . has become.*

392   DIVINE HEALTH

Walking The Walk Cont. >>>

the National AIDS Fund, the Cystic Fibrosis Foundation, Out of the Darkness—The Foundation for Suicide Prevention, the American Cancer Society, and the American Lung Association.

For information about upcoming walking events, local charities, and team training, check with the local chapter or office of a foundation or charity you might like to help.

Just think! Walking may not only improve your health, it might save another person's life!

Righteous Recipes

Poached Pears with Ginger and Peppercorns

Ingredients:

- ☐ 4 cups water
- ☐ 1 tablespoon fresh lemon juice
- ☐ 4–6 ripe (not soft) pears with stems
- ☐ 1 bottle dry red wine
- ☐ 1 cup sugar (or 1 teaspoon Stevia)
- ☐ Juice and grated zest of 1 lemon
- ☐ 4 half-inch slices of peeled fresh gingerroot
- ☐ 10 whole peppercorns

Stir together the water and 1 tablespoon lemon juice in a large bowl. Peel the pears, leaving stems intact, and cut a thin slice from the bottom of each to enable pear to stand upright when served. Place the pears in the lemon water to keep them from browning. Combine the wine and sugar in a pan that is large enough to hold all the pears lying on their sides. Bring just to a boil. Add the lemon juice and zest, ginger slices, and peppercorns.

Remove the pears from the lemon water and arrange them on their sides in the wine poaching liquid; add more water as necessary just to cover the pears. Reduce the heat and simmer 15–20 minutes or until the pears are tender, turning them occasionally. Be careful not to cook the pears too long or they will turn mushy.

Carefully remove the pears to a serving dish. Strain the ginger slices and peppercorns from the poaching liquid. Cook the liquid over high heat until it is reduced to about ¾ cup and is slightly syrupy. Remove from heat. Pour the liquid over the pears. Cover and chill until ready to serve.

Yield: 4–6 servings

"We give You thanks, O Lord God Almighty,
The One who is and who was and who is to come,"
Because You have taken Your great power and reigned.
[18] The nations were angry, and Your wrath has come,
And the time of the dead, that they should be judged,
And that You should reward Your servants the prophets and the
saints,
And those who fear Your name, small and great,
And should destroy those who destroy the earth."

[19] Then the temple of God was opened in heaven, and the ark of His covenant" was seen in His temple. And there were lightnings, noises, thunderings, an earthquake, and great hail.

THE WOMAN, THE CHILD, AND THE DRAGON

12 Now a great sign appeared in heaven a woman clothed with the sun, with the moon under her feet, and on her head a garland of twelve stars. [2] Then being with child, she cried out in labor and in pain to give birth.

[3] And another sign appeared in heaven: behold, a great, fiery red dragon having seven heads and ten horns, and seven diadems on his heads. [4] His tail drew a third of the stars of heaven and threw them to the earth. And the dragon stood before the woman who was ready to give birth, to devour her Child as soon as it was born. [5] She bore a male Child who was to rule all nations with a rod of iron. And her Child was caught up to God and His throne. [6] Then the woman fled into the wilderness, where she has a place prepared by God, that they should feed her there one thousand two hundred and sixty days.

SATAN THROWN OUT OF HEAVEN

[7] And war broke out in heaven: Michael and his angels fought with the dragon; and the dragon and his angels fought, [8] but they did not prevail, nor was a place found for them" in heaven any longer. [9] So the great dragon was cast out, that serpent of old, called the Devil and Satan, who deceives the whole world; he was cast to the earth, and his angels were cast out with him.

11:17 "NU-Text and M-Text omit *and who is to come.* 11:19 "M-Text reads *the covenant of the Lord.* 12:8 "M-Text reads *him.*

Women's Issues
Preconception Counseling

The best time to get counseling about pregnancy and child-bearing is *before conception!* Preconception counseling with an obstetrician/gynecologist should occur at least three months before a couple wants to become pregnant. At this visit, a woman should have a Pap smear and cervical cultures, as well as blood tests to test especially for anemia and immunity to rubella and chicken pox. Vaccinations may be needed.

If there is any history of birth defects or genetic diseases in either the husband or wife's family, targeted tests can be performed to determine whether the couple is at risk for having a child with certain diseases—for example Tay Sach's disease, sickle cell anemia, and cystic fibrosis.

Sexually transmitted diseases can impact fertility. A physician may want to make sure that a woman has no infections that might hinder conception—chlamydia, gonorrhea, and genital herpes can scar the fallopian tubes and make conception difficult or impossible. Mycoplasma, a type of bacteria, can also keep a couple from getting pregnant. Antibiotics can usually clear up infections, and the full round of antibiotics should be completed and all infections cleared before conception.

Preconception counseling is also a time for a woman to check her nutrition and begin supplements of vitamins and minerals if deficiencies exist. A woman definitely needs to take prenatal vitamins that provide between 400 and 800

CONT. NEXT PAGE>>>

[10] Then I heard a loud voice saying in heaven, "Now salvation, and strength, and the kingdom of our God, and the power of His Christ have come, for the accuser of our brethren, who accused them before our God day and night, has been cast down. [11] And they overcame him by the blood of the Lamb and by the word of their testimony, and they did not love their lives to the death. [12] Therefore rejoice, O heavens, and you who dwell in them! Woe to the inhabitants of the earth and the sea! For the devil has come down to you, having great wrath, because he knows that he has a short time."

THE WOMAN PERSECUTED

[13] Now when the dragon saw that he had been cast to the earth, he persecuted the woman who gave birth to the male *Child.* [14] But the woman was given two wings of a great eagle, that she might fly into the wilderness to her place, where she is nourished for a time and times and half a time, from the presence of the serpent. [15] So the serpent spewed water out of his mouth like a flood after the woman, that he might cause her to be carried away by the flood. [16] But the earth helped the woman, and the earth opened its mouth and swallowed up the flood which the dragon had spewed out of his mouth. [17] And the dragon was enraged with the woman, and he went to make war with the rest of her offspring, who keep the commandments of God and have the testimony of Jesus Christ.[a]

THE BEAST FROM THE SEA

13 Then I[a] stood on the sand of the sea. And I saw a beast rising up out of the sea, having seven heads and ten horns,[b] and on his horns ten crowns, and on his heads a blasphemous name. [2] Now the beast which I saw was like a leopard, his feet were like *the feet of* a bear, and his mouth like the mouth of a lion. The dragon gave him his power, his throne, and great authority. [3] And I saw one of his heads as if it had been mortally wounded, and his deadly wound was healed. And all the world marveled and followed the beast. [4] So they worshiped the dragon who gave authority to the beast; and they worshiped the beast, saying, "Who *is* like the beast? Who is able to make war with him?"

[5] And he was given a mouth speaking great things and blasphemies, and he was given authority to continue[a] for forty-two months. [6] Then he opened his mouth in blasphemy against God, to blaspheme His name, His tabernacle, and those who dwell in heaven. [7] It was granted to him to make war with the saints and to overcome them. And authority was given him over every tribe,[a] tongue, and nation. [8] All who dwell on the earth will worship him, whose names have not been written in the Book of Life of the Lamb slain from the foundation of the world.

[9] If anyone has an ear, let him hear. [10] He who leads into captivity shall go into captivity; he who kills with the sword must be killed with the sword. Here is the patience and the faith of the saints.

THE BEAST FROM THE EARTH

[11] Then I saw another beast coming up out of the earth, and he had two horns like a lamb and spoke like a dragon. [12] And he exercises all the authority of the first beast in his presence, and causes the earth

---

12:17 [a]NU-Text and M-Text omit *Christ.*   **13:1** [a]NU-Text reads *he.*   [b]NU-Text and M-Text read *ten horns and seven heads.*   **13:5** [a]M-Text reads *make war.*   **13:7** [a]NU-Text and M-Text add *and people.*

Women's Issues Cont.>>>

micrograms of folic acid to reduce the chance of having a baby with brain or spinal cord malformations.

The body weight of a woman desiring to conceive should be no more than 15 percent above or below her ideal weight. Good fitness throughout a pregnancy makes for an easier labor and delivery for many women.

Stop drinking alcohol and avoid exposure to toxins such as asbestos, lead, and radiation at least three months before trying to conceive. Also stop smoking cigarettes or using illegal drugs. Alcohol, nicotine, drugs, and chemical toxins can have highly adverse effects on a fetus.

The ideal time for conception is usually during a period nine days after a woman begins her period until day nineteen after she begins a period. Daily intercourse during this time period optimizes the chances for conception. No one sexual position has been shown to be advantageous for conception, but it is best for ejaculation to occur deep within the vagina.

Be patient if you are trying to get pregnant. Keep romance alive. Trying to conceive should be enjoyable for both partners. Sometimes it takes a couple six months to a year before conception is successful, especially if a woman has been taking a form of oral contraceptive.

---

and those who dwell in it to worship the first beast, whose deadly wound was healed. [13]He performs great signs, so that he even makes fire come down from heaven on the earth in the sight of men. [14]And he deceives those[a] who dwell on the earth by those signs which he was granted to do in the sight of the beast, telling those who dwell on the earth to make an image to the beast who was wounded by the sword and lived. [15]He was granted *power* to give breath to the image of the beast, that the image of the beast should both speak and cause as many as would not worship the image of the beast to be killed. [16]He causes all, both small and great, rich and poor, free and slave, to receive a mark on their right hand or on their foreheads, [17]and that no one may buy or sell except one who has the mark or[a] the name of the beast, or the number of his name.

[18]Here is wisdom. Let him who has understanding calculate the number of the beast, for it is the number of a man: His number *is* 666.

THE LAMB AND THE 144,000

14 Then I looked, and behold, a[a] Lamb standing on Mount Zion, and with Him one hundred *and* forty-four thousand, having[b] His Father's name written on their foreheads. [2]And I heard a voice from heaven, like the voice of many waters, and like the voice of loud thunder. And I heard the sound of harpists playing their harps. [3]They sang as it were a new song before the throne, before the four living creatures, and the elders; and no one could learn that song except the hundred *and* forty-four thousand

who were redeemed from the earth. [4]These are the ones who were not defiled with women, for they are virgins. These are the ones who follow the Lamb wherever He goes. These were redeemed[a] from *among* men, *being* firstfruits to God and to the Lamb. [5]And in their mouth was found no deceit,[a] for they are without fault before the throne of God.[b]

THE PROCLAMATIONS OF THREE ANGELS

[6]Then I saw another angel flying in the midst of heaven, having the everlasting gospel to preach to those who dwell on the earth—to every nation, tribe, tongue, and people— [7]saying with a loud voice, "Fear God and give glory to Him, for the hour of His judgment has come; and worship Him who made heaven and earth, the sea and springs of water."

[8]And another angel followed, saying, "Babylon[a] is fallen, is fallen, that great city, because she has made all nations drink of the wine of the wrath of her fornication."

[9]Then a third angel followed them, saying with a loud voice, "If any-

Fruit Torte

Ingredients:
- ☐ 8 ounces low-fat cream cheese
- ☐ Fresh berries of your choice
- ☐ Granola

Divide the cream cheese into thirds. Soften these sections individually in the microwave. Spread one section in the bottom of a well-greased loaf pan. Layer ⅓ of the fresh berries over the cream cheese and sprinkle with ⅓ of the granola. Repeat to make two full layers of cream cheese, berries, and granola. Then spread the final third of the cream cheese on top. Reserve the remaining berries and granola. Cover and chill the filled loaf pan for at least an hour or until cream cheese is firm. Loosen the edges of cream cheese with a knife or spatula and invert onto a serving plate. Garnish the top and edges of the torte with the reserved berries and granola. Serve cold.

Yield: 8 servings

Righteous Recipes

13:14 [a]M-Text reads *my own people.* 13:17 [a]NU-Text and M-Text omit *or.* 14:1 [a]NU-Text and M-Text read *the.* [b]NU-Text and M-Text add *His name and.* 14:4 [a]M-Text adds *by Jesus.* 14:5 [a]NU-Text and M-Text read *falsehood.* [b]NU-Text and M-Text omit *before the throne of God.* 14:8 [a]NU-Text reads *Babylon the great is fallen,* is fallen, which has made; M-Text reads *Babylon the great is fallen. She has made.*

WWJE?
[WHAT WOULD JESUS EAT]

[ONIONS AND LEEKS]

Garlic, onions, and leeks—all technically members of the lily family—have been used in cooking and medicine for thousands of years. (Garlic is discussed elsewhere as part of the "Condiment Cabinet.")

In ancient times, onions were considered a food that increased energy and endurance. Slaves, such as the Israelites in Egypt, were fed diets rich in onions to keep them strong for hard manual labor.

Onions have been used externally as an antiseptic and pain reliever, and have been taken internally as a tonic to ease intestinal gas pains and alleviate symptoms of hypertension, high blood sugar, and high cholesterol. Through the centuries, onions have been used to treat kidney and bladder problems. Modern herbalists believe onions to be a good expectorant and an excellent diuretic. George Washington was quoted as saying that he ate a hot roasted onion if he had a cold.

A single tablespoon of cooked onions can help nullify some of the adverse effects of eating a meal high in fat. Onions have antibiotic properties that are effective against a variety of bacteria, fungi, and parasites. Onions are high in vitamins, especially B_1, B_2, and C. They have more than 150 chemicals, some of which appear to help cleanse the blood of bad cholesterol, detoxify the liver, and block tumor growth.

Leeks are a milder, sweeter version of the onion. They have a more delicate flavor than either garlic or onions and form the base for many traditional dishes in ancient Israel. A popular porridge has been made for thousands of years from the white bulb of the leek, whole grains, crushed almonds, and honey as a sweetener. Leeks have been prescribed in quantity for infertility, obesity, kidney complaints, coughs, and intestinal disorders.

REAPING THE EARTH'S HARVEST

[14] Then I looked, and behold, a white cloud, and on the cloud sat *One* like the Son of Man, having on His head a golden crown, and in His hand a sharp sickle. [15] And another angel came out of the temple, crying with a loud voice to Him who sat on the cloud, "Thrust in Your sickle and reap, for the time has come for You[a] to reap, for the harvest of the earth is ripe." [16] So He who sat on the cloud thrust in His sickle on the earth, and the earth was reaped.

REAPING THE GRAPES OF WRATH

[17] Then another angel came out of the temple which is in heaven, he also having a sharp sickle.

[18] And another angel came out from the altar, who had power over fire, and he cried with a loud cry to him who had the sharp sickle, saying, "Thrust in your sharp sickle and gather the clusters of the vine of the earth, for her grapes are fully ripe." [19] So the angel thrust his sickle into the earth and gathered the vine of the earth, and threw *it* into the great winepress of the wrath of God. [20] And the winepress was trampled outside the city, and blood came out of the winepress, up to the horses' bridles, for one thousand six hundred furlongs.

PRELUDE TO THE BOWL JUDGMENTS

15 Then I saw another sign in heaven, great and marvelous: seven angels having the seven last plagues, for in them the wrath of God is complete.

[2] And I saw *something* like a sea of glass mingled with fire, and those who have the victory over the beast, over his image and over his mark[a] *and* over the number of his name, standing on the sea of glass, having harps of God. [3] They sing the song of Moses, the servant of God, and the song of the Lamb, saying:

"Great and marvelous *are* Your works,
   Lord God Almighty!
Just and true *are* Your ways,
   O King of the saints![a]
[4]   Who shall not fear You, O Lord, and
      glorify Your name?

one worships the beast and his image, and receives *his* mark on his forehead or on his hand, [10] he himself shall also drink of the wine of the wrath of God, which is poured out full strength into the cup of His indignation. He shall be tormented with fire and brimstone in the presence of the holy angels and in the presence of the Lamb. [11] And the smoke of their torment ascends forever and ever; and they have no rest day or night, who worship the beast and his image, and whoever receives the mark of his name."

[12] Here is the patience of the saints; here *are* those[a] who keep the commandments of God and the faith of Jesus.

[13] Then I heard a voice from heaven saying to me,[a] "Write: 'Blessed *are* the dead who die in the Lord from now on.' "

"Yes," says the Spirit, "that they may rest from their labors, and their works follow them."

14:12 [a]NU-Text and M-Text omit *here are those*.   14:13 [a]NU-Text and M-Text omit *to me*.   14:15 [a]NU-Text and M-Text omit *for You*.   15:2 [a]NU-Text and M-Text omit *over his mark*.   15:3 [a]NU-Text and M-Text read *nations*.

weighing Less & Enjoying Life More!

[The Calories You Drink]

Don't forget to count the calories you drink! Most people are not aware of the amount of sugar in the beverages they drink. The consumption of soda has jumped 135 percent in the last thirty years. A study done at the Harvard School of Public Health tracked the soft drink consumption of ninety-one thousand women over eight years. Those who drank one or more sodas or fruit punch drinks a day nearly *doubled* their risk of developing type 2 diabetes, a potentially life-threatening disease that can cause heart and kidney damage.

Sweetened ice tea and Frappuccino drinks also pack a lot of sugar, and alcoholic beverages are *all* very high in sugar content!

For *You* alone *are* holy.
For all nations shall come and worship before You,
For Your judgments have been manifested."

⁵After these things I looked, and behold,ᵃ the temple of the tabernacle of the testimony in heaven was opened. ⁶And out of the temple came the seven angels having the seven plagues, clothed in pure bright linen, and having their chests girded with golden bands. ⁷Then one of the four living creatures gave to the seven angels seven golden bowls full of the wrath of God who lives forever and ever. ⁸The temple was filled with smoke from the glory of God and from His power, and no one was able to enter the temple till the seven plagues of the seven angels were completed.

16 Then I heard a loud voice from the temple saying to the seven angels, "Go and pour out the bowlsᵃ of the wrath of God on the earth."

FIRST BOWL: LOATHSOME SORES

²So the first went and poured out his bowl upon the earth, and a foul and loathsome sore came upon the men who had the mark of the beast and those who worshiped his image.

SECOND BOWL: THE SEA TURNS TO BLOOD

³Then the second angel poured out his bowl on the sea, and it became blood as of a dead *man;* and every living creature in the sea died.

THIRD BOWL: THE WATERS TURN TO BLOOD

⁴Then the third angel poured out his bowl on the rivers and springs of water, and they became blood. ⁵And I heard the angel of the waters saying:

"You are righteous, O Lord,ᵃ
The One who is and who was and who is to be,ᵇ
Because You have judged these things.
⁶   For they have shed the blood of saints and prophets,
And You have given them blood to drink.
Forᵃ it is their just due."

⁷And I heard another fromᵃ the altar saying, "Even so, Lord God Almighty, true and righteous *are* Your judgments."

FOURTH BOWL: MEN ARE SCORCHED

⁸Then the fourth angel poured out his bowl on the sun, and power was given to him to scorch men with fire. ⁹And men were scorched with great heat, and they blasphemed the name of God who has power over these plagues; and they did not repent and give Him glory.

FIFTH BOWL: DARKNESS AND PAIN

¹⁰Then the fifth angel poured out his bowl on the throne of the beast, and his kingdom became full of darkness; and they gnawed their tongues because of the pain. ¹¹They blasphemed the God of heaven because of their pains and their sores, and did not repent of their deeds.

"Be sober and temperate, and you will be healthy." —*Benjamin Franklin, American statesman, inventor, and author (1706–1790)*

PREACHING HEALTH

15:5 ᵃNU-Text and M-Text omit *behold.*   16:1 ᵃNU-Text and M-Text read *seven bowls.*   16:5 ᵃNU-Text and M-Text omit *O Lord.*   ᵇNU-Text and M-Text read *who was, the Holy One.*   16:6 ᵃNU-Text and M-Text omit *For.*   16:7 ᵃNU-Text and M-Text omit *another from.*

PEOPLE CALLED "BEAUTIFUL" IN THE BIBLE

Sarai

Beautiful Even in Older Years

Sarai, the wife of Abraham and the woman considered the matriarch of the Jewish race, is one of the women described in the Bible as beautiful. When Abram and those traveling with him went down to Egypt during a time of famine, Abram said to Sarai: "I know that you are a woman of beautiful countenance. Therefore it will happen, when the Egyptians see you, that they will say, 'This is his wife'; and they will kill me, but they will let you live. Please say you are my sister, that it may be well with me for your sake, and that I may live because of you" (Genesis 12:11–13). At the time of this story in the Bible, Sarah was called Sarai and Abraham was called Abram.

As Sarai's brother, Abram would have been able to negotiate her marriage, but as her husband, his life was in danger. If the Egyptians killed him, they could readily take Sarai the widow as their own concubine or wife. In truth, Abram was not asking Sarai to lie, at least not completely. Sarai was Abram's half sister. They had the same father but different mothers, and in the ancient world, that still qualified them for marriage.

Sarai agreed to the ruse but when plagues hit Pharaoh's house as a result of this deception, Pharaoh called Abram and demanded the truth. He then sent Abram away without reprisal. One of the truly amazing aspects of this story is that Sarai was an older woman at this point, likely well into her sixties. She was still considered "a woman of beautiful countenance" and desirable to be part of Pharaoh's harem.

Later, Sarai—who was barren and by this time past the age of normal childbearing—encouraged her husband to have a sexual relationship with Hagar, her Egyptian slave. She wanted Abram to have an heir. Her intent was not malicious—she is applauded throughout the Scriptures as a woman who had her husband's best interests at heart and who was tenaciously devoted to him. God required Sarai to trust Him to give her a son, even as God required Abram to trust Him for a son by Sarai.

When Sarah did conceive, her mothering experience covered a wide gamut of emotions: skepticism, embarrassment, jealousy, exhilaration, and joy. She became the "mother of nations." (See Genesis 17:16.) She is the only woman listed among the heroes of the faith in the Book of Hebrews (Hebrews 11:11).

Sarah's example in the Bible tells us that a woman can remain beautiful and desirable at any age. Beauty is never a matter of cosmetics and fitness alone. It is also a radiant quality that comes with personality, character, and a giving spirit.

SIXTH BOWL: EUPHRATES DRIED UP

[12]Then the sixth angel poured out his bowl on the great river Euphrates, and its water was dried up, so that the way of the kings from the east might be prepared. [13]And I saw three unclean spirits like frogs *coming* out of the mouth of the dragon, out of the mouth of the beast, and out of the mouth of the false prophet. [14]For they are spirits of demons, performing signs, *which* go out to the kings of the earth and[a] of the whole world, to gather them to the battle of that great day of God Almighty.

[15]"Behold, I am coming as a thief. Blessed *is* he who watches, and keeps his garments, lest he walk naked and they see his shame."

[16]And they gathered them together to the place called in Hebrew, Armageddon.[a]

SEVENTH BOWL: THE EARTH UTTERLY SHAKEN

[17]Then the seventh angel poured out his bowl into the air, and a loud voice came out of the temple of heaven, from the throne, saying, "It is done!" [18]And there were noises and thunderings and lightnings; and there was a great earthquake, such a mighty and great earthquake as had not occurred since men were on the earth. [19]Now the great city was divided into three parts, and the cities of the nations fell. And great Babylon was remembered before God, to give her the cup of the wine of the fierceness of His wrath. [20]Then every island fled away, and the mountains were not found. [21]And great hail from heaven fell upon men, *each hailstone* about the weight of a talent. Men blasphemed God because of the plague of the hail, since that plague was exceedingly great.

THE SCARLET WOMAN AND THE SCARLET BEAST

17 Then one of the seven angels who had the seven bowls came and talked with me, saying to me,[a] "Come, I will show you the judgment of the great harlot who sits on many waters, [2]with whom the kings of the earth committed fornication, and the inhabitants of the earth were made drunk with the wine of her fornication."

[3]So he carried me away in the Spirit into the wilderness. And I saw a woman sitting on a scarlet beast *which was* full of names of blas-

16:14 [a]NU-Text and M-Text omit *of the earth and.*   16:16 [a]M-Text reads *Megiddo.*   17:1 [a]NU-Text and M-Text omit *to me.*

phemy, having seven heads and ten horns. ⁴The woman was arrayed in purple and scarlet, and adorned with gold and precious stones and pearls, having in her hand a golden cup full of abominations and the filthiness of her fornication.ᵃ ⁵And on her forehead a name *was* written:

MYSTERY, BABYLON THE GREAT, THE MOTHER OF HARLOTS AND OF THE ABOMINATIONS OF THE EARTH.

⁶I saw the woman, drunk with the blood of the saints and with the blood of the martyrs of Jesus. And when I saw her, I marveled with great amazement.

THE MEANING OF THE WOMAN AND THE BEAST

⁷But the angel said to me, "Why did you marvel? I will tell you the mystery of the woman and of the beast that carries her, which has the seven heads and the ten horns. ⁸The beast that you saw was, and is not, and will ascend out of the bottomless pit and go to perdition. And those who dwell on the earth will marvel, whose names are not written in the Book of Life from the foundation of the world, when they see the beast that was, and is not, and yet is.ᵃ

⁹"Here *is* the mind which has wisdom: The seven heads are seven mountains on which the woman sits. ¹⁰There are also seven kings. Five have fallen, one is, *and* the other has not yet come. And when he comes, he must continue a short time. ¹¹The beast that was, and is not, is himself also the eighth, and is of the seven, and is going to perdition.

¹²"The ten horns which you saw are ten kings who have received no kingdom as yet, but they receive authority for one hour as kings with the beast. ¹³These are of one mind, and they will give their power and authority to the beast. ¹⁴These will make war with the Lamb, and the Lamb will overcome them, for He is Lord of lords and King of kings; and those *who are* with Him *are* called, chosen, and faithful."

¹⁵Then he said to me, "The waters which you saw, where the harlot sits, are peoples, multitudes, nations, and tongues. ¹⁶And the ten horns which you saw onᵃ the beast, these will hate the harlot, make her desolate and naked, eat her flesh and burn her with fire. ¹⁷For God has put it into their hearts to fulfill His purpose, to be of one mind, and to give their kingdom to the beast, until the words of God are fulfilled. ¹⁸And the woman whom you saw is that great city which reigns over the kings of the earth."

THE FALL OF BABYLON THE GREAT

18 After these things I saw another angel coming down from heaven, having great authority, and the earth was illuminated with his glory. ²And he cried mightilyᵃ with a loud voice, saying, "Babylon the great is fallen, is fallen, and has become a dwelling place of demons, a prison for every foul spirit, and a cage for every unclean and hated bird! ³For all the nations have drunk of the wine of the wrath of her fornication, the kings of the earth have committed fornication with her, and the merchants of the earth have become rich through the abundance of her luxury."

⁴And I heard another voice from heaven saying, "Come out of her, my people, lest you share in her sins, and lest you receive of her plagues. ⁵For her sins have reachedᵃ to heaven, and God has remem-

Bible Beverages
Milk—Only for Babies!

Milk was never consumed in Bible times as an adult beverage. It was only for babies and young children. Even today that is a good rule!

While whole milk is not for adult consumption, skim or nonfat milk may be. Some research shows that skim milk lowers the liver's output of LDL (bad) cholesterol. The calcium in skim milk may also have beneficial effects on high blood pressure and mild hypertension. Calcium in milk may also help prevent or slow the development of osteoporosis in older women, and the high calcium and vitamin D content of milk helps prevent colon cancer.

In spite of these benefits, those who have a milk allergy, milk sensitivity, or milk intolerance (lactose intolerance) should avoid milk products and drink soy milk in place of cow's milk.

bered her iniquities. ⁶Render to her just as she rendered to you,ᵃ and repay her double according to her works; in the cup which she has mixed, mix double for her. ⁷In the measure that she glorified herself and lived luxuriously, in the same measure give her torment and sorrow; for she says in her heart, 'I sit *as* queen, and am no widow, and will not see sorrow.' ⁸Therefore her plagues will come in one day—death and mourning and famine. And she will be utterly burned with fire, for strong *is* the Lord God who judgesᵃ her.

17:4 ᵃM-Text reads *the filthiness of the fornication of the earth.* **17:8** ᵃNU-Text and M-Text read *and shall be present.* **17:16** ᵃNU-Text and M-Text read *saw, and the beast.* **18:2** ᵃNU-Text and M-Text omit *mightily.* **18:5** ᵃNU-Text and M-Text read *have been heaped up.* **18:6** ᵃNU-Text and M-Text omit *to you.* **18:8** ᵃNU-Text and M-Text read *has judged.*

DIVINE HEALTH   399

Stress Busters
The Power of Forgiveness

Forgiveness is the supreme stress buster for all stress that is associated with emotional baggage—anger, hatred, bitterness, and resentment. We must be clear, however, about what it means to forgive. Forgiveness is *not* exoneration. When we forgive we are *not* saying that injustice never occurred, that there was or is no pain associated with the injustice, or that the person who committed the wrong was justified in what he or she did. Nor are we saying that a person must never face the consequences for what he or she has done.

What we are saying when we forgive is that we willfully choose no longer to hold on to the pain we have felt and that we refuse to play judge, jury, prison warden, or executioner. Forgiveness is choosing to release a person from the clutches of our heart and place the person and all consequences associated with his or her behavior in the hands of God. Forgiveness is letting go, trusting God to heal us and to deal with the other person as He desires.

When we fail to forgive, to a great extent we tie God's hands. We remain locked in to our own unhealthy emotions, and we cannot receive the fullness of God's blessings, including the blessings of health and wholeness.

THE WORLD MOURNS BABYLON'S FALL

⁹"The kings of the earth who committed fornication and lived luxuriously with her will weep and lament for her, when they see the smoke of her burning, ¹⁰standing at a distance for fear of her torment, saying, 'Alas, alas, that great city Babylon, that mighty city! For in one hour your judgment has come.'

¹¹"And the merchants of the earth will weep and mourn over her, for no one buys their merchandise anymore: ¹²merchandise of gold and silver, precious stones and pearls, fine linen and purple, silk and scar-

let, every kind of citron wood, every kind of object of ivory, every kind of object of most precious wood, bronze, iron, and marble; ¹³and cinnamon and incense, fragrant oil and frankincense, wine and oil, fine flour and wheat, cattle and sheep, horses and chariots, and bodies and souls of men. ¹⁴The fruit that your soul longed for has gone from you, and all the things which are rich and splendid have gone from you,ᵃ and you shall find them no more at all. ¹⁵The merchants of these things, who became rich by her, will stand at a distance for fear of her torment, weeping and wailing, ¹⁶and saying, 'Alas, alas, that great city that was clothed in fine linen, purple, and scarlet, and adorned with gold and precious stones and pearls! ¹⁷For in one hour such great riches came to nothing.' Every shipmaster, all who travel by ship, sailors, and as many as trade on the sea, stood at a distance ¹⁸and cried out when they saw the smoke of her burning, saying, 'What *is* like this great city?'

¹⁹"They threw dust on their heads and cried out, weeping and wailing, and saying, 'Alas, alas, that great city, in which all who had ships on the sea became rich by her wealth! For in one hour she is made desolate.'

²⁰"Rejoice over her, O heaven, and *you* holy apostlesᵃ and prophets, for God has avenged you on her!"

FINALITY OF BABYLON'S FALL

²¹Then a mighty angel took up a stone like a great millstone and threw *it* into the sea, saying, "Thus with violence the great city Babylon shall be thrown down, and shall not be found anymore. ²²The sound of harpists, musicians, flutists, and trumpeters shall not be heard in you anymore. No craftsman of any craft shall be found in you anymore, and the sound of a millstone shall not be heard in you anymore. ²³The light of a lamp shall not shine in you anymore, and the voice of bridegroom and bride shall not be heard in you anymore. For your merchants were the great men of the earth, for by your sorcery all the nations were deceived. ²⁴And in her was found the blood of

[EXPIRATION DATE]

FACT MORSELS

Check the Expiration Date. Many people check the expiration dates on processed and canned foods, and on milk products, but did you know you should also check the expiration date on bottled water?

Try to drink the water within two months of the date printed on the container to decrease your exposure to plasticizers and phthalates.

18:14 ᵃNU-Text and M-Text read *been lost to you.*   18:20 ᵃNU-Text and M-Text read *saints and apostles.*

prophets and saints, and of all who were slain on the earth."

HEAVEN EXULTS OVER BABYLON

19 After these things I heard[a] a loud voice of a great multitude in heaven, saying, "Alleluia! Salvation and glory and honor and power *belong* to the Lord[b] our God! [2]For true and righteous *are* His judgments, because He has judged the great harlot who corrupted the earth with her fornication; and He has avenged on her the blood of His servants *shed* by her." [3]Again they said, "Alleluia! Her smoke rises up forever and ever!" [4]And the twenty-four elders and the four living creatures fell down and worshiped God who sat on the throne, saying, "Amen! Alleluia!" [5]Then a voice came from the throne, saying, "Praise our God, all you His servants and those who fear Him, both[a] small and great!"

[6]And I heard, as it were, the voice of a great multitude, as the sound of many waters and as the sound of mighty thunderings, saying, "Alleluia! For the[a] Lord God Omnipotent reigns! [7]Let us be glad and rejoice and give Him glory, for the marriage of the Lamb has come, and His wife has made herself ready." [8]And to her it was granted to be arrayed in fine linen, clean and bright, for the fine linen is the righteous acts of the saints.

[9]Then he said to me, "Write: 'Blessed *are* those who are called to the marriage supper of the Lamb!' " And he said to me, "These are the true sayings of God." [10]And I fell at his feet to worship him. But he said to me, "See *that you do* not *do that!* I am your fellow servant, and of your brethren who have the testimony of Jesus. Worship God! For the testimony of Jesus is the spirit of prophecy."

CHRIST ON A WHITE HORSE

[11]Now I saw heaven opened, and behold, a white horse. And He who sat on him *was* called Faithful and True, and in righteousness He judges and makes war. [12]His eyes *were* like a flame of fire, and on His head *were* many crowns. He had[a] a name written that no one knew except Himself. [13]He *was* clothed with a robe dipped in blood, and His name is called The Word of God. [14]And the armies in heaven, clothed in fine linen, white and clean,[a] followed Him on white horses. [15]Now

out of His mouth goes a sharp[a] sword, that with it He should strike the nations. And He Himself will rule them with a rod of iron. He Himself treads the winepress of the fierceness and wrath of Almighty God. [16]And He has on *His* robe and on His thigh a name written:

KING OF KINGS AND LORD OF LORDS.

THE BEAST AND HIS ARMIES DEFEATED

[17]Then I saw an angel standing in the sun; and he cried with a loud voice, saying to all the birds that fly in the midst of heaven, "Come and gather together for the supper of the great God,[a] [18]that you may eat the flesh of kings, the flesh of captains, the flesh of mighty men, the flesh of horses and of those who sit on them, and the flesh of all *people,* free[a] and slave, both small and great."

[19]And I saw the beast, the kings of the earth, and their armies, gathered together to make war against Him who sat on the horse and against His army. [20]Then the beast was captured, and with him the false prophet who worked signs in his presence, by which he

---

▲ Striking a New Balance ▲

ULTIMATE HEALTH RESOURCE • ULTIMATE HEALTH RESOURCE

For many people, the pursuit of greater health and wholeness means striking a new balance in their lives, as opposed to giving up something entirely, adding a brand-new discipline, or making radical changes. Consider the benefits of seeking these shifts in balance:

More	Less
More vegetables, fruits, and whole grains	Less red meat
More activity	Less sitting idly
More praise and thanksgiving	Less whining and complaining
More involvement with other believers, more church attendance	Less isolation
More time reading	Less time watching TV
More time spent in a quiet, calm environment	Less time in traffic
More intentional use of resources	Less waste and pollution
More forgiveness	Less pent-up anger, sorrow, resentment, hatred, and bitterness
More expressions of love	Less conflict and estrangement
More words of encouragement	Less criticism, argument, debate, and strife
More good	Less evil

19:1 [a]NU-Text and M-Text add *something like.* [b]NU-Text and M-Text omit *the Lord.* 19:5 [a]NU-Text and M-Text omit *both.* 19:6 [a]NU-Text and M-Text read *our.* 19:12 [a]M-Text adds *names written, and.* 19:14 [a]NU-Text and M-Text read *pure white linen.* 19:15 [a]M-Text adds *two-edged.* 19:17 [a]NU-Text and M-Text read *the great supper of God.* 19:18 [a]NU-Text and M-Text read *both free.*

weighing Less &
ENJOYING LIFE MORE!

[Three Tips for the Obese]

The word *obese* is used these days to refer to people who have more than thirty pounds to lose. If you fall into that category here are some tips that are especially for you.

Walk slowly. According to research, a slower-than-normal walk offers obese men and women better benefits when it comes to burning calories and avoiding knee injuries.

Set incremental goals. Don't think in terms of the "big number" of pounds you have to lose—rather, think in terms of losing eight to ten pounds a month, at an average of two to two-and-a-half pounds a week. Most people do well if they think in terms of a ninety-day time frame, or perhaps a seventy-day or ten-week time frame. Find the time frame that works for you when it comes to keeping yourself motivated. The goal for the time frame must seem "do-able" to you, and be something you will stick with for the duration.

Reward yourself for reaching incremental goals. The problem for many obese people is that they have rewarded themselves in the past with food! Find a new way of rewarding yourself. Think in terms of purchasing something new for your home, going someplace new, or buying tickets to a concert or play.

Be cautious, however, in rewarding yourself with new clothes. You may be more discouraged than encouraged if you go to the store expecting to have lost a dress or jacket size only to find that you haven't. Also, if you are committed to a long-range weight loss of even more pounds, you'll be purchasing clothes that you soon will find too loose. On the other hand, if you set yourself a goal of losing thirty pounds in ninety days and you reach that goal, you'll definitely enjoy shopping for new clothes!

deceived those who received the mark of the beast and those who worshiped his image. These two were cast alive into the lake of fire burning with brimstone. ²¹And the rest were killed with the sword which proceeded from the mouth of Him who sat on the horse. And all the birds were filled with their flesh.

SATAN BOUND 1000 YEARS

20 Then I saw an angel coming down from heaven, having the key to the bottomless pit and a great chain in his hand. ²He laid hold of the dragon, that serpent of old, who is *the* Devil and Satan, and bound him for a thousand years; ³and he cast him into the

Q By what are the just to live?

A Faith *(Romans 1:17).*

bottomless pit, and shut him up, and set a seal on him, so that he should deceive the nations no more till the thousand years were finished. But after these things he must be released for a little while.

THE SAINTS REIGN WITH CHRIST 1000 YEARS

⁴And I saw thrones, and they sat on them, and judgment was committed to them. Then *I saw* the souls of those who had been beheaded for their witness to Jesus and for the word of God, who had not worshiped the beast or his image, and had not received *his* mark on their foreheads or on their hands. And they lived and reigned with Christ for aᵃ thousand years. ⁵But the rest of the dead did not live again until the thousand years were finished. This *is* the first resurrection. ⁶Blessed and holy *is* he who has part in the first resurrection. Over such the second death has no power, but they shall be priests of God and of Christ, and shall reign with Him a thousand years.

SATANIC REBELLION CRUSHED

⁷Now when the thousand years have expired, Satan will be released from his prison ⁸and will go out to deceive the nations which

20:4 ᵃM-Text reads *the.*

are in the four corners of the earth, Gog and Magog, to gather them together to battle, whose number *is* as the sand of the sea. ⁹They went up on the breadth of the earth and surrounded the camp of the saints and the beloved city. And fire came down from God out of heaven and devoured them. ¹⁰The devil, who deceived them, was cast into the lake of fire and brimstone where" the beast and the false prophet *are*. And they will be tormented day and night forever and ever.

THE GREAT WHITE THRONE JUDGMENT

¹¹Then I saw a great white throne and Him who sat on it, from whose face the earth and the heaven fled away. And there was found no place for them. ¹²And I saw the dead, small and great, standing before God," and books were opened. And another book was opened, which is *the Book* of Life. And the dead were judged according to their works, by the things which were written in the books. ¹³The sea gave up the dead who were in it, and Death and Hades delivered up the dead who were in them. And they were judged, each one according to his works. ¹⁴Then Death and Hades were cast into the lake of fire. This is the second death." ¹⁵And anyone not found written in the Book of Life was cast into the lake of fire.

ALL THINGS MADE NEW

21 Now I saw a new heaven and a new earth, for the first heaven and the first earth had passed away. Also there was no more sea. ²Then I, John," saw the holy city, New Jerusalem, coming down out of heaven from God, prepared as a bride adorned for her husband. ³And I heard a loud voice from heaven saying, "Behold, the tabernacle of God *is* with men, and He will dwell with them, and they shall be His people. God Himself will be with them *and be* their God. ⁴And God will wipe away every tear from their eyes; there shall be no more death, nor sorrow, nor crying. There shall be no more pain, for the former things have passed away."

⁵Then He who sat on the throne said, "Behold, I make all things new." And He said to me," "Write, for these words are true and faithful."

⁶And He said to me, "It is done!" I am the Alpha and the Omega, the Beginning and the End. I will give of the fountain of the water of life freely to him who thirsts. ⁷He who overcomes shall inherit all things," and I will be his God and he shall be My son. ⁸But the cowardly, unbelieving," abominable, murderers, sexually immoral, sorcerers, idolaters, and all liars shall have their part in the lake which burns with fire and brimstone, which is the second death."

▲ Overcoming Depression ▲

Are you aware that nearly nineteen million adults in the United States consider themselves to be depressed? Depression can be minor or severe, but the truth is that depressed individuals tend to have generally poor health habits, which places them at even higher risk for developing most types of diseases. Lifestyle choices of the depressed person nearly always result in poor nutrition, little exercise, use of al-cohol or drugs, or overuse of prescription medications. Poor sleep patterns often cause fatigue. The composite result of these bad health habits is a decreased immune function and a greater risk for developing cardiovascular diseases, diabetes, and more frequent infectious diseases. Depressed people tend to experience more severe pain.

Depression has numerous causes—an imbalance in hormones, the death of a loved one, a chronic illness, or a life crisis such as a divorce, the loss of a job, or imprisonment. If you don't know *why* you are depressed, seek out a counselor who can help you discover the reason. Getting to the root cause of your depression is essential in finding a cure.

If you are prone to depression, learn to *HALT*. This word is an acronym for the wise counsel that you should never allow yourself to become too hungry, angry, lonely, or tired.

☐ *Hungry.* Don't allow your blood sugar to drop too low or to get on the roller coaster of eating too much and then starving yourself.

☐ *Angry.* If you feel anger, find a way of expressing your hurt feelings without injuring another person emotionally or physically.

☐ *Lonely.* If you feel isolated and lonely, reach out to volunteer your services to others or attend free classes or church-related studies or functions to socialize with people and make new friends.

☐ *Tired.* Don't allow yourself to get overly tired. Put yourself on a regular schedule of going to bed and getting up, even if you lie in bed awake for a while until your body adjusts to a new bedtime. Exercise during the day will help you establish a regular rhythm of sleeping and waking.

20:10 "NU-Text and M-Text add *also*.   20:12 "NU-Text and M-Text read *the throne*.   20:14 "NU-Text and M-Text add *the lake of fire*.   21:2 "NU-Text and M-Text omit *John*.   21:5 "NU-Text and M-Text omit *to me*.   21:6 "M-Text omits *It is done*.   21:7 "M-Text reads *overcomes, I shall give him these things*.   21:8 "M-Text adds *and sinners*.

THE NEW JERUSALEM

9 Then one of the seven angels who had the seven bowls filled with the seven last plagues came to me" and talked with me, saying, "Come, I will show you the bride, the Lamb's wife."ᵇ 10 And he carried me away in the Spirit to a great and high mountain, and showed me the great city, the holy" Jerusalem, descending out of heaven from God, 11 having the glory of God. Her light *was* like a most precious stone, like a jasper stone, clear as crystal. 12 Also she had a great and high wall with twelve gates, and twelve angels at the gates, and names written on them, which are *the names* of the twelve tribes of the children of Israel: 13 three gates on the east, three gates on the north, three gates on the south, and three gates on the west.

14 Now the wall of the city had twelve foundations, and on them were the names" of the twelve apostles of the Lamb. 15 And he who talked with me had a gold reed to measure the city, its gates, and its wall. 16 The city is laid out as a square; its length is as great as its breadth. And he measured the city with the reed: twelve thousand furlongs. Its length, breadth, and height are equal. 17 Then he measured its wall: one hundred *and* forty-four cubits, *according* to the measure of a man, that is, of an angel. 18 The construction of its wall was *of* jasper; and the city *was* pure gold, like clear glass. 19 The foundations of the wall of the city *were* adorned with all kinds of precious stones: the first foundation *was* jasper, the second sapphire, the third chalcedony, the fourth emerald, 20 the fifth sardonyx, the sixth sardius, the seventh chrysolite, the eighth beryl, the ninth topaz, the tenth chrysoprase, the eleventh jacinth, and the twelfth amethyst. 21 The twelve gates *were* twelve pearls: each individual gate was of one pearl. And the street of the city *was* pure gold, like transparent glass.

THE GLORY OF THE NEW JERUSALEM

22 But I saw no temple in it, for the Lord God Almighty and the Lamb are its temple. 23 The city had no need of the sun or of the moon to shine in it," for the gloryᵇ of God illuminated it. The Lamb *is* its light. 24 And the nations of those who are saved" shall walk in its light, and the kings of the earth bring their glory and honor into it.ᵇ 25 Its gates shall not be shut at all by day (there shall be no night there). 26 And they shall bring the glory and the honor of the nations into it." 27 But there shall by no means enter it anything that defiles, or causes" an abomination or a lie, but only those who are written in the Lamb's Book of Life.

THE RIVER OF LIFE

22 And he showed me a pure" river of water of life, clear as crystal, proceeding from the throne of God and of the Lamb. 2 In the middle of its street, and on either side of the river, *was* the tree of life, which bore twelve fruits, each *tree* yielding its fruit every month. The leaves of the tree *were* for the healing of the nations. 3 And there shall be no more curse, but the throne of God and of the Lamb shall be in it, and His servants shall serve Him. 4 They shall see His face, and His name *shall be* on their foreheads. 5 There shall be no night there: They need no lamp nor light of the sun, for the Lord God gives them light. And they shall reign forever and ever.

THE TIME IS NEAR

6 Then he said to me, "These words *are* faithful and true." And the Lord God of the holy" prophets sent His angel to show His servants the things which must shortly take place.

7 "Behold, I am coming quickly! Blessed *is* he who keeps the words of the prophecy of this book."

8 Now I, John, saw and heard" these things. And when I heard and saw, I fell down to worship before the feet of the angel who showed me these things.

9 Then he said to me, "See *that you do* not *do that.* For" I am your fel-

---

> (Revelation 22:1)

A River of Life! The symbolism of a river is common in the Bible. (See John 4:10, 11 and Psalm 46:4 as examples.) In a vision seen by the prophet Ezekiel, a river brought life everywhere it flowed (Ezekiel 47:1–12). As human beings, our bodies are composed primarily of *water*. We spend the first nine months of our existence, from conception to birth, in a *watery* womb. We need water to maintain life. And note the characteristic of water in Revelation 22:1. It is *a pure river*, clear as crystal.

Spiritually speaking, water is a symbol linked to new life. God hovered over the waters at Creation, spoke, and began the creative process for new life. God called His people to walk through the waters of the Red Sea to a new life of freedom and a new identity as a people. God calls His people to experience baptism in the name of Jesus Christ as they enter a new life of freedom and identity as Christians—new believers are called "new creations" (2 Corinthians 5:17).

The waters that flow ultimately from the throne of God and the Lamb (Jesus) are pure waters that bless the physical and spiritual life of God's people, not only now but forever. These are the *living* waters to which Jesus referred when speaking to a woman by a well in Sychar (John 4:6–14). They are waters that "spring up" and have no end—likened to an artesian spring that produces a deep, full well of clean water.

Ask the Lord today to refresh you and cleanse you with the water that flows directly from Him. Ask Him to help you pour out refreshment and life-giving nourishment to others around you. And in your daily *earthbound* life, seek to bathe in and drink only pure water!

21:9 "NU-Text and M-Text omit *to me.* ᵇM-Text reads *I will show you the woman, the Lamb's bride.* 21:10 "NU-Text and M-Text omit *the great* and read *the holy city, Jerusalem.* 21:14 "NU-Text and M-Text read *twelve names.* 21:23 "NU-Text and M-Text omit *in it.* ᵇM-Text reads *the very glory.* 21:24 "NU-Text and M-Text omit *of those who are saved.* ᵇM-Text reads *the glory and honor of the nations to Him.* 21:26 "M-Text adds *that they may enter in.* 21:27 "NU-Text and M-Text read *anything profane, nor one who causes.* 22:1 "NU-Text and M-Text omit *pure.* 22:6 "NU-Text and M-Text read *spirits of the prophets.* 22:8 "NU-Text and M-Text read *am the one who heard and saw.* 22:9 "NU-Text and M-Text omit *For.*

INSIGHTS INTO THE WORD

> (Revelation 22:2)

A Tree of Life for Healing. One of the two trees at the center of the Garden of Eden was the tree of life (Genesis 3:24). Adam and Eve were never forbidden to eat of that tree—they were to live in a state of eternity on this earth. They were only forbidden to eat of the tree of the knowledge of good and evil (Genesis 2:17). Why? Because God had given them free will to make choices and decisions on their own, but He never wanted them to know evil—only good.

Once they had eaten from the tree of the knowledge of good and evil, God drove them from the garden so they would not eat of the tree of life and remain in a sinful, "fallen" state forever without redemption. At the end of the Bible, in Revelation, we find the tree of life in full force again. It provides constant life for all that eat of its fruit. The life of this new existence with the Lord is a life marked by tremendous goodness—there is no night, no death, no sorrow, no crying, no pain. All of the "former things" are passed away and God wipes the tears from every eye (Revelation 21:3, 4).

While this tree is depicted in heaven, there are also earthly aspects to John's vision in Revelation. There are *twelve* trees, indicative of the twelve apostles and the Christianity that flourished in their ministries and became the body of Christian believers around the world. Christianity is expected to bring about the "healing" of the nations, which will happen when all nations serve God and worship Jesus as the Lamb who sits on the throne of God.

We are to be *whole* as Christians. We are also to be *agents of healing and wholeness* who impact others. This is a message for *now*, not only for eternity. One day we will live again in perfect bodies in a perfect environment and worship God in the perfection of truth and love. Today, we are to seek to heal and to be healed.

---

low servant, and of your brethren the prophets, and of those who keep the words of this book. Worship God." [10]And he said to me, "Do not seal the words of the prophecy of this book, for the time is at hand. [11]He who is unjust, let him be unjust still; he who is filthy, let him be filthy still; he who is righteous, let him be righteous[a] still; he who is holy, let him be holy still."

JESUS TESTIFIES TO THE CHURCHES

[12]"And behold, I am coming quickly, and My reward *is* with Me, to give to every one according to his work. [13]I am the Alpha and the Omega, *the* Beginning and *the* End, the First and the Last."[a]

[14]"Blessed *are* those who do His commandments,[a] that they may have the right to the tree of life, and may enter through the gates into the city. [15]But[a] outside *are* dogs and sorcerers and sexually immoral and murderers and idolaters, and whoever loves and practices a lie.

[16]"I, Jesus, have sent My angel to testify to you these things in the churches. I am the Root and the Offspring of David, the Bright and Morning Star."

[17]And the Spirit and the bride say, "Come!" And let him who hears say, "Come!" And let him who thirsts come. Whoever desires, let him take the water of life freely.

A WARNING

[18]For[a] I testify to everyone who hears the words of the prophecy of this book: If anyone adds to these things, God will add[b] to him the plagues that are written in this book; [19]and if anyone takes away from the words of the book of this prophecy, God shall take away[a] his part from the Book[b] of Life, from the holy city, and *from* the things which are written in this book.

I AM COMING QUICKLY

[20]He who testifies to these things says, "Surely I am coming quickly."

Amen. Even so, come, Lord Jesus!

[21]The grace of our Lord Jesus Christ *be* with you all.[a] Amen.

22:11 [a]NU-Text and M-Text read *do right.*   22:13 [a]NU-Text and M-Text read *the First and the Last, the Beginning and the End.*   22:14 [a]NU-Text reads *wash their robes.*   22:15 [a]NU-Text and M-Text omit *But.*   22:18 [a]NU-Text and M-Text omit *For.* [b]M-Text reads *may God add.*   22:19 [a]M-Text reads *may God take away.* [b]NU-Text and M-Text read *tree of life.*   22:21 [a]NU-Text reads *with all;* M-Text reads *with all the saints.*

Create Your Own Bible-Land Spa

1 Create Your Own Bible-Land Spa

Esther was given a year of pampering beauty treatments before her one-night audience with King Ahasuerus. Talk about spa treatment! All of the latest beauty techniques were no doubt used to help the young women in this king's harem achieve the softest skin, most lustrous hair, most beautiful countenance, and maximum facial and body tone.

There's nothing "vain" about wanting to look your best. Vanity takes root when a person who wants to use their appearance to call attention to themselves so that others will admire them, trust them, or give to them.

Have fun making yourself as beautiful or as handsome as possible using the natural products and simple techniques in this section. These are all ideas you can use at home.

And don't forget: men can enjoy an at-home spa weekend as much as women!

2 Taking Care of Your Skin

Following are some "natural" skin care basics. Many of the products you need for cleansing, toning, moisturizing, exfoliating, and improving your skin can be found in your kitchen cabinets!

Cleansing Your Skin.

If your skin is dry, use a lotion or cream-based product that leaves behind emollients. If your skin is normal to oily, use a gel cleanser or very mild facial soap. If your skin is very oily, use a gentle soap such as Neutrogena or Dove. Never use a deodorant soap on your face or neck. If your skin is particularly sensitive, don't use a deodorant soap at all. You can make a good cleanser by combining equal amounts of clove oil (a natural astringent), chamomile (to maintain skin pigment), and eucalyptus (decongestant for the

skin). Massage this mixture into the skin by making a circular motion with the tips of your fingers and then rinse.

Toning Your Skin.

The purpose of using a toner is to remove residue, soap, moisturizer, and oil. One of the best toners? Lemons! Rose water and witch hazel are also good skin toners. Or, you might try a "tea tonic" as a toner: Mix 2 teaspoons green or chamomile tea with ½ cup water. Saturate a cotton ball with this mixture and apply it to your face. Allow it to remain on the skin until it evaporates. There's no reason to rinse these toners off the skin once they have been applied.

SPA FACT: A Super Hand Lotion Add ½ teaspoon sugar to a dollop of hand cream to enhance the soothing and softening effects on the skin.

Wheat germ oil, which is available in health-food stores and some supermarkets, is effective in keeping the skin elastic and preventing or treating stretch marks. Pregnant women can safely use it on the tummy and breast areas.

One of the simplest toning techniques is to end your shower with a cold-water spray. The colder the water, the better. Turn your face upward so the water runs over your face, neck, and shoulders. The cold will help tighten and tone the skin. Not only does this promote a radiant complexion, it helps avoid wrinkles.

Moisturizing Your Skin.

Moisturizers are more effective when they are applied to damp skin. Evening is the most important time to apply a moisturizer, allowing it to remain on the skin overnight. Don't over-moisturize—use cream on specific areas. Choose the right formula for your skin type and the season of the year. Most people have combination skin—areas of the face that are oily and others that are dry. Use a moisturizer that is right for each type only in the area of the skin you want to moisturize.

Any moisturizer can be stretched for added value by first applying a thin film of natural vitamin E lotion to the skin.

Exfoliating Your Skin.

Exfoliating is necessary to remove grime and the top layer of dead skin cells, as well as to get blood flowing into the face. There are common everyday products that are good for exfoliation:

☐ **Sea salt.** Rub sea salt all over your face and body. The effect is invigorating. It's available in health-food stores.

☐ **Oatmeal.** Open a packet of instant oatmeal and mix it with water to create a paste. Rub this mixture into your face and rinse off the residue. Some beauty experts recommend instant oatmeal on the face and traditional old-fashioned oatmeal for exfoliating the entire body.

☐ **Olive oil and sugar.** Add a couple of drops of olive oil to a packet of raw sugar. Rub it into the creases of your face.

Getting Rid of Age Spots.

To make your own skin-lightening potion, mix the juice of 1 lemon and 1 lime with 2 tablespoons honey and 2 ounces plain yogurt. Gently massage into each spot. Use at least once a week.

3 Take to the Mud!

Mud has been used for facial masks for thousands of years. Mud from the Dead Sea is available in packet form and is preferred by many in the spa business. One of the most popular mud or clay masks, however, is made with nothing but kitty litter (the kind made from "100 Percent Natural Clay"—it must not contain any chemicals, additives, or clumping substances).

Other facial masks can be made with the following:

☐ **Oatmeal.** Grind 1 cup of oatmeal to a powder. Add 3 drops almond oil, ½ cup milk, and 1 egg white. Blend thoroughly and apply to the skin. Rinse off after 20 minutes.

☐ **Tomatoes.** Mash a ripe tomato and leave it on the skin for 15 to 20 minutes. Rinse with warm (not hot) water. This is especially good for oily skin.

☐ **Banana.** Add just enough honey to a very ripe banana to make a soft pulp. Apply it to both face and hair.

☐ **Honey.** Apply pure honey to your face and neck. Allow it to set until dry (about 15 minutes). Rinse with very warm water.

☐ **Cucumbers.** Make a smooth pulp of crushed cucumbers and gently pat the mixture over face and neck. This is good for oily skin and clogged pours.

4 Add More Than Bubbles to Your Bath

Everybody knows the fun of a bubble bath. There are other things you can add to a bath, however, that will be truly therapeutic.

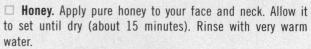

Baking soda. Try adding some baking soda to your bath to soothe itching skin, irritation, and sunburn. Use about half a box.

Honey. Add about a spoonful of honey to a bath to help fight insomnia.

Mustard powder. Add a teaspoon of mustard power to a hot bath to help fend off a cold.

Epsom salts. Using Epsom salts in a bath can help relax muscles and relieve swelling. Use about one half pound.

Instant oatmeal. Grind instant oatmeal to a powder and add to a bath to help with sunburn.

Apple cider vinegar. Add apple cider vinegar to your bath to help invigorate your body and fight fatigue.

Instant milk powder and almond oil. Add a cup of instant milk powder and 3 drops of almond oil to a bath. Soak for at least

15 minutes, then use a coarse washcloth or loofah to exfoliate dead skin.

Orange slices. Orange slices in a bath are uplifting and you'll enjoy the aroma.

5 The Battle Against Cellulite

Cellulite, that cottage-cheese-type appearance to the skin, reflects a general break down in the structure of the skin. In general, creams aimed at eliminating cellulite don't work. Diet and exercise do! There are some simple things you can do to help you in a battle against cellulite:

☐ Drink lots of water to rid cells of toxins.
☐ Stay away from carbonated beverages and avoid alcohol.
☐ Stay away from processed foods—choose to eat lots of fresh fruits and vegetables instead, preferably uncooked.

SPA FACT:
Stay Away from Sharp Objects!
Never use a razor or any other type of cutting device on foot calluses. Use a pumice stone.

☐ Try to walk or jog at least three times a week for 30 to 45 minutes each time.
☐ Scrub the skin with a dry looofah or natural vegetable bristle brush in slow sweeps, always toward the heart. Try to do this for at least 5 minutes a day. Use gentle pressure and increase as tolerated. Follow with a bath or shower. It is important to wash the brush thoroughly every few weeks in warm water to which you've added a few drops of grapefruit seed extract or lavender oil.
☐ Make your own herbal wrap by mixing 1 cup corn oil with ½ cup grapefruit juice and 2 teaspoons dried thyme. Massage it into buttocks, hips, and thighs. Cover with plastic wrap to lock in body heat. For accelerated results lay a heating pad over each area for about 5 minutes.

6 Instant Face Lift Techniques

Egg whites. If you want to tighten your face a bit for an evening out, try this recipe: Beat one egg white to a froth and apply it all over the face, especially the eye area, chin, and jaw. Allow it to dry—about ten minutes, and then rinse lightly.

Potato slices. Raw potato slices contain potassium that can help take away dark circles under the eyes.

Cucumbers. Thin cucumber slices used as a compress can be put over closed eyes to relieve puffiness.

Tea bags. Used cool to the touch, Tea tea bags make good eye refreshers. Don't use herbal tea bags for this purpose-they don't contain enough tannic acid.

7 Lightening Elbows and Knees

Elbows and knees can become discolored. Try a bleaching mask made with the juice of 3 lemons to 1 cup of powdered milk. Add just enough water to make a thick paste. Leave the mixture on for 20 minutes and then scrub it off with a loofah or textured washcloth or sponge.

8 Good for Your Hair!

Egg recipe. Mix 1 egg into your regular shampoo. Or, beat 2 eggs in a cup of warm water and massage the mixture into wet hair. Leave on for 5 to 10 minutes and rinse in lukewarm water. Caution: If you rinse this mix with water that is too hot, the eggs can "scramble" and be nearly impossible to get out!

Powdered gelatin. For thicker hair, add a tablespoon of powdered gelatin to your shampoo.

Lemon juice and vinegar. For shinier hair, blondes can add

¼ cup lemon juice and ½ cup water and use the mix as a hair rinse. Brunettes can add ¼ cup vinegar to ½ cup water.

Egg, honey, and olive oil. To condition dry hair, mix 1 egg, 1 teaspoon honey, and 2 teaspoons olive oil. Apply to wet hair and cover with a shower cap or a layer of plastic wrap. Leave on for about 30 minutes before shampooing out.

Avocado. To nourish "lifeless" hair, mash up an overripe avocado and blend it through dry hair. Leave the mixture on for 30 minutes and shampoo thoroughly.

Banana and almond oil. For damaged hair, mash a ripe banana and mix a few drops of almond oil with it. Massage it over the entire head and leave on for about 15 minutes. Rinse thoroughly.

Aloe vera. For oily hair, add ¼ cup aloe vera gel to ½ cup shampoo. Mix well and apply.

Honey. For overly dry hair, mix 1 tablespoon honey to 2 tablespoons shampoo, and wash your hair as usual.

9 Quick Short-Term Weight Loss

There's no such thing as lasting quick weight loss. All forms of quick weight loss involve diuretics, and the weight lost is water weight. One of the best and most natural means for quick diuretic weight loss is to take 2 garlic tablets and 2 papaya tablets before breakfast, lunch, and dinner. Eat lightly, staying away from carbohydrates and salt. These tablets can be purchased in most health health-food stores and drugstores. A person might lose up to six pounds in a couple of days. Do not take this increased dosage for more than two days. Do not do this frequently.

10 Plant a "Youth Garden"

Herbs known for their rejuvenating anti-aging benefits are calendula, comfrey, elderflower, German chamomile, ginkgo biloba, horsetail, lavender, licorice, oats, parsley, rosemary, and rose petals. These herbs can be used in herbal teas or added to water for a facial steam.

If you have a bathroom with lots of sunlight, or a garden room or greenhouse with a whirlpool tub, this would be an ideal place to plant the herbs of this garden in beautiful containers.

11 A Good Herbal Facial Steam

Herbal facial steams can help heal and rejuvenate the skin. The recipe for a herbal steam is simple: 2 to 3 cups of hot water (not boiling), 2 to 4 tablespoons fresh or dried herbs, and ¼ cup hydrogen peroxide (3 percent solution). Bring the water to a near boil. Add the herbs and hydrogen peroxide. Remove the pot to a place where you can comfortably sit over it. Hold your face 8 inches from the pot and place a towel over your head to create a tent. Steam for 10 to 15 minutes. When you are finished, splash your face with cold water. Then apply a gentle toner and a facial nourishment oil or cream.

12 Exercises to Tone Up Your Facial Muscles

Here are three quick exercises you can do to help tone up facial and neck muscles:

☐ Fill up your mouth with as much water as possible. Hold the water for as long as you can.

☐ Jut out your lower jaw. Gently raise your chin toward your nose, stretching your neck muscles. Then lower your chin back down to the starting position. You can do this while you are talking on the phone or riding in the car.

☐ Open your eyes as wide as possible—try to reach your forehead with your top eyelid! Do this several times.

13 Testing for Skin Allergies

To test for an allergic reaction to a plant or fruit, do a simple skin patch test. Put a drop of the essential oil of the plant or fruit on a cotton ball or swab and swipe the inside of your arm adjacent to the elbow. Leave this on the skin for 15 to 20 minutes. If you note any redness or itching within this time frame, wipe off the oil immediately. The oil is not for you and you likely have an allergy to that particular plant or fruit.

14 Aroma Therapy

Aroma therapy is becoming increasingly popular. Many essential oils fall into certain classifications according to their healing properties:

☐ Citrus aromas are mood elevators and stress relievers. (bitter orange, grapefruit, lemon, lime, blood orange, and sweet orange).
☐ Florals are mood elevators and relaxants. (geranium, lavender, rose, and jasmine).
☐ Grasses are relaxants and skin toners. (lemongrass).

☐ Herbals are anti-infectious, stimulating, and balancing. (Baybay, marjoram, oregano, thyme, and rosemary).
☐ Mints are mental stimulants, refreshing and cooling. (peppermint, and spearmint).
☐ Spices are energizing and warming. (Aniseanise, coriander, cumin, fennel, nutmeg, ginger, cardamom, and black pepper).
☐ Trees are air purifiers and respiratory and breathing facilitators. (fir, pine, sandalwood, eucalyptus, cypress, cedarwood, black spruce, and tea tree).

The World's Most Expensive Scent.

Bulgarian Rose is the most expensive scented oil that can be purchased. It takes approximately four thousand pounds of handpicked flower petals to make one pound of oil. It has been used in aroma therapy by professional practitioners for treatment of depression, grief, sadness, and low self-esteem. Just one very tiny 3-milliliter bottle costs $50–$70.

SPA FACT:

Upward, Upward
When applying products to the skin of the face and neck, always apply them with firm upward strokes!

15 Natural Energy Enhancers

Wheat grass juice is a natural energy enhancer and may assist in healing some diseases.

Ginseng improves energy levels and enhances mental alertness. It has also been shown to help lower LDL (bad) cholesterol while raising levels of HDL (good) cholesterol.

Royal jelly is a high-protein food produced by bees and fed to their offspring. It is available in both capsule and liquid forms in health-food stores. The liquid seems to be more easily absorbed into the body. It is an excellent energy booster. Make sure that your source for royal jelly is reputable. Purity is a must! ■

HEALTH NOTES